The Rites of the Catholic Church
as revised by the
Second Vatican Ecumenical Council

VOLUME ONE

The Roman Ritual revised by
Decree of the
Second Vatican Ecumenical Council
and published by authority
of Pope Paul VI

THE RITES

OF THE

CATHOLIC CHURCH

VOLUME ONE

Prepared by the
International Commission on English in the Liturgy
A Joint Commission of Catholic Bishops' Conferences

Approved for use in the
Dioceses of the United States of America by the
National Conference of Catholic Bishops
and confirmed
by the Apostolic See

STUDY EDITION

A PUEBLO BOOK

The Liturgical Press   Collegeville, Minnesota

1990

Concordat cum originali:
Ronald F. Krisman, Executive Director
Secretariat for the Liturgy
National Conference of Catholic Bishops

Published by authority of the Bishops' Committee on the Liturgy,
National Conference of Catholic Bishops.

Design: Frank Kacmarcik

ISBN 0-8146-6015-0

Printed in the United States of America

CONTENTS

PREFACE

The Roman Ritual has undergone numerous revisions since the edition of Pope Paul V, of 1614. Now, in response to the directives of the Second Vatican Ecumenical Council, a new edition has been undertaken by the Holy See. One of the animating principles that has guided the preparation of the new rites is to encourage the people of God to understand and participate more fully in these sacred celebrations.

The matter is clearly stated in the Instruction on the Proper Implementation of the Constitution on the Sacred Liturgy (*Inter Oecumenici,* September 26, 1964), no. 5:

"It is essential that everybody be persuaded that the scope of the Constitution on the Sacred Liturgy is not limited merely to the changing of liturgical rites and texts. Rather its aim is to foster the formation of the faithful and that pastoral activity of which the liturgy is the summit and source (see Const., Art. 10). The changes in the liturgy which have already been introduced or which will be introduced later, have this same end in view."

The Constitution on the Sacred Liturgy (*Sacrosanctum Concilium*) itself points out:

"Mother Church earnestly desires that all the faithful should be led to that full, conscious, and active participation in liturgical celebrations which is demanded by the very nature of the liturgy, and to which the Christian people, 'a chosen race, a royal priesthood, a holy nation, a redeemed people' (1 Pet. 2:9, 4-5) have a right and obligation by reason of their baptism.

"In the restoration and promotion of the sacred liturgy the full and active participation by all the people is the aim to be considered before all else, for it is the primary and indispensable source from which the faithful are to derive the true Christian spirit. Therefore, in all their apostolic activity, pastors of souls should energetically set about achieving it through the requisite pedagogy" (no. 14).[1]

The Constitution on the Sacred Liturgy goes on to point out the need for liturgical reforms along the following lines:

[1] Unless otherwise noted, the quotations are from the Constitution on the Sacred Liturgy (*Sacrosanctum Concilium*).

"In order that the Christian people may more certainly derive an abundance of graces from the sacred liturgy, holy
Mother Church desires to undertake with great care a general restoration of the liturgy itself. For the liturgy is made
up of unchangeable elements divinely instituted, and elements subject to change. These latter not only may be
changed but ought to be changed with the passage of time,
if they have suffered from the intrusion of anything out of
harmony with the inner nature of the liturgy or have become less suitable. In this restoration both texts and rites
should be drawn up so as to express more clearly the holy
things which they signify. The Christian people, as far as is
possible, should be able to understand them with ease and
take part in them fully, actively, and as a community"
(no. 21).

"The faithful should easily understand the sacramental
signs, and should eagerly frequent those sacraments which
were instituted to nourish the Christian life" (no. 59).

Although the Liturgy "is principally the worship of the divine Majesty, it likewise contains much instruction for the
faithful" (no. 33). Modern courses in religion from the
grades through college as well as advanced studies in
seminaries and graduate schools are careful to give the
study of liturgy a prominent place in the development of the
spiritual and intellectual aspects of Chrisitan life.

The purpose of this book is to bring together for the first
time in one volume those rites which are essential to the
planning of liturgical celebrations and which are frequently
studied and referred to in theology courses and are of special concern to the laity in general. These rites are as follows:

1. Christian Initiation
A. Rite of Christian Initiation of Adults
B. Rite of Baptism for Children
C. Rite of Reception of Baptized Christians into Full
    Communion with the Catholic Church
D. Rite of Confirmation
2. Rite of Penance
3. Holy Communion and Worship of the Eucharist outside
    Mass
4. Blessing of Oils and Consecration of Chrism

5. Rite of Marriage
6. Pastoral Care of the Sick: Rites of Anointing and Viaticum
7. Order of Christian Funerals

As a further aid to the study of these rites a comprehensive outline of each rite precedes the official text.

Here follows a description of the general principles which guided the Fathers of Vatican II in the reforms of the liturgy: The Constitution on the Sacred Liturgy (*Sacrosanctum Concilium*) states:

"With the passage of time . . . there have crept into the rites of the sacraments and sacramentals certain features which have rendered their nature and purpose far from clear to the people of today. Hence some changes are necessary to adapt them to present-day needs" (no. 62).

The purpose and plan of revision of the liturgical books is closely allied to an enlarged view of the importance of sacred scripture as a source of the liturgy.

"Sacred scripture is of the greatest importance in the celebration of the liturgy. For it is from it that lessons are read and explained in the homily, and psalms are sung. It is from the scriptures that the prayers, collects, and hymns draw their inspiration and their force, and that actions derive their meaning. Hence in order to achieve the restoration, progress, and adaptation of the sacred liturgy it is essential to promote that sweet and living love for sacred scripture to which the venerable tradition of Eastern and Western rites gives testimony" (no. 24).

The Constitution closes its section on the general norms for liturgical reforms with a reiteration of its concern for popular participation:

"To promote active participation, the people should be encouraged to take part by means of acclamations, responses, psalms, antiphons, hymns, as well as by actions, gestures and bodily attitudes. And at the proper time a reverent silence should be observed" (no. 30). Also:

"When the liturgical books are being revised, the people's parts must be carefully indicated by the rubrics" (no. 31). The document gives further "Norms Based on the Educative and Pastoral Nature of the Liturgy." Thus:

". . . the visible signs which the sacred liturgy uses to signify invisible divine things have been chosen by Christ or by
the Church. Thus not only when things are read 'which
were written for our instruction' (Rom. 15:4), but also when
the Church prays or sings or acts, the faith of those taking
part is nourished, and their minds are raised to God so that
they may offer him their spiritual homage and receive his
grace more abundantly" (no. 33).

In accordance with the above principles the Council set up
basic guidelines for the reform of specific rites—
requirements which were further elaborated by certain
post-Vatican II documents.

GUIDELINES FOR THE RITE OF BAPTISM

Certain rites which did not appear in the old ritual and yet
stem from the usage of the early Church are restored. Such
is the "catechumenate for adults, comprising several distinct
steps" which is "to be restored and brought into in use at
the discretion of the local ordinary. By this means the time
of the catechumenate, which is intended as a period of suitable instruction, may be sanctified by sacred rites to be
celebrated at successive intervals of time" (no. 64).

"Both rites for the baptism of adults are to be revised, not
only the simpler rite but also, taking into consideration the
restored catechumenate, the more solemn rite. A special
Mass 'For the conferring of Baptism' is to be inserted into
the Roman Missal" (no. 66).

The Constitution continues:

"The rite for the baptism of infants is to be revised, its revision taking into account the fact that those to be baptized are
infants. The roles of parents and godparents, and also their
duties, should be brought out more clearly in the rite itself"
(no. 67).

"The baptismal rite should contain variants, to be used at
the discretion of the local ordinary when a large number are
to be baptized. Likewise a shorter rite is to be drawn up,
especially for mission countries which catechists, and also
the faithful in general, may use when there is danger of
death and neither priest nor deacon is available (no. 68).

"In place of the rite called 'Rite for supplying what was omitted in the baptism of an infant' a new rite is to be drawn up for converts who have already been validly baptized. It should indicate that they are now admitted to communion with the Church" (no. 69).

"Baptismal water, outside of paschal time, may be blessed within the rite of Baptism itself by an approved shorter formula" (no. 70).

GUIDELINES FOR THE RITE OF CONFIRMATION

"Incorporated into the Church by Baptism, the faithful are appointed by their baptismal character to Christian religious worship; reborn as sons of God, they must profess before men the faith they have received from God through the Church. By the sacrament of Confirmation they are more perfectly bound to the Church and are endowed with the special strength of the Holy Spirit. Hence they are, as true witnesses of Christ, more strictly obliged to spread the faith by word and deed" Dogmatic Constitution on the Church (*Lumen Gentium*), no. 11.

The reasons for the changes and adaptations of the rites of both baptism and confirmation lie in the close relationship between the two sacraments and their function in the Christian life. Thus:

"The rite of Confirmation is to be revised also so that the intimate connection of this sacrament with the whole of the Christian initiation may more clearly appear. For this reason the renewal of baptismal promises should fittingly precede the reception of this sacrament. Confirmation may be conferred within Mass when convenient. For conferring outside Mass, a formula introducing the rite should be drawn up" (no. 71).

GUIDELINES FOR THE RITE OF PENANCE

"Those who approach the sacrament of Penance obtain pardon from God's mercy for the offense committed against him, and are, at the same time reconciled with the Church which they have wounded by their sins and which by char-

ity, by example and by prayer labors for their conversion"
Lumen Gentium, no. 11.

In this light, then, the Council decreed as follows:
"The rite and formulae of Penance are to be revised so that
they more clearly express both the nature and effect of the
sacrament" (no. 72).

GUIDELINES FOR THE RITES OF HOLY COMMUNION AND WORSHIP OF THE EUCHARIST OUTSIDE MASS

"Taking part in the eucharist sacrifice, the source and summit of the Christian life, they (the people and priest) offer
the divine victim to God and themselves along with it. And
so it is that, both in the offering and in Holy Communion,
each in his own way, though not of course indiscriminately,
has his own part to play in the liturgical action. Then,
strengthened by the body of Christ in the eucharistic communion, they manifest in a concrete way that unity of the
People of God which this holy sacrament aptly signifies and
admirably realizes" *Lumen Gentium*, no. 11.

Moreover, the decree *Presbyterorum Ordinis*—on the Ministry
and Life of Priests—declares:

"The house of prayer in which the most holy Eucharist is
celebrated and reserved, where the faithful assemble, and
where is worshiped the presence of the Son of God our
Saviour, offered for us on the sacrificial altar for the help
and consolation of the faithful—this house ought to be in
good taste and a worthy place for prayer and sacred ceremonial. In it pastors and faithful are called upon to respond
with grateful hearts to the gifts of him who through his humanity is unceasingly pouring the divine life into the members of his Body" (no. 5).

These views reflect the teaching and traditions of the
Church by stressing the importance of the worship of the
reserved Eucharist and the strengthening and healing flowing from the Sacrament even when received outside Mass.
The document entitled Instruction on the Worship of the
Eucharistic Mystery (S.C.R. *Eucharisticum Mysterium*, May
25, 1967, Chapter II, Section 3C) points out that:

"It is necessary to accustom the faithful to receive communion during the actual celebration of the Eucharist. Even outside Mass, however, priests will not refuse to distribute communion to those who have good reason to ask for it."

A new element in the practice of distributing Communion outside Mass is to give it a more biblical tone. Thus, as noted in the above-mentioned Instruction:

"When, at the prescribed times, communion is distributed outside Mass, if it is judged suitable, a short Bible service may precede it."

The new rite of Holy Communion and Worship of the Eucharist outside Mass clarified some of the traditional practices and encouraged them to be continued as underlined by Pope Paul VI in his encyclical letter *Mysterium Fidei,* September 3, 1965:

"Moreover, in the course of the day the faithful should not omit to visit the Blessed Sacrament, which according to the liturgical laws must be kept in the churches with the greatest possible reverence and in a most honorable location. Such visits are a proof of gratitude, an expression of love to Christ the Lord present in the sacraments, and a duty of the adoration we owe."

The traditional reasons for the reservation of the Eucharist are reiterated and summed up in the document entitled On Holy Communion and the worship of the Eucharistic Mystery Outside Mass (*Eucharistiae Sacramentum*) II, 5:

"The original and primary reason for the reservation of the Eucharist outside Mass is the administration of Viaticum: the distribution of Holy Communion and the adoration of our Lord Jesus Christ present in the Blessed Sacrament are derivative. For in fact the reservation of the sacred species for the benefit of the sick led to the admirable practice of adoring this heavenly food reserved in our churches. This practice of adoration is essentially proper and rational because faith in the real presence of our Lord spontaneously evokes a public and external manifestation of that faith."

GUIDELINES FOR THE RITE OF MARRIAGE

The Dogmatic Constitution on the Church (*Lumen Gentium*) points out:

"Christian married couples help one another to attain holiness in their married life and in the rearing of their children. Hence by reason of their state in life and of their position they have their own gifts in the People of God (cf. 1 Cor. 7:7). From the marriages of Christians there comes the family in which new citizens of human society are born and, by the grace of the Holy Spirit in Baptism, those are made children of God so that the People of God may be perpetuated throughout the centuries. In what might be regarded as the domestic Church, the parents, by word and example, are the first heralds of the faith with regard to their children. They must foster the vocation which is proper to each child, and this with special care if it be to religion" (no. 11).

The Pastoral Constitution on the Church in the Modern World (*Gaudium et Spes*) further illuminates these concepts when it declares:

"Authentic married love is caught up into divine love and is directed and enriched by the redemptive power of Christ and the salvific action of the Church, with the result that the spouses are effectively led to God and are helped and strengthened in their lofty role as fathers and mothers. Spouses, therefore, are fortified and, as it were, consecrated for the duties and dignity of their state by a special sacrament; fulfilling their conjugal and family role by virtue of this sacrament, spouses are penetrated with the spirit of Christ and their whole life is suffused by faith, hope, and charity; thus they increasingly further their own perfection and their mutual sanctification, and together they render glory to God" (no. 48).

It is in the light of these principles which, although traditional in the Church, have received a new impetus through these conciliar pronouncements, that the Council decreed the following:

"The Marriage rite now found in the Roman Ritual is to be revised and enriched so that it will more clearly signify the grace of the sacrament and will emphasize the spouses' duties.

"If any regions use other praiseworthy customs and cere-monies when celebrating the sacrament of Matrimony the sacred Synod earnestly desires that these by all means be retained" (no. 77).

"Matrimony is normally to be celebrated within the Mass after the reading of the gospel and the homily and before 'the prayer of the faithful.' The prayer for the bride, duly amended to remind both spouses of their equal obligation of mutual fidelity, may be said in the vernacular.

"But if the sacrament of Matrimony is celebrated apart from Mass, the epistle and gospel from the nuptial Mass are to be read at the beginning of the rite, and the blessing should always be given to the spouses" (no. 78).

The new rite for the celebration of marriage takes account of the problem of mixed marriages:

"With regard to the liturgical form of the celebration of a mixed marriage, if it is to be taken from the Roman Ritual, use must be made of the ceremonies in the *Rite of Celebration of Marriage* promulgated by our authority, whether it is a question of a marriage between a Catholic and a baptized non-Catholic (39-54) or of a marriage between a Catholic and an unbaptized person (55-66). If, however, the cir-cumstances justify it, a marriage between a Catholic and a baptized non-Catholic can be celebrated, subject to the local Ordinary's consent, according to the rites for the celebration of marriage within Mass (19-38), while respecting the pre-scription of general law with regard to Eucharistic Commu-nion" Apostolic Letter on Mixed Marriages (*Matrimonia Mixta*, Paul VI, January 7, 1970), no. 11.

GUIDELINES FOR THE RITE OF ANOINTING AND PASTORAL CARE OF THE SICK

The sacrament which has been generally called "extreme unction," is placed in focus by the Dogmatic Constitution on the Church (*Lumen Gentium*):

"By the sacred anointing of the sick and the prayer of the priest the whole Church commends those who are ill to the suffering and glorified Lord that he may raise them up and save them (cf. Jas. 5:14-16). And indeed she exhorts them to contribute to the good of the People of God by freely uniting themselves to the passion and death of Christ (cf. Rom. 8:17; Col. 1:24; Tim. 2:11-12; 1 Pet. 4:13)" (no. 11).

The Council also decreed in the Constitution on the Sacred Liturgy (*Sacrosanctum Concilium*) that:

"'Extreme Unction,' which may also and more fittingly be called 'Anointing of the Sick,' is not a sacrament for those only who are at the point of death. Hence, as soon as anyone of the faithful begins to be in danger of death from sickness or old age, the fitting time for him to receive this sacrament has certainly already arrived" (no. 73).

"In addition to the separate rites for Anointing of the Sick and for Viaticum, a continuous rite shall be prepared in which a sick man is anointed after he has made his confession and before he receives Viaticum" (no. 74).

"The number of the anointings is to be adapted to the occasion, and the prayers which belong to the rite of Anointing are to be revised so as to correspond to the varying conditions of the sick who receive the sacrament" (no. 75).

REVISIONS IN THE ORDER OF CHRISTIAN FUNERALS

It has been pointed out that the rites for Christian burial have stressed gloom rather than the paschal mystery. Christ's resurrection and our own future resurrection should be the theme of Christian death and its expression in the rites of the Church.

The Council, acting along these lines, decree as follows: "Funeral rites should express more clearly the paschal character of Christian death, and should correspond more closely to the circumstances and traditions found in various regions. This also applies to the liturgical color to be used" (no. 81).

"The rite for the Burial of Infants is to be revised, and a special Mass for the occasion should be provided" (no. 82).

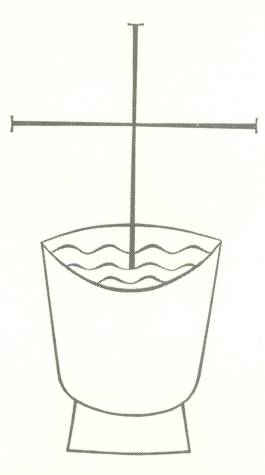

CHRISTIAN INITIATION

CHRISTIAN INITIATION,

GENERAL INTRODUCTION

1. In the sacraments of Christian initiation we are freed from the power of darkness and joined to Christ's death, burial, and resurrection. We receive the Spirit of filial adoption and are part of the entire people of God in the celebration of the memorial of the Lord's death and resurrection.[1]

2. Baptism incorporates us into Christ and forms us into God's people. This first sacrament pardons all our sins, rescues us from the power of darkness, and brings us to the dignity of adopted children,[2] a new creation through water and the Holy Spirit. Hence we are called and are indeed the children of God.[3]

By signing us with the gift of the Spirit, confirmation makes us more completely the image of the Lord and fills us with the Holy Spirit, so that we may bear witness to him before all the world and work to bring the Body of Christ to its fullness as soon as possible.[4]

Finally, coming to the table of the eucharist, we eat the flesh and drink the blood of the Son of Man so that we may have eternal life[5] and show forth the unity of God's people. By offering ourselves with Christ, we share in the universal sacrifice, that is, the entire community of the redeemed offered to God by their High Priest,[6] and we pray for a greater outpouring of the Holy Spirit, so that the whole human race may be brought into the unity of God's family.[7]

[1]See Vatican Council II, Decree on the Church's Missionary Activity *Ad gentes*, no. 14.
[2]See Colossians 1:13; Romans 8:15; Galatians 4:5. See also Council of Trent, sess. 6., *Decr. de iustificatione*, cap. 4: Denz.-Schön. 1524.
[3]See 1 John 3:1.
[4]See Vatican Council II, Decree on the Church's Missionary Activity *Ad gentes*, no. 36.
[5]See John 6:55.
[6]See Augustine, *De civitate Dei* 10,6: PL 41, 284. Vatican Council II, Dogmatic Constitution on the Church *Lumen gentium*, no. 11; Decree on the Ministry and Life of Priests *Presbyterorum Ordinis*, no. 2.
[7]See Vatican Council II, Dogmatic Constitution on the Church *Lumen gentium*, no. 28.

Thus the three sacraments of Christian initiation closely combine to bring us, the faithful of Christ, to his full stature and to enable us to carry out the mission of the entire people of God in the Church and in the world.[8]

DIGNITY OF BAPTISM

3. Baptism, the door to life and to the kingdom of God, is the first sacrament of the New Law, which Christ offered to all, that they might have eternal life.[9] He later entrusted this sacrament and the Gospel to his Church, when he told his apostles: "Go, make disciples of all nations, and baptize them in the name of the Father, and of the Son, and of the Holy Spirit."[10] Baptism is therefore, above all, the sacrament of that faith by which, enlightened by the grace of the Holy Spirit, we respond to the Gospel of Christ. That is why the Church believes that it is its most basic and necessary duty to inspire all, catechumens, parents of children still to be baptized, and godparents, to that true and living faith by which they hold fast to Christ and enter into or confirm their commitment to the New Covenant. In order to enliven such faith, the Church prescribes the pastoral instruction of catechumens, the preparation of the children's parents, the celebration of God's word, and the profession of faith at the celebration of baptism.

4. Further, baptism is the sacrament by which its recipients are incorporated into the Church and are built up together in the Spirit into a house where God lives,[11] into a holy nation and a royal priesthood.[12] Baptism is a sacramental bond of unity linking all who have been signed by it.[13] Because of that unchangeable effect (given expression in the Latin liturgy by the anointing of the baptized person with chrism in the presence of God's people), the rite of baptism is held in highest honor by all Christians. Once it has been validly celebrated, even if by Christians with whom we are not in full communion, it may never lawfully be repeated.

[8]See ibid., no. 31.
[9]See John 3:5.
[10]Matthew 28:19.
[11]See Ephesians 2:22.
[12]See 1 Peter 2:9.
[13]See Vatican Council II, Decree on Ecumenism *Unitatis redintegratio*, no. 22.

5. Baptism, the cleansing with water by the power of the living word,[14] washes away every stain of sin, original and personal, and makes us sharers in God's own life[15] and his adopted children.[16] As proclaimed in the prayers for the blessing of the water, baptism is a cleansing water of re-birth[17] that makes us God's children born from on high. The blessed Trinity is invoked over those who are to be baptized, so that all who are signed in this name are conse-crated to the Trinity and enter into communion with the Father, the Son, and the Holy Spirit. They are prepared for this high dignity and led to it by the scriptural readings, the prayer of the community, and their own profession of belief in the Father, the Son, and the Holy Spirit.

6. Far superior to the purifications of the Old Law, baptism produces these effects by the power of the mystery of the Lord's passion and resurrection. Those who are baptized are united to Christ in a death like his;[18] buried with him in death, they are given life again with him, and with him they rise again.[19] For baptism recalls and makes present the paschal mystery itself, because in baptism we pass from the death of sin into life. The celebration of baptism should therefore re-flect the joy of the resurrection, especially when the celebra-tion takes place during the Easter Vigil or on a Sunday.

OFFICES AND MINISTRIES OF BAPTISM

7. The preparation for baptism and Christian instruction are both of vital concern to God's people, the Church, which hands on and nourishes the faith received from the apostles. Through the ministry of the Church, adults are called to the Gospel by the Holy Spirit and infants are bap-tized in the faith of the Church and brought up in that faith. Therefore it is most important that catechists and other laypersons should work with priests and deacons in the preparation for baptism. In the actual celebration, the people of God (represented not only by the parents, godpar-ents, and relatives, but also, as far as possible, by friends, neighbors, and some members of the local Church) should

[14]See Ephesians 5:26.
[15]See 2 Peter 1:4.
[16]See Romans 8:15; Galatians 4:5.
[17]See Titus 3:5.
[18]See Romans 6:4–5.
[19]See Ephesians 2:5–6.

take an active part. Thus they will show their common faith and the shared joy with which the newly baptized are received into the community of the Church.

8. It is a very ancient custom of the Church that adults are not admitted to baptism without godparents, members of the Christian community who will assist the candidates at least in the final preparation for baptism and after baptism will help them persevere in the faith and in their lives as Christians. In the baptism of children, as well, godparents are to be present in order to represent both the expanded spiritual family of the one to be baptized and the role of the Church as a mother. As occasion offers, godparents help the parents so that children will come to profess the faith and live up to it.

9. At least in the later rites of the catechumenate and in the actual celebration of baptism, the part of godparents is to testify to the faith of adult candidates or, together with the parents, to profess the Church's faith, in which children are baptized.

10. Therefore godparents, chosen by the catechumens or by the families of children to be baptized, must, in the judgment of the parish priest (pastor), be qualified to carry out the proper liturgical functions mentioned in no. 9.

1. Godparents are persons, other than the parents of candidates, who are designated by the candidates themselves or by a candidate's parents or whoever stands in the place of parents, or, in the absence of these, by the pastor or the minister of baptism. Each candidate may have either a godmother or a godfather or both a godmother and a godfather.

2. Those designated must have the capability and intention of carrying out the responsibility of a godparent and be mature enough to do so. A person sixteen years of age is presumed to have the requisite maturity, but the diocesan bishop may have stipulated another age or the pastor or the minister may decide that there is a legitimate reason for allowing an exception.

3. Those designated as godparents must have received the three sacraments of initiation: baptism, confirmation, and eucharist, and be living a life consistent with faith and with the responsibility of a godparent.

4. Those designated as godparents must also be members of the Catholic Church and be canonically free to carry out this office. At the request of parents, a baptized and believing Christian not belonging to the Catholic Church may act as a Christian witness along with a Catholic godparent.[20] In the case of separated Eastern Christians with whom we do not have full communion the special discipline for the Eastern Churches is to be respected.

11. The ordinary ministers of baptism are bishops, priests, and deacons.

1. In every celebration of this sacrament they should be mindful that they act in the Church in the name of Christ and by the power of the Holy Spirit.

2. They should therefore be diligent in the ministry of the word of God and in the manner of celebrating the sacrament. They must avoid any action that the faithful could rightly regard as favoritism.[21]

3. Except in a case of necessity, these ministers are not to confer baptism outside their own territory, even on their own subjects, without the requisite permission.

12. Bishops are the chief stewards of the mysteries of God and leaders of the entire liturgical life in the Church committed to them.[22] This is why they direct the conferring of baptism, which brings to the recipient a share in the kingly priesthood of Christ.[23] Therefore bishops should personally celebrate baptism, especially at the Easter Vigil. They should have a particular concern for the preparation and baptism of adults.

13. It is the duty of pastors to assist the bishop in the instruction and baptism of the adults entrusted to their care, unless the bishop makes other provisions. Pastors, with the assistance of catechists or other qualified laypersons, have the duty of preparing the parents and godparents of

[20]See *Codex Iuris Canonici,* can. 873 and 874, §§ 1 and 2.
[21]See Vatican Council II, Constitution on the Liturgy *Sacrosanctum Concilium,* art. 32; Pastoral Constitution on the Church in the Modern World *Gaudium et spes,* no. 29.
[22]See Vatican Council II, Decree on the Pastoral Office of Bishops *Christus Dominus,* no. 15.
[23]See Vatican Council II, Dogmatic Constitution on the Church *Lumen gentium,* no. 26.

children through appropriate pastoral guidance and of baptizing the children.

14. Other priests and deacons, since they are co-workers in the ministry of bishops and pastors, also prepare candidates for baptism and, by the invitation or consent of the bishop or pastor, celebrate the sacrament.

15. The celebrant of baptism may be assisted by other priests and deacons and also by laypersons in those parts that pertain to them, especially if there are a large number to be baptized. Provision for this is made in various parts of the rituals for adults and for children.

16. In imminent danger of death and especially at the moment of death, when no priest or deacon is available, any member of the faithful, indeed anyone with the right intention, may and sometimes must administer baptism. In a case simply of danger of death the sacrament should be administered, if possible, by a member of the faithful according to one of the shorter rites provided for this situation.[24] Even in this case a small community should be formed to assist at the rite or, if possible, at least one or two witnesses should be present.

17. Since they belong to the priestly people, all laypersons, especially parents and, by reason of their work, catechists, midwives, family or social workers or nurses of the sick, as well as physicians and surgeons, should be thoroughly aware, according to their capacities, of the proper method of baptizing in case of emergency. They should be taught by pastors, deacons, and catechists. Bishops should provide appropriate means within their diocese for such instruction.

REQUIREMENTS FOR THE CELEBRATION OF BAPTISM

18. The water used in baptism should be true water and, both for the sake of authentic sacramental symbolism and for hygienic reasons, should be pure and clean.

---

[24]See *Rite of Christian Initiation of Adults,* nos. 351–375; *Rite of Baptism for Children,* nos. 157–164.

19. The baptismal font, or the vessel in which on occasion the water is prepared for celebration of the sacrament in the sanctuary, should be spotlessly clean and of pleasing design.

20. If the climate requires, provision should be made for the water to be heated beforehand.

21. Except in case of necessity, a priest or deacon is to use only water that has been blessed for the rite. The water blessed at the Easter Vigil should, if possible, be kept and used throughout the Easter season to signify more clearly the relationship between the sacrament of baptism and the paschal mystery. Outside the Easter season, it is desirable that the water be blessed for each occasion, in order that the words of blessing may explicitly express the mystery of salvation that the Church remembers and proclaims. If the baptistery is supplied with running water, the blessing is given as the water flows.

22. As the rite for baptizing, either immersion, which is more suitable as a symbol of participation in the death and resurrection of Christ, or pouring may lawfully be used.

23. The words for conferring baptism in the Latin Church are: I BAPTIZE YOU IN THE NAME OF THE FATHER, AND OF THE SON, AND OF THE HOLY SPIRIT.

24. For celebrating the liturgy of the word of God a suitable place should be provided in the baptistery or in the church.

25. The baptistery or the area where the baptismal font is located should be reserved for the sacrament of baptism and should be worthy to serve as the place where Christians are reborn in water and the Holy Spirit. The baptistery may be situated in a chapel either inside or outside the church or in some other part of the church easily seen by the faithful; it should be large enough to accommodate a good number of people. After the Easter season, the Easter candle should be kept reverently in the baptistery, in such a way that it can be lighted for the celebration of baptism and so that from it the candles for the newly baptized can easily be lighted.

26. In the celebration the parts of the rite that are to be celebrated outside the baptistery should be carried out in different areas of the church that most conveniently suit the size of the congregation and the several parts of the baptismal liturgy. When the baptistery cannot accommodate all the catechumens and the congregation, the parts of the rite that are customarily celebrated inside the baptistery may be transferred to some other suitable area of the church.

27. As far as possible, all recently born babies should be baptized at a common celebration on the same day. Except for a good reason, baptism should not be celebrated more than once on the same day in the same church.

28. Further details concerning the time for baptism of adults and of children will be found in the respective rituals. But at all times the celebration of the sacrament should have a markedly paschal character.

29. Pastors must carefully and without delay record in the baptismal register the names of those baptized, of the minister, parents, and godparents, as well as the place and date of baptism.

ADAPTATIONS BY THE CONFERENCES OF BISHOPS

30. According to the Constitution on the Liturgy (art. 63, b), it is within the competence of the conferences of bishops to compose for their local rituals a section corresponding to this one in the Roman Ritual, adapted to the needs of their respective regions. After it has been reviewed by the Apostolic See, it may be used in the regions for which it was prepared.

In this connection, it is the responsibility of each conference of bishops:

1. to decide on the adaptations mentioned in the Constitution on the Liturgy (art. 39);

2. carefully and prudently to weigh what elements of a people's distinctive traditions and culture may suitably be admitted into divine worship and so to propose to the Apostolic See other adaptations considered useful or necessary that will be introduced with its consent;

3. to retain distinctive elements of any existing local rituals, as long as they conform to the Constitution on the Liturgy and correspond to contemporary needs, or to modify such elements;

4. to prepare translations of the texts that genuinely reflect the characteristics of various languages and cultures and to add, whenever helpful, music suitable for singing;

5. to adapt and augment the Introductions contained in the Roman Ritual, so that the ministers may fully understand the meaning of the rites and carry them out effectively;

6. to arrange the material in the various editions of the liturgical books prepared under the guidance of the conference of bishops, so that these books may better suit pastoral use.

31. Taking into consideration especially the norms in the Constitution on the Liturgy (art. 37-40, 65), the conferences of bishops in mission countries have the responsibility of judging whether the elements of initiation in use among some peoples can be adapted for the rite of Christian baptism and of deciding whether such elements are to be incorporated into the rite.

32. When the Roman Ritual for baptism provides several optional formularies, local rituals may add other formularies of the same kind.

33. The celebration of baptism is greatly enhanced by the use of song, which stimulates in the participants a sense of their unity, fosters their praying together, and expresses the joy of Easter that should permeate the whole rite. The conference of bishops should therefore encourage and help specialists in music to compose settings for those liturgical texts particularly suited to congregational singing.

ADAPTATIONS BY THE MINISTER OF BAPTISM

34. Taking into account existing circumstances and other needs, as well as the wishes of the faithful, the minister should make full use of the various options allowed in the rite.

35. In addition to the adaptations that are provided in the
Roman Ritual for the dialogue and blessings, the minister
may make other adaptations for special circumstances.
These adaptations will be indicated more fully in the Introductions to the rites of baptism for adults and for children.

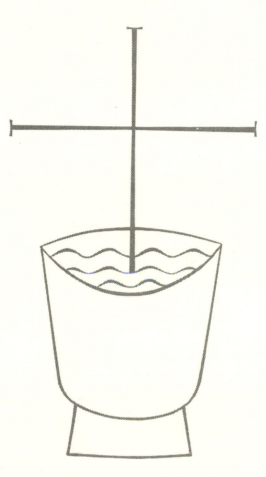

RITE OF CHRISTIAN INITIATION OF ADULTS

RITE OF CHRISTIAN INITIATION OF ADULTS

Decree
FOREWORD
Roman decree
Introduction (1–35)

PART I
CHRISTIAN INITIATION OF ADULTS
Outline for Christian Initiation of Adults

PERIOD OF EVANGELIZATION AND PRECATECHUMENATE (36–40)

FIRST STEP: ACCEPTANCE INTO THE ORDER OF CATECHUMENS (41–47)

Rite of Acceptance into the Order of Catechumens

Receiving the Candidates (48)
Greeting (49)
Opening Dialogue (50–51)
Candidates' First Acceptance of the Gospel (52)
Affirmation By the Sponsors and the Assembly (53)
Signing of the Candidates with the Cross (54)
1. Signing of the Forehead (55)
2. [Signing of the Other Senses] (56)
3. Concluding Prayer (57–59)
Invitation to the Celebration of the Word of God (60)

Liturgy of the Word
Instruction (61)
Readings (62)
Homily (63)
[Presentation of a Bible] (64)
Intercessions for the Catechumens (65)
Prayer over the Catechumens (66)
Dismissal of the Catechumens (67)

Liturgy of the Eucharist (68)

Optional Rites (69)
Exorcism and Renunciation of False Worship (70)
Exorcism (71)
Renunciation of False Worship (72)

Liturgy of the Eucharist (137)

PERIOD OF PURIFICATION AND ENLIGHTENMENT (138–140)

Rites Belonging to the Period of Purification and Enlightenment (138–140)

The Scrutinies (141–146)

Presentations (147–149)

First Scrutiny
(Third Sunday of Lent)

Liturgy of the Word
Readings (150)
Homily (151)
Invitation to Silent Prayer (152)
Intercessions for the Elect (153)
Exorcism (154)
Dismissal of the Elect (155)

Liturgy of the Eucharist (156)

Presentation of the Creed (157)
(Third Week of Lent)

Liturgy of the Word
Readings (158)
Homily (159)
Presentation of the Creed (160)
Prayer over the Elect (161)
Dismissal of the Elect (162)

Liturgy of the Eucharist (163)

Second Scrutiny
(Fourth Sunday of Lent)

Liturgy of the Word
Readings (164)
Homily (165)
Invitation to Silent Prayer (166) (See no. 152, above.)
Intercessions for the Elect (167)
Exorcism (168)
Dismissal of the Elect (169)

Liturgy of the Eucharist (170) (See no. 156, above.)

Third Scrutiny
(Fifth Sunday of Lent)

Liturgy of the Word
Readings (171)
Homily (172)
Invitation to Silent Prayer (173) (See no. 152, above.)
Intercessions for the Elect (174)
Exorcism (175)
Dismissal of the Elect (176)

Liturgy of the Eucharist (177) (See no. 156, above)

Presentation of the Lord's Prayer (178)
(Fifth Week of Lent)

Liturgy of the Word
Readings (179)
Gospel Reading (Presentation of the Lord's Prayer) (180)
Homily (181)
Prayer over the Elect (182)
Dismissal of the Elect (183)

Liturgy of the Eucharist (184)

Preparation Rites on Holy Saturday (185–186)

Model for a Celebration of the Preparation Rites (187–192)
Recitation of the Creed (193)
Reading and Homily (194)
Prayer before the Recitation (195)
Recitation of the Creed (196)

Ephphetha Rite (197)
Reading and Instruction (198)
Ephphetha (199)

[Choosing a Baptismal Name] (200)
Reading and Instruction (201)
Naming of the Elect (202)

Concluding Rites (203)
Prayer of Blessing (204)
Dismissal (205)

THIRD STEP: CELEBRATION OF THE SACRAMENTS OF INITIATION (206–217)

Celebration of the Sacraments of Initiation
(Easter Vigil)

Celebration of Baptism (218)
Presentation of the Candidates (219)
Invitation to Prayer (220)
Litany of the Saints (221)
Prayer over the Water (222)
Profession of Faith (223)
1. Renunciation of Sin (224)
2. Profession of Faith (225)
Baptism (226)
Explanatory Rites (227)
1. [Anointing after Baptism] (228)
2. [Clothing with a Baptismal Garment] (229)
3. Presentation of a Lighted Candle (230)

Celebration of Confirmation (231–232)
Invitation (233)
Laying on of Hands (234)
Anointing with Chrism (235–236)

[Renewal of Baptismal Promises (at the Easter Vigil)]
Invitation (237)
Renewal of Baptismal Promises
1. Renunciation of Sin (238)
2. Profession of Faith (239)
Sprinkling with Baptismal Water (240)

Liturgy of the Eucharist (241–243)

PERIOD OF POSTBAPTISMAL CATECHESIS OF MYSTAGOGY (244–251)

PART II
RITES FOR PARTICULAR CIRCUMSTANCES

1. CHRISTIAN INITIATION OF CHILDREN WHO HAVE REACHED CATECHETICAL AGE (252–259)

FIRST STEP: ACCEPTANCE INTO THE ORDER OF CATECHUMENS (260–261)

Rite of Acceptance into the Order of Catechumens

Receiving the Children (262)
Greeting (263)
Opening Dialogue (264)
Affirmation by the Parents(Sponsors) and the Assembly (265)
Signing of the Candidates with the Cross (266)
Signing of the Forehead (267)
[Signing of the Other Senses] (268)
Invitation to the Celebration of the Word of God (269)

Liturgy of the Word
Instruction (270)
Readings (271)
Homily (272)
[Presentation of a Bible] (273)
Intercessions for the Children (274)
Prayer over the Children (275)
Dismissal (276)

RITE OF ELECTION OR ENROLLMENT OF NAMES [OPTIONAL] (277–280)

Liturgy of the Word
Homily (281)
Presentation of the Children (282)
Affirmation by the (Parents,) Godparents [and the Assembly] (283)
Invitation and Enrollment of Names (284)
Act of Admission or Election (285)
[Recognition of the Godparent(s)] (286)
Intercessions for the Elect (287)
Prayer over the Elect (288)
Dismissal of the Elect (289)

Liturgy of the Eucharist (290)

SECOND STEP: PENITENTIAL RITES (SCRUTINIES) (291–294)

Penitential Rite (Scrutiny)

Liturgy of the Word
Greeting and Introduction (295)
Prayer (296)
Readings (297)
Homily (298)
Intercessions (299)

Exorcism (300)
Anointing with the Oil of Catechumens [or Laying on of Hands] (301)
Dismissal of the Children (302)

Liturgy of Penance (303)

THIRD STEP: CELEBRATION OF THE SACRAMENTS OF INITIATION (304–308)

Celebration of the Sacraments of Initiation

Liturgy of the Word (309)

Celebration of Baptism
Invitation to Prayer (310)
Prayer over the Water (311)
[Community's Profession of Faith] (312)
Children's Profession of Faith (313)
1. Renunciation of Sin (314)
2. [Anointing with the Oil of Catechumens] (315)
3. Profession of Faith (316)
Baptism (317)
Explanatory Rites (318) (See no. 227, above.)
1. [Anointing after Baptism] (319)
2. [Clothing with a Baptismal Garment] (320)
3. Presentation of a Lighted Candle (321)

Celebration of Confirmation (322–323)
Invitation (324)
Laying on of Hands (325) (See no. 234, above.)
Anointing with Chrism (326)

Liturgy of the Eucharist (327–329)

PERIOD OF POSTBAPTISMAL CATECHESIS OR MYSTAGOGY (330)

2. CHRISTIAN INITIATION OF ADULTS IN EXCEPTIONAL CIRCUMSTANCES (331–335)

Christian Initiation of Adults in Exceptional Circumstances (Abbreviated Form) (336–339)

Receiving the Candidate (340)
Greeting (341)
Opening Dialogue (342)
Candidate's Declaration (343)

Affirmation by the Godparents (344)
Invitation to the Celebration of the Word of God (345)

Liturgy of the Word (346)
Readings (347)
Homily (348)
Intercessions for the Candidate (349)
[Penitential Rite] (350)
Prayer of Exorcism (351)
Anointing with the Oil of Catechumens or Laying on of
Hands (352)

Celebration of Baptism
Invitation to Prayer (353)
Prayer over the Water (354)
Profession of Faith (355) (See no. 223, above.)
1. Renunciation of Sin (356)
2. Profession of Faith (357)
Baptism (358)
Explanatory Rites (359)
1. [Clothing with a Baptismal Garment] (360) (See no. 229,
above.)
2. Presentation of a Lighted Candle (361)

Celebration of Confirmation (362–363)
Invitation (364)
Laying on of Hands (365)
Anointing with Chrism (366)

Liturgy of the Eucharist (367–369)

3. CHRISTIAN INITIATION OF A PERSON IN DANGER OF DEATH (370–374)

Christian Initiation of a Person in Danger of Death (375–376)

Introductory Rites
Opening Dialogue (377)
Affirmation by the Godparent and Witnesses (378)

Liturgy of the Word
Gospel Reading (379)
Intercessions for the Candidate (380)
Prayer over the Candidate (381)

Prayer over the Candidates (431)
[Dismissal of the Assembly] (432)

Liturgy of the Eucharist (433)

4B. RITE OF SENDING THE CANDIDATES FOR RECOGNITION BY THE BISHOP AND FOR THE CALL TO CONTINUING CONVERSION (434–437)

Liturgy of the Word
Homily (438)
Presentation of the Candidates (439)
Affirmation by the Sponsors [and the Assembly] (440–441)
General Intercessions (442)
Prayer over the Candidates (443)
[Dismissal of the Assembly] (444)

Liturgy of the Eucharist (445)

4C. RITE OF CALLING THE CANDIDATES TO CONTINUING CONVERSION (446–449)

Liturgy of the Word
Homily (450)
Presentation of the Candidates for Confirmation and Eucharist (451)
Affirmation by the Sponsors [and the Assembly] (452–453)
Act of Recognition (454)
General Intercessions (455)
Prayer over the Candidates (456)
[Dismissal of the Assembly] (457)

Liturgy of the Eucharist (458)

4D. PENITENTIAL RITE (SCRUTINY) (459–463)

PENITENTIAL RITE (Second Sunday of Lent)

Introductory Rite
Greeting and Introduction (464)
Prayer (465)

Liturgy of the Word
Reading (466)
Homily (467)
Invitation to Silent Prayer (468)
Intercessions for the Candidates (469)
Prayer over the Candidates (470)
[Dismissal of the Assembly] (471)

Signing of the Catechumens and of the Candidates with the Cross (514)
1. [Signing of the Forehead] (515)
2. [Signing of the Other Senses of the Catechumens] (516)
3. Signing of the Forehead (518)
4. [Signing of the Other Senses of the Candidates] (519)
5. Concluding Prayer (520)
Invitation to the Celebration of the Word of God (521)

Liturgy of the Word
Instruction (522)
Readings (523)
Homily (524–525)
Intercessions for the Catechumens and Candidates (526)
Prayer over the Catechumens and Candidates (527)
Dismissal of the Catechumens (528)

Liturgy of the Eucharist (529)

RITE 2. PARISH CELEBRATION FOR SENDING CATECHUMENS FOR ELECTION AND CANDIDATES FOR RECOGNITION BY THE BISHOP (OPTIONAL) (530–535)

Liturgy of the Word
Homily (536)
Presentation of the Catechumens (537)
Affirmation by the Godparents [and the Assembly] (538–539)
Presentation of the Candidates (540)
Affirmation by the Sponsors [and the Assembly] (541–542)
Intercessions for the Catechumens and Candidates (543)
Prayer over the Catechumens and Candidates (544)
Dismissal of the Catechumens (545)

Liturgy of the Eucharist (546)

RITE 3. CELEBRATION OF THE RITE OF ELECTION OF CATECHUMENS AND OF THE CALL TO CONTINUING CONVERSION OF CANDIDATES WHO ARE PREPARING FOR CONFIRMATION AND/OR EUCHARIST OR RECEPTION INTO THE FULL COMMUNION OF THE CATHOLIC CHURCH (547–549)

Liturgy of the Word
Homily (550)

Celebration of Election
Presentation of the Catechumens (551)
Affirmation by the Godparents [and the Assembly] (552)
Invitation and Enrollment of Names (553)
Act of Admission or Election (554)

Celebration of the Call to Continuing Conversion
Presentation of the Candidates (555)
Affirmation by the Sponsors [and the Assembly] (556)

Act of Recognition (557)
Intercessions for the Elect and the Candidates (558)
Prayer over the Elect and the Candidates (559)
Dismissal of the Elect (560)

Liturgy of the Eucharist (561)

RITE 4. CELEBRATION AT THE EASTER VIGIL OF THE SACRAMENTS OF INITIATION AND OF THE RITE OF RECEPTION INTO THE FULL COMMUNION OF THE CATHOLIC CHURCH (562–565)

Service of Light

Liturgy of the Word

Celebration of Baptism (567)
Presentation of the Candidates for Baptism (568)
Invitation to Prayer (569)
Litany of the Saints (570) (See no. 221, above.)
Blessing of the Water (571)
Profession of Faith (572)
1. Renunciation of Sin (573) (See no. 224, above.)
2. Profession of Faith (574) (See no. 225, above.)
Baptism (575) (See no. 226, above.)
Explanatory Rites (576) (See no. 227, above.)
1. [Anointing after Baptism] (577) (See no. 228, above)
2. [Clothing with a Baptismal Garment] (578) (See no. 229, above.)
3. Presentation of a Lighted Candle (579)

Renewal of Baptismal Promises
Invitation (580)
Renewal of Baptismal Promises
1. Renunciation of Sin (581)
2. Profession of Faith (582)
Sprinkling with Baptismal Water (583)

NATIONAL CONFERENCE OF CATHOLIC BISHOPS UNITED STATES OF AMERICA

DECREE

In accord with the norms established by decree of the Sacred Congregation of Rites in *Cum, nostra aetate* (27 January 1966), this edition of the *Rite of Christian Initiation of Adults* is declared to be the vernacular typical edition of *Ordo initiationis christianae adultorum* in the dioceses of the United States of America, and is published by authority of the National Conference of Catholic Bishops.

The *Rite of Christian Initiation of Adults* was canonically approved by the National Conference of Catholic Bishops in plenary assembly on 11 November 1986 and was subsequently confirmed by the Apostolic See by decree of the Congregation for Divine Worship on 19 February 1987 (Prot. N. 1192/86).

On 1 July 1988 the *Rite of Christian Initiation of Adults* may be published and used in the liturgy. From 1 September 1988 the use of the *Rite of Christian Initiation of Adults* is mandatory in the dioceses of the United States of America. From that day forward no other English version may be used.

Given at the General Secretariat of the National Conference of Catholic Bishops, Washington, DC, on 18 March 1988, the memorial of Saint Cyril of Jerusalem, bishop and doctor of the Church.

+ John L. May
  Archbishop of Saint Louis
  President
  National Conference of Catholic Bishops

Daniel F. Hoye
General Secretary

FOREWORD

This edition of the *Rite of Christian Initiation of Adults* contains the approved English translation of the 1974 emended second printing of the *Ordo initiationis christianae adultorum* prepared by the International Commission on English in the Liturgy (ICEL) and a number of other rites and liturgical texts approved for use in the dioceses of the United States of America. An English translation of the *Praenotanda de initiatione christiana*, which was also included in the second Latin printing, is also included in this edition and is entitled *"Christian Initiation*, General Introduction." This document has its own self-contained enumeration of paragraphs, to which there are several cross-references in the *Rite of Christian Initiation of Adults*. The ICEL edition incorporates the emendations of the text necessitated by the Code of Canon Law of 1983 and issued by the Congregation for Divine Worship on 12 September 1983.

This final edition of the *Rite of Christian Initiation of Adults* replaces the interim or provisional translation issued by ICEL in 1974. In the United States, the provisional translation had been approved "ad interim" by the Executive Committee of the National Conference of Catholic Bishops and was confirmed by the Apostolic See on 23 September 1974 (Prot. N. 1993/74) and, in the same year, was published by authority of the Bishops' Committee on the Liturgy for use in the dioceses of the United States of America.

The main body of the text of the present edition begins with the Introduction proper to the *Rite of Christian Initiation of Adults*. In the interest of pastoral utility and convenience, the English edition somewhat rearranges the contents of the *praenotanda* of the Latin *editio typica*. The Introduction moves directly from the section entitled "Structure of the Initiation of Adults," which presents a general outline of the steps and periods of the process of Christian initiation, to the section entitled "Ministries and Offices." The paragraphs in the Latin typical edition (nos. 9–40) devoted to a detailed description of each of the steps and periods of the entire catechumenate have been integrated with the correlative paragraphs of the particular introductions to each of those steps and periods, so that all the relevant material is concentrated in its place of application. In the section entitled "Structure of the Initiation of Adults," cross-references are given to these particular introductions. This editorial re-arrangement omits nothing from the Latin original, but it does entail a departure from the paragraph enumeration of the Latin edition. For each paragraph of the English edition bearing the number proper to this edition, the right-hand margin carries the reference number or numbers indicating the corresponding paragraph or paragraphs of the Latin edition. A reference number in the right-hand margin that is preceded by a letter indicates a text from a source other than the *Ordo initiationis christianae adultorum;* numbers that are preceded by the letters "RM" refer to *The Roman Missal;* numbers that are preceded by the letters "PC" refer to *Pastoral Care of the Sick: Rites of Anointing and Viaticum;* numbers preceded by "R" refer to the appendix of the *Ordo initiationis,* "Rite of Reception of Baptized Christians into the Full Communion of the Catholic Church"; and numbers preceded by "P" refer to the *Rite of Penance.* Rites and texts prepared specifically for use in the dioceses of the United States of America are designated "USA" in the margin.

After the introduction to the *Rite of Christian Initiation of Adults,* the new English edition of this ritual presents the contents in two parts:

Part I, entitled "Christian Initiation of Adults," consists of the steps and periods that make up the full and paradigmatic form of Christian initiation, in accord with the restoration of the integral catechumenate decreed by the Second Vatican Council.

Part II, entitled "Rites for Particular Circumstances," consists of material for: the adaptation of the rite to unbaptized children of catechetical age; exceptional circumstances in which the process of Christian initiation is not followed in its complete form; situations in which those already baptized are either to be catechized and complete their Christian initiation or are to become part of the full communion of the Catholic Church.

In accord with the provisions laid down by the *Constitution on the Liturgy* (art. 63, b) and by the Introduction of the *Rite of Christian Initiation of Adults* (nos. 32–33; see also *Christian Initiation,* "General Introduction," nos. 30–33), the National Conference of Catholic Bishops approved a number of adaptations to the *Rite of Christian Initiation of Adults* over which it has discretionary power. Accordingly, the present US edition includes several editorial modifications of the ICEL edition (e.g., all references to the anointing with the oil of catechumens have been removed from *Step Three: Celebration of the Sacraments of Initiation,* since the National Conference of Catholic Bishops determined that in the dioceses of the United States this anointing is to be reserved for use in the period of the catechumenate and in the period of purification and enlightenment, and not be included in the preparation rites on Holy Saturday or in the celebration of initiation at the Easter Vigil or at another time.)

The present edition also contains a number of other rites approved specifically for use in the dioceses of the United States of America. A few of these rites have been incorporated into the ICEL edition as follows.

Part I, "First Step: Acceptance into the Order of Catechumens": inclusion of an optional "Presentation of a Cross"; and "Rite Belonging to the Period of the Catechumenate": inclusion of an optional parish rite, "Sending of the Catechumens for Election," for use when the rite of election is to be celebrated by the bishop at a regional or diocesan celebration.

Part II, "Christian Initiation of Children Who Have Reached Catechetical Age": inclusion of an optional "Rite of Election"; and "Preparation of Uncatechized Adults for Confirmation and Eucharist": inclusion of four (4) optional rites for baptized but previously uncatechized adults— "Welcoming the Candidates," "Sending the Candidates for Recognition by the Bishop," "Calling the Candidates to Continuing Conversion," "Penitential Rite" (Scrutiny).

Appendix I: "Additional (Combined) Rites" contains the "Celebration at the Easter Vigil of the Sacraments of Initiation and of the Rite of Reception into the Full Communion of the Catholic Church." This rite was prepared by ICEL at the request of the conferences of bishops for use in those situations when pastoral circumstances warrant the integration of the rite of reception with the sacraments of initiation in the same celebration of the Easter Vigil. In addition to this order, Appendix I contains three other "combined" rites which may be used in celebrations when both catechumens preparing for Christian initiation and baptized but previously uncatechized candidates preparing either for the sacraments of confirmation and/or eucharist or for reception into the full communion of the Catholic Church are present. All new liturgical rites and texts for this present edition are designated "USA" in the margin to indicate a variance from the ICEL edition.

Careful attention to the convenience of the minister has guided the format and presentation of each of the rites. An outline preceding each rite gives the minister a concise overview of the structure. The various options and alternatives provided within the rites are indicated simply and distinctly; introductory material, rubrics, and liturgical texts for each rite are typographically set off from each other. The full texts of the readings and psalms required for the liturgy of the word in celebrations are not printed out, since it is presumed that, in keeping with liturgical norms, they will be proclaimed from a Lectionary or Bible. Accordingly, either references to the *Lectionary for Mass* are given for the readings and psalms belonging to each celebration or a list of citations of suitable readings is given at the place of their occurrence in the particular rite.

This new edition of the *Rite of Christian Initiation of Adults* was approved for use in the dioceses of the United States of America by the National Conference of Catholic Bishops on 11 November 1986 and confirmed by the Apostolic See on 19 February 1988 (Prot. N. 1192/86).

Baptism is "the door to life and to the kingdom of God" (General Introduction, no. 3). May all those who have already been claimed for Christ draw others to the Lord and, through the rites and prayers of this ritual, forge greater bonds of unity in the Church.

+ Joseph P. Delaney
  Bishop of Fort Worth
  Chairman, Bishops' Committee on the Liturgy
  National Conference of Catholic Bishops

13 March 1988
Fourth Sunday of Lent

CONGREGATION FOR DIVINE WORSHIP

Prot. no. 15/72

DECREE

The Second Vatican Council prescribed the revision of the rite of baptism of adults and decreed that the catechumenate for adults, divided into several steps, should be restored. By this means the time of the catechumenate, which is intended as a period of well-suited instruction, would be sanctified by liturgical rites to be celebrated at successive intervals of time. The Council likewise decreed that both the solemn and simple rites of adult baptism should be revised, with proper attention to the restored catechumenate.

In observance of these decrees, the Congregation for Divine Worship prepared a new rite for the Christian initiation of adults, which Pope Paul VI has approved. The Congregation now publishes it and declares the present edition to be the *editio typica,* to replace the rite of baptism of adults now in the Roman Ritual. It likewise decrees that this new rite may be used in Latin at once and in the vernacular from the day appointed by the conference of bishops, after it has prepared a translation and had it confirmed by the Apostolic See.

All things to the contrary notwithstanding.

From the office of the Congregation for Divine Worship, 6 January 1972, Epiphany.

Arturo Cardinal Tabera
Prefect

A. Bugnini
Secretary

RITE OF CHRISTIAN INITIATION OF ADULTS

There is one Lord, one faith, one baptism, one God, the Father of all

INTRODUCTION

1. The rite of Christian initiation presented here is de-   1
signed for adults who, after hearing the mystery of Christ
proclaimed, consciously and freely seek the living God and
enter the way of faith and conversion as the Holy Spirit
opens their hearts. By God's help they will be strengthened
spiritually during their preparation and at the proper time
will receive the sacraments fruitfully.

2. This rite includes not simply the celebration of the sacra-   2
ments of baptism, confirmation, and eucharist, but also all
the rites belonging to the catechumenate. Endorsed by the
ancient practice of the Church, a catechumenate that would
be suited to contemporary missionary activity in all regions
was so widely requested that the Second Vatican Council
decreed its restoration, revision, and adaptation to local
traditions.[1]

3. So that the rite of initiation will be more useful for the   3
work of the Church and for individual, parochial, and missionary circumstances, the rite is first presented in Part I of
this book in its complete and usual form (nos. 36–251). This
is designed for the preparation of a group of candidates,
but by simple adaptation parish priests (pastors) can devise
a form suited to one person.

Part II provides rites for special circumstances: the Christian
initiation of children (nos. 252–330), a simple form of the
rite for adults to be carried out in exceptional circumstances
(nos. 331–369), and a short form of the rite for those in danger of death (nos. 370–399). Part II also includes guidelines
for preparing uncatechized adults for confirmation and eucharist (nos. 400–410) along with four (4) optional rites
which may be used with such candidates, and the rite of

---

[1]See Vatican Council II, Constitution on the Liturgy *Sacrosanctum Concilium*, art. 64–66; Decree on the Church's Missionary Activity *Ad gentes*, no. 14; Decree on the Pastoral Office of Bishops *Christus Dominus*, no. 14.

reception of baptized Christians into the full communion of the Catholic Church (nos. 473–504).

Rites for catechumens and baptized but previously uncatechized adults celebrated in combination, along with a rite combining the reception of baptized Christians into the full communion of the Catholic Church with the celebration of Christian initiation at the Easter Vigil (nos. 562–594), are contained in Appendix I. The two additional appendices contain acclamations, hymns, and songs, and the National Statutes for the Catechumenate in the Dioceses of the United States of America.

STRUCTURE OF THE INITIATION OF ADULTS

4. The initiation of catechumens is a gradual process that takes place within the community of the faithful. By joining the catechumens in reflecting on the value of the paschal mystery and by renewing their own conversion, the faithful provide an example that will help the catechumens to obey the Holy Spirit more generously. 4

5. The rite of initiation is suited to a spiritual journey of adults that varies according to the many forms of God's grace, the free cooperation of the individuals, the action of the Church, and the circumstances of time and place. 5

6. This journey includes not only the periods for making inquiry and for maturing (see no. 7), but also the steps marking the catechumens' progress, as they pass, so to speak, through another doorway or ascend to the next level. 6

1. The first step: reaching the point of initial conversion and wishing to become Christians, they are accepted as catechumens by the Church.

2. The second step: having progressed in faith and nearly completed the catechumenate, they are accepted into a more intense preparation for the sacraments of initiation.

3. The third step: having completed their spiritual preparation, they receive the sacraments of Christian initiation.

These three steps are to be regarded as the major, more intense moments of initiation and are marked by three liturgical rites: the first by the rite of acceptance into the order of catechumens (nos. 41–74); the second by the rite of election or enrollment of names (nos. 118–137); and the third by the celebration of the sacraments of Christian initiation (nos. 206–243).

7. The steps lead to periods of inquiry and growth; alterna- 7
tively the periods may also be seen as preparing for the en-
suing step.

   1. The first period consists of inquiry on the part of the candidates and of evangelization and the precatechu-menate on the part of the Church. It ends with the rite of acceptance into the order of catechumens.
   2. The second period, which begins with the rite of ac-ceptance into the order of catechumens and may last for several years, includes catechesis and the rites connected with catechesis. It comes to an end on the day of election.
   3. The third and much shorter period, which follows the rite of election, ordinarily coincides with the Lenten prepara-tion for the Easter celebration and the sacraments of initia-tion. It is a time of purification and enlightenment and in-cludes the celebration of the rites belonging to this period.
   4. The final period extends through the whole Easter season and is devoted to the postbaptismal catechesis or mystagogy. It is a time for deepening the Christian experi-ence, for spiritual growth, and for entering more fully into the life and unity of the community.

Thus there are four continuous periods: the precatechu-menate, the period for hearing the first preaching of the Gospel (nos. 36–40); the period of the catechumenate, set aside for a thorough catechesis and for the rites belonging to this period (nos. 75–117); the period of purification and enlightenment (Lenten preparation), designed for a more in-tense spiritual preparation, which is assisted by the celebra-tion of the scrutinies and presentations (nos. 138–205); and the period of postbaptismal catechesis or mystagogy, marked by the new experience of sacraments and commu-nity (nos. 244–251).

8. The whole initiation must bear a markedly paschal char- 8
acter, since the initiation of Christians is the first sacra-mental sharing in Christ's dying and rising and since, in addition, the period of purification and enlightenment ordi-

narily coincides with Lent[2] and the period of postbaptismal catechesis or mystagogy with the Easter season. All the resources of Lent should be brought to bear as a more intense preparation of the elect and the Easter Vigil should be regarded as the proper time for the sacraments of initiation. Because of pastoral needs, however, the sacraments of initiation may be celebrated at other times (see nos. 26–30).

MINISTRIES AND OFFICES

9. In light of what is said in *Christian Initiation*, General Introduction (no. 7), the people of God, as represented by the local Church, should understand and show by their concern that the initiation of adults is the responsibility of all the baptized.[3] Therefore the community must always be fully prepared in the pursuit of its apostolic vocation to give help to those who are searching for Christ. In the various circumstances of daily life, even as in the apostolate, all the followers of Christ have the obligation of spreading the faith according to their abilities.[4] Hence, the entire community must help the candidates and the catechumens throughout the process of initiation: during the period of the precatechumenate, the period of the catechumenate, the period of purification and enlightenment, and the period of postbaptismal catechesis or mystagogy. In particular:

1. During the period of evangelization and precatechumenate, the faithful should remember that for the Church and its members the supreme purpose of the apostolate is that Christ's message is made known to the world by word and deed and that his grace is communicated.[5] They should therefore show themselves ready to give the candidates evidence of the spirit of the Christian community and to welcome them into their homes, into personal conversation, and into community gatherings.

2. At the celebrations belonging to the period of the catechumenate, the faithful should seek to be present when-

[2]See Vatican Council II, Constitution on the Liturgy *Sacrosanctum Concilium*, art. 109.
[3]See Vatican Council II, Decree on the Church's Missionary Activity *Ad gentes*, no. 14.
[4]See Vatican Council II, Dogmatic Constitution on the Church *Lumen gentium*, no. 17.
[5]See Vatican Council II, Decree on the Apostolate of the Laity *Apostolicam actuositatem*, no. 6.

ever possible and should take an active part in the responses, prayers, singing, and acclamations.

3. On the day of election, because it is a day of growth for the community, the faithful, when called upon, should be sure to give honest and carefully considered testimony about the catechumens.

4. During Lent, the period of purification and enlightenment, the faithful should take care to participate in the rites of the scrutinies and presentations and give the elect the example of their own renewal in the spirit of penance, faith, and charity. At the Easter Vigil, they should attach great importance to renewing their own baptismal promises.

5. During the period immediately after baptism, the faithful should take part in the Masses for neophytes, that is, the Sunday Masses of the Easter season (see no. 25), welcome the neophytes with open arms in charity, and help them to feel more at home in the community of the baptized.

10. A sponsor accompanies any candidate seeking admission as a catechumen. Sponsors are persons who have known and assisted the candidates and stand as witnesses to the candidates' moral character, faith, and intention. It may happen that it is not the sponsor for the rite of acceptance and the period of the catechumenate but another person who serves as godparent for the periods of purification and enlightenment and of mystagogy.

11. Their godparents (for each a godmother or godfather, or both) accompany the candidates on the day of election, at the celebration of the sacraments of initiation, and during the period of mystagogy.[6] Godparents are persons chosen by the candidates on the basis of example, good qualities, and friendship, delegated by the local Christian community, and approved by the priest. It is the responsibility of godparents to show the candidates how to practice the Gospel in personal and social life, to sustain the candidates in moments of hesitancy and anxiety, to bear witness, and to guide the candidates' progress in the baptismal life. Chosen before the candidates' election, godparents fulfill this office publicly from the day of the rite of election, when they give testimony to the community about the candidates. They

[6]See *Christian Initiation*, General Introduction, nos. 8 and 10,1.

continue to be important during the time after reception of the sacraments when the neophytes need to be assisted so that they remain true to their baptismal promises.

12. The bishop,[7] in person or through his delegate, sets   44
up, regulates, and promotes the program of pastoral formation for catechumens and admits the candidates to their election and to the sacraments. It is hoped that, presiding if possible at the Lenten liturgy, he will himself celebrate the rite of election and, at the Easter Vigil, the sacraments of initiation, at least for the initiation of those who are fourteen years old or older. Finally, when pastoral care requires, the bishop should depute catechists, truly worthy and properly prepared, to celebrate the minor exorcisms (nos. 90–94) and the blessings of the catechumens (nos. 95–97).

13. Priests, in addition to their usual ministry for any cele-   45
bration of baptism, confirmation, and the eucharist,[8] have the responsibility of attending to the pastoral and personal care of the catechumens,[9] especially those who seem hesitant and discouraged. With the help of deacons and catechists, they are to provide instruction for the catechumens; they are also to approve the choice of godparents and willingly listen to and help them; they are to be diligent in the correct celebration and adaptation of the rites throughout the entire course of Christian initiation (see no. 35).

14. The priest who baptizes an adult or a child of   46
catechetical age should, when the bishop is absent, also confer confirmation,[10] unless this sacrament is to be given at another time (see no. 24). When there are a large number of candidates to be confirmed, the minister of confirmation may associate priests with himself to administer the sacrament. It is preferable that the priests who are so invited:

1. either have a particular function or office in the diocese, being, namely, either vicars general, episcopal vicars, or district or regional vicars;

2. or be the pastors of the places where confirmation is conferred, pastors of the places where the candidates be-

---

[7]See ibid., no. 12.
[8]See ibid., nos. 13–15.
[9]See Vatican Council II, Decree on the Ministry and Life of Priests
Presbyterorum Ordinis, no. 6.
[10]See *Rite of Confirmation*, Introduction, no. 7,b.

long, or priests who have had a special part in the catechetical preparation of the candidates.[11]

15. Deacons should be ready to assist in the ministry to catechumens. Conferences of bishops that have decided in favor of the permanent diaconate should ensure that the number and distribution of permanent deacons are adequate for the carrying out of the steps, periods, and formation programs of the catechumenate wherever pastoral needs require.[12]

47

16. Catechists, who have an important office for the progress of the catechumens and for the growth of the community, should, whenever possible, have an active part in the rites. When deputed by the bishop (see no. 12), they may perform the minor exorcisms and blessings contained in the ritual.[13] When they are teaching, catechists should see that their instruction is filled with the spirit of the Gospel, adapted to the liturgical signs and the cycle of the Church's year, suited to the needs of the catechumens, and as far as possible enriched by local traditions.

48

TIME AND PLACE OF INITIATION

17. As a general rule, pastors should make use of the rite of initiation in such a way that the sacraments themselves are celebrated at the Easter Vigil and the rite of election takes place on the First Sunday of Lent. The rest of the rites are spaced on the basis of the structure and arrangement of the catechumenate as described previously (nos. 6–8). For pastoral needs of a more serious nature, however, it is lawful to arrange the schedule for the entire rite of initiation differently, as will be detailed later (nos. 26–30).

49

PROPER OR USUAL TIMES

18. The following should be noted about the time of celebrating the rite of acceptance into the order of catechumens (nos. 41–74).

50

[11]See ibid., no. 8.
[12]See Vatican Council II, Dogmatic Constitution on the Church *Lumen gentium*, no. 26; Decree on the Church's Missionary Activity *Ad gentes*, no. 16.
[13]See Vatican Council II, Constitution on the Liturgy *Sacrosanctum Concilium*, art. 79.

1. It should not be too early, but should be delayed until the candidates, according to their own dispositions and situation, have had sufficient time to conceive an initial faith and to show the first signs of conversion (see no. 42).

2. In places where the number of candidates is smaller than usual, the rite of acceptance should be delayed until a group is formed that is sufficiently large for catechesis and the liturgical rites.

3. Two dates in the year, or three if necessary, are to be fixed as the usual times for carrying out this rite.

19. The rite of election or enrollment of names (nos. 118–137) should as a rule be celebrated on the First Sunday of Lent. As circumstances suggest or require, it may be anticipated somewhat or even celebrated on a weekday.   51

20. The scrutinies (nos. 150–156, 164–177) should take place on the Third, Fourth, and Fifth Sundays of Lent, or, if necessary, on the other Sundays of Lent, or even on convenient weekdays. Three scrutinies should be celebrated. The bishop may dispense from one of them for serious reasons or, in extraordinary circumstances, even from two (see nos. 34.3; 331). When, for lack of time, the election is held early, the first scrutiny is also to be held early; but in this case care is to be taken not to prolong the period of purification and enlightenment beyond eight weeks.   52

21. By ancient usage, the presentations, since they take place after the scrutinies, are part of the same period of purification and enlightenment. They are celebrated during the week. The presentation of the Creed to the catechumens (nos. 157–163) takes place during the week after the first scrutiny; the presentation of the Lord's Prayer (nos. 178–184) during the week after the third scrutiny. For pastoral reasons, however, to enrich the liturgy in the period of the catechumenate, each presentation may be transferred and celebrated during the period of the catechumenate as a kind of "rite of passage" (see nos. 79, 104–105).   53

22. On Holy Saturday, when the elect refrain from work and spend their time in recollection, the various preparation rites may be celebrated: the recitation or "return" of the Creed by the elect, the ephphetha rite, and the choosing of a Christian name (nos. 185–205).   54

23. The celebration of the sacraments of Christian initiation [55] (nos. 206–243) should take place at the Easter Vigil itself (see nos. 8, 17). But if there are a great many catechumens, the sacraments are given to the majority that night and reception of the sacraments by the rest may be transferred to days within the Easter octave, whether at the principal church or at a mission station. In this case either the Mass of the day or one of the ritual Masses "Christian Initiation: Baptism" may be used and the readings are chosen from those of the Easter Vigil.

24. In certain cases when there is serious reason, confirmation may be postponed until near the end of the period of postbaptismal catechesis, for example, Pentecost Sunday (see no. 249). [56]

25. On all the Sundays of the Easter season after Easter Sunday, the so-called Masses for neophytes are to be scheduled. The entire community and the newly baptized with their godparents should be encouraged to participate (see nos. 247–248). [57]

OUTSIDE THE USUAL TIMES

26. The entire rite of Christian initiation is normally arranged so that the sacraments will be celebrated during the Easter Vigil. Because of unusual circumstances and pastoral needs, however, the rite of election and the rites belonging to the period of purification and enlightenment may be held outside Lent and the sacraments of initiation may be celebrated at a time other than the Easter Vigil or Easter Sunday. [58]

Even when the usual time has otherwise been observed, it is permissible, but only for serious pastoral needs (for example, if there are a great many people to be baptized), to choose a day other than the Easter Vigil or Easter Sunday, but preferably one during the Easter season, to celebrate the sacraments of initiation; the program of initiation during Lent, however, must be maintained.

When the time is changed in either way, even though the rite of Christian initiation occurs at a different point in the liturgical year, the structure of the entire rite, with its properly spaced intervals, remains the same. But the following adjustments are made.

27. As far as possible, the sacraments of initiation are to be 59 celebrated on a Sunday, using, as occasion suggests, the Sunday Mass or one of the ritual Masses "Christian Initiation: Baptism" (see nos. 23, 208).

28. The rite of acceptance into the order of catechumens is 60 to take place when the time is right (see no. 18).

29. The rite of election is to be celebrated about six weeks 61 before the sacraments of initiation, so that there is sufficient time for the scrutinies and the presentations. Care should be taken not to schedule the celebration of the rite of election on a solemnity of the liturgical year.

30. The scrutinies should not be celebrated on solemnities, 62 but on Sundays or even on weekdays, with the usual intervals.

PLACE OF CELEBRATION

31. The rites should be celebrated in the places appropriate 63 to them as indicated in the ritual. Consideration should be given to special needs that arise in secondary stations of mission territories.

ADAPTATIONS BY THE CONFERENCES OF BISHOPS IN THE USE OF THE ROMAN RITUAL

32. In addition to the adaptations envisioned in *Christian* 64 *Initiation*, General Introduction (nos. 30–33), the rite of Christian initiation of adults allows for other adaptations that will be decided by the conference of bishops.

33. Each conference of bishops has discretionary power to 65 make the following decisions:

   1. to establish for the precatechumenate, where it seems advisable, some way of receiving inquirers who are interested in the catechumenate (see no. 39);

   2. to insert into the rite of acceptance into the order of catechumens a first exorcism and a renunciation of false worship, in regions where paganism is widespread (see nos. 69–72) [The National Conference of Catholic Bishops has approved leaving to the discretion of the diocesan bishop this inclusion of a first exorcism and a renunciation of

false worship in the rite of acceptance into the order of catechumens];

3. to decide that in the same rite the tracing of the sign of the cross upon the forehead (nos. 54–55) be replaced by making that sign in front of the forehead, in regions where the act of touching may not seem proper [The National Conference of Catholic Bishops has established as the norm in the dioceses of the United States the tracing of the cross on the forehead. It leaves to the discretion of the diocesan bishop the substitution of making the sign of the cross in front of the forehead for those persons in whose culture the act of touching may not seem proper];

4. to decide that in the same rite candidates receive a new name in regions where it is the practice of non-Christian religions to give a new name to initiates immediately (no. 73) [The National Conference of Catholic Bishops establishes as the norm in the dioceses of the United States that there is to be no giving of a new name. It also approves leaving to the discretion of the diocesan bishop the giving of a new name to persons from those cultures in which it is the practice of non-Christian religions to give a new name];

5. to allow within the same rite, according to local customs, additional rites that symbolize reception into the community (no. 74) [The National Conference of Catholic Bishops has approved the inclusion of an optional presentation of a cross (no. 74) while leaving to the discretion of the diocesan bishop the inclusion of additional rites that symbolize reception into the community];

6. to establish during the period of the catechumenate, in addition to the usual rites (nos. 81–97), "rites of passage": for example, early celebration of the presentations (nos. 157–163, 178–184), the ephphetha rite, the catechumens' recitation of the Creed, or even an anointing of the catechumens (nos. 98–103) [The National Conference of Catholic Bishops approves the use of the anointing with the oil of catechumens during the period of the catechumenate as a kind of "rite of passage" (cf. no. 33.7). In addition it approves, when appropriate in the circumstances, the early celebration of the presentations (nos. 157–163, 178–184), the ephphetha rite (nos. 197–199), and the catechumens' recitation of the Creed (nos. 193–196)];

7. to decide on the omission of the anointing with the oil of catechumens or its transferral to the preparation rites

for Holy Saturday or its use during the period of the catechumenate as a kind of "rite of passage" (nos. 98–103) [The National Conference of Catholic Bishops approves the omission of the anointing with the oil of catechumens both in the celebration of baptism and in the optional preparation rites for Holy Saturday. Thus, anointing with the oil of catechumens is reserved for use in the period of the catechumenate and in the period of purification and enlightenment and is not to be included in the preparation rites on Holy Saturday or in the celebration of initiation at the Easter Vigil or at another time];

8. to make more specific and detailed the formularies of renunciation for the rite of acceptance into the order of catechumens (nos. 70–72) and for the celebration of baptism (no. 224) [The National Conference of Catholic Bishops has established as the norm in the dioceses of the United States that the formularies of renunciation should not be adapted. But for those cases where certain catechumens may be from cultures in which false worship is widespread it has approved leaving to the discretion of the diocesan bishop this matter of making more specific and detailed the formularies of renunciation in the rite of acceptance into the order of catechumens and in the celebration of baptism].

ADAPTATIONS BY THE BISHOP

34. It pertains to the bishop for his own diocese: 66

1. to set up the formation program of the catechumenate and to lay down norms according to local needs (see no. 12);

2. to decide whether and when, as circumstances warrant, the entire rite of Christian initiation may be celebrated outside the usual times (see no. 26);

3. to dispense, on the basis of some serious obstacle, from one scrutiny or, in extraordinary circumstances, even from two (see no. 331);

4. to permit the simple rite to be used in whole or in part (see no. 331);

5. to depute catechists, truly worthy and properly prepared, to give the exorcisms and blessings (see nos. 12, 16);

6. to preside at the rite of election and to ratify, personally or through a delegate, the admission of the elect (see no. 12);

7. in keeping with the provisions of law,[14] to stipulate the requisite age for sponsors (see *Christian Initiation,* General Introduction, no. 10.2).

ADAPTATIONS BY THE MINISTER

35. Celebrants should make full and intelligent use of the freedom given to them either in *Christian Initiation,* General Introduction (no. 34) or in the rubrics of the rite itself. In many places the manner of acting or praying is intentionally left undetermined or two alternatives are offered, so that ministers, according to their prudent pastoral judgment, may accommodate the rite to the circumstances of the candidates and others who are present. In all the rites the greatest freedom is left in the invitations and instructions, and the intercessions may always be shortened, changed, or even expanded with new intentions, in order to fit the circumstances or special situation of the candidates (for example, a sad or joyful event occurring in a family) or of the others present (for example, sorrow or joy common to the parish or civic community).

The minister will also adapt the texts by changing the gender and number as required.

[14]See *Codex Iuris Canonici,* can. 874, §1, 2°.

PART I

CHRISTIAN INITIATION OF ADULTS

Our Savior Jesus Christ has done away with death and brought us life through his Gospel

OUTLINE FOR CHRISTIAN INITIATION OF ADULTS

PERIOD OF EVANGELIZATION AND PRECATECHUMENATE

This is a time, of no fixed duration or structure, for inquiry and introduction to Gospel values, an opportunity for the beginnings of faith.

FIRST STEP: ACCEPTANCE INTO THE ORDER OF CATECHUMENS

This is the liturgical rite, usually celebrated on some annual date or dates, marking the beginning of the catechumenate proper, as the candidates express and the Church accepts their intention to respond to God's call to follow the way of Christ.

PERIOD OF THE CATECHUMENATE

This is the time, in duration corresponding to the progress of the individual, for the nurturing and growth of the catechumens' faith and conversion to God; celebrations of the word and prayers of exorcism and blessing are meant to assist the process.

SECOND STEP: ELECTION OR ENROLLMENT OF NAMES

This is the liturgical rite, usually celebrated on the First Sunday of Lent, by which the Church formally ratifies the catechumens' readiness for the sacraments of initiation and the catechumens, now the elect, express the will to receive these sacraments.

PERIOD OF PURIFICATION AND ENLIGHTENMENT

This is the time immediately preceding the elects' initiation, usually the Lenten season preceding the celebration of this initiation at the Easter Vigil; it is a time of reflection, intensely centered on conversion, marked by celebration of the scrutinies and presentations and of the preparation rites on Holy Saturday.

THIRD STEP: CELEBRATION OF THE SACRAMENTS OF INITIATION

This is the liturgical rite, usually integrated into the Easter Vigil, by which the elect are initiated through baptism, confirmation, and the eucharist.

PERIOD OF POSTBAPTISMAL CATECHESIS OR MYSTAGOGY

This is the time, usually the Easter season, following the celebration of initiation, during which the newly initiated experience being fully a part of the Christian community by means of pertinent catechesis and particularly by participation with all the faithful in the Sunday eucharistic celebration.

PERIOD OF EVANGELIZATION AND PRECATECHUMENATE

I, the light, have come into the world, so that whoever believes in me need not remain in the dark any more

36. Although the rite of initiation begins with admission to the catechumenate, the preceding period or precatechumenate is of great importance and as a rule should not be omitted. It is a time of evangelization: faithfully and constantly the living God is proclaimed and Jesus Christ whom he has sent for the salvation of all. Thus those who are not yet Christians, their hearts opened by the Holy Spirit, may believe and be freely converted to the Lord and commit themselves sincerely to him. For he who is the way, the truth, and the life fulfills all their spiritual expectations, indeed infinitely surpasses them.[1]

37. From evangelization, completed with the help of God, come the faith and initial conversion that cause a person to feel called away from sin and drawn into the mystery of God's love. The whole period of the precatechumenate is set aside for this evangelization, so that the genuine will to follow Christ and seek baptism may mature.

38. During this period, priests and deacons, catechists and other laypersons are to give the candidates a suitable explanation of the Gospel (see no. 42). The candidates are to receive help and attention so that with a purified and clearer intention they may cooperate with God's grace. Opportunities should be provided for them to meet families and other groups of Christians.

39. It belongs to the conference of bishops to provide for the evangelization proper to this period. The conference may also provide, if circumstances suggest and in keeping with local custom, a preliminary manner of receiving those interested in the precatechumenate, that is, those inquirers who, even though they do not fully believe, show some leaning toward the Christian faith (and who may be called "sympathizers").

[1]See Vatican Council II, Decree on the Church's Missionary Activity *Ad gentes*, no. 13.

1. Such a reception, if it takes place, will be carried out without any ritual celebration; it is the expression not yet of faith, but of a right intention.

2. The reception will be adapted to local conditions and to the pastoral situation. Some candidates may need to see evidence of the spirit of Christians that they are striving to understand and experience. For others, however, whose catechumenate will be delayed for one reason or another, some initial act of the candidates or the community that expresses their reception may be appropriate.

3. The reception will be held at a meeting or gathering of the local community, on an occasion that will permit friendly conversation. An inquirer or "sympathizer" is introduced by a friend and then welcomed and received by the priest or some other representative member of the community.

40. During the precatechumenate period, parish priests (pastors) should help those taking part in it with prayers suited to them, for example, by celebrating for their spiritual well-being the prayers of exorcism and the blessings given in the ritual (nos. 94, 97).

13
111
120

FIRST STEP: ACCEPTANCE INTO THE ORDER OF CATECHUMENS

Lord, let your mercy be on us, as we place our trust in you

41. The rite that is called the rite of acceptance into the order of catechumens is of the utmost importance. Assembling publicly for the first time, the candidates who have completed the period of the precatechumenate declare their intention to the Church and the Church in turn, carrying out its apostolic mission, accepts them as persons who intend to become its members. God showers his grace on the candidates, since the celebration manifests their desire publicly and marks their reception and first consecration by the Church. [14] [15] [68]

42. The prerequisite for making this first step is that the beginnings of the spiritual life and the fundamentals of Christian teaching have taken root in the candidates.[1] Thus there must be evidence of the first faith that was conceived during the period of evangelization and precatechumenate and of an initial conversion and intention to change their lives and to enter into a relationship with God in Christ. Consequently, there must also be evidence of the first stirrings of repentance, a start to the practice of calling upon God in prayer, a sense of the Church, and some experience of the company and spirit of Christians through contact with a priest or with members of the community. The candidates should also be instructed about the celebration of the liturgical rite of acceptance. [15] [68]

43. Before the rite is celebrated, therefore, sufficient and necessary time, as required in each case, should be setaside to evaluate and, if necessary, to purify the candidates' motives and dispositions. With the help of the sponsors (see no. 10), catechists and deacons, pastors have the responsibility for judging the outward indications of such dispositions.[2] Because of the effect of baptism once validly received (see *Christian Initiation*, General Introduction, no. 4), it is the duty of pastors to see to it that no baptized person [16] [69]

---

[1] See Vatican Council II, Decree on the Church's Missionary Activity *Ad gentes*, no. 14.
[2] See ibid., no. 13.

seeks for any reason whatever to be baptized a second time.

44. The rite will take place on specified days during the year (see no. 18) that are suited to local conditions. The rite consists in the reception of the candidates, the celebration of the word of God, and the dismissal of the candidates; celebration of the eucharist may follow.

By decision of the conference of bishops, the following may be incorporated into this rite: a first exorcism and renunciation of false worship (nos. 70–72), the giving of a new name (no. 73), and additional rites signifying reception into the community (no. 74). [See no. 33 for the decisions made by the National Conference of Catholic Bishops regarding these matters.]

45. It is desirable that the entire Christian community or some part of it, consisting of friends and acquaintances, catechists and priests, take an active part in the celebration. The presiding celebrant is a priest or a deacon. The sponsors should also attend in order to present to the Church the candidates they have brought.

46. After the celebration of the rite of acceptance, the names of catechumens are to be duly inscribed in the register of the catechumens, along with the names of the sponsors and the minister and the date and place of the celebration.

47. From this time on the Church embraces the catechumens as its own with a mother's love and concern. Joined to the Church, the catechumens are now part of the household of Christ,[3] since the Church nourishes them with the word of God and sustains them by means of liturgical celebrations. The catechumens should be eager, then, to take part in celebrations of the word of God and to receive blessings and other sacramentals. When two catechumens marry or when a catechumen marries an unbaptized person, the appropriate rite is to be used.[4] One who dies during the catechumenate receives a Christian burial.

[3]See Vatican Council II, Dogmatic Constitution on the Church *Lumen gentium*, no. 14; Decree on the Church's Missionary Activity *Ad gentes*, no. 14.
[4] See *Rite of Marriage*, nos. 55–66.

RITE OF ACCEPTANCE INTO THE ORDER OF CATECHUMENS

RECEIVING THE CANDIDATES

48. The candidates, their sponsors, and a group of the 73
faithful gather outside the church (or inside at the entrance
or elsewhere) or at some other site suitable for this rite. As
the priest or deacon, wearing an alb or surplice, a stole,
and, if desired, a cope of festive color, goes to meet them,
the assembly of the faithful may sing a psalm or an appropriate song.

GREETING

49. The celebrant greets the candidates in a friendly man- 74
ner. He speaks to them, their sponsors, and all present,
pointing out the joy and happiness of the Church. He may
also recall for the sponsors and friends the particular experience and religious response by which the candidates, following their own spiritual path, have come to this first
step.

Then he invites the sponsors and candidates to come forward. As they are taking their places before the celebrant,
an appropriate song may be sung, for example, Psalm 63:1–
8.

OPENING DIALOGUE

50. Unless the candidates are already known to all present, 75
the celebrant asks for or calls out their given names. The
candidates answer one by one, even if, because of a large
number, the question is asked only once. One of the following or something similar may be used.

A The celebrant asks:
What is your name?

Candidate:
N.

B The celebrant calls out the name of each candidate.

The candidate answers:
Present.

The celebrant continues with the following questions for the individual candidates or, when there are a large number, for the candidates to answer as a group. The celebrant may use other words than those provided in asking the candidates about their intentions and may let them answer in their own words: for example, to the first question, "What do you ask of the Church of God?" or "What do you desire?" or "For what reason have you come?", he may receive such answers as "The grace of Christ" or "Entrance into the Church" or "Eternal life" or other suitable responses. The celebrant then phrases his next question according to the answer received.

Celebrant:
What do you ask of God's Church?

Candidate:
Faith.

Celebrant:
What does faith offer you?

Candidate:
Eternal life.

---

51. By decision of the diocesan bishop, the candidates' first   USA
acceptance of the Gospel (no. 52) may be replaced by the
rite of exorcism and renunciation of false worship (nos. 70–
72) (see no. 33.2).

CANDIDATES' FIRST ACCEPTANCE OF THE GOSPEL

52. The celebrant addresses the candidates, adapting one   76
of the following formularies or similar words to the answers
received in the opening dialogue.

A
God gives light to everyone who comes into this   76
world; though unseen, he reveals himself through the
works of his hand, so that all people may learn to
give thanks to their Creator.

You have followed God's light and the way of the
Gospel now lies open before you. Set your feet
firmly on that path and acknowledge the living God,
who truly speaks to everyone. Walk in the light of

Christ and learn to trust in his wisdom. Commit your lives daily to his care, so that you may come to believe in him with all your heart.

This is the way of faith along which Christ will lead you in love toward eternal life. Are you prepared to begin this journey today under the guidance of Christ?

Candidates:
I am.

B

God is our Creator and in him all living things have their existence. He enlightens our minds, so that we may come to know and worship him. He has sent his faithful witness, Jesus Christ, to announce to us what he has seen and heard, the mysteries of heaven and earth.   370:1

Since you acknowledge with joy that Christ has come, now is the time to hear his word, so that you may possess eternal life by beginning, in our company, to know God and to love your neighbor. Are you ready, with the help of God, to live this life?

Candidates:
I am.

C

This is eternal life: to know the one true God and Jesus Christ, whom he has sent. Christ has been raised from the dead and appointed by God as the Lord of life and ruler of all things, seen and unseen.   370:2

If, then, you wish to become his disciples and members of his Church, you must be guided to the fullness of the truth that he has revealed to us. You must learn to make the mind of Christ Jesus your own. You must strive to pattern your life on the teachings of the Gospel and so to love the Lord your God and your neighbor. For this was Christ's command and he was its perfect example.

Is each of you ready to accept these teachings of the Gospel?

Candidates:
I am.

AFFIRMATION BY THE SPONSORS AND THE ASSEMBLY

53. Then the celebrant turns to the sponsors and the assembly and asks them in these or similar words.

77
81

Sponsors, you now present these candidates to us; are you, and all who are gathered here with us, ready to help these candidates find and follow Christ?

All:
We are.

With hands joined, the celebrant says:
Father of mercy,
we thank you for these your servants.
You have sought and summoned them in many ways and they have turned to seek you.

82

You have called them today
and they have answered in our presence:
we praise you, Lord, and we bless you.

All sing or say:
We praise you, Lord, and we bless you.

SIGNING OF THE CANDIDATES WITH THE CROSS

54. Next the cross is traced on the forehead of the candidates (or, at the discretion of the diocesan bishop, in front of the forehead for candidates in whose culture the act of touching may not seem proper—see no. 33.3); at the discretion of the celebrant the signing of one, several, or all of the senses may follow. The celebrant alone says the formularies accompanying each signing.

83
85

SIGNING OF THE FOREHEAD

55. One of the following options is used, depending on the number of candidates.

A

If there are only a few candidates, the celebrant invites
them and their sponsors in these or similar words.   83

**Come forward now with your sponsors to receive the
sign of your new way of life as catechumens.**

With their sponsors, the candidates come one by one to the
celebrant; with his thumb he traces a cross on the forehead;
then, if there is to be no signing of the senses, the sponsor
does the same. The celebrant says:
**N., receive the cross on your forehead.
It is Christ himself who now strengthens you
with this sign of his love.
Learn to know him and follow him.**

All sing or say the following or another suitable acclamation.   86
Glory and praise to you, Lord Jesus Christ!

B

If there are a great many candidates, the celebrant speaks   84
to them in these or similar words.*

**Dear candidates, your answers mean that you wish to
share our life and hope in Christ. To admit you as
catechumens I now mark you with the sign of
Christ's cross and call upon your catechists and sponsors to do the same. The whole community welcomes
you with love and stands ready to help you.**

Then the celebrant makes the sign of the cross over all together, as a cross is traced by a sponsor or catechist on the
forehead of each candidate. The celebrant says:
**Receive the cross on your forehead.
It is Christ himself who now strengthens you
with this sign of his love.**
Learn to know him and follow him.

*In those exceptional cases when, at the discretion of the diocesan bishop,
a renunciation of false worship (no. 72) has been included in the rite of
acceptance: "Dear candidates, your answers mean that you have rejected
false worship and wish to share our life and hope in Christ. . . ."
**In those exceptional cases when, at the discretion of the diocesan bishop,
there has been a renunciation of false worship: "with this sign of his victory."
                                                            86

All sing or say the following or another suitable acclamation.
Glory and praise to you, Lord Jesus Christ!

SIGNING OF THE OTHER SENSES

56. The signing is carried out by the catechists or the sponsors. (If required by special circumstances, this may be done by assisting priests or deacons.) The signing of each sense may be followed by an acclamation in praise of Christ, for example, "**Glory and praise to you, Lord Jesus Christ!**" 85 86

While the ears are being signed, the celebrant says:
Receive the sign of the cross on your ears,
that you may hear the voice of the Lord.

While the eyes are being signed:
Receive the sign of the cross on your eyes,
that you may see the glory of God.

While the lips are being signed:
Receive the sign of the cross on your lips,
That you may respond to the word of God.

While the breast is being signed:
Receive the sign of the cross over your heart,
that Christ may dwell there by faith.

While the shoulders are being signed:
Receive the sign of the cross on your shoulders,
that you may bear the gentle yoke of Christ.

[While the hands are being signed: USA
Receive the sign of the cross on your hands,
that Christ may be known in the work which you do.

While the feet are being signed: USA
Receive the sign of the cross on your feet,
that you may walk in the way of Christ.]

Without touching them, the celebrant alone makes the sign of the cross over all the candidates at once (or, if they are few, over each individually), saying:
I sign you with the sign of eternal life
in the name of the Father, and of the Son, ✠
and of the Holy Spirit.

Catechumens:
Amen.

CONCLUDING PRAYER

57. The celebrant concludes the signing of the forehead   87
(and senses) with one of the following prayers.

Let us pray.

A
Lord,   87
we have signed these catechumens
with the sign of Christ's cross.

Protect them by its power,
so that, faithful to the grace which has begun in
   them,
they may keep your commandments
and come to the glory of rebirth in baptism.

We ask this through Christ our Lord.
R̸. Amen.

B
Almighty God,   87
by the cross and resurrection of your Son
you have given life to your people.

Your servants have received the sign of the cross:
make them living proof of its saving power
and help them to persevere in the footsteps of Christ.

We ask this through Christ our Lord.
R̸. Amen.

58. At the discretion of the diocesan bishop, the giving of   USA
a new name (no. 73) may take place at this time.

59. At the discretion of the diocesan bishop, the invitation   USA
to the celebration of the word of God may be preceded or
followed by additional rites signifying reception into the
community, for example, the presentation of a cross (no.
74) or some other symbolic act.

INVITATION TO THE CELEBRATION OF THE WORD OF GOD

60. The célebrant next invites the catechumens and their sponsors to enter the church (or the place where the liturgy of the word will be celebrated). He uses the following or similar words, accompanying them with some gesture of invitation. **90**

**N. and N., come into the church,
to share with us at the table of God's word.**

During the entry an appropriate song is sung or the following antiphon with Psalm 34:2, 3, 6, 9, 10, 11, 16.
**Come, my children, and listen to me;
I will teach you the fear of the Lord.**

LITURGY OF THE WORD

INSTRUCTION

61. After the catechumens have reached their places, the celebrant speaks to them briefly, helping them to understand the dignity of God's word, which is proclaimed and heard in the church. **91**

The Lectionary for Mass or the Bible is carried in procession and placed with honor on the lectern, where it may be incensed.

Celebration of the liturgy of the word follows.

READINGS

62. The readings may be chosen from any of the readings in the Lectionary for Mass that are suited to the new catechumens or the following may be used. **92
372**

FIRST READING

Genesis 12:1–4a—*Leave your country, and come into the land I will show you.*

RESPONSORIAL PSALM

Psalm 33:4–5, 12–13, 18–19, 20 and 22
℟. **(v.12b) Happy the people the Lord has chosen to be his own.**

Or:

℞. (v.22) Lord, let your mercy be on us, as we place our trust in you.

VERSE BEFORE THE GOSPEL

John 1:41, 17b

We have found the Messiah: Jesus Christ, who brings us truth and grace.

GOSPEL

John 1:35–42—*This is the Lamb of God. We have found the Messiah.*

HOMILY

63. A homily follows that explains the readings.   92

PRESENTATION OF A BIBLE

64. A book containing the Gospels may be given to the   93
catechumens by the celebrant; a cross may also be given,
unless this has already been done as one of the additional
rites (see no. 74). The celebrant may use words suited to
the gift presented, for example, "Receive the Gospel of Jesus Christ, the Son of God," and the catechumens may respond in an appropriate way.

INTERCESSIONS FOR THE CATECHUMENS

65. Then the sponsors and the whole congregation join in   94
the following or a similar formulary of intercession for the
catechumens.

[If it is decided, in accord with no. 68, that after the dismissal of the catechumens the usual general intercessions of
the Mass are to be omitted and that the liturgy of the eucharist is to begin immediately, intentions for the Church and
the whole world are to be added to the following intentions
for the catechumens.]

Celebrant:

These catechumens, who are our brothers and sisters, have already traveled a long road. We rejoice with them in the gentle guidance of God who has brought them to this day. Let us pray that they may press on-

wards, until they come to share fully in our way of
life.

Assisting minister:
**That God our Father may reveal his Christ to them
more and more with every passing day, let us pray to
the Lord:**
℟. **Lord, hear our prayer.**

Assisting minister:
**That they may undertake with generous hearts and
souls whatever God may ask of them, let us pray to
the Lord:**
℟. **Lord, hear our prayer.**

Assisting minister:
**That they may have our sincere and unfailing sup-
port every step of the way, let us pray to the Lord:**
℟. **Lord, hear our prayer.**

Assisting minister:
**That they may find in our community compelling
signs of unity and generous love, let us pray to the
Lord:**
℟. **Lord, hear our prayer.**

Assisting minister:
**That their hearts and ours may become more respon-
sive to the needs of others, let us pray to the Lord:**
℟. **Lord, hear our prayer.**

Assisting minister:
**That in due time they may be found worthy to re-
ceive the baptism of new birth and renewal in the
Holy Spirit, let us pray to the Lord:**
℟. **Lord, hear our prayer.**

PRAYER OVER THE CATECHUMENS

66. After the intercessions, the celebrant, with hands outstretched over the catechumens, says one of the following
prayers.
Let us pray.

A

[God of our forebears and] God of all creation,   95
we ask you to look favorably on your servants N.
   and N.;
make them fervent in spirit,
joyful in hope,
and always ready to serve your name.

Lead them, Lord, to the baptism of new birth,
so that, living a fruitful life in the company of your
   faithful,
they may receive the eternal reward that you prom-
   ise.

We ask this in the name of Jesus the Lord.
Ry. Amen.

B

Almighty God,   95
source of all creation,
you have made us in your image.
Welcome with love those who come before you to-
   day.

They have listened among us to the word of Christ;
by its power renew them
and by your grace refashion them,
so that in time they may assume the full likeness of
   Christ,
who lives and reigns for ever and ever.
Ry. Amen.

DISMISSAL OF THE CATECHUMENS

67. If the eucharist is to be celebrated, the catechumens are   96
normally dismissed at this point by use of option A or B; if
the catechumens are to stay for the celebration of the eucharist, option C is used; if the eucharist is not to be celebrated, the entire assembly is dismissed by use of option D.

A

The celebrant recalls briefly the great joy with which the
catechumens have just been received and urges them to
live according to the word of God they have just heard. Af-

ter the dismissal formulary, the group of catechumens goes out but does not disperse. With the help of some of the faithful, the catechumens remain together to share their joy and spiritual experiences. For the dismissal the following or similar words are used.

Catechumens, go in peace, and may the Lord remain with you always.

Catechumens:
Thanks be to God.

B
As an optional formulary for dismissing the catechumens, USA the celebrant may use these or similar words.

My dear friends, this community now sends you forth to reflect more deeply upon the word of God which you have shared with us today. Be assured of our loving support and prayers for you. We look forward to the day when you will share fully in the Lord's Table.

C If for serious reasons the catechumens cannot leave (see 96 no. 75.3) and must remain with the baptized, they are to be instructed that though they are present at the eucharist, they cannot take part in it as the baptized do. They may be reminded of this by the celebrant in these or similar words.

Although you cannot yet participate fully in the Lord's eucharist, stay with us as a sign of our hope that all God's children will eat and drink with the Lord and work with his Spirit to re-create the face of the earth.

D
The celebrant dismisses those present, using these or similar words.

Go in peace, and may the Lord remain with you always.

All:
Thanks be to God.

An appropriate song may conclude the celebration.

LITURGY OF THE EUCHARIST

68. When the eucharist is to follow, intercessory prayer is   97
resumed with the usual general intercessions for the needs
of the Church and the whole world; then, if required, the
profession of faith is said. But for pastoral reasons these
general intercessions and the profession of faith may be
omitted. The liturgy of the eucharist then begins as usual
with the preparation of the gifts.

OPTIONAL RITES

69. By decision of the National Conference of Catholic Bish-   USA
ops the presentation of a cross (no. 74) may be included as
a symbol of reception into the community. At the discretion
of the diocesan bishop, one or more additional rites may be
incorporated into the "Rite of Acceptance into the Order of
Catechumens": a first exorcism and renunciation of false
worship, the giving of a new name, as well as additional
rites that symbolize acceptance into the community (cf. no.
33.2, 33.4, 33.5, 33.8).

EXORCISM AND RENUNCIATION OF FALSE WORSHIP

70. In regions where false worship is widespread, whether   78
in worshiping spiritual powers or in calling on the shades
of the dead or in using magical arts, the diocesan bishop
may permit the introduction of a first exorcism and a renunciation of false worship; this replaces the candidates' first acceptance of the Gospel (no. 52).

EXORCISM

71. After giving a brief introduction to the rite, the cele-   79
brant breathes lightly toward the face of each candidate
and, with a symbolic gesture, for example, holding up his
right hand, or without any gesture, says the formulary of
exorcism.

[If there are a great many candidates, the breathing is omitted and the formulary said only once; the breathing is also
omitted in places where it would be unacceptable.]

Celebrant:
**By the breath of your mouth, O Lord,
drive away the spirits of evil.
Command them to depart,
for your kingdom has come among us.**

RENUNCIATION OF FALSE WORSHIP

72. If the diocesan bishop judges it suitable to have the
candidate openly renounce false worship and spirits or
magical arts, he should see to the preparation of a formulary for the questions and renunciation relevant to the local
situation. As long as the language is not offensive to members of other religious groups, this may be expressed using
one of the following formularies or similar words.   80

A Celebrant: 80
**Dear candidates, you have set out toward your bap-
tism. You have answered God's call and been helped
by his grace; you have decided to serve and worship
him alone and the one he has sent, Jesus Christ.
Since you have made this choice, now is the time to
renounce publicly those powers that are not of God
and those forms of worship that do not rightly honor
him. Are you, therefore, resolved to remain loyal
to God and his Christ, and never to serve ungodly
powers?**

Candidates:
Yes, we are.

Celebrant:
Do you reject the worship of N. and N.?

Candidates:
Yes, we do.

He continues in the same way for each form of worship to
be renounced.

B Celebrant: 371
**Dear candidates, the true God has called you and led
you here. You sincerely desire to worship and serve**

him alone, and his Son Jesus Christ. Now, in the presence of this community, you must reject all rites and forms of worship that do not honor the true God. Are you determined never to abandon him and his Son, Jesus Christ, and never to return to the service of other masters?

Candidates:
We are.

Celebrant:
Christ Jesus, Lord of the living and the dead, has power over all spirits and demons. Are you determined never to abandon him and never again to serve N.*?

Candidates:
We are.

Celebrant:
Christ Jesus alone has the power to protect us. Are you determined never to abandon him and never again to seek [wear/use] N.**?

Candidates:
We are.

Celebrant:
Christ Jesus alone is truth. Are you determined never to abandon him and never to seek out soothsayers, magicians, or witch doctors?

Candidates:
We are.

The celebration then continues with the affirmation by the sponsors and the assembly (no. 53).

GIVING OF A NEW NAME

73. At the discretion of the diocesan bishop, the giving of a new name to persons from cultures in which it is the practice of non-Christian religions to give a new name may fol-

88 USA

*Here mention is made of the images worshiped in false rites, such as fetishes.
**Here mention is made of the objects that are used superstitiously, such as amulets.

low the signing of the candidates with the cross (nos. 54–56).* This may be either a Christian name or one familiar in the culture, provided such a name is not incompatible with Christian beliefs. (In some cases it will suffice to explain the Christian understanding of the catechumens' given names.) If a new name is given, one of the following formularies may be used.

A Celebrant:
By what name do you wish to be called?

Catechumen:
N.

B Celebrant:
N., from now on you will [also] be called N.

The catechumen gives the following or another suitable reply.
Amen.

The celebration then continues with the optional presentation of the cross (no. 74) and/or with an additional rite determined by the diocesan bishop to symbolize acceptance into the community (cf. no. 33.5) or with the invitation to the celebration of the word of God (no. 60).

PRESENTATION OF A CROSS

74. The presentation of a cross on occasion may be incorpo- USA rated into the rite either before or after the invitation to the celebration of the word of God (no. 60).

Celebrant:
You have been marked with the cross of Christ. Receive now the sign of his love.

Catechumens:
Amen.

*If so, this rite is not repeated on Holy Saturday; see no. 200.

PERIOD OF THE CATECHUMENATE

Leave your country, and come into the land I will show you

75. The catechumenate is an extended period during   19
which the candidates are given suitable pastoral formation
and guidance, aimed at training them in the Christian life.[1]
In this way, the dispositions manifested at their acceptance
into the catechumenate are brought to maturity. This is
achieved in four ways.

1. A suitable catechesis is provided by priests or deacons,
or by catechists and others of the faithful, planned to be gradual and complete in its coverage, accommodated to the liturgical year, and solidly supported by celebrations of the word.
This catechesis leads the catechumens not only to an appropriate acquaintance with dogmas and precepts but also to a profound sense of the mystery of salvation in which they desire
to participate.

2. As they become familiar with the Christian way of
life and are helped by the example and support of sponsors, godparents, and the entire Christian community, the
catechumens learn to turn more readily to God in prayer, to
bear witness to the faith, in all things to keep their hopes
set on Christ, to follow supernatural inspiration in their
deeds, and to practice love of neighbor, even at the cost of
self-renunciation. Thus formed, "the newly converted set
out on a spiritual journey. Already sharing through faith in
the mystery of Christ's death and resurrection, they pass
from the old to a new nature made perfect in Christ. Since
this transition brings with it a progressive change of outlook and conduct, it should become manifest by means of
its social consequences and it should develop gradually during the period of the catechumenate. Since the Lord in
whom they believe is a sign of contradiction, the newly converted often experience divisions and separations, but they
also taste the joy that God gives without measure."[2]

3. The Church, like a mother, helps the catechumens
on their journey by means of suitable liturgical rites, which
purify the catechumens little by little and strengthen them
with God's blessing. Celebrations of the word of God are

[1]See Vatican Council II, Decree on the Church's Missionary Activity *Ad
gentes*, no. 14.

[2]Ibid., no. 13.

arranged for their benefit, and at Mass they may also take part with the faithful in the liturgy of the word, thus better preparing themselves for their eventual participation in the liturgy of the eucharist. Ordinarily, however, when they are present in the assembly of the faithful they should be kindly dismissed before the liturgy of the eucharist begins (unless their dismissal would present practical or pastoral problems). For they must await their baptism, which will join them to God's priestly people and empower them to participate in Christ's new worship (see no. 67 for formularies of dismissal).

4. Since the Church's life is apostolic, catechumens should also learn how to work actively with others to spread the Gospel and build up the Church by the witness of their lives and by professing their faith.[3]

76. The duration of the catechumenate will depend on the grace of God and on various circumstances, such as the program of instruction for the catechumenate, the number of catechists, deacons, and priests, the cooperation of the individual catechumens, the means necessary for them to come to the site of the catechumenate and spend time there, the help of the local community. Nothing, therefore, can be settled a priori. [20] [98]

The time spent in the catechumenate should be long enough—several years if necessary—for the conversion and faith of the catechumens to become strong. By their formation in the entire Christian life and a sufficiently prolonged probation the catechumens are properly initiated into the mysteries of salvation and the practice of an evangelical way of life. By means of sacred rites celebrated at successive times they are led into the life of faith, worship, and charity belonging to the people of God.

77. It is the responsibility of the bishop to fix the duration and to direct the program of the catechumenate. The conference of bishops, after considering the conditions of its people and region,[4] may also wish to provide specific guidelines. At the discretion of the bishop, on the basis of the spiritual preparation of the candidate, the period of the [20] [98]

[3]See Vatican Council II, Decree on the Church's Missionary Activity *Ad gentes*, no. 14.
[4]See Vatican Council II, Constitution on the Liturgy *Sacrosanctum Concilium*, art. 64.

catechumenate may in particular cases be shortened (see
nos. 331–335); in altogether extraordinary cases the
catechumenate may be completed all at once (see nos. 332,
336–369).

78. The instruction that the catechumens receive during   99
this period should be of a kind that while presenting Catholic teaching in its entirety also enlightens faith, directs the
heart toward God, fosters participation in the liturgy, inspires apostolic activity, and nurtures a life completely in accord with the spirit of Christ.

79. Among the rites belonging to the period of the   103
catechumenate, then, celebrations of the word of God (nos.
81–89) are foremost. The minor exorcisms (nos. 90–94) and
the blessings of the catechumens (nos. 95–97) are ordinarily
celebrated in conjunction with a celebration of the word. In
addition, other rites may be celebrated to mark the passage
of the catechumens from one level of catechesis to another:
for example, an anointing of the catechumens may be celebrated (nos. 98–103) and the presentations of the Creed and
the Lord's Prayer may be anticipated (see nos. 104–105).

80. During the period of the catechumenate, the catechu-   104
mens should give thought to choosing their godparents   . 105
who will present them to the Church on the day of the election (see no. 11; also *Christian Initiation*, General Introduction, nos. 8–10).

Provision should also be made for the entire community involved in the formation of the catechumens—priests, deacons, catechists, sponsors, godparents, friends and
neighbors—to participate in some of the celebrations belonging to the catechumenate, including any of the optional
"rites of passage" (nos. 98–105).

RITES BELONGING TO THE PERIOD OF THE CATECHUMENATE

CELEBRATIONS OF THE WORD OF GOD

81. During the period of the catechumenate there should be celebrations of the word of God that accord with the liturgical season and that contribute to the instruction of the catechumens and the needs of the community. These celebrations of the word are: first, celebrations held specially for the catechumens; second, participation in the liturgy of the word at the Sunday Mass; third, celebrations held in connection with catechetical instruction. 100

82. The special celebrations of the word of God arranged for the benefit of the catechumens have as their main purpose: 106

   1. to implant in their hearts the teachings they are receiving: for example, the morality characteristic of the New Testament, the forgiving of injuries and insults, a sense of sin and repentance, the duties Christians must carry out in the world;

   2. to give them instruction and experience in the different aspects and ways of prayer;

   3. to explain to them the signs, celebrations, and seasons of the liturgy;

   4. to prepare them gradually to enter the worship assembly of the entire community.

83. From the very beginning of the period of the catechumenate the catechumens should be taught to keep holy the Lord's Day. 107

   1. Care should be taken that some of the special celebrations of the word just mentioned (no. 82) are held on Sunday, so that the catechumens will become accustomed to taking an active and practiced part in these celebrations.

   2. Gradually the catechumens should be admitted to the first part of the celebration of the Sunday Mass. After the liturgy of the word they should, if possible, be dismissed, but an intention for them is included in the general intercessions (see no. 67 for formularies of dismissal).

84. Celebrations of the word may also be held in connec- 108
tion with catechetical or instructional meetings of the catechumens, so that these will occur in a context of prayer.

MODEL FOR A CELEBRATION OF THE WORD OF GOD

85. For the celebrations of the word of God that are held
specially for the benefit of the catechumens (see no. 82), the
following structure (nos. 86–89) may be used as a model.

86. *Song:* An appropriate song may be sung to open the
celebration.

87. *Readings and Responsorial Psalms:* One or more readings
from Scripture, chosen for their relevance to the formation
of the catechumens, are proclaimed by a baptized member
of the community. A sung responsorial psalm should ordinarily follow each reading.

88. *Homily:* A brief homily that explains and applies the
readings should be given.

89. *Concluding Rites:* The celebration of the word may con- USA
clude with a minor exorcism (no. 94) or with a blessing of
the catechumens (no. 97). When the minor exorcism is
used, it may be followed by one of the blessings (no. 97)
or, on occasion, by the rite of anointing (nos. 102–103).*

MINOR EXORCISMS

90. The first or minor exorcisms have been composed in 101
the form of petitions directly addressed to God. They draw
the attention of the catechumens to the real nature of Christian life, the struggle between flesh and spirit, the importance of self-denial for reaching the blessedness of God's
kingdom, and the unending need for God's help.

*Celebrations of the word that are held in connection with instructional ses-
sions may include, along with an appropriate reading, a minor exorcism
(no. 94) or a blessing of the catechumens (no. 97). When the minor exorcism is used, it may be followed by one of the blessings (no. 97) or, on
occasion, by the rite of anointing (nos. 102–103).
The meetings of the catechumens after the liturgy of the word of the Sunday Mass may also include a minor exorcism (no. 94) or a blessing (no.
97). Likewise, when the minor exorcism is used, it may be followed by
one of the blessings (no. 97) or, on occasion, by the rite of anointing (nos.
102–103).

91. The presiding celebrant for the minor exorcisms is a 109
priest, a deacon, or a qualified catechist appointed by the
bishop for this ministry (see no. 16).

92. The minor exorcisms take place within a celebration of 110
the word of God held in a church, a chapel, or in a center
for the catechumenate. A minor exorcism may also be held
at the beginning or end of a meeting for catechesis. When
there is some special need, one of these prayers of exorcism
may be said privately for individual catechumens.

93. The formularies for the minor exorcisms may be used 112
on several occasions, as different situations may suggest.

PRAYERS OF EXORCISM

94. As the catechumens bow or kneel, the celebrant, with 109
hands outstretched over them, says one of the following
prayers.

Let us pray.

A
God of power, 113
who promised us the Holy Spirit through Jesus your
  Son,
we pray to you for these catechumens,
who present themselves before you.

Protect them from the spirit of evil
and guard them against error and sin,
so that they may become the temple of your Holy
  Spirit.

Confirm what we profess in faith,
so that our words may not be empty,
but full of the grace and power
by which your Son has freed the world.

We ask this through Christ our Lord.
R̷. Amen.

B
Lord our God, 114
you make known the true life;

you cut away corruption and strengthen faith,
you build up hope and foster love.

In the name of your beloved Son,
our Lord Jesus Christ,
and in the power of the Holy Spirit,
we ask you to remove from these your servants
all unbelief and hesitation in faith,
[the worship of false gods and magic,
witchcraft and dealings with the dead],
the love of money and lawless passions,
enmity and quarreling,
and every manner of evil.

And because you have called them
to be holy and sinless in your sight,
create in them a spirit of faith and reverence,
of patience and hope,
of temperance and purity,
and of charity and peace.

We ask this through Christ our Lord.
℟. Amen.

C
God of power,
you created us in your image and likeness
and formed us in holiness and justice.

Even when we sinned against you,
you did not abandon us,
but in your wisdom chose to save us
by the incarnation of your Son.

Save these your servants:
free them from evil and the tyranny of the enemy.
Keep far from them the spirit of wickedness, false-
    hood, and greed.

Receive them into your kingdom
and open their hearts to understand your Gospel,
so that, as children of the light,
they may become members of your Church,

115

bear witness to your truth,
and put into practice your commands of love.

We ask this through Christ our Lord.
R̥. Amen.

D

Lord Jesus Christ, 116
when you climbed the mountain to preach,
you turned your disciples from the paths of sin
and revealed to them the beatitudes of your king-
    dom.

Help these your servants, who hear the word of the
    Gospel,
and protect them from the spirit of greed, of lust,
    and of pride.
May they find the blessings of your kingdom
in poverty and in hunger,
in mercy and in purity of heart.
May they work for peace and joyfully endure persecu-
    tion
and so come to share your kingdom
and experience the mercy you promised.
May they finally see God in the joy of heaven
where you live and reign for ever and ever.
R̥. Amen.

E

O God, 117
Creator and Savior of all,
in your love you have formed these your servants;
in your mercy you have called them and received
    them.

Probe their hearts today
and watch over them as they look forward to the com-
    ing of your Son.

Keep them in your providence
and complete in them the plan of your love.
Through their loyalty to Christ
may they be counted among his disciples on earth

and be acknowledged by him in heaven.

We ask this through Christ our Lord.
R̸. Amen.

F
Lord and God,
you know the secrets of our hearts
and reward us for the good we do.

118

Look kindly on the efforts and the progress of your
    servants.
Strengthen them on their way,
increase their faith,
and accept their repentance.
Open to them your goodness and justice
and lead them to share in your sacraments on earth,
until they finally enjoy your presence in heaven.

We ask this through Christ our Lord.
R̸. Amen.

G
Lord Jesus Christ,
loving Redeemer of all,
your name alone has the power to save,
that name before which every knee should bend
in the heavens, on the earth, and under the earth.

373:1

We pray for these your servants,
who worship you as the true God.

Look upon them and enlighten their hearts,
free them from the snares and malice of Satan,
heal their weakness and blot out their sins.

Give them discernment to know what pleases you
and the courage to live by your Gospel,
that they may become the dwelling place of your
    Spirit,
for you live and reign for ever and ever.
R̸. Amen.

H

Lord Jesus Christ,   373:2
sent by the Father and anointed by the Spirit,
when you read in the synagogue at Nazareth
you fulfilled the words of the prophet Isaiah
that proclaimed liberty to captives
and announced a season of forgiveness.

We pray for these your servants
who have opened their ears and hearts to your word.
Grant that they may grasp your moment of grace.

Do not let their minds be troubled
or their lives tied to earthly desires.
Do not let them remain
estranged from the hope of your promises
or enslaved by a spirit of unbelief.
Rather, let them believe in you,
whom the Father has established as universal Lord
and to whom he has subjected all things.
Let them submit themselves to the Spirit of grace,
so that, with hope in their calling,
they may join the priestly people
and share in the abundant joy of the new Jerusalem,
where you live and reign for ever and ever.
℟. Amen.

I

Lord Jesus Christ,   373:3
after calming the storms and freeing the possessed,
you gave us a sign of your mercy
by calling Matthew, the tax collector, to follow you.
You chose him to record for all time
your command to teach all nations.

We pray for these your servants
who confess that they are sinners.

Hold in check the power of the evil one,
and show them your mercy;
heal in them the wounds of sin
and fill their hearts with your peace.

May they delight in their discovery of the Gospel
and generously follow your call,
for you live and reign for ever and ever.
℟. Amen.

J

God of infinite wisdom,   373:4
you chose the apostle Paul
to proclaim your Son to every nation.

We pray that these your servants,
who look forward to baptism,
may follow in the footsteps of Paul
and trust not in flesh and blood,
but in the call of your grace.

Probe their hearts and purify them,
so that, freed from all deception,
they may never look back
but strive always toward what is to come.
May they count everything as loss
compared with the unsurpassed worth of knowing
    your Son,
and so gain him as their eternal reward,
for he is Lord for ever and ever.
℟. Amen.

K

Lord,   373:5
Creator and Redeemer of your holy people,
your great love has drawn these catechumens to seek
    and find you.
Look upon them today,
purify their hearts,
and bring to fulfillment in them the plan of your
    grace,
so that, faithfully following Christ,
they may come to drink the waters of salvation.

We ask this through Christ our Lord.
℟. Amen.

BLESSINGS OF THE CATECHUMENS

95. The blessings of the catechumens are a sign of God's   102
love and of the Church's tender care. They are bestowed on
the catechumens so that, even though they do not as yet
have the grace of the sacraments, they may still receive
from the Church courage, joy, and peace as they proceed
along the difficult journey they have begun.

96. The blessings may be given by a priest, a deacon, or a   119
qualified catechist appointed by the bishop (see no. 16).
The blessings are usually given at the end of a celebration
of the word; they may also be given at the end of a meeting
for catechesis. When there is some special need, the blessings may be given privately to individual catechumens.

PRAYERS OF BLESSING

97. The celebrant, with hands outstretched over the cate-   119
chumens, says one of the following prayers. After the
prayer of blessing, if this can be done conveniently, the
catechumens come before the celebrant, who lays hands on
them individually. Then the catechumens leave.

Let us pray.

A
Lord,   121
form these catechumens by the mysteries of the faith,
that they may be brought to rebirth in baptism
and be counted among the members of your Church.

We ask this through Christ our Lord.
℟. Amen.

B
Father,   122
through your holy prophets
you proclaimed to all who draw near you,
"Wash and be cleansed,"
and through Christ you have granted us rebirth in
   the Spirit.

Bless these your servants
as they earnestly prepare for baptism.

Fulfill your promise:
sanctify them in preparation for your gifts,
that they may come to be reborn as your children
and enter the community of your Church.

We ask this through Christ our Lord.
℟. Amen.

C
God of power, 123
look upon these your servants
as they deepen their understanding of the Gospel.

Grant that they may come to know and love you
and always heed your will
with receptive minds and generous hearts.

Teach them through this time of preparation
and enfold them within your Church,
so that they may share your holy mysteries
both on earth and in heaven.

We ask this through Christ our Lord.
℟. Amen.

D
God our Father, 124
you have sent your only Son, Jesus Christ,
to free the world from falsehood.

Give to your catechumens fullness of understanding,
unwavering faith,
and a firm grasp of your truth.

Let them grow ever stronger,
that they may receive in due time the new birth of
    baptism
that gives pardon of sins,
and join with us in praising your name.

We ask this through Christ our Lord.
℟. Amen.

E

Almighty and eternal God,   374:1
you dwell on high yet look on the lowly;
to bring us your gift of salvation
you sent Jesus your Son,
our Lord and God.

Look kindly on these catechumens,
who bow before you in worship;
prepare them for their rebirth in baptism,
the forgiveness of their sins,
and the garment of incorruptible life.

Enfold them in your holy, catholic, and apostolic
    Church,
that they may join with us
in giving glory to your name.

We ask this through Christ our Lord.
℟. Amen.

F

Lord of all,   374:2
through your only begotten Son
you cast down Satan
and broke the chains that held us captive.

We thank you for these catechumens
whom you have called.

Strengthen them in faith,
that they may know you, the one true God,
and Jesus Christ, whom you have sent.

Keep them clean of heart and make them grow in
    virtue,
that they may be worthy to receive baptism
and enter into the holy mysteries.

We ask this through Christ our Lord.
℟. Amen.

G
Lord God, 374:3
you desire that all be saved
and come to the knowledge of truth.

Enliven with faith those who are preparing for
    baptism;
bring them into the fold of your Church,
there to receive the gift of eternal life.

We ask this through Christ our Lord.
℟. Amen.

H
God of power and Father of our Savior Jesus Christ, 374:4
look kindly upon these your servants.

Drive from their minds all taint of false worship
and stamp your law and commands on their hearts.

Lead them to full knowledge of the truth
and prepare them to be the temple of the Holy Spirit
through their rebirth in baptism.

Grant this through Christ our Lord.
℟. Amen.

I
Lord, 374:5
look with love on your servants,
who commit themselves to your name
and bow before you in worship.

Help them to accomplish what is good;
arouse their hearts,
that they may always remember your works and your
    commands
and eagerly embrace all that is yours.

Grant this through Christ our Lord.
℟. Amen.

ANOINTING OF THE CATECHUMENS

98. During the period of the catechumenate, a rite of anointing the catechumens, through use of the oil of catechumens, may be celebrated wherever this seems beneficial or desirable. The presiding celebrant for such a first anointing of the catechumens is a priest or a deacon.

103
127

99. Care is to be taken that the catechumens understand the significance of the anointing with oil. The anointing with oil symbolizes their need for God's help and strength so that, undeterred by the bonds of the past and overcoming the opposition of the devil, they will forthrightly take the step of professing their faith and will hold fast to it unfalteringly throughout their lives.

212

100. The anointing ordinarily takes place after the homily in a celebration of the word of God (see no. 89), and is conferred on each of the catechumens; this rite of anointing may be celebrated several times during the course of the catechumenate. Further, for particular reasons, a priest or a deacon may confer the anointing privately on individual catechumens.

128

101. The oil used for this rite is to be the oil blessed by the bishop at the chrism Mass, but for pastoral reasons a priest celebrant may bless oil for the rite immediately before the anointing.[1]

129

PRAYER OF EXORCISM OR BLESSING OF OIL

102. When anointing with oil already blessed by the bishop, the celebrant first says the prayer of exorcism given as option A (or one of the other prayers of exorcism in no. 94); a priest celebrant who for pastoral reasons chooses to bless oil for the rite uses the blessing given as option B.

130

A
Prayer of Exorcism

Let us pray.

Lord Jesus Christ,
sent by the Father and anointed by the Spirit,

373:2

[1]See *Rite of the Blessing of Oils, Rite of Consecrating the Chrism,* Introduction, no. 7.

when you read in the synagogue at Nazareth,
you fulfilled the words of the prophet Isaiah
that proclaimed liberty to captives
and announced a season of forgiveness.

We pray for these your servants
who have opened their ears and hearts to your word.
Grant that they may grasp your moment of grace.

Do not let their minds be troubled
or their lives tied to earthly desires.
Do not let them remain
estranged from the hope of your promises
or enslaved by a spirit of unbelief.
Rather, let them believe in you,
whom the Father has established as universal Lord
and to whom he has subjected all things.

Let them submit themselves to the Spirit of grace,
so that, with hope in their calling,
they may join the priestly people
and share in the abundant joy of the new Jerusalem,
where you live and reign for ever and ever.
℟. Amen.

B
Blessing of Oil

Let us pray.

O God,   131
source of strength and defender of your people,
you have chosen to make this oil,
created by your hand,
an effective sign of your power.

Bless ✚ this oil
and strengthen the catechumens who will be
    anointed with it.
Grant them your wisdom to understand the Gospel
    more deeply
and your strength to accept the challenges of Chris-
    tian life.

**Enable them to rejoice in baptism
and to partake of a new life in the Church
as true children of your family.**

**We ask this through Christ our Lord.
℟. Amen.**

ANOINTING

103. Facing the catechumens, the celebrant says: 132

**We anoint you with the oil of salvation
in the name of Christ our Savior.
May he strengthen you with his power,
who lives and reigns for ever and ever.**

Catechumens:
Amen.

The celebrant anoints each catechumen with the oil of catechumens on the breast or on both hands or, if this seems
desirable, even on other parts of the body.

[If there are a great many catechumens, additional priests
or deacons may assist in the anointing.]

The anointing may be followed by a blessing of the catechumens (no. 97).

PRESENTATIONS [OPTIONAL]

104. The presentations normally take place during Lent,   125
the period of purification and enlightenment, after the first
and third scrutinies. But for pastoral advantage and because
the period of purification and enlightenment is rather short,
the presentations may be held during the period of the
catechumenate, rather than at the regular times. But the presentations are not to take place until a point during the
catechumenate when the catechumens are judged ready for
these celebrations.

105. Both the presentation of the Creed and the presenta-   126
tion of the Lord's Prayer may be anticipated; each may be
concluded with the ephphetha rite.[1] When the presenta-

[1]But if the rite of recitation of the Creed (nos. 193–196) is also anticipated
as one of the "rites of passage" (see no. 33.6), the ephphetha rite is used
only to begin this rite of recitation and not with the presentations.

tions are anticipated, care is to be taken to substitute the term "catechumens" for the term "elect" in all formularies.

PRESENTATIONS

Presentation of the Creed: see nos. 157–162.

Presentation of the Lord's Prayer: see nos. 178–183.

Ephphetha Rite: see nos. 197–199.

SENDING OF THE CATECHUMENS FOR ELECTION [OPTIONAL]   USA

106. At the conclusion of the period of the catechumenate, a rite of sending the catechumens to their election by the bishop may be celebrated in parishes wherever this seems beneficial or desirable. When election will take place in the parish, this rite is not used.

107. As the focal point of the Church's concern for the catechumens, admission to election belongs to the bishop who is usually its presiding celebrant. It is within the parish community, however, that the preliminary judgment is made concerning the catechumens' state of formation and progress.

This rite offers that local community the opportunity to express its approval of the catechumens and to send them forth to the celebration of election assured of the parish's care and support.

108. The rite is celebrated in the parish church at a suitable time prior to the rite of election.

109. The rite takes place after the homily in a celebration of the word of God (see no. 89) or at Mass.

110. When the Rite of Sending Catechumens for Election is combined with the rite of sending for recognition by the bishop the (already baptized) adult candidates for the sacraments of confirmation and eucharist (*or:* for reception into the full communion of the Catholic Church), the alternate rite found on page 301 (Appendix I, Rite 2.) is used.

PRESENTATION OF THE CATECHUMENS

111. After the homily, the priest in charge of the catechumens' initiation, or a deacon, a catechist, or a representative of the community, presents the catechumens, using the following or similar words.

Reverend Father, these catechumens, whom I now present to you, are beginning their final period of preparation and purification leading to their initiation. They have found strength in God's grace and support in our community's prayers and example.

Now they ask that they be recognized for the progress they have made in their spiritual formation and that they receive the assurance of our blessings and prayers as they go forth to the rite of election celebrated this afternoon (*or:* next Sunday [*or* specify the day]) **by Bishop N.**

The celebrant replies:
Those who are to be sent to the celebration of election in Christ, come forward, together with those who will be your godparents.

One by one, the catechumens are called by name. Each catechumen, accompanied by a godparent (or godparents), comes forward and stands before the celebrant.

AFFIRMATION BY THE GODPARENTS [AND THE ASSEMBLY]

112. Then the celebrant addresses the assembly in these or similar words:

My dear friends, these catechumens who have been preparing for the sacraments of initiation hope that they will be found ready to participate in the rite of election and be chosen in Christ for the Easter sacraments. It is the responsibility of this community to inquire about their readiness before they are presented to the bishop.

He addresses the godparents:
I turn to you, godparents, for your testimony about these candidates. Have these catechumens taken their

formation in the Gospel and in the Catholic way of life seriously?

Godparents:
They have.

Celebrant:
Have they given evidence of their conversion by the example of their lives?

Godparents:
They have.

Celebrant:
Do you judge them to be ready to be presented to the bishop for the rite of election?

Godparents:
We do.

[When appropriate in the circumstances, the celebrant may also ask the entire assembly to express its approval of the candidates.]

The celebrant concludes the affirmation by the following:
My dear catechumens, this community gladly recommends you to the bishop, who, in the name of Christ, will call you to the Easter sacraments. May God bring to completion the good work he has begun in you.

113. If the signing of the Book of the Elect is to take place in the presence of the bishop, it is omitted here. However, if the signed Book of the Elect is to be presented to the bishop in the rite of election, the catechumens may now come forward to sign it or they should sign it after the celebration or at another time prior to the rite of Election.

INTERCESSIONS FOR THE CATECHUMENS

114. Then the community prays for the catechumens by use of the following or a similar formulary. The celebrant may adapt the introduction and the intentions to fit various circumstances.

[If it is decided, in accord with no. 117, that after the dismissal of the catechumens the usual general intercessions of the Mass are to be omitted and that the liturgy of the eucharist is to begin immediately, intentions for the Church and the whole world are to be added to the following intentions for the catechumens.]

Celebrant:
My brothers and sisters, we look forward to celebrating at Easter the life-giving mysteries of our Lord's suffering, death and resurrection. As we journey together to the Easter sacraments, these catechumens will look to us for an example of Christian renewal. Let us pray to the Lord for them and for ourselves, that we may be renewed by one another's efforts and together come to share the joys of Easter.

Assisting minister:
That these catechumens may be freed from selfishness and learn to put others first, let us pray to the Lord:
R̸. Lord, hear our prayer.

Assisting minister:
That their godparents may be living examples of the Gospel, let us pray to the Lord:
R̸. Lord, hear our prayer.

Assisting minister:
That their teachers may always convey to them the beauty of God's word, let us pray to the Lord:
R̸. Lord, hear our prayer.

Assisting minister:
That these catechumens may share with others the joy they have found in their friendship with Jesus, let us pray to the Lord:
R̸. Lord, hear our prayer.

Assisting minister:
That our community, during this (*or:* the coming) Lenten season, may grow in charity and be constant in prayer, let us pray to the Lord:
R̸. Lord, hear our prayer.

PRAYER OVER THE CATECHUMENS
115. After the intercessions, the celebrant, with hands outstretched over the catechumens, says the following prayer.

Father of love and power,
it is your will to establish everything in Christ
and to draw us into his all-embracing love.

Guide these catechumens in the days and weeks
    ahead:
strengthen them in their vocation,
build them into the kingdom of your Son,
and seal them with the Spirit of your promise.

We ask this through Christ our Lord.
℞. Amen.

DISMISSAL

116. If the eucharist is to be celebrated, the catechumens
are normally dismissed at this point by use of option A or
B; if the catechumens are to stay for the celebration of the
eucharist, option C is used; if the eucharist is not to be celebrated, the entire assembly is dismissed by use of option D.

A   The celebrant dismisses the catechumens in these or
similar words.

My dear friends, you are about to set out on the road
that leads to the glory of Easter. Christ will be your
way, your truth, and your life. In his name we send
you forth from this community to celebrate with the
bishop the Lord's choice of you to be numbered
among his elect. Until we meet again for the scrutinies, walk always in his peace.

Catechumens:
Amen.

B   As an optional formulary for dismissing the catechumens, the celebrant may use these or similar words.

My dear friends, this community now sends you
forth to reflect more deeply upon the word of God
which you have shared with us today. Be assured of
our loving support and prayers for you. We look forward to the day when you will share fully in the
Lord's Table.

C If for serious reasons the catechumens cannot leave (see no. 75.3) and must remain with the rest of the liturgical assembly, they are to be instructed that though they are present at the eucharist, they cannot take part in it as the baptized do. They may be reminded of this by the celebrant in these or similar words.

Although you cannot yet participate fully in the Lord's eucharist, stay with us as a sign of our hope that all God's children will eat and drink with the Lord and work with his Spirit to re-create the face of the earth.

D The celebrant dismisses those present, using these or similar words.

Go in peace, and may the Lord remain with you always.

All:
Thanks be to God.

An appropriate song may conclude the celebration.

LITURGY OF THE EUCHARIST

117. When the eucharist is to follow, intercessory prayer is resumed with the usual general intercessions for the needs of the Church and the whole world; then, if required, the profession of faith is said. But for pastoral reasons these general intercessions and the profession of faith may be omitted. The liturgy of the eucharist then begins as usual with the preparation of the gifts.

SECOND STEP: ELECTION OR ENROLLMENT OF NAMES

Your ways, O Lord, are love and truth to those who keep your covenant

118. The second step in Christian initiation is the liturgical rite called both election and the enrollment of names, which closes the period of the catechumenate proper, that is, the lengthy period of formation of the catechumens' minds and hearts. The celebration of the rite of election, which usually coincides with the opening of Lent, also marks the beginning of the period of final, more intense preparation for the sacraments of initiation, during which the elect will be encouraged to follow Christ with greater generosity. [134]

119. At this second step, on the basis of the testimony of godparents and catechists and of the catechumens' reaffirmation of their intention, the Church judges their state of readiness and decides on their advancement toward the sacraments of initiation. Thus the Church makes its "election," that is, the choice and admission of those catechumens who have the dispositions that make them fit to take part, at the next major celebration, in the sacraments of initiation. [22] [133]

This step is called election because the acceptance made by the Church is founded on the election by God, in whose name the Church acts. The step is also called the enrollment of names because as a pledge of fidelity the candidates inscribe their names in the book that lists those who have been chosen for initiation.

120. Before the rite of election is celebrated, the catechumens are expected to have undergone a conversion in mind and in action and to have developed a sufficient acquaintance with Christian teaching as well as a spirit of faith and charity. With deliberate will and an enlightened faith they must have the intention to receive the sacraments of the Church, a resolve they will express publicly in the actual celebration of the rite. [23]

121. The election, marked with a rite of such solemnity, is the focal point of the Church's concern for the catechu- [135]

mens. Admission to election therefore belongs to the bishop, and the presiding celebrant for the rite of election is the bishop himself or a priest or a deacon who acts as the bishop's delegate (see no. 12).

Before the rite of election the bishop, priests, deacons, catechists, godparents, and the entire community, in accord with their respective responsibilities and in their own way, should, after considering the matter carefully, arrive at a judgment about the catechumens' state of formation and progress. After the election, they should surround the elect with prayer, so that the entire Church will accompany and lead them to encounter Christ.

122. Within the rite of election the bishop celebrant or his delegate declares in the presence of the community the Church's approval of the candidates. Therefore to exclude any semblance of mere formality from the rite, there should be a deliberation prior to its celebration to decide on the catechumens' suitableness. This deliberation is carried out by the priests, deacons, and catechists involved in the formation of the catechumens, and by the godparents and representatives of the local community. If circumstances suggest, the group of catechumens may also take part. The deliberation may take various forms, depending on local conditions and pastoral needs. During the celebration of election, the assembly is informed of the decision approving the catechumens. [23] [137]

123. Before the rite of election godparents are chosen by the catechumens; the choice should be made with the consent of the priest, and the persons chosen should, as far as possible, be approved for their role by the local community (see no. 11). In the rite of election the godparents exercise their ministry publicly for the first time. They are called by name at the beginning of the rite to come forward with the catechumens (no. 130); they give testimony on behalf of the catechumens before the community (no. 131); they may also write their names along with the catechumens in the book of the elect (no. 132). [136]

124. From the day of their election and admission, the catechumens are called "the elect." They are also described as *competentes* ("co-petitioners"), because they are joined together in asking for and aspiring to receive the three sacra- [24]

ments of Christ and the gift of the Holy Spirit. They are also called *illuminandi* ("those who will be enlightened"), because baptism itself has been called *illuminatio* ("enlightenment") and it fills the newly baptized with the light of faith. In our own times, other names may be applied to the elect that, depending on regions and cultures, are better suited to the people's understanding and the idiom of the language.

125. The bishop celebrant or his delegate, however much or little he was involved in the deliberation prior to the rite, has the responsibility of showing in the homily or elsewhere during the celebration the religious and ecclesial significance of the election. The celebrant also declares before all present the Church's decision and, if appropriate in the circumstances, asks the community to express its approval of the candidates. He also asks the catechumens to give a personal expression of their intention and, in the name of the Church, he carries out the act of admitting them as elect. The celebrant should open to all the divine mystery expressed in the call of the Church and in the liturgical celebration of this mystery. He should remind the faithful to give good example to the elect and along with the elect to prepare themselves for the Easter solemnities. [138]

126. The sacraments of initiation are celebrated during the Easter solemnities, and preparation for these sacraments is part of the distinctive character of Lent. Accordingly, the rite of election should normally take place on the First Sunday of Lent and the period of final preparation of the elect should coincide with the Lenten season. The plan arranged for the Lenten season will benefit the elect by reason of both its liturgical structure and the participation of the community. For urgent pastoral reasons, especially in secondary mission stations, it is permitted to celebrate the rite of election during the week preceding or following the First Sunday of Lent. [139]

When, because of unusual circumstances and pastoral needs, the rite of election is celebrated outside Lent, it is to be celebrated about six weeks before the sacraments of initiation, in order to allow sufficient time for the scrutinies and presentations. The rite is not to be celebrated on a solemnity of the liturgical year (see no. 29).

127. The rite should take place in the cathedral/church, in a parish or, if necessary, in some other suitable and fitting place.

140 USA

128. The rite is celebrated within Mass, after the homily, and should be celebrated within the Mass of the First Sunday of Lent. If, for pastoral reasons, the rite is celebrated on a different day, the texts and the readings of the ritual Mass "Christian Initiation: Election or Enrollment of Names" may always be used. When the Mass of the day is celebrated and its readings are not suitable, the readings are those given for the First Sunday of Lent or others may be chosen from elsewhere in the Lectionary.

140 141

When celebrated outside Mass, the rite takes place after the readings and the homily and is concluded with the dismissal of both the elect and the faithful.

[An optional parish rite to send catechumens for election by the bishop precedes the rite of election and is found at no. 106.]

RITE OF ELECTION OR ENROLLMENT OF NAMES

LITURGY OF THE WORD

HOMILY

129. After the readings (see no. 128), the bishop, or the 142
celebrant who acts as delegate of the bishop, gives the homily. This should be suited to the actual situation and should
address not just the catechumens but the entire community
of the faithful, so that all will be encouraged to give good
example and to accompany the elect along the path of the
paschal mystery.

PRESENTATION OF THE CATECHUMENS

130. After the homily, the priest in charge of the catechu- 143
mens' initiation, or a deacon, a catechist, or a representative of the community, presents the candidates, using the
following or similar words.

**Reverend Father, Easter is drawing near, and so these
catechumens, whom I now present to you, are completing their period of preparation. They have found
strength in God's grace and support in our
community's prayers and example.**

**Now they ask that after the celebration of the scruti-
nies, they be allowed to participate in the sacraments
of baptism, confirmation, and the eucharist.**

The celebrant replies:
**Those who are to be chosen in Christ, come forward,
together with your godparents.**

One by one, the candidates and godparents are called by
name. Each candidate, accompanied by a godparent (or godparents), comes forward and stands before the celebrant.

[If there are a great many candidates, all are presented in
groups, for example, each group by its own catechist. But
in this case, the catechists should be advised to have a special celebration beforehand in which they call each candidate forward by name.]

AFFIRMATION BY THE GODPARENTS [AND THE ASSEMBLY]

131. Then the celebrant addresses the assembly. If he has taken part in the earlier deliberation on the candidates' suitableness (see no. 122), he may use either option A or option B or similar words; if he has not taken part in the earlier deliberation, he uses option B or similar words. 144 145

A

My dear friends, these catechumens have asked to be initiated into the sacramental life of the Church this Easter. Those who know them have judged them to be sincere in their desire. During the period of their preparation they have listened to the word of Christ and endeavored to follow his commands; they have shared the company of their Christian brothers and sisters and joined with them in prayer. 145

And so I announce to all of you here that our community has decided to call them to the sacraments. Therefore, I ask their godparents to state their opinion once again, so that all of you may hear.

He addresses the godparents:
As God is your witness, do you consider these candidates worthy to be admitted to the sacraments of Christian initiation?

Godparents:
We do.

When appropriate in the circumstances, the celebrant may also ask the entire assembly to express its approval of the candidates in these or similar words:

Celebrant:
Now I ask you, the members of this community: Are you willing to affirm the testimony expressed about these catechumens and support them in faith, prayer and example as we prepare to celebrate the Easter sacraments? USA

All:
We are.

B

God's holy Church wishes to know whether these   144
candidates are sufficiently prepared to be enrolled
among the elect for the coming celebration of Easter.
And so I speak first of all to you their godparents.

He addresses the godparents:
Have they faithfully listened to God's word proclaimed by the Church?

Godparents:
They have.

Celebrant:
Have they responded to that word and begun to walk
in God's presence?

Godparents:
They have.

Celebrant:
Have they shared the company of their Christian
brothers and sisters and joined with them in prayer?

Godparents:
They have.

When appropriate in the circumstances, the celebrant may
also ask the entire assembly to express its approval of the
candidates in these or similar words:

Celebrant:
And now I speak to you, my brothers and sisters in   USA
this assembly:
Are you ready to support the testimony expressed
about these catechumens and include them in your
prayer and affection as we move toward Easter?

All:
We are.

INVITATION AND ENROLLMENT OF NAMES

132. Then addressing the catechumens in the following or   146
similar words, the celebrant advises them of their accep-   USA
tance and asks them to declare their own intention.

And now, my dear catechumens, I address you. Your own godparents and teachers [and this entire community] have spoken in your favor. The Church in the name of Christ accepts their judgment and calls you to the Easter sacraments.

Since you have already heard the call of Christ, you must now express your response to that call clearly and in the presence of the whole Church.

Therefore, do you wish to enter fully into the life of the Church through the sacraments of baptism, confirmation, and the eucharist?

Catechumens:
We do.

Celebrant:
Then offer your names for enrollment.

The candidates give their names, either going with their godparents to the celebrant or while remaining in place, and the actual inscription of the names may be carried out in various ways. The candidates may inscribe their names themselves or they may call out their names, which are inscribed by the godparents or by the minister who presented the candidates (see no. 130). As the enrollment is taking place, an appropriate song, for example, Psalm 16 or Psalm 33 with a refrain such as, **"Happy the people the Lord has chosen to be his own"** may be sung.

[If there are a great many candidates, the enrollment may simply consist in the presentation of a list of the names to the celebrant, with such words as: **"These are the names of the candidates"** or, when the bishop is celebrant and candidates from several parishes have been presented to him: **"These are the names of the candidates from the parish of *N.*"**]   USA

ACT OF ADMISSION OR ELECTION

133. The celebrant briefly explains the significance of the enrollment that has just taken place. Then, turning to the candidates, he says the following or similar words.   147

N. and N., I now declare you to be members of the elect, to be initiated into the sacred mysteries at the next Easter Vigil.

Candidates:
Thanks be to God.

He continues:
God is always faithful to those he calls: now it is your duty, as it is ours, both to be faithful to him in return and to strive courageously to reach the fullness of truth, which your election opens up before you.

Then the celebrant turns to the godparents and instructs them in the following or similar words.
Godparents, you have spoken in favor of these cate- chumens: accept them now as chosen in the Lord and continue to sustain them through your loving care and example, until they come to share in the sacra- ments of God's life.

He invites them to place their hand on the shoulder of the candidate whom they are receiving into their care, or to make some other gesture to indicate the same intent.

INTERCESSIONS FOR THE ELECT
134. The community may use either of the following for- mularies, options A or B, or a similar formulary to pray for the elect. The celebrant may adapt the introduction and the intentions to fit various circumstances. 148

[If it is decided, in accord with no. 137, that after the dis- missal of the elect the usual general intercessions of the Mass are to be omitted and that the liturgy of the eucharist is to begin immediately, intentions for the Church and the whole world are to be added to the following intentions for the elect.]

Celebrant:
My brothers and sisters, in beginning this period of Lent, we look forward to celebrating at Easter the life-giving mysteries of our Lord's suffering, death, and resurrection. These elect, whom we bring with us to the Easter sacraments, will look to us for an ex- ample of Christian renewal. Let us pray to the Lord for them and for ourselves, that we may be renewed by one another's efforts and together come to share the joys of Easter.

A Assisting minister:

That together we may fruitfully employ this Lenten season to renew ourselves through self-denial and works of holiness, let us pray to the Lord:
℞. **Lord, hear our prayer.**

Assisting minister:

That our catechumens may always remember this day of their election and be grateful for the blessings they have received from heaven, let us pray to the Lord:
℞. **Lord, hear our prayer.**

Assisting minister:

That their teachers may always convey the beauty of God's word to those who search for it, let us pray to the Lord:
℞. **Lord, hear our prayer.**

Assisting minister.

That their godparents may be living examples of the Gospel, let us pray to the Lord:
℞. **Lord, hear our prayer.**

Assisting minister:

That their families, far from placing any obstacles in the way of these catechumens, may help them to follow the promptings of the Spirit, let us pray to the Lord:
℞. **Lord, hear our prayer.**

Assisting minister:

That our community, during this Lenten period, may grow in charity and be constant in prayer, let us pray to the Lord:
℞. **Lord, hear our prayer.**

Assisting minister:

That those who have not yet overcome their hesitation may trust in Christ and come to join our community as our brothers and sisters, let us pray to the Lord:
℞. **Lord, hear our prayer.**

B Assisting minister:
**That these elect may find joy in daily prayer, we
   pray:**
R̶. Lord, hear our prayer.

Assisting minister:
**That, by praying to you often, they may grow ever
closer to you, we pray:**
R̶. Lord, hear our prayer.

Assisting minister:
**That they may read your word and joyfully dwell on
it in their hearts, we pray:**
R̶. Lord, hear our prayer.

Assisting minister:
**That they may humbly acknowledge their faults and
work wholeheartedly to correct them, we pray:**
R̶. Lord, hear our prayer.

Assisting minister:
**That they may dedicate their daily work as a pleasing
offering to you, we pray:**
R̶. Lord, hear our prayer.

Assisting minister:
**That each day of Lent they may do something in
your honor, we pray:**
R̶. Lord, hear our prayer.

Assisting minister:
**That they may abstain with courage from everything
that defiles the heart, we pray:**
R̶. Lord, hear our prayer.

Assisting minister:
**That they may grow to love and seek virtue and holi-
ness of life, we pray:**
R̶. Lord, hear our prayer.

Assisting minister:
**That they may renounce self and put others first, we
pray:**
R̶. Lord, hear our prayer.

Assisting minister:
That you will protect and bless their families, we pray:
℞. **Lord, hear our prayer.**

Assisting minister:
That they may share with others the joy they have found in their faith, we pray:
℞. **Lord, hear our prayer.**

PRAYER OVER THE ELECT

135. After the intercessions, the celebrant, with hands out-stretched over the elect, says one of the following prayers.   149

A
Lord God,   149
you created the human race
and are the author of its renewal.
Bless all your adopted children
and add these chosen ones
to the harvest of your new covenant.
As true children of the promise,
may they rejoice in eternal life,
won, not by the power of nature,
but through the mystery of your grace.

We ask this through Christ our Lord.
℞. **Amen.**

B
Father of love and power,   149
it is your will to establish everything in Christ
and to draw us into his all-embracing love.
Guide the elect of your Church:
strengthen them in their vocation,
build them into the kingdom of your Son,
and seal them with the Spirit of your promise.

We ask this through Christ our Lord.
℞. **Amen.**

DISMISSAL OF THE ELECT

136. If the eucharist is to be celebrated, the elect are nor-mally dismissed at this point by use of option A or B; if the   150

elect are to stay for the celebration of the eucharist, option C is used; if the eucharist is not to be celebrated, the entire assembly is dismissed by use of option D.

A The celebrant dismisses the elect in these or similar words.   150

My dear elect, you have set out with us on the road that leads to the glory of Easter. Christ will be your way, your truth, and your life. Until we meet again for the scrutinies, walk always in his peace.

The elect:
Amen.

B As an optional formulary for dismissing the catechu-   USA mens, the celebrant may use these or similar words.

My dear friends, this community now sends you forth to reflect more deeply upon the word of God which you have shared with us today. Be assured of our loving support and prayers for you. We look forward to the day when you will share fully in the Lord's Table.

C If for serious reasons the elect cannot leave (see no.   150 75.3) and must remain with the baptized, they are to be instructed that though they are present at the eucharist, they cannot take part in it as the baptized do. They may be reminded of this by the celebrant in these or similar words.

Although you cannot yet participate fully in the Lord's eucharist, stay with us as a sign of our hope that all God's children will eat and drink with the Lord and work with his Spirit to re-create the face of the earth.

D The celebrant dismisses those present, using these or similar words.

Go in peace, and may the Lord remain with you always.

All:
Thanks be to God.

An appropriate song may conclude the celebration.

LITURGY OF THE EUCHARIST

137. When the eucharist is to follow, intercessory prayer is 151
resumed with the usual general intercessions for the needs
of the Church and the whole world; then, if required, the
profession of faith is said. But for pastoral reasons these
general intercessions and the profession of faith may be
omitted. The liturgy of the eucharist then begins as usual
with the preparation of the gifts.

PERIOD OF PURIFICATION AND ENLIGHTENMENT

The water that I shall give will turn into a spring of eternal life

138. The period of purification and enlightenment, which the rite of election begins, customarily coincides with Lent. In the liturgy and liturgical catechesis of Lent the reminder of baptism already received or the preparation for its reception, as well as the theme of repentance, renew the entire community along with those being prepared to celebrate the paschal mystery, in which each of the elect will share through the sacraments of initiation.[1] For both the elect and the local community, therefore, the Lenten season is a time for spiritual recollection in preparation for the celebration of the paschal mystery.

21
152

139. This is a period of more intense spiritual preparation, consisting more in interior reflection than in catechetical instruction, and is intended to purify the minds and hearts of the elect as they search their own consciences and do penance. This period is intended as well to enlighten the minds and hearts of the elect with a deeper knowledge of Christ the Savior. The celebration of certain rites, particularly the scrutinies (see nos. 141–146) and the presentations (see nos. 147–149), brings about this process of purification and enlightenment and extends it over the course of the entire Lenten season.

22
153

140. Holy Saturday is the day of proximate preparation for the celebration of the sacraments of initiation and on that day the rites of preparation (see nos. 185–192) may be celebrated.

26

[1]See Vatican Council II, Decree on the Church's Missionary Activity *Ad gentes,* no. 14.

RITES BELONGING TO THE PERIOD OF PURIFICATION AND ENLIGHTENMENT

THE SCRUTINIES

141. The scrutinies, which are solemnly celebrated on Sundays and are reinforced by an exorcism, are rites for self-searching and repentance and have above all a spiritual purpose. The scrutinies are meant to uncover, then heal all that is weak, defective, or sinful in the hearts of the elect; to bring out, then strengthen all that is upright, strong, and good. For the scrutinies are celebrated in order to deliver the elect from the power of sin and Satan, to protect them against temptation, and to give them strength in Christ, who is the way, the truth, and the life. These rites, therefore, should complete the conversion of the elect and deepen their resolve to hold fast to Christ and to carry out their decision to love God above all. 25
154

142. Because they are asking for the three sacraments of initiation, the elect must have the intention of achieving an intimate knowledge of Christ and his Church, and they are expected particularly to progress in genuine self-knowledge through serious examination of their lives and true repentance. 155

143. In order to inspire in the elect a desire for purification and redemption by Christ, three scrutinies are celebrated. By this means, first of all, the elect are instructed gradually about the mystery of sin, from which the whole world and every person longs to be delivered and thus saved from its present and future consequences. Second, their spirit is filled with Christ the Redeemer, who is the living water (gospel of the Samaritan woman in the first scrutiny), the light of the world (gospel of the man born blind in the second scrutiny), the resurrection and the life (gospel of Lazarus in the third scrutiny). From the first to the final scrutiny the elect should progress in their perception of sin and their desire for salvation. 157

144. In the rite of exorcism (nos. 154, 168, 175), which is celebrated by a priest or a deacon, the elect, who have already learned from the Church as their mother the mystery of deliverance from sin by Christ, are freed from the effects of sin and from the influence of the devil. They receive new 156

strength in the midst of their spiritual journey and they
open their hearts to receive the gifts of the Savior.

145. The priest or deacon who is the presiding celebrant   158
should carry out the celebration in such a way that the faithful in the assembly will also derive benefit from the liturgy
of the scrutinies and join in the intercessions for the elect.

146. The scrutinies should take place within the ritual   159
Masses "Christian Initiation: The Scrutinies," which are celebrated on the Third, Fourth, and Fifth Sundays of Lent; the
readings with their chants are those given for these Sundays in the Lectionary for Mass, Year A. When, for pastoral
reasons, these ritual Masses cannot be celebrated on their
proper Sundays, they are celebrated on other Sundays of
Lent or even convenient days during the week.

When, because of unusual circumstances and pastoral
needs, the period of purification and enlightenment takes
place outside Lent, the scrutinies are celebrated on Sundays
or even on weekdays, with the usual intervals between celebrations. They are not celebrated on solemnities of the liturgical year (see no. 30).

In every case the ritual Masses "Christian Initiation: The
Scrutinies" are celebrated and in this sequence: for the first
scrutiny the Mass with the gospel of the Samaritan woman;
for the second, the Mass with the gospel of the man born
blind; for the third, the Mass with the gospel of Lazarus.

PRESENTATIONS

147. The presentations take place after the celebration of   25
the scrutinies, unless, for pastoral reasons, they have been   181
anticipated during the period of the catechumenate (see
nos. 79, 104–105). Thus, with the catechumenal formation
of the elect completed, the Church lovingly entrusts to
them the Creed and the Lord's Prayer, the ancient texts
that have always been regarded as expressing the heart of
the Church's faith and prayer. These texts are presented in
order to enlighten the elect. The Creed, as it recalls the
wonderful deeds of God for the salvation of the human
race, suffuses the vision of the elect with the sure light of
faith. The Lord's Prayer fills them with a deeper realization
of the new spirit of adoption by which they will call God

their Father, especially in the midst of the eucharistic assembly.

148. The first presentation to the elect is the presentation of the Creed, during the week following the first scrutiny. The elect are to commit the Creed to memory and they will recite it publicly (nos. 193–196) prior to professing their faith in accordance with that Creed on the day of their baptism.

183
184

149. The second presentation to the elect is the presentation of the Lord's Prayer, during the week following the third scrutiny (but, if necessary, this presentation may be deferred for inclusion in the preparation rites of Holy Saturday; see no. 185). From antiquity the Lord's Prayer has been the prayer proper to those who in baptism have received the spirit of adoption. When the elect have been baptized and take part in their first celebration of the eucharist, they will join the rest of the faithful in saying the Lord's Prayer.

188
189

FIRST SCRUTINY
(Third Sunday of Lent)

LITURGY OF THE WORD

READINGS

150. The texts and the readings for Mass are always those given for the first scrutiny in the Missal and the Lectionary for Mass among the ritual Masses, "Christian Initiation: The Scrutinies." 160

HOMILY

151. After the readings and guided by them, the celebrant explains in the homily the meaning of the first scrutiny in the light of the Lenten liturgy and of the spiritual journey of the elect. 161

INVITATION TO SILENT PRAYER

152. After the homily, the elect with their godparents come forward and stand before the celebrant. 162

The celebrant first addresses the assembly of the faithful, inviting them to pray in silence and to ask that the elect will be given a spirit of repentance, a sense of sin, and the true freedom of the children of God.

The celebrant then addresses the elect, inviting them also to pray in silence and suggesting that as a sign of their inner spirit of repentance they bow their heads or kneel; he concludes his remarks with the following or similar words.

Elect of God, bow your heads [kneel down] and pray.

The elect bow their heads or kneel, and all pray for some time in silence. After the period of silent prayer, the community and the elect stand for the intercessions.

INTERCESSIONS FOR THE ELECT

153. Either of the following formularies, options A or B, may be used for the intercessions for the elect and both the introduction and the intentions may be adapted to fit various circumstances. During the intercessions the godparents stand with their right hand on the shoulder of the elect. 163

[If it is decided, in accordance with no. 156, that after the dismissal of the elect the usual general intercessions of the

Mass are to be omitted and that the liturgy of the eucharist is to begin immediately, intentions for the Church and the whole world are to be added to the following intentions for the elect.]

Celebrant:
Let us pray for these elect whom the Church has confidently chosen. May they successfully complete their long preparation and at the paschal feast find Christ in his sacraments.

A   Assisting minister: 163
That they may ponder the word of God in their hearts and savor its meaning more fully day by day, let us pray to the Lord:
R̸. Lord, hear our prayer.

Assisting minister:
That they may learn to know Christ, who came to save what was lost, let us pray to the Lord:
R̸. Lord, hear our prayer.

Assisting minister:
That they may humbly confess themselves to be sinners, let us pray to the Lord:
R̸. Lord, hear our prayer.

Assisting minister:
That they may sincerely reject everything in their lives that is displeasing and contrary to Christ, let us pray to the Lord:
R̸. Lord, hear our prayer.

Assisting minister:
That the Holy Spirit, who searches every heart, may help them to overcome their weakness through his power, let us pray to the Lord:
R̸. Lord, hear our prayer.

Assisting minister:
That the same Holy Spirit may teach them to know the things of God and how to please him, let us pray to the Lord:
R̸. Lord, hear our prayer.

Assisting minister:
That their families also may put their hope in Christ and find peace and holiness in him, let us pray to the Lord:
R̸. **Lord, hear our prayer.**

Assisting minister:
That we ourselves in preparation for the Easter feast may seek a change of heart, give ourselves to prayer, and persevere in our good works, let us pray to the Lord:
R̸. **Lord, hear our prayer.**

Assisting minister:
That throughout the whole world whatever is weak may be strengthened, whatever is broken restored, whatever is lost found, and what is found redeemed, let us pray to the Lord:
R̸. **Lord, hear our prayer.**

B Assisting minister: 378
That, like the woman of Samaria, our elect may review their lives before Christ and acknowledge their sins, let us pray to the Lord:
R̸. **Lord, hear our prayer.**

Assisting minister:
That they may be freed from the spirit of mistrust that deters people from following Christ, let us pray to the Lord:
R̸. **Lord, hear our prayer.**

Assisting minister:
That while awaiting the gift of God, they may long with all their hearts for the living water that brings eternal life, let us pray to the Lord:
R̸. **Lord, hear our prayer.**

Assisting minister:
That by accepting the Son of God as their teacher, they may become true worshipers of the Father in spirit and in truth, let us pray to the Lord:
R̸. **Lord, hear our prayer.**

Assisting minister:
That they may share with their friends and neighbors the wonder of their own meeting with Christ, let us pray to the Lord:
℟. **Lord, hear our prayer.**

Assisting minister:
That those whose lives are empty for want of the word of God may come to the Gospel of Christ, let us pray to the Lord:
℟. **Lord, hear our prayer.**

Assisting minister:
That all of us may learn from Christ to do the Father's will in love, let us pray to the Lord:
℟. **Lord, hear our prayer.**

EXORCISM

154. After the intercessions, the rite continues with one of the following exorcisms. 164

A The celebrant faces the elect and, with hands joined, says: 164
God of power,
you sent your Son to be our Savior.
Grant that these catechumens,
who, like the woman of Samaria, thirst for living water,
may turn to the Lord as they hear his word
and acknowledge the sins and weaknesses that weigh them down.

Protect them from vain reliance on self
and defend them from the power of Satan.

Free them from the spirit of deceit,
so that, admitting the wrong they have done,
they may attain purity of heart
and advance on the way to salvation.

We ask this through Christ our Lord.
℟. **Amen.**

Here, if this can be done conveniently, the celebrant lays hands on each one of the elect.

Then, with hands outstretched over all the elect, he continues:

Lord Jesus,
you are the fountain for which they thirst,
you are the Master whom they seek.
In your presence
they dare not claim to be without sin,
for you alone are the Holy One of God.

They open their hearts to you in faith,
they confess their faults
and lay bare their hidden wounds.
In your love free them from their infirmities,
heal their sickness,
quench their thirst, and give them peace.

In the power of your name,
which we call upon in faith,
stand by them now and heal them.
Rule over that spirit of evil,
conquered by your rising from the dead.

Show your elect the way of salvation in the Holy
    Spirit,
that they may come to worship the Father in truth,
for you live and reign for ever and ever.
R̸. Amen.

B The celebrant faces the elect and, with hands joined, says:

379

All-merciful Father,
through your Son you revealed your mercy
to the woman of Samaria;
and moved by that same care
you have offered salvation to all sinners.

Look favorably on these elect,
who desire to become your adopted children
through the power of your sacraments.

Free them from the slavery of sin,
and for Satan's crushing yoke
exchange the gentle yoke of Jesus.

Protect them in every danger,
that they may serve you faithfully in peace and joy
and render you thanks for ever.
℞. Amen.

Here, if this can be done conveniently, the celebrant lays
hands on each one of the elect.

Then, with hands outstretched over all the elect, he
continues:
Lord Jesus,
in your merciful wisdom
you touched the heart of the sinful woman
and taught her to worship the Father
in spirit and in truth.

Now, by your power,
free these elect from the cunning of Satan,
as they draw near to the fountain of living water.

Touch their hearts with the power of the Holy Spirit,
that they may come to know the Father
in true faith, which expresses itself in love,
for you live and reign for ever and ever.
℞. Amen.

An appropriate song may be sung, for example, Psalm 6,
26, 32, 38, 39, 40, 51, 116:1–9, 130, 139, or 142.

DISMISSAL OF THE ELECT

155. If the eucharist is to be celebrated, the elect are normally dismissed at this point by use of option **A** or **B**; if the
elect are to stay for the celebration of the eucharist, option
C is used; if the eucharist is not to be celebrated, the entire
assembly is dismissed by use of option **D**.

A   The celebrant dismisses the elect in these or similar
words. 165
Dear elect, go in peace, and join us again at the next
scrutiny. May the Lord remain with you always.

Elect:
Amen.

B As an optional formulary for dismissing the catechu-   USA
mens, the celebrant may use these or similar words.
**My dear friends, this community now sends you
forth to reflect more deeply upon the word of God
which you have shared with us today. Be assured of
our loving support and prayers for you. We look forward to the day when you will share fully in the
Lord's Table.**

C If for serious reasons the elect cannot leave (see no.
75.3) and must remain with the baptized, they are to be instructed that though they are present at the eucharist, they
cannot take part in it as the baptized do. They may be reminded of this by the celebrant in these or similar words.

**Although you cannot yet participate fully in the
Lord's eucharist, stay with us as a sign of our hope
that all God's children will eat and drink with the
Lord and work with his Spirit to re-create the face of
the earth.**

D The celebrant dismisses those present, using these or
similar words.
**Go in peace, and may the Lord remain with you
always.**

All:
Thanks be to God.

An appropriate song may conclude the celebration.

LITURGY OF THE EUCHARIST

156. When the eucharist is to follow, intercessory prayer is   166
resumed with the usual general intercessions for the needs
of the Church and the whole world; then, if required, the
profession of faith is said. But for pastoral reasons these
general intercessions and the profession of faith may be
omitted. The liturgy of the eucharist then begins as usual
with the preparation of the gifts. In the eucharistic prayer
there is to be a remembrance of the elect and their godparents (see ritual Mass "Christian Initiation: The Scrutinies").

PRESENTATION OF THE CREED
(Third Week of Lent)

157. The presentation of the Creed, which takes place during the week after the first scrutiny, should preferably be celebrated in the presence of a community of the faithful, within Mass after the homily. ^{182 184}

LITURGY OF THE WORD

READINGS

158. In place of the readings assigned for the weekday Mass, the following readings are used, as indicated in the Lectionary for Mass, ritual Masses, "Christian Initiation: Presentation of the Creed." ¹⁸⁵

FIRST READING

Deuteronomy 6:1–7—*Listen, Israel: You shall love the Lord your God with all your heart.*

RESPONSORIAL PSALM

Psalm 19:8, 9, 10, 11

℟. (John 6:68c) **Lord, you have the words of everlasting life.**

SECOND READING

Romans 10:8–13—*The confession of faith of the elect.*

   Or:

1 Corinthians 15:1–8a (longer) or 1–4 (shorter)—*The Gospel will save you only if you keep believing what I preached to you.*

VERSE BEFORE THE GOSPEL

John 3:16
God loved the world so much, he gave us his only Son, that all who believe in him might have eternal life.

GOSPEL

Matthew 16:13–18—*On this rock I will build my Church.*

   Or:

John 12:44–50—*I, the light, have come into the world, so that whoever believes in me need not remain in the dark any more.*

HOMILY

159. After the readings and guided by them, the celebrant   185
explains in the homily the meaning and importance of the
Creed in relation to the teaching that the elect have already
received and to the profession of faith that they must make
at their baptism and uphold throughout their lives.

PRESENTATION OF THE CREED

160. After the homily, a deacon or other assisting minister   186
says:

**Let the elect now come forward to receive the Creed
from the Church.**

Before beginning the Apostles' Creed (option A) or the
Nicene Creed (option B), the celebrant addresses the elect
in these or similar words.

**My dear friends, listen carefully to the words of that
faith by which you will be justified. The words are
few, but the mysteries they contain are great. Receive
them with a sincere heart and be faithful to them.**

A   *Apostles' Creed*
The celebrant alone begins:
I believe in God, the Father almighty,

As the elect listen, he continues with the assembly of the
faithful.
creator of heaven and earth.

I believe in Jesus Christ, his only Son, our Lord.
   **He was conceived by the power of the Holy Spirit
      and born of the Virgin Mary.**
   **He suffered under Pontius Pilate,
      was crucified, died, and was buried.**
   He descended to the dead.
   On the third day he rose again.
   **He ascended into heaven,
      and is seated at the right hand of the Father.**
   **He will come again to judge the living and the
      dead.**
   **I believe in the Holy Spirit,
      the holy catholic Church,
      the communion of saints,
      the forgiveness of sins,**

**the resurrection of the body,
and the life everlasting. Amen.**

B   *Nicene Creed*
The celebrant alone begins:

We believe in one God,

As the elect listen, he continues with the assembly of the
faithful.
   **the Father, the Almighty,
   maker of heaven and earth,
   of all that is seen and unseen.**

**We believe in one Lord, Jesus Christ,
   the only Son of God,
   eternally begotten of the Father,
   God from God, Light from Light,
   true God from true God,
   begotten, not made,
   one in Being with the Father.
   Through him all things were made.
   For us men and for our salvation
      he came down from heaven:
   by the power of the Holy Spirit
      he was born of the Virgin Mary,
         and became man.
   For our sake he was crucified under Pontius Pilate;
      he suffered, died, and was buried.
      On the third day he rose again
         in fulfillment of the Scriptures;
      he ascended into heaven
         and is seated at the right hand of the Father.
   He will come again in glory to judge the living
      and the dead,
      and his kingdom will have no end.
   We believe in the Holy Spirit, the Lord, the giver
      of life,
   who proceeds from the Father and the Son.
   With the Father and the Son he is worshiped and
      glorified.
   He has spoken through the Prophets.**

We believe in one holy catholic and apostolic Church.
We acknowledge one baptism for the forgiveness of sins.
We look for the resurrection of the dead, and the life of the world to come. Amen.

PRAYER OVER THE ELECT

161. Using the following or similar words, the celebrant invites the faithful to pray.   187

Let us pray for these elect, that God in his mercy may make them responsive to his love, so that through the waters of rebirth they may receive pardon for their sins and have life in Christ Jesus our Lord.

All pray in silence.

Then the celebrant, with hands outstretched over the elect, says:
Lord,
eternal source of light, justice, and truth,
take under your tender care
your servants N. and N.

Purify them and make them holy;
give them true knowledge, sure hope, and sound understanding,
and make them worthy
to receive the grace of baptism.

We ask this through Christ our Lord.
R̶. Amen.

DISMISSAL OF THE ELECT

162. If the eucharist is to be celebrated, the elect are normally dismissed at this point by use of option A or B; if the elect are to stay for the celebration of the eucharist, option C is used; if the eucharist is not to be celebrated, the entire assembly is dismissed by use of option D.

LITURGY OF THE EUCHARIST

163. After the elect leave, the celebration of Mass continues in the usual way.

A The celebrant dismisses the elect in these or similar words.
Dear elect, go in peace, and may the Lord remain with you always.

Elect:
Amen.

B As an optional formulary for dismissing the catechumens, the celebrant may use these or similar words.
My dear friends, this community now sends you forth to reflect more deeply upon the word of God which you have shared with us today. Be assured of our loving support and prayers for you. We look forward to the day when you will share fully in the Lord's Table.

C If for serious reasons the elect cannot leave (see no. 75.3) and must remain with the baptized, they are to be instructed that though they are present at the eucharist, they cannot take part in it as the baptized do. They may be reminded of this by the celebrant in these or similar words.

Although you cannot yet participate fully in the Lord's eucharist, stay with us as a sign of our hope that all God's children will eat and drink with the Lord and work with his Spirit to re-create the face of the earth.

D The celebrant dismisses those present, using these or similar words.
Go in peace, and may the Lord remain with you always.

All:
Thanks be to God.

An appropriate song may conclude the celebration.

SECOND SCRUTINY
(Fourth Sunday of Lent)

LITURGY OF THE WORD

READINGS

164. The texts and readings for Mass are always those   167
given for the second scrutiny in the Missal and the
Lectionary for Mass among the ritual Masses, "Christian Initiation: The Scrutinies."

HOMILY

165. After the readings and guided by them, the celebrant   168
explains in the homily the meaning of the second scrutiny
in the light of the Lenten liturgy and of the spiritual journey of the elect.

INVITATION TO SILENT PRAYER

166. See no. 152   169

INTERCESSIONS FOR THE ELECT

167. Either of the following formularies, options A or B,   170
may be used for the intercessions for the elect and both the
introduction and the intentions may be adapted to fit various circumstances. During the intercessions the godparents
stand with their right hand on the shoulder of the elect.

[If it is decided, in accord with no. 170, that after the dismissal of the elect the usual general intercessions of the
Mass are to be omitted and that the liturgy of the eucharist
is to begin immediately, intentions for the Church and the
whole world are to be added to the following intentions for
the elect.]

Celebrant:
**Let us pray for these elect whom God has called, that
they may remain faithful to him and boldly give witness to the words of eternal life.**

A   Assisting minister: 170
**That, trusting in the truth of Christ, they may find
freedom of mind and heart and preserve it always,
let us pray to the Lord:**

℞. Lord, hear our prayer.

Assisting minister:
That, preferring the folly of the cross to the wisdom of the world, they may glory in God alone, let us pray to the Lord:
℞. Lord, hear our prayer.

Assisting minister:
That, freed by the power of the Spirit, they may put all fear behind them and press forward with confidence, let us pray to the Lord:
℞. Lord, hear our prayer.

Assisting minister:
That, transformed in the Spirit, they may seek those things that are holy and just, let us pray to the Lord:
℞. Lord, hear our prayer.

Assisting minister:
That all who suffer persecution for Christ's name may find their strength in him, let us pray to the Lord:
℞. Lord, hear our prayer.

Assisting minister:
That those families and nations prevented from embracing the faith may be granted freedom to believe the Gospel, let us pray to the Lord:
℞. Lord, hear our prayer.

Assisting minister:
That we who are faced with the values of the world may remain faithful to the spirit of the Gospel, let us pray to the Lord:
℞. Lord, hear our prayer.

Assisting minister:
That the whole world, which the Father so loves, may attain in the Church complete spiritual freedom, let us pray to the Lord:
℞. Lord, hear our prayer.

B Assisting minister:

That God may dispel darkness and be the light that shines in the hearts of our elect, let us pray to the Lord:
℟. **Lord, hear our prayer.**

Assisting minister:

That he may gently lead them to Christ, the light of the world, let us pray to the Lord:
℟. **Lord, hear our prayer.**

Assisting minister:

That our elect may open their hearts to God and acknowledge him as the source of light and the witness of truth, let us pray to the Lord:
℟. **Lord, hear our prayer.**

Assisting minister:

That he may heal them and preserve them from the unbelief of this world, let us pray to the Lord:
℟. **Lord, hear our prayer.**

Assisting minister:

That, saved by him who takes away the sin of the world, they may be freed from the contagion and forces of sin, let us pray to the Lord:
℟. **Lord, hear our prayer.**

Assisting minister:

That, enlightened by the Holy Spirit, they may never fail to profess the Good News of salvation and share it with others, let us pray to the Lord:
℟. **Lord, hear our prayer.**

Assisting minister:

That all of us, by the example of our lives, may become in Christ the light of the world, let us pray to the Lord:
℟. **Lord, hear our prayer.**

Assisting minister:

That every inhabitant of the earth may acknowledge the true God, the Creator of all things, who bestows

upon us the gift of Spirit and life, let us pray to the
Lord:
℟. Lord, hear our prayer.

EXORCISM

168. After the intercessions, the rite continues with one of   171
the following exorcisms.

A   The celebrant faces the elect and, with hands joined,   171
says:
Father of mercy,
you led the man born blind
to the kingdom of light
through the gift of faith in your Son.

Free these elect
from the false values that surround and blind them.
Set them firmly in your truth,
children of the light for ever.

We ask this through Christ our Lord.
℟. Amen.

Here, if this can be done conveniently, the celebrant lays
hands on each one of the elect.

Then, with hands outstretched over all the elect, he
continues:
Lord Jesus,
you are the true light that enlightens the world.
Through your Spirit of truth
free those who are enslaved by the father of lies.

Stir up the desire for good in these elect,
whom you have chosen for your sacraments.

Let them rejoice in your light, that they may see,
and, like the man born blind whose sight you
    restored,
let them prove to be staunch and fearless witnesses
    to the faith,
for you are Lord for ever and ever.
℟. Amen.

B The celebrant faces the elect and, with hands joined, says:

Lord God,
source of unfailing light,
by the death and resurrection of Christ
you have cast out the darkness of hatred and lies
and poured forth the light of truth and love
upon the human family.

Hear our prayers for these elect,
whom you have called to be your adopted children.

Enable them to pass from darkness to light
and, delivered from the prince of darkness,
to live always as children of the light.

We ask this through Christ our Lord.
R̷. Amen.

Here, if this can be done conveniently, the celebrant lays hands on each one of the elect.

Then, with hands outstretched over all the elect, he continues:
Lord Jesus,
at your own baptism
the heavens were opened
and you received the Holy Spirit
to empower you to proclaim the Good News to the
    poor
and restore sight to the blind.

Pour out the same Holy Spirit on these elect,
who long for your sacraments.
Guide them along the paths of right faith,
safe from error, doubt, and unbelief,
so that with eyes unsealed
they may come to see you face to face,
for you live and reign for ever and ever.
R̷. Amen.

An appropriate song may be sung, for example, Psalm 6, 26, 32, 38, 39, 40, 51, 116:1–9, 130, 139, or 142.

DISMISSAL OF THE ELECT
169. See no. 155.   172

LITURGY OF THE EUCHARIST
170. See no. 156.   173

THIRD SCRUTINY
(Fifth Sunday of Lent)

LITURGY OF THE WORD

READINGS

171. The texts and readings for Mass are always those   *174*
given for the third scrutiny in the Missal and the Lectionary
for Mass among the ritual Masses, "Christian Initiation: The
Scrutinies."

HOMILY

172. After the readings and guided by them, the celebrant   *175*
explains in the homily the meaning of the third scrutiny in
the light of the Lenten liturgy and of the spiritual journey
of the elect.

INVITATION TO SILENT PRAYER

173. See no. 152.   *176*

INTERCESSIONS FOR THE ELECT

174. Either of the following formularies, options A or B,   *177*
may be used for the intercessions for the elect and both the
introduction and the intentions may be adapted to fit various circumstances. During the intercessions the godparents
stand with their right hand on the shoulder of the elect.

[If it is decided, in accord with no. 177, that after the dismissal of the elect the usual general intercessions of the
Mass are to be omitted and that the liturgy of the eucharist
is to begin immediately, intentions for the Church and the
whole world are to be added to the following intentions for
the elect.]

Celebrant:
**Let us pray for these elect whom God has chosen.
May the grace of the sacraments conform them to
Christ in his passion and resurrection and enable
them to triumph over the bitter fate of death.**

A   Assisting minister: *177*
**That faith may strengthen them against worldly de-
ceits of every kind, let us pray to the Lord:
℟. Lord, hear our prayer.**

Assisting minister:
That they may always thank God, who has chosen to rescue them from their ignorance of eternal life and to set them on the way of salvation, let us pray to the Lord:
℟. **Lord, hear our prayer.**

Assisting minister:
That the example and prayers of catechumens who have shed their blood for Christ may encourage these elect in their hope of eternal life, let us pray to the Lord:
℟. **Lord, hear our prayer.**

Assisting minister:
That they may all have a horror of sin, which distorts life, let us pray to the Lord:
℟. **Lord, hear our prayer.**

Assisting minister:
That those who are saddened by the death of family or friends may find comfort in Christ, let us pray to the Lord:
℟. **Lord, hear our prayer.**

Assisting minister:
That we too at Easter may again be confirmed in our hope of rising to life with Christ, let us pray to the Lord:
℟. **Lord, hear our prayer.**

Assisting minister:
That the whole world, which God has created in love, may flower in faith and charity and so receive new life, let us pray to the Lord:
℟. **Lord, hear our prayer.**

B Assisting minister: 386
That these elect may be given the faith to acknowledge Christ as the resurrection and the life, we pray to the Lord:
℟. **Lord, hear our prayer.**

Assisting minister:
That they may be freed from sin and grow in the holiness that leads to eternal life, we pray to the Lord:
R̸. Lord, hear our prayer.

Assisting minister:
That liberated by repentance from the shackles of sin they may become like Christ by baptism, dead to sin and alive for ever in God's sight, we pray to the Lord:
R̸. Lord, hear our prayer.

Assisting minister:
That they may be filled with the hope of the life-giving Spirit and prepare themselves thoroughly for their birth to new life, we pray to the Lord:
R̸. Lord, hear our prayer.

Assisting minister:
That the eucharistic food, which they are soon to receive, may make them one with Christ, the source of life and of resurrection, we pray to the Lord:
R̸. Lord, hear our prayer.

Assisting minister:
That all of us may walk in newness of life and show to the world the power of the risen Christ, we pray to the Lord:
R̸. Lord, hear our prayer.

Assisting minister:
That all the world may find Christ and acknowledge in him the promises of eternal life, we pray to the Lord:
R̸. Lord, hear our prayer.

EXORCISM

175. After the intercessions, the rite continues with one of the following exorcisms.   178

A The celebrant faces the elect and, with hands joined, says: 178
Father of life and God not of the dead but of the living,

you sent your Son to proclaim life,
to snatch us from the realm of death,
and to lead us to the resurrection.

Free these elect
from the death-dealing power of the spirit of evil,
so that they may bear witness
to their new life in the risen Christ,
for he lives and reigns for ever and ever.
℟. Amen.

Here, if this can be done conveniently, the celebrant lays
hands on each one of the elect.

Then, with hands outstretched over all the elect, he
continues:
Lord Jesus,
by raising Lazarus from the dead
you showed that you came that we might have life
and have it more abundantly.

Free from the grasp of death
those who await your life-giving sacraments
and deliver them from the spirit of corruption.

Through your Spirit, who gives life,
fill them with faith, hope, and charity,
that they may live with you always
in the glory of your resurrection,
for you are Lord for ever and ever.
℟. Amen.

B   The celebrant faces the elect and, with hands joined,
says: 387
Father,
source of all life,
in giving life to the living you seek out the image of
    your glory
and in raising the dead you reveal your unbounded
    power.

Rescue these elect from the tyranny of death,
for they long for new life through baptism.

Free them from the slavery of Satan,
the source of sin and death,
who seeks to corrupt the world you created
and saw to be good.

Place them under the reign of your beloved Son,
that they may share in the power of his resurrection
and give witness to your glory before all.

We ask this through Christ our Lord.
℟. Amen.

Here, if this can be done conveniently, the celebrant lays hands on each one of the elect.

Then, with hands outstretched over all the elect, he continues:
Lord Jesus Christ,
you commanded Lazarus to step forth alive from his
    tomb
and by your own resurrection freed all people from
    death.

We pray for these your servants,
who eagerly approach the waters of new birth
and hunger for the banquet of life.

Do not let the power of death hold them back,
for, by their faith,
they will share in the triumph of your resurrection,
for you live and reign for ever and ever.
℟. Amen.

An appropriate song may be sung, for example, Psalm 6, 26, 32, 38, 39, 40, 51, 116:1–9, 130, 139, or 142.

DISMISSAL OF THE ELECT
176. See no. 162.

LITURGY OF THE EUCHARIST
177. See no. 156.

PRESENTATION OF THE LORD'S PRAYER
(Fifth Week of Lent)

178. The presentation of the Lord's Prayer, which takes   182
place during the week after the third scrutiny, should pref-   189
erably be celebrated in the presence of a community of the
faithful, within Mass.

LITURGY OF THE WORD

READINGS

179. In place of the first reading assigned for the weekday   190
Mass, the following two readings are used, as indicated in
the Lectionary for Mass, ritual Masses, "Christian Initiation:
Presentation of the Lord's Prayer."

FIRST READING

Hosea 11:1b, 3–4, 8c–9—*I have led you with cords of love.*

RESPONSORIAL PSALM

Psalm 23:1–3a, 3b–4, 5, 6
℟. (v.1) **The Lord is my shepherd; there is nothing I
shall want.**

Or:

Psalm 103:1–2, 8 and 10, 11–12, 13 and 18
℟. (v.3) **As a father is kind to his children, so kind is
the Lord to those who fear him.**

SECOND READING

Romans 8:14–17, 26–27—*You have received the Spirit that
makes you God's children and in that Spirit we cry out, "Abba,
Father!"*

Or:

Galatians 4:4–7—*God has sent the Spirit of his Son into our
hearts: the Spirit that cries, "Abba, Father!"*

VERSE BEFORE THE GOSPEL

Romans 8:15
**You have received the Spirit which makes us God's
children, and in that Spirit we call God our Father.**

GOSPEL READING (PRESENTATION OF THE LORD'S PRAYER)

180. After the first and second reading, an assisting dea-   191
con or other minister says:

Let those who are to receive the Lord's Prayer now come forward.

The celebrant first addresses the following or similar words to the elect.
Listen to the gospel reading in which our Lord teaches his followers how to pray.

The gospel reading follows.
A reading from the holy gospel according to Matthew.

At that time Jesus said to his disciples: "Say this when you pray:

**'Our Father,
who art in heaven,
hallowed be thy name;
thy kingdom come;
thy will be done on earth
as it is in heaven.
Give us this day our daily bread
and forgive us our trespasses
as we forgive those
who trespass against us;
and lead us not into temptation,
but deliver us from evil.' "**

HOMILY

181. After the gospel presentation, the celebrant in the   191
homily explains the meaning and importance of the Lord's Prayer.

PRAYER OVER THE ELECT

182. After the homily, the celebrant, using the following   192
or similar words, invites the faithful to pray.

Let us pray for these elect, that God in his mercy may make them responsive to his love, so that through the waters of rebirth they may receive par-

don for their sins and have life in Christ Jesus our
Lord.

All pray in silence.

Then the celebrant, with hands outstretched over the elect,
says:
**Almighty and eternal God,
you continually enlarge the family of your Church.**

**Deepen the faith and understanding
of these elect, chosen for baptism.
Give them new birth in your living waters,
so that they may be numbered among your adopted
   children.**

**We ask this through Christ our Lord.
℟. Amen.**

DISMISSAL OF THE ELECT
183. See no. 162.

LITURGY OF THE EUCHARIST

184. After the elect leave, the celebration of Mass continues in the usual way.

PREPARATION RITES ON HOLY SATURDAY

185. In proximate preparation for the celebration of the sac-   26
raments of initiation: 193

1. The elect are to be advised that on Holy Saturday
they should refrain from their usual activities, spend their
time in prayer and reflection, and, as far as they can, observe a fast.

2. When it is possible to bring the elect together on
Holy Saturday for reflection and prayer, some or all of the
following rites may be celebrated as an immediate preparation for the sacraments: the presentation of the Lord's
Prayer, if it has been deferred (see nos. 149, 178–180), the
"return" or recitation of the Creed (nos. 193–196), the
ephphetha rite (nos. 197–199), the choosing of a baptismal
name (nos. 200–202).

186. The choice and arrangement of these rites should be   195
guided by what best suits the particular circumstances of   197
the elect, but the following should be observed with regard
to their celebration:

1. In cases where celebration of the presentation of the
Creed was not possible, the recitation of the Creed is not
celebrated.

2. When both the recitation of the Creed and the
ephphetha rite are celebrated, the ephphetha rite immediately precedes the "Prayer before the Recitation" (no. 194).

MODEL FOR A CELEBRATION OF THE PREPARATION RITES

187. *Song:* When the elect have gathered, the celebration
begins with a suitable song.

188. *Greeting:* After the singing, the celebrant greets the
elect and any of the faithful who are present, using one of
the greetings for Mass or other suitable words.

189. *Reading of the Word of God:* Where indicated in the particular rites, the reading of the word of God follows; the
readings may be chosen from those suggested for each rite.
If more than one reading is used, a suitable psalm or hymn
may be sung between the readings.

190. *Homily:* Where indicated in the particular rites, a brief homily or an explanation of the text follows the reading of the word of God.

191. *Celebration of the Rites Chosen:* See nos. 193–202.

192. *Concluding Rites:* The celebration may be concluded with the prayer of blessing and dismissal given in nos. 204–205.

RECITATION OF THE CREED

193. The rite of recitation of the Creed prepares the elect   194
for the profession of faith they will make immediately before they are baptized (no. 225); the rite also instructs them
in their duty to proclaim the message of the Gospel.

READING AND HOMILY

194. One of the following readings may be used, or an-   196
other appropriate reading may be chosen:

Matthew 16:13–17—*You are Christ, the Son of the living God.*

    Or:

John 6:35, 63–71—*To whom shall we go? You have the words of
eternal life.*

A brief homily follows.

[If the ephphetha rite (nos. 197–199) is to be included as a
preparation rite, it is celebrated before the following
prayer.]

PRAYER BEFORE THE RECITATION

195. The celebrant, with hands outstretched, says the fol-   198
lowing prayer.

Let us pray.

Lord,
we pray to you for these elect,
who have now accepted for themselves
the loving purpose and the mysteries
that you revealed in the life of your Son.

As they profess their belief with their lips,
may they have faith in their hearts
and accomplish your will in their lives.

We ask this through Christ our Lord.
R̸. Amen.

RECITATION OF THE CREED

196. The elect then recite the Creed. Depending on the ver-   199
sion that was entrusted to them at the presentation, they

recite either the Apostles' Creed, option A, or the Nicene
Creed, option B.

A Apostles' Creed

Elect:

**I believe in God, the Father almighty,
    creator of heaven and earth.**

I believe in Jesus Christ, his only Son, our Lord . . .

The rest of the Creed is recited as in no. 160A.

B Nicene Creed

Elect:

**We believe in one God,
    the Father, the Almighty . . .**

The rest of the Creed is recited as in no. 160B.

EPHPHETHA RITE

197. By the power of its symbolism the ephphetha rite, or 200
rite of opening the ears and mouth, impresses on the elect
their need of grace in order that they may hear the word of
God and profess it for their salvation.

READING AND INSTRUCTION

198. The reading is as indicated for this rite in the 201
Lectionary for Mass; the celebrant gives a brief explanation
of the text.

Mark 7:31–37—*Ephphetha, that is, be opened.*

EPHPHETHA

199. The elect come before the celebrant. A suitable song 202
may be sung as the celebrant touches the right and left ear
and the closed lips of each of the elect with his thumb and
says the following formulary.

[If there are a great many elect, additional priests or deacons may assist in carrying out the rite.]

**Ephphetha: that is, be opened,
that you may profess the faith you hear,
to the praise and glory of God.**

CHOOSING A BAPTISMAL NAME

200. The rite of choosing a baptismal name may be cele- 203
brated on Holy Saturday, unless it was included in the rite
of acceptance into the order of catechumens (see nos. 33.4,
73). The elect may choose a new name, which is either a
traditional Christian name or a name of regional usage that
is not incompatible with Christian beliefs. Where it seems
better suited to the circumstances and the elect are not too
numerous, the naming may consist simply in an explanation of the given name of each of the elect.

READING AND INSTRUCTION

201. There may be a reading—chosen, for example, from 204
the following list—and a brief explanation by the celebrant.

1. Genesis 17:1–7—*You will be called Abraham.*

2. Isaiah 62:1–5—*You will be called by a new name.*

3. Revelation 3:11–13—*I will write my new name upon him.*

4. Matthew 16:13–18—*You are Peter.*

5. John 1:40–42—*You will be called Peter.*

NAMING OF THE ELECT

202. If as baptismal names the elect have chosen new 205
names, option A is used; if they are to use their given
names, option B is used.

A
The celebrant asks each of the elect to state the new name
chosen; then he says the following or similar words.

N., from now on you will [also] be called N.

The elect responds by saying "**Amen**" or in some other suitable way.

B
The celebrant applies some Christian interpretation to the
given name of each of the elect.

CONCLUDING RITES

203. The celebration of the preparation rites may be concluded with a prayer of blessing over the elect and a dismissal.

PRAYER OF BLESSING

204. The celebrant invites those present to pray.
Let us pray.

Then, with hands outstretched over the elect, the celebrant says the following prayer.
Father,   122
through your holy prophets
you proclaimed to all who draw near you,
"Wash and be cleansed,"
and through Christ you have granted us rebirth in
  the Spirit.

Bless these your servants
as they earnestly prepare for baptism.

Fulfill your promise:
sanctify them in preparation for your gifts,
that they may come to be reborn as your children
and enter the community of your Church.

We ask this through Christ our Lord.
R̶. Amen.

DISMISSAL

205. The celebrant may inform the elect of the time and place they are to meet for the Easter Vigil; the celebrant then dismisses them, using the following or another suitable formulary.

May the Lord be with you
until we gather again
to celebrate his paschal mystery.

Elect:
Amen.

THIRD STEP: CELEBRATION OF THE SACRAMENTS OF INITIATION

When we were baptized we joined Jesus in death so that we might walk in the newness of his life

206. The third step in the Christian initiation of adults is the celebration of the sacraments of baptism, confirmation, and eucharist. Through this final step the elect, receiving pardon for their sins, are admitted into the people of God. They are graced with adoption as children of God and are led by the Holy Spirit into the promised fullness of time begun in Christ[1] and, as they share in the eucharistic sacrifice and meal, even to a foretaste of the kingdom of God. | 27

207. The usual time for the celebration of the sacraments of initiation is the Easter Vigil (see no. 23), at which preferably the bishop himself presides as celebrant, at least for the initiation of those who are fourteen years old or older (see no. 12). As indicated in the Roman Missal, "Easter Vigil" (no. 44), the conferral of the sacraments follows the blessing of the water. | 208

208. When the celebration takes place outside the usual time (see nos. 26–27), care should be taken to ensure that it has a markedly paschal character (see *Christian Initiation, General Introduction,* no. 6). Thus the texts for one of the ritual Masses "Christian Initiation: Baptism" given in the Roman Missal are used, and the readings are chosen from those given in the Lectionary for Mass, "Celebration of the Sacraments of Initiation apart from the Easter Vigil." | 209

CELEBRATION OF BAPTISM

209. The celebration of baptism has as its center and high point the baptismal washing and the invocation of the Holy Trinity. Beforehand there are rites that have an inherent relationship to the baptismal washing: first, the blessing of water, then the renunciation of sin by the elect, and their profession of faith. Following the baptismal washing, the effects received through this sacrament are given expression in the explanatory rites: the anointing with chrism (when confirmation does not immediately follow baptism), the | 28 33

[1]See Vatican Council II, Dogmatic Constitution on the Church *Lumen gentium*, no. 48; also Ephesians 1:10.

clothing with a white garment, and the presentation of a lighted candle.

210. *Prayer over the Water:* The celebration of baptism be- 29
gins with the blessing of water, even when the sacraments 210
of initiation are received outside the Easter season. Should
the sacraments be celebrated outside the Easter Vigil but
during the Easter season (see no. 26), the water blessed at
the Vigil is used, but a prayer of thanksgiving, having the
same themes as the blessing, is included. The blessing declares the religious meaning of water as God's creation and
the sacramental use of water in the unfolding of the paschal
mystery, and the blessing is also a remembrance of God's
wonderful works in the history of salvation.

The blessing thus introduces an invocation of the Trinity at
the very outset of the celebration of baptism. For it calls to
mind the mystery of God's love from the beginning of the
world and the creation of the human race; by invoking the
Holy Spirit and proclaiming Christ's death and resurrection,
it impresses on the mind the newness of Christian baptism,
by which we share in his own death and resurrection and
receive the holiness of God himself.

211. *Renunciation of Sin and Profession of Faith:* In their re- 30
nunciation of sin and profession of faith those to be bap- 211
tized express their explicit faith in the paschal mystery that
has already been recalled in the blessing of water and that
will be connoted by the words of the sacrament soon to be
spoken by the baptizing minister. Adults are not saved unless they come forward of their own accord and with the
will to accept God's gift through their own belief. The faith
of those to be baptized is not simply the faith of the
Church, but the personal faith of each one of them and
each one of them is expected to keep it a living faith.

Therefore the renunciation of sin and the profession of faith
are an apt prelude to baptism, the sacrament of that faith
by which the elect hold fast to God and receive new birth
from him. Because of the renunciation of sin and the profession of faith, which form the one rite, the elect will not be
baptized merely passively but will receive this great sacrament with the active resolve to renounce error and to hold
fast to God. By their own personal act in the rite of renouncing sin and professing their faith, the elect, as was prefig-

ured in the first covenant with the patriarchs, renounce sin and Satan in order to commit themselves for ever to the promise of the Savior and to the mystery of the Trinity. By professing their faith before the celebrant and the entire community, the elect express the intention, developed to maturity during the preceding periods of initiation, to enter into a new covenant with Christ. Thus these adults embrace the faith that through divine help the Church has handed down, and are baptized in that faith.

212. *Baptism:* Immediately after their profession of living   31
faith in Christ's paschal mystery, the elect come forward and receive that mystery as expressed in the washing with water; thus once the elect have professed faith in the Father, Son, and Holy Spirit, invoked by the celebrant, the divine persons act so that those they have chosen receive divine adoption and become members of the people of God.

213. Therefore in the celebration of baptism the washing   32
with water should take on its full importance as the sign of that mystical sharing in Christ's death and resurrection through which those who believe in his name die to sin and rise to eternal life. Either immersion or the pouring of water should be chosen for the rite, whichever will serve in individual cases and in the various traditions and circumstances to ensure the clear understanding that this washing is not a mere purification rite but the sacrament of being joined to Christ.

214. *Explanatory Rites:* The baptismal washing is followed   33
by rites that give expression to the effects of the sacrament just received. The anointing with chrism is a sign of the royal priesthood of the baptized and that they are now numbered in the company of the people of God. The clothing with the baptismal garment signifies the new dignity they have received. The presentation of a lighted candle shows that they are called to walk as befits the children of the light.

CELEBRATION OF CONFIRMATION

215. In accord with the ancient practice followed in the Ro-   34
man liturgy, adults are not to be baptized without receiving confirmation immediately afterward, unless some serious reason stands in the way. The conjunction of the two cele-

brations signifies the unity of the paschal mystery, the close link between the mission of the Son and the outpouring of the Holy Spirit, and the connection between the two sacraments through which the Son and the Holy Spirit come with the Father to those who are baptized.

216. Accordingly, confirmation is conferred after the explanatory rites of baptism, the anointing after baptism (no. 228) being omitted.

35

THE NEOPHYTES' FIRST SHARING IN THE CELEBRATION OF THE EUCHARIST

217. Finally in the celebration of the eucharist, as they take part for the first time and with full right, the newly baptized reach the culminating point in their Christian initiation. In this eucharist the neophytes, now raised to the ranks of the royal priesthood, have an active part both in the general intercessions and, to the extent possible, in bringing the gifts to the altar. With the entire community they share in the offering of the sacrifice and say the Lord's Prayer, giving expression to the spirit of adoption as God's children that they have received in baptism. When in communion they receive the body that was given for us and the blood that was shed, the neophytes are strengthened in the gifts they have already received and are given a foretaste of the eternal banquet.

36

CELEBRATION OF THE SACRAMENTS OF INITIATION
(Easter Vigil)

CELEBRATION OF BAPTISM

218. The celebration of baptism begins after the homily. It   213
takes place at the baptismal font, if this is in view of the
faithful; otherwise in the sanctuary, where a vessel of water
for the rite should be prepared beforehand.

PRESENTATION OF THE CANDIDATES

219. Accordingly, one of the following procedures, options   213
A, B, or C, is chosen for the presentation of the candidates.

A *When Baptism Is Celebrated Immediately at the Baptismal Font*
The celebrant accompanied by the assisting ministers goes
directly to the font. An assisting deacon or other minister
calls the candidates forward and their godparents present
them. Then the candidates and the godparents take their
place around the font in such a way as not to block the
view of the congregation. The invitation to prayer (no. 220)
and the Litany of the Saints (no. 221) follow.

[If there are a great many candidates, they and their godparents simply take their place around the font during the singing of the Litany of the Saints.]

B *When Baptism Is Celebrated after a Procession to the Font*
There may be a full procession to the baptismal font. In this
case an assisting deacon or other minister calls the candidates forward and their godparents present them.

[If there are a great many candidates, they and their godparents simply take their place in the procession.]

The procession is formed in this order: a minister carries
the Easter candle at the head of the procession (unless, outside the Easter Vigil, it already rests at the baptismal font),
the candidates with their godparents come next, then the
celebrant with the assisting ministers. The Litany of the
Saints (no. 221) is sung during the procession. When the
procession has reached the font, the candidates and their

godparents take their place around the font in such a way as not to block the view of the congregation. The invitation to prayer (no. 220) precedes the blessing of the water.

C *When Baptism Is Celebrated in the Sanctuary*
An assisting deacon or other minister calls the candidates forward and their godparents present them. The candidates and their godparents take their place before the celebrant in the sanctuary in such a way as not to block the view of the congregation. The invitation to prayer (no. 220) and the Litany of the Saints (no. 221) follow.

[If there are a great many candidates, they and their godparents simply take their place in the sanctuary during the singing of the Litany of the Saints.]

INVITATION TO PRAYER

220. The celebrant addresses the following or a similar invitation for the assembly to join in prayer for the candidates. 213

Dear friends, let us pray to almighty God for our brothers and sisters, N. and N., who are asking for baptism. He has called them and brought them to this moment; may he grant them light and strength to follow Christ with resolute hearts and to profess the faith of the Church. May he give them the new life of the Holy Spirit, whom we are about to call down on this water.

LITANY OF THE SAINTS

221. The singing of the Litany of the Saints is led by cantors and may include, at the proper place, names of other saints (for example, the titular of the church, the patron saints of the place or of those to be baptized) or petitions suitable to the occasion. 214

Lord, have mercy	**Lord, have mercy**
Christ, have mercy	**Christ, have mercy**
Lord, have mercy	**Lord, have mercy**
Holy Mary, Mother of God	**pray for us**
Saint Michael	**pray for us**
Holy Angels of God	**pray for us**

Saint John the Baptist	pray for us
Saint Joseph	pray for us
Saint Peter and Saint Paul	pray for us
Saint Andrew	pray for us
Saint John	pray for us
Saint Mary Magdalene	pray for us
Saint Stephen	pray for us
Saint Ignatius	pray for us
Saint Lawrence	pray for us
Saint Perpetua and Saint Felicity	pray for us
Saint Agnes	pray for us
Saint Gregory	pray for us
Saint Augustine	pray for us
Saint Athanasius	pray for us
Saint Basil	pray for us
Saint Martin	pray for us
Saint Benedict	pray for us
Saint Francis and Saint Dominic	pray for us
Saint Francis Xavier	pray for us
Saint John Vianney	pray for us
Saint Catherine	pray for us
Saint Teresa	pray for us
All holy men and women	pray for us

Lord, be merciful	Lord, save your people
From all evil	Lord, save your people
From every sin	Lord, save your people
From everlasting death	Lord, save your people
By your coming as man	Lord, save your people
By your death and rising to a new life	Lord, save your people
By your gift of the Holy Spirit	Lord, save your people

Be merciful to us sinners	Lord, hear our prayer
Give new life to these chosen ones by the grace of baptism	Lord, hear our prayer
Jesus, Son of the living God	Lord, hear our prayer
Christ, hear us	Christ, hear us
Lord Jesus, hear our prayer	Lord Jesus, hear our prayer

PRAYER OVER THE WATER

222. After the Litany of the Saints, the celebrant blesses   215
the water, using the blessing formulary given in option A.   216

When baptism is celebrated outside the Easter Vigil (see no.
26), the celebrant may use any of the blessing formularies
given in options A, B, and C.

But when baptism is celebrated during the Easter season
(see no. 26) and water already blessed at the Easter Vigil is
available, the celebrant uses either option D or option E, so
that this part of the celebration will retain the themes of
thanksgiving and intercession.

A

Blessing of the Water: Facing the font (or vessel) containing
the water, the celebrant sings the following text:

**Father,
you give us grace through sacramental signs,
which tell us of the wonders of your unseen power.**

**In baptism we use your gift of water,
which you have made a rich symbol of the grace
you give us in this sacrament.**

**At the very dawn of creation
your Spirit breathed on the waters,
making them the wellspring of all holiness.**

**The waters of the great flood
you made a sign of the waters of baptism
that make an end of sin
and a new beginning of goodness.**

**Through the waters of the Red Sea
you led Israel out of slavery
to be an image of God's holy people,
set free from sin by baptism.**

**In the waters of the Jordan
your Son was baptized by John
and anointed with the Spirit.**

**Your Son willed that water and blood should flow
    from his side
as he hung upon the cross.**

After his resurrection he told his disciples:
"Go out and teach all nations,
baptizing them in the name of the Father, and of the
   Son, and of the Holy Spirit."

Father,
look now with love upon your Church
and unseal for it the fountain of baptism.

By the power of the Holy Spirit
give to this water the grace of your Son,
so that in the sacrament of baptism
all those whom you have created in your likeness
may be cleansed from sin
and rise to a new birth of innocence
by water and the Holy Spirit.

Here, if this can be done conveniently, the celebrant before
continuing lowers the Easter candle into the water once or
three times, then holds it there until the acclamation at the
end of the blessing.
We ask you, Father, with your Son
to send the Holy Spirit upon the waters of this font.
May all who are buried with Christ in the death of
   baptism
rise also with him to newness of life.

We ask this through Christ our Lord.

All:
Amen.

The people sing or say the following or some other suitable
acclamation.
Springs of water, bless the Lord.
Give him glory and praise for ever.

B *Blessing of Water:* Facing the font (or vessel) containing
the water, the celebrant says the following.

Praise to you, almighty God and Father,   389
for you have created water to cleanse and to give life.

All sing or say the following or some other suitable
acclamation.
Blessed be God.

Celebrant:
Praise to you, Lord Jesus Christ, the Father's only
   Son,
for you offered yourself on the cross,
that in the blood and water flowing from your side
and through your death and resurrection
the Church might be born.

All:
Blessed be God.

Celebrant:
Praise to you, God the Holy Spirit,
for you anointed Christ at his baptism in the waters
   of the Jordan,
that we might all be baptized in you.

All:
Blessed be God.

Celebrant:
Come to us, Lord, Father of all,
and make holy this water which you have created,
so that all who are baptized in it may be washed
   clean of sin
and be born again to live as your children.

All sing or say the following or some other suitable
invocation.
Hear us, Lord.

Celebrant:
Make this water holy, Lord,
so that all who are baptized into Christ's death and
   resurrection by this water
may become more perfectly like your Son.

All:
Hear us, Lord.

The celebrant touches the water with his right hand and
continues.

Lord,
make holy this water which you have created,
so that all those whom you have chosen
may be born again by the power of the Holy Spirit
and may take their place among your holy people.

All:
Hear us, Lord.

C   *Blessing of Water:* Facing the font (or vessel) containing
the water, the celebrant says the following.

Father, God of mercy,   389
through these waters of baptism
you have filled us with new life as your very own
** children.**

All sing or say the following or some other suitable
acclamation.
Blessed be God.

Celebrant:
From all who are baptized in water and the Holy
** Spirit,**
you have formed one people,
united in your Son, Jesus Christ.

All:
Blessed be God.

Celebrant:
You have set us free and filled our hearts with the
Spirit of your love,
that we may live in your peace.

All:
Blessed be God.

Celebrant:
You call those who have been baptized
to announce the Good News of Jesus Christ to people
** everywhere.**

All:
Blessed be God.

The celebrant concludes with the following.

You have called your children, N. and N.,
to this cleansing water and new birth,
that by sharing the faith of your Church they may
have eternal life.
Bless ✠ this water in which they will be baptized.

We ask this in the name of Jesus the Lord.

All:
Amen.

D *Easter-Season Thanksgiving over Water Already Blessed:* Facing the font (or vessel) containing the blessed water, the celebrant says the following.

Praise to you, almighty God and Father, 389
for you have created water to cleanse and to give life.

All sing or say the following or some other suitable acclamation.
Blessed be God.

Celebrant:
Praise to you, Lord Jesus Christ, the Father's only
Son,
for you offered yourself on the cross,
that in the blood and water flowing from your side
and through your death and resurrection
the Church might be born.

All:
Blessed be God.

Celebrant:
Praise to you, God the Holy Spirit,
for you anointed Christ at his baptism in the waters
of the Jordan,
that we might all be baptized in you.

All:
Blessed be God.

The celebrant concludes with the following prayer.

You have called your children, N. and N., to this cleansing water,
that they may share in the faith of your Church and have eternal life.
By the mystery of this consecrated water
lead them to a new and spiritual birth.

We ask this through Christ our Lord.

All:
Amen.

E *Easter-Season Thanksgiving over Water Already Blessed:* Facing the font (or vessel) containing the blessed water, the celebrant says the following.

Father, God of mercy,   389
through these waters of baptism
you have filled us with new life as your very own children.

All sing or say a suitable acclamation or the following.
Blessed be God.

Celebrant:
From all who are baptized in water and the Holy Spirit,
you have formed one people,
united in your Son, Jesus Christ.

All:
Blessed be God.

Celebrant:
You have set us free and filled our hearts with the Spirit of your love,
that we may live in your peace.

All:
Blessed be God.

Celebrant:
You call those who have been baptized
to announce the Good News of Jesus Christ to people everywhere.

All:
Blessed be God.

The celebrant concludes with the following.
**You have called your children, N. and N., to this
   cleansing water,
that they may share in the faith of your Church and
   have eternal life.
By the mystery of this consecrated water
lead them to a new and spiritual birth.**

We ask this through Christ our Lord.

All:
Amen.

PROFESSION OF FAITH

223. After the blessing of the water (or prayer of thanksgiv-   217
ing), the celebrant continues with the profession of faith,
which includes the renunciation of sin and the profession
itself.

RENUNCIATION OF SIN

224. Using one of the following formularies, the celebrant   217
questions all the elect together; or, after being informed of   USA
each candidate's name by the godparents, he may use the
same formularies to question the candidates individually.

[At the discretion of the diocesan bishop, the formularies
for the renunciation of sin may be made more specific and
detailed as circumstances might require (see no. 33.8).]

A   Celebrant:
**Do you reject sin so as to live in the freedom of
God's children?**

Candidates:
I do.

Celebrant:
**Do you reject the glamor of evil,
and refuse to be mastered by sin?**

Candidates:
I do.

Celebrant:
Do you reject Satan, father of sin and prince of darkness?

Candidates:
I do.

B Celebrant:
Do you reject Satan,
and all his works,
and all his empty promises?

Candidates:
I do.

C Celebrant:
Do you reject Satan?

Candidates:
I do.

Celebrant:
And all his works?

Candidates:
I do.

Celebrant:
And all his empty promises?

Candidates:
I do.

PROFESSION OF FAITH

225. Then the celebrant, informed again of each candidate's name by the godparents, questions the candidates individually. Each candidate is baptized immediately after his or her profession of faith.

[If there are a great many to be baptized, the profession of faith may be made simultaneously either by all together or group by group, then the baptism of each candidate follows.]

Celebrant:
N., do you believe in God, the Father almighty, creator of heaven and earth?

Candidate:
I do.

Celebrant:

Do you believe in Jesus Christ, his only Son, our Lord,
who was born of the Virgin Mary,
was crucified, died, and was buried,
rose from the dead,
and is now seated at the right hand of the Father?

Candidate:
I do.

Celebrant:

Do you believe in the Holy Spirit,
the holy catholic Church, the communion of saints,
the forgiveness of sins, the resurrection of the body,
and the life everlasting?

Candidate:
I do.

BAPTISM

226. The celebrant baptizes each candidate either by immersion, option A, or by the pouring of water, option B. Each baptism may be followed by a short acclamation (Appendix II, no. 595), sung or said by the people. 219 222

[If there are a great number to be baptized, they may be divided into groups and baptized by assisting priests or deacons. In baptizing, either by immersion, option A, or by the pouring of water, option B, these ministers say the sacramental formulary for each candidate. During the baptisms, singing by the people is desirable or readings from Scripture or simply silent prayer.]

A

If baptism is by immersion, of the whole body or of the head only, decency and decorum should be preserved. Either or both godparents touch the candidate. The celebrant, immersing the candidate's whole body or head three times, baptizes the candidate in the name of the Trinity. 220

N., I baptize you in the name of the Father,

He immerses the candidate the first time.

and of the Son,

He immerses the candidate the second time.

and of the Holy Spirit.

He immerses the candidate the third time.

B

If baptism is by the pouring of water, either or both godpar-   221
ents place the right hand on the shoulder of the candidate,
and the celebrant, taking baptismal water and pouring it
three times on the candidate's bowed head, baptizes the
candidate in the name of the Trinity.

N., I baptize you in the name of the Father,

He pours water the first time.

and of the Son,

He pours water the second time.

and of the Holy Spirit.

He pours water the third time.

EXPLANATORY RITES

227. The celebration of baptism continues with the explana-   223
tory rites, after which the celebration of confirmation normally follows.

ANOINTING AFTER BAPTISM

228. If the confirmation of those baptized is separated   224
from their baptism, the celebrant anoints them with chrism
immediately after baptism.

[When a great number have been baptized, assisting priests
or deacons may help with the anointing.]

The celebrant first says the following over all the newly baptized before the anointing.

The God of power and Father of our Lord Jesus
  Christ
has freed you from sin
and brought you to new life
through water and the Holy Spirit.

He now anoints you with the chrism of salvation,
so that, united with his people,

**you may remain for ever a member of Christ
who is Priest, Prophet, and King.**

Newly baptized:
Amen.

In silence each of the newly baptized is anointed with
chrism on the crown of the head.

CLOTHING WITH A BAPTISMAL GARMENT

229. The garment used in this rite may be white or of a 225
color that conforms to local custom. If circumstances suggest, this rite may be omitted.

The celebrant says the following formulary, and at the
words "Receive this baptismal garment" the godparents
place the garment on the newly baptized.

**N. and N., you have become a new creation
and have clothed yourselves in Christ.
Receive this baptismal garment
and bring it unstained to the judgment seat of our
    Lord Jesus Christ,
so that you may have everlasting life.**

Newly baptized:
Amen.

PRESENTATION OF A LIGHTED CANDLE

230. The celebrant takes the Easter candle in his hands or 226
touches it, saying to the godparents:

**Godparents, please come forward to give to the
newly baptized the light of Christ.**

A godparent of each of the newly baptized goes to the celebrant, lights a candle from the Easter candle, then presents
it to the newly baptized.

Then the celebrant says to the newly baptized:
**You have been enlightened by Christ.
Walk always as children of the light
and keep the flame of faith alive in your hearts.
When the Lord comes, may you go out to meet him
with all the saints in the heavenly kingdom.**

Newly baptized:
Amen.

[If the celebration of confirmation is to be deferred, the renewal of baptismal promises, as in the Roman Missal, "Easter Vigil" (no. 46), now takes place; then the neophytes are led back to their places among the faithful.]

[Outside the Easter Vigil, if confirmation is to be deferred, the neophytes are led back to their places among the faithful after the presentation of a lighted candle.]

CELEBRATION OF CONFIRMATION

231. Between the celebration of baptism and confirmation,   227
the congregation may sing a suitable song.

The place for the celebration of confirmation is either at the baptismal font or in the sanctuary, depending on the place where, according to local conditions, baptism has been celebrated.

232. If the bishop has conferred baptism, he should now   228
also confer confirmation. If the bishop is not present, the priest who conferred baptism is authorized to confirm.

[When there are a great many persons to be confirmed, the minister of confirmation may associate priests with himself as ministers of the sacrament (see no. 14).]

INVITATION

233. The celebrant first speaks briefly to the newly bap-   229
tized in these or similar words.

My dear newly baptized, born again in Christ by baptism, you have become members of Christ and of his priestly people. Now you are to share in the outpouring of the Holy Spirit among us, the Spirit sent by the Lord upon his apostles at Pentecost and given by them and their successors to the baptized.

The promised strength of the Holy Spirit, which you are to receive, will make you more like Christ and help you to be witnesses to his suffering, death, and resurrection. It will strengthen you to be active mem-

bers of the Church and to build up the Body of Christ in faith and love.

[The priests who will be associated with the celebrant as ministers of the sacrament now stand next to him.]

With hands joined, the celebrant next addresses the people:
My dear friends, let us pray to God our Father, that he will pour out the Holy Spirit on these newly baptized to strengthen them with his gifts and anoint them to be more like Christ, the Son of God.

All pray briefly in silence.

LAYING ON OF HANDS

234. The celebrant holds his hands outstretched over the entire group of those to be confirmed and says the following prayer.   229

[In silence the priests associated as ministers of the sacrament also hold their hands outstretched over the candidates.]

All-powerful God, Father of our Lord Jesus Christ,   230
by water and the Holy Spirit
you freed your sons and daughters from sin
and gave them new life.

Send your Holy Spirit upon them
to be their helper and guide.

Give them the spirit of wisdom and understanding,
the spirit of right judgment and courage,
the spirit of knowledge and reverence.
Fill them with the spirit of wonder and awe in your
** presence.**

We ask this through Christ our Lord.
℟. Amen.

ANOINTING WITH CHRISM

235. A minister brings the chrism to the celebrant.   231

[When the celebrant is the bishop, priests who are associated as ministers of the sacrament receive the chrism from him.]

Each candidate, with godparent or godparents, goes to the celebrant (or to an associated minister of the sacrament); or, if circumstances require, the celebrant (associated ministers) may go to the candidates.

Either or both godparents place the right hand on the shoulder of the candidate and either a godparent or the candidate gives the candidate's name to the minister of the sacrament. During the conferral of the sacrament a suitable song may be sung.

The minister of the sacrament dips his right thumb in the chrism and makes the sign of the cross on the forehead of the one to be confirmed as he says:

N., be sealed with the Gift of the Holy Spirit.

Newly confirmed:
Amen.

The minister of the sacrament adds:
Peace be with you.

Newly confirmed:
And also with you.

236. At the Easter Vigil the renewal of baptismal promises by the congregation [nos. 237–240 below or in the Roman Missal, "Easter Vigil" (no. 46)] follows the celebration of confirmation. Then the neophytes are led to their places among the faithful.

[Outside the Easter Vigil, the neophytes are led to their places among the faithful immediately after confirmation. The general intercessions then begin (see no. 241).]

RENEWAL OF BAPTISMAL PROMISES (AT THE EASTER VIGIL)   USA
                                                                        RM

INVITATION

237. After the celebration of baptism, the celebrant addresses the community, in order to invite those present to the renewal of their baptismal promises; the candidates for reception into full communion join the rest of the commu-

nity in this renunciation of sin and profession of faith. All stand and hold lighted candles. The celebrant may use the following or similar words.

Dear friends, through the paschal mystery we have been buried with Christ in baptism, so that we may rise with him to newness of life. Now that we have completed our Lenten observance, let us renew the promises we made in baptism, when we rejected Satan and his works and promised to serve God faithfully in his holy catholic Church.

RENEWAL OF BAPTISMAL PROMISES

RENUNCIATION OF SIN

238. The celebrant continues with one of the following formularies of renunciation.

[If circumstances require, the conference of bishops may adapt formulary A in accord with local conditions.]

A Celebrant:
Do you reject sin so as to live in the freedom of God's children?

All:
I do.

Celebrant:
Do you reject the glamor of evil, and refuse to be mastered by sin?

All:
I do.

Celebrant:
Do you reject Satan, father of sin and prince of darkness?

All:
I do.

B Celebrant:
Do you reject Satan?

All:
I do.

Celebrant:
And all his works?

All:
I do.

Celebrant:
And all his empty promises?

All:
I do.

PROFESSION OF FAITH

239. Then the celebrant continues:

**Do you believe in God, the Father Almighty,
   creator of heaven and earth?**

All:
I do.

Celebrant:
**Do you believe in Jesus Christ, his only Son, our
   Lord,
   who was born of the Virgin Mary,
   was crucified, died, and was buried,
   rose from the dead,
   and is now seated at the right hand of the Father?**

All:
I do.

Celebrant:
**Do you believe in the Holy Spirit,
   the holy catholic Church, the communion of saints,
   the forgiveness of sins, the resurrection of the
   body,
   and the life everlasting?**

All:
I do.

SPRINKLING WITH BAPTISMAL WATER

240. The celebrant sprinkles all the people with the blessed baptismal water, while all sing the following song or any other that is baptismal in character.

**I saw water flowing
from the right side of the temple, alleluia.
It brought God's life and his salvation,
and the people sang in joyful praise:
alleluia, alleluia.** (*See* Ezekiel 47:1–2,9)

The celebrant then concludes with the following prayer.

**God, the all-powerful Father of our Lord Jesus
Christ,
has given us a new birth by water and the Holy
Spirit
and forgiven all our sins.
May he also keep us faithful to our Lord Jesus Christ
for ever and ever.**

All:
Amen.

LITURGY OF THE EUCHARIST

241. Since the profession of faith is not said, the general intercessions begin immediately and for the first time the neophytes take part in them. Some of the neophytes also take part in the procession to the altar with the gifts. 232

242. With Eucharistic Prayers I, II, or III the special interpolations given in the Roman Missal, the ritual Masses, "Christian Initiation: Baptism," are used. 233

[Eucharistic Prayer IV, with its special interpolation, indicated in the same ritual Masses, may also be used but outside the Easter Vigil.]

243. It is most desirable that the neophytes, together with their godparents, parents, spouses, and catechists, receive communion under both kinds. 234

Before saying "This is the Lamb of God," the celebrant may briefly remind the neophytes of the preeminence of the eucharist, which is the climax of their initiation and the center of the whole Christian life.

PERIOD OF POSTBAPTISMAL CATECHESIS OR MYSTAGOGY

You are a chosen race, a royal priesthood, a holy people; praise
God who called you out of darkness and into his marvelous light

244. The third step of Christian initiation, the celebration   37
of the sacraments, is followed by the final period, the period of postbaptismal catechesis or mystagogy. This is a
time for the community and the neophytes together to
grow in deepening their grasp of the paschal mystery and
in making it part of their lives through meditation on the
Gospel, sharing in the eucharist, and doing the works of
charity. To strengthen the neophytes as they begin to walk
in newness of life, the community of the faithful, their godparents, and their pastors should give them thoughtful and
friendly help.

245. The neophytes are, as the term "mystagogy" sug-   38
gests, introduced into a fuller and more effective understanding of mysteries through the Gospel message they
have learned and above all through their experience of the
sacraments they have received. For they have truly been renewed in mind, tasted more deeply the sweetness of God's
word, received the fellowship of the Holy Spirit, and grown
to know the goodness of the Lord. Out of this experience,
which belongs to Christians and increases as it is lived,
they derive a new perception of the faith, of the Church,
and of the world.

246. Just as their new participation in the sacraments en-   39
lightens the neophytes' understanding of the Scriptures, so   235
too it increases their contact with the rest of the faithful and
has an impact on the experience of the community. As a
result, interaction between the neophytes and the faithful is
made easier and more beneficial. The period of
postbaptismal catechesis is of great significance for both the
neophytes and the rest of the faithful. Through it the neophytes, with the help of their godparents, should experience a full and joyful welcome into the community and enter into closer ties with the other faithful. The faithful, in
turn, should derive from it a renewal of inspiration and of
outlook.

247. Since the distinctive spirit and power of the period of postbaptismal catechesis or mystagogy derive from the new, personal experience of the sacraments and of the community, its main setting is the so-called Masses for neophytes, that is, the Sunday Masses of the Easter season. Besides being occasions for the newly baptized to gather with the community and share in the mysteries, these celebrations include particularly suitable readings from the Lectionary, especially the readings for Year A. Even when Christian initiation has been celebrated outside the usual times, the texts for these Sunday Masses of the Easter season may be used. 40

248. All the neophytes and their godparents should make an effort to take part in the Masses for the neophytes and the entire local community should be invited to participate with them. Special places in the congregation are to be reserved for the neophytes and their godparents. The homily and, as circumstances suggest, the general intercessions should take into account the presence and needs of the neophytes. 236

249. To close the period of postbaptismal catechesis, some sort of celebration should be held at the end of the Easter season near Pentecost Sunday; festivities in keeping with local custom may accompany the occasion. 237

250. On the anniversary of their baptism the neophytes should be brought together in order to give thanks to God, to share with one another their spiritual experiences, and to renew their commitment. 238

251. To show his pastoral concern for these new members of the Church, the bishop, particularly if he was unable to preside at the sacraments of initiation himself, should arrange, if possible, to meet the recently baptized at least once in the year and to preside at a celebration of the eucharist with them. At this Mass they may receive holy communion under both kinds. 239

PART II

RITES FOR PARTICULAR CIRCUMSTANCES

God loved the world so much, he gave us his only Son, that all who believe in him might have eternal life

1.   CHRISTIAN INITIATION OF CHILDREN WHO HAVE REACHED CATECHETICAL AGE

Do not keep the children from me.

252. This form of the rite of Christian initiation is intended for children, not baptized as infants, who have attained the use of reason and are of catechetical age. They seek Christian initiation either at the direction of their parents or guardians or, with parental permission, on their own initiative. Such children are capable of receiving and nurturing a personal faith and of recognizing an obligation in conscience. But they cannot yet be treated as adults because, at this stage of their lives, they are dependent on their parents or guardians and are still strongly influenced by their companions and their social surroundings.

306

253. The Christian initiation of these children requires both a conversion that is personal and somewhat developed, in proportion to their age, and the assistance of the education they need. The process of initiation thus must be adapted both to their spiritual progress, that is, to the children's growth in faith, and to the catechetical instruction they receive. Accordingly, as with adults, their initiation is to be extended over several years, if need be, before they receive the sacraments. Also as with adults, their initiation is marked by several steps, the liturgical rites of acceptance into the order of catechumens (nos. 260–276) the optional rite of election (nos. 277–290), penitential rites or scrutinies (nos. 291–303), and the celebration of the sacraments of initiation (nos. 304–329); corresponding to the periods of adult initiation are the periods of the children's catechetical formation that lead up to and follow the steps of their initiation.

307
USA

254. The children's progress in the formation they receive 308
depends on the help and example of their companions and
on the influence of their parents. Both these factors should
therefore be taken into account.

1. Since the children to be initiated often belong to a
group of children of the same age who are already baptized
and are preparing for confirmation and eucharist, their initiation progresses gradually and within the supportive setting of this group of companions.

2. It is to be hoped that the children will also receive as
much help and example as possible from the parents,
whose permission is required for the children to be initiated
and to live the Christian life. The period of initiation will
also provide a good opportunity for the family to have contact with priests and catechists.

255. For the celebrations proper to this form of Christian 309
initiation, it is advantageous, as circumstances allow, to
form a group of several children who are in this same situation, in order that by example they may help one another
in their progress as catechumens.

256. In regard to the time for the celebration of the steps 310
of initiation, it is preferable that, if possible, the final period USA
of preparation, begun by the second step, the penitential
rites (or by the optional rite of election), coincide with Lent
and that the final step, celebration of the sacraments of initiation, take place at the Easter Vigil (see no. 8). Nevertheless before the children are admitted to the sacraments at
Easter, it should be established that they are ready for the
sacraments. Celebration at this time must also be consistent
with the program of catechetical instruction they are receiving, since the candidates should, if possible, come to the
sacraments of initiation at the time that their baptized companions are to receive confirmation or eucharist.

257. For children of this age, at the rites during the pro- 311
cess of initiation, it is generally preferable not to have the
whole parish community present, but simply represented.
Thus these rites should be celebrated with the active participation of a congregation that consists of a suitable number
of the faithful, the parents, family, members of the
catechetical group, and a few adult friends.

258. Each conference of bishops may adapt and add to the   312
form of the rite given here, in order that the rite will more
effectively satisfy local needs, conditions, and pastoral requirements. [The National Conference of Catholic Bishops
has done this by providing an optional "Rite of Election" before "Second Step: Penitential Rites (Scrutinies)."] The rites
for the presentation of the Creed (nos. 157–162) and the
Lord's Prayer (nos. 178–183), adapted to the age of the children, may be incorporated. When the form of the rite of initiation for children is translated, the instructions and
prayers should be adapted to their understanding. Furthermore, in addition to any liturgical text translated from the
Latin *editio typica*, the conference of bishops may also approve an original, alternative text that says the same thing
in a way more suited to children (see *Christian Initiation*,
General Introduction, no. 32).

259. In following this form of the rite of Christian initia-   313
tion the celebrant should make full and wise use of the options mentioned in *Christian Initiation*, General Introduction
(nos. 34–35), in the *Rite of Baptism for Children*, Introduction
(no. 31), and in the *Rite of Christian Initiation of Adults*, Introduction (no. 35).

FIRST STEP: ACCEPTANCE INTO THE ORDER OF CATECHUMENS

Happy the people the Lord has chosen to be his own

260. It is important that this rite be celebrated with an actively participating but small congregation, since the presence of a large group might make the children uncomfortable (see no. 257). When possible, the children's parents or guardians should be present. If they cannot come, they should indicate that they have given consent to their children and their place should be taken by "sponsors" (see no. 10), that is, suitable members of the Church who act on this occasion for the parents and present the children. The presiding celebrant is a priest or deacon.

314

261. The celebration takes place in the church or in a place that, according to the age and understanding of the children, can help them to experience a warm welcome. As circumstances suggest, the first part of the rite, "Receiving the Children," is carried out at the entrance of the place chosen for the celebration, and the second part of the rite, "Liturgy of the Word," takes place inside.

315
329

The celebration is not normally combined with celebration of the eucharist.

RITE OF ACCEPTANCE INTO THE ORDER OF CATECHUMENS

RECEIVING THE CHILDREN

262. The priest or deacon, wearing an alb or surplice with stole, comes to the place where the children are waiting with their parents or guardians or, alternatively, with their sponsors. 316

GREETING

263. The celebrant and the community present greet the children simply and in a friendly manner. The celebrant then speaks to the children and their parents or sponsors, pointing out the joy and happiness of the Church at their presence. Next he invites the children and their parents or sponsors to come forward and stand before him. 316 317

OPENING DIALOGUE

264. The celebrant then asks the children individually to express their intention. He may do so by means of such questions and answers as those given here or he may use other words that will allow the children to give such answers as: "I want to do the will of God"; "I want to follow the word of God"; "I want to be baptized"; "I want to be a friend of Jesus Christ"; "I want to join the Christian family." 318

[If there are a great many children, the celebrant may question a few of them and then ask the rest to express agreement with the responses given.]

Celebrant:
What do you want to become?

Children:
A Christian.

Celebrant:
Why do you want to become a Christian?

Children:
Because I believe in Christ.

Celebrant:
What do you gain by believing in Christ?

Children:
Eternal life.

The celebrant concludes this opening dialogue with a brief 319
catechesis, suited to the children's age and circumstances,
on the step they are taking. He may use these or similar
words and may ask the children, as a sign of their assent,
to repeat the final quotation from the words of Christ.

**Since you already believe in Christ and want us to
prepare you for baptism, we welcome you joyfully
into our Christian family, where you will come to
know Christ better day by day. Together with us you
will try to live as children of God, for our Lord has
taught us: "Love God with all your heart and love
one another as I have loved you."**

AFFIRMATION BY THE PARENTS (SPONSORS) AND
THE ASSEMBLY

265. In the following or a similar way, the celebrant asks 320
the children to seek the consent of the parents or sponsors
who are presenting them.

**N. and N., go and ask your parents (sponsors) to
come here and stand with you so that they may give
their assent.**

The children go to their parents or sponsors and bring
them before the celebrant, who continues:
**Dear parents (sponsors), your children have asked to
be prepared for baptism. Do you consent to their
request?**

Parents or sponsors:
We do.

Celebrant:
**Are you willing to do your part in their preparation
for baptism?**

Parents or sponsors:
We are.

Then the celebrant questions the assembly, using these or 321
similar words.

These boys and girls have set out on the road to baptism. They will need the support of our faith and love. Are you, their families and friends, ready to give that help?

All:
We are.

SIGNING OF THE CANDIDATES WITH THE CROSS

266. Next the cross is traced on the forehead of each child (or, at the discretion of the diocesan bishop, in front of the forehead—see nos. 33.3 and 54); at the discretion of the celebrant, and especially if the children are somewhat older, the signing of the other senses may follow. The celebrant alone says the formularies accompanying each signing.

322
USA

SIGNING OF THE FOREHEAD

267. The celebrant first says the following formulary.

322

N. and N., Christ has called you to be his friends. Always remember him and be faithful to him.

Therefore I mark your forehead with the sign of the cross. It is the sign of Christians; let it remind you always of Christ and how much he loves you.

Then the celebrant goes to the children and in silence traces the cross on the forehead of each one.

Then, if there is to be no signing of the other senses, he may, in the following words, invite the parents or sponsors and the catechists to trace the sign of the cross on their candidate's forehead.

And I also invite you, parents (sponsors) and catechists [N. and N.], since you also belong to Christ, to sign the children with the sign of the cross.

All sing or say the following or another suitable acclamation.
Glory and praise to you, Lord Jesus Christ!

SIGNING OF THE OTHER SENSES

268. The signing of the other senses may be carried out by the celebrant, who says the following formulary for each

323

child. The signing of the candidates may also be carried out by their parents or sponsors or by their catechists, as the celebrant says the formulary in the plural over all the children at once. After the signing of each sense the assembly may sing or recite an acclamation in praise of Christ, for example, **"Glory and praise to you, Lord Jesus Christ!"**

While the ears are being signed the celebrant says:
I [we] mark your ears with the sign of the cross: hear the words of Christ.

While the eyes are being signed:
I [we] mark your eyes with the sign of the cross: see the works of Christ.

While the lips are being signed:
I [we] mark your lips with the sign of the cross: speak as Christ would speak.

While the breast is being signed:
I [we] mark the sign of the cross over your heart: make your heart the home of Christ.

While the shoulders are being signed:
I [we] mark your shoulders with the sign of the cross: be strong with the strength of Christ.

[While the hands are being signed:
I (we) mark your hands with the sign of the cross, touch others with the gentleness of Christ.

While the feet are being signed:
I (we) mark your feet with the sign of the cross, walk in the way of Christ.]

While the sign of the cross is traced above the whole person:
**I [we] place you entirely under the sign of Christ's cross
in the name of the Father, and of the Son, ✠
and of the Holy Spirit:
live with Jesus now and for ever.**

Child:
Amen.

INVITATION TO THE CELEBRATION OF THE WORD OF GOD

269. After the signing, the celebrant in the following or   324
similar words invites the children and their parents or sponsors to enter the church or other place chosen for the celebration. Once the invitation has been spoken, the children
enter and take places either with their parents or sponsors
or with the baptized companions of their catechetical group
(see no. 254.1), so that it is clear that they now are a part of
the assembly. During the entrance, Psalm 95 or Psalm 122
is sung or another suitable song.

Celebrant:

**Now you can take your place in the Christian assem-
bly. Come with us to listen to the Lord as he speaks
and to join us in prayer.**

LITURGY OF THE WORD

INSTRUCTION

270. When the children have reached their places, the cele-   325
brant speaks to them briefly, helping them to understand
the dignity of God's word, which is proclaimed and heard
in the Christian assembly.

The Lectionary or the Bible is carried in procession and
placed with honor on the lectern, where it may be incensed.

Celebration of the liturgy of the word follows.

READINGS

271. Scripture readings are chosen that can be adapted to   326
the understanding of the children and to their progress in
the catechetical formation they and their companions have
received. Such readings may be chosen from those given in
the Lectionary for Mass, ritual Masses, "Christian Initiation
apart from the Easter Vigil" or from elsewhere in the
Lectionary; the following texts may also be used.

FIRST READING

Genesis 12:1–4a—*Leave your country, and come into the land I
will show you.*

RESPONSORIAL PSALM

Psalm 33:4–5, 12–13, 18–19, 20 and 22

℟. (v.12b) **Happy the people the Lord has chosen to be his own.**

Or:

℟. (v.22) **Lord, let your mercy be on us, as we place our trust in you.**

VERSE BEFORE THE GOSPEL

John 1:41, 17b

We have found the Messiah: Jesus Christ, who brings us truth and grace.

GOSPEL

John 1:35–42—*This is the Lamb of God. We have found the Messiah.*

HOMILY

272. The celebrant then gives a brief homily in explanation of the readings. 327

It is recommended that after the homily he invite the children to spend a period in silent prayer.

Then a suitable song is sung.

PRESENTATION OF A BIBLE

273. During or after the song, a book containing the Gospels may be presented to the children. They should be prepared for this presentation either beforehand in the homily or by a few words of explanation at this moment. 328

INTERCESSIONS FOR THE CHILDREN

274. The intercessions follow in these or similar words. 329

Celebrant:

Let us pray for these children, your sons and daughters, your companions and friends, as they draw nearer to God.

Assisting minister:
That they may steadily increase their desire to live with Jesus, let us pray to the Lord:
℟. Lord, hear our prayer.

Assisting minister:
That by belonging to the Church they may find true happiness, let us pray to the Lord:
℟. Lord, hear our prayer.

Assisting minister:
That they may be given the strength to persevere in their preparation for baptism, let us pray to the Lord:
℟. Lord, hear our prayer.

Assisting minister:
That they may be preserved from the temptation of discouragement and fear, let us pray to the Lord:
℟. Lord, hear our prayer.

Assisting minister:
That they may rejoice in the happiness of receiving the sacraments of baptism, confirmation, and the eucharist, let us pray to the Lord:
℟. Lord, hear our prayer.

PRAYER OVER THE CHILDREN

275. After the intercessions, the celebrant, with hands out-   329
stretched over the children, says the following prayer.

Lord,
you have filled these children
with the desire to become perfect Christians.
As they grow in wisdom and knowledge,
respond to their hopes
and answer our prayers.

We ask this through Christ our Lord.
℟. Amen.

DISMISSAL

276. After the prayer the children and the community are dismissed and a suitable song concludes the celebration.

But if for some reason the eucharist is to be celebrated (see no. 261), the children are dismissed beforehand.

Celebrant:
Go in peace, and may the Lord remain with you always.

All:
Thanks be to God.

RITE OF ELECTION OR ENROLLMENT OF NAMES (OPTIONAL)

USA

To just such as these the Kingdom of God belongs

277. The (optional) liturgical rite called both election and the enrollment of names may be celebrated with children of catechetical age, especially those whose catechumenate has extended over a long period of time. This celebration, which usually coincides with the beginning of Lent, marks the beginning of the period of final preparation for the sacraments of initiation, during which the children will be encouraged to follow Christ with greater generosity.

278. In the rite of election, on the basis of the testimony of parents, godparents and catechists and of the children's reaffirmation of their intention, the Church judges their state of readiness and decides on their advancement toward the sacraments of initiation. Thus the Church makes its "election," that is, the choice and admission of those children who have the dispositions that make them fit to take part, at the next major celebration, in the sacraments of initiation.

279. The rite should take place in the cathedral church, in a parish church or, if necessary, in some other suitable and fitting place. If the election of children of catechetical age is to take place within a celebration in which older catechumens are also to receive the Church's election, the rite for adults (nos. 129–137) should be used, with appropriate adaptation of the texts to be made by the celebrant.

280. The rite is celebrated within Mass, after the homily, and should be celebrated within the Mass of the First Sunday of Lent. If, for pastoral reasons, the rite is celebrated on a different day, the texts and the readings of the ritual Mass "Christian Initiation: Election or Enrollment of Names" may always be used. When the Mass of the day is celebrated and its readings are not suitable, the readings are those given for the First Sunday of Lent or others may be chosen from elsewhere in the Lectionary.

When celebrated outside Mass, the rite takes place after the readings and the homily and is concluded with the dismissal of both the elect and the faithful.

LITURGY OF THE WORD

HOMILY

281. The bishop, or the celebrant who acts as delegate of the bishop, gives the homily. This should be brief and suitable to the understanding of the children. If the celebrant finds it difficult in the homily to adapt himself to the mentality of the children, one of the adults, for example, the children's catechist, may speak to the children after the gospel. The entire community should be encouraged to give good example to the children and to show their support and interest in them as they prepare to celebrate the Easter sacraments.

PRESENTATION OF THE CHILDREN

282. After the homily, the priest in charge of the childrens' initiation, or a deacon, a catechist, or a representative of the community, presents the children, using the following or similar words.

Reverend Father, these children, whom I now present to you, are completing their preparation for Christian initiation. God's love has strengthened them, and our community has supported them with prayer and good example.

As Easter approaches, they ask to be admitted to the sacraments of baptism, confirmation, and the eucharist.

The celebrant replies:
My dear children who are to be chosen in Christ, come forward now with your parents and godparents.

One by one, the children are called by name. Each candidate, accompanied by one or both parents and/or godparents, comes forward and stands before the celebrant.

[If there are a great many children, all are presented in groups, for example, each group by its own catechist. But in this case, the catechists should be advised to have a special celebration beforehand in which they call each child forward by name.]

AFFIRMATION BY THE (PARENTS,) GODPARENTS
[AND THE ASSEMBLY]

283. Then the celebrant addresses the assembly in these or similar words.

Dear parents, godparents and members of this assembly: These children have asked to be initiated into the sacramental life of the Church this Easter. In the name of God's holy Church, I invite you to give your recommendation on their behalf.

He addresses the parents, godparents (and assembly):
Have these children shown themselves to be sincere in their desire for baptism, confirmation, and the eucharist?

Parents, godparents (and assembly):
They have.

Celebrant:
Have they listened well to the word of God?

Parents, godparents (and assembly):
They have.

Celebrant:
Have they tried to live as his faithful followers?

Parents, godparents (and assembly):
They have.

Celebrant:
Have they taken part in this community's life of prayer and service?

Parents, godparents (and assembly):
They have.

INVITATION AND ENROLLMENT OF NAMES

284. Then addressing the children in the following or similar words, the celebrant advises them of their acceptance and asks them to declare their own intention.

My dear children, your parents and godparents (and this entire community) have spoken in your favor.

The Church in the name of Christ accepts their word and calls you to the Easter sacraments.

Now you must let the whole Church know that you have heard Christ calling you and that you want to follow him.

Therefore, do you wish to enter fully into the life of the Church through the sacraments of baptism, confirmation, and the eucharist?

Children:
We do.

Celebrant:
Then offer your names for enrollment.

The children give their names, either going with their godparents to the celebrant or while remaining in place, and the actual inscription of the names may be carried out in various ways. The candidates may inscribe their names themselves or they may call out their names, which are inscribed by the godparents or by the minister who presented the candidates (see no. 282). As the enrollment is taking place, an appropriate song, for example, Psalm 16 or Psalm 33 with a refrain such as, "**Happy the people the Lord has chosen to be his own,**" may be sung.

[If there are a great many candidates, the enrollment may simply consist in the presentation of a list of the names to the celebrant, with such words as: "**These are the names of the candidates**" or, when the bishop is celebrant and candidates from several parishes have been presented to him: "**These are the names of the candidates from the parish of N.**"]

ACT OF ADMISSION OR ELECTION

285. The celebrant briefly explains the significance of the enrollment that has just taken place. Then, turning to the children, he says the following or similar words.

Celebrant:
My dear children, I am happy to declare you among the elect of God. You have been chosen to be initi-

ated at Easter through the sacraments of baptism, con-firmation, and the eucharist.

Children:
Thanks be to God.

He continues:
God is always faithful to those he calls. On your part, you must strive to know, love, and serve the Lord more and more with each passing day. Continue to rely upon your godparents, parents, and catechists for the help you will need to be faithful to the way of Jesus.

Then the celebrant addresses the parents, godparents, and the entire assembly:
Dear friends, you have spoken in favor of these young catechumens. Accept them as chosen in the Lord. Encourage them to live the way of the Gospel. Offer them the support of your love and concern. And, above all, be a good model to them of Christian living so that by your example they may grow deeper in the faith of the Church.

He invites parents and godparents to place their hand on the shoulder of the candidate whom they are receiving into their care, or to make some other gesture to indicate the same intent.

RECOGNITION OF THE GODPARENT(S)

286. The celebrant may speak briefly of the new relation-ship which will exist between the parents and godparents of the elect. He may conclude by placing his outstretched hands over the parents and godparents while praying in these or similar words.

Celebrant:
May Almighty God bring joy to your hearts as you see the hope of eternal life shine on these elect. Steadfastly bear witness to your faith by what you say and do. May these children grow as faithful mem-bers of God's holy people. And may you be a con-stant support to each other, in Christ Jesus our Lord.

Parent(s) and godparent(s):
Amen.

INTERCESSIONS FOR THE ELECT

287. The community may use the following or a similar formulary to pray for the elect. The celebrant may adapt the introduction and the intentions to fit various circumstances.

[If it is decided, in accord with no. 290, that after the dismissal of the elect the usual general intercessions of the Mass are to be omitted and that the liturgy of the eucharist is to begin immediately, intentions for the Church and the whole world are to be added to the following intentions for the elect.]

Celebrant:
My brothers and sisters, as we begin this Lenten season, we look forward to the initiation of these children at Easter into the mystery of Christ's suffering, death, and resurrection. Let us pray that this Lent will be for them, and for all of us, a time of genuine Christian renewal.

Assisting minister:
That together we may grow this Lent in our love for God and neighbor, let us pray to the Lord:
℟. **Lord, hear our prayer.**

Assisting minister:
That these catechumens may be freed from selfishness and learn to put others first, let us pray to the Lord:
℟. **Lord, hear our prayer.**

Assisting minister:
That their parents, godparents, and catechists may be living examples of the Gospel to inspire these children, let us pray to the Lord:
℟. **Lord, hear our prayer.**

Assisting minister:
That their teachers may always convey to them the beauty of God's word, let us pray to the Lord:
℟. **Lord, hear our prayer.**

Assisting minister:

**That these children may share with others the joy
they have found in their friendship with Jesus, let us
pray to the Lord:**

℟. **Lord, hear our prayer.**

Assisting minister:

**That together with the adults who have been elected,
these children may learn to love the Church and
proudly profess what they believe, let us pray to the
Lord:**

℟. **Lord, hear our prayer.**

Assisting minister:

**That our community, during this Lenten period, may
grow in charity and be constant in prayer, let us pray
to the Lord:**

℟. **Lord, hear our prayer.**

PRAYER OVER THE ELECT

288. After the intercessions, the celebrant, with hands outstretched over the elect, says one of the following prayers.

A

**Lord God,
you created us
and you give us life.
Bless these children
and add them to your family.
May they be joyful in the life you won for us
through Christ our Lord.**

℟. **Amen.**

B

**Father of love and power,
it is your will to establish everything in Christ
and to draw us into his all-embracing love.
Guide the elect of your Church:
strengthen them in their vocation,
build them into the kingdom of your Son,
and seal them with the Spirit of your promise.**

We ask this through Christ our Lord.

℟. **Amen.**

DISMISSAL OF THE ELECT

289. If the eucharist is to be celebrated, the elect are normally dismissed at this point by use of option A or B; if the elect are to stay for the celebration of the eucharist, option C is used; if the eucharist is not to be celebrated, the entire assembly is dismissed by use of option D.

A The celebrant dismisses the elect in these or similar words.

My dear children, elect of God, you have set out with us on the road that leads to the glory of Easter. Christ will be your way, your truth, and your life. Until we meet again, walk always in the Lord's peace.

The elect:
Amen.

B As an optional formulary for dismissing the elect, the celebrant may use these or similar words.

My dear children, go now. Think about God's word and know that we are with you and will pray for you. We look forward to the day when you will join us at the Lord's Table.

C If for serious reasons the elect cannot leave (see no. 75.3) and must remain with the baptized, they are to be instructed that though they are present at the eucharist, they cannot take part in it as the baptized do. They may be reminded of this by the celebrant in these or similar words.

Although you cannot join us at the Lord's Table, stay with us as a sign of our hope that all God's children will eat and drink with the Lord and work with his Spirit to make a new earth.

D The celebrant dismisses those present, using these or similar words.

Go in peace, and may the Lord remain with you always.

All:
Thanks be to God.

An appropriate song may conclude the celebration.

LITURGY OF THE EUCHARIST

290. When the eucharist is to follow, intercessory prayer is resumed with the usual general intercessions for the needs of the Church and the whole world; then, if required, the profession of faith is said. But for pastoral reasons these general intercessions and the profession of faith may be omitted. The liturgy of the eucharist then begins as usual with the preparation of the gifts.

SECOND STEP: PENITENTIAL RITES (SCRUTINIES)

Create in me a new heart and a new spirit

291. These penitential rites, which mark the second step in the children's Christian initiation, are major occasions in their catechumenate. They are held within a celebration of the word of God as a kind of scrutiny, similar to the scrutinies in the adult rite. Thus the guidelines given for the adult rite (nos. 141–146) may be followed and adapted, since the children's penitential rites have a similar purpose.

330

292. Because the penitential rites normally belong to the period of final preparation for baptism, the condition for their celebration is that the children are approaching the maturity of faith and understanding requisite for baptism.

331

293. Along with the children, their godparents and their baptized companions from the catechetical group participate in the celebration of these penitential rites. Therefore the rites are to be adapted in such a way that they also benefit the participants who are not catechumens. In particular, these penitential rites are a proper occasion for baptized children of the catechetical group to celebrate the sacrament of penance for the first time. When this is the case, care should be taken to include explanations, prayers, and ritual acts that relate to the celebration of the sacrament with these children.

332

294. The penitential rites are celebrated during Lent, if the catechumens are to be initiated at Easter; if not, at the most suitable time. At least one penitential rite is to be celebrated, and, if this can be arranged conveniently, a second should follow after an appropriate interval. The texts for a second celebration are to be composed on the model of the first given here, but the texts for the intercessions and prayer of exorcism given in the adult rite (nos. 153–154, 167–168, 174–175) are used, with the requisite modifications.

333

PENITENTIAL RITE (SCRUTINY)

LITURGY OF THE WORD

GREETING AND INTRODUCTION

295. The priest welcomes the assembly and in a few words   334
explains that the rite will have different meanings for the
different participants: the children who are catechumens,
the children who are already baptized, particularly those
who will celebrate the sacrament of penance for the first
time, the parents, godparents, catechists, priests, etc. All
these participants in their own different ways are going to
hear the comforting message of pardon for sin, for which
they will praise the Father's mercy.

A song may be sung that joyfully expresses faith in the
mercy of God our Father.

PRAYER

296. The celebrant then says one of the following prayers.   335

A
God of pardon and mercy,
you reveal yourself in your readiness to forgive
and manifest your glory by making us holy.

Grant that we who repent
may be cleansed from sin
and restored to your life of grace.

We ask this through Christ our Lord.
R̸. Amen.

B
Lord,
grant us your pardon and peace,
so that, cleansed of our sins,
we may serve you with untroubled hearts.

We ask this through Christ our Lord.
R̸. Amen.

READINGS

297. One or several readings may be chosen from those in 336 the following list; if there is more than one reading, one of the responsorial psalms listed here from the ritual Masses, "Christian Initiation apart from the Easter Vigil" (or any of the others from the same Mass) or a song should be used between the readings.

READINGS

1. Ezekiel 36:25–28—*A new heart and a new spirit.*

2. Isaiah 1:16–18—*The cleansing of sin.*

3. Mark 1:1–5, 14–15—*Repent and believe the Good News.*

4. Mark 2:1–12—*Healing of the paralytic.*

5. Luke 15:1–7—*Parable of the lost sheep.*

6. 1 John 1:8—2:2—*Jesus our Savior.*

Or the gospels used in the scrutinies of the adult rite:

7. John 4:1–14—*The Samaritan woman.*

8. John 9:1, 6–9, 13–17, 34–39—*The man born blind.*

9. John 11:3–7, 17, 20–27, 33b–45—*The raising of Lazarus.*

RESPONSORIAL PSALMS

1. Psalm 23:1–3a, 3b–4, 5–6
℞. (v.1) **The Lord is my shepherd; there is nothing I shall want.**

2. Psalm 27:1, 4, 8b–9abc, 13–14
℞. (v.1a) **The Lord is my light and my salvation.**

3. Psalm 32:1–2, 5, 11
℞. (v.1a) **Happy are those whose sins are forgiven.**

4. Psalm 89:3–4, 16–17, 21–22, 25, 27
℞. (v.2a) **For ever I will sing the goodness of the Lord.**

HOMILY

298. After the readings the celebrant explains the sacred texts in a short homily.

During the homily or immediately after it, the celebrant prepares all those in the assembly for conversion and repentance by speaking to them of appropriate themes, then pausing for periods of silent reflection.

If the assembly includes baptized children who will receive the sacrament of penance for the first time, the celebrant turns to them and invites them to show by some external sign their faith in Christ the Savior and their sorrow for their sins.

INTERCESSIONS

299. After a brief interval of silence to lead all present to sincere sorrow for sin, the celebrant introduces the following intercessions with an invitation addressed to the assembly.

For the celebrant's introduction and the intentions of the intercessions the texts in the adult rite (nos. 153, 167, 174) may also be used, with the requisite modifications.

Celebrant:
Let us pray for N. and N., who are preparing themselves for the sacraments of Christian initiation, [for N. and N., who will receive God's forgiveness in the sacrament of penance for the first time,] and for ourselves, who seek the mercy of Christ.

Assisting minister:
That we may open our hearts to the Lord Jesus with gratitude and faith, let us pray to the Lord:
R̸. Lord, hear our prayer.

Assisting minister:
That we may honestly try to know our failures and recognize our sins, let us pray to the Lord:
R̸. Lord, hear our prayer.

Assisting minister:
That, as children of God, we may openly admit our weaknesses and faults, let us pray to the Lord:
R̸. Lord, hear our prayer.

Assisting minister:
That in the presence of Christ we may express sorrow for our sins, let us pray to the Lord:
℟. Lord, hear our prayer.

Assisting minister:
That we may be delivered from present evils and protected against those to come, let us pray to the Lord:
℟. Lord, hear our prayer.

Assisting minister:
That we may learn from our Father in heaven to triumph by his love over the powers of sin, let us pray to the Lord:
℟. Lord, hear our prayer.

EXORCISM

300. Then the celebrant, with hands outstretched over the children, says one of the following. 339

Let us pray.

A
Father of mercies, 339
you sent your only Son
to rescue us from the slavery of sin
and to give us freedom as your children.

Look with love on these young people and fulfill
 their hopes;
they have already experienced temptation
and they acknowledge their faults.

Lead them from darkness into your unfailing light,
cleanse them from sin,
let them know the joy of your peace,
and guide them safely through life.

We ask this through Christ our Lord.
℟. Amen.

B
God of mercy and Father of all, 392
look upon N. and N., who will soon be baptized.

Children:
**We have heard the words of Jesus
and we love them.**

Celebrant:
**Even though they try to live as your children,
they sometimes find this difficult.**

Children:
**Father, we want always to do what pleases you,
but sometimes we find this hard.**

Celebrant:
**Loving Father,
free these young people
from whatever could make them bad
and help them always to walk in your light.**

Children:
**We want to walk with Jesus,
who gave his life for us.
Help us, Father, to follow him.**

Celebrant:
**If they stumble on the way
and do not please you,
help them up with the power of your hand,
that they may rise again
and continue on their journey to you
with Jesus Christ our Lord.**

Children:
Father, give us strength.

ANOINTING WITH THE OIL OF CATECHUMENS [OR LAYING ON OF HANDS]

301. The rite continues with the anointing with the oil of catechumens, option A. But for pastoral reasons, for example, if the children have been anointed already, a laying on of hands, option B, may be used.   340 USA

A *Anointing with the Oil of Catechumens:*

If, for pastoral reasons, the priest chooses to bless oil for the rite, he uses the following blessing.   USA

Let us pray.

O God,   131
source of strength and defender of your people,
you have chosen to make this oil,
created by your hand,
an effective sign of your power.

Bless ✠ this oil
and strengthen the catechumens who will be
  anointed with it.
Grant them your wisdom to understand the Gospel
  more deeply
and your strength to accept the challenges of Chris-
  tian life.

Enable them to rejoice in baptism
and to partake of a new life in the Church
as true children of your family.

We ask this through Christ our Lord.
℟. Amen.

The celebrant faces the children and says: 340
We anoint you with the oil of salvation   132
in the name of Christ our Savior.
May he strengthen you with his power,
who lives and reigns for ever and ever.

Children:
Amen.

Each child is anointed with the oil of catechumens on the
breast or on both hands or even on other parts of the body,
if this seems desirable.

[If there are a great many catechumens, additional priests
or deacons may assist in the anointing.]

The anointing may be followed by a blessing of the catechumens (no. 97).

B *Laying on of Hands:* The celebrant faces the children and
says:

**May Christ our Savior
strengthen you with his power,
for he is Lord for ever and ever.**

Children:
Amen.

Then, in silence, the celebrant lays his hands on the head
of each child.

DISMISSAL OF THE CHILDREN

302. The celebrant dismisses the children, option A, or   341
else sends them back to their places in the church, where
they remain, option B.

A The celebrant dismisses the children, using these or
similar words.
**N. and N., here among us the Lord Jesus has opened
the arms of his mercy to you. Go now in peace.**

Children:
Thanks be to God.

B The celebrant sends the children back to their places in
the church, using these or similar words.
**N. and N., here among us the Lord Jesus has opened
the arms of his mercy to you. Return to your places
now and continue with us in prayer.**

Children:
Thanks be to God.

LITURGY OF PENANCE

303. Next, the liturgy of the sacrament of penance begins   342
for baptized children who will celebrate this sacrament for
the first time. After the celebrant gives a brief instruction,
individual confession, first of the children, then of the others in the assembly, follows.

A suitable song or a prayer of thanksgiving follows the celebration of the sacrament; all then leave.

THIRD STEP: CELEBRATION OF THE SACRAMENTS OF INITIATION

Wake up and rise from death: Christ will shine upon you

304. In order to bring out the paschal character of baptism, celebration of the sacraments of initiation should preferably take place at the Easter Vigil or on a Sunday, the day that the Church devotes to the remembrance of Christ's resurrection (see *Rite of Baptism for Children*, Introduction, no. 9). But the provisions of no. 256 should also guide the choice of time for the celebration of the sacraments of initiation. — 343

305. At this third step of their Christian initiation, the children will receive the sacrament of baptism, the bishop or priest who baptizes them will also confer confirmation, and the children will for the first time participate in the liturgy of the eucharist. — 344

306. If the sacraments of initiation are celebrated at a time other than the Easter Vigil or Easter Sunday, the Mass of the day or one of the ritual Masses in the Roman Missal, "Christian Initiation: Baptism" is used. The readings are chosen from those given in the Lectionary for Mass, "Celebration of the Sacraments of Initiation apart from the Easter Vigil"; but the readings for the Sunday or feast on which the celebration takes place may be used instead. — 345

307. All the children to be baptized are to be accompanied by their own godparent or godparents, chosen by themselves and approved by the priest (see no. 11; *Christian Initiation*, General Introduction, no. 10). — 346

308. Baptized children of the catechetical group may be completing their Christian initiation in the sacraments of confirmation and the eucharist at this same celebration. When the bishop himself will not be the celebrant, he should grant the faculty to confirm such children to the priest who will be the celebrant.[1] For their confirmation, previously baptized children of the catechetical group are to have their own sponsors. If possible, these should be the persons who were godparents for their baptism, but other qualified persons may be chosen.[2]

[1] See *Rite of Confirmation*, Introduction, no. 7, b.
[2] See ibid., nos. 5 and 6.

CELEBRATION OF THE SACRAMENTS OF INITIATION

LITURGY OF THE WORD

309. When the children who are candidates for initiation,   347
their parents or guardians, godparents, other children from
the catechetical group, friends, and members of the parish
have assembled, Mass begins.

The texts for the Mass and the readings in the liturgy of the
word are those already indicated in no. 306. The homily follows the readings.

CELEBRATION OF BAPTISM

INVITATION TO PRAYER

310. After the homily, the celebrant and the children with   348
their parents or guardians and godparents go to the baptismal font, if this is in view of the faithful; otherwise they
gather in the sanctuary, where a vessel of water should be
prepared beforehand. The celebrant speaks to the family,
friends, and the entire assembly in these or similar words.

**Dear friends, N. and N., with the approval of their
parents, have asked to be baptized. Let us call upon
the Father to number them among his adopted children in Christ.**

PRAYER OVER THE WATER

311. Next, the celebrant blesses the water or says a prayer   349
of thanksgiving over the water.   350

When baptism is celebrated at the Easter Vigil, the celebrant blesses the water, using option A; outside the Easter
Vigil, in blessing the water he may use either option A or
the other blessing formularies given in no. 222 as options B
and C.

But when baptism is celebrated during the Easter season
and water already blessed at the Easter Vigil is available,
the celebrant uses option B, so that this part of the celebration will retain the themes of thanksgiving and intercession;

he may also use the second Easter-season thanksgiving formulary given in no. 222 as option E.

A

Blessing of the Water: Facing the font (or vessel) containing the water, the celebrant says the following prayer.

349

Father,
you give us grace through sacramental signs,
which tell us of the wonders of your unseen power.

In baptism we use your gift of water,
which you have made a rich symbol of the grace
you give us in this sacrament.

At the very dawn of creation
your Spirit breathed on the waters,
making them the wellspring of all holiness.

The waters of the great flood
you made a sign of the waters of baptism
that make an end of sin
and a new beginning of goodness.

Through the waters of the Red Sea
you led Israel out of slavery
to be an image of God's holy people,
set free from sin by baptism.

In the waters of the Jordan
your Son was baptized by John
and anointed with the Spirit.

Your Son willed that water and blood should flow
    from his side
as he hung upon the cross.

After his resurrection he told his disciples:
"Go out and teach all nations,
baptizing them in the name of the Father, and of the
    Son, and of the Holy Spirit."

Father,
look now with love upon your Church
and unseal for it the fountain of baptism.

By the power of the Holy Spirit
give to this water the grace of your Son,
so that in the sacrament of baptism
all those whom you have created in your likeness
may be cleansed from sin
and rise to a new birth of innocence
by water and the Holy Spirit.

The celebrant before continuing touches the water with his right hand.

[But at the Easter Vigil, if this can be done conveniently, the celebrant before continuing lowers the Easter candle into the water once or three times, then holds it there until the acclamation at the end of the blessing.]

We ask you, Father, with your Son
to send the Holy Spirit upon the waters of this font.
May all who are buried with Christ in the death of
**   baptism**
rise also with him to newness of life.

We ask this through Christ our Lord.

All:
Amen.

The people sing the following or some other suitable acclamation.

Springs of water, bless the Lord.
Give him glory and praise for ever.

B

Easter-Season Thanksgiving over Water Already Blessed: Facing the font (or vessel) containing the blessed water, the celebrant says the prayer as in no. 222 D.   389

COMMUNITY'S PROFESSION OF FAITH

312. Before the rite of the children's profession of faith, the celebrant may, if this is in keeping with the circumstances, invite the parents or guardians, godparents, and all present to profess their faith.   351

N. and N. have completed a long preparation and are ready for baptism. They will receive new life from God who is love: they will become Christians.

From now on, we will need to help them even more. This is especially true of you, their parents, who have given them permission to be baptized and who have the primary responsibility for their upbringing. But all of us who have in any way prepared them to meet Christ today must always be ready to assist them.

And so, before these children make their profession of faith in our presence, let us in their presence publicly and with a deep sense of responsibility renew our own profession of faith, which is the faith of the Church.

Then together with the celebrant all recite the profession of faith, using either the Apostles' Creed, option A, or the Nicene Creed, option B.

A   Apostles' Creed
All join the celebrant and say:

I believe in God, the Father almighty,
  creator of heaven and earth.

I believe in Jesus Christ, his only Son, our Lord.
  He was conceived by the power of the Holy Spirit
    and born of the Virgin Mary.
  He suffered under Pontius Pilate,
    was crucified, died, and was buried.
  He descended to the dead.
  On the third day he rose again.
  He ascended into heaven,
    and is seated at the right hand of the Father.
  He will come again to judge the living and the
    dead.

I believe in the Holy Spirit,
  the holy catholic Church,
  the communion of saints,
  the forgiveness of sins,
  the resurrection of the body,
  and the life everlasting. Amen.

B Nicene Creed

All join the celebrant and say:

We believe in one God,
   the Father, the Almighty,
   maker of heaven and earth,
   of all that is seen and unseen.

We believe in one Lord, Jesus Christ,
   the only Son of God,
   eternally begotten of the Father,
   God from God, Light from Light,
   true God from true God,
   begotten, not made,
   one in Being with the Father.
   Through him all things were made.
   For us men and for our salvation
      he came down from heaven:
   by the power of the Holy Spirit
      he was born of the Virgin Mary,
         and became man.
   For our sake he was crucified under Pontius Pilate;
      he suffered, died, and was buried.
      On the third day he rose again
         in fulfillment of the Scriptures;
      he ascended into heaven
         and is seated at the right hand of the Father.
   He will come again in glory to judge the living
      and the dead,
      and his kingdom will have no end.

We believe in the Holy Spirit, the Lord, the giver of
   life,
   who proceeds from the Father and the Son.
   With the Father and the Son he is worshiped and
      glorified.
   He has spoken through the Prophets.
   We believe in one holy catholic and apostolic
      Church.
   We acknowledge one baptism for the forgiveness
      of sins.
   We look for the resurrection of the dead,
      and the life of the world to come. Amen.

CHILDREN'S PROFESSION OF FAITH

313. The celebration of baptism continues with the rite of   352
the children's renunciation of sin and profession of faith.

The celebrant first addresses them briefly in these or similar
words.

**Children [N. and N.], you have spent a long time in
preparation and you have now asked to be baptized.
Your parents have agreed to your request; your teachers, companions, and friends have helped you; and
all who have come here today promise you the example of their faith and their loving support.**

**Before you are baptized, reject Satan and profess
your faith here in the presence of God's Church.**

RENUNCIATION OF SIN

314. The celebrant, using one of the following formularies,   353
questions all the children together.

A   Celebrant:
**Do you reject sin so as to live in the freedom of
God's children?**

Children:
I do.

Celebrant:
**Do you reject the glamor of evil,
and refuse to be mastered by sin?**

Children:
I do.

Celebrant:
**Do you reject Satan, father of sin and prince of dark-
ness?**

Children:
I do.

B   Celebrant:
**Do you reject Satan,
and all his works,
and all his empty promises?**

Children:
I do.

ANOINTING WITH THE OIL OF CATECHUMENS

315. If it has not been celebrated at another time during
the catechumenate of the children, particularly within the
penitential rite (no. 301), the anointing with the oil of catechumens now takes place between the renunciation of sin
and the profession of faith. Ordinarily, this rite is to be
omitted, as decreed by the National Conference of Catholic
Bishops (see no. 33.7).

354
USA

The celebrant, facing the children, says:
We anoint you with the oil of salvation
in the name of Christ our Savior.
May he strengthen you with his power,
who lives and reigns for ever and ever.

354

Children:
Amen.

Each of the children is anointed with the oil of catechumens
on both hands, on the breast, or on other parts of the
body, if this seems desirable.

[If there are a great number of children, additional priests
or deacons may assist with the anointings.]

PROFESSION OF FAITH

316. The celebrant, informed by the godparents of the
name of each child, asks the child individually to make the
profession of faith, then immediately baptizes the child.

355

Celebrant:
N., do you believe in God, the Father almighty,
creator of heaven and earth?

Child:
I do.

Celebrant:
Do you believe in Jesus Christ, his only Son, our
Lord,
who was born of the Virgin Mary,

was crucified, died, and was buried,
rose from the dead,
and is now seated at the right hand of the Father?

Child:
I do.

Celebrant:
Do you believe in the Holy Spirit,
the holy catholic Church, the communion of saints,
the forgiveness of sins, the resurrection of the
body,
and the life everlasting?

Child:
I do.

If there are a great many children to be baptized, the profes-   USA
sion of faith may be made simultaneously either by all together or group by group. The baptism of each candidate
follows.

BAPTISM

317. The celebrant baptizes each child either by immer-   356
sion, option A, or by the pouring of water, option B. Each
baptism may be followed by a short acclamation (Appendix
II, no. 595), sung or said by the people.

[If there are a great number of children to be baptized, they
may be divided into groups and baptized by assisting
priests or deacons. In baptizing, either by immersion, option A, or by the pouring of water, option B, these ministers say the sacramental formulary for each child. During
the baptisms, singing by the people is desirable or readings
from Scripture or simply silent prayer.]

A
If baptism is by immersion, of the whole body or of the   220
head only, decency and decorum should be preserved. Either or both godparents touch the child. The celebrant, immersing the child's whole body or head three times, baptizes the child in the name of the Trinity.

N., I baptize you in the name of the Father,

He immerses the child the first time.

and of the Son,

He immerses the child the second time.

and of the Holy Spirit.

He immerses the child the third time.

B

If baptism is by the pouring of water, either or both godpar-   356
ents place the right hand on the shoulder of the child, and
the celebrant, taking baptismal water and pouring it three
times on the child's bowed head, baptizes the child in the
name of the Trinity.

N., I baptize you in the name of the Father,

He pours water the first time.

and of the Son,

He pours water the second time.

and of the Holy Spirit.

He pours water the third time.

EXPLANATORY RITES
318. See no. 227.   357

ANOINTING AFTER BAPTISM

319. If the confirmation of those baptized is separated   358
from baptism, the celebrant anoints them with chrism immediately after baptism.

[When a great number have been baptized, assisting priests
or deacons may help with the anointing.]

The celebrant first says the following over all the newly baptized before the anointing.

**The God of power and Father of our Lord Jesus
   Christ
has freed you from sin
and brought you to new life
through water and the Holy Spirit.**

**He now anoints you with the chrism of salvation,
so that, united with his people,
you may remain for ever a member of Christ
who is Priest, Prophet, and King.**

Children:
Amen.

In silence each of the newly baptized is anointed with
chrism on the crown of the head.

CLOTHING WITH A BAPTISMAL GARMENT

320. The garment used in this rite may be white or of a   359
color that conforms to local custom. If circumstances suggest, this rite may be omitted.

The celebrant says the following formulary and at the
words "Receive this baptismal garment" the godparents
place the garment on the newly baptized children.

**N. and N., you have become a new creation
and have clothed yourselves in Christ.
Receive this baptismal garment
and bring it unstained to the judgment seat of our
   Lord Jesus Christ,
so that you may have everlasting life.**

Children:
Amen.

PRESENTATION OF A LIGHTED CANDLE

321. The celebrant takes the Easter candle in his hands or   360
touches it, saying to the godparents:

**Godparents, please come forward to give to the
newly baptized the light of Christ.**

A godparent of each of the newly baptized goes to the celebrant, lights a candle from the Easter candle, then presents
it to the newly baptized child.

Then the celebrant says to the children:

**You have been enlightened by Christ.
Walk always as children of the light
and keep the flame of faith alive in your hearts.
When the Lord comes, may you go out to meet him
with all the saints in the heavenly kingdom.**

Children:
Amen.

CELEBRATION OF CONFIRMATION

322. Between the celebration of baptism and confirmation, the assembly may sing a suitable song.

361
362

The place for the celebration of confirmation is either at the baptismal font or in the sanctuary, depending on where, according to local conditions, baptism has been celebrated.

If previously baptized children of the catechetical group are to be confirmed, they with their sponsors join the newly baptized children to receive the sacrament.

323. If the bishop has conferred baptism, he should now also confer confirmation. If the bishop is not present, the priest who conferred baptism is authorized to confirm (see no. 308).

362

[When there are a great many children to be confirmed, the minister of confirmation may associate priests with himself as ministers of the sacrament (see no. 14).]

INVITATION

324. The celebrant first speaks briefly to the children in these or similar words.

363

My dear children, by your baptism you have been born again in Christ and you have become members of Christ and of his priestly people. Now you are to share in the outpouring of the Holy Spirit among us, the Spirit sent by the Lord upon his apostles at Pentecost and given by them and their successors to the baptized.

The promised strength of the Holy Spirit, which you are to receive, will make you more like Christ and help you to be witnesses to his suffering, death, and resurrection. It will strengthen you to be active members of the Church and to build up the Body of Christ in faith and love.

[The priests who will be associated with the celebrant as ministers of the sacrament now stand next to him.]

With hands joined, the celebrant next addresses the people:

My dear friends, let us pray to God our Father, that he will pour out the Holy Spirit on these children to strengthen them with his gifts and anoint them to be more like Christ, the Son of God.

All pray briefly in silence.

LAYING ON OF HANDS

325. See no. 234.   364

ANOINTING WITH CHRISM

326. A minister brings the chrism to the celebrant.   365

[When the celebrant is the bishop, priests who are associated as ministers of the sacrament receive the chrism from him.]

Each child to be confirmed, with godparent or godparents, sponsor or sponsors, goes to the celebrant (or to an associated minister of the sacrament); or, if circumstances require, the celebrant (associated ministers) may go to the children.

Either or both godparents or sponsors place the right hand on the shoulder of the child and a godparent or sponsor of each child gives the child's name or the child gives his or her name to the minister of the sacrament. During the conferral of the sacrament an appropriate song may be sung.

The minister of the sacrament dips his right thumb in the chrism and makes the sign of the cross on the forehead of the one to be confirmed as he says:

N., be sealed with the Gift of the Holy Spirit.

Child:
Amen.

The minister of the sacrament adds:
Peace be with you.

Child:
And also with you.

LITURGY OF THE EUCHARIST.

327. Since the profession of faith is not said, the general   366
intercessions begin immediately and for the first time the
newly baptized children take part in them. Some of the children also take part in the procession to the altar with the
gifts.

328. With Eucharistic Prayers I, II or III the special interpo-   367
lations given in the Roman Missal, the ritual Masses, "Christian Initiation: Baptism," are used.

Eucharistic Prayer IV, with its special interpolation indicated in the same ritual Masses, may also be used but outside the Easter Vigil.

329. It is most desirable that the newly baptized children,   368
together with their godparents, parents, and catechists, receive communion under both kinds.

Before saying "This is the Lamb of God," the celebrant may
briefly remind the newly baptized children of the preeminence of the eucharist, which is the climax of their initiation
and the center of the whole Christian life.

The celebrant should also pay special attention to any previously baptized children of the catechetical group who at
this celebration are to receive communion for the first time.
These children, together with their parents, godparents,
sponsors for confirmation, and catechists, may also receive
communion under both kinds.

PERIOD OF POSTBAPTISMAL CATECHESIS OR MYSTAGOGY

The Father chose us to be his adopted children through Jesus Christ

330. A period of postbaptismal catechesis or mystagogy should be provided to assist the young neophytes and their companions who have completed their Christian initiation. This period can be arranged by an adaptation of the guidelines given for adults (nos. 244–251).

369

2.   CHRISTIAN INITIATION OF ADULTS IN EXCEPTIONAL CIRCUMSTANCES

He gave power to become children of God to all who believe in his name

331. Exceptional circumstances may arise in which the lo-   240
cal bishop, in individual cases, can allow the use of a form
of Christian initiation that is simpler than the usual, complete rite (see no. 34.4).

The bishop may permit this simpler form to consist in the
abbreviated form of the rite (nos. 340–369) that is carried
out in one celebration. Or he may permit an expansion of
this abbreviated rite, so that there are celebrations not only
of the sacraments of initiation but also of one or more of
the rites belonging to the period of the catechumenate and
to the period of purification and enlightenment (see nos.
332–335).

The extraordinary circumstances in question are either
events that prevent the candidate from completing all the
steps of the catechumenate or a depth of Christian conversion and a degree of religious maturity that lead the local
bishop to decide that the candidate may receive baptism
without delay.

EXPANDED FORM

332. Extraordinary circumstances, for example, sickness,   274
old age, change of residence, long absence for travel, may
sometimes either prevent a candidate from celebrating the
rite of acceptance that leads to the period of the
catechumenate or, having begun the catechumenate, from
completing it by participation in all the rites belonging to
the period. Yet merely to use the abbreviated form of the
rite given in nos. 340–369 could mean a spiritual loss for
the candidate, who would be deprived of the benefits of a
longer preparation for the sacraments of initiation. It is
therefore important that, with the bishop's permission, an
expanded form of initiation be developed by the incorporation of elements from the complete rite for the Christian initiation of adults.

333. Through such an expansion of the abbreviated rite a   275
new candidate can reach the same level as those who are

already advanced in the catechumenate, since some of the earlier elements from the full rite can be added, for example, the rite of acceptance into the order of catechumens (nos. 48–74) or the minor exorcisms (no. 94) and blessings (no. 97) from the period of the catechumenate. The expansion also makes it possible for a candidate who had begun the catechumenate with others, but was forced to interrupt it, to complete the catechumenate alone by celebrating, in addition to the sacraments of initiation (see nos. 206–217), elements from the full rite, for example, the rite of election (see nos. 118–128) and rites belonging to the period of purification and enlightenment (see nos. 141–149).

334. Pastors can arrange this expanded form of initiation 276
by taking the abbreviated form as a basis, then choosing wisely from the full rite to make adaptations in any of the following ways:

1. supplementing the abbreviated form: for example, adding rites belonging to the period of the catechumenate (nos. 81–102) or adding the presentations (nos. 157–162, 178–182);

2. making the rite of "Receiving the Candidate" or the "Liturgy of the Word" in the abbreviated rite separate or expanded celebrations. As to "Receiving the Candidate" (nos. 340–345), this can be expanded by replacing no. 342 and using elements from the rite of acceptance into the order of catechumens (nos. 48–74); or, depending on the candidate's state of preparation, by celebrating the rite of election (nos. 129–137) in place of nos. 343–344. As to the "Liturgy of the Word," after the readings, the intercessions, penitential rite, and prayer of exorcism, nos. 349–351, can be adapted by use of the elements in the scrutinies (nos. 152–154, 166–168, 173–175);

3. replacing elements of the complete rite with elements of the abbreviated form; or combining the rite of acceptance into the order of catechumens (nos. 48–74) and the rite of election (nos. 129–137) at the time of receiving a properly disposed candidate (which is comparable to the time of receiving interested inquirers in the period of the precatechumenate; see no. 39.3).

335. When this expanded form of initiation is arranged, 277
care should be taken to ensure that:

1. the candidate has received a full catechesis;

2. the rite is celebrated with the active participation of an assembly;

3. after receiving the sacraments the neophyte has the benefit of a period of postbaptismal catechesis, if at all possible.

ABBREVIATED FORM

336. Before the abbreviated form of the rite is celebrated the candidate must have gone through an adequate period of instruction and preparation before baptism, in order to purify his or her motives for requesting baptism and to grow stronger in conversion and faith. The candidate should also have chosen godparents or a godparent (see no. 11) and become acquainted with the local Christian community (see nos. 39, 75.2).   241

337. This rite includes elements that express the presentation and welcoming of the candidate and that also express the candidate's clear and firm resolve to request Christian initiation, as well as the Church's approval of the candidate. A suitable liturgy of the word is also celebrated, then the sacraments of initiation.   242

338. Normally the rite is celebrated within Mass. The choice of readings should be in keeping with the character of the celebration; they may be either those of the day or those in the Lectionary for Mass, ritual Mass, "Christian Initiation apart from the Easter Vigil." The other Mass texts are those of one of the ritual Masses "Christian Initiation: Baptism" or of another Mass. After receiving baptism and confirmation, the candidate takes part for the first time in the celebration of the eucharist.   243

339. If at all possible, the celebration should take place on a Sunday (see no. 27), with the local community taking an active part.   244

CHRISTIAN INITIATION OF ADULTS
IN EXCEPTIONAL CIRCUMSTANCES
(Abbreviated Form)

RECEIVING THE CANDIDATE

340. Before the celebration begins, the candidate with his   245
or her godparents and friends waits outside the church or
inside, at the entrance or some other convenient place. The
celebrant, wearing the vestments for Mass, goes to meet
them, as the faithful sing a psalm or another suitable song.

GREETING

341. The celebrant greets the candidate in a friendly man-   246
ner. He speaks to the candidate, godparents, and friends,
pointing out the joy and happiness of the Church. He recalls for the godparents and friends the particular experience and religious response that have led the candidate, following his or her own spiritual path, to the present celebration.

The celebrant then invites the godparents and the candidate
to come forward. As they are taking their place before him,
an appropriate song may be sung, for example, Psalm
63:1–8.

OPENING DIALOGUE

342. Facing the candidate, the celebrant asks the questions   247
that follow. In asking about the candidate's intention he
may use words other than those provided and may let the
candidate answer in his or her own words: for example, to
the first question, "What do you ask of the Church of
God?" or "What do you desire?" or "For what reason have
you come?", he may receive such answers as "The grace of
Christ" or "Entrance into the Church" or "Eternal life" or
other suitable responses. The celebrant will phrase his next
question according to the answer received.

Celebrant:
What do you ask of God's Church?

Candidate:
Faith.

Celebrant:
What does faith offer you?

Candidate:
Eternal life.

CANDIDATE'S DECLARATION

343. The celebrant addresses the candidate, adapting as re- 248
quired the following or similar words to the answers received in the opening dialogue.

**This is eternal life: to know the one true God and
Jesus Christ, whom he has sent. Christ has been
raised from the dead and appointed by God as the
Lord of life and ruler of all things, seen and unseen.**

**You would not ask for this life or seek baptism to-
day, unless you had already come to know Christ
and wanted to become his disciple. And I ask you,
have you listened to Christ's word and resolved to
keep his commandments? Have you shared our way
of life and joined with us in prayer? Have you done
all these things with the intention of becoming a
Christian?**

Candidate:
I have.

AFFIRMATION BY THE GODPARENTS

344. Then the celebrant turns to the godparents and asks: 249

**You are the candidate's godparents. As God is your
witness, do you consider him/her worthy to be admitted today to the sacraments of Christian initiation?**

Godparents:
I do.

Celebrant:
**You have spoken in N.'s favor. Are you prepared to
help him/her to serve Christ by your words and example?**

Godparents:
I am.

The celebrant, with hands joined, says: 250

Let us pray.

Father of mercy,
we thank you for your servant, N.
You have sought and summoned him/her in many
ways
and he/she has turned to seek you.

You have called him/her today
and he/she has answered in the presence of the
Church.

Look favorably upon him/her
and let your loving purpose be fulfilled within him/
her.

We ask this through Christ our Lord.
R̷. Amen.

INVITATION TO THE CELEBRATION OF THE WORD
OF GOD

345. Using the following or similar words, accompanied by 251
an appropriate gesture, the celebrant invites the candidate
and the godparents to enter the church.

Celebrant:
N., come into the church, to share with us at the ta-
ble of God's word.

During the entrance a suitable song is sung or the following
antiphon, with Psalm 34:2, 3, 6, 9, 10.

Come, my children, and listen to me;
I will teach you the fear of the Lord.

LITURGY OF THE WORD

346. When the candidate and the godparents have taken   252
their place in the church and the celebrant has reached the
sanctuary, the liturgy of the word begins; the usual introductory rites of the Mass are omitted.

READINGS

347. The readings are those already indicated in no. 338.   253

HOMILY

348. The homily follows the gospel reading.   253

INTERCESSIONS FOR THE CANDIDATE

349. After the homily, the candidate and the godparents   254
come before the celebrant. The entire assembly joins in offering the following or similar intercessions.

Celebrant:
**Let us pray for our brother/sister who asks for
Christ's sacraments, and let us pray for ourselves, sin-
ners that we are, that we may all draw nearer to
Christ in faith and repentance and walk untiringly in
newness of life.**

Assisting minister:
**That the Lord may kindle in all of us a spirit of true
repentance, let us pray to the Lord:
R̥. Lord, hear our prayer.**

Assisting minister:
**That we, who have died to sin and been saved by
Christ through baptism, may be living proof of his
grace, let us pray to the Lord:
R̥. Lord, hear our prayer.**

Assisting minister:
**That with trust in God's love and sorrow for sin our
brother/sister may prepare to meet Christ his/her Savior, let us pray to the Lord:
R̥. Lord, hear our prayer.**

Assisting minister:

That by following Christ, who takes away the sin of the world, our brother/sister may be healed of the infection of sin and freed from its power, let us pray to the Lord:

℟. **Lord, hear our prayer.**

Assisting minister:

That by the power of the Holy Spirit, he/she may be cleansed from sin and guided along the paths of holiness, let us pray to the Lord:

℟. **Lord, hear our prayer.**

Assisting minister:

That through burial with Christ in baptism he/she may die to sin and live always for God, let us pray to the Lord:

℟. **Lord, hear our prayer.**

Assisting minister:

That on the day of judgment he/she may come before the Father bearing fruits of holiness and love, let us pray to the Lord:

℟. **Lord, hear our prayer.**

Assisting minister:

That the entire world, for which the Father gave his beloved Son, may believe in his love and turn to him, let us pray to the Lord:

℟. **Lord, hear our prayer.**

PENITENTIAL RITE

350. The penitential rite may be omitted, as circumstances suggest. When it is celebrated, after the intercessions the candidate bows his or her head or kneels and joins the assembly in reciting the general confession of sins. 254

**I confess to almighty God,
and to you, my brothers and sisters,
that I have sinned through my own fault**

All strike their breast

**in my thoughts and in my words,
in what I have done,**

and in what I have failed to do;
and I ask blessed Mary, ever-virgin,
all the angels and saints,
and you, my brothers and sisters,
to pray for me to the Lord our God.

The absolution "**May almighty God**" is not said.

PRAYER OF EXORCISM

351. The celebrant concludes the intercessions (and peni-   255
tential rite) with the following prayer.

Father of mercies,
you sent your only Son
to rescue us from the slavery of sin
and to give us freedom as your children.

We pray for your servant N.;
he/she has faced the temptations of this world
and been tested by the cunning of Satan;
now he/she acknowledges his/her sinfulness
and professes his/her faith.

By the passion and resurrection of your Son
deliver him/her from the powers of darkness
and strengthen him/her through the grace of Christ,
that he/she may journey through life, shielded by
**   your unfailing care.**

We ask this through Christ our Lord.
R̸. Amen.

ANOINTING WITH THE OIL OF CATECHUMENS OR
LAYING ON OF HANDS

352. If it has not been celebrated at another time, the   256
anointing with the oil of catechumens, option A, now takes   USA
place. Ordinarily, this rite is to be omitted, as decreed by
the National Conference of Catholic Bishops (see no. 33.7).
It is always permissible for the celebrant to substitute a laying on of hands, option B.

A   *Anointing with the Oil of Catechumens:* The celebrant
faces the candidate and says:

We anoint you with the oil of salvation
in the name of Christ our Savior.

**May he strengthen you with his power,
who lives and reigns for ever and ever.**

Candidate:
Amen.

The candidate is anointed with the oil of catechumens on
the breast or on both hands or even on other parts of the
body, if this seems desirable.

B   *Laying on of Hands:* The celebrant faces the candidate
and says:

**May Christ our Savior
strengthen you with his power,
for he is Lord for ever and ever.**

Candidate:
Amen.

Then, in silence, the celebrant lays hands on the candidate.

CELEBRATION OF BAPTISM

INVITATION TO PRAYER

353. The candidate with the godparent or the godparents   257
goes to the baptismal font with the celebrant, then the celebrant addresses the following or a similar invitation for the
assembly to join in prayer for the candidate.

**Dear friends, let us pray to almighty God for our
brother/sister N., who is asking for baptism. He has
called N. and brought him/her to this moment; may
he grant N. light and strength to follow Christ with a
resolute heart and to profess the faith of the Church.
May he give N. the new life of the Holy Spirit,
whom we are about to call down on this water.**

PRAYER OVER THE WATER

354. Next, the celebrant blesses the water, using option A;   258
he may also use one of the other blessing formularies given
in no. 222 as option B and C.

But when baptism is celebrated during the Easter season
and water already blessed at the Easter Vigil is available,

the celebrant uses option B, so that this part of the celebration will retain the themes of thanksgiving and intercession; he may also use the second Easter-season thanksgiving formulary given in no. 222 as option E.

A *Blessing of the Water:* Facing the font (or vessel) containing the water, the celebrant says the following prayer.

Father,
you give us grace through sacramental signs,
which tell us of the wonders of your unseen power.

In baptism we use your gift of water,
which you have made a rich symbol of the grace
you give us in this sacrament.

At the very dawn of creation
your Spirit breathed on the waters,
making them the wellspring of all holiness.

The waters of the great flood
you made a sign of the waters of baptism
that make an end of sin
and a new beginning of goodness.

Through the waters of the Red Sea
you led Israel out of slavery
to be an image of God's holy people,
set free from sin by baptism.

In the waters of the Jordan
your Son was baptized by John
and anointed with the Spirit.

Your Son willed that water and blood should flow
   from his side
as he hung upon the cross.

After his resurrection he told his disciples:
"Go out and teach all nations,
baptizing them in the name of the Father, and of the
   Son, and of the Holy Spirit."

Father,
look now with love upon your Church
and unseal for it the fountain of baptism.

By the power of the Holy Spirit
give to this water the grace of your Son,
so that in the sacrament of baptism
all those whom you have created in your likeness
may be cleansed from sin
and rise to a new birth of innocence
by water and the Holy Spirit.

Before continuing, the celebrant pauses and touches the water with his right hand.

We ask you, Father, with your Son
to send the Holy Spirit upon the waters of this font.
May all who are buried with Christ in the death of
    baptism
rise also with him to newness of life.

We ask this through Christ our Lord.

All:
Amen.

B *Easter-Season Thanksgiving over Blessed Water:* See no. 222
D.
389

PROFESSION OF FAITH

355. See no. 223.
259

RENUNCIATION OF SIN

.356. Using one of the following formularies, the celebrant questions the candidate.
259
USA

[At the discretion of the diocesan bishop, the formularies for the renunciation of sin may be made more specific and detailed as circumstances might require (see no. 33.8).]

A Celebrant:
Do you reject sin so as to live in the freedom of
    God's children?

Candidate:
I do.

Celebrant:
**Do you reject the glamor of evil,
and refuse to be mastered by sin?**

Candidate:
I do.

Celebrant:
Do you reject Satan, father of sin and prince of darkness?

Candidate:
I do.

B   Celebrant:
**Do you reject Satan,
and all his works,
and all his empty promises?**

Candidate:
I do.

C   Celebrant:
Do you reject Satan?

Candidate:
I do.

Celebrant:
And all his works?

Candidate:
I do.

Celebrant:
And all his empty promises?

Candidate:
I do.

PROFESSION OF FAITH

357. Then the celebrant asks the candidate: 260

N., do you believe in God, the Father almighty, creator of heaven and earth?

Candidate:
I do.

Celebrant:

**Do you believe in Jesus Christ, his only Son, our
Lord,
who was born of the Virgin Mary,
was crucified, died, and was buried,
rose from the dead,
and is now seated at the right hand of the Father?**

Candidate:

I do.

Celebrant:

**Do you believe in the Holy Spirit,
the holy catholic Church, the communion of saints,
the forgiveness of sins, the resurrection of the
body,
and the life everlasting?**

Candidate:

I do.

BAPTISM

358. Immediately after the profession of faith the celebrant   260
baptizes the candidate either by immersion, option A, or by
the pouring of water, option B. After the baptism it is appropriate for the people to sing a short acclamation (Appendix II, no. 595).

A   See no. 226 A.   261
B   See no. 226 B.   262

EXPLANATORY RITES

359. The celebration of baptism proceeds immediately with
the explanatory rites, after which the celebration of confirmation follows.

CLOTHING WITH A BAPTISMAL GARMENT
360. See no. 229.   264

PRESENTATION OF A LIGHTED CANDLE
361. The celebrant takes the Easter candle in his hands or   265
touches it, saying to the godparent(s):

**Please come forward to give to the newly baptized
the light of Christ.**

A godparent goes to the celebrant and lights a candle from the Easter candle, then presents it to the newly baptized.

Then the celebrant says to the newly baptized:

**You have been enlightened by Christ.
Walk always as a child of the light
and keep the flame of faith alive in your heart.
When the Lord comes, may you go out to meet him
with all the saints in the heavenly kingdom.**

Newly baptized:
Amen.

CELEBRATION OF CONFIRMATION

362. Between the celebration of baptism and confirmation, the assembly may sing an appropriate song.

266

363. If the bishop is not present, the celebrant who conferred baptism confers confirmation.

267

INVITATION

364. The celebrant first speaks briefly to the person newly baptized in these or similar words.

268

N., born again in Christ by baptism, you have become a member of Christ and of his priestly people. Now you are to share in the outpouring of the Holy Spirit among us, the Spirit sent by the Lord upon his apostles at Pentecost and given by them and their successors to the baptized.

The promised strength of the Holy Spirit, which you are to receive, will make you more like Christ and help you to be a witness to his suffering, death, and resurrection. It will strengthen you to be an active member of the Church and to build up the Body of Christ in faith and love.

With hands joined, the celebrant next addresses the people:

My dear friends, let us pray to God our Father, that he will pour out the Holy Spirit on our newly bap-

tized brother/sister to strengthen him/her with his gifts and anoint him/her to be more like Christ, the Son of God.

All pray briefly in silence.

LAYING ON OF HANDS

365. The celebrant then lays hands on the person to be confirmed and says the following prayer. 269

All-powerful God, Father of our Lord Jesus Christ, by water and the Holy Spirit you freed your son/daughter from sin and gave him/her new life.

Send your Holy Spirit upon him/her to be his/her helper and guide.

Give him/her the spirit of wisdom and understanding, the spirit of right judgment and courage, the spirit of knowledge and reverence. Fill him/her with the spirit of wonder and awe in your presence.

We ask this through Christ our Lord. R̄. Amen.

ANOINTING WITH CHRISM

366. A minister brings the chrism to the celebrant. 270

The candidate, with the godparents, goes to the celebrant. Either or both godparents place the right hand on the shoulder of the candidate and either a godparent or the candidate gives the candidate's name to the celebrant. During the conferral of the sacrament an appropriate song may be sung.

The celebrant dips his right thumb in the chrism and makes the sign of the cross on the forehead of the one to be confirmed as he says:

N., be sealed with the Gift of the Holy Spirit.

Newly confirmed:
Amen.

230 CHRISTIAN INITIATION OF ADULTS *367–369*

The celebrant adds:
Peace be with you.

Newly confirmed:
And also with you.

LITURGY OF THE EUCHARIST

367. Since the profession of faith is not said, the general
intercessions begin immediately and for the first time the
neophyte takes part in them. He or she also helps to carry
the gifts when they are brought to the altar.

271

368. The eucharistic prayer is to include the special interpolations given for Eucharistic Prayers I, II, III, and IV in the
Roman Missal, ritual Masses, "Christian Initiation: Baptism."

272

369. It is most desirable that the neophyte, together with
his or her godparents, parents, spouse, and catechists, receive communion under both kinds.

273

Before saying "This is the Lamb of God" the celebrant may
briefly remind the neophyte of the preeminence of the eucharist, which is the climax of Christian initiation and the
center of the whole Christian life.

3. CHRISTIAN INITIATION OF A PERSON IN DANGER OF DEATH

By becoming coheirs with Christ, we share in his sufferings; we will also share in his glory

370. Persons, whether catechumens or not, who are in danger of death but are not at the point of death and so are able to hear and answer the questions involved may be baptized with this short rite.   278

371. Persons who have already been accepted as catechumens must make a promise that upon recovery they will complete the usual catechesis. Persons who are not catechumens must give serious indication of their conversion to Christ and renunciation of pagan worship and must not be seen to be attached to anything that conflicts with the moral life (for example, "simultaneous polygamy"). They must also promise that upon recovery they will go through the complete program of initiation as it applies to them.   279

372. This shorter rite is designed particularly for use by catechists and laypersons; a priest or a deacon may use it in a case of emergency. But normally a priest or a deacon is to use the abbreviated form of Christian initiation given in nos. 340–369, making any changes required by circumstances of place and time.   280

The minister of baptism who is a priest should, when the chrism is at hand and there is time, confer confirmation after the baptism; in this case there is no postbaptismal anointing.

The minister of baptism who is a priest, a deacon, or a catechist or layperson having permission to distribute communion should, if this is possible, give the eucharist to the newly baptized person. In this case before the beginning of the celebration of the rite the blessed sacrament is placed reverently on a table covered with a white cloth.

373. In the case of a person who is at the point of death, that is, whose death is imminent, and time is short, the minister, omitting everything else, pours natural water (even if not blessed) on the head of the sick person, while   281

saying the usual sacramental form (see *Christian Initiation,*
General Introduction, no. 23).

374. If persons who were baptized when in danger of
death or at the point of death recover their health, they are
to be given a suitable formation, be welcomed at the church
in due time, and there receive the other sacraments of initiation. In such cases the guidelines given in nos. 400–410 for
baptized but uncatechized adults are followed, with the necessary changes. The same guidelines should be applied
when sick persons recover after receiving not only baptism
but also confirmation and eucharist as viaticum.

282
294

CHRISTIAN INITIATION OF A PERSON IN DANGER OF DEATH

375. The minister greets the family and then speaks with the sick person about his or her request for baptism and, if the sick person is not a catechumen, about his or her reasons for conversion. After deciding to baptize him or her, the minister should, if necessary, instruct the person briefly.

283

376. Then the minister invites the family, the person designated as godparent, and the friends and neighbors present to gather around the sick person and selects one or two of those present as witnesses. Water, even if it is not blessed, is prepared.

284

INTRODUCTORY RITES

OPENING DIALOGUE

377. The minister addresses the sick person in these or similar words.

285

Dear brother/sister, you have asked to be baptized because you wish to have eternal life. This is eternal life: to know the one, true God and Jesus Christ, whom he has sent. This is the faith of Christians. Do you acknowledge this?

Candidate:
I do.

Minister:
As well as professing your faith in Jesus Christ, you must also be willing to follow his commands, as Christians do. Are you willing to accept this?

Candidate:
I am.

Minister.
Are you prepared to live as Christians do?

Candidate:
I am.

Minister:

Promise, therefore, that once you have recovered your strength, you will try to know Christ better and follow a course of Christian formation. Do you so promise?

Candidate:

I do.

AFFIRMATION BY THE GODPARENT AND WITNESSES

378. Turning to the godparent and to the witnesses, the minister asks them the following questions in these or similar words.   286

You have heard N.'s promise. As his/her godparent do you promise to remind him/her of it and to help him/her to learn the teaching of Christ, to take part in the life of our community, and to bear witness as a true Christian?

Godparent:

I do.

Minister

And will the rest of you, who have witnessed this promise, assist him/her in fulfilling it?

Witnesses:

We will.

Then the minister turns to the sick person and says:

Therefore you will now be baptized into eternal life, in accordance with the command of our Lord Jesus Christ.

LITURGY OF THE WORD

GOSPEL READING

379. According to time and circumstances, the minister reads some words from a gospel and explains them. One of the following may be used.   287

1. John 3:1–6—*Unless you are born again, you will not see the kingdom of heaven.*

2. John 6:44–47—*Whoever believes has eternal life.*

3. Matthew 22:35–40—*This is the greatest and the first commandment.*

4. Matthew 28:18–20—*Go and teach all people my Gospel, baptizing them in the name of the Father, and of the Son, and of the Holy Spirit.*

5. Mark 1:9–11—*Jesus was baptized by John in the Jordan.*

INTERCESSIONS FOR THE CANDIDATE

380. The minister may adapt or shorten the intercessions according to the condition of the sick person. The intercessions may be omitted if the sick person appears to be tiring. The minister begins:
Let us pray to the God of mercy for our sick brother/ sister who has asked for the gift of baptism; let us pray for his/her godparent and for all his/her family and friends.

Assisting minister:
Father, increase his/her faith in Christ, your Son and our Savior; in faith we make our prayer:
℟. Lord, hear us.

Assisting minister:
Grant his/her desire to have eternal life and enter the kingdom of heaven; in faith we make our prayer:
℟. Lord, hear us.

Assisting minister:
Fulfill his/her hope of knowing you, the Creator of the world and the Father of all; in faith we make our prayer:
℟. Lord, hear us.

Assisting minister:
Through baptism forgive his/her sins and make him/ her holy; in faith we make our prayer:
℟. Lord, hear us.

288

Assisting minister:
Grant him/her the salvation that Christ won by his death and resurrection; in faith we make our prayer:
℟. **Lord, hear us.**

Assisting minister:
In your love adopt him/her into your family; in faith we make our prayer:
℟. **Lord, hear us.**

[Assisting minister:
Restore him/her to health so that he/she may have the time to know and imitate Christ more perfectly; in faith we make our prayer:
℟. **Lord, hear us.**]

Assisting minister:
Keep united in faith and love all who have been baptized into the one Body of Christ; in faith we make our prayer:
℟. **Lord, hear us.**

PRAYER OVER THE CANDIDATE

381. The minister concludes the intercessions with the following prayer.   289

Father,
look kindly upon the faith and longing of your servant N.;
through this water
by which you have chosen to give us birth from above,
join him/her to Christ's death and resurrection.

Forgive all his/her sins,
adopt him/her as your own,
and count him/her among your holy people.

[Grant also that he/she may be restored to health, to render you thanks in your Church and grow in faithfulness to the teaching of Christ.]

We ask this through Christ our Lord.
℟. **Amen.**

CELEBRATION OF BAPTISM

RENUNCIATION OF SIN

382. The minister first asks the sick person to renounce sin. The minister may use the following formulary or the longer formulary given in no. 356 and may make pertinent adaptations (see no. 72).   290

Minister:
**Do you reject Satan,
and all his works,
and all his empty promises?**

Candidate:
I do.

PROFESSION OF FAITH

383. A profession of faith is then made. One of the following formularies may be used.   290

A Minister:
N., do you believe in God, the Father almighty, creator of heaven and earth?

Candidate:
I do.

Minister:
**Do you believe in Jesus Christ, his only Son, our Lord,
who was born of the Virgin Mary,
was crucified, died, and was buried,
rose from the dead,
and is now seated at the right hand of the Father?**

Candidate:
I do.

Minister:
**Do you believe in the Holy Spirit,
the holy catholic Church, the communion of saints,
the forgiveness of sins, the resurrection of the body,
and the life everlasting?**

Candidate:
I do.

B Candidate:
I believe in God, the Father almighty,
creator of heaven and earth.

I believe in Jesus Christ, his only Son, our Lord.
He was conceived by the power of the Holy Spirit
and born of the Virgin Mary.
He suffered under Pontius Pilate,
was crucified, died, and was buried.
He descended to the dead.
On the third day he rose again.
He ascended into heaven,
and is seated at the right hand of the Father.
He will come again to judge the living and the
dead.

I believe in the Holy Spirit,
the holy catholic Church,
the communion of saints,
the forgiveness of sins,
the resurrection of the body,
and the life everlasting. Amen.

BAPTISM

384. The minister, using the name the sick person desires   291
to have, baptizes him or her, saying:

N., I baptize you in the name of the Father,

The minister pours water the first time.

and of the Son,

The minister pours water the second time.

and of the Holy Spirit.

The minister pours water the third time.

ANOINTING AFTER BAPTISM

385. If the minister of baptism is a deacon, he says the fol-   292
lowing prayer, then in silence anoints the newly baptized
with chrism on the crown of the head.

**The God of power and Father of our Lord Jesus
    Christ
has freed you from sin
and brought you to new life
through water and the Holy Spirit.**

**He now anoints you with the chrism of salvation,
so that, united with his people,
you may remain for ever a member of Christ
who is Priest, Prophet, and King.**

Newly baptized:
Amen.

386. If the minister is not a priest, the rite continues with the celebration of viaticum (no. 393).

387. If neither confirmation nor viaticum will be celebrated, one of the alternative concluding rites (no. 399) follows baptism.

CELEBRATION OF CONFIRMATION

388. If the minister of baptism is a priest, he should also confer confirmation.   293

If there is not sufficient time because of the condition of the sick person, the "Invitation" (no. 389) may be omitted; it is enough for the priest to anoint with chrism, while saying the words "**N. be sealed, . . .**"; if possible, he first lays hands on the sick person with the prayer "**All-powerful God.**"

INVITATION

389. The priest first speaks briefly to the newly baptized in the following or similar words.   293

N., born again in Christ by baptism, you have become a member of Christ and of his priestly people. Now you are to share in the outpouring of the Holy Spirit among us, the Spirit sent by the Lord upon his

apostles at Pentecost and given by them and their successors to the baptized.

All pray in silence for a short time.

LAYING ON OF HANDS

390. The priest lays hands on the newly baptized and says 293
the following prayer.

All-powerful God, Father of our Lord Jesus Christ,
by water and the Holy Spirit
you freed your son/daughter from sin
and gave him/her new life.

Send your Holy Spirit upon him/her
to be his/her helper and guide.

Give him/her the spirit of wisdom and understand-
ing,
the spirit of right judgment and courage,
the spirit of knowledge and reverence.
Fill him/her with the spirit of wonder and awe in
your presence.

We ask this through Christ our Lord.
R̶/. Amen.

ANOINTING WITH CHRISM

391. The priest dips his right thumb in the chrism and 293
makes the sign of the cross on the forehead of the one to
be confirmed as he says:

N., be sealed with the Gift of the Holy Spirit.

Newly confirmed:
Amen.

The priest adds:
Peace be with you.

Newly confirmed:
And also with you.

392. If viaticum will not be celebrated, one of the alternative concluding rites (no. 399) follows confirmation.

CELEBRATION OF VIATICUM

393. Communion as viaticum is given immediately after 294
confirmation or, if confirmation is not celebrated, immediately after the celebration of baptism.

INVITATION TO PRAYER

394. The minister addresses the sick person: if viaticum follows the celebration of confirmation, the minister uses option A or similar words; if confirmation is not celebrated
and viaticum follows baptism, the minister uses option B or
similar words.

A

N., God our Father has freed you from your sins, has 294
given you a new birth and made you his son/
daughter in Christ. Before you partake of the body of
the Lord and in the spirit of that adoption which you
have received today, join us now in praying as our
Lord himself taught us.

Then the sick person and all present join the minister in the
Lord's Prayer.
Our Father . . .

B

N., God our Father has freed you from your sins, has 294
given you a new birth and made you his son/
daughter in Christ. Soon, God willing, you will re-
ceive the fullness of the Holy Spirit through confir-
mation. Before you partake of the body of the Lord
and in the spirit of that adoption which you have re-
ceived today, join us now in praying as our Lord him-
self taught us.

Then the sick person and all present join the minister in the
Lord's Prayer.
Our Father . . .

COMMUNION AS VIATICUM

395. The minister shows the eucharistic bread to those 294
present, using one of the following formularies.

A
Jesus Christ is the food for our journey;
he calls us to the heavenly table.

B
This is the Lamb of God
who takes away the sins of the world.
Happy are those who are called to his supper.

The sick person and all who are to receive communion say:
Lord, I am not worthy to receive you,
but only say the word and I shall be healed.

The minister goes to the sick person and, showing the
blessed sacrament, says:
The body of Christ.

The sick person answers:
Amen.

Then the minister says:
The blood of Christ.

The sick person answers:
Amen.

Immediately, or after giving communion to the sick person,   PC293
the minister adds the form for viaticum.
May the Lord Jesus Christ protect you and lead you
to eternal life.

The sick person answers:
Amen.

Others present who wish to receive communion then do so
in the usual way.

A short period of silent prayer may follow.

PRAYER AFTER COMMUNION
396. The minister says a concluding prayer.   294

Let us pray.

Pause for silent prayer, if this has not preceded.

Father,
almighty and eternal God,
our brother/sister has received the eucharist
with faith in you and in your healing power.
May the body and blood of Christ
bring him/her eternal healing in mind and body.

We ask this in the name of Jesus the Lord.
℟. Amen.

CONCLUDING RITES

BLESSING

397. The minister blesses the sick person and the others   PC295
present, using one of the following blessings.

A   A minister who is a priest or deacon says:
May the Lord be with you to protect you.
℟. Amen.

May the Lord guide you and give you strength.
℟. Amen.

May the Lord watch over you, keep you in his care,
and bless you with his peace.
℟. Amen.

May almighty God bless you,
the Father, and the Son, ✠ and the Holy Spirit.
℟. Amen.

B   A lay minister invokes God's blessing and signs himself or herself with the sign of the cross, saying:
May the Lord bless us,
protect us from all evil,
and bring us to everlasting life.
℟. Amen.

SIGN OF PEACE

398. The minister and the others present may then give   PC296
the sick person the sign of peace.

ALTERNATIVE CONCLUDING RITES

399. When the celebration is concluded after confirmation and viaticum is not given, the rite is concluded by use of option A. When the celebration concludes immediately after baptism and neither confirmation nor viaticum is celebrated, the rite is concluded by use of option B.

A The minister addresses the sick person in the following words.

N., God our Father has freed you from your sins, has given you a new birth and made you his son/ daughter in Christ. Soon, God willing, you will approach the altar of God to share the food of life at the table of his sacrifice. In the spirit of that adoption which you have received today, join us now in praying as our Lord himself taught us.

Then the sick person and all present join the minister in saying:

Our Father . . .

The blessing (no. 397) and sign of peace (no. 398) may then be given.

B The minister addresses the sick person in the following words.

N., God our Father has freed you from your sins, has given you a new birth and made you his son/ daughter in Christ. Soon, God willing, you will receive the fullness of the Holy Spirit through confirmation and will approach the altar of God to share the food of life at the table of his sacrifice. In his spirit of that adoption which you have received today, join us now in praying as our Lord himself taught us.

Then the sick person and all present join the minister in saying:

Our Father . . .

The blessing (no. 397) and sign of peace (no. 398) may then be given.

4. PREPARATION OF UNCATECHIZED ADULTS FOR CONFIRMATION AND EUCHARIST

If then you have been raised with Christ, seek the things that are above, where Christ is seated at the right hand of God

400. The following pastoral guidelines concern adults who were baptized as infants either as Roman Catholics or as members of another Christian community but did not receive further catechetical formation nor, consequently, the sacraments of confirmation and eucharist. These suggestions may also be applied to similar cases, especially that of an adult who recovers after being baptized in danger of death or at the point of death (see no. 374). 295
USA

Even though uncatechized adults have not yet heard the message of the mystery of Christ, their status differs from that of catechumens, since by baptism they have already become members of the Church and children of God. Hence their conversion is based on the baptism they have already received, the effects of which they must develop.

401. As in the case of catechumens, the preparation of these adults requires a considerable time (see no. 76), during which the faith infused in baptism must grow in them and take deep root through the pastoral formation they receive. A program of training, catechesis suited to their needs, contact with the community of the faithful, and participation in certain liturgical rites are needed in order to strengthen them in the Christian life. 296

402. For the most part the plan of catechesis corresponds to the one laid down for catechumens (see no. 75,1). But in the process of catechesis the priest, deacon, or catechist should take into account that these adults have a special status because they are already baptized. 297

403. Just as it helps catechumens, the Christian community should also help these adults by its love and prayer (see nos. 4 and 75,2) and by testifying to their suitability when it is time for them to be admitted to the sacraments (see nos. 120, 121). 298

404. A sponsor presents these adults to the community (see no. 10). During the period of their catechetical formation, they all choose godparents (a godfather, a godmother, or both) approved by the priest. Their godparents work with these adults as the representatives of the community and have the same responsibilities as the godparents have toward catechumens (see no. 11). The same persons who were the godparents at the baptism of these adults may be chosen as godparents at this time, provided they are truly capable of carrying out the responsibilities of godparents.

299

405. The period of preparation is made holy by means of liturgical celebrations. The first of these is a rite by which the adults are welcomed into the community and acknowledge themselves to be part of it because they have already been marked with the seal of baptism. [The Rite of Welcoming the Candidates, which follows in Part II, 4 A, is provided for this purpose.]

300

406. Once a rite of reception has been celebrated, these adults take part in celebrations of the word of God, both those of the entire Christian assembly and those celebrations arranged specially for the benefit of the catechumens (see nos. 81–84).

301

407. As a sign of God's activity in this work of preparation, some of the rites belonging to the catechumenate, especially suited to the condition and spiritual needs of these baptized adults, can be used to advantage. Among these are the presentation of the Creed (nos. 157–162) and of the Lord's Prayer (nos. 178–182) or also a presentation of a book of the Gospels (no. 64). [The additional rites in Part II, 4 B, 4 C, and 4 D, may also be used in accordance with the individual needs and circumstances of the candidates.]

302
USA

408. The period of catechesis for these adults should be properly coordinated with the liturgical year. This is particularly true of its final phase, which should as a rule coincide with Lent. During the Lenten season penitential services should be arranged in such a way as to prepare these adults for the celebration of the sacrament of penance.

303

409. The high point of their entire formation will normally be the Easter Vigil. At that time they will make a profession of the faith in which they were baptized, receive the sacra-

304

ment of confirmation, and take part in the eucharist. If, because neither the bishop nor another authorized minister is present, confirmation cannot be given at the Easter Vigil, it is to be celebrated as soon as possible and, if this can be arranged, during the Easter season.

410. These adults will complete their Christian formation and become fully integrated into the community by going through the period of postbaptismal catechesis or mystagogy with the newly baptized members of the Christian community.

305

OPTIONAL RITES FOR BAPTIZED BUT UNCATECHIZED ADULTS

4A. RITE OF WELCOMING THE CANDIDATES

Teach us your ways, O Lord

411. This optional rite welcomes baptized but previously uncatechized adults who are seeking to complete their Christian initiation through the sacraments of confirmation and eucharist or to be received into the full communion of the Catholic Church.

412. The prayers and ritual gestures acknowledge that such candidates are already part of the community because they have been marked by baptism. Now the Church surrounds them with special care and support as they prepare to be sealed with the gift of the Spirit in confirmation and take their place at the banquet table of Christ's sacrifice.

413. Once formally welcomed into the life of the community, these adults, besides regularly attending Sunday Eucharist, take part in celebrations of the word of God in the full Christian assembly and in celebrations arranged especially for the benefit of the candidates.

414. The rite will take place on specified days throughout the year (see no. 18) that are suited to local conditions.

415. When the rite of welcoming candidates for the sacraments of confirmation and eucharist is to be combined with the rite of acceptance into the order of catechumens, the alternate rite found on page 287 (Appendix I, Rite 1) is used.

RITE OF WELCOMING THE CANDIDATES

416. When this rite is celebrated within Mass, the entrance song or antiphon is sung as usual. Because they are already numbered among the baptized, the candidates are seated in a prominent place among the faithful.

GREETING

417. The celebrant greets the candidates in a friendly manner. He speaks to them, their sponsors, and all present,

pointing out the joy and happiness of the Church in welcoming them. He reminds the assembly that these candidates have already been baptized. If it seems opportune, he may also indicate briefly the particular path which has led the candidates to seek the completion of their Christian initiation.

Then he invites the sponsors and candidates to come forward. As they are taking their places before the celebrant, an appropriate song may be sung, for example, Psalm 63:1–8.

OPENING DIALOGUE

418. Unless the candidates are already known to all present, the celebrant asks for or calls out their given names. The candidates answer one by one, even if, because of a large number, the question is asked only once. One of the following formularies or similar words may be used.

A   The celebrant asks:
What is your name?

Candidate:
N.

B   The celebrant calls out the name of each candidate.

The candidate answers:
Present.

The celebrant continues with the following question for the individual candidates or, when there are a large number, for the candidates to answer as a group. The celebrant may use other words than those provided in asking the candidates about their intentions and may let them answer in their own words.

Celebrant:
What do you ask of God's Church?

Candidate:
To be accepted as a candidate for catechetical instruction leading to confirmation and eucharist (*or:* reception into the full communion of the Catholic Church).

CANDIDATES' DECLARATION OF INTENT

419. The celebrant addresses the candidates, adapting one of the following formularies or similar words to the answers received in the opening dialogue.

A   Blessed be the God and Father of our Lord Jesus Christ, who, in his great mercy has given us a new birth unto a living hope, a hope which draws its life from Christ's resurrection from the dead. By baptism into Christ Jesus, this hope of glory became your own. Christ opened for you the way of the Gospel that leads to eternal life. Now, under the guidance of the Holy Spirit, you desire to continue that journey of faith.
Are you prepared to reflect more deeply on the mystery of your baptism, to listen with us to the apostles' instruction, and to join with us in a life of prayer and service?

Candidates:
I am.

B   Celebrant:
Please declare before this community the reasons why you desire to enter more fully in the life of the Church.

The candidates respond with a brief personal witness.

AFFIRMATION BY THE SPONSORS AND THE ASSEMBLY

420. Then the celebrant turns to the sponsors and the assembly and asks them in these or similar words.

Sponsors, you now present these candidates to us. Are you, and all who are gathered with us, ready to help these candidates complete their Christian initiation (*or:* prepare for reception into the full communion of the Catholic Church)?

All:
We are.

With hands joined, the celebrant says:

**Father of mercy,
we thank you for these your servants.
You have already consecrated them in baptism
and now you call them
to the fullness of the Church's sacramental life:
we praise you, Lord, and we bless you.**

All sing or say:
We praise you, Lord, and we bless you.

SIGNING OF THE CANDIDATES WITH THE CROSS

421. Next the cross is traced on the forehead of the candidates; at the discretion of the celebrant the signing of one, several, or all of the senses may follow. The celebrant alone says the formularies accompanying each signing.

SIGNING OF THE FOREHEAD

422. The celebrant speaks to the candidates in these or similar words.

Dear candidates, you have expressed your desire to share fully in the life of the Catholic Church. I now mark you with the sign of Christ's cross and call upon your catechists and sponsors to do the same.

Then the celebrant makes the sign of the cross over all together, as a cross is traced by a sponsor or catechist on the forehead of each candidate. The celebrant says:

**Receive the cross on your forehead
as a reminder of your baptism into
Christ's saving death and resurrection.**

All sing or say the following or another suitable acclamation.
Glory and praise to you, Lord Jesus Christ!

SIGNING OF THE OTHER SENSES

423. The signing is carried out by the catechists or the sponsors. (If required by special circumstances, this may be done by assisting priests or deacons.) The signing of each sense may be followed by an acclamation in praise of

Christ, for example, "**Glory and praise to you, Lord Jesus Christ!**"

While the ears are being signed, the celebrant says:
Receive the sign of the cross on your ears,
that you may hear the voice of the Lord.

While the eyes are being signed:
Receive the sign of the cross on your eyes,
that you may see the glory of God.

While the lips are being signed:
Receive the sign of the cross on your lips,
that you may respond to the word of God.

While the breast is being signed:
Receive the sign of the cross over your heart,
that Christ may dwell there by faith.

While the shoulders are being signed:
Receive the sign of the cross on your shoulders,
that you may bear the gentle yoke of Christ.

[While the hands are being signed:
Receive the sign of the cross on your hands,
that Christ may be known in the work which you do.

While the feet are being signed:
Receive the sign of the cross on your feet,
that you may walk in the way of Christ.]

Without touching them the celebrant alone makes the sign of the cross over all the candidates at once (or, if they are few, over each individually), saying:

I sign you with the sign of eternal life
in the name of the Father, and of the Son, ✠
and of the Holy Spirit.

Candidates:
Amen.

CONCLUDING PRAYER

424. The celebrant concludes the signing of the forehead (and senses) with the opening prayer for the Mass of the day or with the following prayer.

Let us pray.

Almighty God,
by the cross and resurrection of your Son
you have given life to your people.

In baptism these your servants accepted the sign of
**   the cross:**
make them living proof of its saving power
and help them to persevere in the footsteps of Christ.

We ask this through Christ our Lord.
R̷. Amen.

LITURGY OF THE WORD

INSTRUCTION

425. The celebrant next speaks briefly to the candidates and their sponsors, helping them to understand the dignity of God's word proclaimed and heard in the church.

READINGS

426. The readings are those assigned for the day. According to the norms of the Lectionary, other appropriate readings may be substituted.

HOMILY

427. A homily follows that explains the readings.

PRESENTATION OF A BIBLE

428. A book containing the Gospels may be given to the candidates by the celebrant. The celebrant may use words suited to the gift presented, for example, "**Receive the Gospel of Jesus Christ, the Son of God.**" The candidates may respond in an appropriate way.

PROFESSION OF FAITH

429. On Sundays and solemnities the profession of faith is recited.

GENERAL INTERCESSIONS

430. Then the sponsors and the whole congregation join in the general intercessions. One or more of the following in-

tentions for the candidates are added to the intentions for
the Church and the whole world.

Assisting minister:
**That God our Father may reveal his Christ to these
candidates more and more with every passing day,
let us pray to the Lord:**
℞. **Lord, hear our prayer.**

Assisting minister:
**That these candidates may come to a deeper apprecia-
tion of the gift of their baptism, which joined them
to Christ, let us pray to the Lord:**
℞. **Lord, hear our prayer.**

Assisting minister:
**That they may find in our community compelling
signs of unity and generous love, let us pray to the
Lord:**
℞. **Lord, hear our prayer.**

Assisting minister:
**That their hearts and ours may become more respon-
sive to the needs of others, let us pray to the Lord:**
℞. **Lord, hear our prayer.**

Assisting minister:
**That in due time these candidates may be (embraced
by the Father's merciful forgiveness,) sealed with the
gift of the Holy Spirit and know the joy of being one
with us at the table of Christ's sacrifice, let us pray to
the Lord:**
℞. **Lord, hear our prayer.**

PRAYER OVER THE CANDIDATES
431. After the intercessions, the celebrant, with hands outstretched over the candidates, says the following prayer.

**Almighty and eternal God,
whose love gathers us together as one,
receive the prayers of your people.**

**Look kindly on these your servants,
already consecrated to you in baptism,
and draw them into the fullness of faith.**

Keep your family one in the bonds of love through Christ our Lord.

R̰. Amen.

DISMISSAL OF THE ASSEMBLY

432. If the eucharist is not to be celebrated, the entire assembly is dismissed by use of the following formulary or similar words.

Celebrant:
Go in peace, and may the Lord remain with you always.

All:
Thanks be to God.

An appropriate song may conclude the celebration.

LITURGY OF THE EUCHARIST

433. The liturgy of the eucharist begins as usual with the preparation of the gifts.

4B. RITE OF SENDING THE CANDIDATES FOR RECOGNITION BY THE BISHOP AND FOR THE CALL TO CONTINUING CONVERSION

My sheep hear my voice and follow me

434. This optional rite is provided for parishes whose candidates seeking to complete their Christian initiation or to be received into the full communion of the Catholic Church will be recognized by the bishop in a subsequent celebration (for example, at the cathedral with the bishop).

435. Because he is the sign of unity within the particular Church, it is fitting for the bishop to recognize these candidates. It is the responsibility of the parish community, however, to prepare the candidates for their fuller life in the Church. Through the experience of worship, daily life and service in the parish community the candidates deepen their appreciation of the Church's tradition and universal character.

This rite offers that local community the opportunity to express its joy in the candidates' decision and to send them forth to the celebration of recognition assured of the parish's care and support.

436. The rite is celebrated in the parish church at a suitable time prior to the rite of recognition and call to continuing conversion.

437. When the rite of sending candidates for recognition is to be combined with the rite of sending catechumens for election, the alternate rite found on page 301 (Appendix I, Rite 2) is used.

RITE OF SENDING THE CANDIDATES FOR RECOGNITION BY THE BISHOP AND FOR THE CALL TO CONTINUING CONVERSION

LITURGY OF THE WORD

HOMILY

438. After the readings the celebrant gives the homily. This should be suited to the actual situation and should address not just the candidates but the entire community of the faithful, so that all will be encouraged to give good example and to accompany the candidates along the path leading to their complete initiation.

PRESENTATION OF THE CANDIDATES

439. After the homily, the priest in charge of the candidates' formation, or a deacon, a catechist, or a representative of the community, presents the candidates, using the following or similar words.

Reverend Father, these candidates, whom I now present to you, are beginning their final period of preparation for the sacraments of confirmation and eucharist (*or:* preparation to be received into the full communion of the Catholic Church). They have found strength in God's grace and support in our community's prayers and example.

Now they ask that they be recognized for the progress they have made in their spiritual formation and that they receive the assurance of our blessings and prayers as they go forth for recognition by Bishop N. this afternoon (*or:* next Sunday [*or:* specify the day]).

The celebrant replies:
Those who are to be recognized, come forward, together with your sponsors.

One by one, the candidates are called by name. Each candidate, accompanied by a sponsor, comes forward and stands before the celebrant.

AFFIRMATION BY THE SPONSORS [AND THE ASSEMBLY]

440. Then the celebrant addresses the assembly in these or similar words.

My dear friends, these candidates, already one with us by reason of their baptism in Christ, have asked to complete their initiation (*or:* to be received into the full communion of the Catholic Church). Those who know them have judged them to be sincere in their desire. During the period of their catechetical formation they have listened to the word of Christ and endeavored to follow his commands more perfectly; they have shared the company of their Christian brothers and sisters in this community and joined with them in prayer.

And so I announce to all of you here that our community ratifies their desire to complete their initiation (*or:* to be received into full communion). Therefore, I ask their sponsors to state their opinion once again, so that all of you may hear.

He addresses the sponsors:
As God is your witness, do you consider these candidates ready to receive the sacraments of confirmation and eucharist?

Sponsors:
We do.

[When appropriate in the circumstances, the celebrant may also ask the entire assembly to express its approval of the candidates.]

441. The celebrant concludes the affirmation by the following:

And now, my dear friends, I address you. Your own sponsors (and this entire community) have spoken in your favor. The Church, in the name of Christ, accepts their testimony and sends you to Bishop N., who will exhort you to live in deeper conformity to the life of Christ.

GENERAL INTERCESSIONS

442. Then the sponsors and the whole congregation join in the general intercessions. One or more of the following intentions for the candidates are added to the intentions for the Church and the whole world.

Assisting minister:

That these candidates may be freed from selfishness and learn to put others first, let us pray to the Lord:
℟. Lord, hear our prayer.

Assisting minister:

That their godparents and sponsors may be living examples of the Gospel, let us pray to the Lord:
℟. Lord, hear our prayer.

Assisting minister:

That their teachers may always convey to them the beauty of God's word, let us pray to the Lord:
℟. Lord, hear our prayer.

Assisting minister:

That these candidates may share with others the joy they have found in their friendship with Jesus, let us pray to the Lord:
℟. Lord, hear our prayer.

Assisting minister:

That our community, during the coming Lenten season, may grow in charity and be constant in prayer, let us pray to the Lord:
℟. Lord, hear our prayer.

PRAYER OVER THE CANDIDATES

443. After the intercessions, the celebrant, with hands outstretched over the candidates, says the following prayer.

Father of love and power,
it is your will to establish everything in Christ
and to draw us into his all-embracing love.

Guide these candidates in the days and weeks ahead:
strengthen them in their vocation,
build them into the kingdom of your Son,
and seal them with the Spirit of your promise.

We ask this through Christ our Lord.

R̷. Amen.

DISMISSAL OF THE ASSEMBLY

444. If the eucharist is not to be celebrated, the entire assembly is dismissed by use of the following formulary or similar words.

Celebrant:
Go in peace, and may the Lord remain with you always.

All:
Thanks be to God.

An appropriate song may conclude the celebration.

LITURGY OF THE EUCHARIST

445. When the eucharist is to follow, intercessory prayer is resumed with the usual general intercessions for the needs of the Church and the whole world; then, if required, the profession of faith is said. But for pastoral reasons these general intercessions and the profession of faith may be omitted. The liturgy of the eucharist then begins as usual with the preparation of the gifts.

4C. RITE OF CALLING THE CANDIDATES TO CONTINUING CONVERSION

USA

As members of one body, you have been called to his peace

446. This rite may be celebrated with baptized but previously uncatechized adults who wish to complete their Christian initiation through the sacraments of confirmation and eucharist or who wish to be received into the full communion of the Catholic Church.

447. The rite is intended for celebrations in communities where there are no catechumens.

448. The rite is celebrated at the beginning of Lent. The presiding celebrant is the pastor of the parish.

449. If the calling of candidates to continuing conversion is to be combined with the rite of election of catechumens (either in a parish celebration or at one in which the bishop is celebrant) the alternate rite given on page 309 (Appendix I, Rite 3) is used.

RITE OF CALLING THE CANDIDATES TO CONTINUING CONVERSION

LITURGY OF THE WORD

HOMILY

450. After the readings, the celebrant gives the homily. This should be suited to the actual situation and should address not just the candidates but the entire community of the faithful, so that all will be encouraged to give good example and to accompany the candidates in their final preparation leading to the celebration of confirmation and eucharist.

PRESENTATION OF THE CANDIDATES FOR CONFIRMATION AND EUCHARIST

451. After the homily, the priest in charge of the candidates' formation, or a deacon, a catechist, or a representative of the community, presents the candidates, using the following or similar words.

Reverend Father, (since Easter is drawing near,) I am pleased to present to you the candidates who seek to complete their Christian initiation (*or:* who are preparing to be received into the full communion of the Catholic Church). They have found strength in God's grace and support in our community's prayers and example.

Now they ask that after this Lenten season, they be admitted to confirmation and the eucharist (*or:* to full eucharistic sharing).

The celebrant replies:
Those who desire to participate fully in the sacramental life of the Church, come forward, together with your sponsors.

One by one, the candidates are called by name. Each candidate, accompanied by a sponsor, comes forward and stands before the celebrant.

AFFIRMATION BY THE SPONSORS [AND THE ASSEMBLY]

452. Then the celebrant addresses the assembly. If he has taken part in the earlier deliberation on the candidates' suitableness (see no. 122), he may use either option A or option B or similar words; if he has not taken part in the earlier deliberation, he uses option B or similar words.

A

My dear friends, these candidates, our brothers and sisters, have asked to be able to participate fully in the sacramental life of the Catholic Church. Those who know them have judged them to be sincere in their desire. During the period of their preparation they have reflected on the mystery of their baptism and have come to appreciate more deeply the presence of Christ in their lives. They have shared the company of their brothers and sisters, joined with them in prayer, and endeavored to follow Christ's commands more perfectly.

And so I am pleased to recognize their desire to participate fully in the sacramental life of the Church. I ask their sponsors now to state their opinion once again, so that all of you may hear.

He addresses the sponsors:
Do you consider these candidates ready to receive the sacraments of confirmation and the eucharist (*or:* to be received into the full communion of the Catholic Church)?

Sponsors:
We do.

453. When appropriate in the circumstances, the celebrant may also ask the entire assembly to express its approval of the candidates in these or similar words:

Celebrant:
Now I ask you, the members of this community: Are you willing to affirm the testimony expressed about these candidates and support them in faith,

prayer, and example as they prepare to participate more fully in the Church's sacraments?

All:
We are.

B
The Christian life and the demands that flow from the sacraments cannot be taken lightly. Therefore, before granting these candidates their request to share fully in the Church's sacraments, it is important that the Church hear the testimony of their sponsors about their readiness.

He addresses the sponsors:
Have they faithfully listened to the apostles' instruction proclaimed by the Church?

Sponsors:
They have.

Celebrant:
Have they come to a deeper appreciation of their baptism, in which they were joined to Christ and his Church?

Sponsors:
They have.

Celebrant:
Have they reflected sufficiently on the tradition of the Church, which is their heritage, and joined their brothers and sisters in prayer?

Sponsors:
They have.

Celebrant:
Have they advanced in a life of love and service of others?

Sponsors:
They have.

When appropriate in the circumstances, the celebrant may also ask the entire assembly to express its approval of the candidates in these or similar words:

Celebrant:

And now I speak to you, my brothers and sisters in this assembly:
Are you ready to support the testimony expressed about these candidates and include them in your prayer and affection as we move toward Easter?

All:
We are.

ACT OF RECOGNITION

454. Then the celebrant says:

N. and N., the Church recognizes your desire (to be sealed with the gift of the Holy Spirit and) to have a place at Christ's eucharistic table. Join with us this Lent in a spirit of repentance. Hear the Lord's call to conversion and be faithful to your baptismal covenant.

Candidates:
Thanks be to God.

Then the celebrant turns to the sponsors and instructs them in the following or similar words.
Sponsors, continue to support these candidates with your guidance and concern. May they see in you a love for the Church and a sincere desire for doing good. Lead them this Lent to the joys of the Easter mysteries.

He invites them to place their hand on the shoulder of the candidate whom they are receiving into their care, or to make some other gesture to indicate the same intent.

GENERAL INTERCESSIONS

455. Then the sponsors and the whole congregation join in the general intercessions. One or more of the following intentions for the candidates are added to the intentions for the Church and the whole world.

Assisting minister:
**That these candidates may come to a deeper apprecia-
tion of their baptism into Christ's death and resurrection, let us pray to the Lord:**
℟. **Lord, hear our prayer.**

Assisting minister:
**That God bless those who have nurtured these candi-
dates in faith, let us pray to the Lord:**
℟. **Lord, hear our prayer.**

Assisting minister:
**That these candidates may embrace the discipline of
Lent as a means of purification and approach the sac-
rament of reconciliation with trust in God's mercy,
let us pray to the Lord:**
℟. **Lord, hear our prayer.**

Assisting minister:
**That they may open their hearts to the promptings of
God's Holy Spirit, let us pray to the Lord:**
℟. **Lord, hear our prayer.**

Assisting minister:
**That they may approach the table of Christ's sacrifice
with thanksgiving and praise, let us pray to the Lord:**
℟. **Lord, hear our prayer.**

Assisting minister:
**That our community, during this Lenten period, may
grow in charity and be constant in prayer, let us pray
to the Lord:**
℟. **Lord, hear our prayer.**

PRAYER OVER THE CANDIDATES

456. After the intercessions, the celebrant, with hands outstretched over the candidates, says the following prayer.

**Lord God,
whose love brings us to life
and whose mercy gives us new birth,
look favorably upon these candidates,
and conform their lives
to the pattern of Christ's suffering.**

May he become their wealth and wisdom,
and may they know in their lives
the power flowing from his resurrection,
who is Lord for ever and ever.

℟. **Amen.**

DISMISSAL OF THE ASSEMBLY

457. If the eucharist is not to be celebrated, the entire assembly is dismissed by use of the following formulary or similar words.

Celebrant:
Go in peace, and may the Lord remain with you
always.

All:
Thanks be to God.

An appropriate song may conclude the celebration.

LITURGY OF THE EUCHARIST

458. The liturgy of the eucharist begins as usual with the preparation of the gifts.

4D. PENITENTIAL RITE (SCRUTINY)   USA

May you all be kept blameless, spirit, soul and body, for the coming of our Lord Jesus Christ

459. This penitential rite can serve to mark the Lenten purification of baptized but previously uncatechized adults who are preparing to receive the sacraments of confirmation and eucharist or to be received into the full communion of the Catholic Church. It is held within a celebration of the word of God as a kind of scrutiny, similar to the scrutinies for catechumens.

460. Because the penitential rite normally belongs to the period of final preparation for the sacraments, its celebration presumes that the candidates are approaching the maturity of faith and understanding requisite for fuller life in the community.

461. Along with the candidates, their sponsors and the larger liturgical assembly also participate in the celebration of the penitential rite. Therefore the rite is to be adapted in such a way that it benefits all the participants. This penitential rite may also help to prepare the candidates to celebrate the sacrament of penance.

462. This penitential rite may be celebrated on the Second Sunday of Lent or on a Lenten weekday, if the candidates are to receive the sacraments of confirmation and eucharist and/or be received into the full communion of the Catholic Church at Easter; if not, at the most suitable time.

463. This penitential rite is intended solely for celebrations with baptized adults preparing for confirmation and eucharist or reception into the full communion of the Catholic Church. Because the prayer of exorcism in the three scrutinies for catechumens who have received the Church's election properly belongs to the elect and uses numerous images referring to their approaching baptism, those scrutinies of the elect and this penitential rite for those preparing for confirmation and eucharist have been kept separate and distinct. Thus, no combined rite has been included in Appendix I.

PENITENTIAL RITE (SCRUTINY)
(SECOND SUNDAY OF LENT)

GREETING AND INTRODUCTION

464. The priest welcomes the assembly and in a few words explains that the rite will have different meanings for the different participants: the candidates who are already baptized, particularly those who are preparing to celebrate the sacrament of penance for the first time, the sponsors, catechists, priests, etc. All these participants in their own different ways are going to hear the comforting message of pardon for sin, for which they will praise the Father's mercy.

A song may be sung that joyfully expresses faith in the mercy of God the Father.

PRAYER

465. The celebrant then says the prayer for the Second Sunday of Lent or, on another day, the following prayer.

**Lord of infinite compassion and steadfast love,
your sons and daughters stand before you
in humility and trust.
Look with compassion on us
as we acknowledge our sinfulness.
Stretch out your hand
to save us and raise us up.
Do not allow the power of darkness
to triumph over us,
but keep us free from sin
as members of Christ's body,
and sheep of your own flock.**

**We ask this through our Lord Jesus Christ, your Son,
who lives and reigns with you and the Holy Spirit,
one God, for ever and ever.**

R̷. Amen.

LITURGY OF THE WORD

READINGS

466. On the Second Sunday of Lent the readings for Mass are those assigned by the Lectionary for Mass. On other days, appropriate readings from the Lectionary are used.

HOMILY

467. After the readings the celebrant explains the sacred texts in the homily. He should prepare all those in the assembly for conversion and repentance and give the meaning of the penitential rite (scrutiny) in the light of the Lenten liturgy and of the spiritual journey of the candidates.

INVITATION TO SILENT PRAYER

468. After the homily, the candidates with their sponsors come forward and stand before the celebrant.

The celebrant first addresses the assembly of the faithful, inviting them to pray in silence and to ask that the candidates will be given a spirit of repentance, a deepened sense of sin, and the true freedom of the children of God.

The celebrant then addresses the candidates, inviting them also to pray in silence and suggesting that as a sign of their inner spirit of repentance they bow their heads or kneel; he concludes his remarks with the following or similar words.

Candidates, bow your heads [kneel down] and pray.

The candidates bow their heads or kneel, and all pray for some time in silence. After the period of silent prayer, the community and the candidates stand for the intercessions.

INTERCESSIONS FOR THE CANDIDATES

469. Then the sponsors and the whole congregation join in the intercessions for the candidates. If the eucharist is to be celebrated, intentions for the Church and for the whole world should be added to the following intentions for the candidates.

Celebrant:
My brothers and sisters, let us pray for these candidates (N. and N.). Christ has already ransomed them in baptism. Now they seek the forgiveness of their

sins and the healing of their weakness, so that they may be ready to be (sealed with the gift of the Father and) fed at the Lord's table. Let us also pray for ourselves, who seek the mercy of Christ.

Assisting minister:
That these candidates may come to a deeper appreciation of their baptism into Christ's death and resurrection, let us pray to the Lord:
R̸. Lord, hear our prayer.

Assisting minister:
That these candidates may embrace the discipline of Lent as a means of purification and approach the sacrament of reconciliation with trust in God's mercy, let us pray to the Lord:
R̸. Lord, hear our prayer.

Assisting minister:
That they may grow to love and seek virtue and holiness of life, let us pray to the Lord:
R̸. Lord, hear our prayer.

Assisting minister:
That they may renounce self and put others first, let us pray to the Lord:
R̸. Lord, hear our prayer.

Assisting minister:
That they may share with others the joy they have found in their faith, let us pray to the Lord:
R̸. Lord, hear our prayer.

Assisting minister:
That they may accept the call to conversion with an open heart and not hesitate to make the personal changes it may require of them, let us pray to the Lord:
R̸. Lord, hear our prayer.

Assisting minister:
That the Holy Spirit, who searches every heart, may help them to overcome their weakness through his power, let us pray to the Lord:
R̸. Lord, hear our prayer.

Assisting minister:
**That their families also may put their hope in Christ
and find peace and holiness in him, let us pray to
the Lord:**
R̦. Lord, hear our prayer.

Assisting minister:
**That we ourselves in preparation for the Easter feast
may seek a change of heart, give ourselves to prayer,
and persevere in our good works, let us pray to the
Lord:**
R̦. Lord, hear our prayer.

PRAYER OVER THE CANDIDATES
470. After the intercessions, the rite continues with the
prayer over the candidates, option A (particularly when
celebrated on the Second Sunday of Lent) or option B.

A The celebrant faces the candidates and, with hands
joined, says:

**Lord God,
in the mystery of the transfiguration
your Son revealed his glory to the disciples
and prepared them for his death and resurrection.**

**Open the minds and hearts of these candidates
to the presence of Christ in their lives.
May they humbly acknowledge their sins and failings
and be freed of whatever obstacles and falsehoods
that
keep them from adhering wholeheartedly to your
kingdom.**

**We ask this through Christ our Lord.
R̦. Amen.**

Here, if this can be done conveniently, the celebrant lays
hands on each one of the candidates.
Then, with hands outstretched over all of them, he continues:

**Lord Jesus,
you are the only-begotten Son,**

whose kingdom these candidates acknowledge
and whose glory they seek.
Pour out upon them the power of your Spirit,
that they may be fearless witnesses to your Gospel
and one with us in the communion of love,
for you are Lord for ever and ever.

℞. Amen.

B   The celebrant faces the candidates and, with hands
joined, says:

Lord our God,
you created us in love
and redeemed us in mercy
through the blood of your Son.
Enlighten these men and women by your grace,
that, clearly seeing their sins and failings,
they may place all their trust in your mercy
and resist all that is deceitful and harmful.

We ask this through Christ our Lord.
℞. Amen.

Here, if this can be done conveniently, the celebrant lays
hands on each one of the candidates.
Then, with hands outstretched over all of them, he continues:

Lord Jesus,
whose love reaches out in mercy
to embrace and heal the contrite of heart,
lead these candidates along the way of holiness,
and heal the wounds of their sins.
May they ever keep safe in all its fullness
the gift your love once gave them
and your mercy now restores,
for you are Lord for ever and ever.

℞. Amen.

An appropriate song may be sung, for example, Psalm 6,
26, 32, 38, 39, 40, 51, 116:1–9, 130, 139, or 142.

DISMISSAL OF THE ASSEMBLY

471. If the eucharist is not to be celebrated, the entire assembly is dismissed by use of the following formulary or similar words.

Celebrant:
Go in peace, and may the Lord remain with you always.

All:
Thanks be to God.

An appropriate song may conclude the celebration.

LITURGY OF THE EUCHARIST

472. When the eucharist is to follow, the profession of faith, if required, is said. But for pastoral reasons it may be omitted. The liturgy of the eucharist then begins as usual with the preparation of the gifts.

5. RECEPTION OF BAPTIZED CHRISTIANS INTO THE FULL COMMUNION OF THE CATHOLIC CHURCH

All of you are one, united in Christ Jesus

473. This is the liturgical rite by which a person born and   R1
baptized in a separated ecclesial Community is received, according to the Latin rite,[1] into the full communion of the
Catholic Church. The rite is so arranged that no greater burden than necessary (see Acts 15:28) is required for the estab-
lishment of communion and unity.[2]

474. In the case of Eastern Christians who enter into the   R2
fullness of Catholic communion, no liturgical rite is required, but simply a profession of Catholic faith, even if
such persons are permitted, in virtue of recourse to the Apostolic See, to transfer to the Latin rite.[3]

475. In regard to the manner of celebrating the rite of   R3
reception:

   1. The rite should appear clearly as a celebration of the
Church and have as its high point eucharistic communion.
For this reason the rite should normally take place within
Mass.
   2. Any appearance of triumphalism should be carefully
avoided and the manner of celebrating this Mass should be
decided beforehand and with a view to the particular circumstances. Both the ecumenical implications and the bond
between the candidate and the parish community should be
considered. Often it will be preferable to celebrate the Mass
with only a few relatives and friends. If for a serious reason
Mass cannot be celebrated, the reception should at least
take place within a liturgy of the word, whenever this is
possible. The person to be received into full communion
should be consulted about the form of reception.

[1]See Vatican Council II, Constitution on the Liturgy *Sacrosanctum
Concilium,* art. 69, b; Decree on Ecumenism *Unitatis redintegratio,* no. 3. Secretariat for Christian Unity, *Ecumenical Directory I,* no. 19: AAS 59 (1967),
581.
[2]See Vatican Council II, Decree on Ecumenism *Unitatis redintegratio,* no. 18.
[3]See Vatican Council II, Decree on the Eastern Catholic Churches
Orientalium Ecclesiarum, nos. 25 and 4.

476. If the rite of reception is celebrated outside Mass, the   R4
Mass in which for the first time the newly received will
take part with the Catholic community should be celebrated
as soon as possible, in order to make clear the connection
between the reception and eucharistic communion.

477. The baptized Christian is to receive both doctrinal   R5
and spiritual preparation, adapted to individual pastoral requirements, for reception into the full communion of the
Catholic Church. The candidate should learn to deepen an
inner adherence to the Church, where he or she will find
the fullness of his or her baptism. During the period of
preparation the candidate may share in worship in conformity with the provisions of the *Ecumenical Directory*.

Anything that would equate candidates for reception with
those who are catechumens is to be absolutely avoided.

478. During the period of their doctrinal and spiritual   USA
preparation individual candidates for reception into the full
communion of the Catholic Church may benefit from the
celebration of liturgical rites marking their progress in formation. Thus, for pastoral reasons and in light of the
catechesis in the faith which these baptized Christians have
received previously, one or several of the rites included in
Part II, 4—"Preparation of Uncatechized Adults for Confirmation and Eucharist"—may be celebrated as they are presented or in similar words. In all cases, however, discernment should be made regarding the length of catechetical
formation required for each individual candidate for reception into the full communion of the Catholic Church.

479. One who was born and baptized outside the visible   R6
communion of the Catholic Church is not required to make
an abjuration of heresy, but simply a profession of faith.[4]

480. The sacrament of baptism cannot be repeated and   R7
therefore it is not permitted to confer it again conditionally,
unless there is a reasonable doubt about the fact or validity
of the baptism already conferred. If serious investigation
raises such prudent doubt and it seems necessary to confer
baptism again conditionally, the minister should explain be-

[4]See Secretariat for Christian Unity, *Ecumenical Directory I*, nos. 19 and 20:
AAS 59 (1967), 581.

forehand the reasons why this is being done and a nonsolemn form of baptism is to be used.[5]

The local Ordinary is to decide in each case what rites are to be included or excluded in conferring conditional baptism.

481. It is the office of the bishop to receive baptized Christians into the full communion of the Catholic Church. But a priest to whom the bishop entrusts the celebration of the rite has the faculty of confirming the candidate within the rite of reception,[6] unless the person received has already been validly confirmed.   R8

482. If the profession of faith and reception take place within Mass, the candidate, according to his or her own conscience, should make a confession of sins beforehand, first informing the confessor that he or she is about to be received into full communion. Any confessor who is lawfully approved may hear the candidate's confession.   R9

483. At the reception, the candidate should be accompanied by a sponsor and may even have two sponsors. If someone has had the principal part in guiding or preparing the candidate, he or she should be the sponsor.   R10

484. In the eucharistic celebration within which reception into full communion takes place or, if the reception takes place outside Mass, in the Mass that follows at a later time, communion under both kinds is permitted for the person received, the sponsor, the parents and spouse who are Catholics, lay catechists who may have instructed the person, and, if the number involved and other circumstances make this feasible, for all Catholics present.   R11

485. The conferences of bishops may, in accord with the provisions of the Constitution on the Liturgy, art. 63, adapt the rite of reception to various circumstances. The local Ordinary, by expanding or shortening the rite, may arrange it to suit the particular circumstances of the persons and place involved.[7]   R12

[5] See ibid., nos. 14–15: AAS 59 (1967), 580.
[6] See *Rite of Confirmation*, Introduction, no. 7,b.
[7] See Secretariat for Christian Unity, *Ecumenical Directory I*, no. 19: AAS 59 (1967), 581.

486. The names of those received into the full communion   R13
of the Catholic Church should be recorded in a special
book, with the date and place of their baptism also noted.

RECEPTION WITHIN MASS

487. If the rite of reception into full communion takes   R14
place on a solemnity or on a Sunday, the Mass of the day
should be celebrated; on other days it is permissible to celebrate the Mass "For the Unity of Christians" from the
Masses for Various Needs.

LITURGY OF THE WORD

READINGS

488. The readings may be taken in whole or in part from   R14
those provided in the Lectionary for Mass for the day, for
the rite of reception into full communion, or for the Mass
"For the Unity of Christians."

HOMILY

489. In the homily following the readings, the celebrant   R14
should express gratitude to God for those being received
and allude to their own baptism as the basis for their reception, to the sacrament of confirmation already received or
about to be received, and to the eucharist, which for the
first time they will celebrate with the Catholic community.

CELEBRATION OF RECEPTION

INVITATION

490. At the end of the homily, the celebrant in the follow-   R14
ing or similar words invites the candidate to come forward
with his or her sponsor and to make the profession of faith
with the community. He may use these or similar words.

**N., of your own free will you have asked to be re-
ceived into the full communion of the Catholic
Church. You have made your decision after careful
thought under the guidance of the Holy Spirit. I now
invite you to come forward with your sponsor and in
the presence of this community to profess the Catholic faith. In this faith you will be one with us for the**

first time at the eucharistic table of the Lord Jesus, the sign of the Church's unity.

PROFESSION OF FAITH

491. The one to be received then joins the community in reciting the Nicene Creed, which is always said at this Mass.   R15

The celebrant then asks the one to be received to add the following profession of faith. The candidate says:

I believe and profess all that the holy Catholic Church believes, teaches, and proclaims to be re- vealed by God.

ACT OF RECEPTION

492. The celebrant lays his right hand on the head of the candidate for reception and says the following. (The gesture is omitted when confirmation is to be conferred immediately.)   R16

N., the Lord receives you into the Catholic Church. His loving kindness has led you here, so that in the unity of the Holy Spirit you may have full communion with us in the faith that you have professed in the presence of his family.

If confirmation is not celebrated, the celebrant's sign of wel- come (no. 495) follows.

CELEBRATION OF CONFIRMATION

LAYING ON OF HANDS

493. If the person being received has not yet received the sacrament of confirmation, the celebrant lays hands on the candidate's head and begins the rite of confirmation with the following prayer.   R17

All-powerful God, Father of our Lord Jesus Christ, by water and the Holy Spirit you freed your son/daughter from sin and gave him/her new life.

**Send your Holy Spirit upon him/her
to be his/her helper and guide.**

**Give him/her the spirit of wisdom and understand-
ing,
the spirit of right judgment and courage,
the spirit of knowledge and reverence.
Fill him/her with the spirit of wonder and awe in
your presence.**

**We ask this through Christ our Lord.
R̃. Amen.**

ANOINTING WITH CHRISM

494. The sponsor places the right hand on the shoulder of R17
the candidate.

The celebrant dips his right thumb in the chrism and makes
the sign of the cross on the forehead of the one to be confirmed as he says:

N., be sealed with the Gift of the Holy Spirit.

Newly confirmed:
Amen.

The celebrant adds:
Peace be with you.

Newly confirmed:
And also with you.

CELEBRANT'S SIGN OF WELCOME

495. The celebrant then takes the hands of the newly re- R18
ceived person into his own as a sign of friendship and acceptance. With the permission of the Ordinary, another suitable gesture may be substituted, depending on local and
other circumstances.

GENERAL INTERCESSIONS

496. In the introduction to the general intercessions the R19
celebrant should mention baptism, (confirmation,) and the
eucharist, and express gratitude to God. The one received
into full communion is mentioned at the beginning of the
intercessions. The celebrant may use these or similar
words.

Brothers and sisters: our brother/sister N. has already been united to Christ through baptism [and confirmation] and now, with thanksgiving to God, we have received him/her into the full communion of the Catholic Church [and confirmed him/her with the gifts of the Holy Spirit]. Soon he/she will share with us at the table of the Lord. As we rejoice at the reception of a new member into the Catholic Church, let us join with him/her in asking for the grace and mercy of our Savior.

Assisting minister:
For N., whom we have welcomed today as one of us, that he/she may have the help and guidance of the Holy Spirit to persevere faithfully in the choice he/she has made, we pray to the Lord:
℟. Lord, hear our prayer.

Assisting minister:
For all who believe in Christ and for the Communities to which they belong, that they may come to perfect unity, we pray to the Lord:
℟. Lord hear our prayer.

Assisting minister:
For the Church [Communion] in which N. was baptized and received his/her formation as a Christian, that it may always grow in knowledge of Christ and proclaim him more effectively, we pray to the Lord:
℟. Lord, hear our prayer.

Assisting minister:
For all in whom the spark of desire for God already burns, that they may be led to the fullness of truth in Christ, we pray to the Lord:
℟. Lord, hear our prayer.

Assisting minister:
For those who do not yet believe in Christ the Lord, that they may enter the way of salvation by the light of the Holy Spirit, we pray to the Lord:
℟. Lord, hear our prayer.

Assisting minister:

**For all people, that they may be freed from hunger
and war and live in peace and tranquility, we pray to
the Lord:**

℟. Lord, hear our prayer.

Assisting minister:

**For ourselves, that as we have received the gift of
faith, so too we may persevere in it to the end of our
lives, we pray to the Lord:**

℟. Lord, hear our prayer.

The celebrant then says:

God our Father,
hear the prayers we offer
that we may continue our loving service to you.

Grant this through Christ our Lord.
℟. Amen.

SIGN OF PEACE

497. After the general intercessions the sponsor and the en-   R20
tire assembly, if not too numerous, may greet the newly received person in a friendly manner. In this case the sign of
peace before communion may be omitted. Finally, the one
who has been received returns to his or her place.

LITURGY OF THE EUCHARIST

498. Then the Mass continues. It is fitting that the person   R21
received and all those mentioned in no. 484 receive communion under both kinds.

RECEPTION OUTSIDE MASS

499. If, for a serious reason, the rite of reception into full   R22
communion takes place outside Mass, a liturgy of the word
is to be celebrated.

[If, in exceptional circumstances, not even a liturgy of the   R28
word is possible, just the celebration of the reception itself
takes place as described in nos. 490–497. It begins with introductory words in which the celebrant quotes from Scripture, for example, a text in praise of the mercy of God that
has guided the candidate, and speaks of the eucharistic
communion that will follow on the earliest day possible.]

500. The celebrant, vested in alb, or at least surplice, with   R23
a stole of festive color, greets those present.

501. A suitable song may be sung, then there are one or   R24
more readings from Scripture, which the celebrant explains
in the homily (see no. 489).

The readings may be chosen from those provided in the
Lectionary for Mass for the day, for the ritual Mass "Christian Initiation apart from the Easter Vigil," or for the Mass
"For the Unity of Christians"; but they are preferably
chosen from those listed here, as indicated for the rite of
reception into full communion.

NEW TESTAMENT READING

1. Romans 8:28–39———*He predestined us to become true images
of his Son.*

2. 1 Corinthians 12:31–13:13—*Love never ends.*

3. Ephesians 1:3–14—*The Father chose us in Christ to be holy
and spotless in love.*

4. Ephesians 4:1–7, 11–13—*There is one Lord, one faith, one
baptism, one God, the Father of all.*

5. Philippians 4:4–8—*Fill your minds with everything that is
holy.*

6. 1 Thessalonians 5:16–24—*May you all be kept blameless, spirit, soul, and body, for the coming of our Lord Jesus Christ.*

RESPONSORIAL PSALM

1. Psalm 27:1, 4, 8–9, 13–14
℟. **(v.1a) The Lord is my light and my salvation.**

2. Psalm 42:2–3; Psalm 43:3,4
℟. **(Psalm 42:3a) My soul is thirsting for the living God.**

3. Psalm 61:2–6, 9
℟. **(v.4a) Lord, you are my refuge.**

4. Psalm 63:2–6, 8–9
℟. **(v.3b) My soul is thirsting for you, O Lord my God.**

5. Psalm 65:2–6
℟. **(v.2a) It is right to praise you in Zion, O God.**

6. Psalm 121
℟. **(v.2a) Our help is from the Lord.**

GOSPEL

1. Matthew 5:2–12a—*Rejoice and be glad, for your reward will be great in heaven.*

2. Matthew 5:13–16—*Let your light shine before all people.*

3. Matthew 11:25–30—*You have hidden these things from the learned and the clever and revealed them to children.*

4. John 3:16–21—*Everyone who believes in him will have everlasting life.*

5. John 14:15–23, 26–27—*My Father will love them, and we will come to them.*

6. John 15:1–6—*I am the vine and you are the branches.*

502. The reception itself, as given in nos. 489–495, follows.   R25

503. Next there are intercessions, in the form given in no.   R26
496 or in a similar form.

504. The rite is concluded as follows: R26

After the concluding prayer of the intercessions, the cele-   R31
brant introduces the Lord's Prayer, in the following or similar words.

**Brothers and sisters, let us join together and pray to
God as our Lord Jesus Christ taught us to pray:**

All:
Our Father . . .

If the person received was accustomed in his or her Community to the final doxology **"For the kingdom . . . ,"** it
should be added here to the Lord's Prayer.

The celebrant gives the blessing in the usual manner. Then   R26
the sponsor and the entire assembly, if not too numerous,   R27
may offer to the newly received person some sign of welcome into the community. All then depart in peace.

APPENDIX I

ADDITIONAL (COMBINED) RITES

My soul is thirsting for the living God

RITE 1: CELEBRATION OF THE RITE OF ACCEPTANCE INTO THE ORDER OF CATECHUMENS AND OF THE RITE OF WELCOMING BAPTIZED BUT PREVIOUSLY UNCATECHIZED ADULTS WHO ARE PREPARING FOR CONFIRMATION AND/OR EUCHARIST OR RECEPTION INTO THE FULL COMMUNION OF THE CATHOLIC CHURCH

USA

I am the good shepherd: I know my sheep and mine know me

505. This rite is for use in communities where catechumens are preparing for initiation and where baptized but previously uncatechized adults are beginning catechetical formation either prior to completing their Christian initiation in the sacraments of confirmation and eucharist or prior to being received into the full communion of the Catholic Church.

506. In the catechesis of the community and in the celebration of these rites, care must be taken to maintain the distinction between the catechumens and the baptized candidates.

CELEBRATION OF THE RITE OF ACCEPTANCE INTO THE ORDER OF CATECHUMENS AND OF THE RITE OF WELCOMING BAPTIZED BUT PREVIOUSLY UNCATECHIZED ADULTS WHO ARE PREPARING FOR CONFIRMATION AND/OR EUCHARIST OR RECEPTION INTO THE FULL COMMUNION OF THE CATHOLIC CHURCH

RECEIVING THE CANDIDATES

507. Those who are to be accepted into the order of catechumens, along with those who are candidates for the sacraments of confirmation and eucharist, their sponsors, and a
group of the faithful gather outside the church (or inside at
the entrance or elsewhere) or at some other site suitable for
this rite. As the priest or deacon, wearing an alb or surplice, a stole, and, if desired, a cope of festive color, goes to
meet them, the assembly of the faithful may sing a psalm
or an appropriate song.

GREETING

508. The celebrant greets the candidates in a friendly manner. He speaks to them, their sponsors, and all present,
pointing out the joy and happiness of the Church. He may
also recall for the sponsors and friends the particular experience and religious response by which the candidates, following their own spiritual path, have come to this celebration. He uses these or similar words.

**Dear friends, the Church joyfully welcomes today
those who will be received into the order of catechumens. In the months to come they will prepare for
their initiation into the Christian faith by baptism,
confirmation, and eucharist.**

**We also greet those who, already one with us by bap-
tism, now wish to complete their Christian initiation
through confirmation and eucharist or to be received
into the full communion of the Catholic Church.**

**For all of these, we give thanks and praise to the
God who has led them by various paths to oneness**

in faith. My dear candidates, you are welcomed in the name of Christ.

Then he invites the sponsors and candidates to come forward. As they are taking their places before the celebrant, an appropriate song may be sung, for example, Psalm 63:1–8.

OPENING DIALOGUE WITH CANDIDATES FOR THE CATECHUMENATE AND WITH CANDIDATES FOR POST-BAPTISMAL CATECHESIS

509. Unless the candidates are already known to all present, the celebrant asks for or calls out their given names. The names of the candidates for the catechumenate are given first, followed by the names of the candidates for post-baptismal catechesis. The candidates answer one by one, even if, because of a large number, the question is asked only once for each group. One of the following formularies or similar words may be used.

A   The celebrant asks:
What is your name?

Candidate:
N.

B   The celebrant calls out the name of each candidate.

The candidate answers:
Present.

The celebrant continues with the following questions for the individual candidates for the catechumenate. When there are a large number the candidates may answer as a group. The celebrant may use other words than those provided in asking the candidates about their intentions and may let them answer in their own words: for example, to the first question, **"What do you ask of the Church of God?"** or **"What do you desire?"** or **"For what reason have you come?"**, he may receive such answers as **"The grace of Christ"** or **"Entrance into the Church"** or **"Eternal life"** or other suitable responses. The celebrant then phrases his next question according to the answer received.

Celebrant:
What do you ask of God's Church?

Candidate:
Faith.

Celebrant:
What does faith offer you?

Candidate:
Eternal life.

The celebrant then addresses the following questions to the individual candidates for post-baptismal catechesis. Again when there are a large number the candidates may answer as a group. The celebrant may use other words than those provided in asking the candidates about their intentions and may let them answer in their own words. The celebrant then phrases his next question according to the answer received.

What do you ask of God's Church?

Candidate:
To be accepted as a candidate for catechetical instruction leading to confirmation and eucharist (*or:* leading to reception into the full communion of the Catholic Church).

Celebrant:
What does this period of formation offer you?

Candidate:
A fuller sharing in the life of the Church.

---

510. At the discretion of the diocesan bishop, the catechumens' first acceptance of the Gospel (which follows in no. 511) may be replaced by the rite of exorcism and renunciation of false worship (nos. 70–72) [see no. 33.2].

CATECHUMENS' FIRST ACCEPTANCE OF THE GOSPEL

511. The celebrant addresses the candidates for the catechumenate, adapting the following formulary to the answers received in the opening dialogue.

God is our Creator and in him all living things have their existence. He enlightens our minds, so that we may come to know and worship him. He has sent his

faithful witness, Jesus Christ, to announce to us what he has seen and heard, the mysteries of heaven and earth.

Since you acknowledge with joy that Christ has come, now is the time to hear his word, so that you may possess eternal life by beginning, in our company, to know God and to love your neighbor. Are you ready, with the help of God, to live this life?

Candidates:
I am.

CANDIDATES' DECLARATION OF INTENT

512. The celebrant then addresses the candidates for post-baptismal catechesis, adapting the following formulary to the answers received in the opening dialogue.

Those of you who seek to complete your Christian initiation (*or:* be received into the full communion of the Catholic Church,) are you prepared to listen to the apostles' instruction, gather with us for prayer, and join us in the love and service of others?

Candidates:
I am.

AFFIRMATION BY THE SPONSORS AND THE ASSEMBLY

513. Then the celebrant turns to the sponsors and the assembly and asks them in these or similar words.

Sponsors, you now present these candidates to us; are you, and all who are gathered with us, ready to help these candidates follow Christ?

All:
We are.

With hands joined, the celebrant says:

Father of mercy,
we thank you for these your servants.
You have sought and summoned them in many ways
and they have turned to seek you.

**You have called them today
and they have answered in our presence:
we praise you, Lord, and we bless you.**

All sing or say:
We praise you, Lord, and we bless you.

SIGNING OF THE CATECHUMENS AND OF THE CANDIDATES WITH THE CROSS

514. Next the cross is traced on the forehead of the catechumens (or, at the discretion of the diocesan bishop, in front of the forehead for those in whose culture the act of touching may not seem proper); at the discretion of the celebrant the signing of one, several, or all of the senses may follow. The celebrant alone says the formularies accompanying each signing.

SIGNING OF THE FOREHEAD OF THE CATECHUMENS

515. The celebrant speaks to the catechumens and their sponsors in these or similar words.*

Celebrant:
Catechumens, come forward now with your sponsors to receive the sign of your new way of life as catechumens.

With their sponsors, the catechumens come one by one to the celebrant; with his thumb he traces a cross on the forehead; then, if there is to be no signing of the senses, the sponsor does the same. The celebrant says:

**N., receive the cross on your forehead.
It is Christ himself who now strengthens you
with this sign of his love.**
Learn to know him and follow him.

All sing or say the following or another suitable acclamation.

Glory and praise to you, Lord Jesus Christ!

*In those exceptional cases when, at the discretion of the diocesan bishop, a renunciation of false worship (no. 72) has been included in the rite of acceptance: "Dear candidates, your answers mean that you have rejected false worship and wish to share our life and hope in Christ. . ."
**In those exceptional cases when, at the discretion of the diocesan bishop, there has been a renunciation of false worship: "with this sign of his victory."

SIGNING OF THE OTHER SENSES OF THE CATECHUMENS

516. The signing is carried out by the catechists or the sponsors. (If required by special circumstances, this may be done by assisting priests or deacons.) The signing of each sense may be followed by an acclamation in praise of Christ, for example, "**Glory and praise to you, Lord Jesus Christ!**"

While the ears are being signed, the celebrant says:
Receive the sign of the cross on your ears,
that you may hear the voice of the Lord.

While the eyes are being signed:
Receive the sign of the cross on your eyes,
that you may see the glory of God.

While the lips are being signed:
Receive the sign of the cross on your lips,
that you may respond to the word of God.

While the breast is being signed:
Receive the sign of the cross over your heart,
that Christ may dwell there by faith.

While the shoulders are being signed:
Receive the sign of the cross on your shoulders,
that you may bear the gentle yoke of Christ.

[While the hands are being signed:
Receive the sign of the cross on your hands,
that Christ may be known in the work which you do.

While the feet are being signed:
Receive the sign of the cross on your feet,
that you may walk in the way of Christ.]

Without touching them the celebrant alone makes the sign of the cross over all the candidates at once (or, if they are few, over each individually), saying:

I sign you with the sign of eternal life
in the name of the Father, and of the Son, ✠
and of the Holy Spirit.

Catechumens:
Amen.

517. Next the cross is traced on the forehead of the candidates for confirmation and eucharist (or reception into the full communion of the Catholic Church); at the discretion of the celebrant the signing of one, several, or all of the senses may follow. The celebrant alone says the formularies accompanying each signing.

SIGNING OF THE FOREHEAD OF THE CANDIDATES

518. The celebrant speaks to the candidates for confirmation and the eucharist and their sponsors in these or similar words.

Celebrant:

Candidates for confirmation and the eucharist (*or:* reception into full communion), come forward now with your sponsors to receive the sign of your life in Christ.

With their sponsors, the candidates come one by one to the celebrant; with his thumb he traces a cross on the forehead; then, if there is to be no signing of the senses, the sponsor does the same. The celebrant says:

**N., receive the cross on your forehead
as a reminder of your baptism
into Christ's saving death and resurrection.**

All sing or say the following or another suitable acclamation.

Glory and praise to you, Lord Jesus Christ!

SIGNING OF THE OTHER SENSES OF THE CANDIDATES

519. The signing is carried out by the catechists or the sponsors. (If required by special circumstances, this may be done by assisting priests or deacons.) The signing of each sense may be followed by an acclamation in praise of Christ, for example, **"Glory and praise to you, Lord Jesus Christ!"**

While the ears are being signed, the celebrant says:
**Receive the sign of the cross on your ears,
that you may hear the voice of the Lord.**

While the eyes are being signed:
**Receive the sign of the cross on your eyes,
that you may see the glory of God.**

While the lips are being signed:
**Receive the sign of the cross on your lips,
that you may respond to the word of God.**

While the breast is being signed:
**Receive the sign of the cross over your heart,
that Christ may dwell there by faith.**

While the shoulders are being signed:
**Receive the sign of the cross on your shoulders,
that you may bear the gentle yoke of Christ.**

[While the hands are being signed:
**Receive the sign of the cross on your hands,
that Christ may be known in the work which you do.**

While the feet are being signed:
**Receive the sign of the cross on your feet,
that you may walk in the way of Christ.]**

Without touching them the celebrant alone makes the sign of the cross over all the candidates at once (or, if they are few, over each individually), saying:

**I sign you with the sign of eternal life
in the name of the Father, and of the Son, ✝
and of the Holy Spirit.**

Candidates:
Amen.

CONCLUDING PRAYER

520. The celebrant concludes the signing of the forehead (and senses) with the following prayer.

Let us pray.

**Almighty God,
by the cross and resurrection of your Son
you have given life to your people.**

Your servants have received the sign of the cross:
make them living proof of its saving power
and help them to persevere in the footsteps of Christ.

We ask this through Christ our Lord.
R̸. Amen.

INVITATION TO THE CELEBRATION OF THE WORD OF GOD

521. The celebrant next invites the catechumens and candidates and their sponsors to enter the church (or the place where the liturgy of the word will be celebrated). He uses the following or similar words, accompanying them with some gesture of invitation.

N. and N., come into the church, to share with us at the table of God's word.

The Lectionary for Mass or the Bible is carried in procession and placed with honor on the lectern, where it may be incensed.

During the entry an appropriate song is sung or the following antiphon, with Psalm 34:2, 3, 6, 9, 10, 11, 16.

Come, my children, and listen to me;
I will teach you the fear of the Lord.

LITURGY OF THE WORD

INSTRUCTION

522. After the catechumens and candidates have reached their places, the celebrant speaks to them briefly, helping them to understand the dignity of God's word, which is proclaimed and heard in the church.

Celebration of the liturgy of the word follows.

READINGS

523. The readings are those assigned for the day. According to the norms of the Lectionary, other appropriate readings, such as the following, may be used.

FIRST READING

Genesis 12:1–4a—*Leave your country, and come into the land I will show you.*

RESPONSORIAL PSALM

Psalm 33:4–5, 12–13, 18–19, 20 and 22
℟. **(v. 12b) Happy the people the Lord has chosen to be his own.**
Or:
℟. **(v. 22) Lord, let your mercy be on us, as we place our trust in you.**

VERSE BEFORE THE GOSPEL

John 1:41, 17b
We have found the Messiah: Jesus Christ, who brings us truth and grace.

GOSPEL

John 1:35–42—*This is the Lamb of God. We have found the Messiah.*

HOMILY

524. A homily follows that explains the readings.

PRESENTATION OF A BIBLE

525. A book containing the Gospels may be given to the catechumens and candidates by the celebrant; a cross may also be given, unless this has already been done as one of the additional rites (see no. 74). The celebrant may use words suited to the gift presented, for example, "**Receive the Gospel of Jesus Christ, the Son of God.**" The catechumens and candidates may respond in an appropriate way.

INTERCESSIONS FOR THE CATECHUMENS AND CANDIDATES

526. Then the sponsors and the whole congregation join in the following or a similar formulary of intercession for the catechumens and candidates.

[If it is decided, in accord with no. 529 that after the dismissal of the catechumens the usual general intercessions of the Mass are to be omitted and that the liturgy of the eucharist is to begin immediately, intentions for the Church and the whole world are to be added to the following intentions for the catechumens and candidates.]

Celebrant:

These catechumens and candidates, who are our brothers and sisters, have already traveled a long road. We rejoice with them in the gentle guidance of God who has brought them to this day. Let us pray that they may press onwards, until they come to share fully in our way of life.

Assisting minister:

That God our Father may reveal his Christ to them more and more with every passing day, let us pray to the Lord:
R̶. Lord, hear our prayer.

Assisting minister:

That they may undertake with generous hearts and souls whatever God may ask of them, let us pray to the Lord:
R̶. Lord, hear our prayer.

Assisting minister:

That they may have our sincere and unfailing support every step of the way, let us pray to the Lord:
R̶. Lord, hear our prayer.

Assisting minister:

That they may find in our community compelling signs of unity and generous love, let us pray to the Lord:
R̶. Lord, hear our prayer.

Assisting minister:

That their hearts and ours may become more responsive to the needs of others, let us pray to the Lord:
R̶. Lord, hear our prayer.

Assisting minister:

That in due time the catechumens may be found worthy to receive the baptism of new birth and renewal in the Holy Spirit and the candidates may be found

worthy to complete their initiation through the sacraments of confirmation and eucharist (*or* be received
into the full communion of the Catholic Church), let
us pray to the Lord:
℟. Lord, hear our prayer.

PRAYER OVER THE CATECHUMENS AND
CANDIDATES

527. After the intercessions, the celebrant, with hands outstretched over the catechumens and candidates, says the following prayer.

Almighty God,
source of all creation,
you have made us in your image.

Receive with love those who come before you.
Lead our catechumens to the baptism of new birth,
and our candidates to a deeper share
   in the paschal mystery,
so that, living a fruitful life
   in the company of your faithful,
they may receive the eternal reward that you
   promise.

We ask this in the name of Jesus the Lord.
℟. Amen.

DISMISSAL OF THE CATECHUMENS

528. If the eucharist is to be celebrated, the catechumens
are normally dismissed at this point by use of option **A** or
B; if the catechumens are to stay for the celebration of the
eucharist, option **C** is used; if the eucharist is not to be celebrated, the entire assembly is dismissed by use of option **D**.

A The celebrant dismisses the catechumens in these or
similar words.

Catechumens, go in peace, and may the Lord remain
with you always.

Catechumens:
Amen.

B As an optional formulary for dismissing the catechumens, the celebrant may use these or similar words.

My dear friends, this community now sends you forth to reflect more deeply upon the word of God which you have shared with us today. Be assured of our loving support and prayers for you. We look forward to the day when you will share fully in the Lord's Table.

C If for serious reasons the catechumens cannot leave (see no. 75.3) and must remain with the rest of the liturgical assembly, they, along with the candidates, are to be instructed that though they are present at the eucharist, they cannot take part in it as the Catholic faithful do. They may be reminded of this by the celebrant in these or similar words.

Although you cannot yet participate fully in the Lord's eucharist, stay with us as a sign of our hope that all God's children will eat and drink with the Lord and work with his Spirit to re-create the face of the earth.

D The celebrant dismisses those present, using these or similar words.

Go in peace, and may the Lord remain with you always.

All:
Thanks be to God.

An appropriate song may conclude the celebration.

LITURGY OF THE EUCHARIST

529. When the eucharist is to follow, intercessory prayer is resumed with the usual general intercessions for the needs of the Church and the whole world; then, if required, the profession of faith is said. But for pastoral reasons these general intercessions and the profession of faith may be omitted. The liturgy of the eucharist then begins as usual with the preparation of the gifts.

RITE 2: PARISH CELEBRATION FOR SENDING CATECHUMENS FOR ELECTION AND CANDIDATES FOR RECOGNITION BY THE BISHOP [OPTIONAL]

The community was of one mind and one heart

530. This optional rite is provided for parishes whose catechumens will celebrate their election and whose adult candidates for confirmation and eucharist or reception into the full communion of the Catholic Church will celebrate their recognition in a subsequent celebration (e.g., at the cathedral with the bishop).

531. As the focal point of the Church's concern for the catechumens, admission to election belongs to the bishop who is usually its presiding celebrant. It is within the parish community, however, that the preliminary judgment is made concerning the catechumens' state of formation and progress.

This rite offers that local community the opportunity to express its approval of the catechumens and to send them forth to the celebration of election assured of the parish's care and support.

532. In addition, those who either are completing their initiation through the sacraments of confirmation and the eucharist or are preparing for reception into the full communion of the Catholic Church are also included in this rite, since they too will be presented to the bishop at the celebration of the rite of election for the catechumens.

533. The rite is celebrated in the parish church at a suitable time prior to the rite of election.

534. The rite takes place after the homily in a celebration of the word of God (see no. 89) or at Mass.

535. In the catechesis of the community and in the celebration of these rites, care must be taken to maintain the distinction between the catechumens and the baptized candidates.

PARISH CELEBRATION FOR SENDING CATECHUMENS FOR ELECTION AND CANDIDATES FOR RECOGNITION BY THE BISHOP [OPTIONAL]

LITURGY OF THE WORD

HOMILY

536. After the readings, the celebrant gives the homily. This should be suited to the actual situation and should address not just the catechumens and candidates but the entire community of the faithful, so that all will be encouraged to give good example and to accompany the candidates along the path of the paschal mystery.

PRESENTATION OF THE CATECHUMENS

537. After the homily, the priest in charge of the catechumens' initiation, or a deacon, a catechist, or a representative of the community, presents the catechumens using the following or similar words.

Reverend Father, these catechumens, N. and N., are beginning their final period of preparation and purification leading to their initiation. They have found strength in God's grace and support in our community's prayers and example.

Now they ask that they be recognized for the progress they have made in their spiritual formation and that they receive the assurance of our blessings and prayers as they go forth to the rite of election celebrated this afternoon (or *next Sunday* or [*specify the day*]) by Bishop N.

The celebrant replies:
Those who are to be sent to the celebration of election in Christ, come forward, together with those who will be your godparents.

One by one, the catechumens are called by name. Each catechumen, accompanied by a godparent (or godparents), comes forward and stands before the celebrant.

AFFIRMATION BY THE GODPARENTS [AND THE ASSEMBLY]

538. Then the celebrant addresses the assembly in these or similar words:

My dear friends, these catechumens who have been preparing for the sacraments of initiation hope that they will be found ready to participate in the rite of election and be chosen in Christ for the Easter sacraments. It is the responsibility of this community to inquire about their readiness before they are presented to the bishop.

He addresses the godparents:

I turn to you, godparents, for your testimony about these candidates. Have these catechumens taken their formation in the Gospel and in the Catholic way of life seriously?

Godparents:
They have.

Celebrant:
Have they given evidence of their conversion by the example of their lives?

Godparents:
They have.

Celebrant:
Do you judge them to be ready to be presented to the bishop for the rite of election?

Godparents:
We do.

[When appropriate in the circumstances, the celebrant may also ask the entire assembly to express its approval of the candidates.]

The celebrant concludes the affirmation by the following:

My dear catechumens, this community gladly recommends you to the bishop, who, in the name of Christ, will call you to the Easter sacraments. May

God bring to completion the good work he has begun in you.

539. If the signing of the Book of the Elect is to take place in the presence of the bishop, it is omitted here. However, if the signed Book of the Elect is to be presented to the bishop in the rite of election, the catechumens may now come forward to sign it or they should sign it after the celebration or at another time prior to the Rite of Election.

PRESENTATION OF THE CANDIDATES

540. The priest in charge of the candidates' formation, or a deacon, a catechist, or a representative of the community, presents the candidates, using the following or similar words.

Reverend Father, I now present to you the candidates who are beginning their final preparation for the sacraments of confirmation and eucharist (*and/or:* reception into the full communion of the Catholic Church). They have found strength in God's grace and support in our community's prayers and example.

Now they ask that they be recognized for the progress they have made in their spiritual formation and that they receive the assurance of our blessings and prayers as they go forth for recognition by Bishop N. this afternoon (or *next Sunday* or [*specify the day*]).

The celebrant replies:
Those who are to be recognized, come forward, together with your sponsors.

One by one, the candidates are called by name. Each candidate, accompanied by a sponsor, comes forward and stands before the celebrant.

AFFIRMATION BY THE SPONSORS [AND THE ASSEMBLY]

541. Then the celebrant addresses the assembly in these or similar words:

My dear friends, these candidates, already one with us by reason of their baptism in Christ, have asked to be able to participate fully in the sacramental life of the Catholic Church. Those who know them have judged them to be sincere in their desire. During the period of their catechetical formation they have listened to the word of Christ and endeavored to follow his commands more perfectly; they have shared the company of their Christian brothers and sisters in this community and joined with them in prayer.

And so I announce to all of you here that our community supports these candidates in their desire. Therefore, I ask their sponsors to state their opinion once again, so that all of you may hear.

He addresses the sponsors:
As God is your witness, do you consider these candidates ready to receive the sacraments of confirmation and eucharist (*or:* ready to be received into the full communion of the Catholic Church)?

Sponsors:
We do.

[When appropriate in the circumstances, the celebrant may also ask the entire assembly to express its approval of the candidates.]

542. The celebrant concludes the affirmation by the following:

And now, my dear friends, I address you. Your own sponsors (and this entire community) have spoken in your favor. The Church, in the name of Christ, accepts their testimony and sends you to Bishop N., who will exhort you to live in deeper conformity to the life of Christ.

INTERCESSIONS FOR THE CATECHUMENS AND CANDIDATES

543. Then the community prays for the catechumens and candidates by use of the following or a similar formulary.

The celebrant may adapt the introduction and the intentions to fit various circumstances.

[If it is decided, in accord with no. 546, that after the dismissal of the catechumens the usual general intercessions of the Mass are to be omitted and that the liturgy of the eucharist is to begin immediately, intentions for the Church and the whole world are to be added to the following intentions for the catechumens and candidates.]

Celebrant:

My brothers and sisters, we look forward to celebrating at Easter the life-giving mysteries of our Lord's suffering, death and resurrection. As we journey together to the Easter sacraments, these catechumens and candidates will look to us for an example of Christian renewal. Let us pray to the Lord for them and for ourselves, that we may be renewed by one another's efforts and together come to share the joys of Easter.

Assisting minister:

That these catechumens and candidates may be freed from selfishness and learn to put others first, let us pray to the Lord:
℟. Lord, hear our prayer.

Assisting minister:

That their godparents and sponsors may be living examples of the Gospel, let us pray to the Lord:
℟. Lord, hear our prayer.

Assisting minister:

That their teachers may always convey to them the beauty of God's word, let us pray to the Lord:
℟. Lord, hear our prayer.

Assisting minister:

That these catechumens and candidates may share with others the joy they have found in their friendship with Jesus, let us pray to the Lord:
℟. Lord, hear our prayer.

Assisting minister:
That our community, during the (coming) Lenten season, may grow in charity and be constant in prayer, let us pray to the Lord:
R̸. Lord, hear our prayer.

PRAYER OVER THE CATECHUMENS AND CANDIDATES

544. After the intercessions, the celebrant, with hands outstretched over the catechumens and candidates, says the following prayer.

Father of love and power,
it is your will to establish everything in Christ
and to draw us into his all-embracing love.

Guide these catechumens and candidates
in the days and weeks ahead:
strengthen them in their vocation,
build them into the kingdom of your Son,
and seal them with the Spirit of your promise.

We ask this through Christ our Lord.
R̸. Amen.

DISMISSAL OF THE CATECHUMENS

545. If the eucharist is to be celebrated, the catechumens are normally dismissed at this point by use of option **A** or **B**; if the catechumens are to stay for the celebration of the eucharist, option **C** is used; if the eucharist is not to be celebrated, the entire assembly is dismissed by use of option **D**.

A The celebrant dismisses the catechumens in these or similar words.

My dear friends, you are about to set out on the road that leads to the glory of Easter. Christ will be your way, your truth, and your life. In his name we send you forth from this community to celebrate with the bishop the Lord's choice of you to be numbered among his elect. Until we meet again for the scrutinies, walk always in his peace.

Catechumens:
Amen.

B   As an optional formulary for dismissing the catechumens, the celebrant may use these or similar words.

My dear friends, this community now sends you forth to reflect more deeply upon the word of God which you have shared with us today. Be assured of our loving support and prayers for you. We look forward to the day when you will share fully in the Lord's Table.

C   If for serious reasons the catechumens cannot leave (see no. 75.3) and must remain with the rest of the liturgical assembly, they, along with the candidates, are to be instructed that though they are present at the eucharist, they cannot take part in it as the Catholic faithful do. They may be reminded of this by the celebrant in these or similar words.

Although you cannot yet participate fully in the Lord's eucharist, stay with us as a sign of our hope that all God's children will eat and drink with the Lord and work with his Spirit to re-create the face of the earth.

D   The celebrant dismisses those present, using these or similar words.

Go in peace, and may the Lord remain with you always.

All:
Thanks be to God.

An appropriate song may conclude the celebration.

LITURGY OF THE EUCHARIST

546. When the eucharist is to follow, intercessory prayer is resumed with the usual general intercessions for the needs of the Church and the whole world; then, if required, the profession of faith is said. But for pastoral reasons these general intercessions and the profession of faith may be omitted. The liturgy of the eucharist then begins as usual with the preparation of the gifts.

RITE 3: CELEBRATION OF THE RITE OF USA ELECTION OF CATECHUMENS AND OF THE CALL TO CONTINUING CONVERSION OF CANDIDATES WHO ARE PREPARING FOR CONFIRMATION AND/OR EUCHARIST OR RECEPTION INTO THE FULL COMMUNION OF THE CATHOLIC CHURCH

The body is one and has many members

547. This rite is for use when the election of catechumens and the call to continuing conversion of candidates preparing either for confirmation and/or eucharist or reception into the full communion of the Catholic Church are celebrated together.

548. The rite should normally take place on the First Sunday of Lent, and the presiding celebrant is the bishop or his delegate.

549. In the catechesis of the community and in the celebration of these rites, care must be taken to maintain the distinction between the catechumens and the baptized candidates.

CELEBRATION OF THE RITE OF ELECTION OF CATECHUMENS AND OF THE CALL TO CONTINUING CONVERSION OF CANDIDATES WHO ARE PREPARING FOR CONFIRMATION AND/OR EUCHARIST OR RECEPTION INTO THE FULL COMMUNION OF THE CATHOLIC CHURCH

LITURGY OF THE WORD

HOMILY

550. After the readings (see no. 128), the bishop, or the celebrant who acts as delegate of the bishop, gives the homily. This should be suited to the actual situation and should address not just the catechumens and the candidates, but the entire community of the faithful, so that all will be encouraged to give good example and to accompany the catechumens and candidates during the time of their Lenten preparation for celebrating the Easter sacraments.

CELEBRATION OF ELECTION

PRESENTATION OF THE CATECHUMENS

551. After the homily, the priest in charge of the catechumens' initiation, or a deacon, a catechist, or a representative of the community, presents the catechumens, using the following or similar words.

Reverend Father, Easter is drawing near, and so these catechumens, whom I now present to you, are completing their period of preparation. They have found strength in God's grace and support in our community's prayers and example.

Now they ask that after the celebration of the scrutinies, they be allowed to participate in the sacraments of baptism, confirmation, and the eucharist.

The celebrant replies:
Those who are to be chosen in Christ, come forward, together with your godparents.

One by one, the catechumens are called by name. Each catechumen, accompanied by a godparent (or godparents), comes forward and stands before the celebrant.

[If there are a great many catechumens, all are presented in groups, for example, each group by its own catechist. But in this case, the catechists should be advised to have a special celebration beforehand in which they call each catechumen forward by name.]

AFFIRMATION BY THE GODPARENTS [AND THE ASSEMBLY]

552. Then the celebrant addresses the assembly. If he has taken part in the earlier deliberation on the catechumens' suitableness (see no. 122), he may use either option **A** or option **B** or similar words; if he has not taken part in the earlier deliberation, he uses option **B** or similar words.

A

My dear friends, these catechumens have asked to be initiated into the sacramental life of the Church this Easter. Those who know them have judged them to be sincere in their desire. During the period of their preparation they have listened to the word of Christ and endeavored to follow his commands; they have shared the company of their Christian brothers and sisters and joined with them in prayer.

And so I announce to all of you here that our community has decided to call them to the sacraments. Therefore, I ask their godparents to state their opinion once again, so that all of you may hear.

He addresses the godparents:
As God is your witness, do you consider these catechumens worthy to be admitted to the sacraments of Christian initiation?

Godparents:
We do.

When appropriate in the circumstances, the celebrant may also ask the entire assembly to express its approval of the catechumens in these or similar words:

Celebrant:
Now I ask you, the members of this community:

Are you willing to affirm the testimony expressed about these catechumens and support them in faith, prayer, and example as we prepare to celebrate the Easter sacraments?

All:
We are.

B
God's holy Church wishes to know whether these catechumens are sufficiently prepared to be enrolled among the elect for the coming celebration of Easter. And so I speak first of all to you their godparents.

He addresses the godparents:
Have they faithfully listened to God's word proclaimed by the Church?

Godparents:
They have.

Celebrant:
Have they responded to that word and begun to walk in God's presence?

Godparents:
They have.

Celebrant:
Have they shared the company of their Christian brothers and sisters and joined with them in prayer?

Godparents:
They have.

When appropriate in the circumstances, the celebrant may also ask the entire assembly to express its approval of the catechumens in these or similar words:

Celebrant:
And now I speak to you, my brothers and sisters in this assembly:
Are you ready to support the testimony expressed about these catechumens and include them in your prayer and affection as we move toward Easter?

All:
We are.

INVITATION AND ENROLLMENT OF NAMES

553. Then addressing the catechumens in the following or similar words, the celebrant advises them of their acceptance and asks them to declare their own intention.

And now, my dear catechumens, I address you. Your own godparents and teachers [and this entire community] have spoken in your favor. The Church in the name of Christ accepts their judgment and calls you to the Easter sacraments.

Since you have already heard the call of Christ, you must now express your response to that call clearly and in the presence of the whole Church.

Therefore, do you wish to enter fully into the life of the Church through the sacraments of baptism, confirmation, and the eucharist?

Catechumens:
We do.

Celebrant:
Then offer your names for enrollment.

The catechumens give their names, either going with their godparents to the celebrant or while remaining in place, and the actual inscription of the names may be carried out in various ways. The catechumens may inscribe their names themselves or they may call out their names, which are inscribed by the godparents or by the minister who presented the catechumens (see no. 117). As the enrollment is taking place, an appropriate song, for example, Psalm 16 or Psalm 33 with a refrain such as, **"Happy the people the Lord has chosen to be his own"** may be sung.

[If there are a great many candidates, the enrollment may simply consist in the presentation of a list of the names to the celebrant, with such words as: **"These are the names of the candidates"** or, when the bishop is celebrant and candidates from several parishes have been presented to him: **"These are the names of the candidates from the parish of N."**]

ACT OF ADMISSION OR ELECTION

554. The celebrant briefly explains the significance of the enrollment that has just taken place. Then, turning to the catechumens, he says the following or similar words.

N. and N., I now declare you to be members of the elect, to be initiated into the sacred mysteries at the next Easter Vigil.

Catechumens:
Thanks be to God.

He continues:
God is always faithful to those he calls: now it is your duty, as it is ours, both to be faithful to him in return and to strive courageously to reach the fullness of truth, which your election opens up before you.

Then the celebrant turns to the godparents and instructs them in the following or similar words.

Godparents, you have spoken in favor of these catechumens: accept them now as chosen in the Lord and continue to sustain them through your loving care and example, until them come to share in the sacraments of God's life.

He invites them to place their hand on the shoulder of the catechumen whom they are receiving into their care, or to make some other gesture to indicate the same intent.

CELEBRATION OF THE CALL TO CONTINUING CONVERSION

PRESENTATION OF THE CANDIDATES

555. The priest in charge of the candidates' formation, or a deacon, a catechist, or a representative of the community, presents the candidates, using the following or similar words.

Reverend Father, I now present to you the candidates who seek to complete their Christian initiation (*or:* who are preparing to be received into the full communion of the Catholic Church). They too have found strength in God's grace and support in our community's prayers and example.

Now they ask that after this Lenten season, they be admitted to confirmation and the eucharist (*or:* to full eucharistic sharing).

The celebrant replies:

Those who desire to participate fully in the sacramental life of the Church, come forward, together with your sponsors.

One by one, the candidates are called by name. Each candidate, accompanied by a sponsor, comes forward and stands before the celebrant.

[If there are a great many candidates, all are presented in groups, for example, each group by its own catechist. But in this case, the catechists should be advised to have a special celebration beforehand in which they call each candidate forward by name.]

AFFIRMATION BY THE SPONSORS [AND THE ASSEMBLY]

556. Then the celebrant addresses the assembly. If he has taken part in the earlier deliberation on the candidates' suitableness (see no. 122), he may use either option **A** or option **B** or similar words; if he has not taken part in the earlier deliberation, he uses option **B** or similar words.

A
My dear friends, these candidates, our brothers and sisters, have asked to be able to participate fully in the sacramental life of the Catholic Church. Those who know them have judged them to be sincere in their desire. During the period of their preparation they have reflected on the mystery of their baptism and have come to appreciate more deeply the presence of Christ in their lives. They have shared the company of their brothers and sisters, joined with them in prayer, and endeavored to follow Christ's commands more perfectly.

And so I am pleased to recognize their desire to participate fully in the sacramental life of the Church. I ask their sponsors now to state their opinion once again, so that all of you may hear.

He addresses the sponsors:
Do you consider these candidates ready to receive the sacraments of confirmation and the eucharist?

Sponsors:
We do.

When appropriate in the circumstances, the celebrant may
also ask the entire assembly to express its approval of the
candidates in these or similar words:

Celebrant:
Now I ask you, the members of this community:
Are you willing to affirm the testimony expressed
about these candidates and support them in faith,
prayer and example as they prepare to participate
more fully in the Church's sacraments?

All:
We are.

B
The Christian life and the demands that flow from
the sacraments cannot be taken lightly. Therefore, be-
fore granting these candidates their request to share
fully in the Church's sacraments, it is important that
the Church hear the testimony of their sponsors
about their readiness.

He addresses the sponsors:
Have they faithfully listened to the apostles' instruc-
tion proclaimed by the Church?

Sponsors:
They have.

Celebrant:
Have they come to a deeper appreciation of their bap-
tism, in which they were joined to Christ and his
Church?

Sponsors:
They have.

Celebrant:
Have they reflected sufficiently on the tradition of
the Church, which is their heritage, and joined their
brothers and sisters in prayer?

Sponsors:
They have.

Celebrant:
Have they advanced in a life of love and service of others?

Sponsors:
They have.

When appropriate in the circumstances, the celebrant may also ask the entire assembly to express its approval of the candidates in these or similar words:

Celebrant:
And now I speak to you, my brothers and sisters in this assembly:

Are you ready to support the testimony expressed about these candidates and include them in your prayer and affection as we move toward Easter?

All:
We are.

ACT OF RECOGNITION

557. The celebrant then says:

N. and N., the Church recognizes your desire (to be sealed with the gift of the Holy Spirit and) to have a place at Christ's eucharistic table. Join with us this Lent in a spirit of repentance. Hear the Lord's call to conversion and be faithful to your baptismal covenant.

Candidates:
Thanks be to God.

Then the celebrant turns to the sponsors and instructs them in the following or similar words.

Sponsors, continue to support these candidates with your guidance and concern. May they see in you a love for the Church and a sincere desire for doing good. Lead them this Lent to the joys of the Easter mysteries.

He invites them to place their hand on the shoulder of the candidate whom they are receiving into their care, or to make some other gesture to indicate the same intent.

INTERCESSIONS FOR THE ELECT AND THE
CANDIDATES

558. The community may use either of the following formularies, options **A** or **B,** or a similar formulary to pray for
the elect and the candidates. The celebrant may adapt the
introduction and the intentions to fit various circumstances.

[If it is decided, in accord with no. 561, that after the dismissal of the elect the usual general intercessions of the
Mass are to be omitted and that the liturgy of the eucharist
is to begin immediately, intentions for the Church and the
whole world are to be added to the following intentions for
the elect and candidates.]

Celebrant:

**My brothers and sisters, in beginning this period of
Lent, we look forward to celebrating at Easter the
life-giving mysteries of our Lord's suffering, death,
and resurrection. These elect and candidates, whom
we bring with us to the Easter sacraments, will look
to us for an example of Christian renewal. Let us
pray to the Lord for them and for ourselves, that we
may be renewed by one another's efforts and together come to share the joys of Easter.**

A   Assisting minister:

**That together we may fruitfully employ this Lenten
season to renew ourselves through self-denial and
works of holiness, let us pray to the Lord:**
R̸. Lord, hear our prayer.

Assisting minister:

**That our catechumens may always remember this day
of their election and be grateful for the blessings
they have received from heaven, let us pray to the
Lord:**
R̸. Lord, hear our prayer.

Assisting minister:

**That our candidates preparing for confirmation and
eucharist (*or:* reception into the full communion of
the Catholic Church) may grow daily in fidelity to
their baptismal covenant, let us pray to the Lord:**
R̸. Lord, hear our prayer.

Assisting minister:
That their teachers may always convey the beauty of God's word to those who search for it, let us pray to the Lord:
℞. **Lord, hear our prayer.**

Assisting minister:
That their godparents and sponsors may be living examples of the Gospel, let us pray to the Lord:
℞. **Lord, hear our prayer.**

Assisting minister:
That their families may help them to follow the promptings of the Spirit, let us pray to the Lord:
℞. **Lord, hear our prayer.**

Assisting minister:
That our community, during this Lenten period, may grow in charity and be constant in prayer, let us pray to the Lord:
℞. **Lord, hear our prayer.**

Assisting minister:
That those who have not yet overcome their hesitation may trust in Christ and come to join our community as our brothers and sisters, let us pray to the Lord:
℞. **Lord, hear our prayer.**

B Assisting minister:
That these elect and candidates may find joy in daily prayer, we pray:
℞. **Lord, hear our prayer.**

Assisting minister:
That by praying to you often, they may grow ever closer to you, we pray:
℞. **Lord, hear our prayer.**

Assisting minister:
That they may read your word and joyfully dwell on it in their hearts, we pray:
℞. **Lord, hear our prayer.**

Assisting minister:
That they may humbly acknowledge their faults and work wholeheartedly to correct them, we pray:
℟. **Lord, hear our prayer.**

Assisting minister:
That they may dedicate their daily work as a pleasing offering to you, we pray:
℟. **Lord, hear our prayer.**

Assisting minister:
That each day of Lent they may do something in your honor, we pray:
℟. **Lord, hear our prayer.**

Assisting minister:
That they may abstain with courage from everything that defiles the heart, we pray:
℟. **Lord, hear our prayer.**

Assisting minister:
That they may grow to love and seek virtue and holiness of life, we pray:
℟. **Lord, hear our prayer.**

Assisting minister:
That they may renounce self and put others first, we pray:
℟. **Lord, hear our prayer.**

Assisting minister:
That you will protect and bless their families, we pray:
℟. **Lord, hear our prayer.**

Assisting minister:
That they may share with others the joy they have found in their faith, we pray:
℟. **Lord, hear our prayer.**

PRAYER OVER THE ELECT AND THE CANDIDATES

559. After the intercessions, the celebrant, with hands outstretched over the elect and the candidates, says one of the following prayers.

A
Lord God,
you created the human race
and are the author of its renewal.

Bless all your adopted children
and add these chosen ones
to the harvest of your new covenant.
As true children of the promise,
may they rejoice in eternal life,
won, not by the power of nature,
but through the mystery of your grace.

We ask this through Christ our Lord.
R̶. Amen.

B
Father of love and power,
it is your will to establish everything in Christ
and to draw us into his all-embracing love.

Guide these chosen ones:
strengthen them in their vocation,
build them into the kingdom of your Son,
and seal them with the Spirit of your promise.

We ask this through Christ our Lord.
R̶. Amen.

DISMISSAL OF THE ELECT

560. If the eucharist is to be celebrated, the elect are normally dismissed at this point by use of option **A** or **B**; if the
elect are to stay for the celebration of the eucharist, option
C is used; if the eucharist is not to be celebrated, the entire
assembly is dismissed by use of option **D**.

A The celebrant dismisses the elect in these or similar
words.

My dear children, you have set out with us on the
road that leads to the glory of Easter. Christ will be
your way, your truth, and your life. Until we meet
again for the scrutinies, walk always in his peace.

The elect:
Amen.

B   As an optional formulary for dismissing the elect, the celebrant may use these or similar words.

My dear friends, this community now sends you forth to reflect more deeply upon the word of God which you have shared with us today. Be assured of our loving support and prayers for you. We look forward to the day when you will share fully in the Lord's Table.

C   If for serious reasons the elect cannot leave (see no. 75.3) and must remain with the rest of the liturgical assembly, they, along with the candidates, are to be instructed that though they are present at the eucharist, they cannot take part in it as the Catholic faithful do. They may be reminded of this by the celebrant in these or similar words.

Although you cannot yet participate fully in the Lord's eucharist, stay with us as a sign of our hope that all God's children will eat and drink with the Lord and work with his Spirit to re-create the face of the earth.

D   The celebrant dismisses those present, using these or similar words.

Go in peace, and may the Lord remain with you always.

All:
Thanks be to God.

An appropriate song may conclude the celebration.

LITURGY OF THE EUCHARIST

561. When this rite is celebrated with the bishop, the liturgy of the eucharist is usually omitted. However, when the eucharist is to follow, intercessory prayer is resumed with the usual general intercessions for the needs of the Church and the whole world; then, if required, the profession of faith is said. But for pastoral reasons these general intercessions and the profession of faith may be omitted. The liturgy of the eucharist then begins as usual with the preparation of the gifts.

RITE 4: CELEBRATION AT THE EASTER VIGIL OF THE SACRAMENTS OF INITIATION AND OF THE RITE OF RECEPTION INTO THE FULL COMMUNION OF THE CATHOLIC CHURCH

The Father chose us in Christ to be holy and spotless in love

562. Pastoral considerations may suggest that along with the celebration of the sacraments of Christian initiation the Easter Vigil should include the rite of reception of already baptized Christians into the full communion of the Catholic Church. But such a decision must be guided by the theological and pastoral directives proper to each rite. The model provided here simply arranges the ritual elements belonging to such a combined celebration. But the model can only be used properly in the light of nos. 206–217, regarding celebration of the sacraments of Christian initiation, and of nos. 473–486, regarding the rite of reception into the full communion of the Catholic Church.

563. Inclusion at the Easter Vigil of the rite of reception into full communion may also be opportune liturgically, especially when the candidates have undergone a lengthy period of spiritual formation coinciding with Lent. In the liturgical year the Easter Vigil, the preeminent commemoration of Christ's paschal mystery, is the preferred occasion for the celebration in which the elect will enter the paschal mystery through baptism, confirmation, and eucharist. Candidates for reception, who in baptism have already been justified by faith and incorporated into Christ,[1] are entering fully into a community that is constituted by its communion both in faith and in the sacramental sharing of the paschal mystery. The celebration of their reception at the Easter Vigil provides the candidates with a privileged opportunity to recall and reaffirm their own baptism, "the sacramental bond of unity [and] foundation of communion between all Christians."[2] At the Easter Vigil these candidates can make their profession of faith by joining the community in the re-

[1]See Secretariat for Christian Unity, *Ecumenical Directory I*, no. 11: AAS 59 (1967), 578–579. Vatican Council II, Decree on Ecumenism *Unitatis redintegratio*, no. 3.
[2]See *Ecumenical Directory I*, no. 11: AAS 59 (1967), 578. Vatican Council II, Decree on Ecumenism *Unitatis redintegratio*, no. 22.

newal of the baptismal promises, and, if they have not yet been confirmed, they can receive the sacrament of confirmation, which is intimately connected with baptism. Since of its nature baptism points to complete entrance into eucharistic communion,[3] the baptismal themes of the Easter Vigil can serve to emphasize why the high point of the candidates' reception is their sharing in the eucharist with the Catholic community for the first time (see no. 475.1).

564. The decision to combine the two celebrations at the Easter Vigil must be guided by the provision in the *Rite of Reception*, Introduction (no. 475.2). The decision should, then, be consistent in the actual situation with respect for ecumenical values and be guided by attentiveness both to local conditions and to personal and family preferences. The person to be received should always be consulted about the form of reception (see no. 475.2).

565. In its actual arrangement the celebration itself must reflect the status of candidates for reception into the full communion of the Catholic Church: such candidates have already been incorporated into Christ in baptism and anything that would equate them with catechumens is to be absolutely avoided (see no. 477).

[3] See Vatican Council II, Decree on Ecumenism *Unitatis redintegratio*, no. 22.

CELEBRATION AT THE EASTER VIGIL OF THE SACRAMENTS OF INITIATION AND OF THE RITE OF RECEPTION INTO THE FULL COMMUNION OF THE CATHOLIC CHURCH

566. Those who will be received into full communion at the Easter Vigil, along with their sponsors, should take places apart from the elect who will be called forward for the celebration of baptism.

The homily should include reference not only to the sacraments of initiation but also to reception into full communion (see no. 489).

CELEBRATION OF BAPTISM

567. The celebration of baptism begins after the homily. It takes place at the baptismal font, if this is in view of the faithful; otherwise in the sanctuary, where a vessel of water for the rite should be prepared beforehand.

PRESENTATION OF THE CANDIDATES FOR BAPTISM

568. Accordingly, one of the following procedures, options A, B, or C, is chosen for the presentation of the candidates for baptism.

A
When Baptism Is Celebrated Immediately at the Baptismal Font
The celebrant accompanied by the assisting ministers goes directly to the font. An assisting deacon or other minister calls the candidates for baptism forward and their godparents present them. Then the candidates and the godparents take their place around the font in such a way as not to block the view of the assembly. The invitation to prayer (no. 569) and the Litany of the Saints (no. 221) follow.

[If there are a great many candidates, they and their godparents simply take their place around the font during the singing of the Litany of the Saints.]

B
When Baptism Is Celebrated after a Procession to the Font
There may be a full procession to the baptismal font. In this case an assisting deacon or other minister calls the candi-

dates for baptism forward and their godparents present
them.

[If there are a great many candidates, they and their godparents simply take their place in the procession].

The procession is formed in this order: a minister carries
the Easter candle at the head of the procession (unless, outside the Easter Vigil, it already rests at the baptismal font),
the candidates with their godparents come next, then the
celebrant with the assisting ministers. The Litany of the
Saints (no. 221) is sung during the procession. When the
procession has reached the font, the candidates and their
godparents take their place around the font in such a way
as not to block the view of the assembly. The invitation to
prayer (no. 569) precedes the blessing of the water.

C
When Baptism Is Celebrated in the Sanctuary
An assisting deacon or other minister calls the candidates
for baptism forward and their godparents present them.
The candidates and their godparents take their place before
the celebrant in the sanctuary in such a way as not to block
the view of the assembly. The invitation to prayer (no. 569)
and the Litany of the Saints (no. 570, see no. 221) follow.

[If there are a great many candidates, they and their godparents simply take their place in the sanctuary during the
singing of the Litany of the Saints.]

INVITATION TO PRAYER

569. The celebrant addresses the following or a similar invitation for the assembly to join in prayer for the candidates
for baptism.

**Dear friends, let us pray to almighty God for our
brothers and sisters, N. and N., who are asking for
baptism. He has called them and brought them to
this moment; may he grant them light and strength to
follow Christ with resolute hearts and to profess the
faith of the Church. May he give them the new life
of the Holy Spirit, whom we are about to call down
on this water.**

LITANY OF THE SAINTS

570. See no. 221.

BLESSING OF THE WATER

571. After the Litany of the Saints, facing the font (or vessel) containing the water, the celebrant sings the following:

**Father,
you give us grace through sacramental signs,
which tell us of the wonders of your unseen power.**

**In baptism we use your gift of water,
which you have made a rich symbol of the grace
you give us in this sacrament.**

**At the very dawn of creation
your Spirit breathed on the waters,
making them the wellspring of all holiness.**

**The waters of the great flood
you made a sign of the waters of baptism
that make an end of sin
and a new beginning of goodness.**

**Through the waters of the Red Sea
you led Israel out of slavery
to be an image of God's holy people,
set free from sin by baptism.**

**In the waters of the Jordan
your Son was baptized by John
and anointed with the Spirit.**

**Your Son willed that water and blood should flow
  from his side
as he hung upon the cross.**

**After his resurrection he told his disciples:
"Go out and teach all nations,
baptizing them in the name of the Father, and of the
  Son, and of the Holy Spirit."**

**Father,
look now with love upon your Church
and unseal for it the fountain of baptism.**

**By the power of the Holy Spirit
give to this water the grace of your Son,
so that in the sacrament of baptism
all those whom you have created in your likeness
may be cleansed from sin
and rise to a new birth of innocence
by water and the Holy Spirit.**

Here, if this can be done conveniently, the celebrant before continuing lowers the Easter candle into the water once or three times, then holds it there until the acclamation at the end of the blessing.

**We ask you, Father, with your Son
to send the Holy Spirit upon the waters of this font.
May all who are buried with Christ in the death of
baptism
rise also with him to newness of life.**

We ask this through Christ our Lord.

All:
Amen.

If the Easter candle has been held in the water, the celebrant then raises it and the people sing the following or another suitable acclamation.

**Springs of water, bless the Lord.
Give him glory and praise for ever.**

PROFESSION OF FAITH

572. After the blessing of the water, the celebrant continues with the profession of faith, which includes the renunciation of sin and the profession itself.

RENUNCIATION OF SIN

573. See no. 224.

PROFESSION OF FAITH

574. See no. 225.

BAPTISM

575. See no. 226.

EXPLANATORY RITES

576. See no. 227.

ANOINTING AFTER BAPTISM

577. See no. 228.

CLOTHING WITH A BAPTISMAL GARMENT

578. See no. 229.

PRESENTATION OF A LIGHTED CANDLE

579. The celebrant takes the Easter candle in his hands or touches it, saying:

Godparents, please come forward to give to the newly baptized the light of Christ.

A godparent of each of the newly baptized goes to the celebrant, lights a candle from the Easter candle, then presents it to the newly baptized.

Then the celebrant says to the newly baptized:
You have been enlightened by Christ.
Walk always as children of the light
and keep the flame of faith alive in your hearts.
When the Lord comes, may you go out to meet him
with all the saints in the heavenly kingdom.

Newly baptized:
Amen.

RENEWAL OF BAPTISMAL PROMISES

INVITATION

580. After the celebration of baptism, the celebrant addresses the community, in order to invite those present to the renewal of their baptismal promises; the candidates for reception into full communion join the rest of the community in this renunciation of sin and profession of faith. All stand and hold lighted candles. The celebrant may use the following or similar words.

Dear friends, through the paschal mystery we have been buried with Christ in baptism, so that we may rise with him to newness of life. Now that we have completed our Lenten observance, let us renew the promises we made in baptism, when we rejected Satan and his works and promised to serve God faithfully in his holy catholic Church.

RENEWAL OF BAPTISMAL PROMISES

RENUNCIATION OF SIN

581. The celebrant continues with one of the following formularies of renunciation.

[If circumstances require, the conference of bishops may adapt formulary A in accord with local conditions.]

A Celebrant:
Do you reject sin so as to live in the freedom of God's children?

All:
I do.

Celebrant:
Do you reject the glamor of evil, and refuse to be mastered by sin?

All:
I do.

Celebrant:
Do you reject Satan, father of sin and prince of darkness?

All:
I do.

B Celebrant:
Do you reject Satan?

All:
I do.

Celebrant:
And all his works?

All:
I do.

Celebrant:
And all his empty promises?

All:
I do.

PROFESSION OF FAITH

582. Then the celebrant continues:

**Do you believe in God, the Father almighty, creator
    of heaven and earth?**

All:
I do.

Celebrant:
**Do you believe in Jesus Christ, his only Son, our
    Lord,
    who was born of the Virgin Mary,
    was crucified, died, and was buried,
    rose from the dead,
    and is now seated at the right hand of the Father?**

All:
I do.

Celebrant:
**Do you believe in the Holy Spirit,
    the holy catholic Church, the communion of saints,
    the forgiveness of sins, the resurrection of the
    body,
    and the life everlasting?**

All:
I do.

SPRINKLING WITH BAPTISMAL WATER

583. The celebrant sprinkles all the people with the
blessed baptismal water, while all sing the following song
or any other that is baptismal in character.

I saw water flowing
from the right side of the temple, alleluia.
It brought God's life and his salvation,
and the people sang in joyful praise:
alleluia, alleluia. (See Ezekiel 47:1–2,9)

The celebrant then concludes with the following prayer.
God, the all-powerful Father of our Lord Jesus
Christ, has given us a new birth by water and the
Holy Spirit and forgiven all our sins.
May he also keep us faithful to our Lord Jesus Christ
for ever and ever.

All:
Amen.

CELEBRATION OF RECEPTION

INVITATION

584. If baptism has been celebrated at the font, the celebrant, the assisting ministers, and the newly baptized with
their godparents proceed to the sanctuary. As they do so
the assembly may sing a suitable song.

Then in the following or similar words the celebrant invites
the candidates for reception, along with their sponsors, to
come into the sanctuary and before the community to make
a profession of faith.

N and N., of your own free will you have asked to
be received into the full communion of the Catholic
Church. You have made your decision after careful
thought under the guidance of the Holy Spirit. I now
invite you to come forward with your sponsors and
in the presence of this community to profess the
Catholic faith. In this faith you will be one with us
for the first time at the eucharistic table of the Lord
Jesus, the sign of the Church's unity.

PROFESSION BY THE CANDIDATES

585. When the candidates for reception and their sponsors
have taken their places in the sanctuary, the celebrant asks
the candidates to make the following profession of faith.
The candidates say:

I believe and profess all that the holy Catholic Church believes, teaches, and proclaims to be revealed by God.

ACT OF RECEPTION

586. Then the candidates with their sponsors go individually to the celebrant, who says to each candidate (laying his right hand on the head of any candidate who is not to receive confirmation):

N., the Lord receives you into the Catholic Church.
His loving kindness has led you here,
so that in the unity of the Holy Spirit
you may have full communion with us
in the faith that you have professed in the presence
of his family.

CELEBRATION OF CONFIRMATION

587. Before the celebration of confirmation begins, the assembly may sing a suitable song.

588. If the bishop has conferred baptism, he should now also confer confirmation. If the bishop is not present, the priest who conferred baptism and received the candidates into full communion is authorized to confirm.

[When there are a great many persons to be confirmed, the minister of confirmation may associate priests with himself as ministers of the sacrament (see no. 14).]

INVITATION

589. The newly baptized with their godparents and, if they have not received the sacrament of confirmation, the newly received with their sponsors, stand before the celebrant. He first speaks briefly to the newly baptized and the newly received in these or similar words.

My dear candidates for confirmation, by your baptism you have been born again in Christ and you have become members of Christ and of his priestly people. Now you are to share in the outpouring of the Holy Spirit among us, the Spirit sent by the Lord

upon his apostles at Pentecost and given by them
and their successors to the baptized.

The promised strength of the Holy Spirit, which you
are to receive, will make you more like Christ and
help you to be witnesses to his suffering, death, and
resurrection. It will strengthen you to be active members of the Church and to build up the Body of
Christ in faith and love.

[The priests who will be associated with the celebrant as
ministers of the sacrament now stand next to him.]

With hands joined, the celebrant next addresses the people:

My dear friends, let us pray to God our Father, that
he will pour out the Holy Spirit on these candidates
for confirmation to strengthen them with his gifts
and anoint them to be more like Christ, the Son of
God.

All pray briefly in silence.

LAYING ON OF HANDS

590. The celebrant holds his hands outstretched over the
entire group of those to be confirmed and says the following prayer.

[In silence the priests associated as ministers of the sacrament also hold their hands outstretched over the
candidates.]

All-powerful God, Father of our Lord Jesus Christ,
by water and the Holy Spirit
you freed your sons and daughters from sin
and gave them new life.

Send your Holy Spirit upon them
to be their helper and guide.

Give them the spirit of wisdom and understanding,
the spirit of right judgment and courage,
the spirit of knowledge and reverence.
Fill them with the spirit of wonder and awe in your
    presence.

We ask this through Christ our Lord.
℟. Amen.

ANOINTING WITH CHRISM

591. A minister brings the chrism to the celebrant.

[When the celebrant is the bishop, priests who are associated as ministers of the sacrament receive the chrism from him.]

Each candidate, with godparent or godparents or with sponsors, goes to the celebrant (or to an associated minister of the sacrament); or, if circumstances require, the celebrant (associated ministers) may go to the candidates.

Either or both godparents and sponsors place the right hand on the shoulder of the candidate; a godparent or a sponsor or the candidate gives the candidate's name to the minister of the sacrament. During the conferral of the sacrament an appropriate song may be sung.

The minister of the sacrament dips his right thumb in the chrism and makes the sign of the cross on the forehead of the one to be confirmed as he says:

N., be sealed with the Gift of the Holy Spirit.

Newly confirmed:
Amen.

The minister of the sacrament adds:
Peace be with you.

Newly confirmed:
And also with you.

After all have received the sacrament, the newly confirmed as well as the godparents and sponsors are led to their places in the assembly.

LITURGY OF THE EUCHARIST

592. Since the profession of faith is not said, the general intercessions begin immediately and for the first time the neophytes take part in them. Some of the neophytes also take part in the procession to the altar with the gifts.

593. With Eucharistic Prayers I, II, or III the special interpolations given in the Roman Missal, the ritual Mass, "Christian Initiation: Baptism" are used.

594. It is most desirable that the neophytes and newly received, together with their godparents, sponsors, parents, spouses, and catechists, receive communion under both kinds.

Before saying "This is the Lamb of God," the celebrant may briefly remind the neophytes of the preeminence of the eucharist, which is the climax of their initiation and the center of the whole Christian life. He may also mention that for those received into full communion this first full sharing with the Catholic community in eucharistic communion is the high point of their reception.

APPENDIX II

ACCLAMATIONS, HYMNS, AND SONGS

Praised be the Father of our Lord Jesus Christ, a God so merciful and kind

ACCLAMATIONS FROM SACRED SCRIPTURE

595. The following are acclamations from Sacred Scripture.   390

1.
Lord God, who is your equal?
Strong, majestic, and holy!
Worthy of praise, worker of wonders! (Exodus 15:11)

2.
God is light: in him there is no darkness. (1 John 1:5)

3.
God is love; those who live in love, live in God.
  (1 John 4:16)

4.
There is one God, one Father of all;
he is over all, and through all;
he lives in all of us. (Ephesians 4:6)

5.
Come to him and receive his light! (Psalm 34:6)

6.
Blessed be God who chose you in Christ. (See Ephesians 1:3–4)

7.
You are God's work of art, created in Christ Jesus.
  (Ephesians 2:10)

8.

**You are now God's children, my dearest friends.
What you shall be in his glory has not yet been revealed.** (1 John 3:2)

9.

**Think of how God loves you!
He calls you his own children,
and that is what you are.** (1 John 3:1)

10.

**Happy are those who have washed their robes clean,
washed in the blood of the Lamb!** (Revelation 22:14)

11.

**All of you are one,
united in Christ Jesus.** (Galatians 3:28)

12.

**Imitate God; walk in his love,
just as Christ loves us.** (Ephesians 5:1–2)

HYMNS IN THE STYLE OF THE NEW TESTAMENT

596. The following are hymns in the style of the New Testament.

1.
Praised be the Father of our Lord Jesus Christ,
a God so merciful and kind!
He has given us a new birth, a living hope,
by raising Jesus his Son from death.
Salvation is our undying inheritance,
preserved for us in heaven,
salvation at the end of time. (1 Peter 1:3–5)

2.
How great the sign of God's love for us,
Jesus Christ our Lord:
promised before all time began,
revealed in these last days.
He lived and suffered and died for us,
but the Spirit raised him to life.
People everywhere have heard his message
and placed their faith in him.
What wonderful blessings he gives his people;
living in the Father's glory;
he fills all creation
and guides it to perfection. (See 1 Timothy 3:16)

SONGS FROM ANCIENT LITURGIES

597. The following are songs from ancient liturgies.

1.
We believe in you, Lord Jesus Christ.
Fill our hearts with your radiance
and make us the children of light!

2.
We come to you, Lord Jesus.
Fill us with your life.
Make us children of the Father
and one in you.

3.
Lord Jesus, from your wounded side
flowed streams of cleansing water;
the world was washed of all its sin,
all life made new again!

4.
The Father's voice calls us above the waters,
the glory of the Son shines on us,
the love of the Spirit fills us with life.

5.
Holy Church of God, stretch out your hand
and welcome your children,
newborn of water
and of the Spirit of God.

6.
Rejoice, you newly baptized,
chosen members of the Kingdom.
Buried with Christ in death,
you are reborn in him by faith.

7.
This is the fountain of life that floods the entire
    world,
the water that took its beginning
from the pierced side of Christ.
You who are born again of this water,
place your hope in the kingdom of heaven.

APPENDIX III

NATIONAL STATUTES FOR THE CATECHUMENATE

Imitate God; walk in his love, just as Christ loves us

NATIONAL STATUTES FOR THE CATECHUMENATE

Approved by the National Conference of Catholic Bishops on November 11, 1986

PRECATECHUMENATE

1. Any reception or service of welcome or prayer for inquirers at the beginning or during a precatechumenate (or in an earlier period of evangelization) must be entirely informal. Such meetings should take into account that the inquirers are not yet catechumens and that the rite of acceptance into the order of catechumens, intended for those who have been converted from unbelief and have initial faith, may not be anticipated.

CATECHUMENATE

2. The term "catechumen" should be strictly reserved for the unbaptized who have been admitted into the order of catechumens; the term "convert" should be reserved strictly for those converted from unbelief to Christian belief and never used of those baptized Christians who are received into the full communion of the Catholic Church.

3. This holds true even if elements of catechumenal formation are appropriate for those who are not catechumens, namely, (a) baptized Catholic Christians who have not received catechetical instruction and whose Christian initiation has not been completed by confirmation and eucharist and (b) baptized Christians who have been members of another Church or ecclesial community and seek to be received into the full communion of the Catholic Church.

4. If the catechumenal preparation takes place in a non-parochial setting such as a center, school, or other institution, the catechumens should be introduced into the Christian life of a parish or similar community from the very beginning of the catechumenate, so that after their initiation and mystagogy they will not find themselves isolated from the ordinary life of the Christian people.

5. In the celebration of the rite of acceptance into the order of catechumens, it is for the diocesan bishop to determine whether the additional rites listed in no. 74, *Rite of Christian Initiation of Adults,* are to be incorporated (see no. 33.5).

6. The period of catechumenate, beginning at acceptance into the order of catechumens and including both the catechumenate proper and the period of purification and enlightenment after election or enrollment of names, should extend for at least one year of formation, instruction, and probation. Ordinarily this period should go from at least the Easter season of one year until the next; preferably it should begin before Lent in one year and extend until Easter of the following year.

7. A thoroughly comprehensive catechesis on the truths of Catholic doctrine and moral life, aided by approved catechetical texts, is to be provided during the period of the catechumenate (see RCIA, no. 75).

CATECHUMENS

8. Catechumens should be encouraged to seek blessings and other suffrages from the Church, since they are of the household of Christ; they are entitled to Christian burial should they die before the completion of their initiation.

9. In this case, the funeral liturgy, including the funeral Mass, should be celebrated as usual, omitting only language referring directly to the sacraments which the catechumen has not received. In view of the sensibilities of the immediate family of the deceased catechumen, however, the funeral Mass may be omitted at the discretion of the pastor.

10. The marriages of catechumens, whether with other catechumens or with baptized Christians or even non-Christians, should be celebrated at a liturgy of the word

and never at the eucharistic liturgy. Chapter III of the *Rite of Marriage* is to be followed, but the nuptial blessing in Chapter I, no. 33, may be used, all references to eucharistic sharing being omitted.

MINISTER OF BAPTISM AND CONFIRMATION

11. The diocesan bishop is the proper minister of the sacraments of initiation for adults, including children of catechetical age, in accord with canon 852:1. If he is unable to celebrate the sacraments of initiation with all the candidates of the local church, he should at least celebrate the rite of election or enrollment of names, ordinarily at the beginning of Lent, for the catechumens of the diocese.

12. Priests who do not exercise a pastoral office but participate in a catechumenal program require a mandate from the diocesan bishop if they are to baptize adults; they then do not require any additional mandate or authorization in order to confirm, but have the faculty to confirm from the law, as do priests who baptize adults in the exercise of their pastoral office.

13. Since those who have the faculty to confirm are bound to exercise it in accord with canon 885:2, and may not be prohibited from using the faculty, a diocesan bishop who is desirous of confirming neophytes should reserve to himself the baptism of adults in accord with canon 863.

CELEBRATION OF THE SACRAMENTS OF INITIATION

14. In order to signify clearly the interrelation or coalescence of the three sacraments which are required for full Christian initiation (canon 842:2), adult candidates, including children of catechetical age, are to receive baptism, confirmation, and eucharist in a single eucharistic celebration, whether at the Easter Vigil or, if necessary, at some other time.

15. Candidates for initiation, as well as those who assist them and participate in the celebration of the Easter Vigil with them, are encouraged to keep and extend the paschal fast of Good Friday, as determined by canon 1251, throughout the day of Holy Saturday until the end of the Vigil itself, in accord with the Constitution on the Liturgy, *Sacrosanctum Concilium*, art. 110.

16. The rite of anointing with the oil of catechumens is to be omitted in the baptism of adults at the Easter Vigil.

17. Baptism by immersion is the fuller and more expressive sign of the sacrament, and, therefore, provision should be made for its more frequent use in the baptism of adults. The provision of the *Rite of Christian Initiation of Adults* for partial immersion, namely, immersion of the candidate's head, should be taken into account.

CHILDREN OF CATECHETICAL AGE

18. Since children who have reached the use of reason are considered, for purposes of Christian initiation, to be adults (canon 852:1), their formation should follow the general pattern of the ordinary catechumenate as far as possible, with the appropriate adaptations permitted by the ritual. They should receive the sacraments of baptism, confirmation, and eucharist at the Easter Vigil, together with the older catechumens.

19. Some elements of the ordinary catechetical instruction of baptized children before their reception of the sacraments of confirmation and eucharist may be appropriately shared with catechumens of catechetical age. Their condition and status as catechumens, however, should not be compromised or confused, nor should they receive the sacraments of initiation in any sequence other than that determined in the ritual of Christian initiation.

ABBREVIATED CATECHUMENATE

20. The abbreviated catechumenate, which the diocesan bishop may permit only in individual and exceptional cases, as described in nos. 307–308 of the *Rite of Christian Initiation of Adults*, should always be as limited as possible. It should extend over a substantial and appropriate period of time. The rites prior to sacramental initiation should not be unduly compressed, much less celebrated on a single occasion. The catechumenate of persons who move from one parish to another or from one diocese to another should not on that account alone be abbreviated.

21. Candidates who have received their formation in an abbreviated catechumenate should receive the sacraments of Christian initiation at the Easter Vigil, if possible, together with candidates who have participated in the more extended catechumenate. They should also participate in the period of mystagogy, to the extent possible.

MYSTAGOGY

22. After the completion of their Christian initiation in the sacraments of baptism, confirmation, and eucharist, the neophytes should begin the period of mystagogy by participating in the principal Sunday Eucharist of the community throughout the Easter season, which ends on Pentecost Sunday. They should do this as a body in company with their godparents and those who have assisted in their Christian formation.

23. Under the moderation of the diocesan bishop, the mystagogy should embrace a deepened understanding of the mysteries of baptism, confirmation, and the eucharist, and especially of the eucharist as the continuing celebration of faith and conversion.

24. After the immediate mystagogy or postbaptismal catechesis during the Easter season, the program for the neophytes should extend until the anniversary of Christian initiation, with at least monthly assemblies of the neophytes for their deeper Christian formation and incorporation into the full life of the Christian community.

UNCATECHIZED ADULT CATHOLICS

25. Although baptized adult Catholics who have never received catechetical instruction or been admitted to the sacraments of confirmation and eucharist are not catechumens, some elements of the usual catechumenal formation are appropriate to their preparation for the sacraments, in accord with the norms of the ritual, "Preparation of Uncatechized Adults for Confirmation and Eucharist."

26. Although it is not generally recommended, if the sacramental initiation of such candidates is completed with confirmation and eucharist on the same occasion as the celebration of the full Christian initiation of candidates for

baptism, the condition and status of those already baptized should be carefully respected and distinguished.

27. The celebration of the sacrament of reconciliation with candidates for confirmation and eucharist is to be carried out at a time prior to and distinct from the celebration of confirmation and the eucharist. As part of the formation of such candidates, they should be encouraged in the frequent celebration of this sacrament.

28. Priests mentioned in canon 883:2 also have the faculty to confirm (a) in the case of the readmission to communion of a baptized Catholic who has been an apostate from the faith and also (b) in the case of a baptized Catholic who has without fault been instructed in a non-Catholic religion or adhered to a non-Catholic religion, but (c) not in the case of a baptized Catholic who without his or her fault never put the faith into practice.

29. In the instance mentioned in no. 28 c, in order to maintain the interrelationship and sequence of confirmation and eucharist as defined in canon 842:2, priests who lack the faculty to confirm should seek it from the diocesan bishop, who may, in accord with canon 884:1, grant the faculty if he judges it necessary.

RECEPTION INTO FULL CATHOLIC COMMUNION

30. Those who have already been baptized in another Church or ecclesial community should not be treated as catechumens or so designated. Their doctrinal and spiritual preparation for reception into full Catholic communion should be determined according to the individual case, that is, it should depend on the extent to which the baptized person has led a Christian life within a community of faith and been appropriately catechized to deepen his or her inner adherence to the Church.

31. Those who have been baptized but have received relatively little Christian upbringing may participate in the elements of catechumenal formation so far as necessary and appropriate, but should not take part in rites intended for the unbaptized catechumens. They may, however, participate in celebrations of the word together with catechumens. In addition they may be included with uncatechized adult

Catholics in such rites as may be appropriate among those included or mentioned in the ritual in Part II, 4, "Preparation of Uncatechized Adults for Confirmation and Eucharist." The rites of presentation of the Creed, the Lord's Prayer, and the book of the Gospels are not proper except for those who have received no Christian instruction and formation. Those baptized persons who have lived as Christians and need only instruction in the Catholic tradition and a degree of probation within the Catholic community should not be asked to undergo a full program parallel to the catechumenate.

32. The reception of candidates into the communion of the Catholic Church should ordinarily take place at the Sunday Eucharist of the parish community, in such a way that it is understood that they are indeed Christian believers who have already shared in the sacramental life of the Church and are now welcomed into the Catholic eucharistic community upon their profession of faith and confirmation, if they have not been confirmed, before receiving the eucharist.

33. It is preferable that reception into full communion not take place at the Easter Vigil lest there be any confusion of such baptized Christians with the candidates for baptism, possible misunderstanding of or even reflection upon the sacrament of baptism celebrated in another Church or ecclesial community, or any perceived triumphalism in the liturgical welcome into the Catholic eucharistic community.

34. Nevertheless if there are both catechumens to be baptized and baptized Christians to be received into full communion at the Vigil, for pastoral reasons and in view of the Vigil's being the principal annual celebration of the Church, the combined rite is to be followed: "Celebration at the Easter Vigil of the Sacraments of Initiation and of the Rite of Reception into the Full Communion of the Catholic Church." A clear distinction should be maintained during the celebration between candidates for sacramental initiation and candidates for reception into full communion, and ecumenical sensitivities should be carefully respected.

35. The "Rite of Reception into the Full Communion of the Catholic Church" respects the traditional sequence of confirmation before eucharist. When the bishop, whose office it

is to receive adult Christians into the full communion of the Catholic Church (*RCIA*, no. 481 [R8]) entrusts the celebration of the rite to a presbyter, the priest receives from the law itself (canon 883:2) the faculty to confirm the candidate for reception and is obliged to use it (canon 885:2); he may not be prohibited from exercising the faculty. The confirmation of such candidates for reception should not be deferred, nor should they be admitted to the eucharist until they are confirmed. A diocesan bishop who is desirous of confirming those received into full communion should reserve the rite of reception to himself.

36. The celebration of the sacrament of reconciliation with candidates for reception into full communion is to be carried out at a time prior to and distinct from the celebration of the rite of reception. As part of the formation of such candidates, they should be encouraged in the frequent celebration of this sacrament.

37. There may be a reasonable and prudent doubt concerning the baptism of such Christians which cannot be resolved after serious investigation into the fact and/or validity of baptism, namely, to ascertain whether the person was baptized with water and with the Trinitarian formula, and whether the minister and the recipient of the sacrament had the proper requisite intentions. If conditional baptism then seems necessary, this must be celebrated privately rather than at a public liturgical assembly of the community and with only those limited rites which the diocesan bishop determines. The reception into full communion should take place later at the Sunday Eucharist of the community.

DOCUMENTATION

The *Rite of Christian Initiation of Adults* incorporates the (slight) emendations of the introduction (*praenotanda*) occasioned by the promulgation of the Code of Canon Law in 1983. It does not, however, include the text of pertinent canons or the underlying conciliar decisions and statements on the catechumenate, although the latter are reflected in the introduction to the ritual. In order to have these texts available in one place, this documentary appendix has been compiled.

A. Conciliar Constitutions and Decrees (Unless otherwise noted all translations are from: *Documents on the Liturgy, 1963–1979: Conciliar, Papal, and Curial Texts* [Collegeville, MN: The Liturgical Press, 1982])

Constitution on the Liturgy *Sacrosanctum Concilium*, art. 64: "The catechumenate for adults, divided into several stages, is to be restored and put into use at the discretion of the local Ordinary. By this means the time of the catechumenate, which is intended as a period of well-suited instruction, may be sanctified by sacred rites to be celebrated at successive intervals of time."

Constitution on the Liturgy *Sacrosanctum Concilium*, art. 65: "With art. 37–40 of this Constitution as the norm, it is lawful in mission lands to allow, besides what is part of Christian tradition, those initiation elements in use among individual peoples, to the extent that such elements are compatible with the Christian rite of initiation."

Constitution on the Liturgy *Sacrosanctum Concilium*, art. 66: "Both of the rites for the baptism of adults are to be revised: not only the simpler rite, but also the more solemn one, with proper attention to the restored catechumenate. A special Mass 'On the Occasion of a Baptism' is to be incorporated into the Roman Missal."

Dogmatic Constitution on the Church *Lumen Gentium*, no. 14: "This holy Council first of all turns its attention to the Catholic faithful. Basing itself on scripture and tradition, it teaches that the Church, a pilgrim now on earth, is necessary for salvation: the one Christ is mediator and the way of salvation; he is present to us in his body which is the Church. He himself explicitly asserted the necessity of faith and baptism (cf. Mk. 16:16; Jn. 3:5), and thereby affirmed at the same time the necessity of the Church which men enter through baptism as through a door. Hence they could not be saved who, knowing that the Catholic Church was founded as necessary by God through Christ, would refuse either to enter it, or to remain in it.

"Fully incorporated into the Church are those who, possessing the Spirit of Christ, accept all the means of salvation given to the Church together with her entire organization, and who—by the bonds constituted by the profession of faith, the sacraments, ecclesiastical government, and

communion—are joined in the visible structure of the
Church of Christ, who rules her through the Supreme Pon-
tiff and the bishops. Even though incorporated into the
Church, one who does not however persevere in charity is
not saved. He remains indeed in the bosom of the Church,
but 'in body' not 'in heart.' All children of the Church
should nevertheless remember that their exalted condition
results, not from their own merits, but from the grace of
Christ. If they fail to respond in thought, word and deed to
that grace, not only shall they not be saved, but they shall
be the more severely judged.

"Catechumens who, moved by the Holy Spirit, desire with
an explicit intention to be incorporated into the Church, are
by that very intention joined to her. With love and solicitude mother Church already embraces them as her own"
(Flannery translation).

Decree on the Church's Missionary Activity *Ad gentes*, no.
13: "Whenever God opens a door for the word in order to
declare the mystery of Christ (cf. Col. 4:3) then the living
God, and he whom he has sent for the salvation of all, Jesus Christ (cf. 1 Th. 1:9–10; 1 Cor. 1:18–21; Gal. 1:31; Acts
14:15–17; 17:22–31), are confidently and perseveringly (cf.
Acts 4:13, 29, 31; 9:27, 28; 13:40; 14:3; 19:8; 26:26; 28:31; 1
Th. 2:2; 2 Cor. 3:12; 7:4; Phil. 1:20; Eph. 3:12; 6:19–20) proclaimed (cf. 1 Cor. 9:15; Rom. 10:14) to all men (cf. Mk.
16:15). And this is in order that non-Christians, whose
heart is being opened by the Holy Spirit (cf. Acts 16:4),
might, while believing, freely turn to the Lord who, since
he is the 'way, the truth and the life' (Jn. 14:6), will satisfy
all their inner hopes, or rather infinitely surpass them.

"This conversion is, indeed, only initial; sufficient however
to make a man realize that he has been snatched from sin,
and is being led into the mystery of God's love, who invites
him to establish a personal relationship with him in Christ.
Under the movement of divine grace the new convert sets
out on a spiritual journey by means of which, while already
sharing through faith in the mystery of the death and resurrection, he passes from the old man to the new man who
has been made perfect in Christ (cf. Col. 3:5–10; Eph. 4:20–
24). This transition, which involves a progressive change of
outlook and morals, should be manifested in its social implications and effected gradually during the period of
catechumenate. Since the Lord in whom he believes is a

sign of contradiction (cf. Lk. 2:34; Mt. 10:34–39) the convert often has to suffer misunderstanding and separation, but he also experiences those joys which are generously granted by God.

"The Church strictly forbids that anyone should be forced to accept the faith, or be induced or enticed by unworthy devices; as it likewise strongly defends the right that no one should be frightened away from the faith by unjust persecutions.

"In accordance with the very ancient practice of the Church, the motives for the conversion should be examined and, if necessary, purified" (Flannery translation).

Decree on the Church's Missionary Activity *Ad gentes*, no. 14: "Those who through the Church have accepted from the Father faith in Christ should be admitted to the catechumenate by means of liturgical ceremonies. The catechumenate means not simply a presentation of teachings and precepts, but a formation in the whole of Christian life and a sufficiently prolonged period of training; by these means the disciples will become bound to Christ as their master. Catechumens should therefore be properly initiated into the mystery of salvation and the practices of gospel living; by means of sacred rites celebrated at successive times, they should be led gradually into the life of faith, liturgy, and charity belonging to the people of God.

"Next, freed from the power of darkness, dying, buried, and risen again together with Christ through the sacraments of Christian initiation, they receive the Spirit of adoption of children, and with the whole people of God celebrate the memorial of the Lord's death and resurrection.

"There is a great need for a reform of the Lenten and Easter liturgy so that it will be a spiritual preparation of the catechumens for the celebration of the paschal mystery, the rites of which will include their being reborn to Christ through baptism.

"Christian initiation during the catechumenate is not the concern of catechists or priests alone, but of the whole community of believers and especially of godparents, so that from the outset the catechumens will have a sense of being part of the people of God. Moreover, because the Church's life is apostolic, catechumens should learn to take an active share in the evangelization and the building up of the Church through the witness of their life and the profession of their faith.

"Finally, the new code of canon law should set out clearly the juridic status of catechumens; they are already joined to the Church, already part of Christ's household, and are in many cases already living a life of faith, hope, and charity."

Decree on the Church's Missionary Activity *Ad gentes,* no. 15: "The Holy Spirit calls all to Christ through the seed of the word and the preaching of the Gospel and inspires in hearts the obedience of faith. When in the womb of the baptismal font the Spirit gives birth into a new life to those who believe in Christ, he gathers them all together into the one people of God, 'a chosen race, a royal priesthood, a holy nation, God's own people' (1 Pt. 2:9).

"As God's co-workers, therefore, missionaries are to create congregations of believers of a kind that, living in a way worthy of their calling, will carry out the divinely appointed offices of priest, prophet, and king. This is how the Christian community becomes a sign of God's presence in the world: by the eucharistic sacrifice it goes constantly with Christ to the Father; strengthened by God's word, it bears witness to Christ; it walks in charity and burns with the apostolic spirit. Right from the beginning the Christian community should be trained to be as far as possible self-sufficient in regard to its own needs."

Decree on the Pastoral Office of Bishops in the Church *Christus Dominus,* no. 14: "[Bishops] should . . . take steps toward restoring the instruction of adult catechumens or toward adapting it more effectively."

Decree on the Ministry and Life of Priests *Presbyterorum ordinis,* no. 5: "God, who alone is holy and the author of holiness, willed to take to himself as companions and helpers men who would humbly dedicate themselves to the work of making others holy. Through the ministry of the bishop God consecrates priests to be sharers by a special title in the priesthood of Christ. In exercising sacred functions they act therefore as the ministers of him who in the liturgy continually fulfills his priestly office on our behalf by the action of his Spirit. By baptism men and women are brought into the people of God and the Church; by the oil of the sick those who are ill find relief; by the celebration of Mass people sacramentally offer the sacrifice of Christ. But in administering all the sacraments, as St. Ignatius the Martyr already attested in the early days of the Church, priests, on various grounds, are linked hierarchically with their bishop and so, in a certain way, bring his presence to every gathering of the faithful.

"The other sacraments, like every ministry of the Church and every work of the apostolate, are linked with the holy eucharist and have it as their end. For the eucharist contains the Church's entire spiritual wealth, that is, Christ, himself. He is our Passover and living bread; through his flesh, made living and life-giving by the Holy Spirit, he is bringing life to people and thereby inviting them to offer themselves together with him, as well as their labors and all created things. The eucharist therefore stands as the source and apex of all evangelization: catechumens are led gradually toward a share in the eucharist and the faithful who already bear the seal of baptism and confirmation enter through the eucharist more fully into the Body of Christ."

Decree on the Ministry and Life of Priests *Presbyterorum ordinis*, no. 6: "The pastor's task is not limited to individual care of the faithful. It extends by right also to the formation of a genuine Christian community. But if a community spirit is to be properly cultivated it must embrace not only the local church but the universal Church. A local community ought not merely to promote the care of the faithful within itself, but should be imbued with the missionary spirit and smooth the path to Christ for all men. But it must regard as its special charge those under instruction and the newly converted who are gradually educated in knowing and living the Christian life" (Flannery translation).

B. Code of Canon Law (Translations are from: *Code of Canon Law: Latin—English Edition* [Washington, DC: The Canon Law Society of America, 1983])

206. *1.* Catechumens are in union with the Church in a special manner, that is, under the influence of the Holy Spirit, they ask to be incorporated into the Church by ex-

plicit choice and are therefore united with the Church by that choice just as by a life of faith, hope and charity which they lead; the Church already cherishes them as its own.
2. The Church has special care for catechumens; the Church invites them to lead the evangelical life and introduces them to the celebration of sacred rites, and grants them various prerogatives which are proper to Christians.

787. *1.* By the witness of their life and words missionaries are to establish a sincere dialogue with those who do not believe in Christ in order that through methods suited to their characteristics and culture avenues may be open to them by which they can be led to an understanding of the gospel message.
2. Missionaries are to see to it that they teach the truths of faith to those whom they judge to be ready to accept the gospel message so that these persons can be admitted to the reception of baptism when they freely request it.

788. *1.* After a period of pre-catechumenate has elapsed, persons who have manifested a willingness to embrace faith in Christ are to be admitted to the catechumenate in liturgical ceremonies and their names are to be registered in a book destined for this purpose.
2. Through instruction and an apprenticeship in the Christian life catechumens are suitably to be initiated into the mystery of salvation and introduced to the life of faith, liturgy, charity of the people of God and the apostolate.
3. It is the responsibility of the conference of bishops to issue statutes by which the catechumenate is regulated; these statutes are to determine what things are to be expected of catechumens and define what prerogatives are recognized as theirs.

789. Through a suitable instruction neophytes are to be formed to a more thorough understanding of the gospel truth and the baptismal duties to be fulfilled; they are to be imbued with a love of Christ and of His Church.

842. *2.* The sacraments of baptism, confirmation, and the Most Holy Eucharist are so interrelated that they are required for full Christian initiation.

851. *1.* An adult who intends to receive baptism is to be admitted to the catechumenate and, to the extent possible, be led through the several stages to sacramental initiation, in accord with the order of initiation adapted by the conference of bishops and the special norms published by it.

852. *1.* What is prescribed in the canons on the baptism of an adult is applicable to all who are no longer infants but have attained the use of reason.

863. The baptism of adults, at least those who have completed fourteen years of age is to be referred to the bishop so that it may be conferred by him, if he judges it expedient.

865. *1.* To be baptized, it is required that an adult have manifested the will to receive baptism, be sufficiently instructed in the truths of faith and in Christian obligations and be tested in the Christian life by means of the catechumenate; the adult is also to be exhorted to have sorrow for personal sins.
2. An adult in danger of death may be baptized if, having some knowledge of the principal truths of faith, the person has in any way manifested an intention of receiving baptism and promises to observe the commandments of the Christian religion.

866. Unless a grave reason prevents it, an adult who is baptized is to be confirmed immediately after baptism and participate in the celebration of the Eucharist, also receiving Communion.

869. *1.* If there is a doubt whether one has been baptized or whether baptism was validly conferred and the doubt remains after serious investigation, baptism is to be conferred conditionally.
2. Those baptized in a non-Catholic ecclesial community are not to be baptized conditionally unless, after an examination of the matter and the form of words used in the conferral of baptism and after a consideration of the intention of an adult baptized person and of the minister of the baptism, a serious reason for doubting the validity of the baptism is present.
3. If the conferral or the validity of the baptism in the cases

mentioned in nos. 1 & 2 remains doubtful, baptism is not to be conferred until the doctrine of the sacrament of baptism is explained to the person, if an adult, and the reasons for the doubtful validity of the baptism have been explained to the adult recipient or, in the case of an infant, to the parents.

883. The following have the faculty of administering confirmation by the law itself:

1. within the limits of their territory, those who are equivalent in law to the diocesan bishop;

2. with regard to the person in question, the presbyter who by reason of office or mandate of the diocesan bishop baptizes one who is no longer an infant or one already baptized whom he admits into the full communion of the Catholic Church;

3. with regard to those in danger of death, the pastor or indeed any presbyter.

884. 1. The diocesan bishop is to administer confirmation personally or see that it is administered by another bishop, but if necessity requires he may give the faculty to administer this sacrament to one or more specified presbyters.
2. For a grave cause, a bishop and likewise a presbyter who has the faculty to confirm by virtue of law or special concession of competent authority may in individual cases associate presbyters with themselves so that they may administer the sacrament.

885. 2. A presbyter who has this faculty must use it for those in whose favor the faculty was granted.

1170. Blessings, to be imparted especially to Catholics, can also be given to catechumens and even to non-Catholics unless a church prohibition precludes this.

1183. 1. As regards funeral rites catechumens are to be considered members of the Christian faithful.

The Rite of Baptism for Children

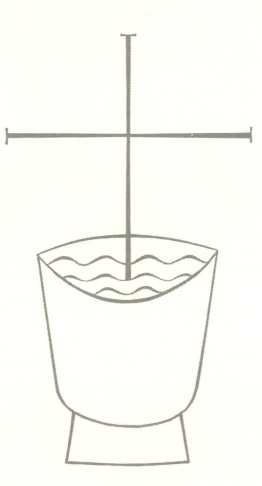

RITE OF BAPTISM FOR CHILDREN

RITE OF BAPTISM FOR CHILDREN

Decree
Baptism of Children (1-31)

CHAPTER I
RITE OF BAPTISM FOR SEVERAL CHILDREN

Reception of the Children (32-43)

Liturgy of the Word
Scripture Readings and Homily (44-46)
Intercessions (Prayer of the Faithful) (47-48)
Prayer of Exorcism and Anointing before Baptism (49-52)

Celebration of the Sacrament (53)
Blessing and Invocation of God over Baptismal Water (54-55)
Renunciation of Sin and Profession of Faith (56-59)
Baptism (60-61)

Explanatory Rites
Anointing after Baptism (62)
Clothing with White Garment (63)
Lighted Candle (64)
Ephphetha or Prayer over Ears and Mouth (65-66)

Conclusion of the Rite (67)
Lord's Prayer (68-69)
Blessing and Dismissal (70-71)

CHAPTER II
RITE OF BAPTISM FOR ONE CHILD

Reception of the Child (72-80)

Liturgy of the Word
Scriptural Readings and Homily (81-83)
Intercessions (Prayer of the Faithful) (84-85)
Prayer of Exorcism and Anointing before Baptism (86-89)

CHAPTER IV
RITE OF BAPTISM FOR CHILDREN
ADMINISTERED BY A CATECHIST WHEN NO
PRIEST OR DEACON IS AVAILABLE

Reception of the Children (132-136)

Liturgy of the Word
Reading and Homily or Short Talk (137-138)
Intercessions (Prayer of the Faithful) (139-140)

Celebration of the Sacrament (141)
Blessing and Invocation of God over Baptismal Water (141-143)
Renunciation of Sin and Profession of Faith (144-147)
Baptism (148-150)

Explanatory Rites (151)
Clothing with White Garment (152)
Lighted Candle (153)

Conclusion of the Rite
Lord's Prayer (154-155)
Blessing and Dismissal (156)

CHAPTER V
RITE OF BAPTISM FOR CHILDREN IN DANGER
OF DEATH WHEN NO PRIEST OR DEACON IS
AVAILABLE (157-164)

CHAPTER VI
RITE OF BRINGING A BAPTIZED CHILD TO
THE CHURCH

Reception of the Child (165-171)

Liturgy of the Word
Readings and Homily (172-174)
Intercessions (Prayer of the Faithful) (175-177)

Explanatory Rites
Anointing after Baptism (178)
Clothing with White Garment (179)
Lighted Candle (180)

Conclusion of the Rite
Lord's Prayer (181-182)
Blessing and Dismissal (183-185)

CHAPTER VII
VARIOUS TEXTS FOR USE IN THE
CELEBRATION OF BAPTISM FOR CHILDREN

I. Scriptural Readings (186-215)
II. Other Forms of the Intercessions (Prayer of the Faithful) (216-220)
III. Another Form of the Prayer of Exorcism (221)
IV. Blessing and Invocation of God over Baptismal Water (222-224)
V. Acclamations and Hymns (225-245)
VI. Forms of the Final Blessing (246-249)

APPENDIX

Litany of the Saints

Special Invocations

SACRED CONGREGATION FOR DIVINE WORSHIP

Prot. n. R 23/969

DECREE

Vatican Council II decreed that the rite of baptism for children in the Roman Ritual was to be revised in order that: the rite might be better adapted to the actual condition of children; the role and responsibilities of parents and godparents might be more clearly expressed; suitable adaptations might be made for the baptism of a large number of people; suitable adaptations might likewise be made for a great number of recipients or for baptism administered by catechists in mission areas or by others in circumstances when the ordinary minister is unavailable; a rite would be composed to make it clear that children baptized according to the shorter rite have already been received into the Church (SC art. 67–69).

This revision has been carried out by the Consilium for the Implementation of the Constitution on the Sacred Liturgy. By his apostolic authority Pope Paul VI has approved and ordered the publication of this new rite of baptism for children to replace the rite given in the Roman Ritual.

Therefore this Sacred Congregation, acting on the express mandate of the Pope, promulgates this rite and sets 8 September 1969 as its effective date.

Anything to the contrary notwithstanding.

From the Congregation for Divine Worship, May 15, 1969, Feast of the Ascension.

Benno Cardinal Gut
Prefect

A. Bugnini
Secretary

INTRODUCTION

I. IMPORTANCE OF BAPTIZING CHILDREN

1. The term "children" or "infants" refers to those who have not yet reached the age of discernment and therefore cannot profess personal faith.

2. From the earliest times, the Church, to which the mission of preaching the Gospel and of baptizing was entrusted, has baptized not only adults but children as well. Our Lord said: "Unless a man is reborn in water and the Holy Spirit, he cannot enter the kingdom of God."[1] The Church has always understood these words to mean that children should not be deprived of baptism, because they are baptized in the faith of the Church, a faith proclaimed for them by their parents and godparents, who represent both the local Church and the whole society of saints and believers: "The whole Church is the mother of all and the mother of each."[2]

3. To fulfill the true meaning of the sacrament, children must later be formed in the faith in which they have been baptized. The foundation of this formation will be the sacrament itself that they have already received. Christian formation, which is their due, seeks to lead them gradually to learn God's plan in Christ, so that they may ultimately accept for themselves the faith in which they have been baptized.

II. MINISTRIES AND ROLES IN THE CELEBRATION OF BAPTISM

4. The people of God, that is, the Church, made present by the local community, has an important part to play in the baptism of both children and adults.

Before and after the celebration of the sacrament, the child has a right to the love and help of the community. During the rite, in addition to the ways of congregational participation mentioned in the General Introduction to Christian Initiation no. 7, the community exercises its duty when it expresses its assent together with the celebrant af-

[1]Jn 3:5.
[2]Augustine, *Ep.* 98, 5: PL 33, 362.

ter the profession of faith by the parents and godparents. In this way it is clear that the faith in which the children are baptized is not the private possession of the individual family, but the common treasure of the whole Church of Christ.

5. Because of the natural relationships, parents have a ministry and a responsibility in the baptism of infants more important than those of the godparents.

1. Before the celebration of the sacrament, it is of great importance that parents, moved by their own faith or with the help of friends or other members of the community, should prepare to take part in the rite with understanding. They should be provided with suitable means such as books, letters addressed to them, and catechisms designed for families. The pastor should make it his duty to visit them or see that they are visited; he should try to gather a group of families together and prepare them for the coming celebration by pastoral counsel and common prayer.

2. It is very important that the parents be present at the celebration in which their child is reborn in water and the Holy Spirit.

3. In the celebration of baptism, the father and mother have special parts to play. They listen to the words addressed to them by the celebrant, they join in prayer along with the congregation, and they exercise a genuine ministry when: a. they publicly ask that the child be baptized; b. they sign their child with the sign of the cross after the celebrant; c. they renounce Satan and recite the profession of faith; d. they (and especially the mother) carry the child to the font; e. they hold the lighted candle; f. they are blessed with the prayers formulated specifically for mothers and fathers.

4. A parent unable to make the profession of faith (for example, not being a Catholic) may keep silent. Such a parent, when making the request for the child's baptism is asked only to make arrangements or at least to give permission for the child's instruction in the faith of its baptism.

5. After baptism it is the responsibility of the parents, in their gratitude to God and in fidelity to the duty they have undertaken, to assist the child to know God, whose adopted child it has become, to prepare the child to receive

confirmation and participate in the holy eucharist. In this duty they are again to be helped by the parish priest (pastor) by suitable means.

6. Each child may have a godfather (*patrinus*) and a godmother (*matrina*), the word "godparents" is used in the rite to describe both.

7. In addition to what is said about the ordinary minister of baptism in the General Introduction to Christian Initiation nos. 11–15, the following should be noted:

1. It is the duty of the priest to prepare families for the baptism of their children and to help them in the task of Christian formation that they have undertaken. It is the duty of the bishop to coordinate such pastoral efforts in the diocese, with the help also of deacons and lay people.

2. It is also the duty of the priest to arrange that baptism is always celebrated with proper dignity and, as far as possible, adapted to the circumstances and wishes of the families concerned. All who perform the rite of baptism should do so with exactness and reverence; they must also try to be understanding and friendly to all.

III. TIME AND PLACE FOR BAPTISM OF CHILDREN

8. As for the time of baptism, the first consideration is the welfare of the child, that it may not be deprived of the benefit of the sacrament; then the health of the mother must be considered, so that, if at all possible, she too may be present. Then, as long as they do not interfere with the greater good of the child, there are pastoral considerations, such as allowing sufficient time to prepare the parents and to plan the actual celebration in order to bring out its true character effectively. Accordingly:

1. If the child is in danger of death, it is to be baptized without delay; this is permitted even when the parents are opposed and even when the infant is the child of non-Catholic parents. The baptism is conferred in the manner laid down in no. 21.

2. In other cases the parents, or at least one of them or whoever stands in the place of the parents, must consent to

the baptism of the infant. So that proper preparation may be made for the celebration of the sacrament, as soon as possible, if need be even before the child is born, the parents should be in touch with the pastor concerning the baptism.

3. An infant should be baptized within the first weeks after birth. In the complete absence of any well-founded hope that the infant will be brought up in the Catholic religion, the baptism is to be delayed, in conformity with the provisions of particular law (see no. 25), and the parents are to be informed of the reasons.

4. In the absence of the conditions laid down in nos. 2 and 3, it is for the pastor, keeping in mind whatever regulations have been laid down by the conference of bishops, to determine the time for the baptism of infants.

9. To bring out the paschal character of baptism, it is recommended that the sacrament be celebrated during the Easter Vigil or on Sunday, when the Church commemorates the Lord's resurrection. On Sunday, baptism may be celebrated even during Mass, so that the entire community may be present and the relationship between baptism and eucharist may be clearly seen; but this should not be done too often. Regulations for the celebration of baptism during the Easter Vigil or at Mass on Sunday will be set out later.

10. So that baptism may clearly appear as the sacrament of the Church's faith and of incorporation into the people of God, it should normally be celebrated in the parish church, which must have a baptismal font.

11. After consulting the local pastor, the local Ordinary may permit or direct that a baptismal font be placed in another church or oratory within the parish boundaries. In these places, too, the right to celebrate baptism belongs ordinarily to the pastor.

However, distance or other circumstances may make it seriously inconvenient for the candidate to go or be brought to the usual place for baptism. In such a case, the sacrament may and should be conferred in another, more accessible church or oratory, or even in some other suitable place. The provisions laid down here, nos. 8–9 and 15–22, on the time and the structure of the celebration are to be followed.

12. Outside a case of necessity, baptism is not to be celebrated in private homes, unless the local Ordinary has, for a serious reason, granted permission.

13. Unless the bishop decides otherwise (see no. 11), baptism should not be celebrated in hospitals, except in cases of emergency or some other compelling pastoral reason. But care should always be taken that the pastor is notified and that the parents are suitably prepared beforehand.

14. While the liturgy of the word is being celebrated, it is desirable that children should be taken to some other place. But provision must be made for the mothers or godmothers to attend the liturgy of the word; the children should therefore be entrusted to the care of other women.

IV. STRUCTURE OF THE RITE OF BAPTIZING CHILDREN

A. ORDER OF BAPTISM CELEBRATED BY THE ORDINARY MINISTER

15. Baptism, whether for one child, or for several, or even for a larger number, should be celebrated by the ordinary minister and with the full rite when there is no immediate danger of death.

16. The rite begins with the reception of the children. This is to indicate the desire of the parents and godparents, as well as the intention of the Church, concerning the celebration of the sacrament of baptism. These purposes are expressed in action when the parents and the celebrant trace the sign of the cross on the foreheads of the children.

17. Then the liturgy of the word is directed toward stirring up the faith of the parents, godparents, and congregation and toward praying in common for the fruits of baptism before the sacrament itself. This part of the celebration consists of the reading of one or more passages from holy Scripture; a homily, followed by a period of silence; the general intercessions, with its concluding prayer, drawn up in the style of an exorcism, to introduce either the anointing with the oil of catechumens or the laying on of hands.

18. In the celebration of the sacrament:

    1. The immediate preparation consists of:

        a. the solemn prayer of the celebrant, which, by invoking God and recalling his plan of salvation, blesses the water of baptism or makes reference to its earlier blessing;

        b. the renunciation of Satan on the part of parents and godparents and their profession of faith, to which is added the assent of the celebrant and the community; and the final interrogation of the parents and godparents.

    2. The sacrament itself consists of the washing in water by way of immersion or infusion, depending on local custom, and the invocation of the blessed Trinity.

    3. The completion of the sacrament consists, first, of the anointing with chrism, which signifies the royal priesthood of the baptized and enrollment into the company of the people of God; then of the ceremonies of the white garment, lighted candle, and *ephphetha* rite (the last of which is optional).

19. Before the altar to prefigure the future sharing in the eucharist, the celebrant introduces and all recite the Lord's Prayer, in which God's children pray to their Father in heaven. Finally, a prayer of blessing is said over the mothers, fathers, and all present, to ask the outpouring of God's grace upon them.

B. SHORTER RITE OF BAPTISM

20. In the shorter rite of baptism designed for the use of catechists,[3] the reception of the children, the celebration of the word of God, or the instruction by the minister, and the general intercessions are retained. Before the font, the minister offers a prayer invoking God and recalling the history of salvation as it relates to baptism. After the baptismal washing, an adapted formulary is recited in place of the anointing with chrism and the whole rite concludes in the customary way. The omissions, therefore, are the exorcism, the anointing with oil of catechumens and with chrism, and the *ephphetha* rite.

[3]See SC art. 68.

21. The shorter rite for baptizing a child in danger of death and in the absence of the ordinary minister has a twofold structure:

   1. At the moment of death or when there is urgency because of imminent danger of death, the minister,[4] omitting all other ceremonies, pours water (not necessarily blessed but real and natural water) on the head of the child and pronounces the customary formulary.[5]

   2. If, however, it is prudently judged that there is sufficient time, several of the faithful may be gathered together and, if one of them is able to lead the others in a short prayer, the following rite may be used: an explanation by the minister of the sacrament, a short set of general intercessions, the profession of faith by the parents or one godparent and the pouring of the water with the customary words. But if those present are uneducated, the minister of the sacrament should recite the profession of faith aloud and baptize according to the rite for use in danger of death.

22. In danger of death, the priest or deacon may also use this shorter form if necessary. If there is time and he has the sacred chrism, the pastor or other priest enjoying the same faculty should not fail to confer confirmation after baptism. In this case he omits the postbaptismal anointing with chrism.

V. ADAPTATIONS BY CONFERENCES OF BISHOPS OR BY BISHOPS

23. In addition to the adaptations provided for (see *Christian Initiation*, General Introduction, nos. 30–33), the baptismal rite for infants admits other variations, to be determined by the conferences of bishops.

24. As is indicated in the Roman Ritual, the following matters are left to the discretion of the conferences:

   1. As local customs may dictate, the questioning about the name of the child may be arranged in different ways: the name may have been given already or may be given during the rite of baptism.

   2. The anointing with oil of catechumens may be omitted (nos. 50, 87).

[4]See General Introduction to Christian Initiation no. 16.
[5]See ibid. no. 23.

3. The formulary of renunciation may be made more pointed and detailed (nos. 57, 94, 121).

4. If the number to be baptized is very great, the anointing with chrism may be omitted (no. 125).

5. The *ephphetha* rite may be retained (nos. 64, 101).

25. In many countries parents are sometimes not ready for the celebration of baptism or they ask for their children to be baptized even though the latter will not afterward receive a Christian education and will even lose the faith. Since to instruct such parents and to inquire about their faith in the course of the rite itself is not enough, conferences of bishops may issue pastoral directives, for the guidance of pastors, to determine a longer interval between birth and baptism.

26. It is for the bishop to decide for his diocese whether catechists may give the homily on their own or only by reading a written text.

VI. ADAPTATIONS BY THE MINISTER

27. During meetings to prepare the parents for the baptism of their children, it is important that the instruction should be supported by prayer and religious rites. For this the various elements provided in the rite of baptism for the celebration of the word of God will prove helpful.

28. When the baptism of children is celebrated as part of the Easter Vigil, the ritual should be arranged as follows:

1. At a convenient time and place before the Easter Vigil the rite of receiving the children is celebrated. The liturgy of the word may be omitted at the end, according to circumstances, and the prayer of exorcism is said, followed by the anointing with oil of catechumens.

2. The celebration of the sacrament (nos. 56–58, 60–63) takes place after the blessing of the water, as is indicated in the rite of the Easter Vigil.

3. The assent of the celebrant and community (no. 59) is omitted, as are the presentation of the lighted candle (no. 64) and the *ephphetha* rite (no. 65).

4. The conclusion of the rite (nos. 67–71) is omitted.

29. If baptism takes place during Sunday Mass, the Mass for that Sunday is used, or, on the Sundays of the Christmas season and of Ordinary Time, the Mass for the Baptism of Children, and the celebration takes place as follows:

1. The rite of receiving the children (nos. 33–43) takes place at the beginning of Mass and the greeting and penitential rite of the Mass are omitted.

2. In the liturgy of the word:

> a. The readings are taken from the Mass of the Sunday. But in the Christmas season and in Ordinary Time they may also be taken from those given in the Lectionary for Mass (757–761) or in this baptismal rite (nos. 44, 186–215).
>
> When a ritual Mass is prohibited, one of the readings may be taken from the texts provided for the celebration of baptism for children, with attention paid to the pastoral benefit of the faithful and the character of the liturgical day.
>
> b. The homily is based on the sacred texts, but should take account of the baptism that is to take place.
>
> c. The *Creed* is not said, since the profession of faith by the entire community before baptism takes its place.
>
> d. The general intercessions are taken from those used in the rite of baptism (nos. 47–48). At the end, however, before the invocation of the saints, petitions are added for the universal Church and the needs of the world.

3. The celebration of baptism continues with the prayer of exorcism, anointing, and other ceremonies described in the rite (nos. 49–66).

4. After the celebration of baptism, the Mass continues in the usual way with the presentation of the gifts.

5. For the blessing at the end of Mass, the priest may use one of the formularies provided in the rite of baptism (nos. 70, 247–249).

30. If baptism is celebrated during Mass on weekdays, it is arranged in basically the same way as on Sunday, but the readings for the liturgy of the word may be taken from those that are provided in the rite of baptism (nos. 44, 186–194, 204–215).

31. In accordance with the General Introduction no. 34, the minister may make some adaptations in the rite as circumstances require, such as:

1. If the child's mother died in childbirth, this should be taken into account in the opening instruction (no. 36), general intercessions (nos. 47, 217–220), and final blessing (nos. 70, 247–248).

2. In the dialogue with the parents (nos. 37–38, 76–77), their answers should be taken into account: if they have not answered *Baptism*, but *Faith*, or *The grace of Christ*, or *Entrance into the Church*, or *Everlasting life*, then the minister does not begin by saying *Baptism*, but uses *Faith*, or *The grace of Christ*, and so forth.

3. The rite of bringing a child already baptized to the church (nos. 165–185), which has been drawn up for use only when the child has been baptized in danger of death, should be adapted to cover other contingencies, for example, when children have been baptized during a time of religious persecution or temporary disagreement between the parents.

(N.B. 1. The texts of the psalms and of the New Testament are taken from the Neo-Vulgate edition of the Bible. 2. Liturgical texts written in the masculine gender can be changed to the feminine; those written in the singular can be changed to the plural.)

CHAPTER I

RITE OF BAPTISM FOR SEVERAL CHILDREN

RECEPTION OF THE CHILDREN

32. If possible, baptism should take place on Sunday, the day on which the Church celebrates the paschal mystery. It should be conferred in a communal celebration for all the recently born children, and in the presence of the faithful, or at least of relatives, friends, and neighbors, who are all to take an active part in the rite.

33. It is the role of the father and mother, accompanied by the godparents, to present the child to the Church for baptism.

34. If there are very many children, and if there are several priests or deacons present, these may help the celebrant in the parts referred to below.

35. The people may sing a psalm or hymn suitable for the occasion. Meanwhile the celebrating priest or deacon, vested in alb or surplice, with a stole (with or without a cope) of festive color, and accompanied by the ministers, goes to the entrance of the church or to that part of the church where the parents and godparents are waiting with those who are to be baptized.

36. The celebrant greets all present, and especially the parents and godparents, reminding them briefly of the joy with which the parents welcomed their children as gifts from God, the source of life, who now wishes to bestow his own life on these little ones.

37. First the celebrant questions the parents of each child.

Celebrant:
What name do you give your child? (or: **have you given?)**
Parents: **N.**

Celebrant:
What do you ask of God's Church for N.?
Parents: **Baptism.**

The celebrant may choose other words for this dialogue.
The first reply may be given by someone other than the parents
if local custom gives him/her the right to name the child.
In the second response the parents may use other words,
e.g., **faith** or **the grace of Christ** or **entrance into the Church**
or **eternal life.**

38. If there are many children to be baptized, the celebrant
asks the names from all the parents together, and each
family replies in turn. The second question may also be
asked of all together.

Celebrant:
What name do you give each of these children? (or:
have you given?)
Parents: **N., N.,** etc.

Celebrant:
What do you ask of God's Church for your children?
All: **Baptism.**

39. The celebrant speaks to the parents in these or similar
words:
**You have asked to have your children baptized. In
doing so you are accepting the responsibility of training them in the practice of the faith. It will be your
duty to bring them up to keep God's commandments
as Christ taught us, by loving God and our neighbor.
Do you clearly understand what you are undertaking?**
Parents: **We do.**

This response is given by each family individually. But if
there are many children to be baptized, the response may be
given by all together.

40. Then the celebrant turns to the godparents and addresses them in these or similar words:

Are you ready to help these parents in their duty as Christian mothers and fathers?
All the godparents: **We are.**

41. The celebrant continues:
N. and N. (or, My dear children), the Christian community welcomes you with great joy. In its name I claim you for Christ our Savior by the sign of the cross. I now trace the cross on your foreheads, and invite your parents (and godparents) to do the same.

He signs each child on the forehead, in silence. Then he invites the parents and, if this seems appropriate, the godparents to do the same.

42. The celebrant invites the parents, godparents, and the others to take part in the liturgy of the word. If circumstances permit, there is a procession to the place where this will be celebrated, during which a song is sung, e.g., Psalm 85:7, 8, 9ab:

**Will you not give us life;
    and shall not your people rejoice in you?
Show us, O Lord, your kindness,
    and grant us your salvation.
I will hear what God proclaims;
    the Lord—for he proclaims peace to his people.**

43. The children to be baptized may be carried to a separate place, where they remain until the end of the liturgy of the word.

LITURGY OF THE WORD

READINGS AND HOMILY
44. One or even two of the following gospel passages are read, during which all may sit if convenient.

John 3:1-6 The meeting with Nicodemus.
Matthew 28:18-20 The apostles are sent to preach the gospel and to baptize.
Mark 1:9-11 The baptism of Jesus.

Mark 10:13-16 Let the little children come to me.

The passages listed in nos. 186-194 and 204-215 may be chosen, or other passages which better meet the wishes or needs of the parents. Between the readings, responsorial psalms or verses may be sung as given in nos. 195-203.

45. After the reading, the celebrant gives a short homily, explaining to those present the significance of what has been read. His purpose will be to lead them to a deeper understanding of the mystery of baptism and to encourage the parents and godparents to a ready acceptance of the responsibilities which arise from the sacrament.

46. After the homily, or in the course of or after the litany, it is desirable to have a period of silence while all pray at the invitation of the celebrant. If convenient, a suitable song follows, e.g., one chosen from nos. 225-245.

INTERCESSIONS (PRAYER OF THE FAITHFUL)

47. Then the intercessions (prayer of the faithful) are said:

Celebrant:

My brothers and sisters,* let us ask our Lord Jesus Christ to look lovingly on these children who are to be baptized, on their parents and godparents, and on all the baptized.

Assisting Minister:

By the mystery of your death and resurrection, bathe these children in light, give them the new life of baptism and welcome them into your holy Church.
All: **Lord, hear our prayer.**

Assisting Minister:

Through baptism and confirmation, make them your faithful followers and witnesses to your gospel.
All: **Lord, hear our prayer.**

---

*At the discretion of the priest, other words which seem more suitable under the circumstances, such as **friends** or **dearly beloved** or **brethren**, may be used. This also applies to parallel instances in the liturgy.

Assisting Minister:
Lead them by a holy life to the joys of God's kingdom.
All: **Lord, hear our prayer.**

Assisting Minister:
Make the lives of their parents and godparents examples of faith to inspire these children.
All: **Lord, hear our prayer.**

Assisting Minister:
Keep their families always in your love.
All: **Lord, hear our prayer.**

Assisting Minister:
Renew the grace of our baptism in each one of us.
All: **Lord, hear our prayer.**

Other forms may be chosen from nos. 217-220.

48. The celebrant next invites all to invoke the saints. At this point, if the children have been taken out, they are brought back.

Holy Mary, Mother of God,	**pray for us.**
Saint John the Baptist,	**pray for us.**
Saint Joseph,	**pray for us.**
Saint Peter and Saint Paul,	**pray for us.**

The names of other saints may be added, especially the patrons of the children to be baptized, and of the church or locality. The litany concludes:

All you saints of God,	**pray for us.**

PRAYER OF EXORCISM AND ANOINTING BEFORE BAPTISM

49. After the invocations, the celebrant says:

A
Almighty and ever-living God,
you sent your only Son into the world
to cast out the power of Satan, spirit of evil,
to rescue man from the kingdom of darkness,

and bring him into the splendor of your kingdom of
     light.
We pray for these children:
set them free from original sin,
make them temples of your glory,
and send your Holy Spirit to dwell within them.
We ask this through Christ our Lord.
All: **Amen.**

Another form of the prayer of exorcism:

B
Almighty God,
you sent your only Son
to rescue us from the slavery of sin,
and to give us the freedom
only your sons and daughters enjoy.
We now pray for these children
who will have to face the world with its temptations,
and fight the devil in all his cunning.
Your Son died and rose again to save us.
By his victory over sin and death,
cleanse these children from the stain of original sin.
Strengthen them with the grace of Christ,
and watch over them at every step in life's journey.
We ask this through Christ our Lord.
All: **Amen.**

50. The celebrant continues:

We anoint you with the oil of salvation
in the name of Christ our Savior;
may he strengthen you with his power,
who lives and reigns for ever and ever.
All: **Amen.**

He anoints each child on the breast with the oil of catechumens. If the number of children is large, the anointing
may be done by several ministers.

51. If, for serious reasons, the conference of bishops so decides, the anointing before baptism may be omitted. [In

the United States, it may be omitted only when the minister of baptism judges the omission to be pastorally necessary or desirable.] In that case the celebrant says once only:

May you have strength in the power of Christ our Savior, who lives and reigns for ever and ever.
All: **Amen.**

And immediately he lays his hand on each child in silence.

52. If the baptistry is located outside the church or is not within view of the congregation, all go there in procession.

If the baptistry is located within view of the congregation, the celebrant, parents, and godparents go there with the children, while the others remain in their places.

If, however, the baptistry cannot accommodate the congregation, the baptism may be celebrated in a suitable place within the church, and the parents and godparents bring the child forward at the proper moment.

Meanwhile, if it can be done suitably, an appropriate song is sung, e.g., Psalm 23:

The Lord is my shepherd; I shall not want.
In verdant pastures he gives me repose;
Beside restful waters he leads me;
he refreshes my soul.
He guides me in right paths
for his name's sake.
Even though I walk in the dark valley
I fear no evil; for you are at my side
With your rod and your staff
that give me courage.
You spread the table before me
in the sight of my foes;
You anoint my head with oil;
my cup overflows.
Only goodness and kindness follow me
all the days of my life;
And I shall dwell in the house of the Lord
for years to come.

CELEBRATION OF THE SACRAMENT

53. When they come to the font, the celebrant briefly reminds the congregation of the wonderful work of God whose plan it is to sanctify man, body and soul, through water. He may use these or similar words:

A
My dear brothers and sisters, we now ask God to give these children new life in abundance through water and the Holy Spirit.

B
My dear brothers and sisters, God uses the sacrament of water to give his divine life to those who believe in him. Let us turn to him, and ask him to pour his gift of life from this font on the children he has chosen.

BLESSING AND INVOCATION OF GOD OVER BAPTISMAL WATER

54. Then, turning to the font, he says the following blessing (outside the Easter season):

A
Father,
you give us grace through sacramental signs,
which tell us of the wonders of your unseen power.

In baptism we use your gift of water,
which you have made a rich symbol of the grace
you give us in this sacrament.

At the very dawn of creation
your Spirit breathed on the waters,
making them the wellspring of all holiness.

The waters of the great flood
you made a sign of the waters of baptism
that make an end of sin
and a new beginning of goodness.

Through the waters of the Red Sea
you led Israel out of slavery

to be an image of God's holy people,
set free from sin by baptism.

In the waters of the Jordan
your Son was baptized by John
and anointed with the Spirit.

Your Son willed that water and blood should flow
    from his side
as he hung upon the cross.

After his resurrection he told his disciples:
"Go out and teach all nations,
baptizing them in the name of the Father, and of the
    Son, and of the Holy Spirit."

Father,
look now with love upon your Church
and unseal for it the fountain of baptism.

By the power of the Holy Spirit
give to this water the grace of your Son,
so that in the sacrament of baptism
all those whom you have created in your likeness
may be cleansed from sin
and rise to a new birth of innocence
by water and the Holy Spirit.

The celebrant touches the water with his right hand and
continues:

We ask you, Father, with your Son
to send the Holy Spirit upon the waters of this font.
May all who are buried with Christ in the death of
    baptism
rise also with him to newness of life.

We ask this through Christ our Lord.

All: **Amen.**

Other forms of the blessing, nos. 223-224, may be chosen.

55. During the Easter season, if there is baptismal water which was consecrated at the Easter Vigil, the blessing and invocation of God over the water are nevertheless included, so that this theme of thanksgiving and petition may find a place in the baptism. The forms of this blessing and invocation are those found in nos. 223-224, with the variation indicated at the end of each text.

RENUNCIATION OF SIN AND PROFESSION OF FAITH

56. The celebrant speaks to the parents and godparents in these words:

Dear parents and godparents: You have come here to present these children for baptism. By water and the Holy Spirit they are to receive the gift of new life from God, who is love.

On your part, you must make it your constant care to bring them up in the practice of the faith. See that the divine life which God gives them is kept safe from the poison of sin, to grow always stronger in their hearts.

If your faith makes you ready to accept this responsibility, renew now the vows of your own baptism. Reject sin; profess your faith in Christ Jesus. This is the faith of the Church. This is the faith in which these children are about to be baptized.

57. The celebrant questions the parents and godparents.

A
Celebrant:
Do you reject Satan?
Parents and godparents: **I do.**

Celebrant:
And all his works?
Parents and godparents: **I do.**

Celebrant:
And all his empty promises?
Parents and godparents: **I do.**

or **B**
Celebrant:
Do you reject sin so as to live in the freedom of God's children?
Parents and godparents: **I do.**

Celebrant:
Do you reject the glamor of evil, and refuse to be mastered by sin?
Parents and godparents: **I do.**

Celebrant:
Do you reject Satan, father of sin and prince of darkness?
Parents and godparents: **I do.**

According to circumstances, this second form may be expressed with greater precision by the conferences of bishops, especially in places where it is necessary for the parents and godparents to reject superstitious and magical practices used with children.

58. Next the celebrant asks for the threefold profession of faith from the parents and godparents:

Celebrant:
Do you believe in God, the Father almighty,
  creator of heaven and earth?
Parents and godparents: **I do.**

Celebrant:
Do you believe in Jesus Christ, his only Son, our Lord,
  who was born of the Virgin Mary,
  was crucified, died, and was buried,
  rose from the dead,
  and is now seated at the right hand of the Father?
Parents and godparents: **I do.**

Celebrant:
Do you believe in the Holy Spirit,
  the holy catholic Church, the communion of saints,

the forgiveness of sins, the resurrection of the body, and the life everlasting?
Parents and godparents: **I do.**

59. The celebrant and the congregation give their assent to the profession of faith:

Celebrant:
This is our faith. This is the faith of the Church. We are proud to profess it, in Christ Jesus our Lord.
All: **Amen.**

If desired, some other formula may be used instead, or a suitable song by which the community expresses its faith with a single voice.

BAPTISM

60. The celebrant invites the first of the families to the font. Using the name of the individual child, he questions the parents and godparents.

Celebrant:
Is it your will that N. should be baptized in the faith of the Church, which we have all professed with you?
Parents and godparents: **It is.**

He baptizes the child, saying:

N., I baptize you in the name of the Father,

He immerses the child or pours water upon it.

and of the Son,

He immerses the child or pours water upon it a second time.

and of the Holy Spirit.

He immerses the child or pours water upon it a third time.

He asks the same question and performs the same action for each child.

After each baptism it is appropriate for the people to sing a short acclamation. (See nos. 225-245).

If the baptism is performed by the pouring of water, it is preferable that the child be held by the mother (or father). Where, however, it is felt that the existing custom should be retained, the godmother (or godfather) may hold the child. If baptism is by immersion, the mother or father (godmother or godfather) lifts the child out of the font.

61. If the number of children to be baptized is large, and other priests or deacons are present, these may baptize some of the children in the way described above, and with the same form.

EXPLANATORY RITES

ANOINTING AFTER BAPTISM

62. Then the celebrant says:

**The God of power and Father of our Lord Jesus
  Christ
has freed you from sin
and brought you to new life
through water and the Holy Spirit.**

**He now anoints you with the chrism of salvation,
so that, united with his people,
you may remain for ever a member of Christ
who is Priest, Prophet, and King.**

All: **Amen.**

Next, the celebrant anoints each child on the crown of the head with chrism, in silence.
If the number of children is large and other priests or deacons are present, these may anoint some of the children with chrism.

CLOTHING WITH WHITE GARMENT

63. The celebrant says:

**(N. and N.,) you have become a new creation, and
have clothed yourselves in Christ.**

See in this white garment the outward sign of your Christian dignity. With your family and friends to help you by word and example, bring that dignity unstained into the everlasting life of heaven.
All: **Amen.**

The white garments are put on the children. A different color is not permitted unless demanded by local custom. It is desirable that the families provide the garments.

LIGHTED CANDLE

64. The celebrant takes the Easter candle and says:

Receive the light of Christ.

Someone from each family (e.g., the father or godfather) lights the child's candle from the Easter candle.

The celebrant then says:

Parents and godparents, this light is entrusted to you to be kept burning brightly. These children of yours have been enlightened by Christ. They are to walk always as children of the light. May they keep the flame of faith alive in their hearts. When the Lord comes, may they go out to meet him with all the saints in the heavenly kingdom.

EPHPHETHA OR PRAYER OVER EARS AND MOUTH

65. If the conference of bishops decides to preserve the practice, the rite of *Ephphetha* follows. [In the United States it may be performed at the discretion of the minister.] The celebrant touches the ears and mouth of each child with his thumb, saying:

The Lord Jesus made the deaf hear and the dumb speak. May he soon touch your ears to receive his word, and your mouth to proclaim his faith, to the praise and glory of God the Father.
All: **Amen.**

66. If the number of children is large, the celebrant says the formula once, but does not touch the ears and mouth.

CONCLUSION OF THE RITE

67. Next there is a procession to the altar, unless the baptism was performed in the sanctuary. The lighted candles are carried for the children.
A baptismal song is appropriate at this time, e.g.:

**You have put on Christ,
in him you have been baptized.
Alleluia, alleluia.**

Other songs may be chosen from nos. 225-245.

LORD'S PRAYER

68. The celebrant stands in front of the altar and addresses the parents, godparents, and the whole assembly in these or similar words:

Dearly beloved, these children have been reborn in baptism. They are now called children of God, for so indeed they are. In confirmation they will receive the fullness of God's Spirit. In holy communion they will share the banquet of Christ's sacrifice, calling God

their Father in the midst of the Church. In their name, in the Spirit of our common sonship, let us pray together in the words our Lord has given us:

69. All present join the celebrant in singing or saying:

Our Father. . . .

BLESSING AND DISMISSAL

70. The celebrant first blesses the mothers, who hold the children in their arms, then the fathers, and lastly the entire assembly:

A
Celebrant:
God the Father, through his Son, the Virgin Mary's child, has brought joy to all Christian mothers, as they see the hope of eternal life shine on their children. May he bless the mothers of these children.

They now thank God for the gift of their children.
May they be one with them in thanking him for ever
in heaven, in Christ Jesus our Lord.
All: **Amen.**

Celebrant:
**God is the giver of all life, human and divine. May he
bless the fathers of these children. With their wives
they will be the first teachers of their children in the
ways of faith. May they be also the best of teachers,
bearing witness to the faith by what they say and do,
in Christ Jesus our Lord.**
All: **Amen.**

Celebrant:
**By God's gift, through water and the Holy Spirit, we
are reborn to everlasting life. In his goodness, may he
continue to pour out his blessings upon all present,
who are his sons and daughters. May he make them
always, wherever they may be, faithful members of
his holy people. May he send his peace upon all who
are gathered here, in Christ Jesus our Lord.**
All: **Amen.**

Celebrant:
**May almighty God, the Father, and the Son, ✝ and
the Holy Spirit, bless you.**
All: **Amen.**

Celebrant: **Go in peace.**
All: **Thanks be to God.**

Other forms of the final blessing, nos. 247, 248, and 249
may be chosen.

B
Celebrant:
**May God the almighty Father, who filled the world
with joy by giving us his only Son, bless these
newly-baptized children. May they grow to be more
fully like Jesus Christ our Lord.**
All: **Amen.**

Celebrant:
May almighty God, who gives life on earth and in heaven, bless the parents of these children. They thank him now for the gift he has given them. May they always show that gratitude in action by loving and caring for their children.
All: **Amen.**

Celebrant:
May almighty God, who has given us a new birth by water and the Holy Spirit, generously bless all of us who are his faithful children. May we always live as his people, and may he bless all here present with his peace.
All: **Amen.**

Celebrant:
May almighty God, the Father, and the Son, ✝ and the Holy Spirit, bless you.
All: **Amen.**

Celebrant:
Go in peace.
All: **Thanks be to God.**

C
Celebrant:
May God, the source of life and love, who fills the hearts of mothers with love for their children, bless the mothers of these newly-baptized children. As they thank God for a safe delivery, may they find joy in the love, growth, and holiness of their children.
All: **Amen.**

Celebrant:
May God, the Father and model of all fathers, help these fathers to give good example, so that their children will grow to be mature Christians in all the fullness of Jesus Christ.
All: **Amen.**

Celebrant:

May God, who loves all people, bless all the relatives and friends who are gathered here. In his mercy, may he guard them from evil and give them his abundant peace.
All: **Amen.**

Celebrant:

And may almighty God, the Father, and the Son, ✝ and the Holy Spirit, bless you.
All: **Amen.**

Celebrant:

Go in peace.
All: **Thanks be to God.**

D

Celebrant:

My brothers and sisters, we entrust you all to the mercy and help of God the almighty Father, his only Son, and the Holy Spirit. May he watch over your life, and may we all walk by the light of faith, and attain the good things he has promised us. And may almighty God, the Father, and the Son, ✝ and the Holy Spirit, bless you.
All: **Amen.**

Celebrant:

Go in peace.
All: **Thanks be to God.**

71. After the blessing, all may sing a hymn which suitably expresses thanksgiving and Easter joy, or they may sing the song of the Blessed Virgin Mary, the Magnificat.

Where there is the practice of bringing the baptized child to the altar of the blessed Virgin, this custom is observed if appropriate.

CHAPTER II

RITE OF BAPTISM FOR ONE CHILD

RECEPTION OF THE CHILD

72. If possible, baptism should take place on Sunday, the day on which the Church celebrates the paschal mystery. It should be conferred in a communal celebration in the presence of the faithful, or at least of relatives, friends, and neighbors, who are all to take an active part in the rite.

73. It is the role of the father and mother, accompanied by the godparents, to present the child to the Church for baptism.

74. The people may sing a psalm or hymn suitable for the occasion. Meanwhile the celebrating priest or deacon, vested in alb or surplice, with a stole (with or without a cope) of festive color, and accompanied by the ministers, goes to the entrance of the church or to that part of the church where the parents and godparents are waiting with the child.

75. The celebrant greets all present, and especially the parents and godparents, reminding them briefly of the joy with which the parents welcomed this child as a gift from God, the source of life, who now wishes to bestow his own life on this little one.

76. First the celebrant questions the parents:

Celebrant:
What name do you give your child? (or: **have you given?**)
Parents: **N.**

Celebrant:
What do you ask of God's Church for N.?
Parents: **Baptism.**

The celebrant may choose other words for this dialogue.
The first reply may be given by someone other than the parents if local custom gives him/her the right to name the child.

In the second response the parents may use other words, such as, **faith** or **the grace of Christ** or **entrance into the Church** or **eternal life.**

77. The celebrant speaks to the parents in these or similar words:

You have asked to have your child baptized. In doing so you are accepting the responsibility of training him (her) in the practice of the faith. It will be your duty to bring him (her) up to keep God's commandments as Christ taught us, by loving God and our neighbor. Do you clearly understand what you are undertaking?
Parents: **We do.**

78. Then the celebrant turns to the godparents and addresses them in these or similar words:

Are you ready to help the parents of this child in their duty as Christian parents?
Godparents: **We are.**

79. The celebrant continues:

N., the Christian community welcomes you with great joy. In its name I claim you for Christ our Savior by the sign of his cross. I now trace the cross on your forehead, and invite your parents (and godparents) to do the same.

He signs the child on the forehead, in silence. Then he invites the parents and (if it seems appropriate) the godparents to do the same.

80. The celebrant invites the parents, godparents, and the others to take part in the liturgy of the word. If circumstances permit, there is a procession to the place where this will be celebrated, during which a song is sung, e.g., Psalm 85:7, 8, 9ab:

Will you not give us life;
    and shall not your people rejoice in you?
Show us, O Lord, your kindness,
    and grant us your salvation.

**I will hear what God proclaims;
the Lord—for he proclaims peace to his people.**

LITURGY OF THE WORD

READINGS AND HOMILY

81. One or even two of the following gospel passages are read, during which all may sit if convenient.

John 3:1-6 The meeting with Nicodemus.
Matthew 28:18-20 The apostles are sent to preach the gospel and to baptize.
Mark 1:9-11 The baptism of Jesus.
Mark 10:13-16 Let the little children come to me.

The passages listed in nos. 186-194 and 204-215 may be chosen, or other passages which better meet the wishes or needs of the parents. Between the readings, responsorial psalms or verses may be sung as given in nos. 195-203.

82. After the reading, the celebrant gives a short homily, explaining to those present the significance of what has been read. His purpose will be to lead them to a deeper understanding of the mystery of baptism and to encourage the parents and godparents to a ready acceptance of the responsibilities which arise from the sacrament.

83. After the homily, or in the course of or after the litany, it is desirable to have a period of silence while all pray at the invitation of the celebrant. If convenient, a suitable song follows, such as one chosen from nos. 225-245.

INTERCESSIONS (PRAYER OF THE FAITHFUL)

84. Then the intercessions (prayer of the faithful) are said:

Celebrant:
My dear brothers and sisters, let us ask our Lord Jesus Christ to look lovingly on this child who is to be baptized, on his (her) parents and godparents, and on all the baptized.

Assisting Minister:

By the mystery of your death and resurrection, bathe this child in light, give him (her) the new life of baptism and welcome him (her) into your holy Church.
All: **Lord, hear our prayer.**

Assisting Minister:

Through baptism and confirmation, make him (her) your faithful follower and a witness to your gospel.
All: **Lord, hear our prayer.**

Assisting Minister:

Lead him (her) by a holy life to the joys of God's kingdom.
All: **Lord, hear our prayer.**

Assisting Minister:

Make the lives of his (her) parents and godparents examples of faith to inspire this child.
All: **Lord, hear our prayer.**

Assisting Minister:

Keep his (her) family always in your love.
All: **Lord, hear our prayer.**

Assisting Minister:

Renew the grace of our baptism in each one of us.
All: **Lord, hear our prayer.**

Other forms may be chosen from nos. 217-220.

85. The celebrant next invites all present to invoke the saints.

Holy Mary, Mother of God,	pray for us.
Saint John the Baptist,	pray for us.
Saint Joseph,	pray for us.
Saint Peter and Saint Paul,	pray for us.

The names of other saints may be added, especially the patrons of the child to be baptized, and of the church or locality. The litany concludes:

All holy men and women,	pray for us.

PRAYER OF EXORCISM AND ANOINTING BEFORE BAPTISM

86. After the invocation, the celebrant says:

Almighty and ever-living God,
you sent your only Son into the world
to cast out the power of Satan, spirit of evil,
to rescue man from the kingdom of darkness,
and bring him into the splendor of your kingdom of
**   light.**
We pray for this child:
set him (her) free from original sin,
make him (her) a temple of your glory,
and send your Holy Spirit to dwell with him (her).
We ask this through Christ our Lord.
All: **Amen.**

For another form of the prayer of exorcism, see no. 221.

87. The celebrant continues:

We anoint you with the oil of salvation
in the name of Christ our Savior;
may he strengthen you with his power,
who lives and reigns for ever and ever.
All: **Amen.**

He anoints the child on the breast with the oil of catechumens.

88. If, for serious reasons, the conference of bishops so decides, the anointing before baptism may be omitted. [In the United States, it may be omitted only when the minister of baptism judges the omission to be pastorally necessary or desirable.] In that case the celebrant says:

May you have strength in the power of Christ our
Savior, who lives and reigns for ever and ever.
All: **Amen.**

And immediately he lays his hand on the child in silence.

89. Then they go to the baptistry, or to the sanctuary when baptism is celebrated there on occasion.

CELEBRATION OF THE SACRAMENT

90. When they come to the font, the celebrant briefly reminds the congregation of the wonderful work of God whose plan it is to sanctify man, body and soul, through water. He may use these or similar words:

A
My dear brothers and sisters, we now ask God to give this child new life in abundance through water and the Holy Spirit.

or **B**
My dear brothers and sisters, God uses the sacrament of water to give his divine life to those who believe in him. Let us turn to him, and ask him to pour his gift of life from this font on this child he has chosen.

BLESSING AND INVOCATION OF GOD OVER BAPTISMAL WATER

91. Then, turning to the font, he says the following blessing (outside the Easter season):

Father,
you give us grace through sacramental signs,
which tell us of the wonders of your unseen power.

In baptism we use your gift of water,
which you have made a rich symbol of the grace
you give us in this sacrament.

At the very dawn of creation
your Spirit breathed on the waters,
making them the wellspring of all holiness.

The waters of the great flood
you made a sign of the waters of baptism
that make an end of sin
and a new beginning of goodness.

Through the waters of the Red Sea
you led Israel out of slavery
to be an image of God's holy people,
set free from sin by baptism.

In the waters of the Jordan
your Son was baptized by John
and anointed with the Spirit.
Your Son willed that water and blood should flow
    from his side
as he hung upon the cross.

After his resurrection he told his disciples:
"Go out and teach all nations,
baptizing them in the name of the Father,
    and of the Son, and of the Holy Spirit."

Father,
look now with love upon your Church
and unseal for it the fountain of baptism.

By the power of the Holy Spirit
give to this water the grace of your Son,
so that in the sacrament of baptism
all those whom you have created in your likeness
may be cleansed from sin
and rise to a new birth of innocence
by water and the Holy Spirit.

The celebrant touches the water with his right hand and
continues:

We ask you, Father, with your Son
to send the Holy Spirit upon the waters of this font.
May all who are buried with Christ in the death of
    baptism
rise also with him to newness of life.

We ask this through Christ our Lord.

All: **Amen.**

Other forms may be chosen from nos. 223-224.

92. During the Easter season, if there is baptismal water
which was consecrated at the Easter Vigil, the blessing and
invocation of God over the water are nevertheless included, so that this theme of thanksgiving and petition
may find a place in the baptism. The forms of this blessing
and invocation are those found in nos. 223-224 with the
variation indicated at the end of the text.

RENUNCIATION OF SIN AND PROFESSION OF FAITH

93. The celebrant speaks to the parents and godparents in these words:

Dear parents and godparents: You have come here to present this child for baptism. By water and the Holy Spirit he (she) is to receive the gift of new life from God, who is love.

On your part, you must make it your constant care to bring him (her) up in the practice of the faith. See that the divine life which God gives him (her) is kept safe from the poison of sin, to grow always stronger in his (her) heart.

If your faith makes you ready to accept this responsibility, renew now the vows of your own baptism. Reject sin; profess your faith in Christ Jesus. This is the faith of the Church. This is the faith in which this child is about to be baptized.

94. The celebrant questions the parents and godparents.

A
Celebrant:
Do you reject Satan?
Parents and godparents: **I do.**

Celebrant:
And all his works?
Parents and godparents: **I do.**

Celebrant:
And all his empty promises?
Parents and godparents: **I do.**

or **B**
Celebrant:
Do you reject sin so as to live in the freedom of God's children?
Parents and godparents: **I do.**

Celebrant:
Do you reject the glamor of evil, and refuse to be mastered by sin?

Parents and godparents: **I do.**

Celebrant:
Do you reject Satan, father of sin and prince of darkness?
Parents and godparents: **I do.**

According to circumstances, this second form may be expressed with greater precision by the conferences of bishops, especially in places where it is necessary for the parents and godparents to reject superstitious and magical practices used with children.

95. Next the celebrant asks for the threefold profession of faith from the parents and godparents:

Celebrant:
Do you believe in God, the Father almighty,
creator of heaven and earth?
Parents and godparents: **I do.**

Celebrant:
Do you believe in Jesus Christ, his only Son, our Lord,
who was born of the Virgin Mary,
was crucified, died, and was buried,
rose from the dead,
and is now seated at the right hand of the Father?
Parents and godparents: **I do.**

Celebrant:
Do you believe in the Holy Spirit,
the holy catholic Church, the communion of saints,
the forgiveness of sins, the resurrection of the body,
and the life everlasting?
Parents and godparents: **I do.**

96. The celebrant and the congregation give their assent to this profession of faith:

Celebrant:
This is our faith. This is the faith of the Church. We are proud to profess it, in Christ Jesus our Lord.
All: **Amen.**

If desired, some other formula may be used instead, or a suitable song by which the community expresses its faith with a single voice.

BAPTISM

97. The celebrant invites the family to the font and questions the parents and godparents:

Celebrant:
Is it your will that N. should be baptized in the faith of the Church, which we have all professed with you?
Parents and godparents: **It is.**

He baptizes the child, saying:

N., I baptize you in the name of the Father,

He immerses the child or pours water upon it.

and of the Son,

He immerses the child or pours water upon it a second time.

and of the Holy Spirit.

He immerses the child or pours water upon it a third time.

After the child is baptized, it is appropriate for the people to sing a short acclamation. (See nos. 225-245.)

If the baptism is performed by the pouring of water, it is preferable that the child be held by the mother (or father). Where, however, it is felt that the existing custom should be retained, the godmother (or godfather) may hold the child. If baptism is by immersion, the mother or father (godmother or godfather) lifts the child out of the font.

EXPLANATORY RITES

ANOINTING AFTER BAPTISM

98. Then the celebrant says:

**The God of power and Father of our Lord Jesus
    Christ
has freed you from sin
and brought you to new life**

through water and the Holy Spirit.

**He now anoints you with the chrism of salvation,
so that, united with his people,
you may remain for ever a member of Christ
who is Priest, Prophet, and King.**

All: **Amen.**

Then the celebrant anoints the child on the crown of the
head with the sacred chrism, in silence.

CLOTHING WITH WHITE GARMENT

99. The celebrant says:

**N., you have become a new creation, and have
clothed yourself in Christ.**

**See in this white garment the outward sign of your
Christian dignity. With your family and friends to
help you by word and example, bring that dignity
unstained into the everlasting life of heaven.**
All: **Amen.**

The white garment is put on the child. A different color is
not permitted unless demanded by local custom. It is desirable that the family provide the garment.

LIGHTED CANDLE

100. The celebrant takes the Easter candle and says:

Receive the light of Christ.

Someone from the family (such as the father or godfather)
lights the child's candle from the Easter candle.

The celebrant then says:

**Parents and godparent (or godparents), this light is
entrusted to you to be kept burning brightly. This
child of yours has been enlightened by Christ. He
(she) is to walk always as a child of the light. May
he (she) keep the flame of faith alive in his (her)
heart. When the Lord comes, may he (she) go out to
meet him with all the saints in the heavenly kingdom.**

EPHPHETHA OR PRAYER OVER EARS AND MOUTH

101. If the conference of bishops decides to preserve the practice, the rite of *Ephphetha* follows. [In the United States it may be performed at the discretion of the minister.] The celebrant touches the ears and mouth of the child with his thumb, saying:

The Lord Jesus made the deaf hear and the dumb speak. May he soon touch your ears to receive his word, and your mouth to proclaim his faith, to the praise and glory of God the Father.
All: **Amen.**

[If baptism is celebrated during Sunday or weekday Mass, the Mass continues in the usual way with preparation of the altar and the gifts.]

CONCLUSION OF THE RITE

102. Next there is a procession to the altar, unless the baptism was performed in the sanctuary. The lighted candle is carried for the child.

A baptismal song is appropriate at this time, e.g.:

**You have put on Christ,
in him you have been baptized.
Alleluia, alleluia.**

Other songs may be chosen from nos. 225-245.

LORD'S PRAYER

103. The celebrant stands in front of the altar, and addresses the parents, godparents, and the whole assembly in these or similar words:

Dearly beloved, this child has been reborn in baptism. He (she) is now called the child of God, for so indeed he (she) is. In confirmation he (she) will receive the fullness of God's Spirit. In holy communion he (she) will share the banquet of Christ's sacrifice, calling God his (her) Father in the midst of the Church. In the name of this child, in the Spirit of our common sonship, let us pray together in the words our Lord has given us:

104. All present join the celebrant in singing or saying:

Our Father. . . .

BLESSING

105. The celebrant first blesses the mother, who holds the child in her arms, then the father, and lastly the entire assembly:

Celebrant:

God the Father, through his Son, the Virgin Mary's child, has brought joy to all Christian mothers, as they see the hope of eternal life shine on their children. May he bless the mother of this child. She now thanks God for the gift of her child. May she be one with him (her) in thanking him for ever in heaven, in Christ Jesus our Lord.
All: **Amen.**

Celebrant:

God is the giver of all life, human and divine. May he bless the father of this child. He and his wife will be the first teachers of their child in the ways of faith. May they be also the best of teachers, bearing witness to the faith by what they say and do, in Christ Jesus our Lord.
All: **Amen.**

Celebrant:

By God's gift, through water and the Holy Spirit, we are reborn to everlasting life. In his goodness, may he continue to pour out his blessings upon these sons and daughters of his. May he make them always, wherever they may be, faithful members of his holy people. May he send his peace upon all who are gathered here, in Christ Jesus our Lord.
All: **Amen.**

Celebrant:

May almighty God, the Father, and the Son, ✠ and the Holy Spirit, bless you.
All: **Amen.**

Celebrant: **Go in peace.**
All: **Thanks be to God.**

For other forms of the blessing, see nos. 247-249.

106. After the blessing, all may sing a hymn which suitably expresses thanksgiving and Easter joy, or they may sing the song of the Blessed Virgin Mary, the Magnificat.

Where there is a practice of bringing the baptized child to the altar of the Blessed Virgin Mary, this custom is observed if appropriate.

CHAPTER III

RITE OF BAPTISM FOR A LARGE NUMBER OF CHILDREN

RECEPTION OF THE CHILDREN

107. The people may sing a psalm or hymn suitable for the occasion. Meanwhile the celebrating priest or deacon, vested in alb or surplice, with a stole (with or without a cope) of festive color, and accompanied by the ministers, goes to the entrance of the church or to that part of the church where the parents and godparents are waiting with those who are to be baptized.

108. The celebrant greets all present, and especially the parents and godparents, reminding them briefly of the joy with which the parents welcomed their children as gifts from God, the source of life, who now wishes to bestow his own life on these little ones.

Then the celebrant questions the parents and godparents together:

A
Celebrant:
What name do you want to give your children?
Each family answers in turn, giving the names of the children.

Celebrant:
What do you ask of God's Church for these children?
All families together: **Baptism.**

But if there is a very large number to be baptized, he omits the first question and asks:

B
Celebrant:
Parents and godparents, what do you ask for these children?
All families together: **Baptism.**

109. The celebrant speaks to the parents in these or similar words:

You have asked to have your children baptized. In doing so you are accepting the responsibility of training them in the practice of the faith. It will be your duty to bring them up to keep God's commandments as Christ taught us, by loving God and our neighbor. Do you clearly understand what you are undertaking?
All parents together: **We do.**

110. Then the celebrant turns to the godparents and addresses them in these or similar words:

Are you ready to help these parents in their duty as Christian mothers and fathers?
All the godparents: **We are.**

111. The celebrant continues:

My dear children, the Christian community welcomes you with great joy. In its name I claim you for Christ our Savior by the sign of his cross.

He makes the sign of the cross over all the children together, and says:

Parents (or godparents), make the sign of Christ our Savior on the foreheads of your children.

Then the parents (or godparents) sign the children on their foreheads.

LITURGY OF THE WORD

READINGS AND HOMILY

112. The celebrant invites the parents, godparents and the others to take part in the liturgy of the word. Matthew 28:18-20 is read, telling how the apostles were sent to preach the gospel and to baptize.

Other passages may also be selected from nos. 44, 186-194, 204-215.

113. After the reading, the celebrant gives a short homily, explaining to those present the significance of what has been read. His purpose will be to lead them to a deeper under- standing of the mystery of baptism and to encourage the parents and godparents to a ready acceptance of the respon- sibilities which arise from the sacrament.

INTERCESSIONS (PRAYER OF THE FAITHFUL)

114. Then the intercessions (prayer of the faithful) are said:

Celebrant:

My dear brothers and sisters, let us ask our Lord Jesus Christ to look lovingly on these children who are to be baptized, on their parents and godparents, and on all the baptized.

Assisting Minister:

By the mystery of your death and resurrection, bathe these children in light, give them the new life of baptism and welcome them into your holy Church.
All: **Lord, hear our prayer.**

Assisting Minister:

Through baptism and confirmation, make them your faithful followers and witnesses to your gospel.
All: **Lord, hear our prayer.**

Assisting Minister:

Lead them by a holy life to the joys of God's king- dom.
All: **Lord, hear our prayer.**

Assisting Minister:

Make the lives of their parents and godparents exam- ples of faith to inspire these children.
All: **Lord, hear our prayer.**

Assisting Minister:

Keep their families always in your love.
All: **Lord, hear our prayer.**

Assisting Minister:
Renew the grace of our baptism in each one of us.
All: **Lord, hear our prayer.**

Other forms may be chosen from nos. 217-220. The invocation of the saints (see no. 48) may be omitted.

PRAYER OF EXORCISM

115. The prayer of the faithful is concluded with the prayer of exorcism:

Almighty and ever-living God,
you sent your only Son into the world
to cast out the power of Satan, spirit of evil,
to rescue man from the kingdom of darkness,
and bring him into the splendor of your kingdom of
    light.
We pray for these children:
set them free from original sin,
make them temples of your glory,
and send your Holy Spirit to dwell within them.
We ask this through Christ our Lord.
All: **Amen.**

For another form of the prayer of exorcism, see no. 221.

Because of the large number of children to be baptized, the celebrant does not anoint them with oil of catechumens. He imposes his hands over all the children at once and says:

May you have strength in the power of Christ our
Savior, who lives and reigns for ever and ever.
All: **Amen.**

116. Then they go to the place where baptism is celebrated.

CELEBRATION OF THE SACRAMENT

117. When they come to the font, the celebrant briefly reminds the congregation of the wonderful work of God whose plan it is to sanctify man, body and soul, through water. He may use these or similar words:

My dear brothers and sisters, God uses the sacrament of water to give his divine life to those who believe in him.

Let us turn to him in our faith, and ask him to pour his gift of life from this font on the children he has chosen.

BLESSING AND INVOCATION OF GOD OVER BAPTISMAL WATER

118. Facing the font (or vessel) containing the water, the celebrant says the following.

Father, God of mercy,
through these waters of baptism
you have filled us with new life as your very own children.

All sing or say a suitable acclamation or the following.
Blessed be God.

Celebrant:
From all who are baptized in water and the Holy Spirit,
you have formed one people,
united in your Son, Jesus Christ.

All: **Blessed be God.**

Celebrant:
You have set us free and filled our hearts with the Spirit of your love,
that we may live in your peace.

All: **Blessed be God.**

Celebrant:
You call those who have been baptized
to announce the Good News of Jesus Christ to people everywhere.

All: **Blessed be God.**

The celebrant concludes with the following.
You have called your children, N. and N.,
to this cleansing water and new birth,

that by sharing the faith of your Church they may
   have eternal life.
Bless ✛ this water in which they will be baptized.

We ask this in the name of Jesus the Lord.

All: **Amen.**

---

119. *Easter-Season Thanksgiving over Water Already Blessed:*
If the baptismal water has already been blessed,
the celebrant omits this last prayer and says:

You have called your children, N. and N., to this
   cleansing water,
that they may share in the faith of your Church and
   have eternal life.
By the mystery of this consecrated water
lead them to a new and spiritual birth.

We ask this through Christ our Lord.

All: **Amen.**

Other forms may be chosen from no. 223.

RENUNCIATION OF SIN AND PROFESSION OF FAITH

120. The celebrant speaks to the parents and godparents in
these words:

**Dear parents and godparents: You have come here to
present these children for baptism. By water and the
Holy Spirit they are to receive the gift of new life
from God, who is love.**

**On your part, you must make it your constant care to
bring them up in the practice of the faith. See that
the divine life which God gives them is kept safe
from the poison of sin, to grow always stronger in
their hearts.**

**If your faith makes you ready to accept this responsi-
bility, renew now the vows of your baptism. Reject
sin; profess your faith in Christ Jesus. This is the
faith of the Church. This is the faith in which these
children are about to be baptized.**

121. The celebrant questions the parents and godparents.

A
Celebrant:
Do you reject Satan?
Parents and godparents: **I do.**

Celebrant:
And all his works?
Parents and godparents: **I do.**

Celebrant:
And all his empty promises?
Parents and godparents: **I do.**

or **B**
Celebrant:
Do you reject sin so as to live in the freedom of God's children?
Parents and godparents: **I do.**

Celebrant:
Do you reject the glamor of evil, and refuse to be mastered by sin?
Parents and godparents: **I do.**

Celebrant:
Do you reject Satan, father of sin and prince of darkness?
Parents and godparents: **I do.**

According to circumstances, this second form may be expressed with greater precision by the conferences of bishops, especially in places where it is necessary for the parents and godparents to reject superstitious and magical practices used with children.

122. Next the celebrant asks for the threefold profession of faith from the parents and godparents:

Celebrant:
**Do you believe in God, the Father almighty,
   creator of heaven and earth?**
Parents and godparents: **I do.**

Celebrant:
Do you believe in Jesus Christ, his only Son, our Lord,

who was born of the Virgin Mary,
was crucified, died, and was buried,
rose from the dead,
and is now seated at the right hand of the Father?
Parents and godparents: **I do.**

Celebrant:
**Do you believe in the Holy Spirit,
the holy catholic Church, the communion of saints,
the forgiveness of sins, the resurrection of the body,
and the life everlasting?**
Parents and godparents: **I do.**

123. The celebrant and the congregation give their assent
to this profession of faith:

Celebrant:
**This is our faith. This is the faith of the Church. We
are proud to profess it, in Christ Jesus our Lord.**
All: **Amen.**

If desired, some other formula may be used instead, or a
suitable song by which the community expresses its faith
with a single voice.

BAPTISM

124. If there are several ministers because of the large
number to be baptized, each of them questions the parents
and godparents, using the name of the individual child:

Celebrant:
**Is it your will that N. should be baptized in the faith
of the Church, which we have all professed with
you?**
Parents and godparents: **It is.**

He baptizes the child, saying:

N., I baptize you in the name of the Father,

He immerses the child or pours water upon it.

and of the Son,

He immerses the child or pours water upon it a second
time.

and of the Holy Spirit.

He immerses the child or pours water upon it a third time.

He asks the same question and performs the same action for each child.

If the baptism is performed by the pouring of water, it is preferable that the child be held by the mother (or father). Where, however, it is felt that the existing custom should be retained, the godmother (or godfather) may hold the child.

If baptism is by immersion, the mother or father (godmother or godfather) lifts the child out of the font.

While the children are being baptized, the community can make acclamations or sing hymns (see nos. 225-245). Some passages from Scripture may also be read, or a sacred silence observed.

EXPLANATORY RITES

ANOINTING AFTER BAPTISM

125. Then the celebrant says the formula of anointing once for all the children:

**The God of power and Father of our Lord Jesus
  Christ
has freed you from sin
and brought you to new life
through water and the Holy Spirit.**

**He now anoints you with the chrism of salvation,
so that, united with his people,
you may remain for ever a member of Christ
who is Priest, Prophet, and King.**

Children: **Amen.**

Then the ministers anoint each child on the crown of the head with the sacred chrism, in silence.

But if the number of children is extremely large, the conferences of bishops may decide that the anointing with chrism may be omitted. [In the United States the anointing may not be omitted.] In this case, an adapted formula is used:

**The God of power and Father of our Lord Jesus
  Christ**

has freed you from sin
and brought you to new life
through water and the Holy Spirit.

He has made you Christians now,
and has welcomed you into his holy people.
As Christ was anointed Priest, Prophet, and King,
so may you live always as members of his body,
sharing everlasting life.

All: **Amen.**

CLOTHING WITH WHITE GARMENT

126. The celebrant says:

My dear children, you have become a new creation, and have clothed yourselves in Christ.

See in this white garment the outward sign of your Christian dignity. With your family and friends to help you by word and example, bring that dignity unstained into the everlasting life of heaven.
All: **Amen.**

The white garments are put on the children. A different color is not permitted unless demanded by local custom. It is desirable that the families provide the garments.

LIGHTED CANDLE

127. The celebrant takes the Easter candle and says:

Receive the light of Christ. Parents and godparents, this light is entrusted to you to be kept burning brightly. These children of yours have been enlightened by Christ. They are to walk always as children of the light. May they keep the flame of faith alive in their hearts. When the Lord comes, may they go out to meet him with all the saints in the heavenly kingdom.

Candles are distributed to the families. The head of one family lights his candle from the Easter candle and passes the flame on to the rest. Meanwhile the community sings a baptismal song, such as:

**You have put on Christ,
in him you have been baptized.
Alleluia, alleluia.**

Other hymns may be chosen from nos. 225-245.

Meanwhile, unless the baptisms were performed in the sanctuary, there is a procession to the altar. The lighted candles are carried for the children.

CONCLUSION OF THE RITE

LORD'S PRAYER

128. The celebrant stands in front of the altar and addresses the parents, godparents, and the whole assembly in these or similar words:

Dearly beloved, these children have been reborn in baptism. They are now called children of God, for so indeed they are. In confirmation they will receive the fullness of God's Spirit. In holy communion they will share the banquet of Christ's sacrifice, calling God their Father in the midst of the Church. In their name, in the spirit of our common sonship, let us pray together in the words our Lord has given us:

129. All present join the celebrant in singing or saying:

Our Father. . . .

BLESSING AND DISMISSAL

130. The celebrant blesses the entire assembly, and dismisses them:

My brothers and sisters, we commend you to the mercy and grace of God our almighty Father, of his only Son, and of the Holy Spirit. May he protect your paths, so that walking in the light of faith, you may come to the good things he has promised us.

May almighty God, the Father, and the Son, ✝ and the Holy Spirit bless you.
All: **Amen.**

Celebrant: **Go in peace.**
All: **Thanks be to God.**

For other forms of the blessing, see nos. 70, 247-248.

131. After the blessing, all may sing a hymn which suitably expresses thanksgiving and Easter joy, or they may sing the song of the Blessed Virgin Mary, the Magnificat.

CHAPTER IV

RITE OF BAPTISM FOR CHILDREN ADMINISTERED BY A CATECHIST WHEN NO PRIEST OR DEACON IS AVAILABLE

RECEPTION OF THE CHILDREN

132. While the faithful sing a suitable psalm or hymn, the catechist and the ministers approach the door of the church or the part of the church where the parents, godparents, and the children to be baptized are waiting.

If there is a large group of persons to be baptized, the catechist may be assisted by others in the act of baptism, as noted below.

133. The catechist greets all present, and especially the parents and godparents, reminding them briefly of the joy with which the parents welcomed their children as gifts from God, the source of life, who now wishes to bestow his own life on these little ones.

Then he questions the parents and godparents together in these or similar words:

A

What name do you give your children? (or: **have you given?**)
Each family answers in turn, giving the names of the children.

Catechist:
What do you ask of God's Church for these children?
All families together: **Baptism.**

If there are many children to be baptized, the first question is omitted and the catechist asks:

B
Parents and godparents, what do you ask for these children?
All families together: **Baptism.**

134. Then the catechist speaks to the parents:

Parents, you have asked to have your children baptized. In doing so you are accepting the responsibility of training them in the practice of the faith. It will be your duty to bring them up to keep God's commandments as Christ taught us, by loving God and our neighbor. Do you clearly understand what you are undertaking?
All parents together: **We do.**

135. Then turning to the godparents, the catechist asks:

Godparents, are you ready to help these parents in their duty as Christian mothers and fathers?
All the godparents: **We are.**

136. The catechist continues:

My dear children, the Christian community welcomes you with great joy. In its name I claim for you Christ our Savior by the sign of his cross.

He makes the sign of the cross over all the children together, and says:

Parents (or godparents), make the sign of Christ our Savior on the foreheads of your children.

Then the parents (or godparents) sign the children on their foreheads.

LITURGY OF THE WORD

READING AND HOMILY OR SHORT TALK

137. The catechist invites the parents, godparents, and the others to take part in the liturgy of the word. Matthew

28:18-20 is read, telling how the apostles were sent to preach the gospel and to baptize.

Other passages may also be selected from nos. 186-194, 204-215. If songs and hymns are sung, see nos. 195-203. After the reading, the catechist can give a brief homily in the way determined by the bishop.

138. In the place of the Scripture reading and the homily, the catechist can, if necessary, give this talk:

In baptism, Christ will come to meet these children. He entrusted this sacrament to his Church when he sent forth his apostles with these words: "Go, make disciples of all nations, and baptize them in the name of the Father, and of the Son, and of the Holy Spirit."

As you know, these children will be given countless gifts in this great sacrament: they will be freed from sin; they will become members of the Church; they will become God's children. But since man is unable to accomplish such wonders, we must pray together with humility and faith for these blessings.

May God our Father see in the fellowship of our community the faith of his Church, and hear in our prayer the voice of Jesus his Son. As he promised us through Christ, may he bless these children by the power of his Holy Spirit.

INTERCESSIONS (PRAYER OF THE FAITHFUL)

139. Then the intercessions (prayer of the faithful) are said:

Catechist:
My dear brothers and sisters, let us ask our Lord Jesus Christ to look lovingly on these children who are to be baptized, on their parents and godparents, and on all the baptized.

Assisting Minister:
By the mystery of your death and resurrection, bathe these children in light, give them the new life of baptism and welcome them into your holy Church.
All: **Lord, hear our prayer.**

Assisting Minister:

Through baptism and confirmation, make them your faithful followers and witnesses to your gospel.
All: **Lord, hear our prayer.**

Assisting Minister:

Lead them by a holy life to the joys of God's kingdom.
All: **Lord, hear our prayer.**

Assisting Minister:

Make the lives of their parents and godparents examples of faith to inspire these children.
All: **Lord, hear our prayer.**

Assisting Minister:

Keep their families always in your love.
All: **Lord, hear our prayer.**

Assisting Minister:

Renew the grace of our baptism in each one of us.
All: **Lord, hear our prayer.**

Other forms may be chosen from nos. 217-220.

Then the catechist invites all present to invoke the saints:

Holy Mary, Mother of God,	pray for us.
Saint John the Baptist,	pray for us.
Saint Joseph,	pray for us.
Saint Peter and Saint Paul,	pray for us.

The names of other saints may be added, especially the patrons of the children to be baptized, and of the church or locality. The litany concludes:

All holy men and women,	pray for us.

140. The prayer of exorcism and the anointing with oil of catechumens are omitted.

CELEBRATION OF THE SACRAMENT

BLESSING AND INVOCATION OF GOD OVER BAPTISMAL WATER

141. With the parents and godparents carrying the children who are to be baptized, the catechist comes to the font. He invites all to pray:

My dear brothers and sisters, let us ask God to give these children new life in abundance through water and the Holy Spirit.

142. If there is no blessed water available, the catechist stands before the font and says this invocation:

A
Catechist:
Father, God of mercy,
through these waters of baptism
you have filled us with new life as your very own
  children.

All sing or say a suitable acclamation or the following.
Blessed be God.

Catechist:
From all who are baptized in water and the Holy
  Spirit,
you have formed one people,
united in your Son, Jesus Christ.

All: **Blessed be God.**

Catechist:
You have set us free and filled our hearts with the
  Spirit of your love,
that we may live in your peace.

All: **Blessed be God.**

Catechist:
You call those who have been baptized
to announce the Good News of Jesus Christ to peo-
  ple everywhere.

All: **Blessed be God.**

The catechist concludes with the following.
Come and bless this water
in which your servants are to be baptized.
You have called them to the washing of new life
in the Faith of your Church,
so that they may have eternal life.
We ask this through Christ our Lord.

All: **Amen.**

143. If blessed water is available, he says the following
invocation:

B
Father of our Lord Jesus Christ,
source of all life and love,
you are glorified throughout the world
by the simple joys and daily cares
of mothers and fathers.

In the beauty of a child's birth
and in the mystery of his rebirth to eternal life,
you give us a glimpse of all creation:
it is guided by your fatherly love,
unfolding in fruitfulness to perfection
in Jesus Christ your Son.

In your kindness
hear the prayers of the Church and of these parents.
Look upon these children with love,
and keep them from the power of sin.
Since they are a gift from you, Father,
welcome them into the kingdom of your Son.

You have created this water,
and made it clean, refreshing, and life-giving.
You have made it holy through the baptism of
  Christ,
that by the power of the Holy Spirit
it may give your people a new birth.

When these children are baptized into the mystery
of Christ's suffering, death, and resurrection,

may they be worthy to become members of your
   Church,
your very own children.
Father, may they rejoice
with Jesus your Son and the Holy Spirit
for ever and ever.
All: **Amen.**

RENUNCIATION OF SIN AND PROFESSION OF FAITH

144. The catechist speaks to the parents and godparents in these words:

Dear parents and godparents: You have come here to present these children for baptism. By water and the Holy Spirit, they are to receive the gift of new life from God, who is love.

On your part, you must make it your constant care to bring them up in the practice of the faith. See that the divine life which God gives them is kept safe from the poison of sin, to grow always stronger in their hearts.

If your faith makes you ready to accept this responsibility, renew now the vows of your baptism. Reject sin; profess your faith in Christ Jesus. This is the faith of the Church. This is the faith in which these children are about to be baptized.

145. Then he asks them:

A
Catechist:
Do you reject Satan?
Parents and godparents: **I do.**

Catechist:
And all his works?
Parents and godparents: **I do.**

Catechist:
And all his empty promises?
Parents and godparents: **I do.**

or **B**
Catechist:
**Do you reject sin so as to live in the freedom of
God's children?**
Parents and godparents: **I do.**

Catechist:
**Do you reject the glamor of evil, and refuse to be
mastered by sin?**
Parents and godparents: **I do.**

Catechist:
**Do you reject Satan, father of sin and prince of
darkness?**
Parents and godparents: **I do.**

According to circumstances, this second form may be expressed with greater precision by the conference of bishops, especially in places where it is necessary for the
parents and godparents to reject superstitious and magical
practices used with children.

146. Then the catechist asks for the threefold profession of
faith from the parents and godparents:

Catechist:
**Do you believe in God, the Father almighty,
   creator of heaven and earth?**
Parents and godparents: **I do.**

Catechist:
**Do you believe in Jesus Christ, his only Son, our Lord,
   who was born of the Virgin Mary,
   was crucified, died, and was buried,
   rose from the dead,
   and is now seated at the right hand of the Father?**
Parents and godparents: **I do.**

Catechist:
**Do you believe in the Holy Spirit,
   the holy catholic Church, the communion of saints,
   the forgiveness of sins, the resurrection of the body,
   and the life everlasting?**
Parents and godparents: **I do.**

147. The catechist and the congregation give their assent to this profession of faith:

Catechist:

This is our faith. This is the faith of the Church. We are proud to profess it, in Christ Jesus our Lord.
All: **Amen.**

If desired, some other formula may be used instead, or a suitable song by which the community expresses its faith with a single voice.

BAPTISM

148. The catechist invites the first of the families to approach the font. Using the name of the individual child, he asks the parents and godparents:

Is it your will that N. should be baptized in the faith of the Church, which we have all professed with you?
Parents and godparents: **It is.**

He baptizes the child, saying:

N., I baptize you in the name of the Father,

He immerses the child or pours water upon it.

and of the Son,

He immerses the child or pours water upon it a second time.

and of the Holy Spirit.

He immerses the child or pours water upon it a third time.

If baptism is performed by the pouring of water, it is preferable that the child be held by the mother or father. Where, however, it is felt that the existing custom should be retained, the godmother or godfather may hold the child. If baptism is by immersion, the parent or godparent lifts the child out of the font.

149. If the number of children to be baptized is large, and other catechists are present, these may baptize some of the children in the way described above, and with the same form (no. 148).

150. While the children are being baptized, the community can make acclamations or sing hymns (see nos. 225-245). Some passages from Scripture may also be read, or a sacred silence observed.

EXPLANATORY RITES

151. The anointing with chrism is omitted. The catechist says once for all the newly-baptized children:

**The God of power and Father of our Lord Jesus
  Christ
has freed you from sin
and brought you to new life
through water and the Holy Spirit.**

**He has made you Christians now,
and has welcomed you into his holy people.
As Christ was anointed Priest, Prophet, and King,
so may you live always as members of his body,
sharing everlasting life.
All: Amen.**

CLOTHING WITH WHITE GARMENT

152. The catechist says:

**My dear children, you have become a new creation,
and have clothed yourselves in Christ.**

**See in this white garment the outward sign of your
Christian dignity. With your family and friends to
help you by word and example, bring that dignity
unstained into the everlasting life of heaven.
All: Amen.**

The white garments are put on the children. A different color is not permitted unless demanded by local custom. It is desirable that the families provide the garments.

LIGHTED CANDLE

153. The catechist takes the Easter candle and says:

Receive the light of Christ. Parents and godparents, this light is entrusted to you to be kept burning brightly. These children of yours have been enlightened by Christ. They are to walk always as children of the light. May they keep the flame of faith alive in their hearts. When the Lord comes, may they go out to meet him with all the saints in the heavenly kingdom.

Candles are distributed to the families. The head of one family lights his candle from the Easter candle and passes the flame on to the rest. Meanwhile the community sings a baptismal song, such as:

**You have put on Christ,
in him you have been baptized.
Alleluia, alleluia.**

Other hymns may be chosen from nos. 225-245.

Meanwhile, unless the baptisms were performed in the sanctuary, there is a procession to the altar. The lighted candles are carried for the children.

CONCLUSION OF THE RITE

LORD'S PRAYER

154. The catechist stands in front of the altar and addresses the parents, godparents, and the whole assembly in these or similar words:

Dearly beloved, these children have been reborn in baptism. They are now called children of God, for so indeed they are. In confirmation they will receive the fullness of God's Spirit. In holy communion they will share the banquet of Christ's sacrifice, calling God their Father in the midst of the Church. In their name, in the spirit of common sonship, let us pray together in the words our Lord has given us:

155. All say together:

Our Father. . . .

BLESSING AND DISMISSAL

156. The catechist invokes the blessing of God and dismisses the assembly.

My brothers and sisters, we commend you to the mercy and grace of God our almighty Father, of his only Son, and of the Holy Spirit. May he protect your paths, so that walking in the light of faith, you may come to the good things he has promised us.

All: **Amen.**

Catechist:
Go in peace.
All: **Thanks be to God.**

After the blessing, all may sing a hymn which suitably expresses thanksgiving and Easter joy, or they may sing the canticle of the Blessed Virgin Mary, the Magnificat.

CHAPTER V

RITE OF BAPTISM FOR CHILDREN IN DANGER OF DEATH WHEN NO PRIEST OR DEACON IS AVAILABLE

157. Water, even though not blessed, is prepared for the rite. The parents, godparents, and if possible, some friends and neighbors of the family gather around the sick child. The minister, who is any suitable member of the Church, begins with this brief prayer of the faithful:

Let us ask almighty God to look with mercy on this child who is about to receive the grace of baptism, on his (her) parents and godparents, and on all baptized persons.
Through baptism, welcome this child into your Church.
℟. **Lord, hear our prayer.**

Through baptism, make him (her) one of your adopted children.
℟. **Lord, hear our prayer.**

Through baptism, he (she) is being buried in the likeness of Christ's death. May he (she) also share in the glory of his resurrection.
℟. **Lord, hear our prayer.**

Renew the grace of our baptism in each one of us.
℟. **Lord, hear our prayer.**

May all the followers of Christ, baptized into one body, always live united in faith and love.
℟. **Lord, hear our prayer.**

158. The prayer of the faithful concludes with this prayer:

Father of our Lord Jesus Christ,
source of all life and love,
you know the anxiety of parents
and you lighten their burden
by your fatherly care for all children in danger.

You reveal the depth of your love
by offering them a new and eternal birth.

In your kindness, hear our prayers:
keep this child from the power of sin,
and welcome him (her) with love into the kingdom of
    your Son.

By water and by the power of the Holy Spirit,
may this child, whom we now call N.,
share in the mystery of Christ's death
so that he (she) may also share in the mystery of
    Christ's resurrection.

May he (she) become your adopted son (daughter),
and share in the inheritance of Christ.
Grant that he (she) may rejoice in the fellowship of
    your Church
with your only Son and the Holy Spirit
for ever and ever.
℟. Amen.

159. Then they make the profession of faith. The minister
says to all present:

A
Let us remember our own baptism, and profess our
faith in Jesus Christ. This is the faith of the Church,
the faith into which children are baptized.

Then the minister asks:

Do you believe in God, the Father almighty,
    creator of heaven and earth?
℟. I do.

Minister:
Do you believe in Jesus Christ, his only Son, our Lord,
    who was born of the Virgin Mary,
    was crucified, died, and was buried,
    rose from the dead,
    and is now seated at the right of the Father?
℟. I do.

Minister:

Do you believe in the Holy Spirit,
the holy catholic Church, the communion of saints,
the forgiveness of sins, the resurrection of the body,
and the life everlasting?

℟. **I do.**

The profession of faith may also be made, if desirable, by reciting the Apostles' Creed:

B

I believe in God, the Father almighty,
Creator of heaven and earth;
and in Jesus Christ, his only Son, our Lord,
who was conceived by the Holy Spirit,
born of the Virgin Mary,
suffered under Pontius Pilate,
was crucified, died, and was buried.
He descended into hell;
the third day he rose again from the dead;
he ascended into heaven,
sitteth at the right hand of God, the Father
almighty,
from thence he shall come to judge the living and
the dead.
I believe in the Holy Spirit,
the holy catholic Church,
the communion of saints,
the forgiveness of sins,
the resurrection of the body,
and the life everlasting. Amen.

160. Then the minister baptizes the child, saying:

N., I baptize you in the name of the Father,

The minister pours water upon the child.

and of the Son,

The minister pours water upon the child a second time.

and of the Holy Spirit.

The minister pours water upon the child a third time.

161. Omitting all other ceremonies, the minister may give the white garment to the child. The minister says:

N., you have become a new creation, and have clothed yourself in Christ.

See in this white garment the outward sign of your Christian dignity. May you bring it unstained into the everlasting life of heaven.

162. The celebration concludes with the recitation of the Lord's Prayer:

Our Father . . .

163. If no one there is capable of directing the prayer, any member of the Church may baptize, after reciting the Apostles' Creed, by pouring water on the child while reciting the customary words (see no. 160, above). The creed may be omitted if necessary.

164. At the moment of death, it is sufficient for the minister to omit all other ceremonies and pour water on the child while saying the usual words (see no. 160, above). It is desirable that the minister, as far as possible, should use one or two witnesses.

CHAPTER VI

RITE OF BRINGING A BAPTIZED CHILD TO THE CHURCH

RECEPTION OF THE CHILD

165. The people may sing a psalm or song suitable for the occasion. Meanwhile the celebrating priest or deacon, vested in alb or surplice, with a stole (with or without a cope) of festive color, and accompanied by the ministers, goes to the entrance of the church where the parents and godparents are waiting with the child.

166. The celebrant greets all present, and especially the parents and godparents. He praises them for having had the child baptized without delay, and thanks God and congratulates the parents on the child's return to health.

167. First the celebrant questions the parents:

Celebrant:
What name have you given the child?
Parents: **N.**

Celebrant:
What do you ask of God's Church, now that your child has been baptized?
Parents: **We ask that the whole community will know that he (she) has been received into the Church.**

The first reply may be given by someone other than the parents if local custom gives him the right to name the child.

In the second response the parents may use other words, such as **that he (she) is a Christian** or **that he (she) has been baptized.**

168. Then the celebrant speaks to the parents in these or similar words:

Celebrant:
Do you realize that in bringing your child to the

Church, you are accepting the duty of raising him (her) in the faith, so that by observing the commandments he (she) will love God and neighbor as Christ taught us?
Parents: **We do.**

169. Then the celebrant turns to the godparents and addresses them in these or similar words:

Are you ready to help the mother and father of this child to carry out their duty as Christian parents?
Godparents: **We are.**

170. The celebrant continues:

N., the Christian community welcomes you with great joy, now that you have recovered your health. We now bear witness that you have been received as a member of the Church. In the name of the community I sign you with the cross of Christ, who gave you a new life in baptism and made you a member of his Church. I invite your parents (and godparents) to do the same.

He signs the child on the forehead, in silence. Then he invites the parents and (if it seems appropriate) the godparents to do the same.

171. The celebrant invites the parents, godparents, and all who are present to take part in the liturgy of the word. If circumstances permit, there is a procession to the place where this will be celebrated, during which a song is sung, such as Psalm 85:7, 8, 9ab:

Will you not give us life;
 and shall not your people rejoice in you?
Show us, O Lord, your kindness,
 and grant us your salvation.
I will hear what God proclaims:
 the Lord—for he proclaims peace to his people.

LITURGY OF THE WORD

READINGS AND HOMILY

172. One or even two of the following gospel passages are read, during which all may sit if convenient.

John 3:1-6 The meeting with Nicodemus..
Matthew 28:18-20 The apostles are sent to preach the gospel and to baptize.
Mark 1:9-11 The baptism of Jesus.
Mark 10:13-16 Let the little children come to me.

The passages listed in nos. 186-194 and 204-215 may also be chosen, or other passages which better meet the wishes or needs of the parents, such as the following:

1 Kings 17:17-24
2 Kings 4:8-37

Between the readings, responsorial psalms or verses may be sung, as given in nos. 195-203.

173. After the reading, the celebrant gives a brief homily, explaining to those present the significance of what has been read. His purpose will be to lead them to a deeper understanding of the mystery of baptism and to encourage parents and godparents to a ready acceptance of the responsibilities which arise from the sacrament.

174. After the homily, or in the course of or after the litany, it is desirable to have a period of silence while all pray at the invitation of the celebrant. A suitable hymn may follow, such as one chosen from nos. 225-245.

INTERCESSIONS (PRAYER OF THE FAITHFUL)

175. Then the intercessions (prayer of the faithful) are said:

Celebrant:
Let us ask our Lord Jesus Christ to look lovingly on this child, on his (her) parents and godparents, and on all the baptized.

Assisting Minister:

May this child always show gratitude to God for his (her) baptism and recovery.
All: **Lord, hear our prayer.**

Assisting Minister:

Help him (her) always to be a living member of your Church.
All: **Lord, hear our prayer.**

Assisting Minister:

Inspire him (her) to hear, follow, and witness to your gospel.
All: **Lord, hear our prayer.**

Assisting Minister:

May he (she) come with joy to the table of your sacrifice.
All: **Lord, hear our prayer.**

Assisting Minister:

Help him (her) to love God and neighbor as you have taught us.
All: **Lord, hear our prayer.**

Assisting Minister:

May he (she) grow in holiness and wisdom by listening to his (her) fellow Christians and following their example.
All: **Lord, hear our prayer.**

Assisting Minister:

Keep all your followers united in faith and love for ever.
All: **Lord, hear our prayer.**

176. The celebrant next invites all present to invoke the saints:

Holy Mary, Mother of God,	**pray for us.**
Saint John the Baptist,	**pray for us.**
Saint Joseph,	**pray for us.**
Saint Peter and Saint Paul,	**pray for us.**

The names of other saints may be added, especially the patrons of the child and of the church or locality. The litany concludes:

All holy men and women,   **pray for us.**

177. Then the celebrant says:

Father of our Lord Jesus Christ,
source of all life and love,
you are glorified by the loving care these parents
  have shown this child.
You rescue children from danger and save them in
  baptism.

Your Church thanks you and prays for your child N.
You have brought him (her) out of the kingdom of
  darkness
and into your marvelous light.
You have made him (her) your adopted child
and a temple of the Holy Spirit.

Help him (her) in all the dangers of this life
and strengthen him (her) in the constant effort to
  reach your kingdom,
through the power of Christ our Savior.
We ask this through Christ our Lord.
All: **Amen.**

EXPLANATORY RITES

ANOINTING AFTER BAPTISM

178. See no. 62.

CLOTHING WITH WHITE GARMENT

179. The celebrant says:

N., you have become a new creation, and have
clothed yourself in Christ.

See in this white garment the outward sign of your
Christian dignity. With your family and friends to
help you by word and example, bring that dignity

unstained into the everlasting life of heaven.
All: **Amen.**

LIGHTED CANDLE

180. The celebrant takes the Easter candle and says:

Receive the light of Christ.

Some'one, such as the father or godfather, lights the child's candle from the Easter candle.

The celebrant then says:

Parents and godparents, this light is entrusted to you to be kept burning brightly. This child of yours has been enlightened by Christ. He (she) is to walk always as a child of the light. May he (she) keep the flame of faith alive in his (her) heart. When the Lord comes, may he (she) go out to meet him with all the saints in the heavenly kingdom.

A baptismal song is appropriate at this time, such as:

You have put on Christ,
in him you have been baptized.
Alleluia, alleluia.

Other songs may be chosen from nos. 225-245.

CONCLUSION OF THE RITE

LORD'S PRAYER

181. The celebrant stands in front of the altar and addresses the parents, godparents, and the whole assembly in these or similar words:

My dear brothers and sisters, this child has been reborn in baptism. He (she) is now called the child of God, for so indeed he (she) is. In confirmation he (she) will receive the fullness of God's Spirit. In holy communion he (she) will share the banquet of Christ's sacrifice, calling God his (her) Father in the midst of the Church. In the name of this child, in the spirit of our common sonship, let us pray together in the words our Lord has given us:

182. All present join the celebrant in singing or saying:

Our Father. . . .

BLESSING AND DISMISSAL

183. The celebrant first blesses the mother, who holds the child in her arms, then the father, and lastly the entire assembly:

Celebrant:

God the Father, through his Son, the Virgin Mary's child, has brought joy to all Christian mothers, as they see the hope of eternal life shine on their children. May he bless the mother of this child. She now thanks God for the gift of her child. May she be one with her son (daughter) in thanking God for ever in heaven, in Christ Jesus our Lord.
All: **Amen.**

Celebrant:

God is the giver of all life, human and divine. May he bless the father of this child. He and his wife will be the first teachers of their child in the ways of faith.

May they also be the best of teachers, bearing witness to the faith by what they say and do, in Christ Jesus our Lord.
All: **Amen.**

Celebrant:

By God's gift, through water and the Holy Spirit, we are reborn to everlasting life. In his goodness, may he continue to pour out his blessings on these sons and daughters of his. May he make them always, wherever they may be, faithful members of his holy people. May he send his peace upon all who are gathered here, in Christ Jesus our Lord.
All: **Amen.**

Celebrant:

May almighty God, the Father, and the Son, ✝ and the Holy Spirit, bless you.
All: **Amen.**

Celebrant:
Go in Peace.
All: **Thanks be to God.**

For other forms of the blessing, see nos. 247-249.

184. After the blessing, all may sing a hymn which suitably expresses thanksgiving and Easter joy, or they may sing the song of the Blessed Virgin Mary, the Magnificat.

Where there is the practice of bringing the baptized child to the altar of the blessed Virgin, this custom is observed if appropriate.

185. The above rite is followed even when the baptized child is brought to the church after other difficulties (such as persecution, disagreement between parents) which prevented the celebration of baptism in the church. In such cases, the celebrant should adapt the explanations, readings, intentions in the prayer of the faithful and other parts of the rite to the child's circumstances.

CHAPTER VII

VARIOUS TEXTS FOR USE IN THE CELEBRATION OF BAPTISM FOR CHILDREN

I. SCRIPTURAL READINGS

OLD TESTAMENT READINGS

186. **Exodus 17:3-7**   Water from the rock.

187. **Ezekiel 36:24-28**   Clean water, a new heart, a renewed spirit.

188. **Ezekiel 47:1-9, 12**   The water of salvation.

NEW TESTAMENT READINGS

189. **Romans 6:3-5**   Baptism: a sharing in Christ's death and resurrection.

190. **Romans 8:28-32**   We have become more perfectly like God's own Son.

191. **1 Corinthians 12:12-13**   Baptized in one Spirit to form one body.

192. **Galatians 3:26-28**   Now that you have been baptized you have put on Christ.

193. **Ephesians 4:1-6**   One Lord, one faith, one baptism.

194. **1 Peter 2:4-5, 9-10**   A chosen race, a royal priesthood.

RESPONSORIAL PSALMS

195. Psalm 23:1-3a, 3b-4, 5, 6
℟. (1) **The Lord is my shepherd; there is nothing I shall want.**

196. Psalm 27:1, 4, 8b-9abc, 13-14
℟. (1a) **The Lord is my light and my salvation.**

Or: Ephesians 5:14
Wake up and rise from death:
Christ will shine upon you!

197. Psalm 34:2-3, 6-7, 8-9, 14-15, 16-17, 18-19
℟. (6a) **Come to him and receive his light!**

Or: (9a) **Taste and see the goodness of the Lord.**

ALLELUIA VERSE AND VERSE BEFORE THE GOSPEL

198. John 3:16
God loved the world so much, he gave us his only
  Son,
that all who believe in him might have eternal life.

199. John 8:12
I am the light of the world, says the Lord;
the man who follows me will have the light of life.

200. John 14:5
I am the way, the truth, and the life, says the Lord;
no one comes to the Father, except through me.

201. Ephesians 4:5-6
One Lord, one faith, one baptism.
One God, the Father of all.

202. 2 Timothy 1:10b
Our Savior Jesus Christ has done away with death,
and brought us life through his gospel.

203. 1 Peter 2:9
You are a chosen race, a royal priesthood, a holy
  people.
Praise God who called you out of darkness and into
  his marvelous light.

GOSPELS

204. **Matthew 22:35-40** The first and most important
commandment.

205. **Matthew 28:18-20** Christ sends his apostles to teach
and baptize.

206. **Mark 1:9-11** The baptism of Jesus.

207. **Mark 10:13-16** Jesus loves children.

208. **Mark 12:28b-34 (longer) or 28b-31 (shorter)** Love God with all your heart.

209. **John 3:1-6** The meeting with Nicodemus.

210. **John 4:5-14** Jesus speaks with the Samaritan woman.

211. **John 6:44-47** Eternal life through belief in Jesus.

212. **John 7:37b-39a** Streams of living water.

213. **John 9:1-7** Jesus heals a blind man who believes in him.

214. **John 15:1-11** Union with Christ, the true vine.

215. **John 19:31-35** The death of Christ, the witness of John the apostle.

II. OTHER FORMS OF THE INTERCESSIONS (PRAYER OF THE FAITHFUL)

Any one of the following forms given in this baptismal ritual may be used for the prayer of the faithful. Petitions may be added or omitted at will, taking into consideration the special circumstances of each family. The prayer always concludes with the invocation of the saints.

216.
As given in no. 47.

217.
We have been called by the Lord to be a royal priesthood, a holy nation, a people he has acquired for himself. Let us ask him to show his mercy to these children, who are to receive the graces of baptism, to their parents and godparents, and to all the baptized everywhere.

Through baptism, bring these children into your Church.
℟. **Lord, hear our prayer.**

Throughout their lives, help them to be faithful witnesses to your Son, Jesus Christ, for they are being marked with his cross.
R̕. Lord, hear our prayer.

As they are being buried in the likeness of Christ's death through baptism, may they also share in the glory of Christ's resurrection.
R̕. Lord, hear our prayer.

Teach them by the words and example of their parents and godparents, and help them to grow strong as living members of the Church.
R̕. Lord, hear our prayer.

Renew the grace of baptism in each of us here.
R̕. Lord, hear our prayer.

May all Christ's followers, baptized into one body, always live united in faith and love.
R̕. Lord, hear our prayer.

The invocation of the saints follows.

218.
My fellow Christians, let us ask the mercy of Jesus Christ our Lord for these children who will receive the gift of baptism, for their parents and godparents, and for all baptized persons.

Through baptism, make these children God's own sons and daughters.
R̕. Lord, hear our prayer.

Help these tender branches grow to be more like you, the true vine, and be your faithful followers.
R̕. Lord, hear our prayer.

May they always keep your commands, walk in your love, and proclaim your Good News to their fellow men.
R̕. Lord, hear our prayer.

May they be counted as God's friends through your

saving work, Lord Jesus, and may they inherit eternal life.
℟. Lord, hear our prayer.

Help their parents and godparents to lead them to know and love God.
℟. Lord, hear our prayer.

Inspire all men to share in the new birth of baptism.
℟. Lord, hear our prayer.

The invocation of the saints follows.

219.

We have been called by the Lord to be a royal priesthood, a holy nation, a people he has acquired for himself. Let us ask him to show his mercy to these children, who are to receive the graces of baptism, to their parents and godparents, and to all the baptized everywhere.

Through baptism may these children become God's own beloved sons and daughters. We pray to the Lord.
℟. Lord, hear our prayer.

Once they are born again of water and the Holy Spirit, may they always live in that Spirit, and make their new life known to their fellow men. We pray to the Lord.
℟. Lord, hear our prayer.

Help them to triumph over the deceits of the devil and the attractions of evil. We pray to the Lord.
℟. Lord, hear our prayer.

May they love you, Lord, with all their heart, soul, mind and strength, and love their neighbor as themselves. We pray to the Lord.
℟. Lord, hear our prayer.

Help all of us here to be models of faith for these children. We pray to the Lord.
℟. Lord, hear our prayer.

May all Christ's faithful people, who receive the sign of the cross at baptism, always and everywhere give witness to him by the way they live. We pray to the Lord.
R̕. Lord, hear our prayer.

The invocation of the saints follows.

220.
Let us ask Christ's mercy for these children, their parents and godparents, and all baptized Christians. Give them a new birth to eternal life through water and the Holy Spirit.
R̕. Lord, hear our prayer.

Help them always to be living members of your Church.
R̕. Lord, hear our prayer.

Inspire them to hear and follow your gospel, and to give witness to you by their lives. We ask this, Lord.
R̕. Lord, hear our prayer.

May they come with joy to the table of your sacrifice.
R̕. Lord, hear our prayer.

Help them to love God and neighbor as you have taught us.
R̕. Lord, hear our prayer.

May they grow in holiness and wisdom by listening to their fellow Christians and by following their example.
R̕. Lord, hear our prayer.

Let all your followers remain united in faith and love.
R̕. Lord, hear our prayer.

The invocation of the saints follows.

III. ANOTHER FORM OF THE PRAYER OF EXORCISM

221.
**Almighty God,
you sent your only Son
to rescue us from the slavery of sin,
and to give us the freedom
only your sons and daughters enjoy.**

**We now pray for these children
who will have to face the world with its temptations,
and fight the devil in all his cunning.**

**Your Son died and rose again to save us.
By his victory over sin and death,
cleanse these children from the stain of original sin.
Strengthen them with the grace of Christ,
and watch over them at every step in life's journey.
We ask this through Christ our Lord.**
All: **Amen.**

IV. BLESSING AND INVOCATION OF GOD OVER BAPTISMAL WATER

222. See the formula in no. 54a.

223. Facing the font (or vessel) containing the water, the celebrant says the following.

**Praise to you, almighty God and Father,
for you have created water to cleanse and to give life.**

All sing or say the following or some other suitable acclamation.

Blessed be God.

Celebrant:
**Praise to you, Lord Jesus Christ, the Father's only
  Son,
for you offered yourself on the cross,
that in the blood and water flowing from your side**

and through your death and resurrection
the Church might be born.

All: **Blessed be God.**

Celebrant:
Praise to you, God the Holy Spirit,
for you anointed Christ at his baptism in the waters
of the Jordan,
that we might all be baptized in you.

All: **Blessed be God.**

A

Celebrant:
Come to us, Lord, Father of all,
and make holy this water which you have created,
so that all who are baptized in it may be washed
clean of sin
and be born again to live as your children.

All sing or say the following or some other suitable invocation.
Hear us, Lord.

Celebrant:
Make this water holy, Lord,
so that all who are baptized into Christ's death and
resurrection by this water
may become more perfectly like your Son.

All: **Hear us, Lord.**

The celebrant touches the water with his right hand and continues.

Lord,
make holy this water which you have created,
so that all those whom you have chosen
may be born again by the power of the Holy Spirit
and may take their place among your holy people.

All: **Hear us, Lord.**

B

During the Easter season, if there is baptismal water already blessed, the celebrant concludes with the following:

You have called your children, N. and N.,
to this cleansing water,
that they may share in the faith of your Church and
have eternal life.
By the mystery of this consecrated water
lead them to a new and spiritual birth.

We ask this through Christ our Lord.

All: Amen.

224. Facing the font (or vessel) containing the water, the celebrant says the following.

Father, God of mercy,
through these waters of baptism
you have filled us with new life as your very own
children.

All sing or say a suitable acclamation or the following.
Blessed be God.

Celebrant:
From all who are baptized in water and the Holy
Spirit,
you have formed one people,
united in your Son, Jesus Christ.

All: Blessed be God.

Celebrant:
You have set us free and filled our hearts with the
Spirit of your love,
that we may live in your peace.

All: Blessed be God.

Celebrant:
You call those who have been baptized
to announce the Good News of Jesus Christ to
people everywhere.

All: Blessed be God.

A

The celebrant concludes with the following.

You have called your children, N. and N.,
to this cleansing water and new birth,
that by sharing the faith of your Church they may
have eternal life.
Bless ✠ this water in which they will be baptized.

We ask this in the name of Jesus the Lord.

All: **Amen.**

B

During the Easter season, if there is baptismal water already blessed, the celebrant concludes with the following:

You have called your children, N. and N.,
to this cleansing water,
that they may share in the faith of your Church and
have eternal life.
By the mystery of this consecrated water
lead them to a new and spiritual birth.

We ask this through Christ our Lord.

All: **Amen.**

V. ACCLAMATIONS AND HYMNS

ACCLAMATIONS FROM SACRED SCRIPTURE

225. Exodus 15:11
**Lord God, who is your equal?
Strong, majestic, and holy!
Worthy of praise, worker of wonders!**

226. 1 John 1:5
God is light: in him there is no darkness.

227. 1 John 4:16
God is love: he who lives in love, lives in God.

228. Ephesians 4:6
**There is one God, one Father of all:
he is over all, and through all:
he lives in all of us.**

229. Psalm 34:6
Come to him and receive his light!

230. see Ephesians 1:4
Blessed be God who chose you in Christ.

231. Ephesians 2:10
You are God's work of art, created in Christ Jesus.

232. 1 John 3:2
**You are now God's children, my dearest friends.
What you shall be in his glory has not yet been
    revealed.**

233. 1 John 3:1
**Think of how God loves you!
He calls you his own children,
and that is what you are.**

234. Revelation 22:14
**Happy are those who have washed their robes clean:
washed in the blood of the Lamb!**

235. Galatians 3:28
**All of you are one:
united in Christ Jesus.**

236. Ephesians 5:1-2
Imitate God, walk in his love,
just as Christ loves us.

HYMNS IN THE STYLE OF THE NEW TESTAMENT

237. 1 Peter 1:3-5
Praised be the Father of our Lord Jesus Christ:
a God so merciful and kind!
He has given us a new birth, a living hope,
by raising Jesus his Son from death.
Salvation is our undying inheritance,
preserved for us in heaven,
salvation at the end of time.

238.
How great the sign of God's love for us,
Jesus Christ our Lord:
promised before all time began,
revealed in these last days.
He lived and suffered and died for us,
but the Spirit raised him to life.
People everywhere have heard his message
and placed their faith in him.
What wonderful blessings he gives his people:
living in the Father's glory,
he fills all creation
and guides it to perfection.

SONGS FROM ANCIENT LITURGIES

239.
We believe in you, Lord Jesus Christ.
Fill our hearts with your radiance,
and make us the children of light!

240.
We come to you, Lord Jesus.
Fill us with your life,
make us children of the Father,
and one in you.

241.

Lord Jesus, from your wounded side
flowed streams of cleansing water:
the world was washed of all its sin,
all life made new again!

242.

The Father's voice calls us above the waters,
the glory of the Son shines on us,
the love of the Spirit fills us with life.

243.

Holy Church of God, stretch out your hand
and welcome your children
newborn of water
and of the Spirit of God.

244.

Rejoice, you newly baptized,
chosen members of the kingdom.
Buried with Christ in death,
you are reborn in him by faith.

245.

This is the fountain of life,
water made holy by the suffering of Christ,
washing all the world.
You who are washed in this water
have hope of heaven's kingdom.

VI. FORMS OF THE FINAL BLESSING

246. See the formula in the rite of baptism for several children, no. 70.

247.
Celebrant:
May God the almighty Father, who filled the world
with joy by giving us his only Son, bless these
newly-baptized children. May they grow to be more
fully like Jesus Christ our Lord.
All: **Amen.**

Celebrant:

May almighty God, who gives life on earth and in heaven, bless the parents of these children. They thank him now for the gift he has given them. May they always show that gratitude in action by loving and caring for their children.
All: **Amen.**

Celebrant:

May almighty God, who has given us a new birth by water and the Holy Spirit, generously bless all of us who are his faithful children. May we always live as his people, and may he bless all here present with his peace.
All: **Amen.**

Celebrant:

May almighty God, the Father, and the Son, ✛ and the Holy Spirit, bless you.
All: **Amen.**

Celebrant: **Go in peace.**
All: **Thanks be to God.**

248.
Celebrant:

May God, the source of life and love, who fills the hearts of mothers with love for their children, bless the mothers of these newly-baptized children. As they thank God for a safe delivery, may they find joy in the love, growth, and holiness of their children.
All: **Amen.**

Celebrant:

May God, the Father and model of all fathers, help these fathers to give good example, so that their children will grow to be mature Christians in all the fullness of Jesus Christ.
All: **Amen.**

Celebrant:

May God, who loves all people, bless all the relatives and friends who are gathered here. In his mercy, may he guard them from evil and give them his abundant peace.
All: **Amen.**

Celebrant:

And may almighty God, the Father, and the Son, ✝ and the Holy Spirit, bless you.
All: **Amen.**

Celebrant: **Go in peace.**
All: **Thanks be to God.**

249.

Celebrant:

My brothers and sisters, we entrust you all to the mercy and help of God the almighty Father, his only Son, and the Holy Spirit. May he watch over your life, and may we all walk by the light of faith, and attain the good things he has promised us.

Go in peace, and may almighty God, the Father, and the Son, ✝ and the Holy Spirit, bless you.
All: **Amen.**

Celebrant: **Go in peace.**
All: **Thanks be to God.**

APPENDIX

LITANY OF THE SAINTS

LITANY FOR SOLEMN INTERCESSIONS

In those sections which contain several sets of invocations
marked by A and B, one or the other may be chosen as
desired. The names of some saints may be added in the
proper place such as the patron saint, title of the church,
name of the founder, but in a different typeface. Some
petitions adapted to the place and need may be added to the
petitions for various needs.

I. PETITIONS TO GOD

A
Lord, have mercy
Lord, have mercy
Christ, have mercy
Christ, have mercy
Lord, have mercy
Lord, have mercy

B

God our Father in heaven	have mercy on us
God the Son, our redeemer	have mercy on us
God the Holy Spirit	have mercy on us
Holy Trinity, one God	have mercy on us

II. PETITIONS TO THE SAINTS

Holy Mary	pray for us.
Mother of God	pray for us.
Most honored of all virgins	pray for us.
Michael, Gabriel, and Raphael	pray for us.
Angels of God	pray for us.

Prophets and Fathers of our Faith

Abraham, Moses and Elijah	pray for us.
Saint John the Baptist	pray for us.
Saint Joseph	pray for us.

Holy patriarchs and prophets   pray for us

Apostles and Followers of Christ

Saint Peter and Saint Paul	pray for us
Saint Andrew	pray for us
Saint John and Saint James	pray for us
Saint Thomas	pray for us
Saint Matthew	pray for us
All holy apostles	pray for us
Saint Luke	pray for us
Saint Mark	pray for us
Saint Barnabas	pray for us
Saint Mary Magdalen	pray for us
All disciples of the Lord	pray for us

Martyrs

Saint Stephen	pray for us
Saint Ignatius	pray for us
Saint Polycarp	pray for us
Saint Justin	pray for us
Saint Lawrence	pray for us
Saint Cyprian	pray for us
Saint Boniface	pray for us
Saint Thomas Becket	pray for us
Saint John Fisher and Saint Thomas More	
	pray for us
Saint Paul Miki	pray for us
Saint Isaac Jogues and Saint John de Brebeuf	
	pray for us
Saint Peter Chanel	pray for us
Saint Charles Lwanga	pray for us
Saint Perpetua and Saint Felicity	pray for us
Saint Agnes	pray for us
Saint Maria Goretti	pray for us
All holy martyrs for Christ	pray for us

Bishops and Doctors

Saint Leo and Saint Gregory	pray for us
Saint Ambrose	pray for us

Saint Jerome	pray for us
Saint Augustine	pray for us
Saint Athanasius	pray for us
Saint Basil and Saint Gregory	pray for us
Saint John Chrysostom	pray for us
Saint Martin	pray for us
Saint Patrick	pray for us
Saint Cyril and Saint Methodius	pray for us
Saint Charles Borromeo	pray for us
Saint Francis de Sales	pray for us
Saint Pius	pray for us

Priests and Religious

Saint Anthony	pray for us
Saint Benedict	pray for us
Saint Bernard	pray for us
Saint Francis and Saint Dominic	pray for us
Saint Thomas Aquinas	pray for us
Saint Ignatius Loyola	pray for us
Saint Francis Xavier	pray for us
Saint Vincent de Paul	pray for us
Saint John Vianney	pray for us
Saint John Bosco	pray for us
Saint Catherine	pray for us
Saint Teresa	pray for us
Saint Rose	pray for us

Laity

Saint Louis	pray for us
Saint Monica	pray for us
Saint Elizabeth	pray for us
All holy men and women	pray for us

III. PETITIONS TO CHRIST

A

Lord, be merciful	Lord, save your people
From all evil	Lord, save your people
From every sin	Lord, save your people
From the snares of the devil	
	Lord, save your people

From anger and hatred	Lord, save your people
From every evil intention	Lord, save your people
From everlasting death	Lord, save your people
By your coming as man	Lord, save your people
By your birth	Lord, save your people
By your baptism and fasting	
	Lord, save your people
By your sufferings and cross	
	Lord, save your people
By your death and burial	Lord, save your people
By your rising to new life	Lord, save your people
By your return in glory to the Father	
	Lord, save your people
By your gift of the Holy Spirit	
	Lord, save your people
By your coming again in glory	
	Lord, save your people

B

Christ, Son of the living God	have mercy on us
You came into this world	have mercy on us
You suffered for us on the cross	have mercy on us
You died to save us	have mercy on us
You lay in the tomb	have mercy on us
You rose from the dead	have mercy on us
You returned in glory to the Father	
	have mercy on us
You sent the Holy Spirit upon your Apostles	
	have mercy on us
You are seated at the right hand of the Father	
	have mercy on us
You will come again to judge the living and the dead.	have mercy on us

IV. PETITIONS FOR VARIOUS NEEDS

A

Lord, be merciful to us	Lord, hear our prayer
Give us true repentance	Lord, hear our prayer
Strengthen us in your service	Lord, hear our prayer

Reward with eternal life all who do good to us
> Lord, hear our prayer

Bless the fruits of the earth and of man's labor
> Lord, hear our prayer

B

Lord, show us your kindness
> Lord, hear our prayer

Raise our thoughts and desires to you
> Lord, hear our prayer

Save us from final damnation
> Lord, hear our prayer

Save our friends and all who have helped us
> Lord, hear our prayer

Grant eternal rest to all who have died in the faith
> Lord, hear our prayer

Spare us from disease, hunger, and war
> Lord, hear our prayer

Bring all peoples together in trust and peace
> Lord, hear our prayer

C — always used

Guide and protect your holy Church
> Lord, hear our prayer

Keep the pope and all the clergy in faithful service to your Church
> Lord, hear our prayer

Bring all Christians together in unity
> Lord, hear our prayer

Lead all men to the light of the Gospel
> Lord, hear our prayer

V. CONCLUSION

A

Christ hear us

Christ hear us

Lord Jesus,   Lord, hear our prayer

Lord Jesus,   Lord, hear our prayer

B

Lamb of God, you take away the sins of the world: have mercy on us

Lamb of God, you take away the sins of the
world: have mercy on us
Lamb of God, you take away the sins of the
world: have mercy on us

PRAYERS

God of love, our strength and protection,
hear the prayers of your Church.
Grant that when we come to you in faith,
our prayers may be answered:
through Christ our Lord.
Or:
Lord God, you know our weakness.
In your mercy
grant that the example of your Saints
may bring us back to love and serve you
through Christ our Lord.

LITANY FOR CONSECRATIONS AND SOLEMN BLESSINGS

In any ceremony, the names of some saints may be added in
the proper place in the litany. This may include the patron
saint, the saints after whom the church is named, the
founder, patrons of those being consecrated, all the apostles
in the ordination of a bishop, and so on. Invocations which
are more appropriate for individual occasions may also be
added to the litany.

Lord, have mercy

Lord, have mercy

Christ, have mercy

Christ, have mercy

Lord, have mercy

Lord, have mercy

Holy Mary, Mother of God pray for us
Saint Michael pray for us
Holy angels of God pray for us
Saint John the Baptist pray for us

Saint Joseph	pray for us
Saint Peter and Saint Paul	pray for us
Saint Andrew	pray for us
Saint John	pray for us
Saint Mary Magdalene	pray for us
Saint Stephen	pray for us
Saint Ignatius	pray for us
Saint Lawrence	pray for us
Saint Perpetua and Saint Felicity	pray for us
Saint Agnes	pray for us
Saint Gregory	pray for us
Saint Augustine	pray for us
Saint Athanasius	pray for us
Saint Basil	pray for us
Saint Martin	pray for us
Saint Benedict	pray for us
Saint Francis and Saint Dominic	pray for us
Saint Francis Xavier	pray for us
Saint John Vianney	pray for us
Saint Catherine	pray for us
Saint Teresa	pray for us
All holy men and women	Lord, save us
Lord, be merciful	Lord, save us
From all evil	Lord, save us
From every sin	Lord, save us
From everlasting death	Lord, save us
By your coming as man	Lord, save us
By your death and rising to new life	Lord, save us
By your gift of the Holy Spirit	Lord, save us

Be merciful to us sinners   Lord, hear our prayer

Guide and protect your holy Church
        Lord, hear our prayer

Keep our pope and all the clergy in faithful service to
    your Church   Lord, hear our prayer

Bring all peoples together in trust and peace
        Lord, hear our prayer

Strengthen us in your service
        Lord, hear our prayer

SPECIAL INVOCATIONS

WHEN THERE IS BAPTISM DURING THE EASTER
VIGIL

**Give new life to these chosen ones by the grace of
baptism**   Lord, hear our prayer

ORDINATIONS

Bless these chosen men   Lord, hear our prayer
Bless these chosen men and make them holy
                    Lord, hear our prayer
Bless these chosen men, make them holy, and consecrate
    them for their sacred duties
                    Lord, hear our prayer

Ordination of one person:

Bless this chosen man   Lord, hear our prayer
Bless this chosen man and make him holy
                    Lord, hear our prayer
Bless this chosen man, make him holy, and consecrate
him for his sacred duties   Lord, hear our prayer

DEDICATION OF A CHURCH

**Make this church holy and consecrate it to your
    worship**   Lord, hear our prayer

Jesus, Son of the living God Lord, hear our prayer
Christ, hear us
                    Christ, hear us

Lord Jesus, hear our prayer
                    Lord Jesus, hear our prayer

RITE OF CONFIRMATION

RITE OF CONFIRMATION

Decree
Apostolic Constitution
Introduction (1-19)

CHAPTER I
RITE OF CONFIRMATION WITHIN MASS

Liturgy of the Word (20)

Sacrament of Confirmation
Presentation of the Candidates (21)
Homily or Instruction (22)
Renewal of Baptismal Promises (23)
The Laying on of Hands (24-25)
The Anointing with Chrism (26-29)
General Intercessions (30)

Liturgy of the Eucharist (31-32)
Blessing and Prayer over the People (33)

CHAPTER II
RITE OF CONFIRMATION OUTSIDE MASS

Entrance Rite
Entrance Song (34-35)
Opening Prayer

Celebration of the Word of God (36-37)

Sacrament of Confirmation
Presentation of the Candidates (38)
Homily or Instruction (39)
Renewal of Baptismal Promises (40)
The Laying on of Hands (41-42)
The Anointing with Chrism (43-46)
General Intercessions (47)
Lord's Prayer (48)
Blessing and Prayer over the People (49)

CHAPTER III
RITE OF CONFIRMATION BY A MINISTER WHO
IS NOT A BISHOP (50-51)

CHAPTER IV
CONFIRMATION OF A PERSON IN DANGER OF
DEATH (52-56)

CHAPTER V
TEXTS FOR THE CELEBRATION OF
CONFIRMATION (57-65)

SACRED CONGREGATION FOR DIVINE WORSHIP

Prot. n. 800/71

DECREE

In the sacrament of confirmation the apostles and the bishops, who are their successors, hand on to the baptized the special gift of the Holy Spirit, promised by Christ the Lord and poured out upon the apostles at Pentecost. Thus the initiation in the Christian life is completed so that believers are strengthened by power from heaven, made true witnesses of Christ in word and deed, and bound more closely to the Church.

To make "the intimate connection of this sacrament with the whole of Christian initiation" clearer, Vatican Council II decreed that the rite of confirmation was to be revised.[1]

Now that this work has been completed and approved by Pope Paul VI in the Apostolic Constitution *Divinae consortium naturae* of 15 August 1971, the Congregation for Divine Worship has published the new *Rite of Confirmation*. It is to replace the rite now in use in the Roman Pontifical and Ritual. The Congregation declares the present edition to be the *editio typica*.

All things to the contrary notwithstanding.

From the Office of the Congregation for Divine Worship, August 22, 1971.

Arturo Cardinal Tabera
Prefect

Annibale Bugnini
Secretary

---

[1] See SC art. 71 [DOL 1 no. 71].

APOSTOLIC CONSTITUTION ON THE SACRAMENT OF CONFIRMATION

PAUL, BISHOP
Servant of the Servants of God For an Everlasting Memorial

The sharing in the divine nature received through the grace of Christ bears a certain likeness to the origin, development, and nourishing of natural life. The faithful are born anew by baptism, strengthened by the sacrament of confirmation, and finally are sustained by the food of eternal life in the eucharist. By means of these sacraments of Christian initiation, they thus receive in increasing measure the treasures of divine life and advance toward the perfection of charity. It has rightly been written: "The body is washed, that the soul may be cleansed; the body is anointed, that the soul may be consecrated; the body is signed, that the soul too may be fortified; the body is overshadowed by the laying on of hands, that the soul may be enlightened by the Spirit; the body is fed on the body and blood of Christ, that the soul may be richly nourished by God."[1]

Conscious of its pastoral charge, the Second Vatican Ecumenical Council devoted special attention to these sacraments of initiation. It prescribed that the rites should be revised in a way that would make them more suited to the understanding of the faithful. Since the *Rite of Baptism for Children*, revised at the mandate of the Council and published at our command, is already in use, it is now fitting to publish a rite of confirmation, in order to show the unity of Christian initiation in its true light.

In fact, careful attention and application have been devoted in these last years to the task of revising the manner of celebrating this sacrament. The aim of this work has been that "the intimate connection of this sacrament with the whole of Christian initiation may stand out more clearly."[2] But the link between confirmation and the other sacraments of initiation is more easily perceived not simply from the fact that their rites have been more closely conjoined; the rite and words by which confirmation is conferred also make this link clear. As a result the rite and words of this

---

[1]Tertullian, *De resurrectione mortuorum* 8, 3: CCL 2, 931.
[2]SC art. 71.

sacrament "express more clearly the holy things they signify and the Christian people, as far as possible, are able to understand them with ease and take part in them fully, actively, and as befits a community."[3]

For that purpose, it has been our wish also to include in this revision what concerns the very essence of the rite of confirmation, through which the faithful receive the Holy Spirit as Gift.

The New Testament shows how the Holy Spirit was with Christ to bring the Messiah's mission to fulfillment. On receiving the baptism of John, Jesus saw the Spirit descending on him (see Mk 1:10) and remaining with him (see Jn 1:32). He was led by the Spirit to undertake his public ministry as the Messiah, relying on the Spirit's presence and assistance. Teaching the people of Nazareth, he showed by what he said that the words of Isaiah, "The Spirit of the Lord is upon me," referred to himself (see Lk 4:17–21).

He later promised his disciples that the Holy Spirit would help them also to bear fearless witness to their faith even before persecutors (see Lk 12:12). The day before he suffered, he assured his apostles that he would send the Spirit of truth from his Father (see Jn 15:26) to stay with them "for ever" (Jn 14:16) and help them to be his witnesses (see Jn 15:26). Finally, after his resurrection, Christ promised the coming descent of the Holy Spirit: "You will receive power when the Holy Spirit comes upon you; then you are to be my witnesses" (Acts 1:8; see Lk 24:49).

On the feast of Pentecost, the Holy Spirit did indeed come down in an extraordinary way on the apostles as they were gathered together with Mary the mother of Jesus and the group of disciples. They were so "filled with" the Holy Spirit (Acts 2:4) that by divine inspiration they began to proclaim "the mighty works of God." Peter regarded the Spirit who had thus come down upon the apostles as the gift of the Messianic age (see Acts 2:17–18). Then those who believed the apostles' preaching were baptized and they too received "the gift of the Holy Spirit" (Acts 2:38). From that time on the apostles, in fulfillment of Christ's wish, imparted to the newly baptized by the laying on of hands the gift of the Spirit that completes the grace of baptism. This is why the Letter to the Hebrews listed among the first ele-

[3]SC art. 21.

ments of Christian instruction the teaching about baptisms and the laying on of hands (Heb 6:2). This laying on of hands is rightly recognized by reason of Catholic tradition as the beginning of the sacrament of confirmation, which in a certain way perpetuates the grace of Pentecost in the Church.

This makes clear the specific importance of confirmation for sacramental initiation, by which the faithful "as members of the living Christ are incorporated into him and configured to him through baptism and through confirmation and the eucharist."[4] In baptism, the newly baptized receive forgiveness of sins, adoption as children of God, and the character of Christ by which they are made members of the Church and for the first time become sharers in the priesthood of their Savior (see 1 Pt 2:5, 9). Through the sacrament of confirmation those who have been born anew in baptism receive the inexpressible Gift, the Holy Spirit himself, by whom "they are endowed . . . with special strength."[5] Moreover, having been signed with the character of this sacrament, they are "more closely bound to the Church"[6] and "they are more strictly obliged to spread and defend the faith, both by word and by deed, as true witnesses of Christ."[7] Finally, confirmation is so closely linked with the holy eucharist[8] that the faithful, after being signed by baptism and confirmation, are incorporated fully into the Body of Christ by participation in the eucharist.[9]

From ancient times the conferring of the gift of the Holy Spirit has been carried out in the Church through various rites. These rites have undergone many changes in the East and the West, but always keeping as their meaning the conferring of the Holy Spirit.

In many Eastern rites it seems that from early times a rite of chrismation, not yet clearly distinguished from baptism,[10] prevailed for the conferring of the Holy Spirit. That rite continues in use today in the greater part of the Churches of the East.

[4]AG no. 36.
[5]LG no. 11.
[6]Ibid.
[7]Ibid. See also AG no. 11.
[8]See PO no. 5.
[9]See ibid.
[10]See Origen, *De principiis* 1, 3, 2: GCS 22, 49ff.; *Comm. in Ep. ad Rom.* 5, 8: PG 14, 1038. Cyril of Jerusalem, *Catech.* 16, 26; 21, 1–7, PG 33, 956; 1088–93.

In the West there are very ancient witnesses concerning the part of Christian initiation that was later distinctly recognized to be the sacrament of confirmation. There are directives for the performance of many rites after the baptismal washing and before the eucharistic meal—for example, anointing, the laying on of the hand, consignation[11]—contained both in liturgical documents[12] and in many testimonies of the Fathers. Consequently, in the course of the centuries, problems and doubts arose as to what belonged with certainty to the essence of the rite of confirmation. Worth mentioning, however, are at least some of the elements that, from the thirteenth century onward, in the ecumenical councils and in papal documents, cast considerable light on the importance of anointing, but at the same time did not allow the laying on of hands to be forgotten.

Our predecessor Innocent III wrote: "The anointing of the forehead with chrism signifies the laying on of the hand, the other name for which is confirmation, since through it the Holy Spirit is given for growth and strength."[13] Another of our predecessors, Innocent IV, mentions that the apostles conferred the Holy Spirit "through the laying on of the hand, which confirmation or the anointing of the forehead with chrism represents."[14] In the profession of faith of Emperor Michael Palaeologus read at the Council of Lyons II mention is made of the sacrament of confirmation, which "bishops confer by the laying on of hands, anointing with chrism those who have been baptized."[15] The Decree for the Armenians, issued by the Council of Florence, declares

[11]See Tertullian, *De Baptismo* 7–8: CCL 1, 282ff. B. Botte, ed., *La tradition apostolique de Saint Hippolyte: Liturgiewissenschaftliche Quellen und Forschungen* 39 (Münster, W., 1963) 52–54. Ambrose, *De Sacramentis* 2, 24; 3, 2, 8; 6, 2, 9; CSEL 73, 36; 42; 74–75; *De mysteriis* 7, 42; CSEL 73, 106.

[12]Mohlberg LibSacr 75, H. Lietzmann, ed., *Das Sacramentarium Gregorianum nach den Aachener Urexemplar: Liturgiegeschichtliche Quellen* 3 (Münster, W., 1921) 53ff. M. Ferotin, ed., *Liber Ordinum: Monumenta Ecclesiae Liturgica* V (Paris, 1904) 33ff. Mohlberg MissGall 67C. Vogel and R. Elze, *Le Pontifical Romano-Germanique du dixième siècle: Le Texte II; Studi e Testi* 227 (Vatican City, 1963) 109. M. Andrieu, *Le Pontifical Romaine du XIIe siecle* in *Le Pontifical Romain au Moyen-Age* v. 1: *Studi e Testi* 86 (Vatican City, 1938) 247ff., 289; *Le Pontifical de la Curie Romaine au XIIIe siècle*, ibid. v. 2: *Studi e Testi* 87 (Vatican City, 1940) 452ff.

[13]Innocent III, *Ep. "Cum venisset"*: PL 215, 285. The profession of faith that the same Pope imposed on the Waldenses has these words: "We regard confirmation by the bishop, that is, the laying on of hands, to be holy and to be received with reverence": PL 215, 1511.

[14]Innocent IV, *Ep. "Sub Catholicae professione"*: Mansi 23, 579.

[15]Council of Lyons II: Mansi 24, 71.

that the "matter" of the sacrament of confirmation is "chrism made of olive oil . . . and balsam"[16] and, quoting the words of the Acts of the Apostles concerning Peter and John, who gave the Holy Spirit through the laying on of hands (see Acts 8:17), it adds: "in the Church in place of that laying on of the hand, confirmation is given."[17] The Council of Trent, though it had no intention of defining the essential rite of confirmation, designated it simply by the term "the holy chrism of confirmation."[18] Benedict XIV made this declaration: "Therefore let this be said, which is beyond dispute: in the Latin Church the sacrament of confirmation is conferred by using the sacred chrism or olive oil mixed with balsam and blessed by the bishop, and by the sacramental minister's tracing the sign of the cross on the forehead of the recipient, while the same minister pronounces the words of the form."[19]

Taking account of these declarations and traditions, many theologians maintained that for valid administration of confirmation only the anointing with chrism, done by placing the hand on the forehead, was required. Nevertheless, in the rites of the Latin Church a laying of hands on those to be confirmed prior to anointing them with chrism was always prescribed.

With regard to the words of the rite by which the Holy Spirit is given, it should be noted that already in the primitive Church Peter and John, in order to complete the initiation of those baptized in Samaria, prayed that they might receive the Holy Spirit and then laid hands on them (see Acts 8:15–17). In the East the first traces of the expression *seal of the gift of the Holy Spirit* appeared in the fourth and fifth centuries.[20] The expression was quickly accepted by the Church of Constantinople and still is a use in Byzantine-Rite Churches.

---

[16]*Epistolae Pontificiae ad Concilium Florentinum spectantes:* G. Hofmann, ed., *Concilium Florentinum* v. 1, ser. A, part II (Rome, 1944) 128.
[17]Ibid, 129.
[18]CT 5, Act. II, 996.
[19]Benedict XIV, *Ep. "Ex quo primum tempore"* 52: *Benedicti XIV . . . Bullarium*, v. 3 (Prati, 1847) 320.
[20]Cyril of Jerusalem, *Catech.* 18, 33: PG 33, 1056. Asterius, Bishop of Amasea, *In parabolam de filio prodigo*, in the "Library of Photius," Cod. 271: PG 104, 213. See also *Epistola cuiusdam Patriarchae Constantinopolitani ad Martyrium, Episcopum Antiochenum:* PG 119, 900.

In the West, however, the words of the rite that completes baptism were less settled until the twelfth and thirteenth centuries. But in the twelfth-century Roman Pontifical the formulary that later became the common one first occurs: "I sign you with the sign of the cross and confirm you with the chrism of salvation. In the name of the Father and of the Son and of the Holy Spirit."[21]

From what we have recalled, it is clear that in the administration of confirmation in the East and the West, though in different ways, the most important place was occupied by the anointing, which in a certain way represents the apostolic laying on of hands. Since this anointing with chrism is an apt sign of the spiritual anointing of the Holy Spirit who is given to the faithful, we wish to confirm its existence and importance.

As regards the words pronounced in confirmation, we have examined with the consideration it deserves the dignity of the respected formulary used in the Latin Church, but we judge preferable the very ancient formulary belonging to the Byzantine Rite. This expresses the Gift of the Holy Spirit himself and calls to mind the outpouring of the Spirit on the day of Pentecost (see Acts 2:1–4, 38). We therefore adopt this formulary, rendering it almost word for word.

Therefore, in order that the revision of the rite of confirmation may, as is fitting, include even the essence of the sacramental rite, by our supreme apostolic authority we decree and lay down that in the Latin Church the following are to be observed for the future.

THE SACRAMENT OF CONFIRMATION IS CONFERRED THROUGH THE ANOINTING WITH CHRISM ON THE FOREHEAD, WHICH IS DONE BY THE LAYING ON OF THE HAND, AND THROUGH THE WORDS: BE SEALED WITH THE GIFT OF THE HOLY SPIRIT.[a]

But the laying of hands on the elect, carried out with the prescribed prayer before the anointing, is still to be regarded as very important, even if it is not of the essence of the sacramental rite: it contributes to the complete perfec-

---

[21]M. Andrieu, *Le Pontifical Romain du XIIe siècle* in *Le Pontifical Romain au Moyen-Age*, v. 1: *Studi e testi* 86 (Vatican City, 1938) 247.
[a]Latin: ACCIPE SIGNACULUM DONI SPIRITUS SANCTI.

tion of the rite and to a more thorough understanding of the sacrament. It is evident that this prior laying on of hands differs from the later laying on of the hand in the anointing of the forehead.

Having established and declared all these elements concerning the essential rite of the sacrament of confirmation, we also approve by our apostolic authority the rite for the same sacrament. This has been revised by the Congregation for Divine Worship, after consultation with the Congregations for the Doctrine of the Faith, for the Discipline of the Sacraments, and for the Evangelization of Peoples on the matters that are within their competence. The Latin edition of the rite containing the new sacramental form will come into effect as soon as it is published; the editions in the vernacular languages, prepared by the conferences of bishops and confirmed by the Apostolic See, will come into effect on the date to be laid down by each conference. The old rite may be used until the end of the year 1972. From 1 January 1973, however, only the new rite is to be used by those concerned.

We intend that everything that we have laid down and prescribed should be firm and effective in the Latin Church, notwithstanding, where relevant, the apostolic constitutions and ordinances issued by our predecessors, and other prescriptions, even those worthy of special mention.

INTRODUCTION

I. DIGNITY OF CONFIRMATION

1. Those who have been baptized continue on the path of Christian initiation through the sacrament of confirmation. In this sacrament they receive the Holy Spirit whom the Lord sent upon the apostles on Pentecost.

2. This giving of the Holy Spirit conforms believers more fully to Christ and strengthens them so that they may bear witness to Christ for the building up of his Body in faith and love. They are so marked with the character or seal of the Lord that the sacrament of confirmation cannot be repeated.

II. OFFICES AND MINISTRIES IN THE CELEBRATION OF CONFIRMATION

3. One of the highest responsibilities of the people of God is to prepare the baptized for confirmation. Pastors have the special responsibility to see that all the baptized reach the completion of Christian initiation and therefore that they are carefully prepared for confirmation.

Adult catechumens who are to be confirmed immediately after baptism have the help of the Christian community and, in particular, the formation that is given to them during the catechumenate. Catechists, sponsors, and members of the local Church participate in the catechumenate by means of catechesis and community celebrations of the rites of initiation. For those who were baptized in infancy and are confirmed only as adults the plan for the catechumenate is used with appropriate adaptations.

The initiation of children into the sacramental life is ordinarily the responsibility and concern of Christian parents. They are to form and gradually increase a spirit of faith in the children and, at times with the help of catechism classes, prepare them for the fruitful reception of the sacraments of confirmation and the eucharist. The role of the parents is also expressed by their active participation in the celebration of the sacraments.

4. Pains should be taken to give the liturgical service the festive and solemn character that its significance for the local Church requires. This will be achieved above all if the candidates are gathered together for a community celebration of the rites. All the people of God, represented by the families and friends of the candidates and by members of the local community, will be invited to take part in such a celebration and will endeavor to express their faith by means of the effects the Holy Spirit has produced in them.

5. As a rule there should be a sponsor for each of those to be confirmed. These sponsors bring the candidates to receive the sacrament, present them to the minister for the anointing, and will later help them to fulfill their baptismal promises faithfully under the influence of the Holy Spirit whom they have received.

In view of contemporary pastoral circumstances, it is desirable that the godparent at baptism, if available, also be the sponsor at confirmation. This change expresses more clearly the link between baptism and confirmation and also makes the function and responsibility of the sponsor more effective.

Nonetheless the option of choosing a special sponsor for confirmation is not excluded. Even the parents themselves may present their children for confirmation. It is for the local Ordinary to determine diocesan practice in the light of local conditions and circumstances.

6. Pastors will see that the sponsors, chosen by the candidates or their families, are spiritually fit to take on this responsibility and have these qualities:

> a. sufficient maturity to fulfill their function;
>
> b. membership in the Catholic Church and their own reception of Christian initiation through baptism, confirmation, and eucharist;
>
> c. freedom from any impediment of law to their fulfilling the office of sponsor.

7. The ordinary minister of confirmation is the bishop. Normally a bishop administers the sacrament so that there will be a clearer reference to the first pouring forth of the Holy Spirit on Pentecost: after the apostles were filled with the

Holy Spirit, they themselves gave the Spirit to the faithful through the laying on of hands. Thus the reception of the Spirit through the ministry of the bishop shows the close bond that joins the confirmed to the Church and the mandate received from Christ to bear witness to him before all.

The law gives the faculty to confirm to the following besides the bishop:

a. territorial prelates and territorial abbots, vicars and prefects apostolic, apostolic administrators and diocesan administrators, within the limits of their territory and while they hold office;

b. in consideration of the person to be confirmed, priests who, in virtue of an office or the mandate of the diocesan bishop, baptize a person who is no longer an infant or receive a person who is already baptized into the full communion of the Catholic Church;

c. in consideration of those who are in danger of death, a pastor or in fact any priest.

8. The diocesan bishop is to administer confirmation himself or to ensure that it is administered by another bishop. But if necessity requires, he may grant to one or several, determinate priests the faculty to administer this sacrament.

For a serious reason, as sometimes is present because of the large number of those to be confirmed, the bishop and also a priest who, in virtue of the law or a particular concession by competent authority, has the faculty to confirm, may in individual cases associate priests with himself so that they may administer the sacrament.

It is preferable that the priests who are so invited:

a. either have a particular function or office in the diocese, being, namely, either vicars general, episcopal vicars, or district or regional vicars;

b. or be the pastors of the places where confirmation is conferred, pastors of the places where the candidates belong, or priests who have had a special part in the catechetical preparation of the candidates.

III. CELEBRATION OF THE SACRAMENT

9. The sacrament of confirmation is conferred through the anointing with chrism on the forehead, which is done by the laying on of the hand, and through the words: BE SEALED WITH THE GIFT OF THE HOLY SPIRIT.

The laying of hands on the candidates with the prayer, *All-powerful God*, does not pertain to the valid giving of the sacrament. But it is still to be regarded as very important: it contributes to the complete perfection of the rite and to a more thorough understanding of the sacrament.

The priests who may at times be associated with the principal minister in conferring the sacrament join him in the laying of hands on all the candidates, but say nothing.

The whole rite presents a twofold symbolism. The laying of hands on the candidates by the bishop and the concelebrating priests represents the biblical gesture by which the gift of the Holy Spirit is invoked and in a manner well suited to the understanding of the Christian people. The anointing with chrism and the accompanying words express clearly the effect of the giving of the Holy Spirit. Signed with the perfumed oil, the baptized receive the indelible character, the seal of the Lord, together with the gift of the Spirit that conforms them more closely to Christ and gives them the grace of spreading "the sweet odor of Christ."

10. The chrism is consecrated by the bishop in the Mass that is celebrated as a rule on Holy Thursday for this purpose.

11. Adult catechumens and children who are baptized at an age when they are old enough for catechesis should ordinarily be admitted to confirmation and the eucharist at the same time as they receive baptism. If this is impossible, they should receive confirmation at another community celebration (see no. 4). Similarly, adults who were baptized in infancy should, after suitable preparation, receive confirmation and the eucharist at a community celebration.

With regard to children, in the Latin Church the administration of confirmation is generally delayed until about the seventh year. For pastoral reasons, however, especially to implant deeply in the lives of the faithful complete obedience to Christ the Lord and a firm witnessing to him, the conferences of bishops may set an age that seems more suitable. This means that the sacrament is given, after the formation proper to it, when the recipients are more mature.

In this case every necessary precaution is to be taken to ensure that in the event of danger of death or serious problems of another kind children receive confirmation in good time, so that they are not left without the benefit of this sacrament.

12. Persons who are to receive confirmation must have already received baptism. Moreover, those possessing the use of reason must be in the state of grace, properly instructed, and capable of renewing the baptismal promises.

The conference of bishops has responsibility for determining more precisely the catechetical resources for the preparation of candidates for confirmation, especially children.

In the case of adults, those principles are to be followed, with the required adaptations, that apply in the individual dioceses to admitting catechumens to baptism and eucharist. Measures are to be taken especially for catechesis preceding confirmation and for the association of the candidates with the Christian community and with individual Christians. Such association is to be of a kind that is effective and sufficient as a practical help for the candidates to achieve formation toward both bearing witness by Christian living and carrying on the apostolate. It should also assist the candidates to have a genuine desire to share in the eucharist (see *Rite of Christian Initiation of Adults,* Introduction no. 19).

Sometimes the preparation of baptized adults for confirmation coincides with preparation for marriage. In such cases, if it is foreseen that the conditions for a fruitful reception of confirmation cannot be satisfied, the local Ordinary will judge whether it is better to defer confirmation until after the marriage.

If one who has the use of reason is confirmed in danger of death, there should, as far as possible, be some spiritual preparation beforehand, suited to the individual situation.

13. Confirmation takes place as a rule within Mass in order that the fundamental connection of this sacrament with all of Christian initiation may stand out in clearer light. Chris-

tian initiation reaches its culmination in the communion of the body and blood of Christ. The newly confirmed therefore participate in the eucharist, which completes their Christian initiation.

If the candidates for confirmation are children who have not received the eucharist and are not being admitted to first communion at this liturgical celebration or if there are other special circumstances, confirmation should be celebrated outside Mass. When this occurs, there is first to be a celebration of the word of God.

When confirmation is given during Mass, it is fitting that the minister of confirmation celebrate the Mass or, better, concelebrate it, especially with those priests who may be joining him in administering the sacrament.

If the Mass is celebrated by someone else, it is proper that the bishop preside over the liturgy of the word, doing all that the celebrant normally does, and that he give the blessing at the end of Mass.

Great emphasis should be placed on the celebration of the word of God that introduces the rite of confirmation. It is from the hearing of the word of God that the many-sided work of the Holy Spirit flows out upon the Church and upon each one of the baptized and confirmed. Through this hearing of his word God's will is made known in the life of Christians.

Great importance is likewise to be attached to the saying of the Lord's Prayer. Those to be confirmed will recite it together with the congregation—either during Mass before communion or outside Mass before the blessing—because it is the Spirit who prays in us and in the Spirit the Christian says, "Abba, Father."

14. The names of those confirmed, as well as the names of the minister, parents, and sponsors, and a notation of the place and date of the confirmation conferred, are to be entered into the registry of confirmations of the diocesan curia, or, where the conference of bishops or the diocesan bishop has so ordered, in a book to be kept in the parish archives. The pastor must inform the pastor of the recipient's place of baptism that confirmation has been conferred, so that this may be recorded in the baptismal register, according to the requirements of the law.

15. If the pastor of the place was not present, the minister should promptly inform him of the confirmation, either personally or through a representative.

IV. ADAPTATIONS PERMITTED IN THE RITE OF CONFIRMATION

16. By virtue of the Constitution of the Liturgy (art. 63 b), conferences of bishops have the right to prepare in particular rituals a section bearing the same title as the present title IV on confirmation in the Roman Pontifical. This is to be adapted to the needs of the individual parts of the world and it is to be used once the *acta* of the conference have been reviewed by the Apostolic See.[1]

17. The conference of bishops will consider whether, in view of local circumstances and the culture and traditions of the people, it is opportune:

> a. to make suitable adaptations of the formularies for the renewal of baptismal promises and professions, either following the text in the rite of baptism or accommodating these formularies so that they are more in accord with the circumstances of the candidates for confirmation;

> b. to introduce a different manner for the minister to give the sign of peace after the anointing, either to each individual or to all the newly confirmed together.

18. The minister of confirmation may introduce some explanations into the rite in individual cases in view of the capacity of the candidates for confirmation. He may also make appropriate accommodations in the existing texts, for example, by expressing these in a kind of dialogue, especially with children.

When confirmation is given by a minister who is not a bishop, whether by concession of the general law or by special indult of the Apostolic See, it is fitting for him to mention in the homily that the bishop is the original minister of the sacrament and to explain the reason why priests receive the

---

[1] See *Rite of Baptism for Children*, General Introduction to Christian Initiation nos. 30–33.

faculty to confirm from the law or by an indult of the Apostolic See.

V. PREPARATIONS

19. The following should be prepared for the administration of confirmation:

a. when confirmation is given within Mass, the vestments prescribed for the celebration of Mass both for the bishop and for any assisting priests who concelebrate with him. If the Mass is celebrated by someone else, the minister of confirmation as well as any priests joining him in administering the sacrament should take part in the Mass wearing the vestments prescribed for administering confirmation: alb, stole, and, for the minister, the cope; these also are the vestments worn when confirmation is given outside Mass;

b. chairs for the bishop and the priests assisting him;

c. vessel (or vessels) for the chrism;

d. Roman Pontifical or Roman Ritual;

e. when confirmation is given within Mass, the requisites for celebration of Mass and for communion under both kinds, if it is to be given;

f. the requisites for the washing of hands after the anointing of those to be confirmed.

CHAPTER I

RITE OF CONFIRMATION WITHIN MASS

LITURGY OF THE WORD

20. The liturgy of the word is celebrated in the ordinary way. The readings may be taken in whole or in part from the Mass of the day or from the texts for confirmation in the *Lectionary for Mass* (nos. 763-767) and listed below (nos. 61-65).

SACRAMENT OF CONFIRMATION

PRESENTATION OF THE CANDIDATES

21. After the gospel the bishop and the priests who will be ministers of the sacrament with him take their seats. The pastor or another priest, deacon, or catechist presents the candidates for confirmation, according to the custom of the region. If possible, each candidate is called by name and comes individually to the sanctuary. If the candidates are children, they are accompanied by one of their sponsors or parents and stand before the celebrant.

If there are very many candidates, they are not called by name, but simply take a suitable place before the bishop.

HOMILY OR INSTRUCTION

22. The bishop then gives a brief homily. He should explain the readings and so lead the candidates, their sponsors and parents, and the whole assembly to a deeper understanding of the mystery of confirmation.
He may use these or similar words:

On the day of Pentecost the apostles received the Holy Spirit as the Lord had promised. They also received the power of giving the Holy Spirit to others and so completing the work of baptism. This we read in the Acts of the Apostles. When Saint Paul placed his hands on those who had been baptized, the Holy Spirit came upon them, and they began to speak in

other languages and in prophetic words.

Bishops are successors of the apostles and have this power of giving the Holy Spirit to the baptized, either personally or through the priests they appoint.

In our day the coming of the Holy Spirit in confirmation is no longer marked by the gift of tongues, but we know his coming by faith. He fills our hearts with the love of God, brings us together in one faith but in different vocations, and works within us to make the Church one and holy.

The gift of the Holy Spirit which you are to receive will be a spiritual sign and seal to make you more like Christ and more perfect members of his Church. At his baptism by John, Christ himself was anointed by the Spirit and sent out on his public ministry to set the world on fire.

You have already been baptized into Christ and now you will receive the power of his Spirit and the sign of the cross on your forehead. You must be witnesses before all the world to his suffering, death, and resurrection; your way of life should at all times reflect the goodness of Christ. Christ gives varied gifts to his Church, and the Spirit distributes them among the members of Christ's body to build up the holy people of God in unity and love.

Be active members of the Church, alive in Jesus Christ. Under the guidance of the Holy Spirit give your lives completely in the service of all, as did Christ, who came not to be served but to serve.

So now, before you receive the Spirit, I ask you to renew the profession of faith you made in baptism or your parents and godparents made in union with the whole Church.

RENEWAL OF BAPTISMAL PROMISES

23. After the homily the candidates stand and the bishop questions them:

Do you reject Satan and all his works and all his empty promises?
The candidates respond together: **I do.**

Bishop:
Do you believe in God the Father almighty, creator of heaven and earth?
Candidates: **I do.**

Bishop:
Do you believe in Jesus Christ, his only Son, our Lord, who was born of the Virgin Mary, was crucified, died, and was buried, rose from the dead, and is now seated at the right hand of the Father?
Candidates: **I do.**

Bishop:
Do you believe in the Holy Spirit, the Lord, the giver of life, who came upon the apostles at Pentecost and today is given to you sacramentally in confirmation?
Candidates: **I do.**

Bishop:
Do you believe in the holy catholic Church, the communion of saints, the forgiveness of sins, the resurrection of the body, and life everlasting?
Candidates: **I do.**

The bishop confirms their profession of faith by proclaiming the faith of the Church:

This is our faith. This is the faith of the Church. We are proud to profess it in Christ Jesus our Lord.

The whole congregation responds: **Amen.**

For **This is our faith,** some other formula may be substituted, or the community may express its faith in a suitable song.

THE LAYING ON OF HANDS
24. The concelebrating priests stand near the bishop. He faces the people and with hands joined, sings or says:

My dear friends:
in baptism God our Father gave the new birth of
**   eternal life**
to his chosen sons and daughters.
Let us pray to our Father
that he will pour out the Holy Spirit
to strengthen his sons and daughters with his gifts
and anoint them to be more like Christ the Son of
**   God.**

All pray in silence for a short time.

25. The bishop and the priests who will minister the sacrament with him lay hands upon all the candidates (by extend-
ing their hands over them). The bishop alone sings or says:

All-powerful God, Father of our Lord Jesus Christ,
by water and the Holy Spirit
you freed your sons and daughters from sin
and gave them new life.
Send your Holy Spirit upon them
to be their Helper and Guide.
Give them the spirit of wisdom and understanding,
the spirit of right judgment and courage,
the spirit of knowledge and reverence.
Fill them with the spirit of wonder and awe in your
**   presence.**
We ask this through Christ our Lord.
R̖. Amen.

THE ANOINTING WITH CHRISM

26. The deacon brings the chrism to the bishop. Each candidate goes to the bishop, or the bishop may go to the
individual candidates. The one who presented the candidate
places his right hand on the latter's shoulder and gives the
candidate's name to the bishop; or the candidate may give
his own name.

27. The bishop dips his right thumb in the chrism and
makes the sign of the cross on the forehead of the one to be
confirmed, as he says:

N., be sealed with the Gift of the Holy Spirit.
The newly confirmed responds: **Amen.**

The bishop says:
Peace be with you.
The newly confirmed responds: **And also with you.**

28. If priests assist the bishop in conferring the sacrament, all the vessels of chrism are brought to the bishop by the deacon or by other ministers. Each of the priests comes to the bishop, who gives him a vessel of chrism.

The candidates go to the bishop or to the priests, or the bishop and priests may go to the candidates. The anointing is done as described above (no. 27).

29. During the anointing a suitable song may be sung. After the anointing the bishop and the priests wash their hands.

GENERAL INTERCESSIONS

30. The general intercessions follow, in this or a similar form determined by the competent authority.

Bishop:
My dear friends:
let us be one in prayer to God our Father
as we are one in the faith, hope, and love his Spirit
    gives.

Deacon or minister:
For these sons and daughters of God,
confirmed by the gift of the Spirit,
that they give witness to Christ
by lives built on faith and love:
let us pray to the Lord.
R̥. Lord, hear our prayer.

Deacon or minister:
For their parents and godparents
who led them in faith,
that by word and example they may always encourage
    them
to follow the way of Jesus Christ:

let us pray to the Lord.
R̸. **Lord, hear our prayer.**

Deacon or minister:
For the holy Church of God,
in union with N. our pope, N. our bishop, and all the
bishops,
that God, who gathers us together by the Holy Spirit,
may help us grow in unity of faith and love
until his Son returns in glory:
let us pray to the Lord.
R̸. **Lord, hear our prayer.**

Deacon or minister:
For all men,
of every race and nation,
that they may acknowledge the one God as Father,
and in the bond of common brotherhood
seek his kingdom,
which is peace and joy in the Holy Spirit:
let us pray to the Lord.
R̸. **Lord, hear our prayer.**

Bishop:
God our Father,
you sent your Holy Spirit upon the apostles,
and through them and their successors
you give the Spirit to your people.
May his work begun at Pentecost
continue to grow in the hearts of all who believe.
We ask this through Christ our Lord.

LITURGY OF THE EUCHARIST

31. After the general intercessions the liturgy of the eucharist is celebrated according to the *Order of Mass,* with these exceptions:
   a) the profession of faith is omitted, since it has already been made;
   b) some of the newly confirmed may join those who bring the gifts to the altar;

c) when Euchaustic Prayer I is used, the special form of **Father, accept this offering** is said.

32. Adults who are confirmed, their sponsors, parents, wives and husbands, and catechists may receive communion under both kinds.

BLESSING

33. Instead of the usual blessing at the end of Mass, the following blessing or prayer over the people is used.

God our Father
made you his children by water and the Holy Spirit:
may he bless you
and watch over you with his fatherly love.
R̰. **Amen.**

Jesus Christ the Son of God
promised that the Spirit of truth
would be with his Church for ever:
may he bless you and give you courage
in professing the true faith.
R̰. **Amen.**

The Holy Spirit
came down upon the disciples
and set their hearts on fire with love:
may he bless you,
keep you one in faith and love
and bring you to the joy of God's kingdom.
R̰. **Amen.**

The bishop adds immediately:
May almighty God bless you,
the Father, and the Son, ✝ and the Holy Spirit.
R̰. **Amen.**

PRAYER OVER THE PEOPLE

Instead of the preceding blessing, the prayer over the people may be used.

The deacon or minister gives the invitation in these or similar words:

Bow your heads and pray for God's blessing.

The bishop extends his hands over the people and sings or says:

**God our Father,
complete the work you have begun
and keep the gifts of your Holy Spirit
active in the hearts of your people.
Make them ready to live his Gospel
and eager to do his will.
May they never be ashamed
to proclaim to all the world Christ crucified
living and reigning for ever and ever.
R̷. Amen.**

The bishop adds immediately:
**And may the blessing of almighty God
the Father, and the Son,✛and the Holy Spirit
come upon you and remain with you
    for ever.
R̷. Amen.**

CHAPTER II

RITE OF CONFIRMATION OUTSIDE MASS

INTRODUCTORY RITES

ENTRANCE SONG

34. When the candidates, their sponsors and parents, and the whole assembly of the faithful have gathered, the bishop goes to the sanctuary with the priests who assist him, one or more deacons, and the ministers. Meanwhile all may sing a psalm or appropriate song.

35. The bishop makes the usual reverence to the altar with the ministers and greets the people:

Peace be with you.
All: **And also with you.**

OPENING PRAYER

Let us pray.

God of power and mercy,
send your Holy Spirit
to live in our hearts
and make us temples of his glory.
We ask this through our Lord Jesus Christ, your
    Son,
who lives and reigns with you and the Holy Spirit,
one God, for ever and ever.
℟. **Amen.**

Or:
Lord,
fulfill your promise:
send your Holy Spirit to make us witnesses before the
    world

to the Good News proclaimed by Jesus Christ, our
    Lord,
who lives and reigns with you and the Holy Spirit,
one God, for ever and ever.
R̷. **Amen.**

Or:
**Lord,
send us your Holy Spirit
to help us walk in unity of faith
and grow in the strength of his love
to the full stature of Christ,
who lives and reigns with you and the Holy Spirit,
one God, for ever and ever.**
R̷. **Amen.**

Or:
**Lord,
fulfill the promise given by your Son
and send the Holy Spirit
to enlighten our minds
and lead us to all truth. Grant this through our Lord
    Jesus Christ,
who lives and reigns with you and the Holy Spirit,
one God, for ever and ever.**
R̷. **Amen.**

CELEBRATION OF THE WORD OF GOD

36. The celebration of the word of God follows. At least one
of the readings suggested for the Mass of confirmation (see
nos. 61-65) is read.

37. If two or three readings are chosen, the traditional order
is followed, that is, the Old Testament, the Apostle, and the
Gospel. After the first and second reading there should be a
psalm or song, or a period of silence may be observed.

SACRAMENT OF CONFIRMATION

PRESENTATION OF THE CANDIDATES

38. After the readings the bishop and the priests who will be ministers of the sacrament with him take their seats. The pastor or another priest, deacon, or catechist presents the candidates for confirmation, according to the custom of the region. If possible, each candidate is called by name and comes individually to the sanctuary. If the candidates are children, they are accompanied by one of their sponsors or parents and stand before the celebrant.

If there are very many candidates, they are not called by name, but simply take a suitable place before the bishop.

HOMILY OR INSTRUCTION

39. The bishop then gives a brief homily. He should explain the readings and so lead the candidates, their sponsors and parents, and the whole assembly to a deeper understanding of the mystery of confirmation.

He may use these or similar words:

On the day of Pentecost the apostles received the Holy Spirit as the Lord had promised. They also received the power of giving the Holy Spirit to others and so completing the work of baptism. This we read in the Acts of the Apostles. When Saint Paul placed his hands on those who had been baptized, the Holy Spirit came upon them, and they began to speak in other languages and in prophetic words.

Bishops are successors of the apostles and have this power of giving the Holy Spirit to the baptized, either personally or through the priests they appoint.

In our day the coming of the Holy Spirit in confirmation is no longer marked by the gift of tongues, but we know his coming by faith. He fills our hearts with the love of God, brings us together in one faith but in different vocations, and works within us to make the Church one and holy.

The gift of the Holy Spirit which you are to receive

will be a spiritual sign and seal to make you more like Christ and more perfect members of his Church. At his baptism by John, Christ himself was anointed by the Spirit and sent out on his public ministry to set the world on fire.

You have already been baptized into Christ and now you will receive the power of his Spirit and the sign of the cross on your forehead. You must be witnesses before all the world to his suffering, death, and resurrection; your way of life should at all times reflect the goodness of Christ. Christ gives varied gifts to his Church, and the Spirit distributes them among the members of Christ's body to build up the holy people of God in unity and love.

Be active members of the Church, alive in Jesus Christ. Under the guidance of the Holy Spirit give your lives completely in the service of all, as did Christ, who came not to be served but to serve.

So now, before you receive the Spirit, I ask you to renew the profession of faith you made in baptism or your parents and godparents made in union with the whole Church.

RENEWAL OF BAPTISMAL PROMISES
40. After the homily the candidates stand and the bishop questions them:

Do you reject Satan and all his works and all his empty promises?
The candidates respond together: **I do.**

Bishop:
Do you believe in God the Father almighty, creator of heaven and earth?
Candidates: **I do.**

Bishop:
**Do you believe in Jesus Christ, his only Son, our Lord, who was born of the Virgin Mary,
was crucified, died, and was buried,
rose from the dead,**

and is now seated at the right hand of the Father?
Candidates: **I do.**

Bishop:
**Do you believe in the Holy Spirit,
the Lord, the giver of life,
who came upon the apostles at Pentecost
and today is given to you sacramentally in
    confirmation?**
Candidates: **I do.**

Bishop:
**Do you believe in the holy catholic Church,
the communion of saints, the forgiveness of sins,
the resurrection of the body, and life everlasting?**
Candidates: **I do.**

The bishop confirms their profession of faith by proclaiming
the faith of the Church:

**This is our faith. This is the faith of the Church.
We are proud to profess it in Christ Jesus our Lord.**
The whole congregation responds: **Amen.**

For **This is our faith,** some other formula may be substituted, or the community may express its faith in a suitable
song.

THE LAYING ON OF HANDS

41. The concelebrating priests stand near the bishop. He
faces the people and with hands joined, sings or says:

**My dear friends:
in baptism God our Father gave the new birth of
    eternal life
to his chosen sons and daughters.
Let us pray to our Father
that he will pour out the Holy Spirit
to strengthen his sons and daughters with his gifts
and anoint them to be more like Christ the Son of
    God.**

All pray in silence for a short time.

42. The bishop and the priests who will minister the sacra-

ment with him lay hands upon all the candidates (by extend-
ing their hands over them). The bishop alone sings or says:

**All-powerful God, Father of our Lord Jesus Christ,
by water and the Holy Spirit
you freed your sons and daughters from sin
and gave them new life.
Send your Holy Spirit upon them
to be their Helper and Guide.
Give them the spirit of wisdom and understanding,
the spirit of right judgment and courage,
the spirit of knowledge and reverence.
Fill them with the spirit of wonder and awe in your
  presence.
We ask this through Christ our Lord.
R̷. Amen.**

THE ANOINTING WITH CHRISM

43. The deacon brings the chrism to the bishop. Each candidate goes to the bishop, or the bishop may go to the individual candidates. The one who presented the candidate
places his right hand on the latter's shoulder and gives the
candidate's name to the bishop; or the candidate may give
his own name.

44. The bishop dips his right thumb in the chrism and
makes the sign of the cross on the forehead of the one to be
confirmed, as he says:

N., be sealed with the Gift of the Holy Spirit.
The newly confirmed responds: **Amen.**

The bishop says:
Peace be with you.
The newly confirmed responds: **And also with you.**

45. If priests assist the bishop in conferring the sacrament,
all the vessels of chrism are brought to the bishop by the
deacon or by other ministers. Each of the priests comes to
the bishop, who gives him a vessel of chrism.
The candidates go to the bishop or to the priests, or the
bishop and priests may go to the candidates. The anointing
is done as described above (no. 44).

46. During the anointing a suitable song may be sung. After the anointing the bishop and the priests wash their hands.

GENERAL INTERCESSIONS

47. The general intercessions follow, in this or a similar form determined by the competent authority.

Bishop:

My dear friends:
let us be one in prayer to God our Father
as we are one in the faith, hope, and love his Spirit
gives.

Deacon or minister:

For these sons and daughters of God,
confirmed by the gift of the Spirit,
that they give witness to Christ
by lives built on faith and love:
let us pray to the Lord.
℟. **Lord, hear our prayer.**

Deacon or minister:

For their parents and godparents
who led them in faith,
that by word and example they may always encourage
them
to follow the way of Jesus Christ:
let us pray to the Lord.
℟. **Lord, hear our prayer.**

Deacon or minister:

For the holy Church of God,
in union with N. our pope, N. our bishop, and all the
bishops,
that God, who gathers us together by the Holy Spirit,
may help us grow in unity of faith and love
until his Son returns in glory:
let us pray to the Lord.
℟. **Lord, hear our prayer.**

Deacon or minister:

For all men,
of every race and nation,

that they may acknowledge the one God as Father,
and in the bond of common brotherhood
seek his kingdom,
which is peace and joy in the Holy Spirit:
let us pray to the Lord.
R̸. Lord, hear our prayer.

Bishop:
God our Father,
you sent your Holy Spirit upon the apostles,
and through them and their successors
you give the Spirit to your people.
May his work begun at Pentecost
continue to grow in the hearts of all who believe.
We ask this through Christ our Lord.

LORD'S PRAYER

48. All then say the Lord's Prayer, which the bishop may
introduce in these or similar words:

Dear friends in Christ,
let us pray together
as the Lord Jesus Christ has taught.

All:
Our Father. . . .

49. After the Lord's Prayer the bishop blesses all present.
Instead of the usual blessing, the following blessing or
prayer over the people is used.

God our Father
made you his children by water and the Holy Spirit:
may he bless you
and watch over you with his fatherly love.
R̸. Amen.

Jesus Christ the Son of God
promised that the Spirit of truth
would be with his Church for ever:
may he bless you and give you courage
in professing the true faith.
R̸. Amen.

The Holy Spirit
came down upon the disciples
and set their hearts on fire with love:
may he bless you,
keep you one in faith and love
and bring you to the joy of God's kingdom.
R̹. **Amen.**

The bishop adds immediately:

May almighty God bless you,
the Father, and the Son, + and the Holy Spirit.
R̹. **Amen.**

PRAYER OVER THE PEOPLE

Instead of the preceding blessing, the prayer over the people
may be used.
The deacon or minister gives the invitation in these or similar words:

Bow your heads and pray for God's blessing.

The bishop extends his hands over the people and sings or
says:

God our Father,
complete the work you have begun
and keep the gifts of your Holy Spirit
active in the hearts of your people.
Make them ready to live his Gospel
and eager to do his will.
May they never be ashamed
to proclaim to all the world Christ crucified
living and reigning for ever and ever.
R̹. **Amen.**

The bishop adds immediately:

And may the blessing of almighty God
the Father, and the Son, + and the Holy Spirit,
Come upon you and remain with you forever.
R̹. **Amen.**

CHAPTER III

RITE OF CONFIRMATION BY A MINISTER WHO IS NOT A BISHOP

50. The minister of confirmation who is not a bishop and who confirms either by concession of the general law or by special indult of the Apostolic See observes the rite described above.

51. If, because of the large number of candidates, other priests join the celebrant in the administration of the sacrament, he chooses them in accord with no. 8 above. These priests should also concelebrate the Mass in which confirmation is conferred.

CHAPTER IV

CONFIRMATION OF A PERSON
IN DANGER OF DEATH

52. It is of the greatest importance that the initiation of every baptized Christian be completed by the sacraments of confirmation and the eucharist. The sick person in danger of death who has reached the age of reason should therefore be strengthened by confirmation before he receives the eucharist as viaticum, after the necessary and possible catechesis.

Confirmation in danger of death and anointing of the sick are not ordinarily to be celebrated in a continuous rite.

In the case of a child who has not yet reached the age of reason, confirmation is given in accord with the same principles and norms as for baptism.

53. When circumstances permit, the entire rite described above is followed.

54. In case of urgent necessity, the minister of confirmation lays his hands upon the sick person as he says:

All-powerful God, Father of our Lord Jesus Christ,
by water and the Holy Spirit
you freed your son (daughter) from sin
and gave him (her) new life.
Send your Holy Spirit upon him (her)
to be his (her) Helper and Guide.
Give him (her) the spirit of wisdom and
    understanding,
the spirit of right judgment and courage,
the spirit of knowledge and reverence.
Fill him (her) with the spirit of wonder and awe in
    your presence.
We ask this through Christ our Lord.
℟. **Amen.**

55. Then the minister dips his right thumb in the chrism and makes the sign of the cross on the forehead of the one to be confirmed, as he says:

N., be sealed with the Gift of the Holy Spirit.

The newly confirmed responds, if he is able: **Amen.**

Other parts of the preparatory and concluding rites may be added in individual cases, depending on the circumstances.

56. In case of extreme necessity, it is sufficient that the anointing be done with the sacramental form:

N., be sealed with the Gift of the Holy Spirit.

CHAPTER V

TEXTS FOR THE CELEBRATION OF CONFIRMATION

I. MASS FOR THE CELEBRATION OF CONFIRMATION

57. One of the following Masses is celebrated where confirmation is given within Mass or immediately before or after it, except on the Sundays of Advent, Lent and Easter, Solemnities, Ash Wednesday, and the weekdays of Holy Week. Red or white vestments are worn.

A
58.

INTRODUCTORY RITES

Ezekiel 36:25-26
I will pour clean water on you and I will give you a new heart, a new spirit within you, says the Lord.

OPENING PRAYER

God of power and mercy,
send your Holy Spirit
to live in our hearts
and make us temples of his glory.

We ask this through our Lord Jesus Christ, your Son,
who lives and reigns with you and the Holy Spirit,
one God, for ever and ever.
℟. Amen.

Or:
Lord,
fulfill your promise.
Send your Holy Spirit
to make us witnesses before the world
to the good news proclaimed by Jesus Christ, our
   Lord,

who lives and reigns with you and the Holy Spirit,
one God, for ever and ever.
R̷. **Amen.**

Another prayer may be chosen from nos. 59, 60.
See Lectionary for Mass, nos. 763–767.

PRAYER OVER THE GIFTS
Pray, brethren ...

**Lord,
we celebrate the memorial of our redemption
by which your Son won for us the gift of the Holy
     Spirit.
Accept our offerings,
and send us your Spirit
to make us more like Christ
in bearing witness to the world.**

We ask this through Christ our Lord.
R̷. **Amen.**

When Eucharistic Prayer I is used, the special form of **Father,
accept this offering** is said.

**Father,
accept this offering
from your whole family
and from those reborn in baptism
and confirmed by the coming of the Holy Spirit.
Protect them with your love and keep them close to
     you.
[Through Christ our Lord.   R̷. Amen.]**

COMMUNION RITE
See Hebrews 6:4
**All you who have been enlightened, who have ex-
perienced the gift of heaven and who have received
your share of the Holy Spirit: rejoice in the Lord.**

PRAYER AFTER COMMUNION
Let us pray.

Pause for silent prayer, if this has not preceded.

Lord,
help those you have anointed by your Spirit
and fed with the body and blood of your Son.
Support them through every trial
and by their works of love.
build up the Church in holiness and joy.
Grant this through Christ our Lord.
℞. Amen.

SOLEMN BLESSING
God our Father
made you his children by water and the Holy Spirit:
may he bless you
and watch over you with his fatherly love.
℞. Amen.

Jesus Christ the Son of God
promised that the Spirit of truth
would be with his Church for ever:
may he bless you and give you courage
in professing the true faith.
℞. Amen.

The Holy Spirit
came down upon the disciples
and set their hearts on fire with love:
may he bless you,
keep you one in faith and love
and bring you to the joy of God's kingdom.
℞. Amen.

May almighty God bless you.
the Father, and the Son, ✝ and the Holy Spirit.
℞. Amen.

Or:

PRAYER OVER THE PEOPLE
God our Father,
complete the work you have begun
and keep the gifts of your Holy Spirit
active in the hearts of your people.
Make them ready to live his gospel
and eager to do his will.

May they never be ashamed
to proclaim to all the world Christ crucified
living and reigning for ever and ever.
R̢. **Amen.**

And may the blessing of Almighty God,
the Father, and the Son, ✛ and the Holy Spirit,
come upon you and remain with you for ever.
R̢. **Amen.**

B
59.

INTRODUCTORY RITES
See Romans 5:5; 8:11
The love of God has been poured into our hearts by
his Spirit living in us.

OPENING PRAYER
Lord,
send us your Holy Spirit
to help us walk in unity of faith
and grow in the strength of his love
to the full stature of Christ,
who lives and reigns with you and the Holy Spirit,
one God, for ever and ever.
R̢. **Amen.**

Another prayer may be chosen from nos. 58, 60.
See Lectionary for Mass, nos. 763–767.

PRAYER OVER THE GIFTS
Pray, brethren . . .

Lord,
you have signed our brothers and sisters
with the cross of your Son
and anointed them with the oil of salvation.
As they offer themselves with Christ,
continue to fill their hearts with your Spirit.
We ask this through Christ our Lord.
R̢. **Amen.**

When Eucharistic Prayer I is used, the special form of **Father, accept this offering** is said, as in the preceding Mass.

COMMUNION RITE

Psalm 34:6, 9

Look up at him with gladness and smile; taste and see the goodness of the Lord.

PRAYER AFTER COMMUNION

Let us pray.

Pause for silent prayer, if this has not preceded.

**Lord,
you give your Son as food
to those you anoint with your Spirit.
Help them to fulfill your law
by living in freedom as your children.
May they live in holiness
and be your witnesses to the world.**

**We ask this through Christ our Lord.
R̷. Amen.**

II. OTHER PRAYERS

60.

OPENING PRAYER

**Lord,
fulfill the promise given by your Son
and send the Holy Spirit
to enlighten our minds and lead us to all truth.
Grant this through our Lord Jesus Christ, your Son,
who lives and reigns with you and the Holy Spirit
one God, for ever and ever.
R̷. Amen.**

PRAYER OVER THE GIFTS

Pray, brethren ...

**Lord,
accept the offering of your family**

and help those who receive the gift of your Spirit
to keep him in their hearts
and come to the reward of eternal life.
We ask this in the name of Jesus the Lord.
R̠. **Amen.**

PRAYER AFTER COMMUNION

Let us pray.

Pause for silent prayer, if this has not preceded.

Lord,
we have shared the one bread of life.
Send the Spirit of your love
to keep us one in faith and peace.

R̠. **Amen.**

III. BIBLICAL READINGS

61. Readings from the Old Testament

1. **Isaiah 11:1-4a**
On him the Spirit of the Lord rests.

2. **Isaiah 42:1-3**
I have endowed my servant with my Spirit.

3. **Isaiah 61:1-3a, 6a, 8b-9**
The Lord God has anointed me and has sent me to bring
Good News to the poor, to give them the oil of gladness.

4. **Ezekiel 36:24-28**
I will place a new Spirit in your midst.

5. **Joel 2:23a, 26-30a**
(Hebrew 2:23a; 3:1-3a)
I will pour out my Spirit on all mankind.

62. Readings from the New Testament

1. **Acts 1:3-8**
You will receive the power of the Holy Spirit, and you will
be my witnesses.

2. **Acts 2:1-6, 14, 22b-23, 32-33**
They were all filled with the Holy Spirit, and began to speak.

3. **Acts 8:1, 4, 14-17**
They laid hands on them, and they received the Holy Spirit.

4. **Acts 10:1, 33-34a, 37-44**
The Holy Spirit came down on all those listening to the word of God.

5. **Acts 19:1b-6a**
Did you receive the Holy Spirit when you became believers?

6. **Romans 5:1-2, 5-8**
The love of God has been poured into our hearts by the Holy Spirit which has been given to us.

7. **Romans 8:14-17**
The Spirit himself and our spirit bear united witness that we are children of God.

8. **Romans 8:26-27**
The Spirit himself will express our plea in a way that could never be put to words.

9. **1 Corinthians 12:4-13**
There is one and the same Spirit giving to each as he wills.

10. **Galatians 5:16-17, 22-23a, 24-25**
If we live in the Spirit, let us be directed by the Spirit.

11. **Ephesians 1:3a, 4a, 13-19a**
You have been signed with the seal of the Holy Spirit of the promise.

12. **Ephesians 4:1-6**
There is one body, one Spirit, and one baptism.

63. Responsorial Psalms

1. Psalm 22:23-24, 26-27, 28 and 31-32
R̶. (23): **I will proclaim your name to my brothers.**
or: (John 15:26-27):
When the Holy Spirit comes to you, you will be my witness.

2. Psalm 23:1-3a, 3b-4, 5-6
R̶. (1): **The Lord is my shepherd; there is nothing I shall want.**

3. Psalm 96:1-2a, 2b-3, 9-10a, 11-12
℟. (3): **Proclaim his marvelous deeds to all the nations.**

4. Psalm 104:1ab and 24, 27-28, 30-31, 33-34
℟. (30): **Lord, send out your Spirit, and renew the face of the earth.**

5. Psalm 117:1, 2
℟. (Acts 1:8): **You will be my witnesses to all the world.**
or: **Alleluia.**

6. Psalm 145:2-3, 4-5, 8-9, 10-11, 15-16, 21
℟. (1b): **I will praise your name for ever, Lord.**

64. Alleluia Verse and Verse before the Gospel

1. John 14:16
The Father will send you the Holy Spirit, says the Lord,
to be with you for ever.

2. John 15:26b, 27a
The Spirit of truth will bear witness to me, says the Lord,
and you also will be my witnesses.

3. John 16:13a; 14:26b
When the Spirit of truth comes, he will teach you all truth
and bring to your mind all I have told you.

4. Revelation 1:5a, 6
Jesus Christ, you are the faithful witness, firstborn from the dead;
you have made us a kingdom of priests to serve our God and Father.

5. **Come, Holy Spirit, fill the hearts of your faithful;**
   and kindle in them the fire of your love.

6. **Come, Holy Spirit;**
   shine on us the radiance of your light.

65. Gospel

1. **Matthew 5:1-12a**
Theirs is the kingdom of heaven.

2. **Matthew 16:24-27**
If anyone wishes to follow me, let him deny himself.

3. **Matthew 25:14-30**
Because you have been faithful in small matters, come into the joy of your master.

4. **Mark 1:9-11**
He saw the Spirit descending and remaining on him.

5. **Luke 4:16-22a**
The Spirit of the Lord is upon me.

6. **Luke 8:4-10a, 11b-15**
Some seed fell into rich soil. These are the people who receive the word and bear fruit in patience.

7. **Luke 10:21-24**
I bless you, Father, for revealing these things to children.

8. **John 7:37b-39**
From the heart of the Lord shall flow fountains of living water.

9. **John 14:15-17**
The Spirit of truth will be with you for ever.

10. **John 14:23-26**
The Holy Spirit will teach you everything.

11. **John 15:18-21, 26-27**
The Spirit of truth who issues from the Father, will be my witness.

12. **John 16:5b-7, 12-13a (Greek 5-7, 12-13a)**
The Spirit of truth will lead you to the complete truth.

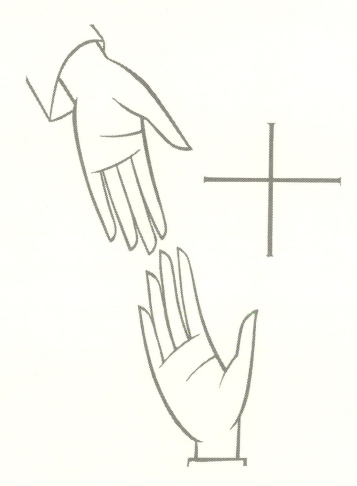

RITE OF PENANCE

RITE OF PENANCE

APPENDIX II
SAMPLE PENITENTIAL SERVICES

APPENDIX III
FORM OF EXAMINATION OF CONSCIENCE

SACRED CONGREGATION FOR DIVINE WORSHIP

Prot. n. 800/73

DECREE

Reconciliation between God and his people was brought about by our Lord Jesus Christ in the mystery of his death and resurrection (see Romans 5:10). The Lord entrusted the ministry of reconciliation to the Church in the person of the apostles (see 2 Corinthians 5:18ff.). The Church carries out this ministry by bringing the good news of salvation to people and by baptizing them in water and the Holy Spirit (see Matthew 28:19).

Because of human weakness, however, Christians "leave [their] first love" (see Revelation 2:4) and even break off their fellowship with God by sinning. The Lord therefore instituted a special sacrament of penance for the pardon of sins committed after baptism (see John 20:21–23) and the Church has faithfully celebrated the sacrament throughout the centuries—in varying ways, but retaining its essential elements.

Vatican Council II decreed that "the rite and formularies for the sacrament of penance are to be revised so that they may more clearly express both the nature and effect of this sacrament."[1] In view of this the Congregation for Divine Worship has carefully prepared the new *Rite of Penance* so that the celebration of the sacrament may be more fully understood by the faithful.

In this new rite, besides the *Rite for Reconciliation of Individual Penitents*, a *Rite for Reconciliation of Several Penitents* has been drawn up to emphasize the relation of the sacrament to the community. This rite places individual confession and absolution in the context of a celebration of the word of God. Furthermore, for special occasions, a *Rite for Reconciliation of Several Penitents with General Confession and Absolution* has been composed in accordance with the Pastoral Norms on General Sacramental Absolution, issued by the Congregation for the Doctrine of the Faith, 16 June 1972.[2]

[1] *SC* art. 72 [*DOL* 1, no. 72].
[2] See *DOL* 361.

The Church is deeply concerned with calling the faithful to continual conversion and renewal. It desires that the baptized who have sinned should acknowledge their sins against God and their neighbor and have heartfelt repentance for them; it takes pains to prepare them to celebrate the sacrament of penance. For this reason the Church urges the faithful to attend penitential celebrations from time to time. This Congregation has therefore made regulations for such celebrations and has proposed examples or models that conferences of bishops may adapt to the needs of their own regions.

Pope Paul VI has by his authority approved the *Rite of Penance* prepared by the Congregation for Divine Worship and ordered it to be published. It is to replace the pertinent titles of the Roman Ritual hitherto in use. The *Rite* in its Latin original is to come into force as soon as it is published; vernacular versions, from the day determined by the conferences of bishops, after they have approved the translation and received confirmation from the Apostolic See.

Anything to the contrary notwithstanding.

From the office of the Congregation for Divine Worship, December 2, 1973, the First Sunday of Advent.

By special mandate of the Pope

✢ Jean Cardinal Villot
Secretary of State

✢ Annibale Bugnini
Titular Archbishop of Diocletiana
Secretary of the Congregation for Divine Worship

INTRODUCTION

1. MYSTERY OF RECONCILIATION IN THE HISTORY OF SALVATION

1. The Father has shown forth his mercy by reconciling the world to himself in Christ and by making peace for all things on earth and in heaven by the blood of Christ on the cross.[1] The Son of God made man lived among us in order to free us from the slavery of sin[2] and to call us out of darkness into his wonderful light.[3] He therefore began his work on earth by preaching repentance and saying: "Repent and believe the Gospel" (Mark 1:15).

This invitation to repentance, which had often been sounded by the prophets, prepared people's hearts for the coming of the kingdom of God through the voice of John the Baptist, who came "preaching a baptism of repentance for the forgiveness of sins" (Mark 1:4).

Jesus, however, not only exhorted people to repentance so that they would abandon their sins and turn wholeheartedly to the Lord,[4] but welcoming sinners, he actually reconciled them with the Father.[5] Moreover, he healed the sick in order to offer a sign of his power to forgive sin.[6] Finally, he himself died for our sins and rose again for our justification.[7] Therefore, on the night he was betrayed and began his saving passion,[8] he instituted the sacrifice of the New Covenant in his blood for the forgiveness of sins.[9] After his resurrection he sent the Holy Spirit upon the apostles, empowering them to forgive or retain sins[10] and sending them forth to all peoples to preach repentance and the forgiveness of sins in his name.[11]

[1]See 2 Corinthians 5:18ff.; Colossians 1:20.
[2]See John 8:34–36.
[3]See 1 Peter 2:9.
[4]See Luke 15.
[5]Luke 5:20 and 27–32, 7:48.
[6]See Matthew 9:2–8.
[7]See Romans 4:25.
[8]See Roman Missal, Eucharistic Prayer III.
[9]See Matthew 26:28.
[10]See John 20:19–23.
[11]See Luke 24:47.

The Lord said to Peter: "I will give you the keys of the kingdom of heaven, and whatever you bind on earth will be
bound in heaven, and whatever you loose on earth will be
loosed also in heaven" (Matthew 16:19). In obedience to
this command, on the day of Pentecost Peter preached the
forgiveness of sins by baptism: "Repent and let every one
of you be baptized in the name of Jesus Christ for the remission of sins" (Acts 2:38).[12] Since then the Church has never
failed to call people from sin to conversion and through the
celebration of penance to show the victory of Christ over
sin.

2. This victory is first brought to light in baptism where
our fallen nature is crucified with Christ so that the body of
sin may be destroyed and we may no longer be slaves to
sin, but rise with Christ and live for God.[13] For this reason
the Church proclaims its faith in "one baptism for the forgiveness of sins."

In the sacrifice of the Mass the passion of Christ is again
made present; his body given for us and his blood shed for
the forgiveness of sins are offered to God again by the
Church for the salvation of the world. For in the eucharist
Christ is present and is offered as "the sacrifice which has
made our peace"[14] with God and in order that "we may be
brought together in unity"[15] by his Holy Spirit.

Furthermore, our Savior Jesus Christ, when he gave to his
apostles and their successors power to forgive sins, instituted in his Church the sacrament of penance. Its purpose
is that the faithful who fall into sin after baptism may be
reconciled with God through the restoration of grace.[16] The
Church "possesses both water and tears: the water of baptism, the tears of penance."[17]

[12]See Acts 3:19 and 26, 17:30.
[13]See Romans 6:4–10.
[14]See Roman Missal, Eucharistic Prayer III.
[15]See Roman Missal, Eucharistic Prayer II.
[16]See Council of Trent, sess. 14, De sacramento Paenitentiae, chapter 1:Denz-
Schön 1668 and 1670; can. 1: Denz-Schön 1701.
[17]Ambrose, Ep. 41, 12; PL 16, 1116.

II. RECONCILIATION OF PENITENTS IN THE CHURCH'S LIFE

THE CHURCH BOTH HOLY AND ALWAYS IN NEED OF PURIFICATION

3. Christ "loved the Church and gave himself up for it to make it holy" (Ephesians 5:25–26) and he united the Church to himself as a bride.[18] He filled it with his divine gifts,[19] because it is his Body and his fullness; through the Church he spreads truth and grace upon all.

The members of the Church, however, are exposed to temptation and often fall into the wretchedness of sin. As a result, "whereas Christ, 'holy, harmless, undefiled' (Hebrews 7:26), knew no sin (see 2 Corinthians 5:21) but came solely to seek pardon for the sins of his people (see Hebrews 2:17), the Church, having sinners in its midst, is at the same time holy and in need of cleansing, and so is unceasingly intent on repentance and reform."[20]

PENANCE IN THE CHURCH'S LIFE AND LITURGY

4. The people of God accomplish and perfect this continual repentance in many different ways. They share in the sufferings of Christ[21] by enduring their own difficulties, carry out works of mercy and charity,[22] and adopt ever more fully the outlook of the Gospel message. Thus the people of God become in the world a sign of conversion to God. All this the Church expresses in its life and celebrates in its liturgy when the faithful confess that they are sinners and ask pardon of God and of their brothers and sisters. This happens in penitential services, in the proclamation of the word of God, in prayer, and in the penitential parts of the eucharistic celebration.[23]

In the sacrament of penance the faithful "obtain from God's mercy pardon for having offended him and at the same

---

[18]See Revelation 19:7.
[19]See Ephesians 1:22–23. *LG* no. 7: *AAS* 57 (1965) 9–11; ConstDecrDecl 100–102.
[20]*LG* no. 8: *AAS* 57 (1965) 12; CosntDecrDecl 106.
[21]See 1 Peter 4:13.
[22]See 1 Peter 4:8.
[23]See Council of Trent, sess. 14, *De sacramento Paenitentiae:* Denz-Schön 1638, 1740, 1743. SCR, Instr. EuchMyst, May 25, 1967, no. 35 [*DOL* 179, no. 1264]; *GIRM,* nos. 29, 30, 56 a, b, g [*DOL* 208, nos. 1419, 1420, 1446].

time reconciliation with the Church, which they have wounded by their sins and which by charity, example, and prayer seeks their conversion."[24]

RECONCILIATION WITH GOD AND WITH THE CHURCH

5. Since every sin is an offense against God that disrupts our friendship with him, "the ultimate purpose of penance is that we should love God deeply and commit ourselves completely to him."[25] Therefore, the sinner who by the grace of a merciful God embraces the way of penance comes back to the Father who "first loved us" (1 John 4:19), to Christ who gave himself up for us,[26] and to the Holy Spirit who has been poured out on us abundantly.[27]

"The hidden and gracious mystery of God unites us all through a supernatural bond: on this basis one person's sin harms the rest even as one person's goodness enriches them."[28] Penance always therefore entails reconciliation with our brethren and sisters who remain harmed by our sins.

In fact, people frequently join together to commit injustice. But it is also true that they help each other in doing penance; freed from sin by the grace of Christ, they become, with all persons of good will, agents of justice and peace in the world.

SACRAMENT OF PENANCE AND ITS PARTS

6. Followers of Christ who have sinned but who, by the prompting of the Holy Spirit, come to the sacrament of penance should above all be wholeheartedly converted to God. This inner conversion embraces sorrow for sin and the intent to lead a new life. It is expressed through confession made to the Church, due expiation, and amendment of life. God grants pardon for sin through the Church, which works by the ministry of priests.[29]

[24]*LG* no. 11 [*DOL* 4, no. 141].

[25]Paul VI, Ap. Const. *Paenitemini*, Feb. 17, 1966: *AAS* 58 (1966) 179. See also *LG* no. 11 [*DOL* 4, no. 141].

[26]See Galatians 2:20; Ephesians 5:25.

[27]See Titus 3:6.

[28]Paul VI, Ap. Const. *Indulgentiarum doctrina*, Jan. 1, 1967, no. 4 [*DOL* 386, no. 3158]. See also Pius XII, Encycl. *Mystici Corporis*, June 29, 1943: *AAS* 35 (1943) 213.

[29]See Council of Trent, sess. 14, *De sacramento Paenitentiae*, Chapter 3: Denz-Schön 1673–1675 [the *ed. typica* erroneously cites Chapter 1].

a) Contrition

The most important act of the penitent is contrition, which is "heartfelt sorrow and aversion for the sin committed along with the intention of sinning no more."[30] "We can only approach the kingdom of Christ by *metanoia*. This is a profound change of the whole person by which we begin to consider, judge, and arrange our life according to the holiness and love of God, made manifest in his Son in the last days and given to us in abundance" (see Hebrews 1:2; Colossians 1:19 and passim; Ephesians 1:23 and passim).[31] The genuineness of penance depends on this heartfelt contrition. For conversion should affect a person from within toward a progressively deeper enlightenment and an ever-closer likeness to Christ.

b) Confession

The sacrament of penance includes the confession of sins, which comes from true knowledge of self before God and from contrition for those sins. However, the inner examination of heart and the outward accusation must be made in the light of God's mercy. Confession requires on the penitent's part the will to open the heart to the minister of God and on the minister's part a spiritual judgment by which, acting in the person of Christ, he pronounces his decision of forgiveness or retention of sins in accord with the power of the keys.[32]

c) Act of Penance

True conversion is completed by expiation for the sins committed, by amendment of life, and also by rectifying injuries done.[33] The kind and extent of the expiation must be suited to the personal condition of penitents so that they may restore the order that they have upset and through the corresponding remedy be cured of the sickness from which they suffered. Therefore, it is necessary that the act of penance really be a remedy for sin and a help to renewal of life. Thus penitents, "forgetting the things that are behind"

---

[30]*Ibid.*, Chapter 4: Denz-Schön 1676.
[31]Paul VI, Ap. Const. *Paenitemini*, Feb. 17, 1966: *AAS* 58 (1966) 179.
[32]See Council of Trent, sess. 14, *De sacramanto Paenitentiae*, Chapter 5: Denz-Schön 1679.
[33]See *ibid.*, Chapter 8: Denz-Schön 1690–1692. Paul VI, Ap. Const. *Indulgentiarum doctrina*, nos. 2–3 [DOL 386, nos. 3156–3157].

(Philippians 3:13), again become part of the mystery of salvation and press on toward the things that are to come.

d) Absolution

Through the sign of absolution God grants pardon to sinners who in sacramental confession manifest their change of heart to the Church's minister; this completes the sacrament of penance. For in God's design the humanity and loving kindness of our Savior have visibly appeared to us[34] and so God uses visible signs to give salvation and to renew the broken covenant.

In the sacrament of penance the Father receives the repentant children who come back to him, Christ places the lost sheep on his shoulders and brings them back to the sheepfold, and the Holy Spirit resanctifies those who are the temple of God or dwells more fully in them. The expression of all this is the sharing in the Lord's table, begun again or made more ardent; such a return of children from afar brings great rejoicing at the banquet of God's Church.[35]

NEED AND BENEFIT OF THIS SACRAMENT

7. Just as the wounds of sin are varied and multiple in the life of individuals and of the community, so too the healing that penance provides is varied. Those who by grave sin have withdrawn from communion with God in love are called back in the sacrament of penance to the life they have lost. And those who, experiencing their weakness daily, fall into venial sins draw strength from a repeated celebration of penance to reach the full freedom of the children of God.

a) To obtain the saving remedy of the sacrament of penance, according to the plan of our merciful God, the faithful must confess to a priest each and every grave sin that they remember after an examination of conscience.[36]

b) Moreover, the frequent and careful celebration of this sacrament is also very useful as a remedy for venial sins. This is not a mere ritual repetition or psychological exercise, but a serious striving to perfect the grace of baptism

[34]See Titus 3:4–5.
[35]See Luke 15:7, 10 and 32.
[36]See Council of Trent, sess. 14, *De sacramento Paenitentiae*, can. 7–8: Denz-Schön 1707–1708.

so that, as we bear in our body the death of Jesus Christ, his life may be seen in us ever more clearly.[37] In confession of this kind, penitents who accuse themselves of venial faults should try to be more closely conformed to Christ and to follow the voice of the Spirit more attentively.

In order that this sacrament of healing may truly achieve its purpose among the faithful, it must take root in their entire life and move them to more fervent service of God and neighbor.

The celebration of this sacrament is thus always an act in which the Church proclaims its faith, gives thanks to God for the freedom with which Christ has made us free,[38] and offers its life as a spiritual sacrifice in praise of God's glory, as it hastens to meet the Lord Jesus.

III. OFFICES AND MINISTRIES IN THE RECONCILIATION OF PENITENTS

ROLE OF THE COMMUNITY IN THE CELEBRATION OF PENANCE

8. The whole Church, as a priestly people, acts in different ways in the work of reconciliation that has been entrusted to it by the Lord. Not only does the Church call sinners to repentance by preaching the word of God, but it also intercedes for them and helps penitents with maternal care and solicitude to acknowledge and confess their sins and to obtain the mercy of God, who alone can forgive sins. Further, the Church becomes itself the instrument of the conversion and absolution of the penitent through the ministry entrusted by Christ to the apostles and their successors.[39]

MINISTER OF THE SACRAMENT OF PENANCE

9. a) The Church exercises the ministry of the sacrament of penance through bishops and priests. By preaching God's word they call the faithful to conversion; in the name of Christ and by the power of the Holy Spirit they declare and grant the forgiveness of sins.

---

[37]See 2 Corinthians 4:10.
[38]See Galatians 4:31.
[39]See Matthew 18:18; John 20:23.

In the exercise of this ministry priests act in communion with the bishop and share in his power and office as the one who regulates the penitential discipline.[40]

b) The competent minister of the sacrament is a priest who has the faculty to absolve in accordance with the provisions of the code of Canon Law, canons 967–975. All priests, however, even though not approved to hear confessions, absolve validly and lawfully any penitents without exception who are in danger of death.

PASTORAL EXERCISE OF THIS MINISTRY

10. a) In order that he may fulfill his ministry properly and faithfully, understand the disorders of souls and apply the appropriate remedies to them, and act as a wise judge, the confessor must acquire the needed knowledge and prudence by constant study under the guidance of the Church's magisterium and especially by praying fervently to God. For the discernment of spirits is indeed a deep knowledge of God's working in the human heart, a gift of the Spirit, and an effect of charity.[41]

b) The confessor should always show himself to be ready and willing to hear the confessions of the faithful whenever they reasonably request this.[42]

c) By receiving repentant sinners and leading them to the light of the truth, the confessor fulfills a paternal function: he reveals the heart of the Father and reflects the image of Christ the Good Shepherd. He should keep in mind that he has been entrusted with the ministry of Christ, who accomplished the saving work of human redemption by mercy and by his power is present in the sacraments.[43]

d) Conscious that he has come to know the secrets of another's conscience only because he is God's minister, the confessor is bound by the obligation of preserving the seal of confession absolutely unbroken.

[40]See *LG* no. 26 [DOL 4, no. 146].
[41]See Philippians 1:9–10.
[42]See *SCDF*, Pastoral Norms for General Absolution, June 16, 1972, Norm XII [*DOL* 361, no. 3050].
[43]See *SC* art. 7 [*DOL* 1, no. 7].

PENITENTS

11. The parts that penitents themselves have in the celebration of the sacrament are of the greatest importance.

When with proper dispositions they approach this saving remedy instituted by Christ and confess their sins, their own acts become part of the sacrament itself, which is completed when the words of absolution are spoken by the minister in the name of Christ.

In this way the faithful, even as they experience and proclaim the mercy of God in their own life, are with the priest celebrating the liturgy of the Church's continual self-renewal.

IV. CELEBRATION OF THE SACRAMENT OF PENANCE

PLACE OF CELEBRATION

12. The sacrament of penance is ordinarily celebrated in a church or oratory, unless a legitimate reason stands in the way.

The conferences of bishops are to establish the norms pertaining to the confessional, which will include provision for clearly visible confessionals that the faithful who wish may readily use and that are equipped with a fixed screen between the penitent and the confessor.

Except for a legitimate reason, confessions are not to be heard outside a confessional.[44]

TIME OF CELEBRATION

13. The reconciliation of penitents may be celebrated in all liturgical seasons and on any day. But it is right that the faithful be informed of the day and hours at which the priest is available for this ministry. They should be encouraged to approach the sacrament of penance at times when Mass is not being celebrated and preferably at the scheduled hours.[45]

Lent is the season most appropriate for celebrating the sacrament of penance. Already on Ash Wednesday the people

[44]See CIC, can. 964.
[45]See SCR, Instr. EuchMyst, May 25, 1967, no. 35 [DOL 179, no. 1264].

of God hear the solemn invitation, "Turn away from sin and be faithful to the Gospel." It is therefore fitting to have several penitential services during Lent, so that all the faithful may have an opportunity to be reconciled with God and their neighbor and so be able to celebrate the paschal mystery in the Easter triduum with renewed hearts.

LITURGICAL VESTMENTS

14. With respect to liturgical vestments in the celebration of penance, the norms laid down by the local Ordinaries are to be followed.

A. RITE FOR RECONCILIATION OF INDIVIDUAL PENITENTS

PREPARATION OF PRIEST AND PENITENT

15. Priest and penitents should prepare themselves above all by prayer to celebrate the sacrament. The priest should call upon the Holy Spirit so that he may receive enlightenment and charity; the penitents should compare their own life with the example and commandments of Christ and then pray to God for the forgiveness of their sins.

WELCOMING THE PENITENT

16. The priest should welcome penitents with fraternal charity and, if need be, address them with friendly words. The penitent then makes the sign of the cross, saying: **In the name of the Father, and of the Son, and of the Holy Spirit. Amen.** The priest may also make the sign of the cross with the penitent. Next the priest briefly urges the penitent to have confidence in God. Penitents who are unknown to the priest are advised to inform him of their state in life, the time of their last confession, their difficulties in leading the Christian life, and anything else that may help the confessor in the exercise of his ministry.

READING OF THE WORD OF GOD

17. Next, the occasion may be taken for the priest, or even the penitent, to read a text of holy Scripture, or this may be done as part of the preparation for the actual celebration of the sacrament. For through the word of God Christians receive light to recognize their sins and are called to conversion and to confidence in God's mercy.

PENITENT'S CONFESSION AND ACCEPTANCE OF THE PENANCE

18. Next comes the penitent's confession of sins, beginning with the general confession formulary, **I confess to almighty God,** if this is the custom. If necessary, the confessor assists the penitent to make a complete confession; he also encourages the penitent to repent sincerely for offenses against God; finally he offers practical advice for beginning a new life, and, where necessary, gives instruction on the duties of the Christian life.

A penitent who has been the cause of harm or scandal to others is to be led by the priest to resolve to make due restitution.

Next, the priest imposes an act of penance or expiation on the penitent; this should serve not only as atonement for past sins but also as an aid to a new life and an antidote for weakness. As far as possible, therefore, the penance should correspond to the seriousness and nature of their sins. This act of penance may suitably take the form of prayer, self-denial, and especially service to neighbor and works of mercy. These will underline the fact that sin and its forgiveness have a social aspect.

PENITENT'S PRAYER AND THE PRIEST'S ABSOLUTION

19. Next, through a prayer for God's pardon the penitent expresses contrition and the resolution to begin a new life. It is advantageous for this prayer to be based on the words of Scripture.

Following the penitent's prayer, the priest extends his hands, or at least his right hand, over the head of the penitent and pronounces the formulary of absolution, in which the essential words are: **I absolve you from your sins in the name of the Father and of the Son and of the Holy Spirit.** As he says the final phrase the priest makes the sign of the cross over the penitent. The form of absolution (see no. 46) indicates that the reconciliation of the penitent comes from the mercy of the Father; it shows the connection between the reconciliation of the sinner and the paschal mystery of Christ; it stresses the role of the Holy Spirit in the forgiveness of sins; finally, it underlines the ecclesial aspect of the sacrament, because reconciliation with God is asked for and given through the ministry of the Church.

PROCLAMATION OF PRAISE AND DISMISSAL OF THE PENITENT

20. After receiving pardon for sin, the penitent praises the mercy of God and gives him thanks in a short invocation taken from Scripture. Then the priest bids the penitent to go in peace.

The penitent continues the conversion thus begun and expresses it by a life renewed according to the Gospel and more and more steeped in the love of God, for "love covers over a multitude of sins" (1 Peter 4:8).

SHORTER RITE

21. When pastoral need dictates, the priest may omit or shorten some parts of the rite but must always retain in their entirety the penitent's confession of sins and acceptance of the act of penance, the invitation to contrition (no. 45), and the formularies of absolution and dismissal. In imminent danger of death, it is sufficient for the priest to say the essential words of the form of absolution, namely: **I absolve you from your sins in the name of the Father, and of the Son, and of the Holy Spirit.**

B. RITE FOR RECONCILIATION OF SEVERAL PENITENTS WITH INDIVIDUAL CONFESSION AND ABSOLUTION

22. When a number of penitents assemble at the same time to receive sacramental reconciliation, it is fitting that they be prepared for the sacrament by a celebration of the word of God.

Those who will receive the sacrament at another time may also take part in the service.

Communal celebration shows more clearly the ecclesial nature of penance. The faithful listen together to the word of God, which as it proclaims his mercy invites them to conversion; at the same time they examine the conformity of their lives with that word of God and help each other through common prayer. After confessing and being absolved individually, all join in praising God together for his wonderful deeds on behalf of the people he has gained for himself through the blood of his Son.

If necessary, several priests should be available in suitable places to hear individual confessions and to reconcile the penitents.

INTRODUCTORY RITES

23. When the faithful have gathered, a suitable hymn may be sung. Then the priest greets them and, if necessary, he or another minister gives a brief introduction to the celebration and explains the order of service. Next he invites all to pray and after a period of silence completes the opening prayer.

CELEBRATION OF THE WORD OF GOD

24. The sacrament of penance should begin with a hearing of God's word, because through his word God calls his people to repentance and leads them to a true conversion of heart.

One or more readings may be chosen. If more than one are read, a psalm, another suitable song, or a period of silence should be inserted between them, so that the word of God may be more deeply understood and heartfelt assent may be given to it. If there is only one reading, it is preferable that it be from a gospel.

Readings should be chosen that will:

a) let God's voice be heard, calling his people back to conversion and ever closer conformity with Christ;

b) call to mind the mystery of our reconciliation through the death and resurrection of Christ and through the gift of the Holy Spirit;

c) bring to bear on people's lives God's judgment of good and evil as a light for the examination of conscience.

25. The homily, taking as its source the scriptural text, should lead the penitents to examine their conscience and to turn away from sin and toward God. It should remind the faithful that sin works against God, against the community and one's neighbors, and against the person of the sinner. Therefore it would be good to recall:

a) the infinite mercy of God, greater than all our sins, by which again and again he calls us back to himself;

b) the need for inner repentance, by which we are genuinely prepared to make reparation for sin;

c) the social dimension of grace and sin whose effect is that in some way the actions of individuals affect the whole Body of the Church;

d) the duty of expiation for sin, which is effective because of Christ's expiation and requires especially, in addition to works of repentance, the exercise of true charity toward God and neighbor.

26. After the homily a suitable period of silence should be allowed for an examination of conscience and the awakening of true contrition for sin. The priest or a deacon or other minister may help the faithful with brief considerations or a litany, adapted to their background, age, etc.

If it should seem suitable, the community's examination of conscience and awakening of contrition may take the place of the homily. But in this case the text of Scripture that has just been read should serve as the starting point.

RITE OF RECONCILIATION

27. At the invitation of the deacon or other minister, all kneel or bow down and say a form of general confession (for example, the prayer, **I confess to almighty God**). Then they stand, if this seems useful, and join in a litany or suitable song to express confession of sins, heartfelt contrition, prayer for forgiveness, and trust in God's mercy. Finally, they say the Lord's Prayer, which is never omitted.

28. After the Lord's Prayer the priests go to the places assigned for confession. The penitents who desire to confess their sins go to the priest of their choice. After they have accepted a suitable act of penance, the priest absolves them, using the formulary for the reconciliation of an individual penitent.

29. When the confessions are over, the priests return to the sanctuary. The priest who presides invites all to make an act of thanksgiving to praise God for his mercy. This may be done in a psalm or hymn or litany. Finally, the priest concludes the celebration with one of the prayers in praise of God for this great love.

DISMISSAL OF THE PEOPLE

30. After the prayer of thanksgiving the priest blesses the faithful. Then the deacon or the priest himself dismisses the congregation.

C. RITE FOR RECONCILIATION OF PENITENTS WITH GENERAL CONFESSION AND ABSOLUTION

DISCIPLINE OF GENERAL ABSOLUTION

31. An individual, complete confession and the receiving of absolution constitute the sole, ordinary means for a member of the faithful who is conscious of serious sin to be reconciled with God and the Church. Physical or moral impossibility alone excuses from this kind of confession; in the case of such impossibility, reconciliation is possible in other ways.

Absolution without prior, individual confession cannot be given collectively to a number of penitents unless:

a) the danger of death is imminent and there is no time for a priest or priests to hear the confessions of the individual penitents;

b) a serious need is present, namely, given the number of penitents, not enough confessors are available to hear the individual confessions properly within a reasonable time, with the result that through no fault of their own, the faithful would be forced to be for a long time without the grace of the sacrament or without communion. The need in question is not regarded as sufficient when the nonavailability of confessors is based solely on there being a large number of penitents, such as may be the case at some great festival or pilgrimage.[46]

32. To make the judgment on whether the requisite conditions already stated in no. 31[b] are verified belongs to the diocesan bishop. After considering the criteria agreed on with the other members of the conference of bishops, he can decide which cases involve the need in question.[47]

[46]See *CIC*, can. 960 and 961, §1.
[47]See *CIC*, can. 961, §2.

33. For the valid reception of general sacramental absolution it is required that the faithful not-only be properly disposed but at the same time have the resolution to confess in due time each of those serious sins that they cannot at the present time confess in this way.

On the occasion of the reception of general absolution, the faithful, to the extent possible, are to be instructed on the requirements just mentioned; even in the case of danger of death when time allows, the imparting of general absolution is to be preceded by an exhortation that each recipient strive to make an act of contrition.[48]

34. Unless there is a good reason preventing it, those who receive pardon for serious sins through general absolution are to go to individual confession as soon as they have the opportunity before any further reception of general absolution. And unless a moral impossibility stands in the way, they are absolutely bound to go to a confessor within one year. For the precept binding every one of the faithful binds them as well, namely, to confess individually to a priest at least once a year all those grave sins not hitherto confessed one by one.[49]

RITE OF GENERAL ABSOLUTION

35. For the reconciliation of penitents by general confession and absolution in the cases provided by law, everything takes place as described already for the reconciliation of several penitents with individual confession and absolution, with the following exceptions.

a) After the homily or during it, the faithful who seek general absolution are to be instructed to dispose themselves properly, that is, to have a personal sorrow for sins committed and the resolve to avoid committing them again; the intention to repair any scandal and harm caused and likewise to confess in due time each one of the grave sins that they cannot confess at present.[50] Some expiatory penance should be proposed for all to perform; individuals may add to this penance if they wish.

[48]See CIC, can. 962, §§1 and 2.
[49]See Congregation for the Doctrine of the Faith, Pastoral Norms on General Absolution, June 16, 1972, Norms VII and VIII: AAS 64 (1972) 512–513, CIC, can. 963, 989.
[50]See ibid. Norm VI [DOL 361, no. 3044].

b) The deacon, another minister, or the priest then calls upon the penitents who wish to receive absolution to show their intention by some sign (for example, by bowing their heads, kneeling, or giving some other sign determined by the conference of bishops). They should also say together a form of general confession (for example, the prayer, **I confess to almighty God**), which may be followed by a litany or a penitential song. Then the Lord's Prayer is sung or said by all, as indicated in no. 27.

c) Then the priest pronounces the invocation that expresses prayer for the grace of the Holy Spirit to pardon sin, proclamation of victory over sin through Christ's death and resurrection, and the sacramental absolution given to the penitents.

d) Finally, the priest invites the people to give thanks, as indicated in no. 29 and, omitting the concluding prayer, he immediately blesses and dismisses them.

V. PENITENTIAL SERVICES

NATURE AND STRUCTURE

36. Penitential services are gatherings of the people of God to hear God's word as an invitation to conversion and renewal of life and as the message of our liberation from sin through Christ's death and resurrection. The structure of these services is the same as that usually followed in celebrations of the word of God[51] and given in the *Rite for Reconciliation of Several Penitents*.

It is appropriate, therefore, that after the introductory rites (song, greeting, and opening prayer) one or more biblical readings be chosen with songs, psalms, or periods of silence inserted between them. In the homily these readings should be explained and applied to the congregation. Before or after the readings from Scripture, readings from the Fathers or other writers may also be selected that will help the community and each person to a true awareness of sin and heartfelt sorrow, in other words, to bring about conversion of life.

After the homily and reflection on God's word, it is desirable that the congregation, united in voice and spirit, pray

[51]See *SCR*, Instr. InterOec, Sept. 26, 1964, nos. 37–39 [*DOL* 23, nos. 329–331].

together in a litany or in some other way suited to general participation. At the end the Lord's Prayer is said, asking God our Father "to forgive us our sins as we forgive those who sin against us . . . and deliver us from evil." The priest or the minister who presides concludes with a prayer and the dismissal of the people.

BENEFIT AND IMPORTANCE

37. Care must be taken to ensure that the faithful do not confuse these celebrations with the celebration of the sacrament of penance.[52] Penitential services are very helpful in promoting conversion of life and purification of heart.[53]

It is desirable to arrange them especially for these purposes:
    —to foster the spirit of penance within the Christian community;
    —to help the faithful to prepare for individual confession that can be made later at a convenient time;
    —to help children gradually form their conscience about sin in human life and about freedom from sin through Christ;
    —to help catechumens during their conversion.

Penitential services, moreover, are very useful in places where no priest is available to give sacramental absolution. They offer help in reaching that perfect contrition that comes from charity and that enables the faithful to receive God's grace through a desire for the sacrament of penance in the future.[54]

VI. ADAPTATIONS OF THE RITE TO VARIOUS REGIONS AND CIRCUMSTANCES

ADAPTATIONS BY THE CONFERENCES OF BISHOPS

38. In preparing particular rituals, the conferences of bishops have the authority to adapt the rite of penance to the needs of individual regions so that, after confirmation of the conference's decisions by the Apostolic See, the rituals

---

[52]See SCDF, Pastoral Norms for General Absolution, Norm X [DOL 361, no. 3048].
[53]Ibid.
[54]See Council of Trent, sess. 14, De sacramento Paenitentiae, Chapter 5: Denz-Schön 1677.

may be used in the respective regions. It is the responsibility of the conferences of bishops in this matter:

a) to establish regulations for the discipline of the sacrament of penance, particularly those affecting the ministry of priests;

b) to determine more precisely regulations about the confessional for the ordinary celebration of the sacrament of penance (see no. 12) and about the signs of repentance to be shown by the faithful before general absolution (see no. 35);

c) to prepare translations of texts adapted to the character and language of each people; also to compose new texts of prayer for use by the faithful and the minister, keeping the essential sacramental formulary intact.

COMPETENCE OF THE BISHOP

39. It is for the diocesan bishop:

a) to regulate the discipline of penance in his diocese,[55] even to the extent of adapting the rite according to the rules proposed by the conference of bishops;

b) to make the decision, after considering the conditions required by the law (see no. 31[b]) and the criteria agreed on with the other members of the conference of bishops, regarding the cases of need in which general absolution may be permitted.[56]

ADAPTATIONS BY THE MINISTER

40. It is for priests, and especially parish priests (pastors):

a) in celebrating reconciliation with individuals or with a community, to adapt the rite to the concrete circumstances of the penitents. They must preserve the essential structure and the entire form of absolution, but if necessary they may omit some parts of the rite for pastoral reasons or enlarge upon them, may select the texts of readings or prayers, and may choose a place more suitable for the celebration according to the regulations of the conference of bishops, so that the entire celebration may be enriching and effective;

---

[55]See *LG* no. 26 [*DOL* 4, no. 146].
[56]See Congregation for the Doctrine of the Faith, Pastoral Norms on General Absolution, June 16, 1972, Norm V: *AAS* 64 (1972) 512. *CIC*, can. 961, §§1 and 2.

b) to celebrate and prepare occasional penitential services during the year especially in Lent. In order that the texts chosen and the order of the celebration may be adapted to the conditions and circumstances of the community or group (for example, children, sick persons, etc.), priests may be assisted by others, including the laity.

CHAPTER I

RITE FOR RECONCILIATION OF INDIVIDUAL PENITENTS

RECEPTION OF THE PENITENT

41. When the penitent comes to confess his sins, the priest welcomes him warmly and greets him with kindness.

42. Then the penitent makes the sign of the cross which the priest may make also.

In the name of the Father, and of the Son, and of the Holy Spirit. Amen.

The priest invites the penitent to have trust in God, in these or similar words:

May God, who has enlightened every heart, help you to know your sins and trust in his mercy.
The penitent answers: **Amen.**

Other forms of reception of the penitent may be chosen from nos. 67-71.

READING OF THE WORD OF GOD (OPTIONAL)

43. Then the priest may read or say from memory a text of Scripture which proclaims God's mercy and calls man to conversion.

A reading may also be chosen from those given in nos. 72-83 and 101-201 for the reconciliation of several penitents. The priest and penitent may choose other readings from scripture.

CONFESSION OF SINS AND ACCEPTANCE OF SATISFACTION

44. Where it is the custom, the penitent says a general formula for confession (for example, **I confess to almighty God**) before he confesses his sins.

If necessary, the priest helps the penitent to make an integral confession and gives him suitable counsel. He urges him to be sorry for his faults, reminding him that through the sacrament of penance the Christian dies and rises with Christ and is thus renewed in the paschal mystery. The priest proposes an act of penance which the penitent accepts to make satisfaction for sin and to amend his life.

The priest should make sure that he adapts his counsel to the penitent's circumstances.

PRAYER OF THE PENITENT AND ABSOLUTION

45. The priest then asks the penitent to express his sorrow, which the penitent may do in these or similar words:

**My God,
I am sorry for my sins with all my heart.
In choosing to do wrong
and failing to do good,
I have sinned against you
whom I should love above all things.
I firmly intend, with your help,
to do penance,
to sin no more,
and to avoid whatever leads me to sin.
Our Savior Jesus Christ
suffered and died for us.
In his name, my God, have mercy.**

Other prayers of the penitent may be chosen from nos. 85-92.

Or:
**Lord Jesus, Son of God
have mercy on me, a sinner.**

46. Then the priest extends his hands over the penitent's head (or at least extends his right hand) and says:

**God, the Father of mercies,
through the death and resurrection of his Son
has reconciled the world to himself**

and sent the Holy Spirit among us
for the forgiveness of sins;
through the ministry of the Church
may God give you pardon and peace,
and I absolve you from your sins
in the name of the Father, and of the Son, ✝
and of the Holy Spirit.
The penitent answers: **Amen.**

PROCLAMATION OF PRAISE OF GOD AND DISMISSAL

47. After the absolution, the priest continues:

Give thanks to the Lord, for he is good.
The penitent concludes: **His mercy endures for ever.**

Then the priest dismisses the penitent who has been reconciled, saying:

The Lord has freed you from your sins. Go in peace.

Or [93]:
May the Passion of our Lord Jesus Christ,
the intercession of the Blessed Virgin Mary,
and of all the saints,
whatever good you do and suffering you endure,
heal your sins,
help you to grow in holiness,
and reward you with eternal life.
Go in peace.

Or:
The Lord has freed you from sin.
May he bring you safely to his kingdom in heaven.
Glory to him for ever.
℞. **Amen.**

Or:

**Blessed are those
whose sins have been forgiven,
whose evil deeds have been forgotten.
Rejoice in the Lord,
and go in peace.**

Or:

**Go in peace,
and proclaim to the world
the wonderful works of God
who has brought you salvation.**

CHAPTER II

RITE FOR RECONCILIATION OF SEVERAL PENITENTS WITH INDIVIDUAL CONFESSION AND ABSOLUTION

INTRODUCTORY RITES

SONG

48. When the faithful have assembled, they may sing a psalm, antiphon, or other appropriate song while the priest is entering the church, for example:

Hear us, Lord,
for you are merciful and kind.
In your great compassion,
look on us with love.

Or:

Let us come with confidence before the throne of
   grace
to receive God's mercy,
and we shall find pardon and strength
in our time of need.

GREETING

49. After the song the priest greets the congregation:
Grace, mercy, and peace be with you
from God the Father
and Christ Jesus our Savior.
R̷. **And also with you.**

Or:
Grace and peace be with you
from God the Father
and from Jesus Christ
who loved us
and washed away our sins in his blood.
R̷. **Glory to him for ever. Amen.**

Or other forms of greeting may be chosen from nos. 94-96.

Then the priest or another minister speaks briefly about the importance and purpose of the celebration and the order of the service.

OPENING PRAYER

50. The priest invites all to pray, using these or similar words:

Brothers and sisters, God calls us to conversion; let us therefore ask him for the grace of sincere repentance.

All pray in silence for a brief period. Then the priest sings or says the prayer:

**Lord,
hear the prayers of those who call on you,
forgive the sins of those who confess to you,
and in your merciful love
give us your pardon and your peace.
We ask this through Christ our Lord.
R̷. Amen.**

Or:
**Lord,
send your Spirit among us
to cleanse us in the waters of repentance.
May he make of us a living sacrifice
so that in every place,
by his life-giving power,
we may praise your glory
and proclaim your loving compassion.
We ask this through Christ our Lord.
R̷. Amen.**

Other forms of the opening prayer may be chosen from nos. 97-100.

CELEBRATION OF THE WORD OF GOD

51. The celebration of the word follows. If there are several readings a psalm or other appropriate song or even a period of silence should intervene between them, so that everyone may understand the word of God more deeply and give it his heartfelt assent. If there is only one reading, it is preferable that it be from the gospel.

FIRST EXAMPLE

Love is the fullness of the law

FIRST READING:

Deuteronomy 5:1-3, 6-7, 11-12, 16-21a; 6:4-6 Love the Lord your God with all your heart.

RESPONSORIAL PSALM:

Baruch 1:15-22 ℟. (3:2) **Listen and have pity, Lord, because you are merciful.**

SECOND READING:

Ephesians 5:1-14 Walk in love, as Christ loved us.

GOSPEL ACCLAMATION:

John 8:12

I am the light of the world.
The man who follows me will have the light of life.

GOSPEL:

Matthew 22:34-40 On these two commandments the whole law and the prophets depend.

Or :
John 13:34-35; 15:10-13 I give you a new commandment: love one another.

SECOND EXAMPLE

Your mind must be renewed

FIRST READING:

Isaiah 1:10-18 Stop doing what is wrong, and learn to do good.

RESPONSORIAL PSALM:

Psalm 51:1-4, 8-17

℟. (19a) **A humbled heart is pleasing to God.**

SECOND READING:

Ephesians 4:23-32   Your mind must be renewed by a spiritual revolution.

GOSPEL ACCLAMATION:

Matthew 11:28

Come to me, all you that labor and are burdened, and I will give you rest.

GOSPEL:

Matthew 5:1-12   Happy the poor in spirit.

Other optional texts are given in nos. 101-201.

HOMILY

52. The homily which follows is based on the texts of the readings and should lead the penitents to examine their consciences and renew their lives.

EXAMINATION OF CONSCIENCE

53. A period of time may be spent in making an examination of conscience and in arousing true sorrow for sins. The priest, deacon, or another minister may help the faithful by brief statements or a kind of litany, taking into consideration their circumstances, age, etc.

RITE OF RECONCILIATION

GENERAL CONFESSION OF SINS

54. The deacon or another minister invites all to kneel or bow, and to join in saying a general formula for confession (for example, **I confess to almighty God**). Then they stand and say a litany or sing an appropriate song. The Lord's Prayer is always added at the end.

FIRST EXAMPLE

Deacon or Minister:
My brothers and sisters, confess your sins and pray

for each other, that you may be healed.

All say:
**I confess to almighty God,
and to you, my brothers and sisters,
that I have sinned through my own fault**
They strike their breast:
**in my thoughts and in my words,
in what I have done,
and in what I have failed to do;
and I ask blessed Mary, ever virgin,
all the angels and saints,
and you, my brothers and sisters,
to pray for me to the Lord our God.**

Deacon or minister:
**The Lord is merciful. He makes us clean of heart and
leads us out into his freedom when we acknowledge
our guilt. Let us ask him to forgive us and bind up the
wounds inflicted by our sins.**

Give us the grace of true repentance.
℟. **We pray you, hear us.**

**Pardon your servants and release them from the debt
of sin.**
℟. **We pray you, hear us.**

**Forgive your children who confess their sins, and
restore them to full communion with your Church.**
℟. **We pray you, hear us.**

**Renew the glory of baptism in those who have lost it
by sin.**
℟. **We pray you, hear us.**

**Welcome them to your altar, and renew their spirit
with the hope of eternal glory.**
℟. **We pray you, hear us.**

**Keep them faithful to your sacraments and loyal in
your service.**
℟. **We pray you, hear us.**

Renew your love in their hearts, and make them bear witness to it in their daily lives.
R⁄. **We pray you, hear us.**

Keep them always obedient to your commandments and protect within them your gift of eternal life.
R⁄. **We pray you, hear us.**

Deacon or minister:
Let us now pray to God our Father in the words Christ gave us, and ask him for his forgiveness and protection from all evil.

All say together:
Our Father . . .

The priest concludes:
Lord,
draw near to your servants
who in the presence of your Church
confess that they are sinners.
Through the ministry of the Church
free them from all sin
so that renewed in spirit
they may give you thankful praise.
We ask this through Christ our Lord.
R⁄. **Amen.**

SECOND EXAMPLE

Deacon or minister:
Brothers and sisters, let us call to mind the goodness of God our Father, and acknowledge our sins, so that we may receive his merciful forgiveness.

All say:
I confess to almighty God,
and to you, my brothers and sisters,
that I have sinned through my own fault

They strike their breast:
in my thoughts and in my words,
in what I have done,
and in what I have failed to do;
and I ask blessed Mary, ever virgin,
all the angels and saints,
and you, my brothers and sisters,
to pray for me to the Lord our God.

Deacon or minister:
Christ our Savior is our advocate with the Father:
with humble hearts let us ask him to forgive us our
  sins
and cleanse us from every stain.

You were sent with good news for the poor and
  healing for the contrite.
R⁊. **Lord, be merciful to me, a sinner. Or: Lord, have mercy.**

You came to call sinners, not the just.
R⁊. **Lord, be merciful to me, a sinner. Or: Lord, have mercy.**

You forgave the many sins of the woman who showed
you great love.
R⁊. **Lord, be merciful to me, a sinner. Or: Lord, have mercy.**

You did not shun the company of outcasts and sin-
ners.
R⁊. **Lord, be merciful to me, a sinner. Or: Lord, have**
mercy.

You carried back to the fold the sheep that had
strayed.
R⁊. **Lord, be merciful to me, a sinner. Or: Lord, have**
mercy.

You did not condemn the woman taken in adultery,
but sent her away in peace.
R⁊. **Lord, be merciful to me, a sinner. Or: Lord, have**
mercy.

You called Zacchaeus to repentance and a new life.
℟. Lord, be merciful to me, a sinner. Or: Lord, have mercy.

You promised Paradise to the repentant thief.
℟. Lord, be merciful to me, a sinner. Or: Lord, have mercy.

You are always interceding for us at the right hand of the Father.
℟. Lord, be merciful to me, a sinner. Or: Lord, have mercy.

Deacon or minister:
Now, in obedience to Christ himself, let us join in prayer to the Father, asking him to forgive us as we forgive others.

All say together:
Our Father . . .

The priest concludes:
Father, our source of life,
you know our weakness.
May we reach out with joy to grasp your hand
and walk more readily in your ways.
We ask this through Christ our Lord.
℟. Amen.

For other texts see numbers 202-205.

INDIVIDUAL CONFESSION AND ABSOLUTION

55. Then the penitents go to the priests designated for individual confession, and confess their sins. Each one receives and accepts a fitting act of satisfaction and is absolved. After hearing the confession and offering suitable counsel, the priest extends his hands over the penitent's head (or at least extends his right hand) and gives him absolution. Everything else which is customary in individual confession is omitted.

God, the Father of mercies,
through the death and resurrection of his Son
has reconciled the world to himself

and sent the Holy Spirit among us
for the forgiveness of sins;
through the ministry of the Church
may God give you pardon and peace,
and I absolve you from your sins
in the name of the Father, and of the Son, ✠
and of the Holy Spirit.

The penitent answers: **Amen.**

PROCLAMATION OF PRAISE FOR GOD'S MERCY

56. When the individual confessions have been completed, the other priests stand near the one who is presiding over the celebration. The latter invites all present to offer thanks and encourages them to do good works which will proclaim the grace of repentance in the life of the entire community and each of its members. It is fitting for all to sing a psalm or hymn or to say a litany in acknowledgment of God's power and mercy, for example, the canticle of Mary (Luke 1:46-55), or Psalm 136:1-9, 13-14, 16, 25-26, or one of the psalms as given in no. 206.

CONCLUDING PRAYER OF THANKSGIVING

57. After the song of praise or the litany, the priest concludes the common prayer:

Almighty and merciful God,
how wonderfully you created man
and still more wonderfully remade him.
You do not abandon the sinner
but seek him out with a father's love.
You sent your Son into the world
to destroy sin and death
by his passion,
and to restore life and joy
by his resurrection.
You sent the Holy Spirit into our hearts
to make us your children
and heirs of your kingdom.
You constantly renew our spirit
in the sacraments of your redeeming love,

freeing us from slavery to sin
and transforming us ever more closely
into the likeness of your beloved Son.
We thank you for the wonders of your mercy,
and with heart and hand and voice
we join with the whole Church
in a new song of praise:
Glory to you
through Christ
in the Holy Spirit,
now and for ever.
R⁷. **Amen.**

Or:
All-holy Father,
you have shown us your mercy
and made us a new creation
in the likeness of your Son.
Make us living signs of your love
for the whole world to see.

We ask this through Christ our Lord.
R⁷. **Amen.**

Other concluding prayers may be chosen from nos 207-211.

CONCLUDING RITE

58. Then the priest blesses all present:

May the Lord guide your hearts in the way of his love
and fill you with Christ-like patience.
R⁷. **Amen.**

May he give you strength
to walk in newness of life
and to please him in all things.
R⁷. **Amen.**

May almighty God bless you,
the Father, and the Son, ✝ **and the Holy Spirit.**
℟. **Amen.**

Other blessings may be selected from nos. 212-214.

59. The deacon or other minister or the priest himself
dismisses the assembly:

The Lord has freed you from your sins. Go in peace.
All answer: **Thanks be to God.**

Any other appropriate form may be used.

CHAPTER III

RITE FOR RECONCILIATION OF SEVERAL PENITENTS WITH GENERAL CONFESSION AND ABSOLUTION

60. For the reconciliation of several penitents with general confession and absolution, in the cases provided for in the law, everything is done as described above for the reconciliation of several penitents with individual absolution, but with the following changes only.

INSTRUCTION

After the homily or as part of the homily, the priest explains to the faithful who wish to receive general absolution that they should be properly disposed. Each one should repent of his sins and resolve to turn away from these sins, to make up for any scandal and harm he may have caused, and to confess individually at the proper time each of the serious sins which cannot now be confessed. Some form of satisfaction should be proposed to all, and each individual may add something if he desires.

GENERAL CONFESSION

61. Then the deacon or other minister or the priest himself invites the penitents who wish to receive absolution to indicate this by some kind of sign. He may say:

Will those of you who wish to receive sacramental absolution please kneel and acknowledge that you are sinners.

Or:

Will those of you who wish to receive sacramental absolution please bow your heads and acknowledge that you are sinners.

Or he may suggest a sign laid down by the episcopal conference.

The penitents say a general formula for confession (for example, **I confess to almighty God**). A litany or appropriate song may follow, as described above for the reconciliation of several penitents with individual confession and absolution (no. 54). The Lord's Prayer is always added at the end.

GENERAL ABSOLUTION

62. The priest then gives absolution, holding his hands extended over the penitents and saying:

God the Father does not wish the sinner to die
but to turn back to him and live.
He loved us first and sent his Son into the world to be
its Savior.
May he show you his merciful love and give you
peace.
RⒷ. **Amen.**

Our Lord Jesus Christ was given up to death for our
sins,
and rose again for our justification.
He sent the Holy Spirit on his apostles
and gave them power to forgive sins.
Through the ministry entrusted to me
may he deliver you from evil
and fill you with his Holy Spirit.
RⒷ. **Amen.**

The Spirit, the Comforter, was given to us for the
forgiveness of sins.
In him we approach the Father.
May he cleanse your hearts and clothe you in his
glory,
so that you may proclaim the mighty acts of God
who has called you out of darkness into the splendor
of his light.
RⒷ. **Amen.**

And I absolve you from your sins
in the name of the Father, and of the Son, ✝

and of the Holy Spirit.
℟. **Amen.**

Or:
God, the Father of mercies,
through the death and resurrection of his Son
has reconciled the world to himself
and sent the Holy Spirit among us
for the forgiveness of sins;
through the ministry of the Church
may God give you pardon and peace,
and I absolve you from your sins
in the name of the Father, and of the Son, ✝
and of the Holy Spirit.
℟. **Amen.**

PROCLAMATION OF PRAISE AND CONCLUSION

63. The priest invites all to thank God and to acknowledge
his mercy. After a suitable song or hymn, he blesses the
people and dismisses them, as described above, nos. 58-59,
but without the concluding prayer (no. 57).

SHORT RITE

64. In case of necessity, the rite for reconciling several
penitents with general confession and absolution may be
shortened. If possible, there is a brief reading from
scripture. After giving the usual instruction (no. 60) and
indicating the act of penance, the priest invites the penitents
to make a general confession (for example, **I confess to
almighty God**), and gives the absolution with the form
which is indicated in no. 62.

65. In imminent danger of death, it is enough for the priest
to use the form of absolution itself. In this case it may be
shortened to the following:

I absolve you from your sins
in the name of the Father, and of the Son, ✛
and of the Holy Spirit.
℟. **Amen.**

66. A person who receives general absolution from grave sins is bound to confess each grave sin at his next individual confession.

CHAPTER IV

VARIOUS TEXTS USED IN THE CELEBRATION OF RECONCILIATION

I. FOR THE RECONCILIATION OF ONE PENITENT

INVITATION TO TRUST IN GOD

67. Ezekiel 33:11
**The Lord does not wish the sinner to die
but to turn back to him and live.
Come before him with trust in his mercy.**

68. Luke 5:32
**May the Lord Jesus welcome you.
He came to call sinners, not the just.
Have confidence in him.**

69.
**May the grace of the Holy Spirit
fill your heart with light,
that you may confess your sins with loving trust
and come to know that God is merciful.**

70.
**May the Lord be in your heart
and help you to confess your sins with true sorrow.**

71. 1 John 2:1-2
**If you have sinned, do not lose heart.
We have Jesus Christ to plead for us with the Father:
he is the Holy One,
the atonement for our sins
and for the sins of the whole world.**

SHORT READINGS FROM SCRIPTURE

**72. Let us look on Jesus
who suffered to save us
and rose again for our justification.**
Isaiah 53:4-6

73. Let us listen to the Lord as he speaks to us:
Ezekiel 11:19-20

74. Let us listen to the Lord as he speaks to us:
Matthew 6:14-15

75. Mark 1:14-15

76. Let us listen to the Lord as he speaks to us:
Luke 6:31-38

77. Luke 15:1-7

78. John 10:19-23

79. Romans 5:8-9

80. Ephesians 5:1-2

81. Colossians 1:12-14

82. Colossians 3:8-10, 12-17

83. 1 John 1:6-7, 9

84. A reading may also be chosen from those given in nos.
101-201 for the reconciliation of several penitents. The priest
and penitent may choose other readings from scripture.

PRAYER OF THE PENITENT
85. Psalm 25:6-7
**Remember, Lord, your compassion and mercy which you
    showed long ago.
Do not recall the sins and failings of my youth.
In your mercy remember me, Lord, because of your
    goodness.**

86. Psalm 50:4-5
Wash me from my guilt
and cleanse me of my sin.
I acknowledge my offense;
my sin is before me always.

87. Luke 15:18; 18:13
Father, I have sinned against you
and am not worthy to be called your son.
Be merciful to me, a sinner.

88.
Father of mercy,
like the prodigal son
I return to you and say:
"I have sinned against you
and am no longer worthy to be called your son."
Christ Jesus, Savior of the world,
I pray with the repentant thief
to whom you promised paradise:
"Lord, remember me in your kingdom."
Holy Spirit, fountain of love,
I call on you with trust:
"Purify my heart,
and help me to walk as a child of the light."

89.
Lord Jesus,
you opened the eyes of the blind,
healed the sick,
forgave the sinful woman,
and after Peter's denial confirmed him in your love.
Listen to my prayer:
forgive all my sins,
renew your love in my heart,
help me to live in perfect unity with my fellow
    Christians
that I may proclaim your saving power to all the
    world.

90.

Lord Jesus,
you chose to be called the friend of sinners.
By your saving death and resurrection
free me from my sins.
May your peace take root in my heart
and bring forth a harvest
of love, holiness, and truth.

91.

Lord Jesus Christ,
you are the Lamb of God;
you take away the sins of the world.
Through the grace of the Holy Spirit
restore me to friendship with your Father,
cleanse me from every stain of sin
in the blood you shed for me,
and raise me to new life
for the glory of your name.

92.

Lord God,
in your goodness have mercy on me:
do not look on my sins,
but take away all my guilt.
Create in me a clean heart
and renew within me an upright spirit.

Or:

Lord Jesus, Son of God,
have mercy on me, a sinner.

AFTER THE ABSOLUTION

93. In place of the proclamation of God's praise and the
dismissal, the priest may say:

May the Passion of our Lord Jesus Christ,
the intercession of the Blessed Virgin Mary and of all
**   the saints,**
whatever good you do and suffering you endure,
heal your sins,

help you grow in holiness,
and reward you with eternal life.
Go in peace.

Or:
The Lord has freed you from sin.
May he bring you safely to his kingdom in heaven.
Glory to him for ever.
R℣. Amen.

Or:
Blessed are those
whose sins have been forgiven,
whose evil deeds have been forgotten.
Rejoice in the Lord,
and go in peace.

Or:
Go in peace,
and proclaim to the world
the wonderful works of God,
who has brought you salvation.

II. FOR THE RECONCILIATION OF SEVERAL PENITENTS

GREETING
94.
Grace, mercy, and peace
from God the Father and Jesus Christ his Son
be with you in truth and love.
R℣. Amen.

95.
May God open your hearts to his law
and give you peace;
may he answer your prayers
and restore you to his friendship.
R℣. Amen.

96.

Grace and peace be with you
from God our Father
and from the Lord Jesus Christ
who laid down his life for our sins.
R̷. **Glory to him for ever. Amen.**

The greetings from the introductory rites of Mass may also
be used.

OPENING PRAYERS

97.

Lord,
turn to us in mercy
and forgive us all our sins
that we may serve you in true freedom.

We ask this through Christ our Lord.
R̷. **Amen.**

98.

Lord our God,
you are patient with sinners
and accept our desire to make amends.
We acknowledge our sins
and are resolved to change our lives.
Help us to celebrate this sacrament of your mercy
so that we may reform our lives
and receive from you the gift of everlasting joy.

We ask this through Christ our Lord.
R̷. **Amen.**

99.

Almighty and merciful God,
you have brought us together in the name of your Son
to receive your mercy and grace in our time of need.
Open our eyes to see the evil we have done.
Touch our hearts and convert us to yourself.

Where sin has divided and scattered,
may your love make one again;
where sin has brought weakness,

may your power heal and strengthen;
where sin has brought death,
may your Spirit raise to new life.

Give us a new heart to love you,
so that our lives may reflect the image of your Son.
May the world see the glory of Christ
revealed in your Church,
and come to know
that he is the one whom you have sent,
Jesus Christ, your Son, our Lord.
R̷. **Amen.**

100.
Father of mercies
and God of all consolation,
you do not wish the sinner to die
but to be converted and live.
Come to the aid of your people,
that they may turn from their sins
and live for you alone.
May we be attentive to your word,
confess our sins, receive your forgiveness,
and be always grateful for your loving kindness.
Help us to live the truth in love
and grow into the fullness of Christ, your Son,
who lives and reigns for ever and ever.
R̷. **Amen.**

BIBLICAL READINGS

The following readings are proposed as a help for pastors and
others involved in the selection of readings. For diversity, and
according to the nature of the group, other readings may be
selected.

READINGS FROM THE OLD TESTAMENT

101. **Genesis 3:1-19** She took the fruit of the tree and ate it.

102. **Genesis 4:1-15**   Cain set on his brother and killed him.

103. **Genesis 18:17-33**   The Lord said: I will not destroy the city for the sake of ten good men.

104. **Exodus 17:1-7**   They tempted the Lord saying: Is the Lord here or not?

105. **Exodus 20:1-21**   I am the Lord your God . . . you will not have other gods.

106. **Deuteronomy 6:3-9**   Love the Lord your God with your whole heart.

107. **Deuteronomy 9:7-19**   Your people quickly turned away from the wrong you had showed them.

108. **Deuteronomy 30:15-20**   I set before you life and prosperity, death and evil.

109. **2 Samuel 12:1-9, 13**   David said to Nathan: I have sinned against the Lord God. Nathan said to David: The Lord has forgiven your sin; you will not die.

110. **Nehemiah 9:1-20**   The sons of Israel assembled for a fast and confessed their sins.

111. **Wisdom 1:1-16**   Love justice, for wisdom will not enter an evil soul nor live in a body subjected to sin.

112. **Wisdom 5:1-16**   The hope of the wicked is like down flying on the wind. The just, however, live for ever.

113. **Sirach 28:1-7**   Forgive your neighbor when he hurts you, and then your sins will be forgiven when you pray.

114. **Isaiah 1:2-6, 15-18**   I have nourished and educated sons; however they have rebelled against me.

115. **Isaiah 5:1-7**   The vineyard became my delight. He looked for grapes, but it yielded wild grapes.

116. **Isaiah 43:22-28**   On account of me your iniquities are blotted out.

117. **Isaiah 53:1-12**   The Lord laid upon him our guilt.

118. **Isaiah 55:1-11**   Let the wicked man forsake his way and return to the Lord, and he will have mercy on him because he is generous in forgiving.

119. **Isaiah 58:1-11**   When you give your soul to the hungry and fulfill the troubled soul, your light will rise like dawn from the darkness, and your darkness will be like midday.

120. **Isaiah 59:1-4, 9-15**   Your iniquities divide you and your God.

121. **Jeremiah 2:1-13**   My people have done two evils: they have abandoned me, the fountain of living water, and have dug for themselves broken cisterns which hold no water.

122. **Jeremiah 7:21-26**   Listen to my voice, and I will be your God, and you will be my people.

123. **Ezekiel 11:14-21**   I will take the heart of stone from their bodies, and I will give them a heart of flesh, so that they may walk according to my laws.

124. **Ezekiel 18:20-32**   If a wicked man turns away from his sins, he shall live and not die.

125. **Ezekiel 36:23-28**   I shall sprinkle upon you clean water, put my spirit within you, and make you walk according to my commands.

126. **Hosea 2:16-25**   I will make a covenant for them on that day.

127. **Hosea 11:1-11**   I took them in my arms, and they did not know that I cured them.

128. **Hosea 14:2-10**   Israel, return to the Lord your God.

129. **Joel 2:12-19**   Return to me with your whole heart.

130. **Micah 6:1-4, 4-6** Do right and love mercy, and walk humbly with your God.

131. **Micah 7:2-7, 18-20** The Lord will turn back and have mercy on us; he will cast all our sins into the depths of the sea.

132. **Zechariah 1:1-6** Return to me, and I shall return to you.

RESPONSORIAL PSALM

133. Psalm 13

R⁒. (6a): **All my hope, O Lord, is in your loving kindness.**

134. Psalm 25

R⁒. (16a): **Turn to me, Lord, and have mercy.**

135. Psalm 31:2-6

R⁒. (6b): **You have redeemed us, Lord, God of truth.**

136. Psalm 32

R⁒. (5c): **Lord, forgive the wrong I have done.**

137. Psalm 36

R⁒. (8): **How precious is your unfailing love, Lord.**

138. Psalm 50: 7-8, 14-23

R⁒. (23b): **To the upright I will show the saving power of God.**

139. Psalm 51

R⁒. (14a): **Give back to me the joy of your salvation.**

140. Psalm 73

R⁒. (28a): **It is good for me to be with the Lord.**

141. Psalm 90

R⁒. (14): **Fill us with your love, O Lord, and we will sing for joy!**

142. Psalm 95

R⫶ (8a): **If today you hear his voice, harden not your hearts.**

143. Psalm 119:1, 10-13, 15-16

R⫶ (1): **Happy are they who follow the law of the Lord!**

144. Psalm 123

R⫶ (2c): **Our eyes are fixed on the Lord.**

145. Psalm 130

R⫶ (7bc): **With the Lord there is mercy, and fullness of redemption.**

146. Psalm 139:1-18, 23-24

R⫶ (23a): **You have searched me, and you know me, Lord.**

147. Psalm 143: 1-11

R⫶ (10): **Teach me to do your will, my God.**

READINGS FROM THE NEW TESTAMENT

148. **Romans 3:22-26**   All men are justified by the gift of God through redemption in Christ Jesus.

149. **Romans 5:6-11**   We give glory to God through our Lord Jesus Christ, through whom we have received reconciliation.

150. **Romans 6:2b-13**   Consider yourselves dead to sin but alive to God.

151. **Romans 6:16-23**   The wages of sin is death; the gift of God is eternal life in Christ Jesus our Lord.

152. **Romans 7:14-25**   Unhappy man that I am! Who will free me? Thanks to God through Jesus Christ our Lord.

153. **Romans 12:1-2, 9-19**   Be transformed by the renewal of your mind.

154. **Romans 13:8-14** Let us cast away the works of darkness and put on the weapons of light.

155. **2 Corinthians 5:17-21** God reconciled the world to himself through Christ.

156. **Galatians 5:16-24** You cannot belong to Christ unless you crucify the flesh with its passions and concupiscence.

157. **Ephesians 2:1-10** When we were dead to sin, God, on account of his great love for us, brought us to life in Christ.

158. **Ephesians 4:1-3, 17-32** Renew yourself and put on the new man.

159. **Ephesians 5:1-14** You were once in darkness; now you are light in the Lord, so walk as children of light.

160. **Ephesians 6:10-18** Put God's armor on so that you will be able to stand firm against evil.

161. **Colossians 3:1-10, 12-17** If you were raised to life with Christ, aspire to the realm above. Put to death what remains in this earthly life.

162. **Hebrews 12:1-5** You have not resisted to the point of shedding your blood in your struggle against sin.

163. **James 1:22-27** Be doers of the word and not merely listeners.

164. **James 2:14-26** What use is it if someone says that he believes and does not manifest it in works?

165. **James 3:1-12** If someone does not offend in word, he is a perfect man.

166. **1 Peter 1:13-23** You have been redeemed not by perishable goods, gold or silver, but by the precious blood of Jesus Christ.

167. **2 Peter 1:3-11** Be careful so that you may make firm your calling and election.

168. **1 John 1:5-10, 2:1-2**   If we confess our sins, he is faithful and just and will forgive our sins and cleanse us from all injustice.

169. **1 John 2:3-11**   Whoever hates his brother remains in darkness.

170. **1 John 3:1-24**   We know that we have crossed over from death to life because we love our brothers.

171. **1 John 4:16-21**   God is love, and he who lives in love, lives in God, and God in him.

172. **Revelation 2:1-5**   Do penance and return to your former ways.

173. **Revelation 3:14-22**   Because you are lukewarm, neither hot or cold, I will vomit you out of my mouth.

174. **Revelation 20:11-15**   All have been judged according to their works.

175. **Revelation 21:1-8**   Whoever conquers will inherit all this, and I will be his God, and he will be my son.

176. **Matthew 3:1-12**   Repent, for the kingdom of heaven is close at hand.

177. **Matthew 4:12-17**   Repent, for the kingdom of heaven is close at hand.

178. **Matthew 5:1-12**   When he saw the crowds, he went up to the hill and taught his disciples.

179. **Matthew 5:13-16**   Let your light shine before men.

180. **Matthew 5:17-47**   But I am speaking to you.

181. **Matthew 9:1-8**   Have confidence, my son, your sins are forgiven.

182. **Matthew 9:9-13**   I did not come to call the just, but sinners.

183. **Matthew 18:15-20** You have won back your brother.

184. **Matthew 18:21-35** This is the way my heavenly Father will deal with you unless each one forgives his brother from his heart.

185. **Matthew 25:31-46** Whatever you have done to the very least of my brothers, you have done to me.

186. **Matthew 26:69-75** Peter went outside and wept bitterly.

187. **Mark 12:28-34** This is the first commandment.

188. **Luke 7:36-50** Her many sins must have been forgiven her, because she loved much.

189. **Luke 13:1-5** Unless you repent you will all perish as they did.

190. **Luke 15:1-10** Heaven is filled with joy when one sinner turns back to God.

191. **Luke 15:11-32** When he was still far away, his father saw him and was moved with mercy. He ran to him and embraced and kissed him.

192. **Luke 17:1-4** If your brother sins against you seven times a day and returns to you seven times a day and says I am sorry, you must forgive him.

193. **Luke 18:9-14** God, be merciful to me, a sinner.

194. **Luke 19:1-10** The Son of Man has come to seek out and save what was lost.

195. **Luke 23:39-43** Today you will be with me in paradise.

196. **John 8:1-11** Go and sin no more.

197. **John 8:31-36** Everyone who commits sin is a slave of sin.

198. **John 15:1-8** The Father prunes every barren branch, and every branch that bears fruit he makes it bear even more.

199. **John 15:9-14** You are my friends if you do what I command you.

200. **John 19:13-37** They shall look upon him whom they pierced.

201. **John 20:19-23** Receive the Holy Spirit; whose sins you forgive, they are forgiven.

INVITATION OF THE MINISTER FOR THE GENERAL CONFESSION OF SINS

202. If the prayer is directed to the Father:

1
Dear friends in Christ, our merciful Father does not desire the death of the sinner but rather that he should turn back to him and have life. Let us pray that we who are sorry for our past sins may fear no future evil and sin no more.
℟. **Spare us, Lord; spare your people.**

2
God who is infintely merciful pardons all who are repentant and takes away their guilt. Confident in his goodness, let us ask him to forgive all our sins as we confess them with sincerity of heart.
℟. **Lord, hear our prayer.**

3
God gave us his Son for our sins and raised him up to make us holy. Let us humbly pray to the Father.
℟. **Lord, have mercy on your people.**

4
God our Father waits for the return of those who are lost and welcomes them back as his children. Let us pray that we may turn back to him and be received with kindness into his house.
℟. **Lord, do not hold our sins against us.**

Or:

Father, we have sinned in your sight; we are un-worthy to be called your children.

5

Our God seeks out what is lost, leads home the abandoned, binds up what is broken and gives strength to the weak; let us ask him to help us.
R̷. **Lord, heal our weakness.**

203. If the prayer is directed to Christ:

1

Jesus Christ is the victor over sin and death: in his mercy may he pardon our offenses against God and reconcile us with the Church we have wounded by our sins.
R̷. **Lord Jesus, be our salvation.**

2

In his great love Christ willingly suffered and died for our sins and for the sins of all mankind. Let us come before him with faith and hope to pray for the salvation of the world.
R̷. **Christ, graciously hear us.**

3

Let us pray with confidence to Christ, the Good Shepherd, who seeks out the lost sheep and carries it back with joy.
R̷. **Lord, seek us out and bring us home.**

4

Christ our Lord bore our sins upon the cross and by his suffering has brought us healing, so that we live for God and are dead to sin. Let us pray with humility and trust.
R̷. **Lord, to whom shall we go? You have the words of eternal life. We have come to believe and to know that you are the Christ, the Son of God.**

Or:
Have pity on us, and help us.

5
Christ our Lord was given up to death for our sins and rose again for our justification. Let us pray to him with confidence in his goodness.
℟. **You are our Savior**

Or:
Jesus Christ, Son of the living God, have pity on us.

PENITENTIAL INTERCESSIONS

(At least one of the intercessions should always be a petition for a true conversion of heart.)

204. If the prayer is addressed to the Father:

1
—By human weakness we have disfigured the holiness of the Church: pardon all our sins and restore us to full communion with our brethren.
℟. **Lord, hear our prayer.** Or: **Lord, hear us.**

Or another suitable response may be used.

—Your mercy is our hope: welcome us to the sacrament of reconciliation. ℟.

—Give us the will to change our lives, and the lives of others, by charity, good example and prayer. ℟.

—As we make our confession, rescue us from slavery to sin and lead us to the freedom enjoyed by your children. ℟.

—Make us a living sign of your love for all to see: people reconciled with you and with each other. ℟.

—Through the sacrament of reconciliation may we grow in your peace and seek to spread it throughout the world. ℟.

—In this sign of your love you forgive us our sins: may it teach us to love others and to forgive their sins against us. R̥.

—In your mercy clothe us in the wedding garment of grace and welcome us to your table. R̥.

—Forgive us our sins, lead us in the ways of goodness and love, and bring us to the reward of everlasting peace. R̥.

—Give light to our darkness and lead us by your truth. R̥.

—In justice you punish us: in your mercy set us free for the glory of your name. R̥.

—May your power keep safe from all danger those whom your love sets free from the chains of sin. R̥.

—Look on our weakness: do not be angry and condemn, but in your love cleanse, guide and save us. R̥.

—In your mercy free us from the past and enable us to begin a new life of holiness. R̥.

—When we stray from you, guide us back into the way of holiness, love and peace. R̥.

—By your redeeming love overcome our sinfulness and the harm it has brought us. R̥.

—Blot out the sins of the past and fit us for the life that is to come. R̥.

2
The following intercessions may be used with a variable response or with an invariable response as in the *Liturgy of the Hours*.

In your goodness, forgive our sins against the unity of your family,
—make us one in heart, one in spirit.

We have sinned, Lord, we have sinned,
—take away our sins by your saving grace.

Give us pardon for our sins,
—and reconciliation with your Church.

Touch our hearts and change our lives, make us grow always in your friendship,
—help us to make up for our sins against your wisdom and goodness.

Cleanse and renew your Church, Lord,
—may it grow in strength as a witness to you.

Touch the hearts of those who have abandoned you through sin and scandal,
—call them back to you and keep them faithful in your love.

May we show forth in our lives the sufferings of your Son,
—you raised us up to life when you raised him from the dead.

Have mercy on us, Lord, as we praise and thank you,
—with your pardon give us also your peace.

Lord, our sins are many, but we trust in your mercy,
—call us, and we shall turn to you.

Receive us as we come before you with humble and contrite hearts,
—those who trust in you shall never trust in vain.

We have turned away from you and fallen into sin,
—we have followed evil ways and rejected your commandments.

Turn to us, Lord, and show us your mercy; blot out our sins,
—cast them into the depths of the sea.

Restore us, Lord, to your favor, and give us joy in your presence,
—may our glory be to serve you with all our hearts.

205. If the prayer is addressed to Christ:

1
Romans 5:10
—**By your death you reconciled us with the Father
and brought us salvation.**
R̷. **Lord, have mercy.** Or: **Christ, hear us.**

Or another suitable response may be used.

Romans 8:34
—**You died and rose again, and sit at the right hand of
the Father, to make intercession for us.** R̷.

1 Corinthians 1:30
—**You came from God as our wisdom and justice, our
sanctification and redemption.** R̷.

1 Corinthians 6:11
—**You washed mankind in the Spirit of our God; you
made us holy and righteous.** R̷.

1 Corinthians 8:12
—**You warned us that if we sin against each other we
sin against you.** R̷.

2 Corinthians 8:9
—**Though you were rich you became poor for our
sake, so that by your poverty we might become rich.**
R̷.

Galatians 1:4
—**You gave yourself up for our sins to save us from
this evil world.** R̷.

1 Thessalonians 1:10
—**You rose from the dead to save us from the anger
that was to come.** R̷.

1 Timothy 1:15
—**You came into the world to save sinners.** R̷.

1 Timothy 2:6
—**You gave yourself up to bring redemption to all.** R̷.

2 Timothy 1:10
—**You destroyed death and gave light to life.** R̷.

2 Timothy 4:1
—You will come to judge the living and the dead. R̕.

Titus 2:14
—You gave yourself up for us to redeem us from all sin and to prepare for yourself a holy people, marked as your own, devoted to good works. R̕.

Hebrews 2:17
—You showed us your mercy, and as a faithful high priest in the things of God you made atonement for the sins of the people. R̕.

Hebrews 5:9
—You became the source of salvation for all who obey you. R̕.

Hebrews 9:15
—Through the Holy Spirit you offered yourself to God as a spotless victim, cleansing our consciences from lifeless works. R̕.

Hebrews 9:28
—You were offered in sacrifice to undo the sins of the many. R̕.

1 Peter 3:18
—Once and for all you died for our sins, the innocent one for the guilty. R̕.

1 John 2:2
—You are the atonement for our sins and for the sins of the world. R̕.

John 3:16, 35
—You died that those who believe in you may not perish but have eternal life. R̕.

Matthew 18:11
—You came into the world to seek and save what was lost. R̕.

John 3:17
—You were sent by the Father, not to judge the world but to save it. R̕.

Mark 2:10
—**You have power on earth to forgive sins.** ℞.

Matthew 11:28
—**You invite all who labor and are burdened to come to you to be refreshed.** ℞.

Matthew 16:19, 18:18
—**You gave your apostles the keys to the kingdom of heaven, the power to bind and to loose.** ℞.

Matthew 22:38-40
—**You told us that the whole law depends on love of God and of our neighbor.** ℞.

John 10:10
—**Jesus, life of all mankind, you came into the world to give us life, life in its fullness.** ℞.

John 10:11
—**Jesus, Good Shepherd, you gave your life for your sheep.** ℞.

John 14:6; 8:32, 36
—**Jesus, eternal truth, you give us true freedom.** ℞.

John 14:6
—**Jesus, you are the way to the Father.** ℞.

John 11:25
—**Jesus, you are the resurrection and life; those who believe in you, even if they are dead, will live.** ℞.

John 15:1-2
—**Jesus, true vine, the Father prunes your branches to make them bear even greater fruit.** ℞.

2
The following intercessions may be used with a variable response or with an invariable response as in the *Liturgy of the Hours*.

Healer of the body and soul, bind up the wounds of our hearts,
—**that our lives may grow strong through grace.**

Help us to strip ourselves of sin,
—and put on the new life of grace.

Redeemer of the world, give us the spirit of penance
and a deeper devotion to your passion,
—so that we may have a fuller share in your risen
    glory.

May your Mother, the refuge of sinners, intercede for
    us,
—and ask you in your goodness to pardon our sins.

You forgave the woman who repented,
—show us also your mercy.

You brought back the lost sheep on your shoulders,
—pity us and lead us home.

You promised paradise to the good thief,
—take us with you into your Kingdom.

You died for us and rose again,
—make us share in your death and resurrection.

PROCLAMATION OF PRAISE
206.
Psalm 32:1-7, 10-11

℞. Rejoice in the Lord and sing for joy, friends of
God.

Psalm 98: 1-9

℞. The Lord has remembered his mercy.

Psalm 100:2-5

℞. The Lord is loving and kind: his mercy is for ever.

Psalm 119:1, 10-13, 15-16, 18, 33, 105, 169, 170, 174-175.

℞. Blessed are you, Lord; teach me your decrees.

Psalm 103:1-4, 8-18

℞. The mercy of the Lord is from everlasting to
everlasting on those who revere him.

Psalm 145:1-21

℟. **Day after day I will bless you, Lord: I will praise your name for ever.**

Psalm 146:2-10

℟. **I will sing to my God all the days of my life.**

Isaiah 12:1b-6

℟. **Praise the Lord and call upon his name.**

Isaiah 61:10-11

℟. **My spirit rejoices in my God.**

Jeremiah 31:10-14

℟. **The Lord has redeemed his people.**

Daniel 3:52-57

℟. **Bless the Lord, all the works of his hand: praise and glorify him for ever.**

Luke 1:46-55

℟. **The Lord has remembered his mercy.**

Ephesians 1:3-10

℟. **Blessed be God who chose us in Christ.**

Revelation 15:3-4

℟. **Great and wonderful are all your works, Lord.**

CONCLUDING PRAYERS

207.
Father, all-powerful and ever-living God,
we do well always and everywhere to give you
thanks.

When you punish us, you show your justice;
when you pardon us, you show your kindness;
yet always your mercy enfolds us.

When you chastise us, you do not wish to condemn
    us;
when you spare us, you give us time to make amends
    for our sins
through Christ our Lord.
R⁊. **Amen.**

208.
Lord God,
creator and ruler of your kingdom of light,
in your great love for this world
you gave up your only Son
for our salvation.
His cross has redeemed us,
his death has given us life,
his resurrection has raised us to glory.
Through him we ask you
to be always present among your family.
Teach us to be reverent in the presence of your glory;
fill our hearts with faith,
our days with good works,
our lives with your love;
may your truth be on our lips
and your wisdom in all our actions,
that we may receive the reward of everlasting life.

We ask this through Christ our Lord.
R⁊. **Amen.**

209.
Lord Jesus Christ,
your loving forgiveness knows no limits.
You took our human nature
to give us an example of humility
and to make us faithful in every trial.
May we never lose the gifts you have given us,
but if we fall into sin
lift us up by your gift of repentance,
for you live and reign for ever and ever.
R⁊. **Amen.**

210.
Father,
in your love you have brought us
from evil to good and from misery to happiness.
Through your blessings
give the courage of perseverance
to those you have called and justified by faith.

Grant this through Christ our Lord.
R̷. **Amen.**

211.
God and Father of us all,
you have forgiven our sins
and sent us your peace.
Help us to forgive each other
and to work together to establish peace in the world.

We ask this through Christ our Lord.
R̷. **Amen.**

212.
And may the blessing of almighty God,
the Father, and the Son, ✛ and the Holy Spirit,
come upon you and remain with you for ever.
R̷. **Amen.**

213.
May the Father bless us,
for we are his children, born to eternal life.
R̷. **Amen.**

May the Son show us his saving power,
for he died and rose for us.
R̷. **Amen.**

May the Spirit give us his gift of holiness
and lead us by the right path,
for he dwells in our hearts.
R̷. **Amen.**

214.
May the Father bless us,
for he has adopted us as his children.
R̷. **Amen.**

May the Son come to help us,
for he has received us as brothers and sisters.
R̷. **Amen.**

May the Spirit be with us,
for he has made us his dwelling place.
R̷. **Amen.**

APPENDIX I

ABSOLUTION FROM CENSURES

1. The form of absolution is not to be changed when a priest, in keeping with the provision of law, absolves a properly disposed penitent within the sacramental forum from a censure *latae sententiae*. It is enough that the confessor intend to absolve also from censures. Before absolving from sins, however, the confessor may absolve from the censure, using the formula which is given below for absolution from censure outside the sacrament of penance.

2. When a priest, in accordance with the law, absolves a penitent from a censure outside the sacrament of penance, he uses the following formula:

By the power granted to me,
I absolve you
from the bond of excommunication (or **suspension** or
interdict).
In the name of the Father, and of the Son, ✝
and of the Holy Spirit.
The penitent answers: **Amen.**

DISPENSATION FROM IRREGULARITY

3. When, in accordance with the law, a priest dispenses a penitent from an irregularity, either during confession, after absolution has been given, or outside the sacrament of penance, he says:

By the power granted to me
I dispense you from the irregularity
which you have incurred.
In the name of the Father, and of the Son, ✝
and of the Holy Spirit.
The penitent answers: **Amen.**

APPENDIX II

SAMPLE PENITENTIAL SERVICES

These services have been prepared by the Congregation for Divine Worship to help those who prepare or lead penitential celebrations.

PREPARING PENITENTIAL CELEBRATIONS

1. Penitential celebrations, mentioned in the *Rite of Penance* (nos. 36-37), are beneficial in fostering the spirit and virtue of penance among individuals and communities; they also help in preparing for a more fruitful celebration of the sacrament of penance. However, the faithful must be reminded of the difference between these celebrations and sacramental confession and absolution.[1]

2. The particular conditions of life, the manner of speaking, and the educational level of the congregation or special group should be taken into consideration. Thus liturgical commissions[2] and individual Christian communities preparing these celebrations should choose the texts and format most suited to the circumstances of each particular group.

3. To this end, several examples of penitential celebrations are given below. These are models and should be adapted to the specific conditions and needs of each community.

4. When the sacrament of penance is celebrated in these services, it follows the readings and homily, and the rite of reconciling several penitents with individual confession and absolution is used (nos. 54-59, *Rite of Penance*); when permitted by law, the rite for general confession and absolution is used (nos. 60-63, *Rite of Penance*).

I. PENITENTIAL CELEBRATIONS DURING LENT

5. Lent is the principal time of penance both for individual Christians and for the whole Church. It is therefore desira-

[1] See Congregation for the Doctrine of the Faith, *Normae pastorales circa absolutionem sacramentalem generali modo impertiendam*, June 16, 1972, no. X: *AAS* 64 (1972) 513.

[2] See Congregation of Rites, Instruction *Inter Oecumenici*, September 26, 1964, no. 39: *AAS* (1964) 110.

ble to prepare the Christian community for a fuller sharing in the paschal mystery by penitential celebrations during Lent.[1]

6. Texts from the lectionary and sacramentary may be used in these penitential celebrations; the penitential nature of the liturgy of the word in the Masses for Lent should be considered.

7. Two outlines of penitential celebrations suitable for Lent are given here. The first emphasizes penance as strengthening or restoring baptismal grace; the second shows penance as a preparation for a fuller sharing in the Easter mystery of Christ and his Church.

FIRST EXAMPLE

PENANCE LEADS TO A STRENGTHENING OF BAPTISMAL GRACE

8. a) After an appropriate song and the greeting by the minister, the meaning of this celebration is explained to the people. It prepares the Christian community to recall their baptismal grace at the Easter Vigil and to reach newness of life in Christ through freedom from sins.

9. b) Prayer

My brothers and sisters, we have neglected the gifts of our baptism and fallen into sin. Let us ask God to renew his grace within us as we turn to him in repentance.

Let us kneel (or: **Bow your heads before God).**
All pray in silence for a brief period.
Let us stand (or: **Raise your heads).**

Lord Jesus,
you redeemed us by your passion
and raised us to new life in baptism.
Protect us with your unchanging love
and share with us the joy of your resurrection,
for you live and reign for ever and ever.
R̸. Amen.

[1]See Second Vatican Council, constitution *Sacrosanctum concilium*, no. 109; Paul VI, Apostolic Constitution *Paenitemini*, February 17, 1966, no. IX: *AAS* 58 (1966) 185.

10. c) Readings

First Reading
1 Corinthians 10:1-13
All this that happened to the people of Moses in the desert was written for our benefit.

Responsorial Psalm
Psalm 106:6-10, 13-14, 19-22
℟. (4): **Lord, remember us,**
for the love you bear your people.

Gospel
Luke 15:4-7
Share my joy: I have found my lost sheep.

or
Luke 15:11-32
Your brother here was dead, and has come to life.

11. d) Homily
The celebrant may speak about:
—the need to fulfill the grace of baptism by living faithfully the Gospel of Christ (see 1 Corinthians 10:1-13);
—the seriousness of sin committed after baptism (see Hebrews 6:4-8);
—the unlimited mercy of our God and Father who continually welcomes those who turn back to him after having sinned (see Luke 15);
—Easter as the feast when the Church rejoices over the Christian initiation of catechumens and the reconciliation of penitents.

12. e) Examination of conscience.
After the homily, the examination of conscience takes place; a sample text is given in Appendix III. A period of silence should always be included so that each person may personally examine his conscience. In a special way the people should examine their conscience on the baptismal promises which will be renewed at the Easter Vigil.

13. f) Act of repentance
The deacon (or another minister, if there is no deacon) speaks to the assembly:

My brothers and sisters, the hour of God's favor
draws near, the day of his mercy and of our salvation,
when death was destroyed and eternal life began.
This is the season for planting new vines in God's
vineyard, the time for pruning the vines to ensure a
richer harvest.

We all acknowledge that we are sinners. We are
moved to penance, encouraged by the example and
prayers of our brothers and sisters. We admit our guilt
and say: "Lord, I acknowledge my sins; my offenses
are always before me. Turn away your face, Lord,
from my sins, and blot out all my wrong-doing. Give
me back the joy of your salvation and give me a new
and steadfast spirit."

We are sorry for having offended God by our sins.
May he be merciful and hear us as we ask to be
restored to his friendship and numbered among the
living who share the joy of Christ's risen life.

Then the priest sprinkles the congregation with holy water,
while all sing (say):

Cleanse us, Lord, from all our sins;
Wash us, and we shall be whiter than snow.

Then the priest says:
Lord our God,
you created us in love
and redeemed us in mercy.
While we were exiled from heaven
by the jealousy of the evil one,
you gave us your only Son,
who shed his blood to save us.
Send now your Holy Spirit
to breathe new life into your children,
for you do not want us to die
but to live for you alone.
You do not abandon those who abandon you;
correct us as a Father
and restore us to your family.

Lord,
your sons and daughters stand before you
in humility and trust.
Look with compassion on us
as we confess our sins.
Heal our wounds;
stretch out a hand of pity
to save us and raise us up.
Keep us free from harm
as members of Christ's body,
as sheep of your flock,
as children of your family.
Do not allow the enemy
to triumph over us
or death to claim us for ever,
for you raised us to new life in baptism.

Hear, Lord, the prayers we offer from contrite hearts.
Have pity on us as we acknowledge our sins.
Lead us back to the way of holiness.
Protect us now and always
from the wounds of sin.
May we ever keep safe in all its fullness
the gift your love once gave us
and your mercy now restores.

We ask this through our Lord Jesus Christ, your Son,
who lives and reigns with you and the Holy Spirit,
one God for ever and ever.
℟. Amen.

The celebration ends with an appropriate song and the
dismissal of the people.

SECOND EXAMPLE

PENANCE PREPARES FOR A FULLER SHARING IN THE PASCHAL MYSTERY OF CHRIST FOR THE SALVATION OF THE WORLD

14. a) After an appropriate song and the greeting by the

minister, the faithful are briefly reminded that they are linked with each other in sin and in repentance so that each should take his calling to conversion as an occasion of grace for the whole community.

15. b) Prayer

My brothers and sisters, let us pray that by penance we may be united with Christ, who was crucified for our sins, and so share with all mankind in his resurrection.

Let us kneel (or: Bow your heads before God).
All pray in silence for a brief period.
Let us stand (or: Raise your heads).

Lord, our God and Father,
through the passion of your Son
you gave us new life.
By our practice of penance
make us one with him in his dying
so that we and all mankind
may be one with him
in his resurrection.

We ask this through Christ our Lord.
R̲. Amen.

Or:
Almighty and merciful Father,
send your Holy Spirit
to inspire and strengthen us,
so that by always carrying
the death of Jesus in our bodies
we may also show forth the power of his risen life.

We ask this through Christ our Lord.
R̲. Amen.

16. c) Readings

First Reading
Isaiah 53:1-7, 10-12
He is the one who bore our sufferings.

Responsorial Psalm
Psalm 22:2-3, 7-9, 18-28
R̶. **Father, your will be done.**

Second Reading
1 Peter 2:20-25
You had gone astray but now you have come back to the
shepherd and guardian of your souls.

Gospel
Verse before the gospel
**Glory to you, Lord; you were given up to death for
our sins and rose again for our justification. Glory to
you, Lord.**
Or an appropriate song may be sung.

Mark 10:32-45 (or short form: **Mark 10:32-34, 42-45**)
Now we are going up to Jerusalem, and the Son of Man will
be handed over.

17. d) Homily
The celebrant may speak about:
—sin, by which we offend God and also Christ's body, the
Church, whose members we became in baptism;
—sin as a failure of love for Christ who in the paschal
mystery showed his love for us to the end;
—the way we affect each other when we do good or choose
evil;
—the mystery of vicarious satisfaction by which Christ bore
the burden of our sins, so that by his wounds we would be
healed (see Isaiah 53; 1 Peter 2:24);
—the social and ecclesial dimension of penance by which
individual Christians share in the work of converting the
whole community;
—the celebration of Easter as the feast of the Christian
community which is renewing itself by the conversion or
repentance of each member, so that the Church may become
a clearer sign of salvation in the world.

18. e) Examination of conscience
After the homily, the examination of conscience takes place;
a sample text is given in Appendix III. A period of
silence should always be included so that each person may
personally examine his conscience.

19. f) Act of repentance
After the examination of conscience, all say together:

I confess to almighty God,
and to you, my brothers and sisters,
that I have sinned through my own fault.
They strike their breast:
in my thoughts and in my words,
in what I have done,
and in what I have failed to do;
and I ask blessed Mary, ever virgin,
all the angels and saints,
and you, my brothers and sisters,
to pray for me to the Lord our God.

As a sign of conversion and charity toward others, it should be suggested that the faithful give something to help the poor to celebrate the feast of Easter with joy; or they might visit the sick, or make up for some injustice in the community, or perform similar works.

Then the Lord's Prayer may be said, which the priest concludes in this way:

Deliver us, Father, from every evil
as we unite ourselves through penance
with the saving passion of your Son.
Grant us a share
in the joy of the resurrection of Jesus
who is Lord for ever and ever.
R̰. **Amen.**

Depending on circumstances, the general confession may be followed by a form of devotion such as adoration of the cross or the way of the cross, according to local customs and the wishes of the people.

At the end, an appropriate song is sung, and the people are sent away with a greeting or blessing.

II. PENITENTIAL CELEBRATIONS DURING ADVENT

20. a) After an appropriate song and the greeting by the minister, the meaning of the celebration is explained in these or similar words:

My brothers and sisters, Advent is a time of preparation, when we make ready to celebrate the mystery of our Lord's coming as man, the beginning of our redemption. Advent also moves us to look forward with renewed hope to the second coming of Christ, when God's plan of salvation will be brought to fulfillment. We are reminded too of our Lord's coming to each one of us at the hour of our death. We must make sure that he will find us prepared for his coming, as the gospel tells us: "Blessed are those servants who are found awake when the Lord comes" Luke 12:37. **This service of penance is meant to make us ready in mind and heart for the coming of Christ, which we are soon to celebrate in the Mass of Christmas.**

Or:
Now it is time for you to wake from sleep, for our salvation is nearer to us than it was when we first believed. The night is ending; the day draws near. Let us then cast off the deeds of darkness and put on the armor of light. Let us live honestly as people do in the daylight, not in carousing and drunkenness, not in lust and debauchery, not in quarreling and jealousy. But rather let us put on the Lord Jesus Christ and give no thought to the desires of the flesh. Romans 13:11-12.

21. b) Prayer

My brothers and sisters, we look forward to celebrating the mystery of Christ's coming on the feast of Christmas. Let us pray that when he comes he may find us awake and ready to receive him.
All pray in silence for a brief period.

Lord our God,
maker of the heavens,
as we look forward to the coming of our redeemer
grant us the forgiveness of our sins.

We ask this through Christ our Lord.
R̰. **Amen.**

Or:
Eternal Son of God,
creator of the human family
and our redeemer,
come at last among us
as the child of the immaculate Virgin,
and redeem the world.
Reveal your loving presence
by which you set us free from sin
in becoming one like us
in all things but sin,
for you live and reign for ever and ever.
R̰. **Amen.**

22. c) Readings

First Reading
Malachi 3:1-7a
The Lord whom you seek will come to his temple.

Responsorial Psalm
Psalm 85:1-13
R̰. (8) **Lord, let us see your kindness, and grant us your salvation.**

Second Reading
Revelation 21:1-12
He will wipe away all the tears from their eyes.

Gospel
Verse before the gospel
I am coming quickly, says the Lord, and I will repay each man.
Come, Lord Jesus.

Or:
The Spirit and the Bride say: "Come."
Let all who hear answer: "Come."
Come, Lord Jesus.

Or another appropriate song may be sung.

Matthew 3:1-12
Repent, for the kingdom of heaven is close at hand.

Or:
Luke 3:3-17
All mankind shall see the salvation of God.

23. d) Examination of conscience
After the homily, the examination of conscience takes place;
a sample text is given in Appendix III. A period of
silence should always be included so that each person may
personally examine his conscience.

24. e) Act of repentance
The act of repentance follows the examination of conscience.
All may say the **I confess to almighty God** or the inter-
cessions as in no. 60.

The Lord's Prayer is said or sung, and is concluded by the
presiding minister in this way:

Lord our God,
on the first day of creation
you made the light
that scatters all darkness.
Let Christ, the light of lights,
hidden from all eternity,
shine at last on your people
and free us from the darkness of sin.
Fill our lives with good works
as we go out to meet your Son,
so that we may give him a fitting welcome.

We ask this through Christ our Lord.
R̶. **Amen.**

Or:
**Almighty and eternal God,
you sent your only-begotten Son
to reconcile the world to yourself.
Lift from our hearts
the oppressive gloom of sin,
so that we may celebrate
the approaching dawn of Christ's birth
with fitting joy.**

**We ask this through Christ our Lord.
R⁄. Amen.**

At the end, a song is sung, and the people are sent away
with a greeting or blessing.

III. COMMON PENITENTIAL CELEBRATIONS

I. SIN AND CONVERSION

25. a) After an appropriate song (for example Psalm
139:1-12, 16, 23-24) and greeting, the minister who presides
briefly explains the meaning of the readings. Then he invites
all to pray. After a period of silence, he concludes the prayer
in this way:

**Lord Jesus,
you turned and looked on Peter
when he denied you for the third time.
He wept for his sin
and turned again to you in sincere repentance.
Look now on us and touch our hearts,
so that we also may turn back to you
and be always faithful in serving you,
for you live and reign for ever and ever.
R⁄. Amen.**

26. b) Readings

First Reading
Luke 22:31-34
I tell you, Peter: the cock will not crow today before you
deny me three times.

A short period of silence follows the reading.

Second Reading
Luke 22:54-62
Peter went out and wept bitterly.

Responsorial Psalm
Psalm 32:10, 15-27, 20 or Psalm 52 or another
appropriate song.
R⁊. **My trust is in you, O Lord.**

Gospel
John 21:15-19
Simon, son of John, do you love me?

27. c) Homily
The celebrant may speak about:
—the trust we must put in God's grace, not in our own
powers;
—the faithfulness by which we as baptized Christians must
live as true and faithful followers of the Lord;
—our weakness by which we often fall into sin and refuse to
give witness to the gospel;
—the mercy of the Lord, who welcomes as a friend the one
who turns to him with his whole heart.

28. d) Examination of conscience
After the homily, the examination of conscience takes place;
a sample text is given in Appendix III. A period of
silence should always be included so that each person may
personally examine his conscience.

29. e) Act of repentance
After the examination of conscience, the presiding minister
invites all to prayer in these or similar words:

God gives us an example of love: when we were
sinners he first loved us and took pity on us. Let us
turn to him with a sincere heart, and in the words of
Peter say to him:
R⁊. **Lord, you know all things; you know that I love**
you.

A short period of silence should follow each invocation.

Each invocation may be said by different individuals, the rest answering.

—Lord, like Peter we have relied on our own strength rather than on grace. Look on us, Lord, and have mercy.
℟. Lord, you know all things; you know that I love you.

—Our pride and foolishness have led us into temptation. Look on us, Lord, and have mercy.
℟. Lord, you know all things; you know that I love you.

—We have been vain and self-important. Look on us, Lord, and have mercy.
℟. Lord, you know all things; you know that I love you.

—We have at times been pleased rather than saddened by the misfortunes of others. Look on us, Lord, and have mercy.
℟. Lord, you know all things; you know that I love you.

—We have shown indifference for those in need instead of helping them. Look on us, Lord, and have mercy.
℟. Lord, you know all things; you know that I love you.

—We have been afraid to stand up for justice and truth. Look on us, Lord, and have mercy.
℟. Lord, you know all things; you know that I love you.

—We have repeatedly broken the promises of our baptism and failed to be your disciples. Look on us, Lord, and have mercy.
℟. Lord, you know all things; you know that I love you.

—Let us now pray to the Father in the words Christ gave us and ask forgiveness for our sins:
Our Father . . .

30. f) After an appropriate song, the presiding minister says the final prayer and dismisses the people:

Lord Jesus, our Savior,
you called Peter to be an apostle;
when he repented of his sin
you restored him to your friendship
and confirmed him as first of the apostles.
Turn to us with love
and help us to imitate Peter's example.
Give us strength to turn from our sins
and to serve you in the future
with greater love and devotion,
for you live and reign for ever and ever.
℟. **Amen.**

II. THE SON RETURNS TO THE FATHER

31. a) After an appropriate song and the greeting by the minister, the theme of the celebration is explained to the community. Then he invites all to pray. After a period of silence, he says:

Almighty God,
you are the Father of us all.
You created the human family
to dwell for ever with you
and to praise your glory.
Open our ears to hear your voice
so that we may return to you
with sincere repentance for our sins.
Teach us to see in you our loving Father,
full of compassion for all who call to you for help.
We know that you punish us only to set us free from evil
and that you are ready to forgive us our sins.

Restore your gift of salvation
which alone brings true happiness,
so that we may all return to our Father's house
and share your table
now and for ever.
℟. **Amen.**

32. b) Readings

First Reading
Ephesians 1:3-7
He chose us from all eternity to be his adopted sons and
daughters.

Responsorial Psalm
Psalm 27:1, 4, 7-10, 13-14
℟. **The Lord is my light and my help.**

Gospel
Luke 15:11-32
His father saw him and was filled with pity.

33. c) Homily
The minister may speak about:
—sin as a turning away from the love that we should have
for God our Father;
—the limitless mercy of our Father for his children who
have sinned;
—the nature of true conversion;
—the forgiveness we should extend to our brothers;
—the eucharistic banquet as the culmination of our reconciliation with the Church and with God.

34. d) Examination of conscience
After the homily, the examination of conscience takes place;
a sample text is given in Appendix III. A period of
silence should always be included so that each person may
personally examine his conscience.

35. e) Act of repentance
After the examination of conscience, the presiding minister
invites all to pray:

Our God is a God of mercy, slow to anger and full of patience. He is the father who welcomes his son when he returns from a distant country. Let us pray to him with trust in his goodness:
R̷. We are not worthy to be called your children.

—By our misuse of your gifts we have sinned against you.
R̷. We are not worthy to be called your children.

—By straying from you in mind and heart we have sinned against you.
R̷. We are not worthy to be called your children.

—By forgetting your love we have sinned against you.
R̷. We are not worthy to be called your children.

—By indulging ourselves, while neglecting our true good and the good of our neighbor, we have sinned against you.
R̷. We are not worthy to be called your children.

—By failing to help our neighbor in his need we have sinned against you.
R̷. We are not worthy to be called your children.

—By being slow to forgive we have sinned against you.
R̷. We are not worthy to be called your children.

—By failing to remember your repeated forgiveness we have sinned against you.
R̷. We are not worthy to be called your children.

Members of the congregation may add other invocations. A brief period of silence should follow each invocation. It may be desirable to have different individuals say each invocation.

—Let us now call upon our Father in the words that Jesus gave us, and ask him to forgive us our sins:
Our Father . . .

36. f) After an appropriate song, the presiding minister says the final prayer and dismisses the people:

God our Father,
you chose us to be your children,
to be holy in your sight
and happy in your presence.
Receive us as a loving Father
so that we may share the joy and love
of your holy Church.

We ask this through Christ our Lord.
℟. **Amen.**

III. THE BEATITUDES

37. a) After an appropriate song and greeting of the minister, the person presiding explains briefly the meaning of the readings. Then he invites all to pray. After a period of silence, he says:

Lord,
open our ears and our hearts today
to the message of your Son,
so that through the power of his death and
resurrection
we may walk in newness of life.

We ask this through Christ our Lord.
℟. **Amen.**

38. b) Readings

First Reading
1 John 1:5-9
If we say that we have no sin, we are deceiving ourselves.

Responsorial Psalm (See Isaiah 35:4)
Psalm 146:5-10
℟. **Lord, come and save us.**

Gospel
Matthew 5:1-10
Happy are the poor in spirit, for theirs is the kingdom of heaven.

39. c) Homily
The minister may speak about:
—sin, by which we ignore the commandments of Christ and
act contrary to the teaching of the beatitudes;
—the firmness of our faith in the words of Jesus;
—our faithfulness in imitating Christ in our private lives, in
the Christian community, and in human society;
—each beatitude.

40. d) Examination of conscience
After the homily, the examination of conscience takes place;
a sample text is given in Appendix III. A period of
silence should always be included so that each person may
personally examine his conscience.

41. e) Act of repentance
After the examination of conscience, the presiding minister
invites all to pray in these or similar words:

**My brothers and sisters, Jesus Christ has left an
example for us to follow. Humbly and confidently let
us ask him to renew us in spirit so that we may shape
our lives according to the teaching of his Gospel.**

**—Lord Jesus Christ, you said:
"Blessed are the poor in spirit,
for theirs is the kingdom of heaven."
Yet we are preoccupied with money and worldly
goods
and even try to increase them at the expense of
justice.
Lamb of God, you take away the sin of the world:
R̶. Have mercy on us.**

**—Lord Jesus Christ, you said:
"Blessed are the gentle,
for they shall inherit the earth."
Yet we are ruthless with each other,
and our world is full of discord and violence.
Lamb of God, you take away the sin of the world:
R̶. Have mercy on us.**

—Lord Jesus Christ, you said:
"Blessed are those who mourn,
for they shall be comforted."
Yet we are impatient under our own burdens
and unconcerned about the burdens of others.
Lamb of God, you take away the sin of the world:
℟. Have mercy on us.

—Lord Jesus Christ, you said:
"Blessed are those who hunger and thirst for justice,
for they shall be filled."
Yet we do not thirst for you, the fountain of all
    holiness,
and are slow to spread your influence
in our private lives or in society.
Lamb of God, you take away the sin of the world:
℟. Have mercy on us.

—Lord Jesus Christ, you said:
"Blessed are the merciful,
for they shall receive mercy."
Yet we are slow to forgive
and quick to condemn.
Lamb of God, you take away the sin of the world:
℟. Have mercy on us.

—Lord Jesus Christ, you said:
"Blessed are the clean of heart,
for they shall see God."
Yet we are prisoners of our senses and evil desires
and dare not raise our eyes to you.
Lamb of God, you take away the sin of the world:
℟. Have mercy on us.

—Lord Jesus Christ, you said:
"Blessed are the peacemakers,
for they shall be called children of God."
Yet we fail to make peace in our families,
in our country, and in the world.
Lamb of God, you take away the sin of the world:
℟. Have mercy on us.

—Lord Jesus Christ, you said:
"Blessed are those who are persecuted
for the sake of justice,
for the kingdom of heaven is theirs."
Yet we prefer to practice injustice
rather than suffer for the sake of right;
we discriminate against our neighbors
and oppress and persecute them.
Lamb of God, you take away the sin of the world:
℟. Have mercy on us.

—Now let us turn to God our Father and ask him to
free us from evil and prepare us for the coming of his
kingdom:
Our Father . . .

42. f) After an appropriate song, the presiding minister says
the final prayer and dismisses the people:

Lord Jesus Christ,
gentle and humble of heart,
full of compassion and maker of peace,
you lived in poverty
and were persecuted in the cause of justice.
You chose the cross as the path to glory
to show us the way to salvation.
May we receive with joyful hearts
the word of your Gospel
and live by your example
as heirs and citizens of your kingdom,
where you live and reign for ever and ever.
℟. Amen.

IV. FOR CHILDREN

43. This service is suitable for younger children, including
those who have not yet participated in the sacrament of
penance.

Theme:

GOD COMES TO LOOK FOR US

44. The penitential celebration should be prepared with the children so that they will understand its meaning and purpose, be familiar with the songs, have at least an elementary knowledge of the biblical text to be read, and know what they are to say and in what order.

45. a) Greeting
When the children have come together in the church or some other suitable place, the celebrant greets them in a friendly manner. Briefly he reminds them why they have come together and recounts the theme of the service. After the greeting, an opening song may be sung.

46. b) Reading
The celebrant may give a short introduction to the reading in these or similar words:

My dear children, each one of us has been baptized, and so we are all sons and daughters of God. God loves us as a Father, and he asks us to love him with all our hearts. He also wants us to be good to each other, so that we may all live happily together.

But people do not always do what God wants. They say: "I will not obey! I am going to do as I please." They disobey God and do not want to listen to him. We, too, often act like that.

That is what we call sin. When we sin we turn our backs on God. If we do something really bad we cut ourselves off from God; we are complete strangers to him.

What does God do when someone turns away from him? What does he do when we leave the path of goodness that he has shown us, when we run the risk of losing the life of grace he has given us? Does God turn away from us when we turn away from him by our sins?

Here is what God does, in the words of Jesus himself:

47. Only one text of Scripture should be read.

Luke 15:1-7
Heaven is filled with joy when one sinner turns back to
God.

48. c)   Homily
The homily should be short, proclaiming God's love for us
and preparing the ground for the examination of conscience.

49. d)   Examination of conscience
The celebrant should adapt the examination to the children's
level of understanding by brief comments. There should be
a suitable period of silence (see Appendix III).

50. e)   Act of repentance
This litany may be said by the celebrant or by one or more of
the children, alternating with all present. Before the response, which may be sung, all should observe a brief
pause.

God our Father,

**——Sometimes we have not behaved as your children
should.**
R7. **But you love us and come to us.**

**——We have given trouble to our parents and
teachers.**
R7. **But you love us and come to us.**

——We have quarrelled and called each other names.
R7. **But you love us and come to us.**

**——We have been lazy at home and in school, and
have not been helpful to our parents (brothers, sisters,
friends).**
R7. **But you love us and come to us.**

**——We have thought too much of ourselves and have
told lies.**
R7. **But you love us and come to us.**

——We have not done good to others when we had the chance.
℟. **But you love us and come to us.**

Now with Jesus, our brother, we come before our Father in heaven and ask him to forgive our sins: Our Father . . .

51. f) Act of contrition and purpose of amendment
Sorrow may be shown by some sign, for example, individual children may come to the altar or another suitable place with a candle, and light it there; if necessary, a server may help. Each child says in his own words:

Father,
I am sorry for all my sins:
for what I have done
and for what I have failed to do.
I will sincerely try to do better
especially . . .
(he mentions his particular resolution).
Help me to walk by your light.

In place of the candle, or in addition to it, the children may prepare a written prayer or resolution and place it on the altar or on a table designated for this purpose.

If the number of children or other circumstances do not allow for this, the celebrant asks the children present to say the above prayer together, along with a general resolution.

52. g) Prayer of the celebrant

God our Father always seeks us out
when we walk away from the path of goodness.
He is always ready to forgive
when we have sinned.
May almighty God have mercy on us,
forgive us our sins,
and bring us to everlasting life.
℟. **Amen.**

53. The minister invites the children to express their thanks to God. They may do this by an appropriate hymn.

Then he dismisses them.

V. FOR YOUNG PEOPLE

54. The penitential celebration should be prepared with the young people so that with the celebrant, they may choose or compose the texts and songs. The readers, cantors or choir should be chosen from among them.

Theme:

RENEWAL OF OUR LIVES ACCORDING TO THE CHRISTIAN VOCATION

55. a)   Greeting
This may be given in these or similar words:

Dear friends, we have come here to do penance and to make a fresh start as Christians. Many people see in penance only its difficult side, and its emphasis on sorrow. But it has also a more joyful side, and it looks more to the future than to the past.

Through penance God calls us to a new beginning. He helps us to find our true freedom as his sons and daughters. When Jesus invites us to repentance, he is inviting us to take our place in his Father's kingdom. This is what he teaches us in the parable about the merchant who came across a pearl of great value and sold everything he had in order to buy it.

If we follow our Lord's advice we exchange our past life for one far more valuable.

Then a song is sung; it should stress the call to a new life or following God's call with an eager heart (for example, Psalm 40:1-9).
℞. **Here am I, Lord; I come to do your will.**

56. b)   Prayer

**Lord our God,
you call us out of darkness into light,**

out of self-deception into truth,
out of death into life.
Send us your Holy Spirit
to open our ears to your call.
Fill our hearts with courage
to be true followers of your Son.
We ask this through Christ our Lord.
R℣. **Amen.**

57. c) Readings

First Reading
Romans 7:18-25
Unhappy man am I! Who will free me? Thanks to God
through Jesus Christ our Lord.

or:
Romans 8:19-23
We know that by turning everything to their good, God
cooperates with all those who love him.

A song is sung, or a brief period of silence is observed.

Gospel
Matthew 13:44-46
He sold all that he had and bought the field.

58. d) Homily
The celebrant may speak about:
——the law of sin which in us struggles against God;
——the necessity of giving up the way of sin so that we may
enter the kingdom of God.

59. e) Examination of conscience
After the homily, the examination of conscience takes place;
a sample text is given in Appendix III. A period of
silence should always be included so that each person may
personally examine his conscience.

60. f) Act of repentance
Christ our Lord came to call sinners into his Father's
kingdom. Let us now make an act of sorrow in our
hearts and resolve to avoid sin in the future.

After a brief period of silence, all say together:
I confess to almighty God,
and to you, my brothers and sisters,
that I have sinned through my own fault
They strike their breast:
in my thoughts and in my words,
in what I have done,
and in what I have failed to do;
and I ask blessed Mary, ever virgin,
all the angels and saints,
and you, my brothers and sisters,
to pray for me to the Lord our God.

Minister:
Lord our God,
you know all things.
You know that we want to be more generous
in serving you and our neighbor.
Look on us with love and hear our prayer.

Reader:
Give us the strength to turn away from sin.
R̘. Hear our prayer.

Help us to be sorry for our sins and to keep our
resolutions.
R̘. Hear our prayer.

Forgive our sins and have pity on our weakness.
R̘. Hear our prayer.

Give us trust in your goodness and make us generous
in serving you.
R̘. Hear our prayer.

Help us to be true followers of your Son and living
members of his Church.

Minister:
God does not want the sinner to die, but to turn to
him and live. May he be pleased that we have
confessed our sinfulness, and may he show us his
mercy as we pray in obedience to his Son.

All say together:
Our Father . . .

61. The celebration ends with an appropriate song and the dismissal.

VI. FOR THE SICK

62. According to the condition of the sick people and the suitability of the place, the minister goes to the sick, gathered in one room, or else he brings them together in the sanctuary or church. He should adapt carefully the texts and their number to the condition of those who take part in the service. Since in most instances none of the sick will be able to act as reader, the minister should, if possible, invite another person to carry out this office.

Theme:

THE TIME OF SICKNESS IS A TIME OF GRACE

63. a) Greeting
He may greet them in these or similar words:

My dear friends, when Jesus came to preach repentance, he was bringing us good news, for he was proclaiming to us God's love and mercy. Again and again God comes to our help so that we may turn to him and live our lives entirely in his service. Penance is his gift, a gift we should accept with gratitude. Keeping this in mind, let us open our hearts to God with great simplicity and humility and ask to be reconciled with him as we now forgive each other.

If possible, a penitential song is sung by the sick persons, or by a choir.

64. b) Prayer
**Lord our God,
source of all goodness and mercy,
we come together as your family
to ask your forgiveness**

and the forgiveness of each other.
Give us true sorrow for our sins
and loving trust in your compassion
so that we may acknowledge our sins
with sincere hearts.
Through this celebration
restore us to fuller union with yourself
and with our neighbor
so that we may serve you with greater generosity.

We ask this through Christ our Lord.
R̷. Amen.

65. c) Readings
The readings may be introduced in these or similar words:

Many people enjoy good health and other blessings
and accept them as a matter of course, with no sense
of gratitude. In time of sickness we discover that all
these are great gifts, and that without them we easily
lose heart. God allows us to experience sickness in
order to test our faith. What is more, if we see our
suffering as a share in Christ's suffering, it can be of
great value both to ourselves and to the Church. The
time of sickness is not then wasted or meaningless. It
is in fact a time of grace if we accept it as God wants
us to accept it. This celebration is meant to help us to
do so. We shall therefore listen to God's word,
examine our conscience, and pray with sincere hearts.

66. First Reading
James 5:13-16
The prayer of faith will save the sick man.

Responsorial Psalm
Between the readings, a psalm may be said or sung
alternately, for example, Psalm 130 or Psalm 51.

Gospel
Mark 2:1-12
The Son of Man has authority on earth to forgive sins.

67. d) Homily
It is fitting that the celebrant speak of sickness, dwelling not
so much on sickness of the body as on sickness of the soul.
He should emphasize the power of Jesus and his Church to
forgive sins and the value of suffering offered for others.

68. e) Examination of conscience
After the homily, the examination of conscience takes place;
a sample text is given in Appendix III. A period of
silence should always be included so that each person may
personally examine his conscience.

The following questions may be added but adapted to the
condition of the sick:

**——Do I trust God's goodness and providence, even
in times of stress and illness?**
**——Do I give in to sickness, to despair, to other
unworthy thoughts and feelings?**
**——Do I fill my empty moments with reflection on
life and with prayer to God?**
**——Do I accept my illness and pain as an opportunity
for suffering with Christ, who redeemed us by his
passion?**
**——Do I live by faith, confident that patience in
suffering is of great benefit to the Church?**
**——Am I thoughtful of others and attentive to my
fellow patients and their needs?**
**——Am I grateful to those who look after me and visit
me?**
——Do I give a good Christian example to others?
**——Am I sorry for my past sins, and do I try to make
amends for them by my patient acceptance of
weakness and illness.**

69. f) Act of repentance
After a moment of silence, all say together:

**I confess to almighty God,
and to you, my brothers and sisters,
that I have sinned through my own fault**

They strike their breast:
**in my thoughts and in my words,
in what I have done,
and in what I have failed to do;
and I ask blessed Mary, ever virgin,
all the angels and saints,
and you, my brothers and sisters,
to pray for me to the Lord our God.**

Reader:
**Lord our God, we bear the name of your Son and call
you Father. We are sorry for our sins against you and
against our brothers and sisters.
R̸. Give us true repentance and sincere love for you
and for our neighbor.**

**Lord Jesus Christ, you redeemed us by your passion
and cross and gave us an example of patience and
love. We are sorry for our sins against you, and
especially for failing to serve you and our brothers
and sisters.
R̸. Give us true repentance and sincere love for you
and for our neighbor.**

**Holy Spirit, Lord, you speak to us in the Church and
in our conscience and inspire within us the desire to
do good. We are sorry for our sins against you, and
especially for our obstinate refusal to obey you.
R̸. Give us true repentance and sincere love for you
and for our neighbor.**

Minister:
**Let us ask God our Father to forgive us and to free us
from evil:
Our Father . . .**

70. Then, if possible, the choir or the assembled people sing
a song, and the service concludes with a prayer of
thanksgiving:

71.
God of consolation and Father of mercies,

you forgive the sinner who acknowledges his guilt:
R̷. **We praise you and thank you.**

God of consolation and Father of mercies,
you give to those who suffer hardship or pain
a share in the sufferings of your Son
for the salvation of the world:
R̷. **We praise you and thank you.**

God of consolation and Father of mercies,
you look with love on those who are troubled or in
      sorrow;
you give them hope of salvation
and the promise of eternal life:
R̷. **We praise you and thank you.**

Let us pray.
Lord,
your goodness and mercy are boundless.
Look on your sons and daughters
gathered here in the name of your Son.
We thank you for all your gifts
and ask you to keep us always as your family,
full of living faith, firm hope,
and sincere love for you and for our neighbor.
We ask this through Christ our Lord.
R̷. **Amen.**

72. In place of the prayer, the service may end with a blessing.

May the God of peace
fill your hearts with every blessing.
May he sustain you
with his gifts of hope and consolation,
help you to offer your lives in his service,
and bring you safely to eternal glory.
May almighty God,
the Father, and the Son, ✠ and the Holy Spirit,
grant you all that is good.
R̷. **Amen.**

73. The minister dismisses the assembly, or invites those present to a friendly visit with the sick.

APPENDIX III

FORM OF EXAMINATION OF CONSCIENCE

1. This suggested form for an examination of conscience should be completed and adapted to meet the needs of different individuals and to follow local usages.

2. In an examination of conscience, before the sacrament of penance, each individual should ask himself these questions in particular:

1. **What is my attitude to the sacrament of penance? Do I sincerely want to be set free from sin, to turn again to God, to begin a new life, and to enter into a deeper friendship with God? Or do I look on it as a burden, to be undertaken as seldom as possible?**

2. **Did I forget to mention, or deliberately conceal, any grave sins in past confessions?**

3. **Did I perform the penance I was given? Did I make reparation for any injury to others? Have I tried to put into practice my resolution to lead a better life in keeping with the Gospel?**

3. Each individual should examine his life in the light of God's word.

I. The Lord says: "You shall love the Lord your God with your whole heart."

1. **Is my heart set on God, so that I really love him above all things and am faithful to his commandments, as a son loves his father? Or am I more concerned about the things of this world? Have I a right intention in what I do?**

2. **God spoke to us in his Son. Is my faith in God firm and secure? Am I wholehearted in accepting the Church's teaching? Have I been careful to grow in my understanding of the faith, to hear God's word, to**

listen to instructions on the faith, to avoid dangers to faith? Have I been always strong and fearless in professing my faith in God and the Church? Have I been willing to be known as a Christian in private and public life?

3. Have I prayed morning and evening? When I pray, do I really raise my mind and heart to God or is it a matter of words only? Do I offer God my difficulties, my joys, and my sorrows? Do I turn to God in time of temptation?

4. Have I love and reverence for God's name? Have I offended him in blasphemy, swearing falsely, or taking his name in vain? Have I shown disrespect for the Blessed Virgin Mary and the saints?

5. Do I keep Sundays and feast days holy by taking a full part, with attention and devotion, in the liturgy, and especially in the Mass? Have I fulfilled the precept of annual confession and of communion during the Easter season?

6. Are there false gods that I worship by giving them greater attention and deeper trust than I give to God: money, superstition, spiritism, or other occult practices?

II. The Lord says: "Love one another as I have loved you."

1. Have I a genuine love for my neighbors? Or do I use them for my own ends, or do to them what I would not want done to myself? Have I given grave scandal by my words or actions?

2. In my family life, have I contributed to the well-being and happiness of the rest of the family by patience and genuine love? Have I been obedient to parents, showing them proper respect and giving them help in their spiritual and material needs? Have I been careful to give a Christian upbringing to my children, and to help them by good example and by

exercising authority as a parent? Have I been faithful to my husband (wife) in my heart and in my relations with others?

3. Do I share my possessions with the less fortunate? Do I do my best to help the victims of oppression, misfortune, and poverty? Or do I look down on my neighbor, especially the poor, the sick, the elderly, strangers, and people of other races?

4. Does my life reflect the mission I received in confirmation? Do I share in the apostolic and charitable works of the Church and in the life of my parish? Have I helped to meet the needs of the Church and of the world and prayed for them: for unity in the Church, for the spread of the Gospel among the nations, for peace and justice, etc.?

5. Am I concerned for the good and prosperity of the human community in which I live, or do I spend my life caring only for myself? Do I share to the best of my ability in the work of promoting justice, morality, harmony, and love in human relations? Have I done my duty as a citizen? Have I paid my taxes?

6. In my work or profession am I just, hard-working, honest, serving society out of love for others? Have I paid a fair wage to my employees? Have I been faithful to my promises and contracts?

7. Have I obeyed legitimate authority and given it due respect?

8. If I am in a position of responsibility or authority, do I use this for my own advantage or for the good of others, in a spirit of service?

9. Have I been truthful and fair, or have I injured others by deceit, calumny, detraction, rash judgment, or violation of a secret?

10. Have I done violence to others by damage to life or limb, reputation, honor, or material possessions? Have I involved them in loss? Have I been responsi-

ble for advising an abortion or procuring one? Have I kept up hatred for others? Am I estranged from others through quarrels, enmity, insults, anger? Have I been guilty of refusing to testify to the innocence of another because of selfishness?

11. Have I stolen the property of others? Have I desired it unjustly and inordinately? Have I damaged it? Have I made restitution of other people's property and made good their loss?

12. If I have been injured, have I been ready to make peace for the love of Christ and to forgive, or do I harbor hatred and the desire for revenge?

III. Christ our Lord says: "Be perfect as your Father is perfect."

1. Where is my life really leading me? Is the hope of eternal life my inspiration? Have I tried to grow in the life of the Spirit through prayer, reading the word of God and meditating on it, receiving the sacraments, self-denial? Have I been anxious to control my vices, my bad inclinations and passions, e.g., envy, love of food and drink? Have I been proud and boastful, thinking myself better in the sight of God and despising others as less important than myself? Have I imposed my own will on others, without respecting their freedom and rights?

2. What use have I made of time, of health and strength, of the gifts God has given me to be used like the talents in the Gospel? Do I use them to become more perfect every day? Or have I been lazy and too much given to leisure?

3. Have I been patient in accepting the sorrows and disappointments of life? How have I performed mortification so as to "fill up what is wanting to the sufferings of Christ"? Have I kept the precept of fasting and abstinence?

4. Have I kept my senses and my whole body pure and chaste as a temple of the Holy Spirit consecrated for resurrection and glory, and as a sign of God's faithful love for men and women, a sign that is seen most perfectly in the sacrament of matrimony? Have I dishonored my body by fornication, impurity, un- worthy conversation or thoughts, evil desires, or ac- tions? Have I given in to sensuality? Have I indulged in reading, conversation, shows, and entertainments that offend against Christian and human decency? Have I encouraged others to sin by my own failure to maintain these standards? Have I been faithful to the moral law in my married life?

5. Have I gone against my conscience out of fear or hypocrisy?

6. Have I always tried to act in the true freedom of the sons of God according to the law of the Spirit, or am I the slave of forces within me?

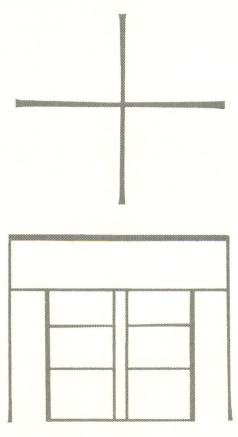

HOLY COMMUNION
AND WORSHIP OF THE EUCHARIST
OUTSIDE MASS

HOLY COMMUNION AND WORSHIP OF THE EUCHARIST OUTSIDE MASS

The Short Rite with the Celebration of the Word (42–53)

Introductory Rites (43)
Greeting (43)
Penitential Rite (43)

The Short Form of the Reading of the Word (44)

Holy Communion (45–50)
Lord's Prayer (45)
Invitation to Communion (46)
Communion (47–49)
Silence, Psalm, or Song of Praise (49)
Concluding Prayer (50)

Concluding Rite (51–53)
Blessing (51–52)
Dismissal (53)

CHAPTER II
ADMINISTRATION OF COMMUNION AND
VIATICUM TO THE SICK BY AN
EXTRAORDINARY MINISTER (54–78)

The Ordinary Rite of Communion of the Sick (56–63)

Introductory Rite (56–57)
Greeting (56)
Penitential Rite (57)

The Short Form of the Reading of the Word (58)

Holy Communion (59–62)
Lord's Prayer (59)
Invitation to Communion (60)
Communion (61)
Concluding Prayer (62)

Concluding Rite (63)
Blessing (63)

Short Rite of Communion of the Sick (64–67)
Antiphon (65)
Invitation to Communion (66)
Distribution of Communion (66)
Concluding Prayer (67)

Viaticum (68–78)

Introductory Rite (68–70)
Greeting (68)

SACRED CONGREGATION FOR DIVINE WORSHIP

Prot. no. 900/73

DECREE

The sacrament of the eucharist was entrusted by Christ to his bride, the Church, as spiritual nourishment and as a pledge of eternal life. The Church continues to receive this gift with faith and love.

The celebration of the eucharist in the sacrifice of the Mass is the true origin and purpose of the worship shown to the eucharist outside Mass. The principal reason for reserving the sacrament after Mass is to unite, through sacramental communion, the faithful unable to participate in the Mass, especially the sick and the aged, with Christ and the offering of his sacrifice.

In turn, eucharistic reservation, which became customary in order to permit the reception of communion, led to the practice of adoring this sacrament and offering to it the worship which is due to God. This cult of adoration is based upon valid and solid principles. Moreover, some of the public and communal forms of this worship were instituted by the Church itself.

The rite of Mass has been revised and, in the instruction *Eucharisticum mysterium* of May 25, 1967, regulations have been published "on the practical arrangements for the cult of this sacrament even after Mass and its relationship to the proper ordering of the sacrifice of the Mass in the light of the regulations of the Second Vatican Council, and of other documents of the Apostolic See on this matter."[1] Now the Congregation for Divine Worship has revised the rites, "Holy Communion and the Worship of the Eucharist Outside Mass."

These rites, approved by Pope Paul VI, are now published in this edition, which is declared to be the *editio typica*. They are to replace the rites which appear in the Roman Ritual at

---

[1]See Congregation of Rites, instruction *Eucharisticum mysterium*, no. 3g: *AAS* 59 (1967) 543.

the present time. They may be used at once in Latin; they may be used in the vernacular from the day set by the episcopal conferences for their territory, after the conferences have prepared a vernacular version and have obtained the confirmation of the Holy See.

Anything to the contrary notwithstanding.

From the office of the Congregation for Divine Worship, June 21, 1973, the feast of Corpus Christi.

Arturo Cardinal Tabera
Prefect

✝ Annibale Bugnini
Titular Archbishop of Diocletiana
Secretary

HOLY COMMUNION AND WORSHIP OF THE EUCHARIST OUTSIDE MASS

GENERAL INTRODUCTION

I. RELATIONSHIP BETWEEN EUCHARISTIC WORSHIP OUTSIDE MASS AND THE EUCHARISTIC CELEBRATION

1. The celebration of the eucharist is the center of the entire Christian life, both for the universal Church and for the local congregations of the Church. "The other sacraments, like every other ministry of the Church and every work of the apostolate, are linked with the holy eucharist and have it as their end. For the eucharist contains the Church's entire spiritual wealth, that is, Christ himself. He is our Passover and living bread; through his flesh, made living and life-giving by the Holy Spirit, he is bringing life to people and in this way inviting and leading them to offer themselves together with him, as well as their labors and all created things."[1]

2. "The celebration of the eucharist in the sacrifice of the Mass," moreover, "is truly the origin and purpose of the worship that is shown to the eucharist outside Mass."[2] Christ the Lord "is offered in the sacrifice of the Mass when he begins to be sacramentally present as the spiritual food of the faithful under the appearances of bread and wine"; "after the sacrifice has been offered . . . as long as the eucharist is reserved in churches and oratories, Christ is truly the Emmanuel, that is, 'God with us.' Day and night he is in our midst; full of grace and truth, he dwells among us."[3]

3. No one therefore may doubt "that all the faithful show this holy sacrament the veneration and adoration that is due to God himself, as has always been the practice recognized in the Catholic Church. Nor is the sacrament to be less the object of adoration on the grounds that it was instituted by Christ the lord to be received as food."[4]

[1]*PO* no. 5 [*DOL* 18, no. 260].
[2]*SCR*, Instr. EuchMyst no. 3 e [*DOL* 179, no. 1232].
[3]*Ibid.*, no. 3 b and Paul VI, Encycl. *Mysterium fidei*, no. 67 [DOL 176, no. 1211].
[4]*SCR*, Instr. EuchMyst no. 3 f [*DOL* 179, no. 1232].

4. In order to give right direction and encouragement to devotion to the sacrament of the eucharist, the eucharistic mystery must be considered in all its fullness, both in the celebration of Mass and in the worship of the sacrament reserved after Mass in order to extend the grace of the sacrifice.[5]

II. PURPOSE OF EUCHARISTIC RESERVATION

5. The primary and original reason for reservation of the eucharist outside Mass is the administration of viaticum. The secondary ends are the giving of communion and the adoration of our Lord Jesus Christ present in the sacrament. The reservation of the sacrament for the sick led to the praiseworthy practice of adoring this heavenly food that is reserved in churches. This cult of adoration has a sound and firm foundation, especially since faith in the real presence of the Lord has as its natural consequence the outward, public manifestation of that belief.[6]

6. In the celebration of Mass the chief ways in which Christ is present in his Church emerge clearly one after the other. First, he is present in the very assembly of the faithful, gathered together in his name; next, he is present in his word, with the reading and explanation of Scripture in the church; also in the person of the minister; finally, and above all, in the eucharistic elements. In a way that is completely unique, the whole and entire Christ, God and man, is substantially and permanently present in the sacrament. This presence of Christ under the appearance of bread and wine "is called real, not to exclude the other kinds of presence as though they were not real, but because it is real par excellence."[7]

Consequently, on the grounds of the sign value, it is more in keeping with the nature of the celebration that, through reservation of the sacrament in the tabernacle, Christ not be present eucharistically from the beginning on the altar where Mass is celebrated. That presence is the effect of the consecration and should appear as such.[8]

---

[5]See *ibid.*, no. 3 g [*DOL* 179, no. 1232].
[6]See *ibid.*, no. 49 [*DOL* 179, no. 1278].
[7]Paul VI, Encycl. *Mysterium fidei*, no. 39 [*DOL* 176, no. 1183].
[8]See *SCR*, Instr. EuchMyst 55 [*DOL* 179, no. 1284].

7. The consecrated hosts are to be frequently renewed and reserved in a ciborium or other vessel in a number sufficient for the communion of the sick and of others outside Mass.[9]

8. Pastors should see that, unless a serious reason stands in the way, churches where, in conformity with the law, the holy eucharist is reserved, are open every day for at least several hours at a convenient time, so that the faithful may easily pray in the presence of the blessed sacrament.[10]

III. PLACE OF EUCHARISTIC RESERVATION

9. The place for the reservation of the eucharist should be truly preeminent. It is highly recommended that the place be suitable also for private adoration and prayer so that the faithful may readily and fruitfully continue to honor the Lord, present in the sacrament, through personal worship.

This will be achieved more readily if the chapel is separate from the body of the church, especially in churches where marriages and funerals are celebrated frequently and in churches where there are many visitors because of pilgrimages or the artistic and historical treasures.

10. The holy eucharist is to be reserved in an immovable and solid tabernacle. It must be opaque and locked in such a way as to provide every possible security against the danger of desecration. Ordinarily there should be only one tabernacle in a church or in an oratory. This tabernacle is to be placed in some noble and prominent part of the church that is properly ornamented and suited to prayer.

The one in charge of the church or oratory is to see to it that the key to the tabernacle where the eucharist is reserved is safeguarded most carefully.[11]

---

[9]See *GIRM* nos, 285, 292 [*DOL* 208, nos. 1675, 1682].
[10]See SCR, Instr. EuchMyst no. 51 [*DOL* 179, no. 1280].
[R1]See *DOL* 179, no. 1281, note R4.
[11]See Congregation of Rites, Instruction *Eucharisticum mysterium*, nos. 52–53: *AAS* 59 (1967) 567–568. *CIC*, can. 938.
[R2]On this point Not 9 (1973) 333 comments on the relationship between the reformed ritual and the canonical rules now in force: The norms contained in the reformed Roman Ritual and approved by Pope Paul VI amend, as required, the prescriptions of the *Codex Iuris Canonici* and other laws hith-

11. The presence of the eucharist in the tabernacle is to be shown by a veil or another suitable way determined by the competent authority.

As an indication of Christ's presence and as a mark of reverence, a special lamp should burn continuously before a tabernacle in which the eucharist is reserved.

According to traditional usage, the lamp should, if at all possible, be an oil lamp or a lamp with a wax candle.[12]

IV. COMPETENCE OF THE CONFERENCE OF BISHOPS

12. It is for the conference of bishops, in the preparation of particular rituals in accord with the Constitution on the Liturgy (art. 63, b),[c] to accommodate this title of the Roman Ritual to the needs of individual regions so that, once the *acta* of the conferences have been approved by the Apostolic See, the ritual may be followed in the respective regions.

In this matter it will be up to the conferences:

a) to consider carefully what elements, if any, from the traditions of individual peoples may be retained or introduced, provided they are compatible with the spirit of the liturgy; the conferences are then to propose to the Apostolic See adaptations considered useful or necessary that will be introduced with its consent;

b) to prepare translations of texts that are truly accommodated to the character of various languages and the mentality of various cultures; they may add texts, especially for singing with appropriate melodies.[†]

---

erto in force or repeal them; other laws that are neither repealed nor amended in the new Ritual remain valid and firm. Accordingly, in regard to the custody of the eucharist [see Introduction no. 10] the May 26, 1938 Instruction of the Congregation of the Sacraments, *Nullo unquam* (*AAS* 30 [1938] 198), continues to apply.

[12]See Congregation of Rites, Instruction *Eucharisticum mysterium*, no. 57: *AAS* 59 (1967) 569. CIC, can. 940.

[c]See *DOL* 1, no. 63.

[†]The Latin text has the following footnote here: The text of the psalms and New Testament books are quoted from the edition by the Pontifical Commission for the Neo-Vulgate [see *DOL* 237]. Liturgical texts that are used in respect of a man, may be used with a change of gender for a woman also. And in either case the singular may be changed into the plural.

CHAPTER I
HOLY COMMUNION OUTSIDE MASS

INTRODUCTION

I. THE RELATIONSHIP BETWEEN COMMUNION OUTSIDE MASS AND THE SACRIFICE

13. Sacramental communion received during Mass is a more complete participation in the eucharistic celebration. This truth stands out more clearly, by force of the sign value, when after the priest's communion the faithful receive the Lord's body and blood from the same sacrifice.[1] Therefore, recently baked bread should ordinarily be consecrated in every eucharistic celebration for the communion of the faithful.

14. The faithful are to be led to the practice of receiving communion during the actual eucharist celebration.

Priests, however, are not to refuse to give communion to the faithful who for a legitimate reason ask for it even outside Mass.[2]

In fact it is proper that those who are prevented from being present at the community's celebration should be refreshed with the eucharist. In this way they may realize that they are united not only with the Lord's sacrifice but also with the community itself and are supported by the love of their brothers and sisters.

Pastors should take care that the sick and the elderly be given the opportunity even if they are not gravely ill or in imminent danger of death, to receive the eucharist often, even daily, especially during the Easter season. It is lawful to minister communion under the form of wine to those who cannot receive the consecrated bread.[3]

15. The faithful should be instructed carefully that, even when they receive communion outside Mass, they are

[1] See SC art. 55 [DOL 1, no. 55].
[2] See SCR, Instr. EuchMyst no. 33 a [DOL 179, no. 1262].
[3] See ibid., nos. 40–41 [DOL 179, no. 1269–1270].

closely united with the sacrifice that perpetuates the sacrifice of the cross. They are sharers in the sacred banquet in which "through the communion of the body and blood of the Lord, the people of God share the benefits of the paschal sacrifice, renew the new covenant with us made once and for all by God in Christ's blood, and in faith and hope foreshadow and anticipate the eschatological banquet in the Father's kingdom, as they proclaim the death of the Lord, until he comes."[4]

II. THE TIME OF COMMUNION OUTSIDE MASS

16. Communion may be given outside Mass on any day and at any hour. It is proper, however, to schedule the hours for giving communion, with a view to the convenience of the faithful, so that the celebration may take place in a fuller form and with greater spiritual benefit. Nevertheless:

a) On Holy Thursday communion may be given only during Mass; communion may be brought to the sick at any hour of the day.

b) On Good Friday communion may be given only during the celebration of the passion of the Lord; communion may be brought at any hour of the day to the sick who cannot participate in the celebration.

c) On Holy Saturday communion may be given only as viaticum.[5]

III. THE MINISTER OF COMMUNION

17. It belongs first of all to the priest and the deacon to minister holy communion to the faithful who ask to receive it.[6] It is most fitting, therefore, that they give a suitable part of their time to this ministry of their order, depending on the needs of the faithful.

---

[4] *Ibid.*, no. 3 a [*DOL* 179, no. 1232].
[5] See *MR, Missa vespertina in Cena Domini*, 243; *Celebratio Passionis Domini* 250, no. 3; *Sabbato Sancto* 265 [*RM*, Holy Thursday, *Evening Mass of the Lord's Supper;* Good Friday, *Celebration of the Lord's Passion* no. 3; Holy Saturday].
[6] See *SCR*, Instr. EuchMyst no. 31 [*DOL* 179, no. 1260].

It also belongs to an acolyte who has been properly instituted to give communion as a special minister when the priest and deacon are absent or impeded by sickness, old age, or pastoral ministry or when the number of the faithful at the holy table is so great that the Mass or other service may be unreasonably prolonged.[7]

The local Ordinary may give other special ministers the faculty to give communion whenever it seems necessary for the pastoral benefit of the faithful and no priest, deacon, or acolyte is available.[8]

IV. THE PLACE OF COMMUNION OUTSIDE MASS

18. The place where communion outside Mass is ordinarily given is a church or oratory in which the eucharist is regularly celebrated or reserved, or a church, oratory, or other place where the local community regularly gathers for the liturgical assembly on Sundays or other days. Communion may be given, however, in other places, including private homes, when it is a question of the sick, prisoners, or others who cannot leave the place without danger or serious difficulty.

V. REGULATIONS FOR GIVING COMMUNION

19. When communion is given in a church or oratory, a corporal is to be placed on the altar, which is already covered with a cloth, and there are to be two lighted candles as a sign of reverence and festiveness.[9] A communion plate is to be used.

When communion is given in other places, a suitable table is to be prepared and covered with a cloth; candles are also to be provided.

---

[7]See Paul VI, Motu Proprio *Ministeria quaedam*, Aug. 15, 1972, no. VI [*DOL* 340, no. 2931].
[8]See *SCDS*, Instr. *Immensae caritatis*, January 29, 1973, 1, nos. I and II [*DOL* 264, nos. 2075–2076].
[9]See *GIRM* no. 269 [*DOL* 208, no. 1659].

20. The minister of communion if he is a priest or deacon, is to be vested in an alb, or a surplice over a cassock, and a stole.

Other ministers should wear either the liturgical vesture that may be traditional in their region or attire that is in keeping with this ministry and has been approved by the Ordinary.

The eucharist for communion outside a church is to be carried in a pyx or other covered vessel; the vesture of the minister and the manner of carrying the eucharist should be appropriate and in accord with local circumstances.

21. In giving communion, the custom of placing the particle of consecrated bread on the tongue of the communicant is to be maintained because it is based on a tradition of several centuries.

Conferences of bishops, however, may decree, once their decision has been confirmed by the Apostolic See, that communion may also be given in their territories by placing the consecrated bread in the hand of the faithful, provided any danger is prevented of engendering in the attitudes of the faithful irreverence or false ideas about the eucharist.[10]

The faithful, furthermore, must be taught that Jesus Christ is Lord and Savior and that therefore the worship of *latria* or adoration belonging to God is owed to Christ present in this sacrament.[11]

In either case, communion must be given by the authorized minister, who shows the particle of consecrated bread to the communicants and gives it to them, saying: **The body of Christ,** to which the communicants reply: **Amen.**

In the case of communion under the appearance of wine, the liturgical regulations are to be followed exactly.[12]

22. Fragments remaining after communion are to be gathered and placed in a ciborium or in a vessel with water.

---

[10]See *SCDW*, Instr. *Memoriale Domini*, May 29, 1969, [*DOL* 260, no. 2060].
[11]See *SCDS*, Instr. *Immensae caritatis* no. 4 [*DOL* 264, no. 2088].
[12]See General Instruction of the Roman Missal, no. 242. Congregation for Divine Worship, Instruction *Sacramentali Communione*, June 29, 1970, no. 6: *AAS* 62 (1970) 665–666.

Likewise, if communion is given under the appearance of wine, the chalice or other vessel is to be washed with water.

The water used for cleansing the vessels may be drunk or poured out in a suitable place.

VI. DISPOSITIONS FOR COMMUNION

23. The eucharist, which continuously makes the paschal mystery of Christ to be present among us, is the source of every grace and of the forgiveness of sins. Nevertheless, those who intend to receive the body of the Lord must approach it with a pure conscience and proper dispositions of soul if they are to receive the effects of the paschal sacrament.

On this account the Church prescribes "that those conscious of mortal sin, even though they think themselves to be contrite, must not go to the holy eucharist without sacramental confession beforehand."[13] When there is a serious reason and no opportunity for confession, they are to make an act of perfect contrition with the intention of confessing individually, as soon as possible, the mortal sins that they cannot confess at present.

It is desirable that those who receive communion daily or very often go to the sacrament of penance at regular intervals, depending on their circumstances.

The faithful also should look upon the eucharist as a remedy that frees them from their daily faults and preserves them from mortal sins; they should also receive an explanation of how to make use of the penitential parts of the liturgy, especially at Mass.[14]

24. Communicants are not to receive the sacrament unless they have fasted for at least one hour from food and beverages, with the exception only of water and medicine.

---

[13]See Council of Trent, sess. 13, *Decr. de Eucharistia* 7: Denz-Schön 1646–1647; sess. 14, *Canones de sacramento Paenitentiae 9*: Denz-Schön 1709. *SCDF, Pastoral Norms on Giving General Sacramental Absolution,* June 16, 1972, Preface and Norm VI [*DOL* 361, nos. 3038 and 3044].
[14]See *SCR,* Instr. EuchMyst no. 35 [*DOL* 179, no. 1264].

The elderly and those suffering from any kind of infirmity, as well as those who take care of such persons, may receive the eucharist even if they have taken something within the hour before communion.[15]

25. The union with Christ, to which the sacrament is directed, should be extended to the whole of Christian life. Thus the faithful, constantly reflecting upon the gift they have received, should carry on their daily work with thanksgiving, under the guidance of the Holy Spirit, and should bring forth fruits of rich charity.

In order to continue more surely in the thanksgiving that in the Mass is offered to God in an eminent way, those who have been nourished by communion should be encouraged to remain for some time in prayer.[16]

[15]See CIC, can. 919, §§1 and 3.
[16]See SCR, Instr. EuchMyst no. 38 [DOL 179, no. 1267].

RITE OF DISTRIBUTING HOLY COMMUNION OUTSIDE MASS

1. THE LONG RITE WITH THE CELEBRATION OF THE WORD

26. This rite is to be used chiefly when Mass is not celebrated or when communion is not distributed at scheduled times. The purpose is that the people should be nourished by the word of God. By hearing it they learn that the marvels it proclaims reach their climax in the paschal mystery of which the Mass is a sacramental memorial and in which they share by communion. Nourished by God's word, they are led on to grateful and fruitful participation in the saving mysteries.

INTRODUCTORY RITES

27. After the people have assembled and preparations for the service (see nos. 19-20) are complete, all stand for the greeting of the minister.

GREETING

If he is a priest or deacon, he says:

The grace of our Lord Jesus Christ and the love of God and the fellowship of the Holy Spirit be with you all.
The people answer: **And also with you.**

Or:
The Lord be with you.
The people answer: **And also with you.**

If the minister is not a priest or deacon, he greets those present with these or similar words:

Brothers and sisters,
the Lord invites us (you) to his table
to share in the body of Christ:
bless him for his goodness.
The people answer: **Blessed be God for ever.**

Another form of greeting, no. 189, may be chosen.

Any other customary forms of greeting from scripture may be used.

PENITENTIAL RITE

28. The penitential rite follows, and the minister invites the people to recall their sins and to repent of them in these words:

**My brothers and sisters,
to prepare ourselves for this celebration,
let us call to mind our sins.**

A pause for silent reflection follows.

All say:
**I confess to almighty God,
and to you, my brothers and sisters,
that I have sinned through my own fault**
They strike their breast:
**in my thoughts and in my words,
in what I have done,
and in what I have failed to do;
and I ask blessed Mary, ever virgin,
all the angels and saints,
and you, my brothers and sisters,
to pray for me to the Lord our God.**

The minister concludes:
**May almighty God have mercy on us,
forgive us our sins,
and bring us to everlasting life.**
The people answer: **Amen.**

Other forms of the penitential rite, no. 190 or 191, may be chosen.

CELEBRATION OF THE WORD OF GOD

29. The Liturgy of the Word now takes place as at Mass. Texts are chosen for the occasion either from the Mass of the day or from the votive Masses of the Holy Eucharist or the Precious Blood, the readings from which are in the Lection-

ary. A list of these passages can be found in nos. 113-153 of this Ritual. The Lectionary offers a wide range of readings which may be drawn upon for particular needs, such as the votive Mass of the Sacred Heart. See nos. 154-158 below.

There may be one or more readings, the first being followed by a psalm or some other chant or by a period of silent prayer.

The celebration of the word ends with the general intercessions.

HOLY COMMUNION

LORD'S PRAYER

30. After the prayer the minister goes to the place where the sacrament is reserved, takes the ciborium or pyx containing the body of the Lord, places it on the altar and genuflects. He then introduces the Lord's Prayer in these or similar words:

Let us pray with confidence to the Father in the words our Savior gave us:

He continues with the people:

Our Father. . . .

SIGN OF PEACE

31. The minister may invite the people in these or similar words:

Let us offer each other the sign of peace.

All make an appropriate sign of peace, according to local custom.

INVITATION TO COMMUNION

32. The minister genuflects. Taking the host, he raises it slightly over the vessel or pyx and, facing the people, says:

**This is the Lamb of God
who takes away the sins of the world.
Happy are those who are called to his supper.**

The communicants say once:

**Lord, I am not worthy to receive you,
but only say the word and I shall be healed.**

COMMUNION

33. If the minister receives communion, he says quietly:

May the body of Christ bring me to everlasting life.

He reverently consumes the body of Christ.

34. Then he takes the vessel or pyx and goes to the communicants. He takes a host for each one, raises it slightly, and says:

The body of Christ.

The communicant answers: **Amen,**
and receives communion.

COMMUNION SONG

35. During the distribution of communion, a hymn may be sung.

36. After communion the minister puts any particle left on the plate into the pyx, and he may wash his hands. He returns any remaining hosts to the tabernacle and genuflects.

SILENCE, PSALM, OR SONG OF PRAISE

37. A period of silence may now be observed, or a psalm or song of praise may be sung.

CONCLUDING PRAYER

38. The minister then says the concluding prayer:
Let us pray.

**Lord Jesus Christ,
you gave us the eucharist
as the memorial of your suffering and death.
May our worship of this sacrament of your body and
   blood**

help us to experience the salvation you won for us
and the peace of the kingdom
where you live with the Father and the Holy Spirit,
one God, for ever and ever.
The people answer: **Amen.**
Other prayers, nos. 210-222, may be chosen.

CONCLUDING RITE

BLESSING

39. If the minister is a priest or deacon, he extends his
hands and, facing the people, says:

The Lord be with you.
The people answer: **And also with you.**

He blesses the people with these words:

**May almighty God bless you,
the Father, and the Son, ✛ and the Holy Spirit.**
The people answer: **Amen.**

Instead of this formula a solemn blessing or prayer over the
people may be used, as in the concluding rite of Mass in the
Roman Missal.

40. If the minister is not a priest or deacon, he invokes
God's blessing and, crossing himself, says:

**May the Lord bless us,
protect us from all evil
and bring us to everlasting life.**

or:
**May the almighty and merciful God bless and protect
     us,
the Father, and the Son, ✛ and the Holy Spirit.**
The people answer: **Amen.**

DISMISSAL

41. Finally the minister says:

Go in the peace of Christ.
The people answer: **Thanks be to God.**

Then after the customary reverence, the minister leaves.

2. THE SHORT RITE WITH THE CELEBRATION OF THE WORD

42. This form of service is used when the longer, more elaborate form is unsuitable, especially when there are only one or two for communion and a true community celebration is impossible.

INTRODUCTORY RITES

43. When everything is ready (see nos. 19-20), the minister greets the communicants.

GREETING

[27]

If he is a priest or deacon, he says:

The grace of our Lord Jesus Christ and the love of God and the fellowship of the Holy Spirit be with you all.
The people answer: **And also with you.**

Or:
The Lord be with you.
The people answer: **And also with you.**

If the minister is not a priest or deacon, he greets those present with these or similar words:

Brothers and sisters,
the Lord invites us (you) to his table
to share in the body of Christ:
bless him for his goodness.
The people answer: **Blessed be God for ever.**

Another form of greeting, no. 189, may be chosen:

The grace and peace of God our Father and the Lord Jesus Christ be with you.
The people answer: **Blessed be the God and Father of our Lord Jesus Christ.**
or:
And also with you.

Any other customary forms of greeting from scripture may be used.

PENITENTIAL RITE

The penitential rite follows, and the minister invites the people to recall their sins and to repent of them in these words [28]:

My brothers and sisters,
to prepare ourselves for this celebration,
let us call to mind our sins.

A pause for silent reflection follows.

All say:
I confess to almighty God,
and to you, my brothers and sisters,
that I have sinned through my own fault
They strike their breast:
in my thoughts and in my words,
in what I have done,
and in what I have failed to do;
and I ask blessed Mary, ever virgin,
all the angels and saints,
and you, my brothers and sisters,
to pray for me to the Lord our God.

The minister concludes:
May almighty God have mercy on us,
forgive us our sins,
and bring us to everlasting life.
The people answer: **Amen.**

Other forms of the penitential rite, no. 190 or 191, may be chosen.

THE SHORT FORM OF THE READING OF THE WORD

44. Omitting the celebration of the word of God, the minister or other person should read a short scriptural text referring to the bread of life.
John 6:54-55
John 6:54-58

John 14:6
John 14:23
John 15:4
1 Corinthians 11:26
1 John 4:16

See nos. 133ff. for a further selection of texts.

HOLY COMMUNION

LORD'S PRAYER

45. The minister takes the ciborium or pyx containing the body of the Lord, places it on the altar, and genuflects. He then introduces the Lord's Prayer in these or similar words:

**Let us pray with confidence to the Father
in the words our Savior gave us:**

He continues with the people:

Our Father. . . .

INVITATION TO COMMUNION

46. The minister genuflects. Taking the host, he raises it slightly over the vessel or pyx and, facing the people, says:

**This is the Lamb of God
who takes away the sins of the world.
Happy are those who are called to his supper.**

The communicants say once:
**Lord, I am not worthy to receive you,
but only say the word and I shall be healed.**

COMMUNION

47. If the minister receives communion, he says quietly:

May the body of Christ bring me to everlasting life.

He reverently consumes the body of Christ.

48. Then he takes the vessel or pyx and goes to the communicants. He takes a host for each one, raises it slightly, and says:

The body of Christ.

The communicant answers: **Amen,** and receives communion.

49. After communion the minister puts any particles left on the plate into the pyx, and he may wash his hands. He returns any remaining hosts to the tabernacle and genuflects.

SILENCE, PSALM, OR SONG OF PRAISE

A period of silence may now be observed, or a psalm or song of praise may be sung.

CONCLUDING PRAYER

50. The minister then says the concluding prayer:

Let us pray.

Lord Jesus Christ,
you gave us the eucharist as the memorial of your
**   suffering and death.**
May our worship of this sacrament of your body and
**   blood**
help us to experience the salvation you won for us
and the peace of the kingdom
where you live with the Father and the Holy Spirit,
one God, for ever and ever.
The people answer: **Amen.**

Other prayers, nos. 210-222, may be chosen.

CONCLUDING RITE

BLESSING

51. If the minister is a priest or deacon, he extends his hands and, facing the people, says:

The Lord be with you.
The people answer: **And also with you.**

He blesses the people with these words:

May almighty God bless you,
the Father, and the Son, ✠ and the Holy Spirit.
The people answer: **Amen.**

52. If the minister is not a priest or deacon, he invokes God's blessing, and crossing himself says:

May the Lord bless us,
protect us from all evil
and bring us to everlasting life.
or:
May the almighty and merciful God bless and protect
      us,
the Father, and the Son, and the Holy Spirit.
The people answer: **Amen.**

DISMISSAL

53. Finally the minister says:

Go in the peace of Christ.
The people answer: **Thanks be to God.**

Then after the customary reverence, the minister leaves.

CHAPTER II

ADMINISTRATION OF COMMUNION AND VIATICUM TO THE SICK BY AN EXTRAORDINARY MINISTER

54. A priest or deacon administers communion or viaticum to the sick in the manner prescribed by the *Rite of Anointing and Pastoral Care of the Sick.* When an acolyte or an extraordinary minister, duly appointed, gives communion to the sick, the rite here described is followed.

55. Those who cannot receive communion in the form of bread may receive it in the form of wine. The precioius blood must be carried to the sick person in a vessel so secured as to eliminate all danger of spilling. The sacrament should be administered with due regard to the individual concerned, and the rite for giving communion under both kinds provides a choice of methods. If all the precious blood is not consumed, the minister himself must consume it and then wash the vessel as required.

1. THE ORDINARY RITE OF COMMUNION OF THE SICK

INTRODUCTORY RITE

GREETING

56. Wearing the appropriate vestments (see no. 20), the minister approaches the sick person and greets him and the others present in a friendly manner. He may use this greeting:

Peace to this house and to all who live in it.

Any other customary form of greeting from scripture may be used. Then he places the sacrament on the table, and all adore it.

PENITENTIAL RITE

57. The minister invites the sick person and those present to recall their sins and to repent of them in these words:

My brothers and sisters,
to prepare ourselves for this celebration,
let us call to mind our sins.

A pause for silent reflection follows.

All say:
I confess to almighty God,
and to you, my brothers and sisters,
that I have sinned through my own fault
They strike their breast:
in my thoughts and in my words,
in what I have done,
and in what I have failed to do;
and I ask blessed Mary, ever virgin,
all the angels and saints,
and you, my brothers and sisters,
to pray for me to the Lord our God.

The minister concludes:
May almighty God have mercy on us,
forgive us our sins,
and bring us to everlasting life.
The people answer: **Amen.**

Other forms of the penitential rite, no. 190 or 191, may be chosen.

THE SHORT FORM OF THE READING OF THE WORD

58. A brief passage from sacred scripture (see no. 71) may then be read by one of those present or by the minister himself.
John 6:54-58
John 14:6
John 14:23

John 15:4
John 15:5
1 Corinthians 11:26
1 John 4:16

See the *Rite of Anointing and Pastoral Care of the Sick* (nos. 247ff. or 153ff.) for a further selection of texts.

HOLY COMMUNION

LORD'S PRAYER

59. The minister then introduces the Lord's Prayer in these or similar words:

Now let us pray together to the Father in the words given us by our Lord Jesus Christ.

He continues with the people:
Our Father. . . .

INVITATION TO COMMUNION

60. Then the minister shows the holy eucharist, saying:

This is the Lamb of God
who takes away the sins of the world.
Happy are those who are called to his supper.

The sick person and the other communicants say once:

Lord, I am not worthy to receive you,
but only say the word and I shall be healed.

COMMUNION

61. The minister goes to the sick person and, showing him the sacrament, says:

The body of Christ (or: The blood of Christ).

The sick person answers: **Amen,** and receives communion.

Others present then receive in the usual manner.

CONCLUDING PRAYER

62. After communion the minister washes the vessel as

usual. A period of silence may now be observed.

The minister then says the concluding prayer:

Let us pray.

**God our Father, almighty and eternal,
we confidently call upon you,
that the body [and blood] of Christ
which our brother (sister) has received
may bring him (her)
lasting health in mind and body.**

We ask this through Christ our Lord.
The people answer: **Amen.**

Other prayers, nos. 210-222, may be chosen.

CONCLUDING RITE

BLESSING

63. Then the minister invokes God's blessing, and crossing him or herself says:

**May the Lord bless us,
protect us from all evil
and bring us to everlasting life.**

or:

**May the almighty and merciful God bless and protect
us, the Father, and the Son, and the Holy Spirit.**
The people answer: **Amen.**

2. SHORT RITE OF COMMUNION OF THE SICK

64. This shorter rite is to be used when communion is given in different rooms of the same building, such as a hospital. Elements taken from the ordinary rite may be added according to circumstances.

ANTIPHON

65. The rite may begin in the church or chapel or in the first room, where the minister says the following antiphon:

**How holy this feast
in which Christ is our food:
his passion is recalled,
grace fills our hearts,
and we receive a pledge of the glory to come.**

Other antiphons, nos. 201-203, may be chosen.

INVITATION TO COMMUNION

66. Then the minister may be escorted by someone carrying a candle. He says to all the sick persons in the same room or to each communicant individually:

**This is the Lamb of God
who takes away the sins of the world.
Happy are those who are called to his supper.**

The one who is to receive communion then says once:

**Lord, I am not worthy to receive you,
but only say the word and I shall be healed.**

DISTRIBUTION OF COMMUNION

He receives communion in the usual manner.

CONCLUDING PRAYER

67. The rite is concluded with a prayer (see no. 62) which may be said in the church or chapel or in the last room:

Let us pray.

**God our Father, almighty and eternal,
we confidently call upon you,
that the body [and blood] of Christ
which our brother (sister) has received
may bring him (her)
lasting health in mind and body.**

We ask this through Christ our Lord.
The people answer: **Amen.**

Other prayers, nos. 210-222, may be chosen.

3. VIATICUM

INTRODUCTORY RITE

GREETING

68. Wearing the appropriate vestments (see no. 20) the minister approaches the sick person and greets him and the others present in a friendly manner. He may use this greeting:

Peace to this house and to all who live in it.

Any other customary form of greeting from scripture may be used. Then he places the sacrament on the table, and all adore it.

INSTRUCTION

69. Afterward the minister addresses those present, using the following instruction or one better suited to the sick person's condition:

My brothers and sisters:

Before our Lord Jesus Christ passed from this world to return to his Father, he gave us the sacrament of his body and blood. This is the promise of our resurrection, the food and drink for our journey as we pass from this life to join him. United in the love of Christ, let us ask God to give strength to our brother (sister).

A period of silent prayer then follows.

PENITENTIAL RITE

70. The minister invites the sick person and all present to recall their sins and to repent of them in these words:

**My brothers and sisters,
to prepare ourselves for this celebration,
let us call to mind our sins.**

A pause for silent reflection follows.

All say:
**I confess to almighty God,
and to you, my brothers and sisters,**

that I have sinned through my own fault
They strike their breast:
in my thoughts and in my words,
in what I have done,
and in what I have failed to do;
and I ask blessed Mary, ever virgin,
all the angels and saints,
and you, my brothers and sisters,
to pray for me to the Lord our God.
The minister concludes:
May almighty God have mercy on us,
forgive us our sins,
and bring us to everlasting life.
The people answer: **Amen.**

Other forms of the penitential rite, no. 190 or 191, may be chosen.

THE SHORT FORM OF THE READING OF THE WORD

71. It is most fitting that one of those present or the minister himself read a brief text from scripture:
John 6:54-58
John 14:6
John 14:23
John 15:4
1 Corinthians 11:26
1 John 4:16

See the *Rite of Anointing and Pastoral Care of the Sick* (nos. 247ff. or 153ff.) for a further selection of texts.

PROFESSION OF BAPTISMAL FAITH

72. It is desirable that the sick person renew his baptismal profession of faith before he receives viaticum. The minister gives a brief instruction and then asks the following questions:

Do you believe in God, the Father almighty, creator of heaven and earth?
R̷. **I do.**

Do you believe in Jesus Christ, his only Son, our
Lord, who was born of the Virgin Mary, was
crucified, died, and was buried, rose from the dead,
and is now seated at the right hand of the Father?
R̽. I do.

Do you believe in the Holy Spirit, the holy Catholic
Church, the communion of saints, the forgiveness
of sins, the resurrection of the body, and life everlasting?
R̽. I do.

PRAYER FOR THE SICK PERSON

73. If the condition of the sick person permits, a brief litany
is recited in these or similar words. The sick person, if he is
able, and all present respond:

My brothers and sisters, let us pray with one mind
and heart to our Lord Jesus Christ:

Lord, you loved us to the end, and you accepted death
that we might have life: hear our prayer for our
brother (sister).
R̽. Lord, hear our prayer.

Lord, you said: "He who eats my flesh and drinks my
blood has eternal life": hear our prayer for our brother
(sister).
R̽. Lord, hear our prayer.

Lord, you invite us to the banquet of your kingdom,
where there will be no more pain or mourning, no
more sorrow or separation: hear our prayer for our
brother (sister).
R̽. Lord, hear our prayer.

VIATICUM

LORD'S PRAYER

74. The minister introduces the Lord's Prayer in these or
similar words:

Now let us pray together to the Father in the words given us by our Lord Jesus Christ.

All continue:
Our Father. . . .

INVITATION TO COMMUNION
75. Then the minister shows the holy eucharist to those present, saying:

**This is the Lamb of God
who takes away the sins of the world.
Happy are those who are called to his supper.**

The sick person and all who are to receive communion say once:

**Lord, I am not worthy to receive you,
but only say the word and I shall be healed.**

COMMUNION
76. The minister goes to the sick person and, showing him the sacrament, says:

The body of Christ (or: The blood of Christ).

The sick person answers: **Amen.**
Immediately, or after giving communion, the minister adds:

May the Lord Jesus Christ protect you and lead you to eternal life.
The sick person answers: **Amen.**

Others present then receive communion in the usual manner.

77. After communion the minister washes the vessel as usual. Then a period of silence may be observed.

CONCLUDING RITE

CONCLUDING PRAYER
78. The minister says the concluding prayer:
Let us pray.

Father,
your son, Jesus Christ, is our way, our truth, and our
  life.
Our brother (sister) N. entrusts himself (herself) to
  you
with full confidence in all your promises.
Refresh him (her) with the body and blood of your
  Son
and lead him (her) to your kingdom in peace.
We ask this through Christ our Lord.
The people answer: **Amen.**

For another prayer, no. 223 may be chosen.

CHAPTER III
FORMS OF WORSHIP OF THE EUCHARIST

79. The eucharistic sacrifice is the source and culmination of the whole Christian life. Therefore, devotion, both private and public, toward the eucharist even outside Mass that conforms to the norms laid down by lawful authority is strongly advocated.

In structuring these devotional exercises account should be taken of the liturgical seasons so that they accord with the liturgy, are in some way derived from it, and lead the people back to it.[1]

80. When the faithful adore Christ present in the sacrament, they should remember that this presence derives from the sacrifice and has as its purpose both sacramental and spiritual communion.

Therefore, the devotion prompting the faithful to visit the blessed sacrament draws them into an ever deeper share in the paschal mystery and leads them to respond gratefully to the gift of him who through his humanity constantly pours divine life into members of his Body. Abiding with Christ the Lord, they enjoy his intimate friendship and pour out their hearts before him for themselves and for those dear to them and they pray for the peace and salvation of the world. Offering their entire lives with Christ to the Father in the Holy Spirit, they derive from this sublime colloquy an increase of faith, hope, and charity. Thus they foster those right dispositions that enable them with due devotion to celebrate the memorial of the Lord and receive frequently the bread given us by the Father.

Therefore, the faithful should strive to worship Christ the Lord in the blessed sacrament in a manner fitting in with their own way of life. Pastors should show the way by example and by word encourage their people.[2]

81. Prayer before Christ the Lord sacramentally present extends the union with Christ that the faithful have reached in communion. It renews the covenant that in turn moves

---

[1]See *SCR*, Instr. EuchMyst no. 58 [*DOL* 179, no. 1287].
[2]See *ibid.*, no. 50 [*DOL* 179, no. 1279].

them to maintain by the way they live what they have received through faith and the sacrament. They should strive to lead their whole lives in the strength of this heavenly food, as sharers in the death and resurrection of the Lord. All should be eager to do good works and to please God, so that they may seek to imbue the world with the Christian spirit and, in all things, even in the midst of human affairs, to become witnesses of Christ.[3]

[3] See *ibid.*, no. 13 [*DOL* 179, no. 1242].

1. EXPOSITION OF THE HOLY EUCHARIST

INTRODUCTION

I. RELATIONSHIP BETWEEN EXPOSITION AND MASS

82. Exposition of the holy eucharist, either in a ciborium or in a monstrance, leads us to acknowledge Christ's marvelous presence in the sacrament and invites us to the spiritual union with him that culminates in sacramental communion. Therefore it is a strong encouragement toward the worship owed to Christ in spirit and in truth.

In such exposition care must be taken that everything clearly brings out the meaning of eucharistic worship in its correlation with the Mass. There must be nothing about the appointments used for exposition that could in any way obscure Christ's intention of instituting the eucharist above all to be near us to feed, to heal, and to comfort us.[4]

83. During the exposition of the blessed sacrament, celebration of Mass in the body of the church or oratory is prohibited.

In addition to the reasons given in no. 6, the celebration of the eucharistic mystery includes in a higher way that inner communion to which exposition is meant to lead the faithful.

If exposition of the blessed sacrament goes on for a day or for several successive days, it should be interrupted during the celebration of Mass, unless it is celebrated in a chapel separate from the area of exposition and at least some of the faithful remain in adoration.[5]

II. REGULATIONS FOR EXPOSITION

84. Genuflection in the presence of the blessed sacrament, whether reserved in the tabernacle or exposed for public adoration, is on one knee.

---

[4]See *ibid.*, no. 60 [*DOL* 179, no. 1289].
[5]See *ibid.*, no. 61 [*DOL* 179, no. 1290].

85. For exposition of the blessed sacrament in the monstrance, four to six candles are lighted, as at Mass, and incense is used. For exposition of the blessed sacrament in the ciborium, at least two candles should be lighted and incense may be used.

LENGTHY EXPOSITION

86. In churches and oratories where the eucharist is reserved, it is recommended that solemn exposition of the blessed sacrament for an extended period of time should take place once a year, even though this period is not strictly continuous. In this way the local community may meditate on this mystery more deeply and adore.

This kind of exposition, however, may take place only if there is assurance of the participation of a reasonable number of the faithful.[6]

87. For any serious and general need, the local Ordinary is empowered to order prayer before the blessed sacrament exposed for a more extended period of time in those churches to which the faithful come in large numbers.[7]

88. Where there cannot be uninterrupted exposition because there is not a sufficient number of worshipers, it is permissible to replace the blessed sacrament in the tabernacle at fixed hours that are announced ahead of time. But this may not be done more than twice a day, for example, at midday and at night.

The following form of simple reposition may be observed: the priest or deacon, vested in an alb, or a surplice over a cassock, and a stole, replaces the blessed sacrament in the tabernacle after a brief period of adoration and a prayer said with those present. The exposition of the blessed sacrament may take place again, in the same manner and at a scheduled time.[8]

BRIEF PERIOD OF EXPOSITION

89. Shorter expositions of the eucharist are to be arranged in such a way that the blessing with the eucharist is pre-

---

[6]See *ibid.*, no. 63 [DOL 179, no. 1292].
[7]See *ibid.*, no. 64 [DOL 179, no. 1293].
[8]See *ibid.*, no. 65 [DOL 179, no. 1294].

ceded by a reasonable time for readings of the word of God, songs, prayers, and a period for silent prayer.[9]

Exposition merely for the purpose of giving benediction is prohibited.

ADORATION IN RELIGIOUS COMMUNITIES

90. According to the constitutions and regulations of their institute, some religious communities and other groups have the practice of perpetual eucharistic adoration or adoration over extended periods of time. It is strongly recommended that they pattern this holy practice in harmony with the spirit of the liturgy. Then, with the whole community taking part, the adoration before Christ the Lord, will consist of readings, songs, and religious silence to foster effectively the spiritual life of the community. This promotes between the members of the religious house the spirit of unity and mutual love that the eucharist signifies and effects, and gives the worship due the sacrament a more sublime expression.

The form of adoration in which one or two members of the community take turns before the blessed sacrament is also to be maintained and is highly commended. Through it, in accordance with the nature of the institute as approved by the Church, the worshipers adore Christ the Lord in the sacrament and pray to him in the name of the entire community and Church.

III. MINISTER OF EXPOSITION

91. The ordinary minister for exposition of the eucharist is a priest or deacon. At the end of the period of adoration, before the reposition, he blesses the congregation with the sacrament.

In the absence of a priest or deacon or if they are lawfully impeded, an acolyte, another special minister of communion, or another person appointed by the local Ordinary may publicly expose and later repose the eucharist for the adoration of the faithful.

Such ministers may open the tabernacle and also, as required, place the ciborium on the altar or place the host in

[9]See *ibid.*, no. 66 [DOL 179, no. 1295].

the monstrance. At the end of the period of adoration, they replace the blessed sacrament in the tabernacle. It is not lawful, however, for them to give the blessing with the sacrament.

92. The minister, if he is a priest or deacon, should vest in an alb, or a surplice over a cassock, and a stole. Other ministers should wear either the liturgical vestments that are used in the region or the vesture that is befitting this ministry and is approved by the Ordinary.

The priest or deacon should wear a white cope and humeral veil to give the blessing at the end of adoration, when the exposition takes place with the monstrance; in the case of exposition in the ciborium, he should put on the humeral veil.

RITE OF EUCHARISTIC EXPOSITION AND BENEDICTION

EXPOSITION

93. After the people have assembled, a song may be sung while the minister comes to the altar. If the holy eucharist is not reserved at the altar where the exposition is to take place, the minister puts on a humeral veil and brings the sacrament from the place of reservation; he is accompanied by servers or by the faithful with lighted candles.

The ciborium or monstrance should be placed upon the table of the altar which is covered with a cloth. If exposition with the monstrance is to extend over a long period, a throne in an elevated position may be used, but this should not be too lofty or distant.[10] After exposition, if the monstrance is used, the minister incenses the sacrament. If the adoration is to be lengthy, he may then withdraw.

94. In the case of more solemn and lengthy exposition, the host should be consecrated in the Mass which immediately precedes the exposition and after communion should be placed in the monstrance upon the altar. The Mass ends with the prayer after communion, and the concluding rites are omitted. Before the priest leaves, he may place the blessed sacrament on the throne and incense it.

ADORATION

95. During the exposition there should be prayers, songs, and readings to direct the attention of the faithful to the worship of Christ the Lord.

To encourage a prayerful spirit, there should be readings from scripture with a homily or brief exhortations to develop a better understanding of the eucharistic mystery. It is also desirable for the people to respond to the word of God by singing and to spend some periods of time in religious silence.

96. Part of the liturgy of the hours, especially the principal

---

[10]See ibid., no. 62[DOL 179, no. 1291].

hours, may be celebrated before the blessed sacrament when there is a lengthy period of exposition. This liturgy extends the praise and thanksgiving offered to God in the eucharistic celebration to the several hours of the day; it directs the prayers of the Church to Christ and through him to the Father in the name of the whole world.

BENEDICTION

EUCHARISTIC HYMN AND INCENSATION

97. Toward the end of the exposition the priest or deacon goes to the altar, genuflects, and kneels. Then a hymn or other eucharistic song is sung.[11] Meanwhile the minister, while kneeling, incenses the sacrament if the exposition has taken place with the monstrance.

PRAYER

98. Afterward the minister rises and sings or says:

Let us pray.

After a brief period of silence, the minister continues:

Lord Jesus Christ,
you gave us the eucharist
as the memorial of your suffering and death.
May our worship of this sacrament of your body and
blood
help us to experience the salvation you won for us
and the peace of the kingdom
where you live with the Father and the Holy Spirit,
one God, for ever and ever.
All respond: **Amen.**

Other prayers, nos. 224-229, may be chosen.

EUCHARISTIC BLESSING

99. After the prayer the priest or deacon puts on the humeral veil, genuflects, and takes the monstrance or ciborium. He makes the sign of the cross over the people with the monstrance or ciborium, in silence.

[11]See below, nos. 192-199.

REPOSITION

100. After the blessing the priest or deacon who gave the blessing, or another priest or deacon, replaces the blessed sacrament in the tabernacle and genuflects. Meanwhile the people may sing or say an acclamation, and the minister then leaves.

2. EUCHARISTIC PROCESSIONS

101. In processions in which the eucharist is carried through the streets solemnly with singing, the Christian people give public witness to faith and to their devotion toward this sacrament.

But it is for the diocesan bishop to decide on both the advisability of such processions in today's conditions and on the time, place, and plan for them that will ensure their being carried out with decorum and without any loss of reverence toward this sacrament.[12]

102. The annual procession on the solemnity of Corpus Christi, or on a convenient day near this feast, has a special importance and meaning for the pastoral life of the parish or city. It is therefore desirable to continue this procession, in accordance with the law, when today's circumstances permit and when it can truly be a sign of common faith and adoration.

In the principal districts of large cities there may be additional eucharistic processions for pastoral reasons at the discretion of the diocesan bishop. If the procession cannot be held on the solemnity of Corpus Christi, it is fitting to hold some kind of public celebration for the entire city or its principal districts in the cathedral church or other convenient places.

103. It is fitting that a eucharistic procession begin after the Mass and the host to be carried in the procession is consecrated at this Mass. A procession may also take place, however, at the end of a lengthy period of public adoration that has been held after Mass.

104. Eucharistic processions should be arranged in accordance with local customs in regard to the decoration of the streets and the order followed by the participants. In the course of the procession there may be stations where the eucharistic blessing is given, if there is such a custom and some pastoral advantage recommends it. Songs and prayers should be planned with the purpose of expressing the faith of the participants and the centering of their attention on the Lord alone.

[12]See *SCR* Inst. EuchMyst no. 59 [*DOL* 179, no. 1288].

105. The priest who carries the blessed sacrament may wear the vestments used for the celebration of Mass if the procession takes place immediately afterward, or he may vest in a white cope.

106. Lights, incense, and the canopy under which the priest carrying the blessed sacrament walks should be used in accordance with local customs.

107. It is fitting that the procession should go from one church to another. Nevertheless, if local circumstances require, the procession may return to the same church where it began.

108. At the end of the procession benediction with the blessed sacrament should be given in the church where the procession ends or at another appropriate place. Then the blessed sacrament is reposed.

3. EUCHARISTIC CONGRESSES

109. Eucharistic congresses have been introduced into the life of the Church in recent years as a special manifestation of eucharistic worship. They should be considered as a kind of "station" to which a particular community invites an entire local Church or to which an individual local Church invites other Churches of a single region or nation or even of the entire world. The purpose is that together the members of the Church join in the deepest profession of some aspect of the eucharistic mystery and express their worship publicly in the bond of charity and unity.

Such congresses should be a genuine sign of faith and charity by reason of the total participation of the local Church and the association with it of the other Churches.

110. Both the local Church and other churches should undertake studies beforehand concerning the place, theme, and program of the congress. These studies are meant to lead to the consideration of genuine needs and to foster the progress of theological studies and the good of the local Church. Specialists in theological, biblical, liturgical, pastoral, and humane studies should help in this research.

111. In preparation for a eucharistic congress, the concentration should be on the following:

a) a thorough catechesis, accommodated to the capacity of different groups, concerning the eucharist, especially as the mystery of Christ living and working in the Church;

b) more active participation in the liturgy in order to encourage a reverent hearing of the word of God and the spirit of mutual love and community[13];

c) research into the means and the pursuit of social action for human development and the just distribution of goods, including the temporal, following the example of the primitive Christian community.[14] The goal is that every eucharistic table may be a center from which the leaven of the Gospel spreads as a force in the growth of contemporary society and as the pledge of the future kingdom.[15]

[13]See *SC* art. 41–52 [*DOL* 1, nos. 41–52].
[14]See Acts 4:32.
[15]See *SC*, art. 47 [*DOL* 1, no. 47]; *UR* no. 15 [*DOL* 6, no. 187].

112. The celebration of the congress should be planned on the basis of the following criteria:[16]

a) The celebration of the eucharist should be the true center and high point of the congress, to which all the programs and the various devotional services should be directed.

b) Celebrations of the word of God, catechetical meetings, and public conferences should be planned to investigate thoroughly the theme of the congress and to set out more clearly the ways for carrying out its practical implications.

c) There should be an opportunity for common prayers and extended adoration in the presence of the blessed sacrament exposed at designated churches that are especially suited to this form of piety.

d) The regulations concerning eucharistic processions[17] should be observed for the procession in which the blessed sacrament is carried through the streets of the city to the accompaniment of public hymns and prayers, taking into account local, social, and religious conditions.

[16]See *SCR*, Instr. EuchMyst no. 67 [*DOL* 179, no. 1296].
[17]See nos. 101–108 of this document.

CHAPTER IV

TEXTS FOR USE IN THE RITE OF DISTRIBUTING HOLY COMMUNION OUTSIDE MASS AND IN THE WORSHIP AND PROCESSION OF THE BLESSED SACRAMENT

1. BIBLICAL READINGS

READINGS FROM THE OLD TESTAMENT

113. Genesis 14:18-20
Melchisedech brought bread and wine.

114. Exodus 12:21-27
When the Lord sees the blood on the door, he will pass over your home.

115. Exodus 16:2-4, 12-15
I will rain bread from heaven upon you.

116. Exodus 24:3-8
This is the blood of the covenant that the Lord God has made with you.

117. Deuteronomy 8:2-3, 15b-16a
He gave you food which you and your fathers did not know.

118. 1 Kings 19:4-8
Strengthened by the food, he walked to the mountain of the Lord.

119. Proverbs 9:1-6
Come and eat my bread, drink the wine I have prepared.

READINGS FROM THE NEW TESTAMENT

120. Acts 2:42-47
They continued in fellowship with the apostles and in the breaking of the bread.

121. Acts 10:34a, 37-43
After he was raised from the dead, we ate and drank with him.

122. 1 Corinthians 10:16-17
Though we are many, we are one bread and one body.

123. 1 Corinthians 11:23-26
Each time you eat this bread and drink this cup, you are proclaiming the death of the Lord Jesus.

124. Hebrews 9:11-15
The blood of Christ purifies our hearts from sin.

125. Hebrews 12:18-19, 22-24
Jesus brings you to the Father by shedding his blood for you.

126. 1 Peter 1:17-21
You have been redeemed by the precious blood of Jesus Christ.

127. 1 John 5:4-7a, 8b
The Spirit, the water, and the blood give witness.

128. Revelation 1:5-8
Because he loves us, he has saved us from sin with his blood.

129. Revelation 7:9-14
They have washed their robes in the blood of the Lamb.

RESPONSORIAL PSALM

130. Psalm 23:1-3, 4, 5, 6
R̂. (1): **The Lord is my shepherd; there is nothing I shall want.**

131. Psalm 34:2-3, 4-5, 6-7, 8-9
R̂. (9a): **Taste and see the goodness of the Lord.**

132. Psalm 40:2 and 4ab, 7-8a, 8b-9, 10
R̂. (8a and 9a): **Here I am, Lord; I come to do your will.**

133. Psalm 78:3-4a and 7ab, 23-24, 25, 54
R̂. (24b): **The Lord gave them bread from heaven.**

134. Psalm 110: 1, 2, 3, 4
R̂. (4bc): **You are a priest for ever, in the line of Melchisedech.**

135. Psalm 116:12-13, 15 and 16bc, 17-18
R̂. (13): **I will take the cup of salvation, and call on the name of the Lord.**

or (1 Corinthians 10:16): **Our blessing-cup is a communion with the blood of Christ.**

136. Psalm 145:10-11, 15-16, 17-18
R̰. (see 16): **The hand of the Lord feeds us; he answers all our needs.**

137. Psalm 148:12-13, 14-15, 19-20
R̰. (12a): **Praise the Lord, Jerusalem.**
or (John 6:58c): **Whoever eats this bread will live for ever.**

ALLELUIA VERSE AND VERSE BEFORE THE GOSPEL
138. John 6:51
**I am the living bread from heaven, says the Lord;
if anyone eats this bread he will live for ever.**

139. John 6:56
Whoever eats my flesh and drinks my blood, says the Lord, will live in me and I in him.

140. John 6:57
As the living Father sent me, and I live because of the Father, so he who eats me will live because of me.

141. See Revelation 1:5ab
Jesus Christ, you are the faithful witness, firstborn from the dead.

142. Revelation 5:9
You are worthy, O Lord, to receive the book and open its seals.

GOSPEL
143. **Mark 14:12-16, 22-26**
This is my body. This is my blood.

144. **Mark 15:16-20**
They dressed Jesus up in purple and put a crown of thorns on him.

145. **Luke 9:11b-17**
All the people ate and were satisfied.

146. **Luke 22:39-44**
His sweat became like drops of blood falling to the ground.

147. **Luke 24:13-35** (longer) **or 13-16, 28-35** (shorter)
They recognized him at the breaking of the bread.

148. John 6:1-15
They gave the people all the food they wanted.

149. John 6:24-35
If you come to me, you will never be hungry. He who believes in me will never know thirst.

150. John 6:41-51
I am the living bread from heaven.

151. John 6:51-58
My flesh and blood are true food and drink.

152. John 19:31-37
When they pierced his side with a spear, blood and water flowed out.

153. John 21:1-14
Jesus took the bread and gave it to them.

READING FROM THE VOTIVE MASS OF THE SACRED HEART

READINGS FROM THE OLD TESTAMENT

154. Exodus 34:4b-7a, 8-9
Our God is merciful and compassionate.

155. Deuteronomy 7:6-11
God has chosen you because he loves you.

156. Deuteronomy 10:12-22
God loves his chosen ones and their children.

157. Isaiah 49:13-15
Even if a mother forgets her child, I will never forget you.

158. Jeremiah 31:1-4
I have loved you with a love that will never end.

159. Ezekiel 34:11-16
I will take care of my flock.

160. Hosea 11:1b, 3-4, 8c-9 (Hebrew 1, 3-4, 8c-9)
My heart is saddened at the thought of parting.

READINGS FROM THE NEW TESTAMENT

161. Romans 5:5-11
God has poured out his love into our hearts.

162. Ephesians 1:3-10
He has lavished his rich graces upon us.

163. Ephesians 3:8-12
God has given me the privilege of proclaiming the riches of
Christ to all the nations.

164. Ephesians 3:14-19
I pray that you will grasp the unbounded love of Christ.

165. Philippians 1:8-11
May your life be filled with the perfection which comes
through Jesus Christ.

166. 1 John 4:7-16
We love God because he has loved us first.

167. Revelation 3:14b, 20-22
I will come to eat with you.

168. Revelation 5:6-12
You brought us back to God by shedding your blood for us.

RESPONSORIAL PSALM

169. Isaiah 12:2-3, 4bcd, 5-6
R⁷. (3): **You will draw water joyfully from the springs
of salvation.**

170. Psalm 23:1-3, 4, 5, 6
R⁷. (1): **The Lord is my shepherd; there is nothing I
shall want.**

171. Psalm 25:4bc-5ab, 6-7bc, 8-9, 10, 14
R⁷. (6a): **Remember your mercies, O Lord.**

172. Psalm 33:1-2, 4-5, 11-12, 18-19, 20-21
R⁷. (5b): **The earth is full of the goodness of the Lord.**

173. Psalm 34:2-3, 4-5, 6-7
R⁷. (9a): **Taste and see the goodness of the Lord.**

174. Psalm 103:1-2, 3-4, 6-7, 8, 10
R⁷. (17): **The Lord's kindness is everlasting to those
who fear him.**

ALLELUIA VERSE AND VERSE BEFORE THE GOSPEL

175. See Matthew 11:25
**Blessed are you, Father, Lord of heaven and earth;
you have revealed to little ones the mysteries of the
      kingdom.**

176. Matthew 11:28
**Come to me, all you that labor and are burdened,
and I will give you rest, says the Lord.**

177. Matthew 11:29ab
**Take my yoke upon you;
learn from me, for I am gentle and lowly in heart.**

178. John 10:14
**I am the good shepherd, says the Lord;
I know my sheep, and mine know me.**

179. John 15:9
**As the Father has loved me, so have I loved you;
remain in my love.**

180. 1 John 4:10b
**God first loved us
and sent his Son to take away our sins.**

GOSPEL

181. **Matthew 11:25-30**
I am gentle and humble of heart.

182. **Luke 15:1-10**
Heaven is filled with joy when one sinner turns back to
God.

183. **Luke 15:1-3, 11-32**
We are celebrating because your brother has come back from
death.

184. **John 10:11-18**
A good shepherd is ready to die for his flock.

185. **John 15:1-8**
Live in me as I live in you.

186. **John 15:9-17**
Love one another as much as I love you.

187. John 17:20-26
Father, you loved them as you loved me.

188. John 19:31-37
When they pierced his side with a spear, blood and water flowed out.

2. FORMS OF GREETING

189.

The grace and peace of God our Father and the Lord Jesus Christ be with you.

The people answer:
Blessed be the God and Father of our Lord Jesus Christ.

or:
And also with you.

3. FORMS OF THE PENITENTIAL RITE

190. The minister invites the people to recall their sins and to repent of them in these words:

My brothers and sisters,
to prepare ourselves for this celebration,
let us call to mind our sins.

A pause for silent reflection follows.

The minister says:
Lord, we have sinned against you.
The people answer: **Lord, have mercy.**

Minister:
Lord, show us your mercy and love.
The people answer: **And grant us your salvation.**

The minister concludes:
May almighty God have mercy on us,
forgive us our sins,
and bring us to everlasting life.
The people answer: **Amen.**

191. The minister invites the people to recall their sins and to repent of them in these words:

My brothers and sisters,
to prepare ourselves for this celebration,
let us call to mind our sins.

After a brief silence the minister, or someone else, makes the following or other invocations:

Minister:
You brought us to salvation by your paschal mystery:
Lord, have mercy.
The people answer: **Lord, have mercy.**

Minister:
You renew among us the wonders of your passion:
Christ, have mercy.
The people answer: **Christ, have mercy.**

Minister:
You give us your body to make us one with your
**   Easter sacrifice:**
Lord, have mercy.
The people answer: **Lord, have mercy.**

The minister concludes:
May almighty God have mercy on us,
forgive us our sins,
and bring us to everlasting life.
The people answer: **Amen.**

4. HYMNS

At benediction, which concludes the service of adoration, especially the short form, singing may be confined to the last part, beginning with the words: **Tantum ergo.**

Pange, Lingua
192. Pange, lingua, gloriosi

Sacris sollemniis
193. Sacris sollemniis iuncta sint gaudia

Verbum Supernum
194. Verbum supernum prodiens

Jesu, Nostra Redemptio
195. Jesu, nostra redemptio

Aeterne Rex Altissime
196. Aeterne rex altissime

Lauda, Sion
197. This sequence may be sung either in its entirety or beginning at the words: Ecce panis.

Adoro Te Devote
198. Adoro te devote, latens veritas,

Ubi Caritas
199. Ubi caritas est vera, Deus ibi est
A further choice of chants can be found in the Liturgy of the Hours.

5. ANTIPHONS

200.
**How holy this feast
in which Christ is our food:
his passion is recalled,
grace fills our hearts,
and we receive a pledge of the glory to come.**

201.
**How gracious you are, Lord:
your gift of bread from heaven
reveals a Father's love and brings us perfect joy.
You fill the hungry with good things
and send away empty the rich in their pride.**

202.
**Body of Jesus, born of the Virgin Mary,
body bowed in agony,
raised upon the cross
and offered for us in sacrifice,
body pierced and flowing with blood and water,
come at the hour of our death**

as our living bread,
the foretaste of eternal glory:
come, Lord Jesus,
loving and gracious Son of Mary.

203.
I am the living bread
come down from heaven.
If anyone eats this bread
he shall live for ever.
The bread I will give is my flesh
for the life of the world.

6. RESPONSORIES

204.
While they were at table, Jesus took bread,
said the blessing, broke the bread,
and gave it to his disciples saying:
Take this, all of you, and eat it: this is my body.

℣. Those who dwell with me said: Who will give us
    flesh to eat?
Take this, all . . .

205.
I am the bread of life: your fathers ate the manna in
    the desert and they are dead;
this is the bread which comes down from heaven;
    whoever eats it will not die.

℣. I am the living bread which has come down from
    heaven;
whoever eats this bread will live for ever.
This is the . . .

206.
See in this bread the body that hung on the cross;
see in this cup the blood that flowed from his side.
Take and eat the body of Christ; take and drink his
    blood.

For now you are members of Christ.

℣. **Receive the bond of love and be united; receive the price of your salvation and know your worth.**
For now you . . .

207.

We though many are one bread, one body; for we all share one bread and one cup.

℣. **You have made us live in peace in your house, O Lord;**
in your kindness you have prepared a banquet for the poor.
For we all . . .

208.

A man prepared a banquet and sent his servants to tell the guests:
Come, all is ready.

℣. **Eat my bread and drink my wine.**
Come, all is ready.

209.

The living Father has sent me and I have life from the Father.
He who eats me, has life from me.

℣. **The Lord has fed him on the bread of life and understanding.**
He who eats . . .

7. PRAYERS AFTER COMMUNION

210.
Father,
you have brought to fulfillment the work of our redemption
through the Easter mystery of Christ your Son.
May we who faithfully proclaim his death and resurrection in these sacramental signs

experience the constant growth of your salvation in
our lives.

We ask this through Christ our Lord.

211.
Lord,
you have nourished us with one bread from heaven.
Fill us with your Spirit,
and make us one in peace and love.

We ask this through Christ our Lord.

212.
Lord,
may our sharing at this holy table make us holy.
By the body and blood of Christ
join all your people in brotherly love.

We ask this through Christ our Lord.

213.
Father,
you give us food from heaven.
By our sharing in this mystery
teach us to judge wisely the things of earth
and to love the things of heaven.

Grant this through Christ our Lord.

214.
Lord,
we give thanks for these holy mysteries
which bring to us here on earth
a share in the life to come,
through Christ our Lord.

215.
All-powerful God,
you renew us with your sacraments.
Help us to thank you by lives of faithful service.

We ask this through Christ our Lord.

216.

God our Father,
you give us a share in the one bread and the one cup
and make us one in Christ.
Help us to bring your salvation and joy
to all the world.

We ask this through Christ our Lord.

217.

Lord,
you renew us at your table with the bread of life.
May this food strengthen us in love
and help us to serve you in each other.

We ask this in the name of Jesus the Lord.

218.

Lord,
we thank you for the nourishment you give us
through your holy gift.
Pour out your Spirit upon us
and in the strength of this food from heaven
keep us single-minded in your service.

We ask this in the name of Jesus the Lord.

219.

Lord,
we are renewed by the breaking of one bread.
Keep us in your love
and help us to live the new life Christ won for us.

Grant this in the name of Jesus the Lord.

During the Easter Season the prayers in nos. 220-222 are
preferred:

220.

Lord,
you have nourished us with your Easter sacraments.
Fill us with your Spirit
and make us one in peace and love.

We ask this through Christ our Lord.

221.
Lord,
may this sharing in the sacrament of your Son
free us from our old life of sin
and make us your new creation.

We ask this in the name of Jesus the Lord.

222.
Almighty and ever-living Lord,
you restored us to life
by raising Christ from death.
Strengthen us by this Easter sacrament;
may we feel its saving power in our daily life.

We ask this through Christ our Lord.

223. Another prayer after Viaticum:

Lord,
you are the source of eternal health
for those who believe in you.
May our brother (sister) N.,
who has been refreshed
with food and drink from heaven,
safely reach your kingdom of light and life.

We ask this through Christ our Lord.

8. PRAYERS AT BENEDICTION OF THE BLESSED SACRAMENT

224.
Lord our God,
in this great sacrament
we come into the presence of Jesus Christ, your Son,
born of the Virgin Mary
and crucified for our salvation.
May we who declare our faith in this fountain of love
    and mercy
drink from it the water of everlasting life.

We ask this through Christ our Lord.

225.
Lord our God,
may we always give due honor
to the sacramental presence of the Lamb who was
    slain for us.
May our faith be rewarded
by the vision of his glory,
who lives and reigns for ever and ever.

226.
Lord our God,
you have given us the true bread from heaven.
In the strength of this food
may we live always by your life
and rise in glory on the last day.

We ask this through Christ our Lord.

227.
Lord,
give to our hearts
the light of faith and the fire of love,
that we may worship in spirit and in truth
our God and Lord, present in this sacrament,
who lives and reigns for ever and ever.

228.
Lord,
may this sacrament of new life
warm our hearts with your love
and make us eager
for the eternal joy of your kingdom.

We ask this through Christ our Lord.

229.
Lord our God,
teach us to cherish in our hearts
the paschal mystery of your Son
by which you redeemed the world.
Watch over the gifts of grace
your love has given us

**and bring them to fulfillment
in the glory of heaven.**

We ask this through Christ our Lord.

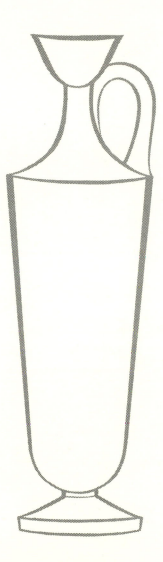

RITE OF THE BLESSING OF OILS

RITE OF CONSECRATING THE CHRISM

RITE OF THE BLESSING OF OILS
RITE OF CONSECRATING THE CHRISM

Decree
Introduction (1–12)

BLESSING OF OILS AND CONSECRATION
OF THE CHRISM (13–28)

Preparations (13)
Liturgy of the Word
Renewal of Priestly Commitment

Rite of Blessing (14–18)
Procession with the Oils and the Gifts (16)
Hymn (17)
Presentation of the Oils and the Gifts (18)

Liturgy of the Eucharist (19–20)
Preparation of the Altar and the Gifts
Eucharistic Prayer
Blessing of the Oil of the Sick (20)
Communion Rite
Lord's Prayer
Prayer After Communion

Blessing of the Oil of Catechumens (21–22)

Consecration of the Chrism (23–26)
Invitation (24)
Consecratory Prayer (25)

Concluding Rite (27–28)
Blessing
Dismissal

SACRED CONGREGATION FOR DIVINE WORSHIP

Prot. n. 3133/70

DECREE

Since the Holy Week rites of the Roman Missal have been revised, it seemed appropriate to make the necessary adaptations in the rites of the blessing of the oil of catechumens and the oil of the sick and of consecrating the chrism, for use in the chrism Mass.

Therefore the Sacred Congregation for Divine Worship has revised these rites and, with the approval of Pope Paul VI, publishes them to be used in place of those now given in the Roman Pontifical.

It is the responsibility of the conferences of bishops to prepare vernacular editions of these rites and to present them to this Congregation for confirmation.

Anything to the contrary notwithstanding.

From the Sacred Congregation for Divine Worship, December 3, 1970.

Benno Cardinal Gut
prefect

A. Bugnini
secretary

INTRODUCTION

1. The bishop is to be considered as the high priest of his flock. The life in Christ of his faithful is in some way derived and dependent upon the bishop.[1]

The chrism Mass is one of the principal expressions of the fullness of the bishop's priesthood and signifies the close unity of the priests with him. During the Mass, which he concelebrates with priests from various sections of the diocese, the bishop consecrates the chrism and blesses the other oils. The newly baptized are anointed and confirmed with the chrism consecrated by the bishop. Catechumens are prepared and disposed for baptism with the second oil. And the sick are anointed in their illness with the third oil.

2. The Christian liturgy has assimilated this Old Testament usage of anointing kings, priests, and prophets with consecratory oil because the name of Christ, whom they prefigured, means "the anointed of the Lord."

Chrism is a sign: by baptism Christians are plunged into the paschal mystery of Christ; they die with him, are buried with him, and rise with him;[2] they are sharers in his royal and prophetic priesthood. By confirmation Christians receive the spiritual anointing of the Spirit who is given to them.

By the oil of catechumens the effect of the baptismal exorcisms is extended. Before they go to the font of life to be reborn the candidates for baptism are strengthened to renounce sin and the devil.

By the use of the oil of the sick, to which Saint James is a witness,[3] the sick receive a remedy for the illness of mind and body, so that they may have strength to bear suffering and resist evil and obtain the forgiveness of sins.

I. THE OILS

3. The matter proper for the sacraments is olive oil or, ac-

---

[1]See II Vatican Council, Constitution on the Sacred Liturgy, *Sacrosanctum Concilium*, no. 42.
[2]*Ibid.*, no. 6.
[3]James 5:14

cording to circumstances, other plant oil.

4. Chrism is made of oil and perfumes or other sweet smelling matter.

5. The preparation of the chrism may take place privately before the rite of consecration or may be done by the bishop during the liturgical service.

II. THE MINISTER

6. The consecration of the chrism belongs to the bishop alone.

7. If the use of the oil of catechumens is retained by the conferences of bishops, it is blessed by the bishop with the other oils during the chrism Mass.

In the case of the baptism of adults, however, priests have the faculty to bless the oil of catechumens before the anointing in the designated stage of the catechumenate.

8. The oil used for anointing the sick must be blessed for this purpose by the bishop or by a priest who has this faculty, either from the law or by special concession of the Apostolic See.

The law itself permits the following to bless the oil of the sick:
    a) those whom the law equates with diocesan bishops;
    b) in case of true necessity, any priest.

III. TIME OF BLESSING

9. The blessing of the oil and the consecration of the chrism are ordinarily celebrated by the bishop at the chrism Mass celebrated on Holy Thursday morning.

10. If it is difficult for the clergy and people to assemble with the bishop on Holy Thursday morning, the blessing may be held on an earlier day, near Easter, with the celebration of the proper chrism Mass.

IV. PLACE OF THE BLESSING IN THE MASS

11. According to the tradition of the Latin liturgy, the blessing of the oil of the sick takes place before the end of the eucharistic prayer; the blessing of the oil of catechumens and the consecration of the chrism, after communion.

12. For pastoral reasons, however, the entire rite of blessing may be celebrated after the liturgy of the word, according to the order described below.

BLESSING OF OILS AND CONSECRATION OF THE CHRISM

PREPARATIONS

13. For the blessing of oils the following preparations are made in addition to what is needed for Mass:

In the sacristy or other appropriate place:
—vessels of oils;
—balsam or perfume for the preparation of the chrism if the bishop wishes to mix the chrism during the liturgical service;
—bread, wine, and water for Mass, which are carried with the oils before the preparation of the gifts.

In the sanctuary:
—table for the vessels of oil, placed so that the people may see the entire rite easily and take part in it;
—chair for the bishop, if the blessing takes place in front of the altar.

RITE OF BLESSING

14. The chrism Mass is always concelebrated. It is desirable that there be some priests from the various sections of the diocese among the priests who concelebrate with the bishop and are his witnesses and the co-workers in the ministry of the holy chrism.

15. The preparation of the bishop, the concelebrants, and other ministers, their entrance into the church, and everything from the beginning of Mass until the end of the liturgy of the word take place as indicated in the rite of concelebration. The deacons who take part in the blessing of oils walk ahead of the concelebrating priests to the altar.

PROCESSION WITH THE OILS AND THE GIFTS

16. After the renewal of commitment to priestly service the deacons and ministers appointed to carry the oils or, in their absence, some priests and ministers together with the faithful who will carry the bread, wine, and water, go in procession to the sacristy or other place where the oils and other offerings have been prepared. Returning to the altar, they follow this order: first the minister carrying the vessel of

balsam, if the bishop wishes to prepare the chrism, then the minister with the vessel for the oil of the catechumens, if it is to be blessed, the minister with the vessel for the oil of the sick, lastly a deacon or priest carrying the oil for the chrism. The ministers who carry the bread, wine, and water for the celebration of the eucharist follow them.

HYMN

17. During the procession through the church, the choir leads the singing of the hymn "O Redeemer" or some other appropriate song, in place of the offertory song.

PRESENTATION OF THE OILS AND THE GIFTS

18. When the procession comes to the altar or the chair, the bishop receives the gifts. The deacon who carries the vessel of oil for the chrism shows it to the bishop, saying in a loud voice: **The oil for the holy chrism.** The bishop takes the vessel and gives it to one of the assisting deacons to place on the table. The same is done by those who carry the vessels for the oil of the sick and the oil of the catechumens. The first says: **The oil of the sick;** the second says: **The oil of catechumens.** The bishop takes the vessels in the same way, and the ministers place them on the table.

LITURGY OF THE EUCHARIST

19. Then the Mass continues, as in the rite of concelebration, until the end of the eucharistic prayer, unless the entire rite of blessing takes place immediately (see no. 12). In this case everything is done as described below (no. 26).

BLESSING OF THE OIL OF THE SICK

20. Before the bishop says **Through Christ our Lord/you give us all these gifts** in Eucharistic Prayer I, or the doxology **Through him** in the other eucharistic prayers, the one who carried the vessel for oil of the sick brings it to the altar and holds it in front of the bishop while he blesses the oil. The bishop says or sings this prayer:

Lord God, loving Father,
you bring healing to the sick
through your Son Jesus Christ.

Hear us as we pray to you in faith,
and send the Holy Spirit, man's Helper and Friend,
upon this oil, which nature has provided
to serve the needs of men.
May your blessing ✛
come upon all who are anointed with this oil,
that they may be freed from pain and illness
and made well again in body, mind, and soul.
Father, may this oil be blessed for our use
in the name of our Lord Jesus Christ
(who lives and reigns with you for ever and ever.
℟. Amen.)

The conclusion **Who lives and reigns with you** is said only when this blessing takes place outside the eucharistic prayer.

When Eucharistic Prayer I is used, the beginning of the prayer **Through Christ our Lord/you give us all these gifts** is changed to: **Through whom you give us all these gifts.**

After the blessing, the vessel with the oil of the sick is returned to its place, and the Mass continues until the communion rite is completed.

BLESSING OF THE OIL OF CATECHUMENS

21. After the prayer after communion, the ministers place the oils to be blessed on a table suitably located in the center of the sanctuary. The concelebrating priests stand around the bishop on either side, in a semicircle, and the other ministers stand behind him. The bishop then blesses the oil of catechumens, if it is to be blessed, and consecrates the chrism.

22. When everything is ready, the bishop faces the people and, with his hands extended, sings or says the following prayer:

Lord God, protector of all who believe in you,
bless ✛ this oil
and give wisdom and strength
to all who are anointed with it

in preparation for their baptism.
Bring them to a deeper understanding of the gospel,
help them to accept the challenge of Christian living,
and lead them to the joy of new birth
in the family of your Church.
We ask this through Christ our Lord.
℟. Amen.

CONSECRATION OF THE CHRISM

23. Then the bishop pours the balsam or perfume in the oil
and mixes the chrism in silence, unless this was done
beforehand.

INVITATION

24. After this he sings or says the invitation:

Let us pray
that God our almighty Father
will bless this oil
so that all who are anointed with it
may be inwardly transformed
and come to share in eternal salvation.

CONSECRATORY PRAYER

25. Then the bishop may breathe over the opening of the
vessel of chrism. With his hands extended, he sings or says
one of the following consecratory prayers.

God our maker,
source of all growth in holiness,
accept the joyful thanks and praise
we offer in the name of your Church.

In the beginning, at your command,
the earth produced fruit-bearing trees.
From the fruit of the olive tree
you have provided us with oil for holy chrism.
The prophet David sang of the life and joy
that the oil would bring us in the sacraments of your
    love.

After the avenging flood,
the dove returning to Noah with an olive branch
announced your gift of peace.
This was a sign of a greater gift to come.
Now the waters of baptism wash away the sins of
     men,
and by the anointing with olive oil
you make us radiant with your joy.

At your command,
Aaron was washed with water,
and your servant Moses, his brother,
anointed him priest.
This too foreshadowed greater things to come.
After your Son, Jesus Christ our Lord,
asked John for baptism in the waters of Jordan,
you sent the Spirit upon him
in the form of a dove
and by the witness of your own voice
you declared him to be your only, well-beloved Son.
In this you clearly fulfilled the prophecy of David,
that Christ would be anointed with the oil of gladness
beyond his fellow men.

All the celebrants extend their right hands toward the
chrism, without saying anything, until the end of the
prayer.

And so, Father, we ask you to bless ✝ this oil you
     have created.
Fill it with the power of your Holy Spirit
through Christ your Son.
It is from him that chrism takes its name
and with chrism you have anointed
for yourself priests and kings,
prophets and martyrs.

Make this chrism a sign of life and salvation
for those who are to be born again in the waters of
     baptism.
Wash away the evil they have inherited from sinful
     Adam,

and when they are anointed with this holy oil
make them temples of your glory,
radiant with the goodness of life
that has its source in you.

Through this sign of chrism
grant them royal, priestly, and prophetic honor,
and clothe them with incorruption.
Let this be indeed the chrism of salvation
for those who will be born again of water and the Holy Spirit.
May they come to share eternal life
in the glory of your kingdom.
We ask this through Christ our Lord.
℟. Amen.

Or:

Father, we thank you for the gifts
you have given us in your love:
we thank you for life itself and for the sacraments
that strengthen it and give it fuller meaning.

In the Old Covenant you gave your people
a glimpse of the power of this holy oil
and when the fullness of time had come
you brought that mystery to perfection
in the life of our Lord Jesus Christ, your Son.

By his suffering, dying, and rising to life
he saved the human race.
He sent your Spirit to fill the Church
with every gift needed to complete your saving work.

From that time forward,
through the sign of holy chrism,
you dispense your life and love to men.
By anointing them with the Spirit,
you strengthen all who have been reborn in baptism.
Through that anointing
you transform them into the likeness of Christ your Son
and give them a share

in his royal, priestly, and prophetic work.

All the concelebrants extend their right hands toward the chrism without saying anything, until the end of the prayer.

And so, Father, by the power of your love,
make this mixture of oil and perfume
a sign and source ✛ of your blessing.
Pour out the gifts of your Holy Spirit
on our brothers and sisters who will be anointed with
**   it.**
Let the splendor of holiness shine on the world
from every place and thing
signed with this oil.

Above all, Father, we pray
that through this sign of your anointing
you will grant increase to your Church
until it reaches the eternal glory
where you, Father, will be the all in all,
together with Christ your Son,
in the unity of the Holy Spirit,
for ever and ever.
℞. Amen.

26. When the entire rite of blessing of oils is to be celebrated after the liturgy of the word, at the end of the renewal of commitment to priestly service the bishop goes with the concelebrants to the table where the blessing of the oil of the sick and of the oil of the chrism are to take place, and everything is done as described above (nos. 20-25).

27. After the final blessing of the Mass, the bishop puts incense in the censer, and the procession to the sacristy is arranged.

The blessed oils are carried by the ministers immediately after the cross, and the choir and people sing some verses of the hymn "O Redeemer" or some other appropriate song.

28. In the sacristy the bishop may instruct the priests about the reverent use and safe custody of the holy oils.

RITE OF MARRIAGE

RITE OF MARRIAGE

SACRED CONGREGATION OF RITES

Prot. n. R 23/969

DECREE

The rite for celebrating marriage has been revised according to the norms of the Constitution on the Liturgy, in order that this rite might be enriched, more clearly signify the grace of the sacrament, and impart a knowledge of the obligation of the married couple.[a] This revision has been carried out by the Consilium for the Implementation of the Constitution on the Sacred Liturgy. By his apostolic authority, Pope Paul VI has approved this rite and ordered its publication. Therefore this Congregation, acting on the express mandate of the Pope, publishes this rite and directs that it be used from July 1, 1969.

Anything to the contrary notwithstanding.

From the Congregation of Rites, March 19, 1969, solemnity of Saint Joseph, husband of the Blessed Virgin Mary.

Benno Card. Gut
Prefect of S.R.C.
President of the Consilium

✝ Ferdinando Antonelli
Titular Archbishop of Idicra
Secretary of S.R.C.

[a]See *DOL* 1, no. 77.

INTRODUCTION

IMPORTANCE AND DIGNITY OF THE SACRAMENT OF MARRIAGE

1. In virtue of the sacrament of marriage, married Christians signify and share in the mystery of the unity and fruitful love that exists between Christ and his Church[1]; they thus help each other to attain holiness in their married life and in welcoming and rearing children; and they have their own special place and gift among the people of God.[2]

2. A marriage is established by the marriage covenant, the irrevocable consent that the spouses freely give to and receive from each other. This unique union of a man and woman and the good of the children impose total fidelity on each of them and the unbreakable unity of their bond. To make the indissoluble marriage covenant a clearer sign of this full meaning and a surer help in its fulfillment, Christ the Lord raised it to the dignity of a sacrament, modeled on his own nuptial bond with the Church.[3]

3. Christian couples, therefore, are to strive to nourish and develop their marriage by undivided affection, which wells up from the fountain of divine love: in a merging of the human and the divine, they remain faithful in body and in mind, in good times as in bad.[4]

4. By their very nature, the institution of marriage and wedded love have as their purpose the procreation and education of children and find in them their ultimate crown. Children are the most precious gift of a marriage and contribute most to the well-being of the parents. Therefore, married Christians, without in any way considering the other purposes of marriage of less account, should be steadfast and ready to cooperate with the love of the Creator and Savior, who through them will constantly enrich and enlarge his own family.[5]

---

[1] See Ephesians 5:32.
[2] See 1 Corinthians 7:7. LG no. 11 [DOL 4, no. 141].
[3] See GS no. 48 [DOL 19, no. 271].
[4] See GS nos. 48, 49 [DOL 19, nos. 271, 272].
[5] See GS nos. 48 [DOL 19, no. 271], 50.

5. A priest should bear in mind these doctrinal principles, both in his instructions to those preparing to be married and when giving the homily during the marriage ceremony; he should relate the homily to the text of the sacred readings.[6]

The bridal couple should, if necessary, be given a review of these fundamentals of Christian doctrine; then the catechesis for marriage should include the teachings on marriage and the family, on the sacrament itself and its rites, prayers, and readings. In this way the bridegroom and the bride will receive far greater benefit from the celebration of the sacrament.

6. In the celebration of marriage (which normally should be within Mass), certain elements should be stressed. The first is the liturgy of the word, which brings out the importance of Christian marriage in the history of salvation and the duties and responsibilities it involves in the sanctification of the couple and their children. Also to be emphasized are: the consent of the contracting parties, which the priest asks and receives; the special nuptial blessing on the bride, by which the priest implores God's blessing on the wedding covenant; and, finally, the reception of holy communion by the groom and the bride and by others present, which above all is the source of love and lifts us up into communion with our Lord and with one another.[7]

7. Priests should first of all strengthen and nourish the faith of those about to be married, for the sacrament of marriage presupposes and demands faith.[8]

CHOICE OF RITE

8. In a marriage between a Catholic and a baptized person who is not a Catholic, the rite of marriage outside Mass (nos. 39–54) shall be used. If the situation warrants and if the local Ordinary gives permission, the rite for celebrating marriage within Mass (nos. 19–38) may be used, except that communion is not given to the non-Catholic, since the general law does not allow it.

[6]See SC art. 52 [DOL 1, no. 52], SCR, Instr. InterOec, Sept. 26, 1964, no. 54 [DOL 23, no. 346].
[7]See AA no. 3 [DOL 16, no. 232]; LG no. 12 [DOL 4, no. 142].
[8]See SC art. 59 [DOL 1, no. 59].

In a marriage between a Catholic and one who is not baptized, the rite in nos. 55–66 of the ritual is to be followed.

9. Furthermore, priests should show special consideration for those who take part in liturgical celebrations or hear the Gospel only on the occasion of a wedding, either because they are not Catholics or because they are Catholics who rarely if ever take part in the eucharist or who apparently have lost their faith. Priests after all are ministers of Christ's Gospel to everyone.

10. In the celebration of marriage, apart from the liturgical laws providing for due honors to civil authorities, there is to be no preferential treatment of any private persons or classes of person, whether in the ceremonies or by external display.[9]

11. Whenever marriage is celebrated during Mass, white vestments are worn and the wedding Mass is used. If the marriage is celebrated on a Sunday or solemnity, the Mass of the day is used with the nuptial blessing and the special final blessing according to the circumstances.

The liturgy of the word as adapted to the marriage celebration, however, is a highly effective means for the catechesis on the sacrament of marriage and its duties. Therefore when the wedding Mass may not be held, one of the readings from the texts provided for the marriage celebration (nos. 67–105) may be chosen, except from Holy Thursday to Easter, on the solemnities of Epiphany, Ascension, Pentecost, or Corpus Christi, or on holydays of obligation. On the Sundays of the Christmas season and in Ordinary Time, the entire wedding Mass may be used in Masses that are not parish Masses.

When a marriage is celebrated during Advent or Lent or other days of penance, the parish priest should advise the couple to take into consideration the special nature of these liturgical seasons.

[9]See *SC* art. 32 [*DOL* 1, no. 32].

PREPARATION OF LOCAL RITUALS

12. Without prejudice to the faculty spoken of in no. 17 for regions where the Roman Ritual for marriage is used, particular rituals shall be prepared, suitable for the customs and needs of individual areas, in conformity with the norms of the Constitution on the Liturgy art. 63 b and 77.[a] Decisions on this matter are to be reviewed by the Apostolic See.

In making adaptations, the following points must be remembered.

13. The formularies of the Roman Ritual may be adapted or, as the case may be, supplemented (including the questions before the consent and the actual words of consent).

When the Roman Ritual has several optional formularies, local rituals may add others of the same type.

14. Within the actual rite of the sacrament of marriage, the arrangement of parts may be varied. If it seems more suitable, even the questions before the consent may be omitted as long as the assisting priest asks for and receives the consent of the contracting parties.

15. After the exchange of rings, the crowning or veiling of the bride may take place according to local custom.

In any region where the joining of hands or the blessing or exchange of rings does not fit in with the practice of the people, the conference of bishops may allow these rites to be omitted or other rites substituted.

16. As for the marriage customs of nations that are now receiving the Gospel for the first time, whatever is good and is not indissolubly bound up with superstition and error should be sympathetically considered and, if possible, preserved intact. Such things may in fact be taken over into the liturgy itself, as long as they harmonize with its true and authentic spirit.[10]

[a] See *DOL* 1, nos. 63 and 77.
[10] See *SC* art. 37 [*DOL* 1, no. 37].

RIGHT TO PREPARE A COMPLETELY NEW RITE

17. Each conference of bishops may draw up its own marriage rite suited to the usages of the place and people and approved by the Apostolic See. A necessary condition, however, is that in the rite the priest assisting at such marriages must ask for and receive the consent of the contracting parties[11] and the nuptial blessing should always be given.[12]

18. Among peoples where the marriage ceremonies customarily take place in the home, sometimes over a period of several days, their customs should be adapted to the Christian spirit and to the liturgy. In such cases the conference of bishops, according to the pastoral needs of the people, may allow the sacramental rite to be celebrated in the home.

[11]See SC art. 77 [DOL 1, no. 77].
[12]See SC art. 78 [DOL 1, no. 78].

CHAPTER I
RITE FOR CELEBRATING MARRIAGE
DURING MASS

ENTRANCE RITE

19. At the appointed time, the priest, vested for Mass, goes with the ministers to the door of the church or, if more suitable, to the altar. There he meets the bride and bridegroom in a friendly manner, showing that the Church shares their joy.

Where it is desirable that the rite of welcome be omitted, the celebration of marriage begins at once with the Mass.

20. If there is a procession to the altar, the ministers go first, followed by the priest, and then the bride and the bridegroom. According to local custom, they may be escorted by at least their parents and the two witnesses. Meanwhile, the entrance song is sung.

LITURGY OF THE WORD

21. The liturgy of the word is celebrated according to the rubrics. There may be three readings, the first of them from the Old Testament.

22. After the gospel, the priest gives a homily drawn from the sacred text. He speaks about the mystery of Christian marriage, the dignity of wedded love, the grace of the sacrament and the responsibilities of married people, keeping in mind the circumstances of this particular marriage.

RITE OF MARRIAGE

INTRODUCTION

23. All stand, including the bride and bridegroom, and the priest addresses them in these or similar words:

My dear friends,* you have come together in this church so that the Lord may seal and strengthen your love in the presence of the Church's minister and this community. Christ abundantly blesses this love. He has already consecrated you in baptism and now he enriches and strengthens you by a special sacrament so that you may assume the duties of marriage in mutual and lasting fidelity. And so, in the presence of the Church, I ask you to state your intentions.

QUESTIONS

24. The priest then questions them about their freedom of choice, faithfulness to each other, and the acceptance and upbringing of children:

N. and N., have you come here freely and without reservation to give yourselves to each other in marriage?

Will you love and honor each other as man and wife for the rest of your lives?

The following question may be omitted if, for example, the couple is advanced in years.

Will you accept children lovingly from God, and bring them up according to the law of Christ and his Church?

Each answers the questions separately.

CONSENT

25. The priest invites the couple to declare their consent:

Since it is your intention to enter into marriage, join your right hands, and declare your consent before God and his Church.

They join hands.

*At the discretion of the priest, other words which seem more suitable under the circumstances, such as **friends** or **dearly beloved** or **brethren** may be used. This also applies to parallel instances in the liturgy.

The bridegroom says:

I, N., take you, N., to be my wife. I promise to be true to you in good times and in bad, in sickness and in health. I will love you and honor you all the days of my life.

The bride says:

I, N., take you, N., to be my husband. I promise to be true to you in good times and in bad, in sickness and in health. I will love you and honor you all the days of my life.

If, however, it seems preferable for pastoral reasons, the priest may obtain consent from the couple through questions.

First he asks the bridegroom:
N., do you take N. to be your wife? Do you promise to be true to her in good times and in bad, in sickness and in health, to love her and honor her all the days of your life?
The bridegroom: **I do.**

Then he asks the bride:
N., do you take N. to be your husband? Do you promise to be true to him in good times and in bad, in sickness and in health, to love him and honor him all the days of your life?
The bride: **I do.**

If pastoral necessity demands it, the conference of bishops may decree, in virtue of the faculty in no. 17, that the priest should always obtain the consent of the couple through questions.

In the dioceses of the United States, the following form may also be used:

I, N., take you, N., for my lawful wife, to have and to hold, from this day forward, for better, for worse, for

richer, for poorer, in sickness and in health, until death do us part.

I, N., take you, N., for my lawful husband, to have and to hold, from this day forward, for better, for worse, for richer, for poorer, in sickness and in health, until death do us part.

If it seems preferable for pastoral reasons for the priest to obtain consent from the couple through questions, in the dioceses of the United States the following alternative form may be used:

N., do you take N. for your lawful wife (husband), to have and to hold, from this day forward, for better, for worse, for richer, for poorer, in sickness and in health, until death do you part?
The bride (bridegroom): I do.

26. Receiving their consent, the priest says:

You have declared your consent before the Church.
May the Lord in his goodness strengthen your consent
and fill you both with his blessings.
What God has joined, men must not divide.
R̷. Amen.

BLESSING OF RINGS
27. Priest:

May the Lord bless ✛ these rings
which you give to each other
as the sign of your love and fidelity.
R̷. Amen.

Other forms of the blessing of the rings, nos. 110 or 111, may be chosen.

EXCHANGE OF RINGS
28. The bridegroom places his wife's ring on her ring finger. He may say:

N., take this ring as a sign of my love and fidelity. In

the name of the Father, and of the Son, and of the Holy Spirit.

The bride places her husband's ring on his ring finger. She may say:

N., take this ring as a sign of my love and fidelity. In the name of the Father, and of the Son, and of the Holy Spirit.

GENERAL INTERCESSIONS

29. The general intercessions (prayer of the faithful) follow, using formulas approved by the conference of bishops. If the rubrics call for it, the profession of faith is said after the general intercessions.

LITURGY OF THE EUCHARIST

30. The Order of Mass is followed, with the following changes. During the offertory, the bride and bridegroom may bring the bread and wine to the altar.

31. Proper preface (see nos. 115-117).

32. When the Roman canon is used, the special **Hanc igitur** is said (no. 118).

NUPTIAL BLESSING

33. After the Lord's Prayer, the prayer **Deliver us** is omitted. The priest faces the bride and bridegroom and, with hands joined, says:

My dear friends, let us turn to the Lord and pray that he will bless with his grace this woman (or N.) now married in Christ to this man (or N.) and that (through the sacrament of the body and blood of Christ,) he will unite in love the couple he has joined in this holy bond.

All pray silently for a short while. Then the priest extends his hands and continues:

Father, by your power you have made everything out
    of nothing.
In the beginning you created the universe
and made mankind in your own likeness.
You gave man the constant help of woman
so that man and woman should no longer be two,
    but one flesh,
and you teach us that what you have united
may never be divided.

Or:

Father, you have made the union of man and wife so
    holy a mystery
that it symbolizes the marriage of Christ and his
    Church.

Or:

Father, by your plan man and woman are united,
and married life has been established
as the one blessing that was not forfeited by original
    sin
or washed away in the flood.

Look with love upon this woman, your daughter,
now joined to her husband in marriage.
She asks your blessing.
Give her the grace of love and peace.
May she always follow the example of the holy
    women
whose praises are sung in the scriptures.

May her husband put his trust in her
and recognize that she is his equal
and the heir with him to the life of grace.
May he always honor her and love her
as Christ loves his bride, the Church.

Father, keep them always true to your
    commandments.
Keep them faithful in marriage
and let them be living examples of Christian life.

Give them the strength which comes from the gospel
so that they may be witnesses of Christ to others.
(Bless them with children
and help them to be good parents.
May they live to see their children's children.)
And, after a happy old age,
grant them fullness of life with the saints
in the kingdom of heaven.

We ask this through Christ our Lord.
R̷. **Amen.**

34. If one or both of the parties will not be receiving
communion, the words in the introduction to the nuptial
blessing, **through the sacrament of the body and blood of
Christ,** may be omitted.

If desired, in the prayer **Father, by your power,** two of the
first three paragraphs may be omitted, keeping only the
paragraph which corresponds to the reading of the Mass.

In the last paragraph of this prayer, the words in parentheses may be omitted whenever circumstances suggest it,
if, for example, the couple is advanced in years.

Other forms of the nuptial blessing, no. 120 or 121, may be
chosen.

SIGN OF PEACE

35. At the words **Let us offer each other the sign of peace,**
the married couple and all present show their peace and
love for one another in an appropriate way.

COMMUNION

36. The married couple may receive communion under
both kinds.

SOLEMN BLESSING

37. Before blessing the people at the end of Mass, the priest
blesses the bride and bridegroom, using one of the forms
in nos. 125-127.

Or:
In the dioceses of the United States, the following form
may be used:

May almighty God, with his Word of blessing, unite
your hearts in the never-ending bond of pure love.
℟. Amen.

May your children bring you happiness, and may
your generous love for them be returned to you, many
times over.
℟. Amen.

May the peace of Christ live always in your hearts and
in your home.
May you have true friends to stand by you, both in
joy and in sorrow.
May you be ready and willing to help and comfort all
who come to you in need.
And may the blessings promised to the compassionate
be yours in abundance.
℟. Amen.

May you find happiness and satisfaction in your
work.
May daily problems never cause you undue anxiety,
nor the desire for earthly possessions dominate
your lives.
But may your hearts' first desire be always the good
things waiting for you in the life of heaven.
℟. Amen.

May the Lord bless you with many happy years
together, so that you may enjoy the rewards of a
good life.
And after you have served him loyally in his kingdom
on earth, may he welcome you to his eternal
kingdom in heaven.
℟. Amen.

And may almighty God bless you all, the Father, and
the Son, ✛ and the Holy Spirit.
℟. Amen.

38. If two or more marriages are celebrated at the same
time, the questioning before the consent, the consent itself,

and the acceptance of consent shall always be done individually for each couple; the rest, including the nuptial blessing, is said once for all, using the plural form.

CHAPTER II
RITE FOR CELEBRATING MARRIAGE OUTSIDE MASS [13]

ENTRANCE RITE

39. At the appointed time, the priest, wearing surplice and white stole (or a white cope, if desired), proceeds with the ministers to the door of the church, or, if more suitable, to the altar. There he greets the bride and bridegroom in a friendly manner, showing that the Church shares their joy.

Where it is desirable that the rite of welcome be omitted, the celebration of matrimony begins at once with the liturgy of the word.

40. If there is a procession to the altar, the ministers go first, followed by the priest, and then the bride and the bridegroom. According to local custom, they may be escorted by at least their parents and the two witnesses. Meanwhile, the entrance song is sung.

Then the people are greeted, and the prayer is offered, unless a brief pastoral exhortation seems more desirable. [14] See nos. 106-109.

LITURGY OF THE WORD

41. The liturgy of the word takes place in the usual manner. There may be three readings, the first of them from the Old Testament. See nos. 67-105.

42. After the gospel, the priest gives a homily drawn from the sacred text. He speaks about the mystery of Christian marriage, the dignity of wedded love, the grace of the

---

[13] According to the words of the Constitution on the Sacred Liturgy, *Sacrosanctum Concilium*, repeated in no. 6 of the introduction above, the celebration of marriage normally takes place during Mass. Nevertheless, a good reason can excuse from the celebration of Mass (Sacred Congregation of Rites, Instruction, *Inter Oecumenici*, no. 70: *AAS* 56 [1964] 893), and sometimes even urges that Mass should be omitted. In this case the rite for celebrating marriage outside Mass should be used.

[14] Sacred Congregation of Rites, Instruction, *Inter Oecumenici*, no. 74: *AAS* 56 (1964) 894.

sacrament, and the responsibilities of married people, keeping in mind the circumstances of this particular marriage.

RITE OF MARRIAGE

43. All stand, including the bride and bridegroom, and the priest addresses them in these or similar words:

INTRODUCTION

My dear friends, you have come together in this church so that the Lord may seal and strengthen your love in the presence of the Church's minister and this community. Christ abundantly blesses this love. He has already consecrated you in baptism and now he enriches and strengthens you by a special sacrament so that you may assume the duties of marriage in mutual and lasting fidelity. And so, in the presence of the Church, I ask you to state your intentions.

QUESTIONS

44. The priest then questions them about their freedom of choice, faithfulness to each other, and the acceptance and upbringing of children:

If two or more marriages are celebrated at the same time, see no. 38, above.

N. and N., have you come here freely and without reservation to give yourselves to each other in marriage?

Will you love and honor each other as man and wife for the rest of your lives?

The following question may be omitted if, for example, the couple is advanced in years.

Will you accept children lovingly from God, and bring them up according to the law of Christ and his Church?

Each answers the questions separately.

CONSENT

45. The priest invites them to declare their consent:

Since it is is your intention to enter into marriage, join your right hands, and declare your consent before God and his Church.

They join hands.

The bridegroom says:
I, N., take you, N., to be my wife. I promise to be true to you in good times and in bad, in sickness and in health. I will love you and honor you all the days of my life.

The bride says:
I, N., take you, N., to be my husband. I promise to be true to you in good times and in bad, in sickness and in health. I will love you and honor you all the days of my life.

If, however, it seems preferable for pastoral reasons, the priest may obtain consent from the couple through questions. First he asks the bridegroom:

N., do you take N. to be your wife? Do you promise to be true to her in good times and in bad, in sickness and in health, to love her and honor her all the days of your life?
The bridegroom: **I do.**

Then he asks the bride:
N., do you take N. to be your husband? Do you promise to be true to him in good times and in bad, in sickness and in health, to love him and honor him all the days of your life?
The bride: **I do.**

If pastoral necessity demands it, the conference of bishops may decree, in virtue of the faculty in no. 17, that the priest should always obtain the consent of the couple through questions.

In the dioceses of the United States, the following form may also be used:

I, N., take you, N., for my lawful wife, to have and to

hold, from this day forward, for better, for worse, for richer, for poorer, in sickness and in health, until death do us part.

I, N., take you N., for my lawful husband, to have and to hold, from this day forward, for better, for worse, for richer, for poorer, in sickness and in health, until death do us part.

If it seems preferable for pastoral reasons for the priest to obtain consent from the couple through questions, in the dioceses of the United States the following alternative form may be used:

N., do you take N. for your lawful wife (husband), to have and to hold, from this day forward, for better, for worse, for richer, for poorer, in sickness and in health, until death do you part?
The bride (bridegroom): **I do.**

46. Receiving their consent, the priest says:

You have declared your consent before the Church. May the Lord in his goodness strengthen your consent and fill you both with his blessings.

What God has joined, men must not divide.
R⁷. Amen.

BLESSING OF RINGS
47. Priest:

May the Lord bless ✝ these rings which you give to each other as the sign of your love and fidelity.
R⁷. Amen.

For other forms of the blessing of rings, see nos. 110, 111.

EXCHANGE OF RINGS
48. The bridegroom places his wife's ring on her ring finger. He may say:

N., take this ring as a sign of my love and fidelity. In the name of the Father, and of the Son, and of the Holy Spirit.

The bride places her husband's ring on his ring finger. She may say:

N., take this ring as a sign of my love and fidelity. In the name of the Father, and of the Son, and of the Holy Spirit.

GENERAL INTERCESSIONS AND NUPTIAL BLESSING

49. The general intercessions (prayer of the faithful) and the blessing of the couple take place in this order:

a) First the priest uses the invitatory of any blessing of the couple [see the first part of no. 33, 120, and 121] or any other, taken from the approved formulas for the general intercessions.

b) Immediately after the invitatory, there can be either a brief silence, or a series of petitions from the prayer of the faithful with responses by the people. All the petitions should be in harmony with the blessing which follows, but should not duplicate it.

c) Then, omitting the prayer that concludes the prayer of the faithful, the priest extends his hands and blesses the bride and bridegroom.

50. This blessing may be **Father, by your power,** (no. 33) or another from nos. 120 or 121.

CONCLUSION OF THE CELEBRATION

LORD'S PRAYER AND BLESSING

51. The entire rite can be concluded with the Lord's Prayer and the blessing, whether with the simple form, **May almighty God,** or with one of the forms in nos. 125-127.

52. If two or more marriages are celebrated at the same time, the questioning before the consent, the consent itself and the acceptance of consent shall always be done individually for each couple; the rest, including the nuptial blessing, is said once for all using the plural form.

53. The rite described above should be used by a deacon who, when a priest cannot be present, has been delegated by the bishop or pastor to assist at the celebration of marriage, and to give the Church's blessing.[15]

---

[15]Paul VI, motu proprio, *Sacrum Diaconatus Ordinem*, June 18, 1967, no. 22, 4: *AAS* 59 (1967) 702.

54. If Mass cannot be celebrated and communion is to be distributed during the rite, the Lord's Prayer is said first. After communion, a reverent silence may be observed for a while, or a psalm or song of praise may be sung or recited. Then comes the prayer, **Lord, we who have shared** (no. 123, if only the bride and bridegroom receive), or the prayer, **God, who in this wondrous sacrament** or other suitable prayer.

The rite ends with a blessing, either the simple formula, **May almighty God bless you,** or one of the forms in nos. 125-127.

CHAPTER III
RITE FOR CELEBRATING MARRIAGE BETWEEN A CATHOLIC AND AN UNBAPTIZED PERSON

If marriage is celebrated between a Catholic and unbaptized person (either a catechumen or a non-Christian), the rite may be performed in the church or some other suitable place and takes the following form.

RITE OF WELCOME

55. At the appointed time, the priest, wearing surplice and white stole (or a white cope if desired), proceeds with the ministers to the door of the church or to another appropriate place and greets the bride and the bridegroom.

Where it is desirable that the rite of welcome be omitted, the celebration of marriage begins at once with the liturgy of the word.

LITURGY OF THE WORD

56. The liturgy of the word takes place in the usual manner. There may be three readings, the first of them from the Old Testament. If circumstances make it more desirable, there may be a single reading. See nos. 67-105.

HOMILY

57. A homily, drawn from the sacred text, is given and should speak of the obligations of marriage and other appropriate points.

RITE OF MARRIAGE

INTRODUCTION

58. All stand, including the bride and the bridegroom. The priest addresses them in these or similar words:

My dear friends, you have come together in this church so that the Lord may seal and strengthen your love in the presence of the Church's minister and this community.

In this way you will be strengthened to keep mutual and lasting faith with each other and to carry out the other duties of marriage. And so, in the presence of the Church, I ask you to state your intentions.

QUESTIONS

59. The priest then questions them about their freedom of choice, faithfulness to each other, and the acceptance and upbringing of children:

N. and N., have you come here freely and without reservation to give yourselves to each other in marriage?

Will you love and honor each other as man and wife for the rest of your lives?

The following question may be omitted if, for example, the couple is advanced in years.

Will you accept children lovingly from God, and bring them up according to the law of Christ and his Church?

Each answers the questions separately.

CONSENT

60. The priest invites them to declare their consent:

Since it is your intention to enter into marriage, join your right hands, and declare your consent before God and his Church.

They join hands.

The bridegroom says:
I, N., take you, N., to be my wife. I promise to be true to you in good times and in bad, in sickness and in health. I will love you and honor you all the days of my life.

The bride says:
I, N., take you, N., to be my husband. I promise to be true to you in good times and in bad, in sickness and in health. I will love you and honor you all the days of my life.

If, however, it seems perferable for pastoral reasons, the priest may obtain consent from the couple through questions. First he asks the bridegroom:

N., do you take N. to be your wife? Do you promise to be true to her in good times and in bad, in sickness and in health, to love her and honor her all the days of your life?
The bridegroom: **I do.**

Then he asks the bride:
N., do you take N. to be your husband? Do you promise to be true to him in good times and in bad, in sickness and in health, to love him and honor him all the days of your life?
The bride: **I do.**

If pastoral necessity demands it, the conference of bishops may decree, in virtue of the faculty in no. 17, that the priest should always obtain the consent of the couple through questions.

In the dioceses of the United States, the following form may also be used:

I, N., take you, N., for my lawful wife, to have and to hold, from this day forward, for better, for worse, for richer, for poorer, in sickness and in health, until death do us part.

I, N., take you, N., for my lawful husband, to have and to hold, from this day forward, for better, for worse, for richer, for poorer, in sickness and in health, until death do us part.

If it seems preferable for pastoral reasons for the priest to obtain consent from the couple through questions, in the dioceses of the United States the following alternative form may be used:

N., do you take N. for your lawful wife (husband), to have and to hold, from this day forward, for better, for worse, for richer, for poorer, in sickness and in health, until death do you part?
The bride (bridegroom): **I do.**

61. Receiving their consent, the priest says:

You have declared your consent before the Church. May the Lord in his goodness strengthen your consent and fill you both with his blessings.

What God has joined, men must not divide.
R̷. Amen.

BLESSING OF RINGS

62. If circumstances so require, the blessing and exchange of rings can be omitted. If this rite is observed, the priest says:

May the Lord bless ✝ these rings which you give to each other as the sign of your love and fidelity.
R̷. Amen.

For other forms of the blessing of rings, see nos. 110-111.

EXCHANGE OF RINGS

63. The bridegroom places his wife's ring on her ring finger. He may say:

N., take this ring as a sign of my love and fidelity. In the name of the Father, and of the Son, and of the Holy Spirit.

The bride places her husband's ring on his ring finger. She may say:

N., take this ring as a sign of my love and fidelity. In the name of the Father, and of the Son, and of the Holy Spirit.

GENERAL INTERCESSIONS AND NUPTIAL BLESSING

64. If circumstances so require, the blessing of the bride and bridegroom can be omitted. If used, it is combined with the general intercessions (prayer of the faithful) in this order:

a) First the priest uses the invitatory of any blessing of the couple (see the first part of nos. 33, 120, and 121) or any other, taken from any approved formula for the general intercessions.

b) Immediately after the invitatory, there can be either a brief period of silence, or a series of petitions from the prayer of the faithful with responses by the people. All the petitions should be in harmony with the blessing which follows, but should not duplicate it.

c) Then, omitting the prayer that concludes the prayer of the faithful, the priest blesses the bride and the bridegroom:

65. Facing them, he joins his hands and says:

My brothers and sisters, let us ask God for his continued blessings upon this bridegroom and his bride.

All pray silently for a short while. Then the priest extends his hands and continues:

**Holy Father, creator of the universe,
maker of man and woman in your likeness,
source of blessing for married life,
we humbly pray to you for this bride
who today is united with her husband in the bond of
      marriage.**

**May your fullest blessing come upon her and her
      husband
so that they may together rejoice in your gift of
      married love.
May they be noted for their good lives,
(and be parents filled with virtue).**

**Lord, may they both praise you when they are happy
and turn to you in their sorrows.
May they be glad that you help them in their work,
and know that you are with them in their need.
May they reach old age in the company of their
      friends,
and come at last to the kingdom of heaven.
We ask this through Christ our Lord.
R̷. Amen.**

CONCLUSION OF THE CELEBRATION

LORD'S PRAYER AND BLESSING

66. The rite may be concluded with the Lord's Prayer (or, if

the nuptial blessing has been omitted, another prayer by the priest) and a blessing using the customary form, **May almighty God bless you** or another formula from nos. 125-127.

CHAPTER IV

TEXTS FOR USE IN THE MARRIAGE RITE AND IN THE WEDDING MASS

I. SCRIPTURE READINGS

In the wedding Mass and in marriages celebrated without Mass, the following selections may be used:

OLD TESTAMENT READINGS

67. Genesis 1:26-28, 31a
Male and female he created them.

68. Genesis 2:18-24
And they will be two in one flesh.

69. Genesis 24:48-51, 58-67
Isaac loved Rebekah, and so he was consoled for the loss of his mother.

70. Tobit 7:9-10, 11-15
May God join you together and fill you with his blessings.

71. Tobit 8:5-10
May God bring us to old age together.

72. Song of Songs 2:8-10, 14, 16a; 8:6-7a
For love is as strong as death.

73. Ecclesiasticus 26:1-4, 16-21 (Greek 1-4, 13-16)
Like the sun rising is the beauty of a good wife in a well-kept house.

74. Jeremiah 31:31-32a, 33-34a
I will make a new covenant with the House of Israel and Judah.

NEW TESTAMENT READINGS

75. Romans 8:31b-35, 37-39
Who will separate us from the love of Christ?

76. Romans 12:1-2, 9-18 (longer) or **Romans 12:1-2, 9-13** (shorter)

Offer to God your bodies as a living and holy sacrifice, truly
pleasing to him.

77. 1 Corinthians 6:13c-15a, 17-20
Your body is a temple of the Spirit.

78. 1 Corinthians 12:31; 13:8a
If I am without love, it will do me no good whatever.

79. Ephesians 5:2a, 21-33 (longer) or 2a, 25-32 (shorter)
This mystery has many implications, and I am saying it
applies to Christ and the Church.

80. Colossians 3:12-17
Above all have love, which is the bond of perfection.

81. 1 Peter 3:1-9
You should agree with one another, be sympathetic and
love the brothers.

82. 1 John 3:18-24
Our love is to be something real and active.

83. 1 John 4:7-12
God is love.

84. Revelation 19:1, 5-9a
Happy are those who are invited to the wedding feast of the
Lamb.

RESPONSORIAL PSALMS

85. Psalm 33:12 and 18, 20-21, 22
R̶. (5b) **The earth is full of the goodness of the Lord.**

86. Psalm 34:2-3, 4-5, 6-7, 8-9
R̶. (2a) **I will bless the Lord at all times.**
Or: (9a) **Taste and see the goodness of the Lord.**

87. Psalm 103:1-2, 8 and 13, 17-18a
R̶. (8a) **The Lord is kind and merciful.**
Or: (17) **The Lord's kindness is everlasting to those
who fear him.**

88. Psalm 112:1-2, 3-4, 5-7a, 7bc-8, 9
R̶. (1b) **Happy are those who do what the Lord commands.**
Or: **Alleluia.**

89. Psalm 128:1-2, 3, 4-5
R̶. (1a) **Happy are those who fear the Lord.**

Or: (4) **See how the Lord blesses those who fear him.**

90. Psalm 145:8-9, 10 and 15, 17-18
R⁷. (9a) **The Lord is compassionate to all his creatures.**

91. Psalm 148:1-2, 3-4, 9-10, 11-12ab, 12c-14a
R⁷. (12c) **Let all praise the name of the Lord.**
Or: **Alleluia.**

ALLELUIA VERSE AND VERSE BEFORE THE GOSPEL

92. 1 John 4:8 and 11
God is love;
let us love one another as he has loved us.

93. 1 John 4:12
If we love one another
God will live in us in perfect love.

94. 1 John 4:16
He who lives in love, lives in God, and God in him.

95. 1 John 4:7b
Everyone who loves is born of God and knows him.

GOSPELS

96. **Matthew 5:1-12**
Rejoice and be glad, for your reward will be great in heaven.

97. **Matthew 5:13-16**
You are the light of the world.

98. **Matthew 7:21, 24-29** (longer) or **21, 24-25** (shorter)
He built his house on rock.

99. **Matthew 19:3-6**
So then, what God has united, man must not divide.

100. **Matthew 22:35-40**
This is the greatest and the first commandment. The second
is similar to it.

101. **Mark 10:6-9**
They are no longer two, therefore, but one body.

102. **John 2:1-11**
This was the first of the signs given by Jesus; it was given at
Cana in Galilee.

103. **John 15:9-12**
Remain in my love.

104. **John 15:12-16**
This is my commandment: love one another.

105. **John 17:20-26** (longer) or **20-23** (shorter)
May they be completely one.

II. OPENING PRAYERS

106.
Father,
you have made the bond of marriage
a holy mystery,
a symbol of Christ's love for his Church.
Hear our prayers for N. and N.
With faith in you and in each other
they pledge their love today.
May their lives always bear witness
to the reality of that love.

We ask this through our Lord Jesus Christ, your Son,
who lives and reigns with you and the Holy Spirit,
one God, for ever and ever.

107.
Father,
hear our prayers for N. and N.,
who today are united in marriage before your altar.
Give them your blessing.
and strengthen their love for each other.

We ask this through our Lord Jesus Christ, your Son,
who lives and reigns with you and the Holy Spirit,
one God, for ever and ever.

108.
Almighty God,
hear our prayers for N. and N.,
who have come here today

to be united in the sacrament of marriage.
Increase their faith in you and in each other,
and through them bless your Church (with Christian
    children).

We ask this through our Lord Jesus Christ, your Son,
who lives and reigns with you and the Holy Spirit,
one God, for ever and ever.

109.
Father,
when you created mankind
you willed that man and wife should be one.
Bind N. and N.
in the loving union of marriage;
and make their love fruitful
so that they may be living witnesses
to your divine love in the world.

We ask this through our Lord Jesus Christ, your Son,
who lives and reigns with you and the Holy Spirit,
one God, for ever and ever.

III. BLESSING OF RINGS

110.
Lord, bless these rings which we bless ✝ in your
    name.
Grant that those who wear them
may always have a deep faith in each other.
May they do your will
and always live together
in peace, good will, and love.

We ask this through Christ our Lord.
℟. Amen.

111.
Lord,
bless ✝ and consecrate N. and N.

in their love for each other.
May these rings be a symbol
of true faith in each other,
and always remind them of their love.

We ask this through Christ our Lord.
R̷. Amen.

IV. PRAYERS OVER THE GIFTS

112.
Lord,
accept our offering
for this newly-married couple, N. and N.
By your love and providence you have brought them
      together;
now bless them all the days of their married life.

We ask this through Christ our Lord.

113.
Lord,
accept the gifts we offer you
on this happy day.
In your fatherly love
watch over and protect N. and N.,
whom you have united in marriage.

We ask this through Christ our Lord.

114.
Lord,
hear our prayers
and accept the gifts we offer for N. and N.
Today you have made them one in the sacrament of
      marriage.
May the mystery of Christ's unselfish love,
which we celebrate in this eucharist,
increase their love for you and for each other.

We ask this through Christ our Lord.

V. PREFACES

115.

Father, all-powerful and ever-living God,
we do well always and everywhere to give you
     thanks.
By this sacrament your grace unites man and woman
in an unbreakable bond of love and peace.

You have designed the chaste love of husband and
     wife
for the increase both of the human family
and of your own family born in baptism.

You are the loving Father of the world of nature;
you are the loving Father of the new creation of grace.
In Christian marriage you bring together the two
     orders of creation:
nature's gift of children enriches the world
and your grace enriches also your Church.

Through Christ the choirs of angels
and all the saints
praise and worship your glory.
May our voices blend with theirs
as we join in their unending hymn:

116.

Father, all-powerful and ever-living God,
we do well always and everywhere to give you thanks
through Jesus Christ our Lord.

Through him you entered into a new covenant with
     your people.
You restored man to grace in the saving mystery of
     redemption.
You gave him a share in the divine life
through his union with Christ.
You made him an heir of Christ's eternal glory.

This outpouring of love in the new covenant of grace

is symbolized in the marriage covenant
that seals the love of husband and wife
and reflects your divine plan of love.

And so, with the angels and all the saints in heaven
we proclaim your glory
and join in their unending hymn of praise:

117.
Father, all-powerful and ever-living God,
we do well always and everywhere to give you
    thanks.

You created man in love to share your divine life.
We see his high destiny in the love of husband
    and wife,
which bears the imprint of your own divine love.

Love is man's origin,
love is his constant calling,
love is his fulfillment in heaven.

The love of man and woman
is made holy in the sacrament of marriage,
and becomes the mirror of your everlasting love.

Through Christ the choirs of angels
and all the saints
praise and worship your glory.
May our voices blend with theirs
as we join in their unending hymn:

VI. HANC IGITUR

118. The words in parentheses may be omitted if desired.

Father, accept this offering
from your whole family
and from N. and N., for whom we now pray.
You have brought them to their wedding day:
grant them (the gift and joy of children and)

a long and happy life together.

[Through Christ our Lord. Amen.]

VII. NUPTIAL BLESSING

119.

Father, by your power, with the proper invitatory, as in no. 33.

120. In the following prayer, either the paragraph **Holy Father, you created mankind,** or the paragraph **Father, to reveal the plan of your love,** may be omitted, keeping only the paragraph which corresponds to the reading of the Mass.

The priest faces the bride and bridegroom and, with hands joined, says:

Let us pray to the Lord for N. and N.
who come to God's altar at the beginning of their
married life
so that they may always be united in love for each
other
(as now they share in the body and blood of Christ).

All pray silently for a short while. Then the priest extends his hands and continues:

Holy Father, you created mankind in your own image
and made man and woman to be joined as husband
and wife
in union of body and heart
and so fulfill their mission in this world.

Father, to reveal the plan of your love,
you made the union of husband and wife
an image of the covenant between you and your
people.
In the fulfillment of this sacrament,
the marriage of Christian man and woman
is a sign of the marriage between Christ and the
Church.

Father, stretch out your hand, and bless N. and N.

Lord, grant that as they begin to live this sacrament
they may share with each other the gifts of your love
and become one in heart and mind
as witnesses to your presence in their marriage.
Help them to create a home together
(and give them children to be formed by the gospel
and to have a place in your family).

Give your blessings to N., your daughter,
so that she may be a good wife (and mother),
caring for the home,
faithful in love for her husband,
generous and kind.
Give your blessings to N., your son,
so that he may be a faithful husband
(and a good father).
Father, grant that as they come together to your table
    on earth,
so they may one day have the joy of sharing your feast
    in heaven.

We ask this through Christ our Lord.
R⁷. Amen.

121. The priest faces the bride and bridegroom and, with
hands joined, says:

My dear friends, let us ask God
for his continued blessings upon this bridegroom and
    his bride (or N. and N.).

All pray silently for a short while. Then the priest extends
his hands and continues:

Holy Father, creator of the universe,
maker of man and woman in your own likeness,
source of blessing for married life,
we humbly pray to you for this woman
who today is united with her husband in this
    sacrament of marriage.

May your fullest blessing come upon her and her
    husband
so that they may together rejoice in your gift of
    married love
(and enrich your Church with their children).

Lord, may they both praise you when they are happy
and turn to you in their sorrows.
May they be glad that you help them in their work
and know that you are with them in their need.
May they pray to you in the community of the
    Church,
and be your witnesses in the world.
May they reach old age in the company of their
    friends,
and come at last to the kingdom of heaven.

We ask this through Christ our Lord.
℟. Amen.

VIII. PRAYERS AFTER COMMUNION

122.
Lord,
in your love
you have given us this eucharist
to unite us with one another and with you.
As you have made N. and N.
one in this sacrament of marriage
(and in the sharing of the one bread and the one cup),
so now make them one in love for each other.

We ask this through Christ our Lord.

123.
Lord,
we who have shared the food of your table
pray for our friends N. and N.,
whom you have joined together in marriage.
Keep them close to you always.
May their love for each other

proclaim to all the world
their faith in you.

We ask this through Christ our Lord.

124.
Almighty God,
may the sacrifice we have offered
and the eucharist we have shared
strengthen the love of N. and N.,
and give us all your fatherly aid.

We ask this through Christ our Lord.

IX. BLESSING AT THE END OF MASS

125.
God the eternal Father keep you in love with each
    other,
so that the peace of Christ may stay with you
and be always in your home.
R̷. Amen.

May (your children bless you,)
your friends console you
and all men live in peace with you.
R̷. Amen.

May you always bear witness to the love of God in
    this world
so that the afflicted and the needy
will find in you generous friends,
and welcome you into the joys of heaven.
R̷. Amen.

And may almighty God bless you all,
the Father, and the Son, ✝ and the Holy Spirit.
R̷. Amen.

126.
May God, the almighty Father,
give you his joy

and bless you (in your children).
R̷. Amen.

May the only Son of God have mercy on you
and help you in good times and in bad.
R̷. Amen.

May the Holy Spirit of God
always fill your hearts with his love.
R̷. Amen.

And may almighty God bless you all,
the Father, and the Son, ✝ and the Holy Spirit.
R̷. Amen.

127.

May the Lord Jesus, who was a guest at the wedding
      in Cana,
bless you and your families and friends.
R̷. Amen.

May Jesus, who loved his Church to the end,
always fill your hearts with his love.
R̷. Amen.

May he grant that, as you believe in his resurrection,
so you may wait for him in joy and hope.
R̷. Amen.

And may almighty God bless you all,
the Father, and the Son, ✝ and the Holy Spirit.
R̷. Amen.

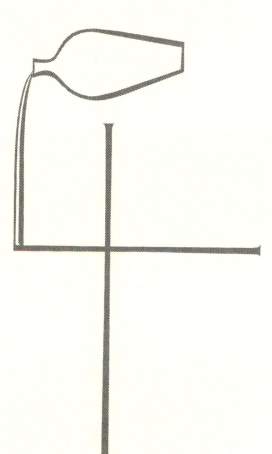

PASTORAL CARE OF THE SICK:
RITES OF ANOINTING AND VIATICUM

PASTORAL CARE OF THE SICK:
RITES OF ANOINTING AND VIATICUM

Decree
Apostolic Constitution
Decree of the National Conference of Catholic Bishops
Foreword
General Introduction (1–41)

PART I
PASTORAL CARE OF THE SICK (42–160)

Introduction (42–53)

CHAPTER I
VISITS TO THE SICK (54–61)

Introduction (54–61)
Reading (57)
Response (58)
The Lord's Prayer (59)
Concluding Prayer (60)
Blessing (61)

CHAPTER II
VISITS TO A SICK CHILD (62–70)

Introduction (62–70)
Reading (66)
Response (67)
The Lord's Prayer (68)
Concluding Prayer (69)
Blessing (70)

CHAPTER III
COMMUNION OF THE SICK (71–96)

Introduction (71–80)

COMMUNION IN ORDINARY CIRCUMSTANCES (81–91)

Introductory Rites (81–83)
Greeting (81)
Sprinkling with Holy Water (82)
Penitential Rite (83)

Laying on of Hands (122)
Prayer over the Oil (123)
Anointing (124)
Prayer after Anointing (125)
The Lord's Prayer (126)

Liturgy of Holy Communion (127–129)
Communion (127)
Silent Prayer (128)
Prayer after Communion (129)

Concluding Rite (130)
Blessing (130)

ANOINTING WITHIN MASS (131–148)

Introduction (131–134)

Introductory Rites (135–136)
Reception of the Sick (135)
Opening Prayer (136)

Liturgy of the Word (137)

Liturgy of Anointing (138–146)
Litany (138)
Laying on of Hands (139)
Prayer over the Oil (140)
Anointing (141)
Prayer after Anointing (142)
Liturgy of the Eucharist (143)
   Prayer over the Gifts (144)
   Eucharistic Prayer (145)
Prayer after Communion (146)

Concluding Rites (147–148)
Blessing (147)
Dismissal (148)

ANOINTING IN A HOSPITAL OR INSTITUTION
(149–160)

Introduction (149–153)

Introductory Rites (154–155)
Greeting (154)
Instruction (155)

Liturgy of Anointing (156–159)
Laying on of Hands (156)
Anointing (157)
The Lord's Prayer (158)
Prayer after Anointing (159)

Concluding Rite (160)
Blessing (160)

PART II
PASTORAL CARE OF THE DYING (161–296)

Introduction (161–174)

CHAPTER V
CELEBRATION OF VIATICUM (175–211)

Introduction (175–188)

VIATICUM WITHIN MASS (189–196)

Liturgy of the Word (189–191)
Homily (189)
Baptismal Profession of Faith (190)
Litany (191)

Liturgy of the Eucharist (192–193)
Sign of Peace (192)
Communion as Viaticum (193)

Concluding Rites (194–196)
Blessing (194)
Apostolic Pardon (195)
Dismissal (196)

VIATICUM OUTSIDE MASS (197–211)

Introductory Rites (197–201)
Greeting (197)
Sprinkling with Holy Water (198)
Instruction (199)
Penitential Rite (200)
Apostolic Pardon (201)

Liturgy of the Word (202–205)
Reading (202)
Homily (203)

CONTINUOUS RITES OF PENANCE AND ANOINTING (236–258)

Introduction (236–238)

Introductory Rites (239–240)
Greeting (239)
Instruction (240)

Liturgy of Penance (241–245)
Sacrament of Penance (241)
Penitential Rite (242)
Apostolic Pardon (243)
Baptismal Profession of Faith (244)
Litany (245)

Liturgy of Confirmation (246)

Liturgy of Anointing (247–250)
Laying on of Hands (247)
Prayer over the Oil (248)
Anointing (249)
Prayer after Anointing (250)

Liturgy of Viaticum (251–254)
The Lord's Prayer (251)
Communion as Viaticum (252)
Silent Prayer (253)
Prayer after Communion (254)

Concluding Rites (255–258)
Blessing (255)
Sign of Peace (256–258)

RITE FOR EMERGENCIES (259–274)

Introduction (259–263)

Sacrament of Penance (264)

Apostolic Pardon (265)

The Lord's Prayer (266)

Communion as Viaticum (267)

Prayer before Anointing (268)

Anointing (269)

Concluding Prayer (270)

SACRED CONGREGATION FOR DIVINE WORSHIP

Prot. no. 1501/72

DECREE

When the Church cares for the sick, it serves Christ himself in the suffering members of his Mystical Body. When it follows the example of the Lord Jesus, who "went about doing good and healing all" (Acts 10:38), the Church obeys his command to care for the sick (see Mark 16:18).

The Church shows this solicitude not only by visiting those who are in poor health but also by raising them up through the sacrament of anointing and by nourishing them with the eucharist during their illness and when they are in danger of death. Finally, the Church offers prayers for the sick to commend them to God, especially in the last crisis of life.

To make the meaning of the sacrament of anointing clearer and more evident, Vatican Council II decreed: "The number of the anointings is to be adapted to the circumstances; the prayers that belong to the rite of anointing are to be so revised that they correspond to the varying conditions of the sick who receive the sacrament."[1] The Council also directed that a continuous rite be prepared according to which the sick person is anointed after the sacrament of penance and before receiving viaticum.[2]

In the Apostolic Constitution *Sacram Unctionem infirmorum* of 30 November 1972, Pope Paul VI established a new sacramental form of anointing and approved the *Ordo Unctionis infirmorum eorumque pastoralis curae*. The Congregation for Divine Worship prepared this rite and now issues it, declaring this to be the *editio typica* so that it may replace the pertinent sections that are now in the Roman Ritual.

Anything to the contrary notwithstanding.

---

[1]Vatican Council II, Constitution on the Liturgy, art. 75: *Acta Apostolicae Sedis* (AAS) 56 (1964) 119.
[2]See ibid., art. 74: AAS 119.

From the office of the Congregation for Divine Worship,
7 December 1972.

+ Arturo Cardinal Tabera
Prefect

+ Annibale Bugnini
Titular Archbishop of Diocletiana
Secretary

APOSTOLIC CONSTITUTION

SACRAMENT OF THE ANOINTING OF THE SICK

PAUL, BISHOP

Servant of the Servants of God
For an Everlasting Memorial

The Catholic Church professes and teaches that the anointing of the sick is one of the seven sacraments of the New Testament, that it was instituted by Christ our Lord, "intimated in Mark (6:13) and through James, the apostle and brother of the Lord, recommended to the faithful and made known: 'Is there anyone sick among you? Let him send for the presbyters of the Church and let them pray over him, anointing him with oil in the name of the Lord. The prayer of faith will save the sick man and the Lord will raise him up. If he has committed any sins, they will be forgiven him' (James 5:14-15)."[1]

From ancient times there is evidence of the anointing of the sick in the Church's tradition, particularly in the liturgical tradition, both in the East and in the West. Worthy of special note are the letter which Innocent I, our predecessor, addressed to Decentius, Bishop of Gubbio,[2] and also the ancient prayer used for blessing the oil of the sick, "Lord, . . . send the Holy Spirit, our Helper and Friend. . . ." This prayer was inserted in the eucharistic prayer[3] and is still preserved in the Roman Pontifical.[4]

In the course of centuries of liturgical tradition, the parts of the body to be anointed with holy oil were more explicitly defined in different ways. Several formularies of prayer were

[1]Council of Trent, sess. 14, De Extrema Unctione, cap. 1 (see also can. 1): *Concilium Tridentinum* (CT), vol. 7, pt. 1, 355-356; Denz.-Schön. 1695, 1716.
[2]See Innocent I, Ep. *Si Instituta Ecclesiastica*, cap. 8:PL 20, 559-561; Denz.-Schön. 216.
[3]See L.C. Mohlberg, ed., *Liber Sacramentorum Romanae Aecclesiae Ordinis Anni Circuli* in *Rerum Ecclesiasticarum Documenta, Fontes* 4 (Rome, 1960) 61; J. Deshusses, ed., *Le Sacramentaire Grégorien*, in *Spicilegium Friburgense* 16 (Fribourg, 1971) 172. See also B. Botte, ed., *La Tradition Apostolique de Saint Hippolyte* in *Liturgiewissenschaftliche Quellen und Forschungen* 39 (Münster-W., 1963) 18-19; E. Lanne, ed., *Le Grand Euchologie du Monastère Blanc* in *Patrologia Orientalis* 28, pt. 2 (Paris, 1958) 392-395.
[4]See Roman Pontifical, *Rite of Blessing Oils, Rite of Consecrating the Chrism*, no. 20 [*The Sacramentary* (*The Roman Missal*) Appendix II].

added to accompany the anointings and these are contained in the liturgical books of various Churches. In the Church of Rome during the Middle Ages the custom prevailed of anointing the sick on the senses with the formulary: *Per istam sanctam Unctionem, et suam piissimam misericordiam, indulgeat tibi Dominus quidquid deliquisti,* with the name of each sense added.[5]

In addition, the teaching concerning the sacrament of anointing is expounded in the documents of the ecumenical Councils of Florence, Trent especially, and Vatican II.

After the Council of Florence had described the essential elements of the sacrament of the anointing of the sick,[6] the Council of Trent declared that it was of divine institution and explained what is taught in the Letter of James concerning holy anointing, especially about the reality signified and the effects of the sacrament: "This reality is in fact the grace of the Holy Spirit, whose anointing takes away sins, if any still remain, and the remnants of sin; this anointing also raises up and strengthens the soul of the sick person, arousing a great confidence in the divine mercy; thus sustained, the sick person may more easily bear the trials and hardships of sickness, more easily resist the temptations of the devil 'lying in wait for his heel' (Genesis 3:15), and sometimes regain bodily health, if this is expedient for the health of the soul."[7] The same Council also declared that these words of the apostle state with sufficient clarity that "this anointing is to be given to the sick, especially those who are in such a serious condition as to appear to have reached the end of their life. For this reason it is also called the sacrament of the dying."[8] Finally, the Council declared that the presbyter is the proper minister of the sacrament.[9]

Vatican Council II adds the following: " 'Extreme unction,' which may also and more properly be called 'anointing of the sick,' is not a sacrament for those only who are at the point of

[5]See M. Andrieu, *Le Pontifical Romain au Moyen-Age*, vol. 1, *Le Pontifical Romain du XII siècle* in *Studi e Testi* 86 (Vatican City, 1938) 267-268; vol. 2, *Le Pontifical de la Curie Romaine au XIIIe siècle* in *Studi e Testi* 87 (Vatican City, 1940) 491-492.
[6]See Council of Florence, *Decr. pro Armeniis*: G. Hofmann, *Concilium Florentinum*, vol. 1, pt. 2 (Rome, 1944) 130; Denz.-Schön. 1324-1325.
[7]Council of Trent, sess. 14, De Extrema Unctione, cap. 2: CT 7, 1, 356; Denz.-Schön. 1696.
[8]Ibid., cap. 3: CT, ibid.; Denz.-Schön. 1698.
[9]See ibid., cap. 3, can. 4: CT, ibid.; Denz-Schön. 1697, 1719.

death. Hence, as soon as any one of the faithful begins to be in danger of death from sickness or old age, the fitting time for that person to receive this sacrament has certainly already arrived."[10] The use of this sacrament is a concern of the whole Church: "By the sacred anointing of the sick and the prayer of its presbyters, the whole Church commends the sick to the suffering and glorified Lord so that he may raise them up and save them (see James 5:14-16). The Church exhorts them, moreover, to contribute to the welfare of the whole people of God by associating themselves willingly with the passion and death of Christ (see Romans 8:17; Colossians 1:24; 2 Timothy 2:11-12; 1 Peter 4:13)."[11]

All these considerations had to be weighed in revising the rite of anointing in order better to adapt to present-day conditions those elements which were subject to change.[12]

We have thought fit to modify the sacramental form in such a way that, by reflecting the words of James, it may better express the effects of the sacrament.

Since olive oil, which has been prescribed until now for the valid celebration of the sacrament, is unobtainable or difficult to obtain in some parts of the world, we have decreed, at the request of a number of bishops, that from now on, according to circumstances, another kind of oil can also be used, provided it is derived from plants, and is thus similar to olive oil.

As regards the number of anointings and the parts of the body to be anointed, it has seemed opportune to simplify the rite.

Therefore, since this revision in certain points touches upon the sacramental rite itself, by our apostolic authority we establish that the following is to be observed for the future in the Latin rite:

The sacrament of the anointing of the sick is given to those who are seriously ill by anointing them on the forehead and hands with blessed olive oil or, according to circumstances, with another blessed plant oil and saying once only these words:

[10]Vatican Council II, Constitution on the Liturgy, art. 73: AAS 56 (1964) 118-119.
[11]Vatican Council II, Dogmatic Constitution on the Church, no. 11: AAS 57 (1965) 15.
[12]See Vatican Council II, Constitution on the Liturgy, art. 1: AAS 56 (1964) 97.

"Through this holy anointing
May the Lord in His love and mercy help you
with the grace of the Holy Spirit.

"May the Lord who frees you from sin
save you and raise you up."*

In the case of necessity, however, it is sufficient that a single anointing be given on the forehead or, because of the particular condition of the sick person, on another suitable part of the body, while the whole sacramental form is said.

The sacrament may be repeated if the sick person recovers after being anointed and then again falls ill or if during the same illness the person's condition becomes more serious.

Having made these decisions and declarations about the essential rite of the sacrament of the anointing of the sick, by our apostolic authority we also approve the *Ordo Unctionis infirmorum eorumque pastoralis curae*, which has been revised by the Congregation for Divine Worship. At the same time, where necessary we amend the prescriptions of the Code of Canon Law or other laws hitherto in force or we repeal them; other prescriptions and laws, which are neither repealed nor amended by the above-mentioned rite, remain valid and in force. The Latin edition containing the new rite will come into force as soon as it is published; the vernacular editions, prepared by the conferences of bishops and confirmed by the Apostolic See, will come into force on the dates to be laid down by the individual conferences. The old rite may be used until 31 December 1973. From 1 January 1974, however, only the new rite is to be used by those concerned.

We intend that everything we have laid down and prescribed should be firm and effective in the Latin rite, notwithstanding, where relevant, the apostolic constitutions and ordinances issued by our predecessors and other prescriptions, even if worthy of special mention.

Given at Rome, at Saint Peter's, 30 November 1972, the tenth year of our pontificate.

PAUL VI

Latin: Per istam sanctam unctionem et suam piissimam misericordiam, adiuvette Dominus gratia Spiritus Sancti, ut a peccatis liberatum te salvet atque propitius allevet.

NATIONAL CONFERENCE OF CATHOLIC BISHOPS UNITED STATES OF AMERICA

DECREE

In accord with the norms established by decree of the Sacred Congregation of Rites *"Cum, nostra aetate"* (27 January 1966), *Pastoral Care of the Sick: Rites of Anointing and Viaticum* is declared to be the vernacular *editio typica* of the *Ordo Unctionis Infirmorum eorumque pastoralis curae* for the dioceses of the United States of America, and may be published by authority of the National Conference of Catholic Bishops.

Pastoral Care of the Sick: Rites of Anointing and Viaticum was canonically approved by the National Conference of Catholic Bishops in plenary assembly on 18 November 1982 and was subsequently confirmed by the Apostolic See by decree of the Sacred Congregation for the Sacraments and Divine Worship on 11 December 1982 (Prot. CD 1207/82).

On 1 September 1983 *Pastoral Care of the Sick: Rites of Anointing and Viaticum* may be published and used in celebrations for the sick and dying. The mandatory effective date has been established by the conference of bishops as 27 November 1983, the First Sunday of Advent. From that day forward no other vernacular versions of these rites may be used.

Given at the General Secretariat of the National Conference of Catholic Bishops, Washington, D.C., on 28 January 1983, the Memorial of Saint Thomas Aquinas, priest and doctor.

✝ John R. Roach
Archbishop of Saint Paul and Minneapolis
President
National Conference of Catholic Bishops

Daniel F. Hoye
General Secretary

FOREWORD

The purpose of this Foreword is to draw attention to the special features of *Pastoral Care of the Sick: Rites of Anointing and Viaticum,* approved by the National Conference of Catholic Bishops on November 18, 1982 and confirmed by the Sacred Congregation for the Sacraments and Divine Worship on December 11, 1982 (Prot. CD 1207/82).

While the material in this volume is substantially a translation of the Latin *editio typica* of the *Ordo Unctionis Infirmorum eorumque pastoralis curae* promulgated by the Apostolic Constitution of Paul VI, *Sacram Unctionem infirmorum,* of November 30, 1972, at the request of the member and associate member episcopal conferences of the Joint International Commission on English in the Liturgy, the Latin edition has been expanded and adapted for greater pastoral effectiveness.

This expansion and adaptation includes original English texts which address pastoral circumstances not foreseen in the Latin edition nor in the provisional English edition of 1973. Also included in this volume are texts from other approved parts of the Roman Ritual, e.g. *Rite of Funerals, Rite of Christian Initiation of Adults*, etc.

The texts in this volume have been arranged "in a format that will be as suitable as possible for pastoral use" (General Introduction 38*f.*). Finally, as the General Introduction notes, "whenever the Roman Ritual gives several alternative texts, particular rituals may add other texts of the same kind" (no. 39).

In undertaking the pastoral rearrangement of *Ordo Unctionis Infirmorum eorumque pastoralis curae* it was necessary to depart from the numbering system employed in the Latin edition. The General Introduction corresponds exactly to the Latin introduction. Beginning with number 42, however, the present numbering system diverges from the Latin system. The new numbering system appears at the left-hand side of the page. The corresponding reference number from the Latin edition appears in the right-hand margin.

1. In the case of the rubrics or the introduction to the parts or chapters of this book, the reference number from the Latin edition indicates that the text is either a direct translation or

that it is derived from the numbered material in the Latin. In the case of liturgical texts, the reference number from the Latin edition indicates that the text is translated from the Latin text cited. Reference numbers from the Latin edition appear only once, at the beginning of the appropriate material, unless this is interrupted by material from another reference number or by the insertion of a newly composed text. In this case, the previous reference number is repeated.

2. A text having a number on the left but no reference number in the right-hand margin is newly composed.

3. A reference number in the right-hand margin that is preceded by a letter indicates a text which has been taken from a rite other than the *Ordo Unctionis Infirmorum eorumque pastoralis curae.*

a. Texts with reference numbers preceded by the letter "E" are taken from *Holy Communion and Worship of the Eucharist outside Mass.*
b. "F" indicates texts from the *Rite of Funerals.*
c. "I" indicates texts from *Christian Initiation of Adults.*
d. "P" indicates texts taken from the *Rite of Penance.*

This new edition of *Pastoral Care of the Sick: Rites of Anointing and Viaticum* is commended to the Church and its ministers who care for the sick and dying members of the Body of Christ in the confident hope of the Lord's constant compassionate love for them.

> John S. Cummins, Bishop of Oakland
> Chairman
> The Bishops' Committee on the Liturgy
> National Conference of Catholic Bishops

27 November 1983
First Sunday of Advent

GENERAL INTRODUCTION

HUMAN SICKNESS AND ITS MEANING IN THE MYSTERY OF SALVATION

1. Suffering and illness have always been among the greatest problems that trouble the human spirit. Christians feel and experience pain as do all other people; yet their faith helps them to grasp more deeply the mystery of suffering and to bear their pain with greater courage. From Christ's words they know that sickness has meaning and value for their own salvation and for the salvation of the world. They also know that Christ, who during his life often visited and healed the sick, loves them in their illness.

2. Although closely linked with the human condition, sickness cannot as a general rule be regarded as a punishment inflicted on each individual for personal sins (see John 9:3). Christ himself, who is without sin, in fulfilling the words of Isaiah took on all the wounds of his passion and shared in all human pain (see Isaiah 53:4–5). Christ is still pained and tormented in his members, made like him. Still, our afflictions seem but momentary and slight when compared to the greatness of the eternal glory for which they prepare us (see 2 Corinthians 4:17).

3. Part of the plan laid out by God's providence is that we should fight strenuously against all sickness and carefully seek the blessings of good health, so that we may fulfill our role in human society and in the Church. Yet we should always be prepared to fill up what is lacking in Christ's sufferings for the salvation of the world as we look forward to creation's being set free in the glory of the children of God (see Colossians 1:24; Romans 8:19–21).

Moreover, the role of the sick in the Church is to be a reminder to others of the essential or higher things. By their witness the sick show that our mortal life must be redeemed through the mystery of Christ's death and resurrection.

4. The sick person is not the only one who should fight against illness. Doctors and all who are devoted in any way to caring for the sick should consider it their duty to use all the means which in their judgment may help the sick, both

physically and spiritually. In so doing, they are fulfilling the command of Christ to visit the sick, for Christ implied that those who visit the sick should be concerned for the whole person and offer both physical relief and spiritual comfort.

CELEBRATION OF THE SACRAMENTS FOR THE SICK AND THE DYING

ANOINTING OF THE SICK

5. The Lord himself showed great concern for the bodily and spiritual welfare of the sick and commanded his followers to do likewise. This is clear from the gospels, and above all from the existence of the sacrament of anointing, which he instituted and which is made known in the Letter of James. Since then the Church has never ceased to celebrate this sacrament for its members by the anointing and the prayer of its priests, commending those who are ill to the suffering and glorified Lord, that he may raise them up and save them (see James 5:14-16). Moreover, the Church exhorts them to associate themselves willingly with the passion and death of Christ (see Romans 8:17),[1] and thus contribute to the welfare of the people of God.[2]

Those who are seriously ill need the special help of God's grace in this time of anxiety, lest they be broken in spirit and, under the pressure of temptation, perhaps weakened in their faith.

This is why, through the sacrament of anointing, Christ strengthens the faithful who are afflicted by illness, providing them with the strongest means of support.[3]

The celebration of this sacrament consists especially in the laying on of hands by the priests of the Church, the offering of the prayer of faith, and the anointing of the sick with oil made holy by God's blessing. This rite signifies the grace of the sacrament and confers it.

---

[1] See also Colossians 1:24; 2 Timothy 2:11-12; 1 Peter 4:13.
[2] See Council of Trent, sess. 14, De Extrema Unctione, cap. 1: Denz.-Schön. 1695; Vatican Council II, Dogmatic Constitution on the Church, no. 11: AAS 57 (1965) 15.
[3] See Council of Trent, sess. 14, De Extrema Unctione, cap. 1: Denz-Schön. 1694.

6. This sacrament gives the grace of the Holy Spirit to those who are sick: by this grace the whole person is helped and saved, sustained by trust in God, and strengthened against the temptations of the Evil One and against anxiety over death. Thus the sick person is able not only to bear suffering bravely, but also to fight against it. A return to physical health may follow the reception of this sacrament if it will be beneficial to the sick person's salvation. If necessary, the sacrament also provides the sick person with the forgiveness of sins and the completion of Christian penance.[4]

7. In the anointing of the sick, which includes the prayer of faith (see James 5:15), faith itself is manifested. Above all this faith must be made actual both in the minister of the sacrament and, even more importantly, in the recipient. The sick person will be saved by personal faith and the faith of the Church, which looks back to the death and resurrection of Christ, the source of the sacrament's power (see James 5:15),[5] and looks ahead to the future kingdom that is pledged in the sacraments.

Recipients of the Anointing of the Sick

8. The Letter of James states that the sick are to be anointed in order to raise them up and save them.[6] Great care and concern should be taken to see that those of the faithful whose health is seriously* impaired by sickness or old age receive this sacrament.[7]

A prudent or reasonably sure judgment, without scruple, is sufficient for deciding on the seriousness of an illness;[8] if necessary a doctor may be consulted.

[4]See ibid., prooem. and cap. 2: Denz.-Schön. 1694 and 1696.
[5]See St. Thomas Aquinas, In 4 Sententiarum, d. 1, q. 1, a. 4, quaestiuncula 3.
[6]See Council of Trent, sess. 14, De Extrema Unctione, cap. 2: Denz.-Schön. 1698.
[7]See Vatican Council II, Constitution on the Liturgy, art, 73: AAS 56 (1964) 118-119.
[8]See Pius XI, Epist. Explorata res, 2 February 1923: AAS 15 (1923) 103-107.
*The word periculose has been carefully studied and rendered as "seriously," rather than as "gravely," "dangerously," or "perilously." Such a rendering will serve to avoid restrictions upon the celebration of the sacrament. On the one hand, the sacrament may and should be given to anyone whose health is seriously impaired; on the other hand, it may not be given indiscriminately or to any person whose health is not seriously impaired.

9. The sacrament may be repeated if the sick person recovers after being anointed and then again falls ill or if during the same illness the person's condition becomes more serious.

10. A sick person may be anointed before surgery whenever a serious illness is the reason for the surgery.

11. Elderly people may be anointed if they have become notably weakened even though no serious illness is present.

12. Sick children are to be anointed if they have sufficient use of reason to be strengthened by this sacrament. In case of doubt whether a child has reached the use of reason, the sacrament is to be conferred.[9]

13. In public and private catechesis, the faithful should be educated to ask for the sacrament of anointing and, as soon as the right time comes, to receive it with full faith and devotion. They should not follow the wrongful practice of delaying the reception of the sacrament. All who care for the sick should be taught the meaning and purpose of the sacrament.

14. The sacrament of anointing is to be conferred on sick people who, although they have lost consciousness or the use of reason, would, as Christian believers, have at least implicitly asked for it when they were in control of their faculties.[10]

15. When a priest has been called to attend those who are already dead, he should not administer the sacrament of anointing. Instead, he should pray for them, asking that God forgive their sins and graciously receive them into the kingdom. But if the priest is doubtful whether the sick person is dead, he is to confer the sacrament, using the rite given in no. 269.[11]

The anointing of the sick is not to be conferred on anyone who remains obdurately in open and serious sin.

[9]See CIC, can. 1005.
[10]See CIC, can. 1006.
[11]See CIC, can. 1005.

Minister of the Anointing of the Sick

16. The priest is the only proper minister of the anointing of the sick.[12]

This office is ordinarily exercised by bishops, parish priests (pastors) and their assistants, chaplains of health care facilities, and superiors of clerical religious institutes.[13]

17. These ministers have the pastoral responsibility both of preparing and helping the sick and others who are present, with the assistance of religious and laity, and of celebrating the sacrament.

The diocesan bishop has the responsibility of supervising celebrations at which many sick persons may come together to receive the sacrament.

18. For a reasonable cause any other priest may confer this sacrament with at least the presumed consent of the minister mentioned in no. 16, whom the priest need only inform later.

19. When two or more priests are present for the anointing of a sick person, one of them may say the prayers and carry out the anointings, saying the sacramental form. The others may take the remaining parts, such as the introductory rites, readings, invocations, or instructions. Each priest may lay hands on the sick person.

Requirements for Celebrating the Anointing of the Sick

20. The matter proper for the sacrament is olive oil or, according to circumstances, other oil derived from plants.[14]

21. The oil used for the anointing of the sick must be blessed for this purpose by the bishop or by a priest who has the faculty, either from the law or by special concession of the Apostolic See.

---

[12]See Council of Trent, sess. 14, *De extrema unctione*, chapter 3 and can. 4: Denziger-Schönmetzer 1697 and 1719; CIC, can. 1003, §1.
[13]See CIC, can. 1003, §2.
[14]See Roman Pontifical, *Rite of Blessing of Oils, Rite of Consecrating the Chrism*, Introduction, no. 3. [*The Sacramentary (The Roman Missal)* Appendix II].

The law itself permits the following, besides a bishop, to bless the oil of the sick:

a) those whom the law equates with diocesan bishops;

b) in case of necessity, any priest, but only within the celebration of the sacrament.[15]

The oil of the sick is ordinarily blessed by the bishop on Holy Thursday.[16]

22. If a priest in accord with no. 21b, is to bless the oil during the rite, he may bring the unblessed oil with him, or the family of the sick person may prepare the oil in a suitable vessel. If any of the oil is left after the celebration of the sacrament, it should be absorbed in cotton (cotton wool) and burned.

If the priest uses oil that has already been blessed (either by the bishop or by a priest), he brings it with him in the vessel in which it is kept. This vessel, made of suitable material, should be clean and should contain sufficient oil (soaked in cotton [cotton wool] for convenience). In this case, after celebrating the sacrament the priest returns the vessel to the place where it is kept with proper respect. He should make sure that the oil remains fit for use and should replenish it from time to time, either yearly when the bishop blesses the oil on Holy Thursday or more frequently if necessary.

23. The sick person is anointed on the forehead and on the hands. It is appropriate to divide the sacramental form so that the first part is said while the forehead is anointed, the latter part while the hands are anointed.

In case of necessity, however, it is sufficient that a single anointing be given on the forehead or, because of the particular condition of the sick person, on another suitable part of the body, while the whole sacramental form is said.

24. Depending on the culture and traditions of different peoples, the number of anointings may be increased and the place of anointing may be changed. Directives on this should be included in the preparation of particular rituals.

---

[15]See CIC, can. 999.
[16]See Roman Pontifical, *Rite of Blessing of Oils*, . . . , no. 9 [*The Roman Missal* (*The Sacramentary*)], Appendix II].

25. The following is the sacramental form with which the anointing of the sick is given in the Latin rite:

**Through this holy anointing
may the Lord in his love and mercy help you
with the grace of the Holy Spirit.**

**May the Lord who frees you from sin
save you and raise you up.**

VIATICUM FOR THE DYING

26. When in their passage from this life Christians are strengthened by the body and blood of Christ in viaticum, they have the pledge of the resurrection that the Lord promised "Those who eat my flesh and drink my blood have eternal life, and I will raise them up on the last day" (John 6:54).

When possible, viaticum should be received within Mass so that the sick person may receive communion under both kinds. Communion received as viaticum should be considered a special sign of participation in the mystery which is celebrated in the eucharist: the mystery of the death of the Lord and his passage to the Father.[17]

27. All baptized Christians who are able to receive communion are bound to receive viaticum by reason of the precept to receive communion when in danger of death from any cause. Priests with pastoral responsibility must see that the celebration of this sacrament is not delayed, but that the faithful are nourished by it while still in full possession of their faculties.[18]

28. It is also desirable that during the celebration of viaticum, Christians renew the faith professed at their baptism, by which they became adopted children of God and coheirs of the promise of eternal life.

---

[17]See Congregation of Rites, Instruction *Eucharisticum mysterium*, May 25, 1967, nos. 36, 39, 41[DOL 179, nos. 1265, 1268, 1270].

[18]See Congregation of Rites, Instruction *Eucharisticum Mysterium*, May 25, 1967, no. 39[DOL 179, no. 1268].

29. The ordinary ministers of viaticum are the parish priest (pastor) and his assistants, chaplains, and, for all staying in the house, the superior in clerical religious institutes or societies of apostolic life.

In case of necessity or with at least the presumed permission of the competent minister, any priest or deacon is to give viaticum, or, if no ordained minister is available, any member of the faithful who has been duly appointed.

A deacon and other ministers follow the rite provided for "Viaticum outside Mass," nos. 197–211.

CONTINUOUS RITE

30. For special cases, when sudden illness or some other cause has unexpectedly placed one of the faithful in proximate danger of death, a continuous rite is provided by which the sick person may be given the sacraments of penance, anointing, and the eucharist as viaticum in a single celebration.

If death is imminent and there is not enough time to celebrate the three sacraments in the manner already described, the sick person should be given an opportunity to make a sacramental confession, even if it has to be a generic confession. After this the person should be given viaticum, since all the faithful are bound to receive this sacrament if they are in danger of death. Then, if there is sufficient time, the sick person should be anointed.

The sick person who, because of the nature of the illness, cannot receive communion should be anointed.

31. If the sick person is to be strengthened by the sacrament of confirmation, nos. 238, 246, 276, 290, and 291 of this ritual should be consulted.

In danger of death, the law gives the faculty to confirm to parish priests (pastors) and in fact to any priest.[19]

OFFICES AND MINISTRIES FOR THE SICK

32. If one member suffers in the Body of Christ, which is the Church, all members suffer with that member (1 Corin-

---

[19]See Roman Pontifical, *Rite of Confirmation*, Introduction, no. 7c.

thians 12:26).[20] For this reason, kindness shown toward the sick and works of charity and mutual help for the relief of every kind of human want are held in special honor.[21] Every scientific effort to prolong life[22] and every act of care for the sick, on the part of any person, may be considered a preparation for the Gospel and a sharing in Christ's healing ministry.[23]

33. It is thus especially fitting that all baptized Christians share in this ministry of mutual charity within the Body of Christ by doing all that they can to help the sick return to health, by showing love for the sick, and by celebrating the sacraments with them. Like the other sacraments, these too have a community aspect, which should be brought out as much as possible when they are celebrated.

34. The family and friends of the sick and those who take care of them in any way have a special share in this ministry of comfort. In particular, it is their task to strengthen the sick with words of faith and by praying with them, to commend them to the suffering and glorified Lord, and to encourage them to contribute to the well-being of the people of God by associating themselves willingly with Christ's passion and death.[24] If the sickness grows worse, the family and friends of the sick and those who take care of them have the responsibility of informing the parish priest (pastor) and by their kind words of prudently disposing the sick for the reception of the sacraments at the proper time.

35. Priests, particularly parish priests (pastors) and the others mentioned in no. 16, should remember that it is their duty to care for the sick by personal visits and other acts of kindness.[25] Especially when they give the sacraments,

[20]See Vatican Council II, Dogmatic Constitution on the Church, no. 7[DOL 4, no. 139].

[21]See Vatican Council II, Decree on the Apostolate of the Laity, no. 8[DOL 16, no. 235].

[22]See Vatican Council II, Pastoral Constitution on the Church in the Modern World, no. 18[DOL 19, no. 269].

[23]See Vatican Council II, Dogmatic Constitution on the Church, no. 28[DOL 4, no. 148].

[24]see *ibid*. no. 21[DOL 4, no. 145].

[25]See CIC, can. 529, §1.

priests should stir up the hope of those present and strengthen their faith in Christ who suffered and is glorified. By bringing the Church's love and the consolation of faith, they comfort believers and raise the minds of others to God.

36. It is important that all the faithful, and above all the sick, be aided by suitable catechesis in preparing for and participating in the sacraments of anointing and viaticum, especially if the celebration is to be carried out communally. In this way they will understand more fully what has been said about the anointing of the sick and about viaticum, and the celebration of these sacraments will nourish, strengthen, and manifest faith more effectively. For the prayer of faith which accompanies the celebration of the sacrament is nourished by the profession of this faith.

37. When the priest prepares for the celebration of the sacraments, he should ask about the condition of the sick person. He should take this information into account, for example, in planning the rite, in choosing readings and prayers, and in deciding whether he will celebrate Mass when viaticum is to be given. As far as possible, he should arrange all this with the sick person and the family beforehand, when he explains the meaning of the sacraments.

ADAPTATIONS BELONGING TO THE CONFERENCES OF BISHOPS

38. In virtue of the Constitution on the Liturgy (art. 63b), the conferences of bishops have the right to prepare a section in particular rituals corresponding to the present section of the Roman Ritual and adapted to the needs of the different parts of the world. This section is for use in the regions concerned once the *acta* have been reviewed by the Apostolic See.

The following are the responsibilities of the conferences of bishops in this regard:

a. to decide on the adaptations dealt with in the Constitution on the Liturgy, article 39;

b. to weigh carefully and prudently what elements from the

traditions and culture of individual peoples may be appropriately admitted into divine worship, then to propose to the Apostolic See adaptations considered useful or necessary that will be introduced with its consent;

c. to retain elements in the rites of the sick that now exist in particular rituals, as long as they are compatible with the Constitution on the Liturgy and with contemporary needs; or to adapt any of these elements;

d. to prepare translations of the texts so that they are truly adapted to the genius of different languages and cultures and to add, whenever appropriate, suitable melodies for singing;

e. to adapt and enlarge, if necessary, this Introduction in the Roman Ritual in order to encourage the conscious and active participation of the faithful;

f. to arrange the material in the editions of liturgical books prepared under the direction of the conferences of bishops in a format that will be as suitable as possible for pastoral use.

39. Whenever the Roman Ritual gives several alternative texts, particular rituals may add other texts of the same kind.

ADAPTATIONS BY THE MINISTER

40. The minister should take into account the particular circumstances, needs, and desires of the sick and of other members of the faithful and should willingly use the various opportunities that the rites provide.

a. The minister should be especially aware that the sick tire easily and that their physical condition may change from day to day and even from hour to hour. For this reason the celebration may be shortened if necessary.

b. When there is no group of the faithful present, the priest should remember that the Church is already present in his own person and in the one who is ill. For this reason he should try to offer the sick person the love and help of the Christian community both before and after the celebration of the sacrament. He may ask another Christian from the local community to do this if the sick person will accept this help.

c. Sick persons who regain their health after being anointed should be encouraged to give thanks for the favor received by participating in a Mass of thanksgiving or by some other suitable means.

41. The priest should follow the structure of the rite in the celebration, while accommodating it to the place and the people involved. The penitential rite may be part of the introductory rite or take place after the reading from Scripture. In place of the thanksgiving over the oil, the priest may give an instruction. This alternative should be considered when the sick person is in a hospital and other sick people present do not take part in the celebration of the sacrament.

PART I

PASTORAL CARE OF THE SICK

INTRODUCTION
Lord, your friend is sick.

42. The rites in Part I of *Pastoral Care of the Sick: Rites of Anointing and Viaticum* are used by the Church to comfort the sick in time of anxiety, to encourage them to fight against illness, and perhaps to restore them to health. These rites are distinct from those in the second part of this book, which are provided to comfort and strengthen a Christian in the passage from this life.

43. The concern that Christ showed for the bodily and spiritual welfare of those who are ill is continued by the Church in its ministry to the sick. This ministry is the common responsibility of all Christians, who should visit the sick, remember them in prayer, and celebrate the sacraments with them. The family and friends of the sick, doctors and others who care for them, and priests with pastoral responsibilities have a particular share in this ministry of comfort. Through words of encouragement and faith they can help the sick to unite themselves with the sufferings of Christ for the good of God's people.

Remembrance of the sick is especially appropriate at common worship on the Lord's Day, during the general intercessions at Mass and in the intercessions at Morning Prayer and Evening Prayer. Family members and those who are dedicated to the care of the sick should be remembered on these occasions as well.

44. Priests have the special task of preparing the sick to celebrate the sacrament of penance (individually or in a communal celebration), to receive the eucharist frequently if their condition permits, and to celebrate the sacrament of anointing at the appropriate time. During this preparation it will be especially helpful if the sick person, the priest, and the family become accustomed to praying together. The priest should provide leadership to those who assist him in the care of the sick, especially deacons and other ministers of the eucharist.

The words "priest," "deacon," and "minister" are used advisedly. Only in those rites which must be celebrated by a priest is the word "priest" used in the rubrics (that is, the sacrament of penance, the sacrament of the anointing of the sick, the celebration of viaticum within Mass). Whenever it is clear that, in the absence of a priest, a deacon may preside at a particular rite, the words "priest or deacon" are used in the rubrics. Whenever another minister is permitted to celebrate a rite in the absence of a priest or deacon, the word "minister" is used in the rubrics, even though in many cases the rite will be celebrated by a priest or deacon.

45. The pastoral care of the sick should be suited to the nature and length of the illness. An illness of short duration in which the full recovery of health is a possibility requires a more intensive ministry, whereas illness of a longer duration which may be a prelude to death requires a more extensive ministry. An awareness of the attitudes and emotional states which these different situations engender in the sick is indispensable to the development of an appropriate ministry.

VISITS TO THE SICK

46. Those who visit the sick should help them to pray,   45
sharing with them the word of God proclaimed in the assembly from which their sickness has separated them. As the occasion permits, prayer drawn from the psalms or from other prayers or litanies may be added to the word of God. Care should be taken to prepare for a future visit during which the sick will receive the eucharist.

VISITS TO A SICK CHILD

47. What has already been said about visiting the sick and praying with them (see no. 46) applies also in visits to a sick child. Every effort should be made to know the child and to accommodate the care in keeping with the age and comprehension of the child. In these circumstances the minister should also be particularly concerned to help the child's family.

48. If it is appropriate, the priest may discuss with the parents the possibility of preparing and celebrating with the child the sacraments of initiation (baptism, confirmation, eucharist). The priest may baptize and confirm the child (see *Rite of Confirmation*, no. 7b). To complete the process of

initiation, the child should also receive first communion. (If the child is a proper subject for confirmation, then he or she may receive first communion in accordance with the practice of the Church.) There is no reason to delay this, especially if the illness is likely to be a long one.

49. Throughout the illness the minister should ensure that the child receives communion frequently, making whatever adaptations seem necessary in the rite for communion of the sick (Chapter III).

50. The child is to be anointed if he or she has sufficient use of reason to be strengthened by the sacrament of anointing. The rites provided (Chapter IV) are to be used and adapted.

COMMUNION OF THE SICK

51. Because the sick are prevented from celebrating the eucharist with the rest of the community, the most important visits are those during which they receive holy communion. In receiving the body and blood of Christ, the sick are united sacramentally to the Lord and are reunited with the eucharistic community from which illness has separated them.

ANOINTING OF THE SICK

52. The priest should be especially concerned for those whose health has been seriously impaired by illness or old age. He will offer them a new sign of hope: the laying on of hands and the anointing of the sick accompanied by the prayer of faith (James 5:14). Those who receive this sacrament in the faith of the Church will find it a true sign of comfort and support in time of trial. It will work to overcome the sickness, if this is God's will.

56
8

53. Some types of mental sickness are now classified as serious. Those who are judged to have a serious mental illness and who would be strengthened by the sacrament may be anointed (see no. 5). The anointing may be repeated in accordance with the conditions for other kinds of serious illness (see no. 9).

5
9

CHAPTER I

VISITS TO THE SICK

INTRODUCTION
I was sick, and you visited me.

54. The prayers contained in this chapter follow the common   45
pattern of reading, response, prayer, and blessing. This
pattern is provided as an example of what can be done and
may be adapted as necessary. The minister may wish to invite
those present to prepare for the reading from Scripture,
perhaps by a brief introduction or through a moment of
silence. The laying on of hands may be added by the priest, if
appropriate, after the blessing is given.

55. The sick should be encouraged to pray when they are   44
alone or with their families, friends, or those who care for
them. Their prayer should be drawn primarily from
Scripture. The sick person and others may help to plan the
celebration, for example, by choosing the prayers and
readings. Those making these choices should keep in mind
the condition of the sick person.

The passages found in this chapter and those included in Part
III speak of the mystery of human suffering in the words,
works, and life of Christ. Occasionally, for example, on the
Lord's Day, the sick may feel more involved in the worship of
the community from which they are separated if the readings
used are those assigned for that day in the lectionary. Prayers
may also be drawn from the psalms or from other prayers or
litanies. The sick should be helped in making this form of
prayer, and the minister should always be ready to pray with
them.

56. The minister should encourage the sick person to offer his   43
or her sufferings in union with Christ and to join in prayer for
the Church and the world. Some examples of particular
intentions which may be suggested to the sick person are: for
peace in the world; for a deepening of the life of the Spirit in
the local Church; for the pope and the bishops; for people
suffering in a particular disaster.

READING

57. The word of God is proclaimed by one of those present or by the minister. An appropriate reading from Part III or one of the following readings may be used:

A   Acts of the Apostles 3:1-10   162
In the name of Jesus and the power of his Church, there is salvation—even liberation from sickness.

B   Matthew 8:14-17   206
Jesus fulfills the prophetic figure of the servant of God taking upon himself and relieving the sufferings of God's people.

RESPONSE

58. A brief period of silence may be observed after the reading of the word of God. An appropriate psalm from Part III or one of the following psalms may be used:

A   Psalm 102   193
℟. **O Lord, hear my prayer and let my cry come to you.**

B   Psalm 27   186
℟. **The Lord is my light and my salvation.**

The minister may then give a brief explanation of the reading, applying it to the needs of the sick person and those who are looking after him or her.

THE LORD'S PRAYER

59. The minister introduces the Lord's Prayer in these or similar words:

Now let us offer together the prayer our Lord Jesus Christ taught us:

All say:

Our Father . . .

60. The minister says a concluding prayer. One of the following may be used:

A
Father,
your Son accepted our sufferings
to teach us the virtue of patience in human illness.
Hear the prayers we offer for our sick brother/sister.

May all who suffer pain, illness, or disease
realize that they have been chosen to be saints
and know that they are joined to Christ
in his suffering for the salvation of the world.

We ask this through Christ our Lord.
R̲. Amen.

B
All-powerful and ever-living God,
the lasting health of all who believe in you,
hear us as we ask your loving help for the sick;
restore their health,
that they may again offer joyful thanks in your Church.

Grant this through Christ our Lord.
R̲. Amen.

C
All-powerful and ever-living God,
we find security in your forgiveness.
Give us serenity and peace of mind;
may we rejoice in your gifts of kindness
and use them always for your glory and our good.

We ask this in the name of Jesus the Lord.
R̲. Amen.

BLESSING

61. The minister may give a blessing. One of the following
may be used:

A
All praise and glory is yours, Lord our God,
for you have called us to serve you in love.
Bless N.
so that he/she may bear this illness
in union with your Son's obedient suffering.
Restore him/her to health,
and lead him/her to glory.

We ask this through Christ our Lord.
R̲. Amen.

B   For an elderly person
All praise and glory are yours, Lord our God,
for you have called us to serve you in love.
Bless all who have grown old in your service
and give N. strength and courage
to continue to follow Jesus your Son.

We ask this through Christ our Lord.
R̸. Amen.

If the minister is a priest or deacon, he immediately
concludes:

May the blessing of almighty God,   238
the Father, and the Son, ✝ and the Holy Spirit,
come upon you and remain with you for ever.
R̸. Amen.

The priest may lay hands upon the sick person's head.   45

A minister who is not a priest or deacon invokes God's
blessing and makes the sign of the cross on himself or herself,
while saying:

May the Lord bless us,
protect us from all evil,
and bring us to everlasting life.
R̸. Amen.

The minister may then trace the sign of the cross on the sick   E40
person's forehead.

CHAPTER II

VISITS TO A SICK CHILD

INTRODUCTION
Let the children come to me; do not keep them back from me.

62. The following readings, prayers, and blessings will help the minister to pray with sick children and their families. They are provided as an example of what can be done and may be adapted as necessary. The minister may wish to invite those present to prepare for the reading from Scripture, perhaps by a brief introduction or through a moment of silence.

63. If the child does not already know the minister, the latter should seek to establish a friendly and easy relationship with the child. Therefore, the greeting which begins the visit should be an informal one.

64. The minister should help sick children to understand that the sick are very special in the eyes of God because they are suffering as Christ suffered and because they can offer their sufferings for the salvation of the world.

65. In praying with the sick child the minister chooses, together with the child and the family if possible, suitable elements of common prayer in the form of a brief liturgy of the word. This may consist of a reading from Scripture, simple one-line prayers taken from Scripture which can be repeated by the child, other familiar prayers such as the Lord's Prayer, the Hail Mary, litanies, or a simple form of the general intercessions. The laying on of hands may be added by the priest, if appropriate, after the child has been blessed.

READING
66. One of the following readings may be used for a brief liturgy of the word. Other readings may be chosen, for example: Mark 5:21-23, 35-43, *Jesus raises the daughter of Jairus and gives her back to her parents;* Mark 9:14-27, *Jesus cures a boy and gives him back to his father;* Luke 7:11-15, *Jesus raises a young*

man, the only son of his mother, and gives him back to her; John 4:46-53, *Jesus gives his second sign by healing an official's son.* In addition, other stories concerning the Lord's healing ministry may be found suitable, especially if told with the simplicity and clarity of one of the children's versions of Scripture.

A   Mark 9:33-37
Jesus proposes the child as the ideal of those who would enter the kingdom.

B   Mark 10:13-16
Jesus welcomes the children and lays his hands on them.

RESPONSE

67. After the reading of the word of God, time may be set apart for silent reflection if the child is capable of this form of prayer. The minister should also explain the meaning of the reading to those present, adapting it to their circumstances.

The minister may then help the child and the family to respond to the word of God. The following short responsory may be used:

Jesus, come to me.
—Jesus, come to me.

Jesus, put your hand on me.
—Jesus, put your hand on me.

Jesus, bless me.
—Jesus, bless me.

THE LORD'S PRAYER

68. The minister introduces the Lord's Prayer in these or similar words:

Let us pray to the Father using those words which Jesus himself used:

All say:

Our Father . . .

CONCLUDING PRAYER

69. The minister says a concluding prayer. One of the following may be used:

A
God of love,
ever caring,
ever strong,
stand by us in our time of need.

Watch over your child N. who is sick,
look after him/her in every danger,
and grant him/her your healing and peace.

We ask this in the name of Jesus the Lord.
R̷. Amen.

B
Father,
in your love
you gave us Jesus
to help us rise triumphant over grief and pain.

Look on your child N. who is sick
and see in his/her sufferings those of your Son.

Grant N. a share in the strength you granted your Son
that he/she too may be a sign
of your goodness, kindness, and loving care.

We ask this in the name of Jesus the Lord.
R̷. Amen.

BLESSING

70. The minister makes a sign of the cross on the child's
forehead, saying one of the following:

A
N., when you were baptized,
you were marked with the cross of Jesus.
I (we) make this cross + on your forehead
and ask the Lord to bless you,
and restore you to health.
R̷. Amen.

B
All praise and glory is yours, heavenly God,
for you have called us to serve you in love.

Have mercy on us and listen to our prayer
as we ask you to help N.

Bless + your beloved child,
and restore him/her to health
in the name of Jesus the Lord.
R/. Amen.

Each one present may in turn trace the sign of the cross on the child's forehead, in silence.

If the minister is a priest or deacon, he concludes as described in no. 61.

The priest may then lay hands upon the sick child, in silence.   45

A minister who is not a priest or deacon concludes as described in no. 61.

CHAPTER III

COMMUNION OF THE SICK

INTRODUCTION
Whoever eats this bread will live for ever.

71. This chapter contains two rites: one for use when communion can be celebrated in the context of a liturgy of the word; the other, a brief communion rite for use in more restrictive circumstances, such as in hospitals.

59

72. Priests with pastoral responsibilities should see to it that the sick or aged, even though not seriously ill or in danger of death, are given every opportunity to receive the eucharist frequently, even daily, especially during the Easter season. They may receive communion at any hour. Those who care for the sick may receive communion with them, in accord with the usual norms. To provide frequent communion for the sick, it may be necessary to ensure that the community has a sufficient number of ministers of communion. The communion minister should wear attire appropriate to this ministry.

43
46
47
49

The sick person and others may help to plan the celebration, for example, by choosing the prayers and readings. Those making these choices should keep in mind the condition of the sick person. The readings and the homily should help those present to reach a deeper understanding of the mystery of human suffering in relation to the paschal mystery of Christ.

73. The faithful who are ill are deprived of their rightful and accustomed place in the eucharistic community. In bringing communion to them the minister of communion represents Christ and manifests faith and charity on behalf of the whole community toward those who cannot be present at the eucharist. For the sick the reception of communion is not only a privilege but also a sign of support and concern shown by the Christian community for its members who are ill.

The links between the community's eucharistic celebration, especially on the Lord's Day, and the communion of the sick are intimate and manifold. Besides remembering the sick in the general intercessions at Mass, those present should be reminded occasionally of the significance of communion in the lives of those who are ill: union with Christ in his struggle with evil, his prayer for the world, and his love for the Father, and union with the community from which they are separated.

The obligation to visit and comfort those who cannot take part in the eucharistic assembly may be clearly demonstrated by taking communion to them from the community's eucharistic celebration. This symbol of unity between the community and its sick members has the deepest significance on the Lord's Day, the special day of the eucharistic assembly.

74. When the eucharist is brought to the sick, it should be carried in a pyx or small closed container. Those who are with the sick should be asked to prepare a table covered with a linen cloth upon which the blessed sacrament will be placed. Lighted candles are prepared and, where it is customary, a vessel of holy water. Care should be taken to make the occasion special and joyful. [46] [47] [48] [95]

Sick people who are unable to receive communion under the form of bread may receive it under the form of wine alone. If the wine is consecrated at a Mass not celebrated in the presence of the sick person, the blood of the Lord is kept in a properly covered vessel and is placed in the tabernacle after communion. The precious blood should be carried to the sick in a vessel which is closed in such a way as to eliminate all danger of spilling. If some of the precious blood remains, it should be consumed by the minister, who should also see to it that the vessel is properly purified.

75. If the sick wish to celebrate the sacrament of penance, it is preferable that the priest make himself available for this during a previous visit. [60] [65]

76. If it is necessary to celebrate the sacrament of penance during the rite of communion, it takes the place of the penitential rite. [51] [65]

COMMUNION IN ORDINARY CIRCUMSTANCES

77. If possible, provision should be made to celebrate Mass in the homes of the sick, with their families and friends gathered

around them. The Ordinary determines the conditions and requirements for such celebrations.

COMMUNION IN A HOSPITAL OR INSTITUTION

78. There will be situations, particularly in large institutions with many communicants, when the minister should consider alternative means so that the rite of communion of the sick is not diminished to the absolute minimum. In such cases the following alternatives should be considered: (a) where possible, the residents or patients may be gathered in groups in one or more areas; (b) additional ministers of communion may assist.   59

When it is not possible to celebrate the full rite, the rite for communion in a hospital or institution may be used. If it is convenient, however, the minister may add elements from the rite for ordinary circumstances, for example, a Scripture reading.

79. The rite begins with the recitation of the eucharistic antiphon in the church, the hospital chapel, or the first room visited. Then the minister gives communion to the sick in their individual rooms.   61

80. The concluding prayer may be said in the church, the hospital chapel, or the last room visited. No blessing is given.   63

COMMUNION IN ORDINARY CIRCUMSTANCES

INTRODUCTORY RITES

GREETING

81. The minister greets the sick person and the others   49
present. One of the following may be used:

A

The peace of the Lord be with you always.
R7. And also with you.

B

Peace be with you (this house) and with all who live
here.
R7. And also with you.

C

The grace of our Lord Jesus Christ and the love of God   230
and the fellowship of the Holy Spirit be with you all.
R7. And also with you.

D

The grace and peace of God our Father and the Lord   231
Jesus Christ be with you.
R7. And also with you.

The minister then places the blessed sacrament on the table   49
and all join in adoration.

SPRINKLING WITH HOLY WATER

82. If it seems desirable, the priest or deacon may sprinkle the   50
sick person and those present with holy water. One of the
following may be used:

A

Let this water call to mind our baptism into Christ,
who by his death and resurrection has redeemed us.

B

Like a stream in parched land,
may the grace of the Lord
refresh our lives.

If the sacrament of penance is now celebrated (see Appendix, nos. 299–305), the penitential rite is omitted.

PENITENTIAL RITE

83. The minister invites the sick person and all present to join in the penitential rite, using these or similar words:

A

My brothers and sisters, to prepare ourselves for this celebration, let us call to mind our sins.

B

My brothers and sisters, let us turn with confidence to the Lord and ask his forgiveness for all our sins.

After a brief period of silence, the penitential rite continues, using one of the following:

A

Lord Jesus, you healed the sick:
Lord, have mercy.
R̰. **Lord, have mercy.**

Lord Jesus, you forgave sinners:
Christ, have mercy.
R̰. **Christ, have mercy.**

Lord Jesus, you give us yourself to heal us and bring us
    strength:
Lord, have mercy.
R̰. **Lord, have mercy.**

B All say:
I confess to almighty God,
and to you, my brothers and sisters,
that I have sinned through my own fault

They strike their breast.

in my thoughts and in my words,
in what I have done,
and in what I have failed to do;
and I ask blessed Mary, ever virgin,
all the angels and saints,
and you, my brothers and sisters,
to pray for me to the Lord our God.

The minister concludes the penitential rite with the following:

May almighty God have mercy on us,
forgive us our sins,
and bring us to everlasting life.
R̷. **Amen.**

LITURGY OF THE WORD

READING

84. The word of God is proclaimed by one of those present or   53
by the minister. An appropriate reading from Part III or one
of the following readings may be used:

A **John 6:51**
B **John 6:54-58**
C **John 14:6**
D **John 15:5**
E **John 4:16**

RESPONSE

85. A brief period of silence may be observed after the   53
reading of the word of God.

The minister may then give a brief explanation of the reading,
applying it to the needs of the sick person and those who are
looking after him or her.

GENERAL INTERCESSIONS

86. The general intercessions may be said. With a brief
introduction the minister invites all those present to pray.
After the intentions the minister says the concluding prayer.
It is desirable that the intentions be announced by someone
other than the minister.

LITURGY OF HOLY COMMUNION

THE LORD'S PRAYER

87. The minister introduces the Lord's Prayer in these or   54
similar words:

A
Now let us pray as Christ the Lord has taught us:

B
And now let us pray with confidence as Christ our Lord commanded:

All say:

Our Father . . .

COMMUNION

88. The minister shows the eucharistic bread to those present, saying: 55

A
This is the bread of life.
Taste and see that the Lord is good.

B
This is the Lamb of God 55
who takes away the sins of the world.
Happy are those who are called to his supper.

The sick person and all who are to receive communion say:

Lord, I am not worthy to receive you,
but only say the word and I shall be healed.

The minister goes to the sick person and, showing the blessed 56
sacrament, says:

The body of Christ.

The sick person answers: "Amen," and receives communion.

Then the minister says:

The blood of Christ.

The sick person answers: "Amen," and receives communion.

Others present who wish to receive communion then do so in the usual way.

After the conclusion of the rite, the minister cleanses the 57
vessel as usual.

SILENT PRAYER

89. Then a period of silence may be observed. 57

PRAYER AFTER COMMUNION

90. The minister says a concluding prayer. One of the 57
following may be used:

Let us pray.

Pause for silent prayer, if this has not preceded.

A
God our Father, 235
you have called us to share the one bread and one cup
and so become one in Christ.

Help us to live in him
that we may bear fruit,
rejoicing that he has redeemed the world.

We ask this through Christ our Lord.
R̰. Amen.

B
All-powerful God, 236
we thank you for the nourishment you give us
through your holy gift.

Pour out your Spirit upon us
and in the strength of this food from heaven
keep us single-minded in your service.

We ask this in the name of Jesus the Lord.
R̰. Amen.

C
All-powerful and ever-living God, 57
may the body and blood of Christ your Son
be for our brother/sister N.
a lasting remedy for body and soul.

We ask this through Christ our Lord.
R̰. Amen.

CONCLUDING RITE

BLESSING

91. The priest or deacon blesses the sick person and the others present, using one of the following blessings. If, however, any of the blessed sacrament remains, he may bless the sick person by making a sign of the cross with the blessed sacrament, in silence.

58

A

May God the Father bless you.
℟. **Amen.**

79

May God the Son heal you.
℟. **Amen.**

May God the Holy Spirit enlighten you.
℟. **Amen.**

May almighty God bless you,
the Father, and the Son, ✝ and the Holy Spirit,
℟. **Amen.**

B

May the Lord be with you to protect you.
℟. **Amen.**

237

May he guide you and give you strength.
℟. **Amen.**

May he watch over you, keep you in his care,
and bless you with his peace.
℟. **Amen.**

May almighty God bless you,
the Father, and the Son, ✝ and the Holy Spirit.
℟. **Amen.**

C

May the blessing of almighty God,
the Father, and the Son, ✝ and the Holy Spirit,
come upon you and remain with you for ever.
℟. **Amen.**

238

A minister who is not a priest or deacon invokes God's   E40
blessing and makes the sign of the cross on himself or herself,
while saying:

A
May the Lord bless us,
protect us from all evil,
and bring us to everlasting life.
R̲. **Amen.**

B
May the almighty and merciful God bless and protect
**   us,**
the Father, and the Son, + and the Holy Spirit.
R̲. **Amen.**

COMMUNION IN A HOSPITAL OR INSTITUTION

INTRODUCTORY RITE

ANTIPHON

92. The rite may begin in the church, the hospital chapel, or the first room, where the minister says one of the following antiphons:

A

**How holy this feast
in which Christ is our food:
his passion is recalled;
grace fills our hearts;
and we receive a pledge of the glory to come.**

B

**How gracious you are, Lord:
your gift of bread from heaven
reveals a Father's love and brings us perfect joy.
You fill the hungry with good things
and send the rich away empty.**

C

**I am the living bread
come down from heaven.
If you eat this bread
you will live for ever.
The bread I will give is my flesh
for the life of the world.**

If it is customary, the minister may be accompanied by a person carrying a candle.

LITURGY OF HOLY COMMUNION

GREETING

93. On entering each room, the minister may use one of the following greetings:

A

The peace of the Lord be with you always.
R̷. And also with you.

B

The grace of our Lord Jesus Christ and the love of God 230
and the fellowship of the Holy Spirit be with you all.
R̷. And also with you.

The minister then places the blessed sacrament on the table, 49
and all join in adoration.

If there is time and it seems desirable, the minister may 59
proclaim a Scripture reading from those found in no. 84 or
those appearing in Part III.

THE LORD'S PRAYER

94. When circumstances permit (for example, when there are 59
not many rooms to visit), the minister is encouraged to lead
the sick in the Lord's Prayer. The minister introduces the
Lord's Prayer in these or similar words:

A

Jesus taught us to call God our Father, and so we have
the courage to say:

B

Now let us pray as Christ the Lord has taught us:

All say:

Our Father . . .

COMMUNION

95. The minister shows the eucharistic bread to those 62
present, saying:

A

This is the Lamb of God
who takes away the sins of the world.
Happy are those who hunger and thirst,
for they shall be satisfied.

B

This is the bread of life,
Taste and see that the Lord is good.

The rite then continues as described in no. 88.

CONCLUDING RITE

CONCLUDING PRAYER

96. The concluding prayer may be said either in the last room 63
visited, in the church, or chapel. One of the following may be
used.

Let us pray.

Pause for silent prayer.

A

God our Father, 235
you have called us to share the one bread and one cup
and so become one in Christ.

Help us to live in him
that we may bear fruit,
rejoicing that he has redeemed the world.

We ask this through Christ our Lord.
R̷. Amen.

B

All-powerful and ever-living God, 57
may the body and blood of Christ your Son
be for our brothers and sisters
a lasting remedy for body and soul.
We ask this through Christ our Lord.
R̷. Amen.

C

All-powerful God, 236
we thank you for the nourishment you give us
through your holy gift.

Pour out your Spirit upon us
and in the strength of this food from heaven
keep us single-minded in your service.

We ask this in the name of Jesus the Lord.
R̷. Amen.

The blessing is omitted and the minister cleanses the vessel as 63
usual.

CHAPTER IV

ANOINTING OF THE SICK

INTRODUCTION
Do not be worried or distressed. Have faith in God, and faith in me.

97. The sacrament of anointing is the proper sacrament for those Christians whose health is seriously impaired by sickness or old age. It may be celebrated in the home, in a hospital or institution, or in church. This chapter contains three rites for use in these varying circumstances: anointing outside Mass, anointing within Mass, and anointing in a hospital or institution. Several sick persons may be anointed within the rite especially if the celebration takes place in a church or hospital. While the sacrament will be celebrated more frequently outside Mass, the celebration may also take place within Mass.

8
80

98. In the course of his visits to the sick, the priest should try to explain two complementary aspects of this sacrament: through the sacrament of anointing the Church supports the sick in their struggle against illness and continues Christ's messianic work of healing. All who are united in the bond of a common baptism and a common faith are joined together in the body of Christ since what happens to one member affects all. The sacrament of anointing effectively expresses the share that each one has in the sufferings of others. When the priest anoints the sick, he is anointing in the name and with the power of Christ himself (see Mark 6:13). On behalf of the whole community, he is ministering to those members who are suffering. This message of hope and comfort is also needed by those who care for the sick, especially those who are closely bound in love to them. There should be opportunity for suitable preparation over a period of time for the benefit of the sick themselves and of those who are with them.

3
5
64
85

99. The priest should ensure that the abuse of delaying the reception of the sacrament does not occur, and that the celebration takes place while the sick person is capable of active participation. However, the intent of the conciliar

8
13

reform (Constitution on the Liturgy, art. 73) that those needing the sacrament should seek it at the beginning of a serious illness should not be used to anoint those who are not proper subjects for the sacrament. The sacrament of the anointing of the sick should be celebrated only when a Christian's health is seriously impaired by sickness or old age.

Because of its very nature as a sign, the sacrament of the anointing of the sick should be celebrated with members of the family and other representatives of the Christian community whenever this is possible. Then the sacrament is seen for what it is—a part of the prayer of the Church and an encounter with the Lord. The sign of the sacrament will be further enhanced by avoiding undue haste in prayer and action.

100. The priest should inquire about the physical and spiritual condition of the sick person and he should become acquainted with the family, friends, and others who may be present. The sick person and others may help to plan the celebration, for example, by choosing the readings and prayers. It will be especially helpful if the sick person, the priest, and the family become accustomed to praying together.

In the choice of readings the condition of the sick person should be kept in mind. The readings and the homily should help those present to reach a deeper understanding of the mystery of human suffering in relation to the paschal mystery of Christ.

The sick person who is not confined to bed may take part in the sacrament of anointing in a church, chapel, or other appropriate place. He or she should be made comfortable and there should be room for relatives and friends. In hospitals and other institutions the priest should consider all who will be present for the celebration: whether they are able to take part; whether they are very weak; and, if they are not Catholic, whether they might be offended.

101. If the sick person wishes to celebrate the sacrament of penance, it is preferable that the priest make himself available for this during a previous visit. If it is necessary to celebrate

the sacrament of penance during the rite of anointing, it takes the place of the penitential rite. The priest should also arrange for the continued pastoral care of the sick, especially for frequent opportunities to receive communion.

102. The sacrament of anointing may be repeated: 9

a. when the sick person recovers after being anointed and, at   11
a later time, becomes sick again;
b. when during the same illness the condition of the sick person becomes more serious.

In the case of a person who is chronically ill, or elderly and in a weakened condition, the sacrament of anointing may be repeated when in the pastoral judgment of the priest the condition of the sick person warrants the repetition of the sacrament.

103. A sick person who recovers after being anointed should   40c
be encouraged to give thanks for the favors received, especially by participating in a Mass of thanksgiving.

CELEBRATING THE SACRAMENT OF ANOINTING

104. There are three distinct and integral aspects to the celebration of this sacrament: the prayer of faith, the laying on of hands, and the anointing with oil.

105. *Prayer of faith:* The community, asking God's help for the sick, makes its prayer of faith in response to God's word and in a spirit of trust (see James 5:14-15). In the rites for the sick, it is the people of God who pray in faith. The entire Church is made present in this community—represented by at least the priest, family, friends, and others—assembled to pray for those to be anointed. If they are able, the sick persons should also join in this prayer.

106. *Laying on of hands:* The gospels contain a number of instances in which Jesus healed the sick by the laying on of hands or even by the simple gesture of touch. The ritual has restored to major significance the gesture of the laying on of hands with its several meanings. With this gesture the priest indicates that this particular person is the object of the Church's prayer of faith. The laying on of hands is clearly a

sign of blessing, as we pray that by the power of God's healing grace the sick person may be restored to health or at least strengthened in time of illness. The laying on of hands is also an invocation: the Church prays for the coming of the Holy Spirit upon the sick person. Above all, it is the biblical gesture of healing and indeed Jesus' own usual manner of healing: "They brought the sick with various diseases to him; and he laid hands on every one of them and healed them" (Luke 4:40).

107. *Anointing with oil:* The practice of anointing the sick with oil signifies healing, strengthening, and the presence of the Spirit.

In the gospel of Mark the disciples were sent out by the Lord to continue his healing ministry: "They anointed many sick people with oil and cured them" (Mark 6:13). And Saint James witnesses to the fact that the Church continued to anoint the sick with oil as both a means and a sign of healing (James 5:14). The Church's use of oil for healing is closely related to its remedial use in soothing and comforting the sick and in restoring the tired and the weak. Thus the sick person is strengthened to fight against the physically and spiritually debilitating effects of illness. The prayer for blessing the oil of the sick reminds us, furthermore, that the oil of anointing is the sacramental sign of the presence, power, and grace of the Holy Spirit.

If the anointing is to be an effective sacramental symbol, there should be a generous use of oil so that it will be seen and felt by the sick person as a sign of the Spirit's healing and strengthening presence. For the same reason, it is not desirable to wipe off the oil after the anointing.

ANOINTING OF THE SICK WITH A LARGE
CONGREGATION

108. The rites for anointing outside Mass and anointing within Mass may be used to anoint a number of people within the same celebration. These rites are appropriate for large gatherings of a diocese, parish, or society for the sick, or for pilgrimages. These celebrations should take place in a church, chapel, or other appropriate place where the sick and others can easily gather. On occasion, they may also take place in hospitals and other institutions.

67
83
84
85

If the diocesan bishop decides that many people are to be anointed in the same celebration, either he or his delegate should ensure that all disciplinary norms concerning anointing are observed, as well as the norms for pastoral preparation and liturgical celebration. In particular, the practice of indiscriminately anointing numbers of people on these occasions simply because they are ill or have reached an advanced age is to be avoided. Only those whose health is seriously impaired by sickness or old age are proper subjects for the sacrament. The diocesan bishop also designates the priests who will take part in the celebration of the sacrament.

The full participation of those present must be fostered by every means, especially through the use of appropriate songs, so that the celebration manifests the Easter joy which is proper to this sacrament.

109. The communal rite begins with a greeting followed by a reception of the sick (see no. 135), which is a sympathetic expression of Christ's concern for those who are ill and of the role of the sick in the people of God. [87] [91]

Before the rite of dismissal the blessing is given. The celebration may conclude with an appropriate song.

110. If there are large numbers of sick people to be anointed, other priests may assist the celebrant. Each priest lays hands on some of the sick and anoints them, using the sacramental form. Everything else is done once for all, and the prayers are said in the plural by the celebrant. After the sacramental form has been heard at least once by those present, suitable songs may be sung while the rest of the sick are being anointed. [67] [90]

ANOINTING OUTSIDE MASS

INTRODUCTION
He has borne our sickness and endured our suffering.

111. The rite which follows provides for the celebration of the   68
sacrament of anointing outside Mass. This celebration takes
place in the home, in a hospital or institution, or in church.
Appropriate vestments should be worn by the priest.

112. The priest should inquire beforehand about the physical   64
and spiritual condition of the sick person and he should   85
become acquainted with the family, friends, and others who
may be present. If possible, he should involve them in the
preparation for the celebration, for example, in the choice of
the readings and prayers, and he should explain to them the
significance of the sacrament. Since the liturgical texts appear
in the singular, they must be adapted in gender and number
for a celebration in which two or more people are anointed.

113. If the sick person wishes to celebrate the sacrament of   65
penance, it is preferable that the priest make himself available   86
for this during a previous visit. If it is necessary for the sick
person to confess during the celebration of the sacrament of
anointing, this takes the place of the penitential rite.

114. If communion is to be given during the celebration, this   78
occurs after the liturgy of anointing.

INTRODUCTORY RITES

GREETING
115. The priest greets the sick person and the others present.   68
One of the greetings in no. 81 may be used.

If communion is to take place during the rite, the priest then   68
places the blessed sacrament on the table, and all join in
adoration.

SPRINKLING WITH HOLY WATER
116. If it seems desirable, the priest may sprinkle the sick   69
person and those present with holy water. One of the
following may be used:

A

**The Lord is our shepherd
and leads us to streams of living water.**

B

**Like a stream in parched land,
may the grace of the Lord
refresh our lives.**

C

Let this water call to mind our baptism into Christ, 69
who by his death and resurrection has redeemed us.

INSTRUCTION

117. Then he addresses those present in these or similar 70
words:

**My dear friends, we are gathered here in the name of
our Lord Jesus Christ who is present among us. As the
gospels relate, the sick came to him for healing;
moreover, he loves us so much that he died for our
sake. Through the apostle James, he has commanded
us: "Are there any who are sick among you? Let them
send for the priests of the Church, and let the priests
pray over them, anointing them with oil in the name of
the Lord; and the prayer of faith will save the sick
persons, and the Lord will raise them up; and if they
have committed any sins, their sins will be forgiven
them."**

**Let us therefore commend our sick brother/sister N. to
the grace and power of Christ, that he may save
him/her and raise him/her up.**

If the sacrament of penance is now celebrated (see Appen- 65
dix, nos. 299–305) the penitential rite is omitted.

PENITENTIAL RITE

118. The priest invites the sick person and all present to join 52
in the penitential rite, using these or similar words: 88

A

**My brothers and sisters, to prepare ourselves for this
holy anointing, let us call to mind our sins.**

B

My brothers and sisters, as we prepare to celebrate this holy sacrament, let us acknowledge our failings and ask the Lord for pardon and strength.

C

My brothers and sisters, let us turn with confidence to the Lord and ask his forgiveness for all our sins.

D

Coming together as God's family, with confidence let us ask the Lord's forgiveness, for he is full of gentleness and compassion.

After a brief period of silence, the penitential rite continues, using one of the following:

A All say:

I confess to almighty God,
and to you, my brothers and sisters,
that I have sinned through my own fault

52
74

They strike their breast.

in my thoughts and in my words,
in what I have done,
and in what I have failed to do;
and I ask blessed Mary, ever virgin,
all the angels and saints,
and you, my brothers and sisters,
to pray for me to the Lord our God.

B

Lord Jesus, you healed the sick:
Lord, have mercy.
℞. Lord, have mercy.

Lord Jesus, you forgave sinners:
Christ, have mercy.
℞. Christ, have mercy.

Lord Jesus, you give us yourself to heal us and bring us
    strength:
Lord, have mercy.
℞. Lord, have mercy.

C

By your paschal mystery   233
   you have won for us salvation:
Lord, have mercy.
R̸. Lord, have mercy.

You renew among us now
   the wonders of your passion:
Christ, have mercy.
R̸. Christ, have mercy.

When we receive your body,
you share with us your paschal sacrifice:
Lord, have mercy.
R̸. Lord, have mercy.

The priest concludes the penitential rite with the following: 52

May almighty God have mercy on us,
forgive us our sins,
and bring us to everlasting life.
R̸. Amen.

LITURGY OF THE WORD

READING

119. The word of God is proclaimed by one of those present
or by the priest. An appropriate reading from Part III or one
of the following readings may be used:

A
Matthew 11:25-30   207
Childlike confidence in the goodness of God will bring us the
"rest" that only Jesus can give.

B
Mark 2:1-12   210
Much more important than the health of our bodies is the
peace and consolation of the presence of Jesus who can
forgive us our sins and reconcile us with God.

C
Luke 7:18b-23   214
The healing hand of Christ is a sign of the presence of God;
that same hand is extended to us in this sacrament now, to
console and strengthen us.

RESPONSE

120. A brief period of silence may be observed after the reading of the word of God.

72
89

The priest may then give a brief explanation of the reading, applying it to the needs of the sick person and those who are looking after him or her.

LITURGY OF ANOINTING

LITANY

121. The priest may adapt or shorten the litany according to the condition of the sick person.

73
90

My brothers and sisters, in our prayer of faith let us appeal to God for our brother/sister N.

70

Come and strengthen him/her through this holy anointing: Lord, have mercy.
R̷. Lord, have mercy.

Free him/her from all harm: Lord, have mercy. R̷.

Free him/her from sin and all temptation: Lord, have mercy. R̷.

Relieve the sufferings of all the sick [here present]: Lord, have mercy. R̷.

Assist all those dedicated to the care of the sick: Lord, have mercy. R̷.

Give life and health to our brother/sister N., on whom we lay our hands in your name: Lord, have mercy. R̷.

LAYING ON OF HANDS

122. In silence, the priest lays his hands on the head of the sick person.

74
90

PRAYER OVER THE OIL

123. The priest says a prayer of thanksgiving over blessed oil or he may bless the oil himself (see no. 21), using one of the following:

75

Thanksgiving over Blessed Oil—If the oil is already blessed, the priest says the following prayer of thanksgiving over it:

Praise to you, God, the almighty Father.
You sent your Son to live among us
and bring us salvation.
℟. Blessed be God who heals us in Christ.

Praise to you, God, the only-begotten Son.
You humbled yourself to share in our humanity
and you heal our infirmities. ℟.

Praise to you, God, the Holy Spirit, the Consoler.
Your unfailing power gives us strength
in our bodily weakness. ℟.

God of mercy,
ease the sufferings and comfort the weakness of your
    servant N.,
whom the Church anoints with this holy oil.

We ask this through Christ our Lord.
℟. Amen.

Blessing of Oil—When the priest blesses the oil during the rite,
he uses the following blessing:

Let us pray.

God of all consolation,
you chose and sent your Son to heal the world.
Graciously listen to our prayer of faith:
send the power of your Holy Spirit, the Consoler,
into this precious oil, this soothing ointment,
this rich gift, this fruit of the earth.

Bless this oil ✝ and sanctify it for our use.

Make this oil a remedy for all who are anointed with it;
heal them in body, in soul, and in spirit,
and deliver them from every affliction.

We ask this through our Lord Jesus Christ, your Son,
who lives and reigns with you and the Holy Spirit,
one God, for ever and ever.
℟. Amen.

Other forms of the blessing may be found in nos. 140 and
248.

ANOINTING

124. The priest anoints the sick person with the blessed oil.   76

First he anoints the forehead, saying:

Through this holy anointing
may the Lord in his love and mercy help you
with the grace of the Holy Spirit.
R̲̅. Amen.

Then he anoints the hands, saying:

May the Lord who frees you from sin
save you and raise you up.
R̲̅. Amen.

The sacramental form is said only once, for the anointing of the forehead and hands, and is not repeated.

Depending upon the culture and traditions of the place, as   23
well as the condition of the sick person, the priest may also   24
anoint additional parts of the body, for example, the area of
pain or injury. He does not repeat the sacramental form.

PRAYER AFTER ANOINTING

125. The priest says one of the following prayers: 77
    90

Let us pray.

A General
Father in heaven,
through this holy anointing
grant N. comfort in his/her suffering.

When he/she is afraid, give him/her courage,
when afflicted, give him/her patience,
when dejected, afford him/her hope,
and when alone, assure him/her of the support
    of your holy people.

We ask this through Christ our Lord.
R̲̅. Amen.

B General
Lord Jesus Christ, our Redeemer,   77
by the grace of your Holy Spirit
cure the weakness of your servant N.

Heal his/her sickness and forgive his/her sins;
expel all afflictions of mind and body;
mercifully restore him/her to full health,
and enable him/her to resume his/her former duties,
for you are Lord for ever and ever.
℟. **Amen.**

C In extreme or terminal illness
Lord Jesus Christ,   77
you chose to share our human nature,
to redeem all people, and to heal the sick.

Look with compassion upon your servant N.,
whom we have anointed in your name with this holy
**   oil**
for the healing of his/her body and spirit.

Support him/her with your power,
comfort him/her with your protection,
and give him/her the strength to fight against evil.

Since you have given him/her a share in your own
**   passion,**
help him/her to find hope in suffering,
for you are Lord for ever and ever.
℟. **Amen.**

D In advanced age
God of mercy,   243
look kindly on your servant
who has grown weak under the burden of years.
In this holy anointing
he/she asks for healing in body and soul.

Fill him/her with the strength of your Holy Spirit.
Keep him/her firm in faith and serene in hope,
so that he/she may give us all an example of patience
and joyfully witness to the power of your love.

We ask this through Christ our Lord.
℟. **Amen.**

E Before surgery
God of compassion,
our human weakness lays claim to your strength.

We pray that through the skills of surgeons and nurses
your healing gifts may be granted to N.

May your servant respond to your healing will
and be reunited with us at your altar of praise.

Grant this through Christ our Lord.
R⁷. Amen.

F   For a child
God our Father,
we have anointed your child N.
with the oil of healing and peace.

Caress him/her,
Shelter him/her,
and keep him/her in your tender care.

We ask this in the name of Jesus the Lord.
R⁷. Amen

G   For a young person
God our healer,
in this time of sickness you have come
to bless N. with your grace.

Restore him/her to health and strength,
make him/her joyful in spirit,
and ready to embrace your will.

Grant this through Christ our Lord.
R⁷. Amen.

THE LORD'S PRAYER

126. The priest introduces the Lord's Prayer in these or
similar words: 78

A
Now let us offer together the prayer our Lord Jesus
Christ taught us:

B
And now let us pray with confidence as Christ our Lord
commanded:

All say:

Our Father . . .

If the sick person does not receive communion, the rite   79
concludes with a blessing as in no. 130.

LITURGY OF HOLY COMMUNION

COMMUNION
127. The priest shows the eucharistic bread to those present,   55
saying:

A

**This is the Lamb of God
who takes away the sins of the world.
Come to me, all you that labor and are burdened,
and I will refresh you.**

B

**These are God's holy gifts to his holy people:
receive them with thanksgiving.**

C

**This is the bread of life.
Taste and see that the Lord is good.**

The rite then continues as described in no. 88.

SILENT PRAYER
128. Then a period of silence may be observed.   57

PRAYER AFTER COMMUNION
129. The priest says a concluding prayer. One of the   57
following may be used:

Let us pray.

Pause for silent prayer, if this has not preceded.

A

**All-powerful God,
through the paschal mystery of Christ your Son**   234
you have completed the work of our redemption.

**May we, who in these sacramental signs
proclaim his death and resurrection,
grow in the experience of your saving power.**

We ask this through Christ our Lord.
℟. Amen.

B

All-powerful God, 236
we thank you for the nourishment you give us
through your holy gift.

Pour out your Spirit upon us
and in the strength of this food from heaven
keep us single-minded in your service.

We ask this in the name of Jesus the Lord.
℟. Amen.

C

All-powerful and ever-living God, 57
may the body and blood of Christ your Son
be for our brother/sister N.
a lasting remedy for body and soul.

We ask this through Christ our lord.
℟. Amen.

CONCLUDING RITE

BLESSING

130. The priest blesses the sick person and the others 58
present, using one of the following blessings. If, however, 79
any of the blessed sacrament remains, he may bless the sick
person by making a sign of the cross with the blessed
sacrament, in silence.

A

May the Lord be with you to protect you. 237
℟. Amen.

May he guide you and give you strength.
℟. Amen.

May he watch over you, keep you in his care,
and bless you with his peace.
℟. Amen.

May almighty God bless you,
the Father, and the Son, ✝ and the Holy Spirit.
℟. Amen.

B

May God the Father bless you.   79
℟. Amen.

May God the Son heal you.
℟. Amen.

May God the Holy Spirit enlighten you.
℟. Amen.

May almighty God bless you,
the Father, and the Son, ✝ and the Holy Spirit.
℟. Amen.

C

May the God of all consolation   79
bless you in every way
and grant you hope all the days of your life.
℟. Amen.

May God restore you to health
and grant you salvation.
℟. Amen.

May God fill your heart with peace
and lead you to eternal life.
℟. Amen.

May almighty God bless you,
the Father, and the Son, ✝ and the Holy Spirit.
℟. Amen.

D

May the blessing of almighty God,   238
the Father, and the Son, ✝ and the Holy Spirit,
come upon you and remain with you for ever.
℟. Amen.

ANOINTING WITHIN MASS

INTRODUCTION
If one member suffers, all share in those sufferings.

131. When the condition of the sick person permits, and especially when communion is to be received, the sacrament of anointing may be celebrated within Mass. The following rite provides for such a celebration, which takes place in a church or in a suitable place in the home of the sick person or in the hospital.

80

132. This rite may be used to anoint a number of people within the same celebration (see nos. 108-110). It is especially appropriate for large gatherings of a diocese, parish, or society for the sick, or for pilgrimages. Since the liturgical texts appear in the plural, they must be adapted in gender and number for a celebration in which one person is anointed.

67
83

133. The priest should ensure that the sick who wish to celebrate the sacrament of penance have a convenient opportunity to do so before Mass.

65
86

134. When the ritual Mass for the anointing of the sick is celebrated, the priest wears white vestments. The readings are taken from *The Lectionary for Mass* (2nd edition, nos. 790-795) or from Part III, unless the sick person and those involved with the priest in planning the liturgy choose other readings from Scripture.

81

The ritual Mass for the anointing of the sick is not permitted during the Easter triduum, on the solemnities of Christmas, Epiphany, Ascension, Pentecost, Corpus Christi, or on a solemnity which is a holy day of obligation. On these occasions, the texts and readings are taken from the Mass of the day. Although the ritual Mass is also excluded on the Sundays of Advent, Lent, and the Easter season, on solemnities, Ash Wednesday, and the weekdays of Holy Week, one of the readings may be taken from the Scripture texts indicated above, and the special form of the final blessing may be used.

INTRODUCTORY RITES

RECEPTION OF THE SICK

135. After the greeting the priest welcomes the sick in these   92
or similar words:

A

We have come together to celebrate the sacraments of anointing and eucharist. Christ is always present when we gather in his name; today we welcome him especially as physician and healer. We pray that the sick may be restored to health by the gift of his mercy and made whole in his fullness.

B

Christ taught his disciples to be a community of love. In praying together, in sharing all things, and in caring for the sick, they recalled his words: "Insofar as you did this to one of these, you did it to me." We gather today to witness to this teaching and to pray in the name of Jesus the healer that the sick may be restored to health. Through this eucharist and anointing we invoke his healing power.

OPENING PRAYER

136. Afterward the priest, with hands joined, sings or says:

Let us pray.

All pray in silence for a brief period.

A
Father,
you raised your Son's cross
as the sign of victory and life.

May all who share in his suffering
find in these sacraments
a source of fresh courage and healing.

We ask this through our Lord Jesus Christ, your Son, who lives and reigns with you and the Holy Spirit, one God, for ever and ever.
R̰. Amen.

B
God of compassion,
you take every family under your care
and know our physical and spiritual needs.

Transform our weakness by the strength of your grace
and confirm us in your covenant
so that we may grow in faith and love.

We ask this through our Lord Jesus Christ, your Son,
who lives and reigns with you and the Holy Spirit,
one God, for ever and ever.
℞. Amen.

LITURGY OF THE WORD

137. The liturgy of the word is celebrated in the usual way
according to the instructions in no. 134. The general
intercessions are omitted since they are included in the litany.

92
82a
89

In the homily the celebrant should show how the sacred text
speaks of the meaning of illness in the history of salvation
and of the grace given by the sacrament of anointing.

A brief period of silence may follow the homily.

LITURGY OF ANOINTING

LITANY

138. The priest may adapt or shorten the litany according to
the condition of the sick persons.

73
82b

Let us pray to God for our brothers and sisters and for
all those who devote themselves to caring for them.

241

Bless N. and N. and fill them with new hope and
strength: Lord, have mercy.
℞. Lord, have mercy.

Relieve their pain: Lord, have mercy. ℞.

Free them from sin and do not let them give way to
temptation: Lord, have mercy. ℞.

Sustain all the sick with your power: Lord, have mercy.
R̠̂.

Assist all who care for the sick: Lord, have mercy. R̠̂.

Give life and health to our brothers and sisters on whom we lay our hands in your name: Lord, have mercy. R̠̂.

LAYING ON OF HANDS

139. In silence, the priest lays his hands on the head of each sick person. If there are several priests present, each one lays hands on some of the sick.   74 82b 90

PRAYER OVER THE OIL

140. The priest says a prayer of thanksgiving over blessed oil or he may bless the oil himself (see no. 21), using one of the following: 75 75b 82b

Thanksgiving over Blessed Oil—If the oil is already blessed, the priest says the following prayer of thanksgiving over it:

Praise to you, God, the almighty Father.
You sent your Son to live among us
and bring us salvation.
R̠̂. Blessed be God who heals us in Christ.

Praise to you, God, the only-begotten Son.
You humbled yourself to share in our humanity
and you heal our infirmities. R̠̂.

Praise to you, God, the Holy Spirit, the Consoler.
Your unfailing power gives us strength
in our bodily weakness. R̠̂.

God of mercy,
ease the sufferings and comfort the weakness of your
   servants
whom the Church anoints with this holy oil.

We ask this through Christ our Lord.
R̠̂. Amen.

Blessing of Oil—When the priest blesses the oil during the rite, he uses one of the following blessings: 75

A

This blessing is found in no. 123.

B

Praise to you, God, the almighty Father.
You sent your Son to live among us
and bring us salvation.
R̸. Blessed be God who heals us in Christ.

Praise to you, God, the only-begotten Son.
You humbled yourself to share in our humanity
and you heal our infirmities. R̸.

Praise to you, God, the Holy Spirit, the Consoler.
Your unfailing power gives us strength
in our bodily weakness. R̸.

Almighty God,
come to our aid and sanctify this oil
which has been set apart for healing your people.
May the prayer of faith and the anointing with oil
free them from every affliction.

We ask this through Christ our Lord.
R̸. Amen.

242

ANOINTING

141. The priest anoints the sick person with the blessed oil. If
there are large numbers of sick people to be anointed, other
priests may assist the celebrant. Each priest anoints some of
the sick, using the sacramental form as described in no. 124.

76
90

PRAYER AFTER ANOINTING

142. The priest says one of the following prayers A–D, as in
no. 125.

82c

LITURGY OF THE EUCHARIST

143. The Order of Mass then continues with the liturgy of the
eucharist.

82c

PRAYER OVER THE GIFTS

144. With hands extended, the priest sings or says:

A
Merciful God,
as these simple gifts of bread and wine
will be transformed into the risen Lord,
so may he unite our sufferings with his
and cause us to rise to new life.

We ask this through Christ our Lord.
R̕. Amen.

B
Lord,
we bring you these gifts,
to become the health-giving body and blood of your
    Son.

In his name
heal the ills which afflict us
and restore to us the joy of life renewed.

We ask this through Christ our Lord.
R̕. Amen.

EUCHARISTIC PRAYER

145. The priest begins the eucharistic prayer. With hands extended he sings or says:

The Lord be with you.
R̕. And also with you.

Lift up your hearts.
R̕. We lift them up to the Lord.

Let us give thanks to the Lord our God.
R̕. It is right to give him thanks and praise.

Father, all-powerful and ever-living God,
we do well always and everywhere to give you thanks,
for you have revealed to us
in Christ the healer
your unfailing power and steadfast compassion.

In the splendor of his rising
your Son conquered suffering and death
and bequeathed to us his promise
of a new and glorious world,

where no bodily pain will afflict us
and no anguish of spirit.

Through your gift of the Spirit,
you bless us, even now,
with comfort and healing,
strength and hope,
forgiveness and peace.

In this supreme sacrament of your love
you give us the risen body of your Son:
a pattern of what we shall become
when he returns again at the end of time.

In gladness and joy
we unite with the angels and saints
in the great canticle of creation,
as we say (sing):

Holy, holy, holy Lord, God of power and might,
heaven and earth are full of your glory.
   Hosanna in the highest.
Blessed is he who comes in the name of the Lord.
   Hosanna in the highest.

Special Intercessions—The following embolisms may be used
with Eucharistic Prayers I, II, and III.

When Eucharistic Prayer I is used, the special form of
"Father, accept this offering," is said:

Father, accept this offering
from your whole family,
and especially from those who ask for healing
of body, mind, and spirit.
Grant us your peace in this life,
save us from final damnation,
and count us among those you have chosen.

When Eucharistic Prayer II is used, after the words "and all
the clergy," there is added:

Remember also those who ask for healing
in the name of your Son,
that they may never cease to praise you
for the wonders of your power.

When Eucharistic Prayer III is used, after the words "the family you have gathered here," there is added:

Hear especially the prayers of those who ask for healing
in the name of your Son,
that they may never cease to praise you
for the wonders of your power.

PRAYER AFTER COMMUNION

146. With hands extended, the priest sings or says:

Let us pray.

Pause for silent prayer, if this has not preceded.

A
Merciful God,
in celebrating these mysteries
your people have received the gifts of unity and peace.

Heal the afflicted
and make them whole
in the name of your only Son,
who lives and reigns for ever and ever.
R̲͆. Amen.

B
Lord,
through these sacraments
you offer us the gift of healing.

May this grace bear fruit among us
and make us strong in your service.

We ask this through Christ our Lord.
R̲͆. Amen.

CONCLUDING RITES

BLESSING

147. Then the priest blesses the sick persons and others present, using one of the following:

A

May the God of all consolation 79
bless you in every way
and grant you hope all the days of your life.
R̷. Amen.

May God restore you to health
and grant you salvation.
R̷. Amen.

May God fill your heart with peace
and lead you to eternal life.
R̷. Amen.

May almighty God bless you,
the Father, and the Son, ✛ and the Holy Spirit.
R̷. Amen.

B

May the Lord be with you to protect you. 237
R̷. Amen.

May he guide you and give you strength.
R̷. Amen.

May he watch over you, keep you in his care,
and bless you with his peace.
R̷. Amen.

May almighty God bless you,
the Father, and the Son, ✛ and the Holy Spirit.
R̷. Amen.

C

May the blessing of almighty God, 238
the Father, and the Son, ✛ and the Holy Spirit,
come upon you and remain with you for ever.
R̷. Amen.

DISMISSAL

148. The deacon (or the priest) then dismisses the people and
commends the sick to their care.

ANOINTING IN A HOSPITAL OR INSTITUTION

INTRODUCTION
Have faith in God, and faith in me.

149. Although the sacrament of anointing should be celebrated whenever possible in accordance with the full rites already given, the special circumstances of hospital ministry often make it necessary to abbreviate the rite. The rite which follows is a simplification of the anointing rite and preserves its central elements. It is intended for those occasions when only the priest and sick person are present and the complete rite cannot be celebrated.

150. The priest should inquire beforehand about the physical and spiritual condition of the sick person in order to plan the celebration properly and choose the appropriate prayers. If possible he should involve the sick person in this preparation, and should explain the significance of the sacrament.   64

151. If the sick person wishes to celebrate the sacrament of penance, it is preferable that the priest make himself available for this during a previous visit. If it is necessary, this may take place during the introductory rites.   65

152. The circumstances of an emergency room or casualty ward of a hospital may make the proper celebration of the sacrament difficult. If the condition of the sick person does not make anointing urgent, the priest may find it better to wait for a more appropriate time to celebrate the sacrament.

153. The priest should arrange for the continued pastoral care of the sick person, especially for frequent opportunities to receive communion.

INTRODUCTORY RITES

GREETING

154. The priest greets the sick person. One of the following may be used: 68

A

The peace of the Lord be with you always.

℟. **And also with you.**

B

The grace and peace of God our Father and the Lord 231
Jesus Christ be with you.

℟. **And also with you.**

INSTRUCTION

155. The priest may prepare the sick person for the liturgy of 70
anointing with an instruction (see no. 117) or with the
following prayer:

Lord God, 239
you have said to us through your apostle James:
"Are there people sick among you?
Let them send for the priests of the Church,
and let the priests pray over them
anointing them with oil in the name of the Lord.
The prayer of faith will save the sick persons,
and the Lord will raise them up.
If they have committed any sins,
their sins will be forgiven them."

Lord,
we have gathered here in your name
and we ask you to be among us,
to watch over our brother/sister N.
We ask this with confidence,
for you live and reign for ever and ever.
℟. **Amen.**

If the sick person so wishes, the sacrament of penance may 65
now be celebrated (see Appendix, p. 737).

LITURGY OF ANOINTING

LAYING ON OF HANDS

156. In silence, the priest lays his hands on the head of the 74
sick person.

ANOINTING

157. The rite is as described in no. 124.   76

THE LORD'S PRAYER

158. The priest introduces the Lord's Prayer in these or   78
similar words:

A

**Now let us pray to God as our Lord Jesus Christ taught
us:**

B

**And now let us pray with confidence as Christ our Lord
    commanded:**

All say:

Our Father . . .

PRAYER AFTER ANOINTING

159. The priest says one of the prayers given in no. 125.   77

CONCLUDING RITE

BLESSING

160. Then the priest blesses the sick person, using one of the   79
following:

A

May the blessing of almighty God,   238
the Father, and the Son, ✝ and the Holy Spirit,
come upon you and remain with you for ever.
R̸. Amen.

B

May God the Father bless you.   79
R̸. Amen.

May God the Son heal you.
R̸. Amen.

May God the Holy Spirit enlighten you.
R̸. Amen.

May almighty God bless you,
the Father, and the Son, ✛ and the Holy Spirit.
℟. **Amen.**

PART II

PASTORAL CARE OF THE DYING

INTRODUCTION
When we were baptized in Christ Jesus we were baptized into his death . . . so that as Christ was raised from the dead by the Father's glory, we too might live a new life.

161. The rites in Part II of *Pastoral Care of the Sick: Rites of Anointing and Viaticum* are used by the Church to comfort and strengthen a dying Christian in the passage from this life. The ministry to the dying places emphasis on trust in the Lord's promise of eternal life rather than on the struggle against illness which is characteristic of the pastoral care of the sick.

The first three chapters of Part II provide for those situations in which time is not a pressing concern and the rites can be celebrated fully and properly. These are to be clearly distinguished from the rites contained in Chapter Eight, "Rites for Exceptional Circumstances," which provide for the emergency situations sometimes encountered in the ministry to the dying.

162. Priests with pastoral responsibilities are to direct the efforts of the family and friends as well as other ministers of the local Church in the care of the dying. They should ensure that all are familiar with the rites provided here.

The words "priest," "deacon," and "minister" are used advisedly. Only in those rites which must be celebrated by a priest is the word "priest" used in the rubrics (that is, the sacrament of penance, the sacrament of the anointing of the sick, the celebration of viaticum within Mass). Whenever it is clear that, in the absence of a priest, a deacon may preside at a particular rite, the words "priest or deacon" are used in the rubrics. Whenever another minister is permitted to celebrate a rite in the absence of a priest or deacon, the word "minister" is used in the rubrics, even though in many cases the rite will be celebrated by a priest or deacon.

163. The Christian community has a continuing responsibility to pray for and with the person who is dying. Through its sacramental ministry to the dying the community

helps Christians to embrace death in mysterious union with
the crucified and risen Lord, who awaits them in the fullness
of life.

CELEBRATION OF VIATICUM

164. A rite for viaticum within Mass and another for viati-   94
cum outside Mass are provided. If possible, viaticum
should take place within the full eucharistic celebration,
with the family, friends, and other members of the Christian community taking part. The rite for viaticum outside
Mass is used when the full eucharistic celebration cannot
take place. Again, if it is possible, others should take part.

COMMENDATION OF THE DYING

165. The second chapter of Part II contains a collection of
prayers for the spiritual comfort of the Christian who is close
to death. These prayers are traditionally called the
commendation of the dying to God and are to be used
according to the circumstances of each case.

PRAYERS FOR THE DEAD

166. A chapter has also been provided to assist a minister   15
who has been called to attend a person who is already dead.
A priest is not to administer the sacrament of anointing.
Instead, he should pray for the dead person, using prayers
such as those which appear in this chapter. He may find it
necessary to explain to the family of the person who is dead
that sacraments are celebrated for the living, not for the dead,
and that the dead are effectively helped by the prayers of the
living.

RITES FOR EXCEPTIONAL CIRCUMSTANCES

167. Chapter VIII, "Rites for Exceptional Circumstances,"
contains rites which should be celebrated with a person who
has suddenly been placed in proximate or immediate danger
of death. They are for emergency circumstances and should
be used only when such pressing conditions exist.

CARE OF A DYING CHILD

168. In its ministry to the dying the Church must also
respond to the difficult circumstances of a dying child.
Although no specific rites appear in Part II for the care of a

dying child, these notes are provided to help bring into focus the various aspects of this ministry.

169. When parents learn that their child is dying, they are often bewildered and hurt. In their love for their son or daughter, they may be beset by temptations and doubts and find themselves asking: Why is God taking this child from us? How have we sinned or failed that God would punish us in this way? Why is this innocent child being hurt?

Under these trying circumstances, much of the Church's ministry will be directed to the parents and family. While pain and suffering in an innocent child are difficult for others to bear, the Church helps the parents and family to accept what God has allowed to happen. It should be understood by all beforehand that this process of acceptance will probably extend beyond the death of the child. The concern of the Christian community should continue as long as necessary.

Concern for the child must be equal to that for the family. Those who deal with dying children observe that their faith matures rapidly. Though young children often seem to accept death more easily than adults, they will often experience a surprisingly mature anguish because of the pain which they see in their families.

170. At such a time, it is important for members of the Christian community to come to the support of the child and the family by prayer, visits, and other forms of assistance. Those who have lost children of their own have a ministry of consolation and support to the family. Hospital personnel (doctors, nurses, aides) should also be prepared to exercise a special role with the child as caring adults. Priests and deacons bear particular responsibility for overseeing all these elements of the Church's pastoral ministry. The minister should invite members of the community to use their individual gifts in this work of communal care and concern.

171. By conversation and brief services of readings and prayers, the minister may help the parents and family to see that their child is being called ahead of them to enter the kingdom and joy of the Lord. The period when the child is dying can become a special time of renewal and prayer for the family and close friends. The minister should help them to see that the child's sufferings are united to those of Jesus for the salvation of the whole world.

172. If it is appropriate, the priest should discuss with the parents the possibility of preparing and celebrating with the child the sacraments of initiation (baptism, confirmation, eucharist). The priest may baptize and confirm the child (see *Rite of Confirmation*, no. 7b). To complete the process of initiation, the child should also receive first communion.

According to the circumstances, some of these rites may be celebrated by a deacon or lay person. So that the child and family may receive full benefit from them, these rites are normally celebrated over a period of time. In this case, the minister should use the usual rites, that is, the *Rite of Baptism for Children*, the *Rite of Confirmation*, and if suitable, the *Rite of Penance*. Similarly, if time allows, the usual rites for anointing and viaticum should be celebrated.

173. If sudden illness or an accident has placed an uninitiated child in proximate danger of death, the minister uses "Christian Initiation for the Dying" (nos. 275–296), adapting it for use with a child.

174. For an initiated child or a child lacking only the sacrament of confirmation, who is in proximate danger of death, the "Continuous Rite of Penance, Anointing, and Viaticum" (nos. 236–258) may be used and adapted to the understanding of the child. If death is imminent it should be remembered that viaticum rather than anointing is the sacrament for the dying.

CHAPTER V

CELEBRATION OF VIATICUM

INTRODUCTION

I am going to prepare a place for you; I shall come back and take you with me.

175. This chapter contains a rite for viaticum within Mass and a rite for viaticum outside Mass. The celebration of the eucharist as viaticum, food for the passage through death to eternal life, is the sacrament proper to the dying Christian. It is the completion and crown of the Christian life on this earth, signifying that the Christian follows the Lord to eternal glory and the banquet of the heavenly kingdom.

The sacrament of the anointing of the sick should be celebrated at the beginning of a serious illness. Viaticum, celebrated when death is close, will then be better understood as the last sacrament of Christian life.

176. Priests and other ministers entrusted with the spiritual   93
care of the sick should do everything they can to ensure that those in proximate danger of death receive the body and blood of Christ as viaticum. At the earliest opportunity, the necessary preparations should be given to the dying person, family, and others who may take part.

177. Whenever it is possible, the dying Christian should be   36
able to receive viaticum within Mass. In this way he or she   101
shares fully, during the final moments of this life, in the eucharistic sacrifice, which proclaims the Lord's own passing through death to life. However, circumstances, such as confinement to a hospital ward or the very emergency which makes death imminent, may frequently make the complete eucharistic celebration impossible. In this case, the rite for viaticum outside Mass is appropriate. The minister should wear attire appropriate to this ministry.

178. Because the celebration of viaticum ordinarily takes place in the limited circumstances of the home, a hospital, or other institution, the simplifications of the rite for Masses in small gatherings may be appropriate. Depending on the condition of the dying person, every effort should be made to

involve him or her, the family, friends, and other members of the local community in the planning and celebration. Appropriate readings, prayers, and songs will help to foster the full participation of all. Because of this concern for participation, the minister should ensure that viaticum is celebrated while the dying person is still able to take part and respond.

179. A distinctive feature of the celebration of viaticum, whether within or outside Mass, is the renewal of the baptismal profession of faith by the dying person. This occurs after the homily and replaces the usual form of the profession of faith. Through the baptismal profession at the end of earthly life, the one who is dying uses the language of his or her initial commitment, which is renewed each Easter and on other occasions in the Christian life. In the context of viaticum, it is a renewal and fulfillment of initiation into the Christian mysteries, baptism leading to the eucharist.

28
108

180. The rites of viaticum within and outside Mass may include the sign of peace. The minister and all who are present embrace the dying Christian. In this and in other parts of the celebration the sense of leave-taking need not be concealed or denied, but the joy of Christian hope, which is the comfort and strength of the one near death, should also be evident.

99d
114

181. As an indication that the reception of the eucharist by the dying Christian is a pledge of resurrection and food for the passage through death, the special words proper to viaticum are added: "May the Lord Jesus Christ protect you and lead you to eternal life." The dying person and all who are present may receive communion under both kinds. The sign of communion is more complete when received in this manner because it expresses more fully and clearly the nature of the eucharist as a meal, one which prepares all who take part in it for the heavenly banquet (see General Instruction of *The Roman Missal*, no. 240).

26
95
96

The minister should choose the manner of giving communion under both kinds which is suitable in the particular case. If the wine is consecrated at a Mass not celebrated in the presence of the sick person, the blood of the Lord is kept in a properly covered vessel and is placed in the tabernacle after communion. The precious blood should be carried to the sick person in a vessel which is closed in such a way as to eliminate all danger of spilling. If some of the precious blood remains after communion, it should be consumed by the minister, who should also see to it that the vessel is properly purified.

The sick who are unable to receive under the form of bread may receive under the form of wine alone. If the wine is consecrated at a Mass not celebrated in the presence of the sick person, the instructions given above are followed.

182. In addition to these elements of the rites which are to be given greater stress, special texts are provided for the general intercessions or litany and the final solemn blessing.

183. It often happens that a person who has received the eucharist as viaticum lingers in a grave condition or at the point of death for a period of days or longer. In these circumstances he or she should be given the opportunity to receive the eucharist as viaticum on successive days, frequently if not daily. This may take place during or outside Mass as particular conditions permit. The rite may be simplified according to the condition of the one who is dying.

VIATICUM WITHIN MASS

184. When viaticum is received within Mass, the ritual Mass for Viaticum or the Mass of the Holy Eucharist may be celebrated. The priest wears white vestments. The readings may be taken from *The Lectionary for Mass* (2nd edition, nos. 796-800) or from Part III of this ritual, unless the dying person and those involved with the priest in planning the liturgy choose other readings from Scripture.

97
99f

A ritual Mass is not permitted during the Easter triduum, on the solemnities of Christmas, Epiphany, Ascension, Pentecost, Corpus Christi, or on a solemnity which is a holy day of obligation. On these occasions, the texts and readings are taken from the Mass of the day. Although the Mass for Viaticum or the Mass of the Holy Eucharist are also excluded on the Sundays of Advent, Lent, and the Easter season, on solemnities, Ash Wednesday, and the weekdays of Holy Week, one of the readings may be taken from the biblical texts indicated above. The special form of the final blessing may be used and, at the discretion of the priest, the apostolic pardon may be added.

185. If the dying person wishes to celebrate the sacrament of penance, it is preferable that the priest make himself available for this during a previous visit. If this is not possible, the sacrament of penance may be celebrated before Mass begins (see Appendix, nos. 299–305). 98

VIATICUM OUTSIDE MASS

186. Although viaticum celebrated in the context of the full eucharistic celebration is always preferable, when it is not possible the rite for viaticum outside Mass is appropriate. This rite includes some of the elements of the Mass, especially a brief liturgy of the word. Depending on the circumstances and the condition of the dying person, this rite should also be a communal celebration. Every effort should be made to involve the dying person, family, friends, and members of the local community in the planning and celebration. The manner of celebration and the elements of the rite which are used should be accommodated to those present and the nearness of death.

187. If the dying person wishes to celebrate the sacrament of penance and this cannot take place during a previous visit, it should be celebrated before the rite of viaticum begins, especially if others are present. Alternatively, it may be celebrated during the rite of viaticum, replacing the penitential rite. At the discretion of the priest, the apostolic pardon may be added after the penitential rite or after the sacrament of penance. 100

188. An abbreviated liturgy of the word, ordinarily consisting of a single biblical reading, gives the minister an opportunity to explain the word of God in relation to viaticum. The sacrament should be described as the sacred food which strengthens the Christian for the passage through death to life in sure hope of the resurrection. 107

VIATICUM WITHIN MASS

LITURGY OF THE WORD

HOMILY

189. After the gospel a brief homily on the sacred text may be given in which the priest explains the meaning and importance of viaticum.   99a

BAPTISMAL PROFESSION OF FAITH

190. If the sick person is to renew his or her baptismal profession of faith, this should be done at the conclusion of the homily. This renewal takes the place of the usual profession of faith in the Mass.   99b

The priest gives a brief introduction and then asks the following questions: 108

N., do you believe in God, the Father almighty, creator of heaven and earth?
R̠⃠. I do.

Do you believe in Jesus Christ, his only Son, our Lord, who was born of the Virgin Mary, was crucified, died, and was buried, rose from the dead, and is now seated at the right hand of the Father?
R̠⃠. I do.

Do you believe in the Holy Spirit, the holy catholic Church, the communion of saints, the forgiveness of sins, the resurrection of the body, and life everlasting?
R̠⃠. I do.

LITANY

191. The priest may adapt or shorten the litany according to the condition of the sick person. The litany may be omitted if the sick person has made the profession of faith and appears to be tiring.   99c

My brothers and sisters, with one heart let us call on our Savior Jesus Christ.   109

You loved us to the very end and gave yourself over to death in order to give us life. For our brother/sister, Lord, we pray:

R̶. **Lord, hear our prayer.**

You said to us: "All who eat my flesh and drink my blood will live forever." For our brother/sister, Lord, we pray: R̶.

You invite us to join in the banquet where pain and sorrow, sadness and separation will be no more. For our brother/sister, Lord, we pray: R̶.

LITURGY OF THE EUCHARIST

SIGN OF PEACE

192. The priest and those present may give the sick person the sign of peace at the usual place in the Order of Mass. `99d`

COMMUNION AS VIATICUM

193. The sick person and all present may receive communion under both kinds. When the priest gives communion to the sick person, he uses the form for viaticum. `99e`

The priest genuflects, takes the eucharistic bread, raises it slightly and, facing those present, says:

A

**Jesus Christ is the food for our journey;
he calls us to the heavenly table.**

B

**This is the Lamb of God
who takes away the sins of the world.
Happy are those who are called to his supper.** `111`

C

**These are God's holy gifts to his holy people:
receive them with thanksgiving.**

The sick person and all who are to receive communion say: `111`

**Lord, I am not worthy to receive you,
but only say the word and I shall be healed.**

The priest goes to the sick person and, showing the blessed sacrament, says: 112

The body of Christ.

The sick person answers: "Amen."

Then the priest says:

The blood of Christ.

The sick person answers: "Amen."

Immediately, or after giving communion to the sick person, the priest adds:

**May the Lord Jesus Christ protect you
and lead you to eternal life.
R̰. Amen.**

Others present who wish to receive communion then do so in the usual way.

CONCLUDING RITES

BLESSING

194. At the end of Mass the priest may use one of the blessings A, B, or C, in no. 91. 99f

APOSTOLIC PARDON

195. The priest may add the apostolic pardon for the dying. 99f

**Through the holy mysteries of our redemption, 106
may almighty God release you from all punishments
in this life and in the life to come.**

**May he open to you the gates of paradise
and welcome you to everlasting joy.
R̰. Amen.**

DISMISSAL

196. The deacon (or priest) then dismisses the people.

VIATICUM OUTSIDE MASS

INTRODUCTORY RITES

GREETING

197. The minister greets the sick person and the others   101
present as described in no. 115.

The minister then places the blessed sacrament on the table,   101
and all join in adoration.

SPRINKLING WITH HOLY WATER

198. If it seems desirable, the priest or deacon may sprinkle   102
the sick person and those present with holy water. One of the
following may be used:

A
Let this water call to mind our baptism into Christ,
who by his death and resurrection has redeemed us.

B
The Lord is our shepherd
and leads us to streams of living water.

INSTRUCTION

199. Afterward the minister addresses those present, using   103
the following instruction or one better suited to the sick
person's condition.

My brothers and sisters, before our Lord Jesus Christ
passed from this world to return to the Father, he left
us the sacrament of his body and blood. When the hour
comes for us to pass from this life and join him, he
strengthens us with this food for our journey and
comforts us by this pledge of our resurrection.

If the sacrament of penance is now celebrated (see Appen-   104
dix, nos. 299–305), the penitential rite is omitted. In case
of necessity, this may be a generic confession.

PENITENTIAL RITE

200. The minister invites the sick person and all present to   105
join in the penitential rite, using these or similar words:

A

My brothers and sisters, to prepare ourselves for this celebration, let us call to mind our sins.

B

My brothers and sisters, let us turn with confidence to the Lord and ask his forgiveness for all our sins.

After a brief period of silence, the penitential rite continues, 105
using prayer A or C in no. 118.

The minister concludes the penitential rite with the following: 105

May almighty God have mercy on us,
forgive us our sins,
and bring us to everlasting life.
R̶ . Amen.

APOSTOLIC PARDON

201. At the conclusion of the sacrament of penance or the 106
penitential rite, the priest may give the apostolic pardon for
the dying, using one of the following:

A

Through the holy mysteries of our redemption,
may almighty God release you from all punishments
in this life and in the life to come.

May he open to you the gates of paradise
and welcome you to everlasting joy.
R̶ . Amen.

B

By the authority which the Apostolic See has given me,
I grant you a full pardon and the remission of all your
**   sins**
in the name of the Father, and of the Son, ✛ and of the
**   Holy Spirit.**
R̶ . Amen.

LITURGY OF THE WORD

READING

202. The word of God is proclaimed by one of those present 107

or by the minister. An appropriate reading from Part III or one of the following may be used:

A **John 6:54-55**
B **John 14:23**
C **John 15:4**
D **1 Corinthians 11:26**

HOMILY

203. Depending on circumstances, the minister may then give a brief explanation of the reading. [107]

BAPTISMAL PROFESSION OF FAITH

204. The rite is as described in no. 190. [108]

LITANY

205. The rite is as described in no. 191. [109]

LITURGY OF VIATICUM

THE LORD'S PRAYER

206. The minister introduces the Lord's Prayer as in no. 126. [110]

COMMUNION AS VIATICUM

207. The sick person and all present may receive communion under both kinds. When the minister gives communion to the sick person, the form for viaticum is used. [99e]

The minister shows the eucharistic bread to those present, saying: [111]

A
**Jesus Christ is the food for our journey;
he calls us to the heavenly table.**

B
**This is the bread of life.
Taste and see that the Lord is good.**

The rite then proceeds as described in no. 193. [111] [112]

After the conclusion of the rite, the minister cleanses the vessel as usual. [113]

SILENT PRAYER

208. Then a period of silence may be observed. [113]

PRAYER AFTER COMMUNION

209. The minister says a concluding prayer. One of the
following may be used:

Let us pray.

Pause for silent prayer, if this has not preceded.

A

God of peace,
you offer eternal healing to those who believe in you;
you have refreshed your servant N.
with food and drink from heaven:
lead him/her safely into the kingdom of light.

We ask this through Christ our Lord.
R͡. Amen.

B

All-powerful and ever-living God,
may the body and blood of Christ your Son
be for our brother/sister N.
a lasting remedy for body and soul.

We ask this through Christ our Lord.
R͡. Amen.

C

Father,
your son, Jesus Christ, is our way, our truth, and our
life.
Look with compassion on your servant N.
who has trusted in your promises.
You have refreshed him/her with the body and blood of
your Son:
may he/she enter your kingdom in peace.

We ask this through Christ our Lord.
R͡. Amen.

CONCLUDING RITES

BLESSING

210. The priest or deacon blesses the sick person and the
others present, using one of the blessings in no. 91. If,

however, any of the blessed sacrament remains, he may bless the sick person by making a sign of the cross with the blessed sacrament, in silence.

A minister who is not a priest or deacon invokes God's E40 blessing and makes the sign of the cross on himself or herself, as described in no. 91.

SIGN OF PEACE
211. The minister and the others present may then give the 114 sick person the sign of peace.

CHAPTER VI

COMMENDATION OF THE DYING

INTRODUCTION
Into your hands, Lord, I commend my spirit.

212. In viaticum the dying person is united with Christ in his passage out of this world to the Father. Through the prayers for the commendation of the dying contained in this chapter, the Church helps to sustain this union until it is brought to fulfillment after death.

213. Christians have the responsibility of expressing their union in Christ by joining the dying person in prayer for God's mercy and for confidence in Christ. In particular, the presence of a priest or deacon shows more clearly that the Christian dies in the communion of the Church. He should assist the dying person and those present in the recitation of the prayers of commendation and, following death, he should lead those present in the prayer after death. If the priest or deacon is unable to be present because of other serious pastoral obligations, other members of the community should be prepared to assist with these prayers and should have the texts readily available to them. 138
142

214. The minister may choose texts from among the prayers, litanies, aspirations, psalms, and readings provided in this chapter, or others may be added. In the selection of these texts the minister should keep in mind the condition and piety of both the dying person and the members of the family who are present. The prayers are best said in a slow, quiet voice, alternating with periods of silence. If possible, the minister says one or more of the brief prayer formulas with the dying person. These may be softly repeated two or three times. 139
140

215. These texts are intended to help the dying person, if still conscious, to face the natural human anxiety about death by imitating Christ in his patient suffering and dying. The Christian will be helped to surmount his or her fear in the hope of heavenly life and resurrection through the power of Christ, who destroyed the power of death by his own dying. 139

Even if the dying person is not conscious, those who are

present will draw consolation from these prayers and come to
a better understanding of the paschal character of Christian
death. This may be visibly expressd by making the sign of the
cross on the forehead of the dying person, who was first
signed with the cross at baptism.

216. Immediately after death has occurred, all may kneel 141
while one of those present leads the prayers given in nos.
221–222.

SHORT TEXTS

217. One or more of the following short texts may be recited 140
with the dying person. If necessary, they may be softly
repeated two or three times.

Romans 8:35 143
Who can separate us from the love of Christ?

Romans 14:8
Whether we live or die, we are the Lord's.

2 Corinthians 5:1
We have an everlasting home in heaven.

1 Thessalonians 4:17
We shall be with the Lord for ever.

1 John 3:2
We shall see God as he really is.

1 John 3:14
We have passed from death to life
because we love each other.

Psalm 25:1
To you, Lord, I lift up my soul.

Psalm 27:1
The Lord is my light and my salvation.

Psalm 27:13
I believe that I shall see the goodness of the Lord
in the land of the living.

Psalm 42:3
My soul thirsts for the living God.

Psalm 23:4
Though I walk in the shadow of death,
I will fear no evil,
for you are with me.

Matthew 25:34
Come, blessed of my Father,
says the Lord Jesus,
and take possession of the kingdom
prepared for you.

Luke 23:43
The Lord Jesus says,
today you will be with me in paradise.

John 14:2
In my Father's home
there are many dwelling places,
says the Lord Jesus.

John 14:2-3
The Lord Jesus says,
I go to prepare a place for you,
and I will come again to take you to myself.

John 17:24
I desire that where I am,
they also may be with me,
says the Lord Jesus.

John 6:40
Everyone who believes in the Son
has eternal life.

Psalm 31:5a
Into your hands, Lord,
I commend my spirit.

Acts 7:59
Lord Jesus, receive my spirit.

Holy Mary, pray for me.

Saint Joseph, pray for me.

Jesus, Mary, and Joseph,
assist me in my last agony.

READING

218. The word of God is proclaimed by one of those present 144
or by the minister. Selections from Part III or from the
following readings may be used:

A Job 19:23-27a
Job's act of faith is a model for our own; God is the God of the
living.

B **Psalm 23**
C **Psalm 25**
D **Psalm 91**
E **Psalm 121**
F **1 John 4:16**

G Revelation 21:1-5a, 6-7

God our Father is the God of newness and life; it is his desire
that we should come to share his life with him.

H Matthew 25:1-13

Jesus bid us be prepared for our ultimate destiny, which is
eternal life.

I Luke 22:39-46

Jesus is alive to our pain and sorrow, because faithfulness to
his Father's will cost him life itself.

J Luke 23:44-49

Jesus' death is witnessed by his friends.

K Luke 24:1-8

Jesus is alive; he gives us eternal life with the Father.

L John 6:37-40

Jesus will raise his own from death and give them eternal life.

M John 14:1-6, 23, 27

The love of Jesus can raise us up from the sorrow of death to
the joy of eternal life.

LITANY OF THE SAINTS

219. When the condition of the dying person calls for the use 145
of brief forms of prayer, those who are present are
encouraged to pray the litany of the saints—or at least some
of its invocations—for him or her. Special mention may be
made of the patron saints of the dying person, of the family,
and of the parish. The litany may be said or sung in the usual
way. Other customary prayers may also be used.

One of the following litanies may be used:

A

Lord, have mercy	**Lord, have mercy**
Christ, have mercy	**Christ, have mercy**
Lord, have mercy	**Lord, have mercy**
Holy Mary, Mother of God	pray for him/her
Holy angels of God	pray for him/her

Abraham, our father in faith	pray for him/her
David, leader of God's people	pray for him/her
All holy patriarchs and prophets	pray for him/her
Saint John the Baptist	pray for him/her
Saint Joseph	pray for him/her
Saint Peter and Saint Paul	pray for him/her
Saint Andrew	pray for him/her
Saint John	pray for him/her
Saint Mary Magdalene	pray for him/her
Saint Stephen	pray for him/her
Saint Ignatius	pray for him/her
Saint Lawrence	pray for him/her
Saint Perpetua and Saint Felicity	pray for him/her
Saint Agnes	pray for him/her
Saint Gregory	pray for him/her
Saint Augustine	pray for him/her
Saint Athanasius	pray for him/her
Saint Basil	pray for him/her
Saint Martin	pray for him/her
Saint Benedict	pray for him/her
Saint Francis and Saint Dominic	pray for him/her
Saint Francis Xavier	pray for him/her
Saint John Vianney	pray for him/her
Saint Catherine	pray for him/her
Saint Teresa	pray for him/her

Other saints may be included here.

All holy men and women	pray for him/her
Lord, be merciful	Lord, save your people
From all evil	Lord, save your people
From every sin	Lord, save your people
From Satan's power	Lord, save your people
At the moment of death	Lord, save your people
From everlasting death	Lord, save your people
On the day of judgment	Lord, save your people
By your coming as man	Lord, save your people
By your suffering and cross	Lord, save your people

By your death and rising to new life	Lord, save your people
By your return in glory to the Father	Lord, save your people
By your gift of the Holy Spirit	Lord, save your people
By your coming again in glory	Lord, save your people
Be merciful to us sinners	Lord, hear our prayer
Bring N. to eternal life, first promised to him/her in baptism	Lord, hear our prayer
Raise N. on the last day, for he/she has eaten the bread of life	Lord, hear our prayer
Let N. share in your glory, for he/she has shared in your suffering and death	Lord, hear our prayer
Jesus, Son of the living God	Lord, hear our prayer
Christ, hear us	Christ, hear us
Lord Jesus, hear our prayer	Lord Jesus, hear our prayer

B

A brief form of the litany may be prayed. Other saints may be added, including the patron saints of the dying person, of the family, and of the parish; saints to whom the dying person may have a special devotion may also be included.

Holy Mary, Mother of God	pray for him/her
Holy angels of God	pray for him/her
Saint John the Baptist	pray for him/her
Saint Joseph	pray for him/her
Saint Peter and Saint Paul	pray for him/her

Other saints may be included here.

| All holy men and women | pray for him/her |

PRAYER OF COMMENDATION

220. When the moment of death seems near, some of the following prayers may be said: 145

A

Go forth, Christian soul, from this world   146
in the name of God the almighty Father,
who created you,
in the name of Jesus Christ, Son of the living God,
who suffered for you,
in the name of the Holy Spirit,
who was poured out upon you,
go forth, faithful Christian.

May you live in peace this day,
may your home be with God in Zion,
with Mary, the virgin Mother of God,
with Joseph, and all the angels and saints.

B

I commend you, my dear brother/sister, to almighty   147
   God,
and entrust you to your Creator.
May you return to him
who formed you from the dust of the earth.
May holy Mary, the angels, and all the saints
come to meet you as you go forth from this life.
May Christ who was crucified for you
bring you freedom and peace.
May Christ who died for you,
admit you into his garden of paradise.
May Christ, the true Shepherd,
acknowledge you as one of his flock.
May he forgive all your sins,
and set you among those he has chosen.
May you see your Redeemer face to face,
and enjoy the vision of God for ever.
℟. Amen.

C

Welcome your servant, Lord, into the place of salvation   148
which because of your mercy he/she rightly hoped for.
℟. Amen, or ℟. Lord, save your people.

Deliver your servant, Lord, from every distress. ℟.

Deliver your servant, Lord, as you delivered Noah
from the flood. ℟.

Deliver your servant, Lord, as you delivered Abraham from Ur of the Chaldees. ℟.

Deliver your servant, Lord, as you delivered Job from his sufferings. ℟.

Deliver your servant, Lord, as you delivered Moses from the hand of the Pharaoh. ℟.

Deliver your servant, Lord, as you delivered Daniel from the den of lions. ℟.

Deliver your servant, Lord, as you delivered the three young men from the fiery furnace. ℟.

Deliver your servant, Lord, as you delivered Susanna from her false accusers. ℟.

Deliver your servant, Lord, as you delivered David from the attacks of Saul and Goliath. ℟.

Deliver your servant, Lord, as you delivered Peter and Paul from prison. ℟.

Deliver your servant, Lord, through Jesus our Savior, who suffered death for us and gave us eternal life. ℟.

D

Lord Jesus Christ, Savior of the world,   149
we pray for your servant N.,
and commend him/her to your mercy.
For his/her sake you came down from heaven;
receive him/her now into the joy of your kingdom.

For though he/she has sinned,
he/she has not denied the Father, the Son, and the Holy
    Spirit,
but has believed in God
and has worshiped his/her Creator.
℟. Amen.

E   The following antiphon may be said or sung: 150
Hail, holy Queen, Mother of mercy,
hail, our life, our sweetness, and our hope.
To you we cry, the children of Eve;
to you we send up our sighs,
mourning and weeping in this land of exile.
Turn, then, most gracious advocate,

your eyes of mercy toward us;
lead us home at last
and show us the blessed fruit of your womb, Jesus:
O clement, O loving, O sweet Virgin Mary.

PRAYER AFTER DEATH

221. When death has occurred, one or more of the following   151
prayers may be said:

A
Saints of God, come to his/her aid!
Come to meet him/her, angels of the Lord!
R̸. **Receive his/her soul and present him/her to God the**
    Most High.

May Christ, who called you, take you to himself;
may angels lead you to Abraham's side. R̸.

Give him/her eternal rest, O Lord,
and may your light shine on him/her for ever. R̸.

The following prayer is added:

Let us pray.

All-powerful and merciful God,
we commend to you N., your servant.
In your mercy and love,
blot out the sins he/she has committed
    through human weakness.
In this world he/she has died:
let him/her live with your for ever.

We ask this through Christ our Lord.
R̸. **Amen.**

B Psalm 130   F163
R̸. **My soul hopes in the Lord.**

The following prayer is added: F30

Let us pray.

God of love,
welcome into your presence
your son/daughter N., whom you have called from this
    life.
Release him/her from all his/her sins,

bless him/her with eternal light and peace,
raise him/her up to live for ever with all your saints
in the glory of the resurrection.

We ask this through Christ our Lord.
R̸. **Amen.**

C   Psalm 23
R̸. **Lord, remember me in your kingdom.**   F145

The following prayer is added: F33

Let us pray.

God of mercy,
hear our prayers and be merciful
to your son/daughter N., whom you have called from
  this life.
Welcome him/her into the company of your saints,
in the kingdom of light and peace.

We ask this through Christ our Lord.
R̸. **Amen.**

D
Almighty and eternal God,   F167
hear our prayers for your son/daughter N.,
whom you have called from this life to yourself.

Grant him/her light, happiness, and peace.
Let him/her pass in safety through the gates of death,
and live for ever with all your saints
in the light you promised to Abraham
and to all his descendants in faith.

Guard him/her from all harm
and on that great day of resurrection and reward
raise him/her up with all your saints.
Pardon his/her sins
and give him/her eternal life in your kingdom.

We ask this through Christ our Lord.
R̸. **Amen.**

E
Loving and merciful God,   F168
we entrust our brother/sister to your mercy.

You loved him/her greatly in this life:
now that he/she is freed from all its cares,
give him/her happiness and peace for ever.

The old order has passed away:
welcome him/her now into paradise
where there will be no more sorrow,
no more weeping or pain,
but only peace and joy
with Jesus, your Son,
and the Holy Spirit
for ever and ever
R⁄. Amen.

F
God of our destiny,   F48
into your hands we commend our brother/sister.
We are confident that with all who have died in Christ
he/she will be raised to life on the last day
and live with Christ for ever.

[We thank you for all the blessings
you gave him/her in this life
to show your fatherly care for all of us
and the fellowship which is ours with the saints
in Jesus Christ.]

Lord, hear our prayer:
welcome our brother/sister to paradise
and help us to comfort each other
with the assurance of our faith
until we all meet in Christ
to be with you and with our brother/sister for ever.

We ask this through Christ our Lord.
R⁄. Amen.

PRAYER FOR THE FAMILY AND FRIENDS
222. One of the following prayers may be said:

Let us pray.   834

A   For the family and friends   F34
God of all consolation,
in your unending love and mercy for us

you turn the darkness of death
into the dawn of new life.
Show compassion to your people in their sorrow.

[Be our refuge and our strength
to lift us from the darkness of this grief
to the peace and light of your presence.]

Your Son, our Lord Jesus Christ,
by dying for us, conquered death
and by rising again, restored life.

May we then go forward eagerly to meet him,
and after our life on earth
be reunited with our brothers and sisters
where every tear will be wiped away.

We ask this through Christ our Lord.
R̷. **Amen.**

B For the deceased person and for the family and friends   F169
Lord Jesus, our Redeemer,
you willingly gave yourself up to death
so that all people might be saved
and pass from death into a new life.
Listen to our prayers,
look with love on your people
who mourn and pray for their brother/sister N.

Lord Jesus, holy and compassionate:
forgive N. his/her sins.
By dying you opened the gates of life
for those who believe in you:
do not let our brother/sister be parted from you,
but by your glorious power
give him/her light, joy, and peace in heaven
where you live for ever and ever.
R̷. **Amen.**

For the solace of those present the minister may conclude
these prayers with a simple blessing or with a symbolic
gesture, for example, signing the forehead with the sign of
the cross. A priest or deacon may sprinkle the body with holy
water.

CHAPTER VII

PRAYERS FOR THE DEAD

INTRODUCTION
I want those you have given me to be with me where I am.

223. This chapter contains prayers for use by a minister who   15
has been called to attend a person who is already dead. A
priest is not to administer the sacraments of penance or
anointing. Instead, he should pray for the dead person using
these or similar prayers.

224. It may be necessary to explain to the family of the person
who is dead that sacraments are celebrated for the living, not
for the dead, and that the dead are effectively helped by the
prayers of the living.

225. To comfort those present the minister may conclude
these prayers with a simple blessing or with a symbolic
gesture, for example, making the sign of the cross on the
forehead. A priest or deacon may sprinkle the body with holy
water.

GREETING
226. The minister greets those who are present, offering
them sympathy and the consolation of faith, using one of the
following or similar words:

A
In this moment of sorrow
the Lord is in our midst
and comforts us with his word:
Blessed are the sorrowful; they shall be consoled.

B
Praised be God, the Father of our Lord Jesus Christ,
the Father of mercies,
and the God of all consolation!
He comforts us in all our afflictions
and thus enables us to comfort those who are in
   trouble,
with the same consolation
we have received from him.

PRAYER

227. The minister then says one of prayers D or E in no. 221.

READING

228. The word of God is proclaimed by one of those present or by the minister. An appropriate reading from Part III or one of the following readings may be used:

A   Luke 23:44-46
B   John 11:3-7, 17, 20-27, 33-36, 41-44

LITANY

229. Then one of those present may lead the others in praying a brief form of the litany of the saints. (The full form of the litany of the saints may be found in no. 219.) Other saints may be added, including the patron saints of the dead person, of the family, and of the parish; saints to whom the deceased person may have had a special devotion may also be included.

Saints of God, come to his/her aid!
Come to meet him/her, angels of the Lord!

Holy Mary, Mother of God	**pray for him/her**
Saint Joseph	**pray for him/her**
Saint Peter and Saint Paul	**pray for him/her**

The following prayer is added:

God of mercy,   F33
hear our prayers and be merciful
to your son/daughter N., whom you have called from
**   this life.**
Welcome him/her into the company of your saints,
in the kingdom of light and peace.

We ask this through Christ our Lord.
R̷. Amen.

THE LORD'S PRAYER

230. The minister introduces the Lord's Prayer in these or similar words:

A
With God there is mercy and fullness of redemption;
let us pray as Jesus taught us to pray:

B
Let us pray for the coming of the kingdom as Jesus taught us:

All say:

Our Father . . .

PRAYER OF COMMENDATION

231. The minister then concludes with the following prayer:

Lord Jesus, our Redeemer,   F169
you willingly gave yourself up to death
so that all people might be saved
and pass from death into a new life.
Listen to our prayers,
look with love on your people
who mourn and pray for their brother/sister N.

Lord Jesus, holy and compassionate:
forgive N. his/her sins.
By dying you opened the gates of life
for those who believe in you:
do not let our brother/sister be parted from you,
but by your glorious power
give him/her light, joy, and peace in heaven
where you live for ever and ever.
R̸. Amen.

For the solace of those present the minister may conclude these prayers with a simple blessing or with a symbolic gesture, for example, signing the forehead with the sign of the cross. A priest or deacon may sprinkle the body with holy water.

CHAPTER VIII

RITES FOR EXCEPTIONAL CIRCUMSTANCES

INTRODUCTION

I am the gateway. Whoever enters through me will be safe.

232. The rites contained in this section are exclusively for use in exceptional circumstances. In all other cases, the more developed forms of pastoral care ought to be employed for the greater benefit of those members of the community who are dying and for the greater consolation of those who are close to them.

The exceptional circumstances for which these rites are provided arise when there is a genuine necessity, for example, when sudden illness or an accident or some other cause has placed one of the faithful in the proximate or immediate danger of death.

CONTINUOUS RITE

233. A "Continuous Rite of Penance, Anointing, and Viaticum" has been set out so that these sacraments may be given together in a single celebration. If the person is unable to receive holy communion, the priest can use this rite, omitting the liturgy of viaticum.

RITE FOR EMERGENCIES

234. If death seems imminent and there is not enough time to celebrate the three sacraments in the manner given in the continuous rite, the priest should proceed with the "Rite for Emergencies." 116

CHRISTIAN INITIATION

235. This chapter also includes "Christian Initiation for the Dying," which contains the rites for baptism, confirmation, and viaticum. It is to be used when ministering to an uninitiated or partially initiated person.

CONTINUOUS RITE OF PENANCE, ANOINTING, AND VIATICUM

INTRODUCTION
He will wipe away all tears from their eyes; there will be no more death, and no more mourning or sadness.

236. This rite has been provided for use when sudden illness, an accident, or some other cause has placed one of the faithful in danger of death. It makes possible the reception of the three sacraments of penance, anointing, and viaticum in a single celebration. It is not only for use at the point of death, but even possibly a day or so before when time or the condition of the dying person will not allow a more developed celebration of these sacraments over a period of time. In its pastoral ministry the Church always seeks to be as complete as possible, and with this continuous rite those who are in danger of death are prepared to face it sustained by all the spiritual means available to the Church.

30

237. The priest should be guided by the condition of the dying person in deciding how much of this rite should be celebrated and where it should be appropriately shortened or adapted. If the dying person wishes to celebrate the sacrament of penance, this should take place before the anointing and reception of communion as viaticum. If necessary, the dying person may confess at the beginning of the celebration, before the anointing. Otherwise, the penitential rite should be celebrated.

115
116

If the danger of death is imminent, the priest should anoint immediately with a single anointing and then give viaticum. If the circumstances are extreme, he should give viaticum immediately (see no. 30), without the anointing. The "Rite for Emergencies" has been designed for this situation. Christians in danger of death are bound by the precept of receiving communion so that in their passage from this life, they may be strengthened by the body of Christ, the pledge of the resurrection.

238. It is preferable not to celebrate the sacrament of confirmation and the sacrament of the anointing of the sick in

117

a continuous rite. The two anointings can cause some confusion between the two sacraments. However, if the dying person has not been confirmed this sacrament may be celebrated immediately before the blessing of the oil of the sick. In this case, the imposition of hands which is part of the liturgy of anointing is omitted.

INTRODUCTORY RITES

GREETING

239. The priest greets the sick person and the others present. One of the following may be used as described in no. 81.   118

If communion as viaticum is celebrated during the rite, the priest then places the blessed sacrament on the table, and all join in adoration.   118

INSTRUCTION

240. If the occasion requires, the priest speaks to the sick person about the celebration of the sacraments.   119

Depending on the circumstances, he reads a brief gospel text or an instruction to invite the sick person to repentance and the love of God.

A   **Matthew 11:28-30**
B   **John 6:40**

C   The priest may use the following instruction, or one   119
    better adapted to the sick person's condition:

Beloved in Christ, the Lord Jesus is with us at all times, warming our hearts with his sacramental grace. Through his priests he forgives the sins of the repentant; he strengthens the sick through holy anointing; to all who watch for his coming, he gives the food of his body and blood to sustain them on their last journey, confirming their hope of eternal life. Our brother/sister has asked to receive these three sacraments: let us help him/her with our love and our prayers.

LITURGY OF PENANCE

SACRAMENT OF PENANCE

241. If the sick person so wishes, the sacrament of penance is   120
celebrated; in case of necessity, the confession may be
generic.

The priest extends his hands over the penitent's head (or at   F46
least extends his right hand) and says:

God, the Father of mercies,
through the death and resurrection of his Son
has reconciled the world to himself
and sent the Holy Spirit among us
for the forgiveness of sins;
through the ministry of the Church
may God give you pardon and peace,
and I absolve you from your sins
in the name of the Father, and of the Son, +
and of the Holy Spirit.
R̸. **Amen.**

PENITENTIAL RITE

242. If there is no celebration of the sacrament of penance,   121
the penitential rite takes place as usual. The priest invites the
sick person and all present to join in the penitential rite using
these or similar words:

A
My brothers and sisters, let us turn with confidence to
the Lord and ask his forgiveness for all our sins.

B
My brothers and sisters, to prepare ourselves for this
celebration, let us call to mind our sins.

After a brief period of silence, the penitential rite continues,
as described in no. 118, A or C.

APOSTOLIC PARDON

243. At the conclusion of the sacrament of penance or the   122
penitential rite, the priest may give the apostolic pardon for
the dying, as described in no. 201.

BAPTISMAL PROFESSION OF FAITH

244. If the condition of the sick person permits, the baptismal profession of faith follows. The priest gives a brief introduction and then asks the following questions, as described in no. 190.

108
123

The priest may sprinkle the sick person with holy water after the renewal of the baptismal profession of faith.

LITANY

245. The litany may be adapted to express the intentions of the sick person and of those present. The sick person, if able, and all present respond. One of the following may be used:

A

You bore our weakness and carried our sorrows:
Lord, have mercy.
R̥. Lord, have mercy.

240

You felt compassion for the crowd,
and went about doing good and healing the sick:
Christ, have mercy.
R̥. Christ, have mercy.

You commanded your apostles
to lay their hands on the sick in your name:
Lord, have mercy.
R̥. Lord, have mercy.

B

Let us pray, dear friends, for our brother/sister N.,
whom the Lord at this hour is refreshing with the
sacraments.

123

That the Lord may look on our brother/sister and see in
him/her the face of his own suffering Son, we pray:
R̥. Lord, hear our prayer.

That the Lord may help N. in this moment of trial, we
pray: R̥.

That the Lord may watch over N., and keep him/her
ever in his love, we pray: R̥.

That the Lord may give N. strength and peace, we pray:
R̥.

LITURGY OF CONFIRMATION

246. It is highly appropriate that the initiation of every   124
baptized Christian be completed by the sacraments of
confirmation and the eucharist. If the sacrament of
confirmation is celebrated in the same rite, the priest
continues as indicated in "Christian Initiation for the Dying,"
no. 290. In such a case, the laying on of hands which belongs
to the anointing of the sick (see no. 247) is omitted.

LITURGY OF ANOINTING

LAYING ON OF HANDS

247. In silence, the priest then lays his hands on the head of   125
the sick person.

PRAYER OVER THE OIL

248. In some situations the priest may bless the oil himself   75
(see no. 21). Otherwise, he says a prayer of thanksgiving over
oil already blessed.

Thanksgiving over Blessed Oil—If the oil is already blessed, the   127
priest says the following prayer of thanksgiving over it, as
described in no. 123.

Blessing of Oil—When the priest is to bless the oil during the   126
rite, he uses the following blessing:

Bless, + Lord, your gift of oil
and our brother/sister N.
that it may bring him/her relief.

Other forms of the blessing may be found in nos. 123 and 140.

ANOINTING

249. The priest anoints the sick person with the blessed oil, as   128
described in no. 124.

When viaticum is celebrated the following prayer is omitted.   134

PRAYER AFTER ANOINTING

250. The priest says one of the following prayers: 134

A
Lord Jesus Christ, Redeemer of the world,   244
you have shouldered the burden of our weakness

and borne our sufferings in your own passion and
   death.

Hear this prayer for our sick brother/sister N.
whom you have redeemed.
Strengthen his/her hope of salvation
and sustain him/her in body and soul,
for you live and reign for ever and ever.
R̹. Amen.

B   See Prayer D, in no. 125.   243

LITURGY OF VIATICUM

THE LORD'S PRAYER

251. The priest introduces the Lord's Prayer in these or   129
similar words:

A
**Jesus taught us to call God our Father, and so we have
the courage to say:**

B
**And now let us pray with confidence as Christ our Lord
commanded:**

All say:

Our Father . . .

COMMUNION AS VIATICUM

252. The sick person and all present may receive communion   99e
under both kinds. When the priest gives communion to the   130
sick person, the form for viaticum is used, as described in no.   131
193.

After the conclusion of the rite, the priest cleanses the vessel   132
as usual.

SILENT PRAYER

253. Then a period of silence may observed.   132

PRAYER AFTER COMMUNION

254. The priest says a concluding prayer. One of the   133
following may be used:

Let us pray.

Pause for silent prayer, if this has not preceded.

A   See Prayer C, in no. 209.
B   See Prayer A, in no. 209.

CONCLUDING RITES

BLESSING

255. The priest blesses the sick person and the others   133
present, using one of the following blessings. If, however,
any of the blessed sacrament remains, he may bless the sick
person by making a sign of the cross with the blessed
sacrament, in silence.

A   See Blessing A in no. 91.
B   See Blessing C in no. 91.

SIGN OF PEACE

256. The priest and the others present may then give the sick   133
person the sign of peace.

257. If the person recovers somewhat, the priest or other
minister may continue to give further pastoral care, bringing
viaticum frequently, and using other prayers and blessings
from the rite of visiting the sick.

258. When death has occurred, prayers may be offered for
the dead person and for the family and friends. These are
given in nos. 221–222. This may be done in any suitable
place, including a hospital chapel or prayer room.

RITE FOR EMERGENCIES

INTRODUCTION
I am at your side always.

259. There are extreme circumstances in which not even the continuous rite can be celebrated. These occur when the danger of death from injury or illness is sudden and unexpected or when the priest is not called to exercise his ministry until the person is at the point of death.

260. In such a situation of emergency the priest should offer every possible ministry of the Church as reverently and expeditiously as he can. He may be able to provide only the barest minimum of sacramental rites and forms of prayer, but even then he should add other appropriate prayers from the ritual to help the dying person and those who may be present.

261. If the dying person wishes, the sacrament of penance is celebrated first. If necessary, the confession may be generic. Because of the emergency situation, viaticum follows immediately. Christians in danger of death are bound by the precept to receive communion. If there is still sufficient time, the anointing of the sick may then be celebrated. The brief rite which follows has been provided for the celebration of these sacraments in such a situation. The priest should judge, in light of the particular circumstances, how much or how little of this rite is possible. 30 116

262. After the celebration of the abbreviated rite for emergencies, the priest should continue in prayer with the dying person, if possible, and with the family and friends, as suggested in the "Commendation of the Dying" (nos. 212–222). When death has occurred, some of the prayers suggested at the end of the "Commendation of the Dying" may be said with the family and friends.

263. When a priest has been called to attend a person who is already dead, he is not to administer the sacrament of anointing. Instead, he should pray for the dead person, asking that God forgive his or her sins and graciously receive him or her into the kingdom. It is appropriate that he lead the 15 135

family and friends, if they are present, in some of the prayers suggested at the end of the "Commendation of the Dying," as already mentioned. Sometimes the priest may find it necessary to explain to the family of the person who has died that sacraments are celebrated for the living, not for the dead, and that the dead are effectively helped by the prayers of the living.

If the priest has reason to believe that the person is still living, he anoints him or her, saying the usual sacramental form.

SACRAMENT OF PENANCE

264. If the sick person so wishes, the sacrament of penance is celebrated; in case of necessity, the confession may be generic.   120

The rite is as described in no. 241.

APOSTOLIC PARDON

265. The priest may give the apostolic pardon for the dying, as described in no. 195.   122

THE LORD'S PRAYER

266. The priest introduces the Lord's Prayer: 129

Jesus taught us to call God our Father, and so we have the courage to say:

All say:

Our Father . . .

COMMUNION AS VIATICUM

267. The priest goes to the sick person and, showing the blessed sacrament, says: 131

The body of Christ,

The sick person answers: "Amen."

Then the priest says:

The blood of Christ.

The sick person answers: "Amen."

Immediately, or after giving communion to the sick person, the priest adds the form for viaticum:

May the Lord Jesus Christ protect you
and lead you to eternal life.
R̷. Amen.

Others present who wish to receive communion then do so in the usual way.

PRAYER BEFORE ANOINTING

268. The priest says: 135

Let us ask the Lord to come to our brother/sister N.
with his merciful love, and grant him/her relief
through this holy anointing. In faith we pray:
R̷. Lord, hear our prayer.

ANOINTING

269. The priest anoints the sick person with the blessed   128
oil.   135

CONCLUDING PRAYER

270. The priest says one of the following prayers: 134b

A
Father,   246
you readily take into account
every stirring of good will,
and you never refuse to pardon the sins
of those who seek your forgiveness.

Have mercy on your servant N.,
who has now entered the struggle of his/her final
    agony.
May this holy anointing and our prayer of faith
comfort and aid him/her in body and soul.
Forgive all his/her sins,
and protect him/her with your loving care.

We ask this, Father, through your Son Jesus Christ,
because he has won the victory over death,
opened the way to eternal life,
and now lives and reigns with you for ever and ever.
R̝. Amen.

B   When anointing and viaticum are given together: 245
Lord God, merciful Father,
comforter of the afflicted,
look kindly on your servant N., who trusts in you.
Though now weighed down with grievous distress,
may he/she find relief through this holy anointing;
and may the food he/she has received,
the body and blood of your Son, Jesus Christ,
refresh and strengthen him/her for his/her journey to
    life.

We ask this through Christ our Lord.
R̝. Amen.

BLESSING

271. The priest blesses the sick person: 133

May the blessing of almighty God,   238
the Father, and the Son, + and the Holy Spirit,
come upon you and remain with you for ever.
R̝. Amen.

SIGN OF PEACE

272. The priest and the others present may then give the sick   133
person the sign of peace.

273. If the person recovers somewhat, the priest or other
minister may continue to give further pastoral care, bringing
viaticum frequently, and using other prayers and blessings
from the rite of visiting the sick.

274. When death has occurred, prayers may be offered for
the dead person and for the family and friends. These are
given in nos. 221-222. This may be done in any suitable
place, including a hospital chapel or prayer room.

CHRISTIAN INITIATION FOR THE DYING

INTRODUCTION
By becoming coheirs with Christ, we share in his sufferings; we will also share in his glory.

275. The rites of Christian initiation are normally celebrated over a period of time. This allows the dying person, family, and friends to benefit fully from their celebration. In such circumstances the rite of *Christian Initiation of Adults* should be used.

276. Anyone, catechumen or not, who is in danger of death may be baptized with the short rite that follows, as long as such a person is not at the point of death and is able to hear and answer the questions. When no priest or deacon is available, any member of the faithful may baptize.

1278
1280

If the sacred chrism is at hand and there is time, a priest who baptizes should confer confirmation after the baptism; in this case the postbaptismal anointing with chrism is omitted.

Also whenever possible the priest or deacon, as well as a catechist or layperson having permission to distribute communion, should give the eucharist to the person newly baptized (with the special words proper to viaticum). In this case the sacrament may be brought before the celebration of the rite and placed reverently on a table covered with a white cloth.

277. When a person is at the point of death or when time is pressing because death is imminent, the minister, omitting everything else, pours natural water (even if not blessed) on the head of the sick person, while saying the usual sacramental form (see General Introduction to *Christian Initiation*, no. 23).

1281

278. One already admitted as a catechumen must make a promise to complete the usual catechesis upon recovering. One not a catechumen must give serious indication of being converted to Christ and of renouncing pagan worship and must not be seen to be attached to anything that conflicts with the moral life (for example, "simultaneous" polygamy, etc.). The person must also make a promise to go through the complete cycle of initiation upon recovering.

1279

279. If persons who were baptized in proximate danger of   1282
death or at the point of death should recover their health,
they should be given a suitable formation, be received at the
church at a fitting time, and be given the rest of the
sacraments of initiation.

CARE OF A DYING CHILD

280. As far as possible, the *Rite of Baptism for Children* and the
Rite of Confirmation are celebrated in the usual way. The
eucharist completes the sacraments of initiation. A dying
child with the use of reason shares the common responsibility
of receiving viaticum. It is also desirable that an even younger
child complete his or her initiation by reception of the
eucharist, in accord with the practice of the Church.

INTRODUCTORY RITES

GREETING

281. The minister greets the family and then speaks with the   1283
sick person about the request for baptism and, if the sick   1284
person is not a catechumen, about the reasons for conversion.
After deciding to baptize him or her, the minister should, if
necessary, instruct the person briefly.

Then the minister invites the family, the godparent, and
some friends and neighbors to gather around the sick person,
and selects one or two of these as witnesses. Water, even if it
is not blessed, is prepared.

DIALOGUE

282. The minister addresses the sick person in these or   1285
similar words:

**Dear brother/sister, you have asked to be baptized
because you wish to have eternal life. This is eternal
life: to know the one, true God and Jesus Christ, whom
he has sent. This is the faith of Christians. Do you
acknowledge this?**
R̸. **I do.**

**As well as professing your faith in Jesus Christ, you
must also be willing to follow his commands, as
Christians do. Are you willing to accept this?**
R̸. **I am.**

And are you prepared to live as Christians do?
℞. **I am.**

[Promise, therefore, that once you have recovered your strength, you will try to know Christ better and follow a course of Christian formation. Do you so promise?
℞. **I do.]**

Turning to the godparent and to the witnesses, the minister asks them the following questions in these or similar words: 1286

You have heard N.'s promise. As his/her godparent do you promise to remind him/her of it and to help him/her to learn the teaching of Christ, to take part in the life of our community, and to bear witness as a true Christian?
℞. **I do.**

And will the rest of you, who have witnessed this promise, assist him/her in fulfilling it?
℞. **We will.**

The minister turns to the sick person and says: 1287

Therefore you will now be baptized into eternal life, in accordance with the command of our Lord Jesus.

LITURGY OF THE WORD

GOSPEL

283. According to time and circumstances, the minister reads some words from the gospel and explains them. One of the following may be used: 1287

A
Matthew 22:35-40
This is the greatest and first commandment.

B
John 6:44-47
Whoever believes has eternal life.

LITANY

284. The minister may adapt or shorten the litany according to the condition of the sick person. The litany may be omitted if the sick person appears to be tiring. 1288

Let us pray to the God of mercy for our sick brother/sister who has asked for the gift of baptism; let us pray for his/her godparent and for all his/her family and friends.

Father, increase his/her faith in Christ, your Son and our Saviour; in faith we make our prayer:
℟. Lord, hear us.

Grant his/her desire to have eternal life and enter the kingdom of heaven; in faith we make our prayer: ℟.

Fulfill his/her hope of knowing you, the creator of the world and the Father of all; in faith we make our prayer: ℟.

Through baptism forgive his/her sins and make him/her holy; in faith we make our prayer: ℟.

Grant him/her the salvation which Christ won by his death and resurrection; in faith we make our prayer: ℟.

In your love adopt him/her into your family; in faith we make our prayer: ℟.

[Restore him/her to health so that he/she may have the time to know and imitate Christ more perfectly; in faith we make our prayer: ℟.]

Keep united in faith and love all who have been baptized into the one body of Christ; in faith we make our prayer: ℟.

The minister concludes with the following prayer: 1289

Father,
look kindly upon the faith and longing of your servant,
   N.;
through this water
by which you have chosen to give us new birth
join him/her to Christ's death and resurrection.

Forgive all his/her sins,
adopt him/her as your own,
and count him/her among your holy people.

[Grant also that he/she may be restored to health,
to render you thanks in your Church,
and grow in faithfulness to the teaching of Christ.]

We ask this through Christ our Lord.
R̂. Amen.

LITURGY OF CHRISTIAN INITIATION

RENUNCIATION OF SIN

285. The minister first asks the sick person to renounce sin.   1290

Do you reject Satan,
and all his works,
and all his empty promises?
R̂. I do.

PROFESSION OF FAITH

286. A profession of faith is then made. One of the following   1290
may be used. In the case of a child, the Apostles' Creed may
be more appropriate.

A   See no. 190

B

I believe in God, the Father almighty, creator of heaven
   and earth.

I believe in Jesus Christ, his only Son, our Lord.
   He was conceived by the power of the Holy Spirit
      and born of the Virgin Mary.
   He suffered under Pontius Pilate, was crucified,
      died, and was buried.
   He descended to the dead.
   On the third day he rose again.
   He ascended into heaven, and is seated at the right
      hand of the Father.
   He will come again to judge the living and the dead.

I believe in the Holy Spirit,
   the holy catholic Church,
   the communion of saints,

the forgiveness of sins,
the resurrection of the body,
and the life everlasting. Amen

BAPTISM

287. The minister, using the name which the sick person   1291
desires to receive, baptizes him or her, saying:

N., I baptize you in the name of the Father,

The minister pours water a first time.

and of the Son,

The minister pours water a second time.

and of the Holy Spirit.

The minister pours water a third time.

ANOINTING AFTER BAPTISM

288. If the minister of baptism is a priest or deacon and   1263
confirmation does not take place, he should now anoint the   1291
neophyte with chrism in the usual way. He says the following
prayer over the newly baptized:

God, the Father of our Lord Jesus Christ,   1263
has freed you from sin,
given you a new birth by water and the Holy Spirit,
and welcomed you into his holy people.

He now anoints you with the chrism of salvation.

As Christ was anointed Priest, Prophet, and King, so
may you live always as a member of his body,
sharing everlasting life.
R̰. Amen.

289. If neither confirmation nor viaticum can be given, after   1292
baptizing, the minister says:

N., God our Father has freed you from your sins, has
given you a new birth, and made you his son/daughter
in Christ. Soon, God willing, you will receive the
fullness of the Holy Spirit through confirmation, and
will approach the altar of God to share the food of life
at the table of his sacrifice. In the spirit of that

adoption which you have received today, join us now in praying as our Lord himself taught us:

All say:

Our Father . . .

The rite concludes with the blessing, no. 295.

CONFIRMATION

290. If baptism was conferred by a priest, he may also confirm (see rite of *Christian Initiation of Adults*, no. 280), beginning with an instruction in these or similar words:　1293

My dear newly baptized, born again in Christ by baptism, you have become a member of Christ and of his priestly people. Now you are to share in the outpouring of the Holy Spirit among us, the Spirit sent by the Lord upon his apostles at Pentecost and given by them and their successors to the baptized.

All pray in silence for a short time. The priest lays hands upon the candidate and says:　136

All-powerful God, Father of our Lord Jesus Christ,
by water and the Holy Spirit
you freed your son/daughter from sin
and gave him/her new life.

Send your Holy Spirit upon him/her
to be his/her helper and guide.

Give him/her the spirit of wisdom and understanding,
the spirit of right judgment and courage,
the spirit of knowledge and reverence.
Fill him/her with the spirit of wonder and awe in your
presence.

Then the priest dips his right thumb in chrism and makes the sign of the cross on the forehead of the person to be confirmed as he says:

N., be sealed with the Gift of the Holy Spirit.
R̰. Amen.

The priest adds:　1293

Peace be with you.
R̰. And also with you.

291. In a case of necessity, it is enough to anoint with chrism, while saying the words: "N., be sealed with the Gift of the Holy Spirit." If possible, the priest should first lay hands upon the sick person with the prayer: "All-powerful God." After confirmation, viaticum, if possible, should be given to the neophyte. Otherwise, the celebration ends with the recitation of the Lord's Prayer by all present.

137
1293

THE LORD'S PRAYER

292. The minister instructs the sick person in these or similar words. If confirmation was given, the words in brackets are omitted.

1294

N., God our Father has freed you from your sins, has given you a new birth, and made you his son/daughter in Christ. [Soon, God willing, you will receive the fullness of the Holy Spirit through confirmation.] Before you partake of the body of the Lord, and in the spirit of that adoption which you have received today, join us now in praying as our Lord himself taught us:

All say:

Our Father . . .

COMMUNION AS VIATICUM

293. The minister shows the eucharistic bread to those present, saying:

130

A

Jesus Christ is the food for our journey; he calls us to the heavenly table.

B

This is the Lamb of God who takes away the sins of the world. Happy are those who are called to his supper.

130
131

The rite then proceeds as described in no. 193.

PRAYER AFTER COMMUNION

294. The minister says a concluding prayer.

133

Let us pray.

Pause for silent prayer, if this has not preceded. 1294

Father,
almighty and eternal God,
our brother/sister has received the eucharist
with faith in you and in your healing power.
May the body and blood of Christ
bring him/her eternal healing in mind and body.

We ask this in the name of Jesus the Lord.
R̷. Amen.

CONCLUDING RITES

BLESSING

295. The priest or deacon blesses the sick person and the 133
others present, using one of the following blessings. If,
however, any of the blessed sacrament remains, he may bless
the sick person by making a sign of the cross with the blessed
sacrament, in silence.

A Blessing B, no. 147.
B Blessing C, no. 147.

A minister who is not a priest or deacon invokes God's E40
blessing and makes the sign of the cross on himself or herself, as described in no. 91.

SIGN OF PEACE

296. The minister and the others present may then give the 133
sick person the sign of peace.

PART III

READINGS, RESPONSES, AND VERSES FROM SACRED SCRIPTURE

297. The following readings may be used in the Mass for the sick, in the visitation of the sick, or when praying for the sick. The selection should be made according to pastoral need, and special attention should be given to the physical and spiritual condition of the sick persons for whom the readings are used. Certain readings are indicated as more suitable for the dying.   152

OLD TESTAMENT READINGS

A **1 Kings 19:4-8**   153
God strengthens and sustains his servants.

B **Job 3:3, 11-17, 20-23**   154
Why should the sufferer be born to see the light?

C **Job 7:1-4, 6-11**   155
Remember that our life is like the wind, and yet we are destined for eternal life with God.

D **Job 7:12-21**   156
What are we, that you make much of us?

E **(For the dying) Job 19:23-27a**   157
I know that my Redeemer lives.

F **Wisdom 9:1, 9-18**   158
Who could know your counsel? We ask to share in God's wisdom.

G **Isaiah 35:1-10**   159
Strengthen the feeble hands.

H **Isaiah 52:13-53:12**   160
He bore our sufferings himself.

I **Isaiah 61:1-3a**   161
The spirit of the Lord is upon me to comfort all who mourn.

NEW TESTAMENT READINGS

EASTER SEASON

A Acts 3:1-10   162
In the name of Jesus, stand up and walk.

B Acts 3:11-16   163
Faith in Jesus has given this man perfect health.

C Acts 4:8-12   164
There is no other name but the name of Jesus by which we
are saved.

D Acts 13:32-39   165
The one whom God raised from the dead will never see
corruption of the flesh.

OTHER SEASONS

E Romans 8:14-17   166
If we suffer with him, we will be glorified with him.

F Romans 8:18-27   167
We groan while we wait for the redemption of our bodies.
The Spirit enables us to pray in our suffering.

G Romans 8:31b-35, 37-39   168
Nothing can come between us and the love of Christ.

H Romans 12:1-2
All our lives, even our suffering and pain, are caught up
in the offering of Christ in obedience to the will of our
Father.

I   1 Corinthians 1:18-25   169
God's weakness is stronger than human strength.

J   1 Corinthians 12:12-22, 24b-27   170
If one member suffers, all the members suffer.

K 1 Corinthians 15:1-4
The death and resurrection of Christ, the basis of our
faith.

L (for the dying) **1 Corinthians 15:12-20**   171
Christ has been raised from the dead; through him has
come the resurrection of us all.

M **2 Corinthians 4:16-18**   172
Though our body is being weakened, our spirit is
renewed.

N (for the dying) **2 Corinthians 5:1, 6-10**   173
We have an everlasting home in heaven.

O **Galatians 4:12-19**   174
My illness gave me the opportunity to bring the Gospel to
you.

P **Philippians 2:25-30**   175
He was ill and almost died but God took pity on him.

Q **Colossians 1:22-29**   176
In my flesh I fill up what is lacking in the sufferings of
Christ for the sake of his body.

R **Hebrews 4:14-16; 5:7-9**   177
Jesus identified himself with us totally; he suffered, and
through his suffering discovered the will of the Father.

S **James 5:13-16**   178
This prayer, made in faith, will save the sick person.

T **1 Peter 1:3-9**   179
You will rejoice even though for a short time you must
suffer.

U **1 John 3:1-2**   180
What we shall be has not yet been revealed.

V **Revelation 21:1-7**   181
There will be no more death or mourning, sadness or
pain.

W (for the dying) **Revelation 22:17, 20-21**   182
Come, Lord Jesus.

RESPONSORIAL PSALMS

A Isaiah 38: The cry of a suffering person and joy in God's   183
strength.
℟. **You saved my life, O Lord; I shall not die.**

B Psalm 6: A suffering person who cries to God for strength. 184
℟. **Have mercy on me, Lord; my strength is gone.**

C Psalm 25: A prayer for forgiveness and salvation. 185
℟. **To you, O Lord, I lift my soul.**

D Psalm 27: Trust in God in time of suffering. 186
℟. **Put your hope in the Lord; take courage and be strong.**

E Psalm 34: God is the salvation of those who trust in him. 187
℟. **The Lord is near to broken hearts.**
or: **Taste and see the goodness of the Lord.**

F Psalms 42 and 43: Nostalgia and longing to be with God. 188
℟. **Like a deer that longs for running streams, my soul longs for you, my God.**

G Psalm 63: A prayer of desire to be with God. 189
℟. **My soul is thirsting for you, O Lord my God.**

H Psalm 71: God is our hope in all our trials. 190
℟. **My God, come quickly to help me.**
or: **My lips, my very soul will shout for joy: you have redeemed me!**

I Psalm 86: Prayer of those who are in distress. 191
℟. **Listen, Lord, and answer me.**
or: **God, you are merciful and kind; turn to me and have mercy.**

J Psalm 90: Our God is eternal, strong, with power to save us. 192
℟. **In every age, O Lord, you have been our refuge.**

K Psalm 102: The prayer of those who want to be united with God. 193
℟. **O Lord, hear my prayer and let my cry come to you.**

L Psalm 103: Praise and thanks to God for his merciful love. 194
℟. **O bless the Lord, my soul.**
or: **The Lord is kind and merciful; slow to anger, and rich in compassion.**

M Psalm 123: God is the hope of his people. 195
℟. **Our eyes are fixed on the Lord, pleading for his mercy.**

N Psalm 143: A prayer for help in time of trouble.   196
R̰. **O Lord, hear my prayer.**
or: **For the sake of your name, O Lord, save my life.**

ALLELUIA VERSE AND VERSE BEFORE THE
GOSPEL

A Psalm 33   192
Lord, let your mercy be on us,
as we place our trust in you.

B Matthew 5:4   198
Happy are they who mourn;
they shall be comforted.

C Matthew 8:17   199
He bore our sickness,
and endured our suffering.

D Matthew 11:28   200
Come to me, all you that labor and are burdened,
and I will give you rest, says the Lord.

E 2 Corinthians 1:3b-4a   201
Blessed be the Father of mercies and the God of all
**   comfort,**
who consoles us in all our afflictions.

F Ephesians 1:3   202
Blessed be God, the Father of our Lord Jesus Christ,
for he has blessed us with every spiritual gift in Christ.

G James 1:12   203
Blessed are they who stand firm when trials come;
when they have stood the test, they will win the crown
**   of life.**

GOSPELS

A **Matthew 5:1-12a**   204
   Rejoice and be glad, for your reward is great in heaven.

B **Matthew 8:1-4**   205
   If you wish to do so, you can cure me.

C **Matthew 8:5-17**   206
He bore our infirmities.

D **Matthew 11:25-30**   207
Come to me, all you who labor.

E **Matthew 15:29-31**   208
Jesus heals large crowds.

F **Matthew 25:31-40**   209
As often as you did it to the least of these who belong to
me, you did it to me.

G **Mark 2:1-12**   210
Seeing their faith, Jesus said to the sick man: Your sins are
forgiven.

H **Mark 4:35-41**   211
Why are you so fearful? Why do you not have faith?

I **Mark 10:46-52**   212
Jesus, Son of David, have mercy on me.

J **Mark 16:15-20**   213
They will place their hands on the sick and they will
recover.

K **Luke 7:18b-23**   214
Go tell John what you have seen.

L **Luke 10:5-6, 8-9**   215
Heal the sick, Jesus commanded his followers.

M **Luke 10:25-37**   216
Who is my neighbor?

N **Luke 11:5-13**   217
Ask and it will be given to you.

O **Luke 12:35-44**   218
Happy are those whom the master finds watching when
he returns.

P **Luke 18:9-14**   219
O God, be merciful to me, a sinner.

Q (for the dying) **John 6:35-40**   220
It is the will of my Father that what he has given me will
not perish.

R (for the dying) **John 6:53-58**   221
Whoever eats this bread has eternal life.

S John 9:1-7 222

The blind man has not sinned; it was to let God's work show forth in him.

T John 10:11-18 223

The good shepherd lays down his life for his sheep.

MASS FOR VIATICUM

298. The following texts may be used when celebrating the Mass for Viaticum.

OLD TESTAMENT READINGS

A **1 Kings 19:4-8**   247
Strengthened by that food, he walked to the mountain of God.

B **Job 19:23-27a**
Job's act of faith is a model for our own: God is the God of the living.

NEW TESTAMENT READINGS

A **1 Corinthians 10:16-17**
Though we are many, we are one bread and body.

B **1 Corinthians 11:23-26**   248
When you eat this bread and drink this cup, you proclaim the death of the Lord.

C **Revelation 3:14b, 20-22**
I will come and share his meal, side by side.

D **Revelation 22:17, 20-21**
Come, Lord Jesus!

RESPONSORIAL PSALMS

A Psalm 23   249
℟. **Though I walk in the valley of darkness, I fear no evil, for you are with me.**
or: **The Lord is my shepherd; there is nothing I shall want.**

B Psalm 34   250
℟. **Taste and see the goodness of the Lord.**

C Psalms 42 and 43   251
℟. **My soul is thirsting for the living God: when shall I see him face to face?**

D Psalm 116 252

℟. **I will walk in the presence of the Lord, in the land of the living.**

or: **I will take the cup of salvation and call on the name of the Lord.**

or: **Alleluia.**

E Psalm 145

℟. **The Lord is near to all who call on him.**

ALLELUIA VERSE AND VERSE BEFORE THE GOSPEL

A John 6:51 253

I am the living bread from heaven, says the Lord; whoever eats this bread will live for ever.

B John 6:54 254

All who eat my flesh and drink my blood have eternal life, says the Lord; and I will raise them up on the last day.

C John 10:9 255

I am the gate, says the Lord; whoever enters through me will be safe and find pasture.

D John 11:25; 14:6 256

I am the resurrection and the life, says the Lord; no one comes to the Father except through me.

GOSPELS

A John 6:41-51a 257

I am the bread of life that comes down from heaven.

B John 6:51-58 258

All who eat this bread will live for ever and I will raise them up on the last day.

APPENDIX

RITE FOR RECONCILIATION OF INDIVIDUAL PENITENTS

299. This form for celebrating the sacrament of penance is for use when it is necessary in the following cases: during communion of the sick; during the celebration of anointing; during the celebration of viaticum. As far as possible, the indications contained in the pastoral notes preceding these various rites should be observed.

RECEPTION OF THE PENITENT

INVITATION TO TRUST

300. Using one of the following forms, or other similar words, the priest invites the sick person to have trust in God: P42

A

May the grace of the Holy Spirit P69
fill your heart with light,
that you may confess your sins with loving trust
and come to know that God is merciful.
R⁊. Amen.

B

May the Lord be in your heart P70
and help you to confess your sins with true sorrow.
R⁊. Amen.

C

The Lord does not wish the sinner to die P67
but to turn back to him and live.
Come before him with trust in his mercy.
R⁊. Amen.

REVELATION OF STATE OF LIFE

301. At this point, if the sick person is unknown to the priest, it is proper for the sick person to indicate his or her state in life, the time of the last confession, difficulties in leading the Christian life, and anything else which may help the priest to exercise his ministry.

LITURGY OF RECONCILIATION

CONFESSION OF SINS

302. Where it is the custom, the sick person may say a   P44
general formula for confession (for example, "I confess to
almighty God . . .") before confessing his or her sins.

The sick person then confesses his or her sins. If
circumstances call for it, a generic confession is sufficient.

If necessary, the priest helps the person to make an integral
confession and gives suitable counsel; he should make sure
that such counsel is adapted to the circumstances.

The priest urges the sick person to sorrow for sins,
underlining that through the sacrament of penance the
Christian dies and rises with Christ and is thus renewed in
the paschal mystery.

ACCEPTANCE OF SATISFACTION

303. Where it is opportune, the priest proposes an act of   P44
penance which the sick person accepts to make satisfaction
for sin and to amend his or her life. The act of penance should
serve not only to make up for the past, but also to help begin
a new life and provide an antidote to weakness.

As far as possible, the penance should correspond to the
seriousness and nature of the sins.

This act of penance may suitably take the form of prayer,
self-denial, and especially the uniting of sufferings with those
of Christ for the salvation of the world. This will underline
the fact that sins and their forgiveness have a social aspect,
and will emphasize the important role the sick have in
praying with and for the rest of the community.

PENITENT'S PRAYER OF SORROW

304. The priest then asks the sick person to express his or her   P45
sorrow; this may be done using one of the following prayers
or any other act of contrition which may be familiar to the
penitent.

A

Lord Jesus, P89
you opened the eyes of the blind,
healed the sick,
forgave the sinful woman,
and after Peter's denial confirmed him in your love.
Listen to my prayer, forgive all my sins,
renew your love in my heart,
help me to live in perfect unity with my fellow
    Christians
that I may proclaim your saving power to all the world.

B

Father of mercy, P88
like the prodigal son I return to you and say:
"I have sinned against you and am no longer worthy to
    be called your son."
Christ Jesus, Savior of the world,
I pray with the repentant thief to whom you promised
    Paradise:
"Lord, remember me in your Kingdom."
Holy Spirit, fountain of love, I call on you with trust:
"Purify my heart, and help me to walk as a child of
    light."

ABSOLUTION

305. Then the priest extends his hands over the head of the P46
penitent (or at least extends his right hand); care should be
taken that this gesture is not confused with the laying on of
hands during anointing. He says:

God, the Father of mercies,
through the death and resurrection of his Son
has reconciled the world to himself
and sent the Holy Spirit among us
for the forgiveness of sins;
through the ministry of the Church
may God give you pardon and peace,
and I absolve you from your sins
in the name of the Father, and of the Son, +
and of the Holy Spirit.
R̊. Amen.

He concludes by saying: P47

The Lord has freed you from sin.   P93
May he bring you safely to his kingdom in heaven.
Glory to him for ever.
R̶. **Amen.**

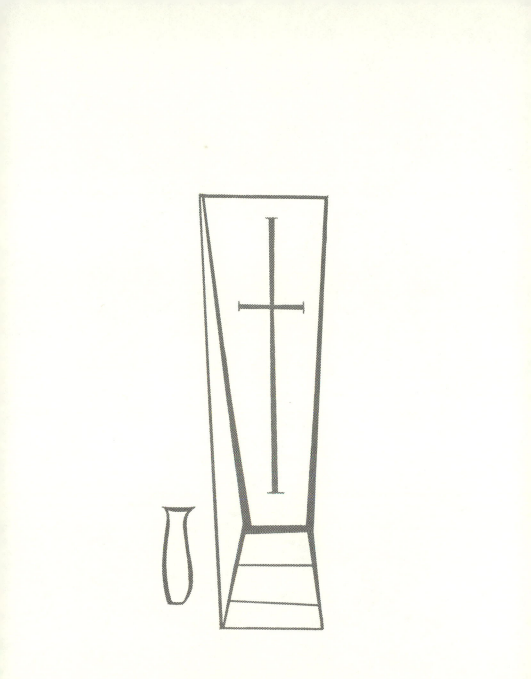

ORDER OF CHRISTIAN FUNERALS

ORDER OF CHRISTIAN FUNERALS

Editorial Note
Decree
Decree of National Conference of Catholic Bishops
General Introduction (1–49)

PART I
FUNERAL RITES (50)

Vigil and Related Rites and Prayers (51–127)

VIGIL FOR THE DECEASED (54–81)

Introductory Rites (69–72)
Greeting (69)
Opening Song (70)
Invitation to Prayer (71)
Opening Prayer (72)

Liturgy of the Word (73–77)
First Reading (74)
Responsorial Psalm (75)
Gospel (76)
Homily (77)

Prayer of Intercession (78–80)
Litany (78)
The Lord's Prayer (79)
Concluding Prayer (80)

Concluding Rite (81)
Blessing (81)

VIGIL FOR THE DECEASED WITH RECEPTION AT THE
CHURCH (82–97)

Reception at the Church

Introductory Rites (82–88)
Greeting (82) (See no. 69, above.)
Sprinkling with Holy Water (83)
[Placing of the Pall] (84)
Entrance Procession (85)
[Placing of Christian Symbols] (86)

Invitation to Prayer (87)
Opening Prayer (88)

Liturgy of the Word (89–93)
First Reading (90)
Responsorial Psalm (91)
Gospel (92)
Homily (93)

Prayer of Intercession (94–96)
Litany (94) (See no. 78, above.)
The Lord's Prayer (95) (See no. 79, above.)
Concluding Prayer (96)

Concluding Rite (97)
Blessing (97) (See no. 81, above.)

RELATED RITES AND PRAYERS (98–127)

Prayers after Death (101–108)
Invitation to Prayer (104)
Reading (105)
The Lord's Prayer (106)
Concluding Prayers (107)
Blessing (108) (See no. 81, above.)

Gathering in the Presence of the Body (109–118)
Sign of the Cross (112)
Scripture Verse (113)
Sprinkling with Holy Water (114)
Psalm (115)
The Lord's Prayer (116) (See no. 106, above.)
Concluding Prayer (117)
Blessing (118)

Transfer of the Body to the Church or to the Place of Committal (119–127)
Invitation (121)
Scripture Verse (122)
Litany (123)
The Lord's Prayer (124)
Concluding Prayer (125)
Invitation to the Procession (126)
Procession to the Church or to the Place of Committal (127)

Funeral Liturgy (128–203)

FUNERAL MASS (154–176)

Introductory Rites (159–164)
Greeting (159)
Sprinkling with Holy Water (160) (See no. 83, above.)
[Placing of the Pall] (161)
Entrance Procession (162)
[Placing of Christian Symbols] (163) (See no. 86, above.)
Opening Prayer (164)

Liturgy of the Word (165–167)
Readings (165)
Homily (166)
General Intercessions (167)

Liturgy of the Eucharist (168–169)

Final Commendation (170–175)
Invitation to Prayer (171)
Silence (172)
[Signs of Farewell] (173)
Song of Farewell (174)
Prayer of Commendation (175)

Procession to the Place of Committal (176)

FUNERAL LITURGY OUTSIDE MASS (177–203)

Introductory Rites (184–190)
Greeting (184)
Sprinkling with Holy Water (185) (See no. 83, above.)
[Placing of the Pall] (186)
Entrance Procession (187)
[Placing of Christian Symbols] (188) (See no. 86, above.)
Invitation to Prayer (189)
Opening Prayer (190)

Liturgy of the Word (191–196)
Readings (191)
Homily (192)
General Intercessions (193)
The Lord's Prayer (194)
[Holy Communion] (195)
[Procession] (196)

Final Commendation (197–202)
Invitation to Prayer (198) (See no. 171, above.)
Silence (199)
[Signs of Farewell] (200)
Song of Farewell (201) (See no. 174, above.)
Prayer of Commendation (202) (See no. 175, above.)

Procession to the Place of Committal (203)

Rite of Committal (204–233)

RITE OF COMMITTAL (216–223)

Invitation (216–218)
Scripture Verse (217)
Prayer over the Place of Committal (218)

Committal (219–222)
Intercessions (220)
The Lord's Prayer (221)
Concluding Prayer (222)

Prayers over the People (223)

RITE OF COMMITTAL WITH FINAL COMMENDATION
(224–233)

Invitation (224–226)
Scripture Verse (225) (See no. 217, above.)
Prayer over the Place of Committal (226)

Invitation to Prayer (227–232)
Silence (228)
[Signs of Farewell] (229) (See no. 173, above.)
Song of Farewell (230) (See no. 174, above.)
Prayer of Commendation (231) (See no. 175, above.)
Committal (232)

Prayer over the People (233) (See no. 223, above.)

PART II
FUNERAL RITES FOR CHILDREN (234–342)

Vigil (243–263)

VIGIL FOR A DECEASED CHILD (243–263)

Introductory Rites (248–254)
Greeting (248)
Sprinkling with Holy Water or Brief Address (249)
[Placing of the Pall] (250)
Entrance Procession (251)
[Placing of Christian Symbols] (252)
Invitation to Prayer (253)
Opening Prayer (254)

Liturgy of the Word (255–259)
First Reading (256)
Responsorial Psalm (257)
Gospel (258)
Homily (259)

Prayer of Intercession (260–262)
Litany (260)
The Lord's Prayer (261)
Concluding Prayer (262)

Concluding Rite (263)
Blessing (263)

Funeral Liturgy (264–315)

FUNERAL MASS (276–294)

Introductory Rites (277–282)
Greeting (277)
Sprinkling with Holy Water or Brief Address (278)
[Placing of the Pall] (279) (See no. 250, above.)
Entrance Procession (280)
[Placing of Christian Symbols] (281) (See no. 252, above.)
Opening Prayer (282)

Liturgy of the Word (283–285)
Readings (283)
Homily (284)
General Intercessions (285)

Liturgy of the Eucharist (286–287)
[Procession] (287)

Final Commendation (288–293)
Invitation to Prayer (289)
Silence (290)
[Signs of Farewell] (291)
Song of Farewell (292)
Prayer of Commendation (293)

Procession to the Place of Committal (294)

FUNERAL LITURGY OUTSIDE MASS (295–315)

Introductory Rites (296–302)
Greeting (296) (See no. 277, above.)
Sprinkling with Holy Water or Brief Address (297)
[Placing of the Pall] (298)
Entrance Procession (299)
[Placing of Christian Symbols] (300) (See no. 252, above.)
Invitation to Prayer (301)
Opening Prayer (302)

Liturgy of the Word (303–308)
Readings (303)
Homily (304)
General Intercessions (305)
The Lord's Prayer (306)
[Holy Communion] (307) (See nos. 409–410, below.)
[Procession] (308)

Final Commendation (309–314)
Invitation to Prayer (310) (See no. 289, above.)
Silence (311)
[Signs of Farewell] (312)
Song of Farewell (313) (See no. 292, above.)
Prayer of Commendation (314)

Procession to the Place of Committal (315)

Rite of Committal (316–342)

RITE OF COMMITTAL (316–326)

Invitation (319–321)
Scripture Verse (320)
Prayer over the Place of Committal (321)

Committal (322–325)
Intercessions (323)
The Lord's Prayer (324)
Concluding Prayer (325)

Prayer over the People (326) (See no. 223, above.)

RITE OF COMMITTAL WITH FINAL COMMENDATION (327–336)

Invitation (327–329)
Scripture Verse (328) (See no. 217, above.)
Prayer over the Place of Committal (329)

Invitation to Prayer (330–335)
Silence (331)
[Signs of Farewell] (332)
Song of Farewell (333) (See no. 292, above.)
Prayer of Commendation (334)
Committal (335)

Prayer over the People (336)

RITE OF FINAL COMMENDATION FOR AN INFANT (337–342)

Brief Address (337)
Scripture Verse (338)
Blessing of the Body (339)
The Lord's Prayer (340)
Prayer of Commendation (341)
Blessing (342)

PART III
TEXTS OF SACRED SCRIPTURE (343–347)

FUNERALS FOR ADULTS (345)

FUNERALS FOR BAPTIZED CHILDREN (346)

FUNERALS FOR CHILDREN WHO DIED BEFORE BAPTISM

ANTIPHONS AND PSALMS (347)

PART IV
OFFICE FOR THE DEAD (348–395)

MORNING PRAYER (373–384)*

Introductory Verse (374)
Hymn (375)
Psalmody (376)
Reading (377)
Responsory (378)
Canticle of Zechariah (379)
Intercessions (380)
The Lord's Prayer (381)
Concluding Prayer (382)
Dismissal (383)
Procession to the Place of Committal (384)

EVENING PRAYER (385–395)*

Introductory Verse (386)
Hymn (387)
Psalmody (388)
Reading (389)
Responsory (390)
Canticle of Mary (391)
Intercessions (392)
The Lord's Prayer (393)
Concluding Prayer (394)
Dismissal (395)

PART V
ADDITIONAL TEXTS (397–410)

PRAYERS AND TEXTS IN PARTICULAR
CIRCUMSTANCES (397–408)

Prayers for the Dead (398)
Prayers for Mourners (399)
Placing of Christian Symbols (400)
General Intercessions and Litanies (401)

Final Commendation and Farewell (402–404)
Invitation to Prayer (402)
Song of Farewell (403)
Prayer of Commendation (404)

* The texts are found in the Liturgy of the Hours, Office of the Dead.

EDITORIAL NOTE

Beginning with the General Introduction, the numbering system in this book diverges from the Latin edition of *Ordo Exsequiarum*. The new numbering system appears at the left-hand side of the page. The corresponding number from the Latin edition appears in the right-hand margin. A text having a number on the left but no reference number in the righthand margin is either newly composed or is a text from *The Roman Missal, Holy Communion and Worship of the Eucharist outside Mass, The Liturgy of the Hours,* or *Pastoral Care of the Sick: Rites of Anointing and Viaticum.*

"Funeral rites" is a general designation used of all the liturgical celebrations in this book. "Funeral liturgy" is a more particular designation applied to the two forms of liturgical celebration presented under the headings "Funeral Mass" and "Funeral Liturgy outside Mass."

Part IV presents morning prayer and evening prayer of the office for the dead from *The Liturgy of the Hours.*

Part V contains "Holy Communion outside Mass," which is an excerpt from *Holy Communion and Worship of the Eucharist outside Mass.*

CONGREGATION FOR DIVINE WORSHIP

Prot. no. 720/69

DECREE

By means of the funeral rites it has been the practice of the Church, as a tender mother, not simply to commend the dead to God but also to raise high the hopes of its children and to give witness to its own faith in the future resurrection of the baptized with Christ.

Vatican Council II accordingly directed in the Constitution on the Liturgy that the funeral rites be revised in such a way that they would more clearly express the paschal character of the Christian's death and also that the rites for the burial of children would have a proper Mass (art. 81–82).

The Consilium prepared the desired rites and put them into trial use in different parts of the world. Now Pope Paul VI by his apostolic authority has approved and ordered the publication of these rites as henceforth obligatory for all those using the Roman Ritual.

Also by order of Pope Paul this Congregation for Divine Worship promulgates the *Order of Funerals,* stipulating that its effective date is 1 June 1970.

The Congregation further establishes that until 1 June 1970, when Latin is used in celebrating funerals there is an option to use either the present rite or the rite now in the Roman Ritual; after 1 June 1970 only this new *Order of Funerals* is to be used.

Once the individual conferences of bishops have prepared a vernacular version of the rite and received its confirmation from this Congregation, they have authorization to fix any other, feasible effective date prior to 1 June 1970 for use of the *Order of Funerals.*

All things to the contrary notwithstanding.

Congregation for Divine Worship, 15 August 1969, the solemnity of the Assumption.

Benno Cardinal Gut
Prefect

A. Bugnini
Secretary

NATIONAL CONFERENCE OF CATHOLIC BISHOPS UNITED STATES OF AMERICA

DECREE

In accord with the norms established by decree of the Sacred Congregation of Rites *"Cum, nostra aetate"* (27 January 1966), the *Order of Christian Funerals* is declared to be the vernacular *editio typica* of the *Ordo Exsequiarum* for the dioceses of the United States of America, and may be published by authority of the National Conference of Catholic Bishops.

The *Order of Christian Funerals* was canonically approved by the National Conference of Catholic Bishops in plenary assembly on 14 November 1985 and was subsequently confirmed by the Apostolic See by decree of the Congregation for Divine Worship on 29 April 1987 (Prot. N. CD 1550/85).

On 1 October 1989 the *Order of Christian Funerals* may be published and used in funeral celebrations. From All Souls Day, 2 November 1989, its use is mandatory in the dioceses of the United States of America. From that date forward no other English version of these rites may be used.

Given at the General Secretariat of the National Conference of Catholic Bishops, Washington, D.C., on 15 August 1989, the Solemnity of the Assumption.

+ John L. May
   Archbishop of Saint Louis
   President
   National Conference of Catholic Bishops

   Robert N. Lynch
   General Secretary

ORDER OF CHRISTIAN FUNERALS
Why do you search for the Living One among the dead?

GENERAL INTRODUCTION

1. In the face of death, the Church confidently proclaims that God has created each person for eternal life and that Jesus, the Son of God, by his death and resurrection, has broken the chains of sin and death that bound humanity. Christ "achieved his task of redeeming humanity and giving perfect glory to God, principally by the paschal mystery of his blessed passion, resurrection from the dead, and glorious ascension."[1]

2. The proclamation of Jesus Christ "who was put to death for our sins and raised to life to justify us" (Romans 4:25) is at the center of the Church's life. The mystery of the Lord's death and resurrection gives power to all of the Church's activity. "For it was from the side of Christ as he slept the sleep of death upon the cross that there came forth the sublime sacrament of the whole Church."[2] The Church's liturgical and sacramental life and proclamation of the Gospel make this mystery present in the life of the faithful. Through the sacraments of baptism, confirmation, and eucharist, men and women are initiated into this mystery. "You have been taught that when we were baptized in Christ Jesus we were baptized into his death; in other words when we were baptized we went into the tomb with him and joined him in death, so that as Christ was raised from the dead by the Father's glory, we too might live a new life. If in union with Christ we have imitated his death, we shall also imitate him in his resurrection" (Romans 6:3–5).

3. In the eucharistic sacrifice, the Church's celebration of Christ's Passover from death to life, the faith of the baptized in the paschal mystery is renewed and nourished. Their union with Christ and with each other is strengthened: "Because there is one bread, we who are many, are one body, for we all partake of the one bread" (1 Corinthians 10:17).

[1] Vatican Council II, Constitution on the Liturgy *Sacrosanctum Concilium*, art. 5.
[2] Ibid.

4. At the death of a Christian, whose life of faith was begun in the waters of baptism and strengthened at the eucharistic table, the Church intercedes on behalf of the deceased because of its confident belief that death is not the end nor does it break the bonds forged in life. The Church also ministers to the sorrowing and consoles them in the funeral rites with the comforting word of God and the sacrament of the eucharist.

5. Christians celebrate the funeral rites to offer worship, praise, and thanksgiving to God for the gift of a life which has now been returned to God, the author of life and the hope of the just. The Mass, the memorial of Christ's death and resurrection, is the principal celebration of the Christian funeral.

6. The Church through its funeral rites commends the dead to God's merciful love and pleads for the forgiveness of their sins. At the funeral rites, especially at the celebration of the eucharistic sacrifice, the Christian community affirms and expresses the union of the Church on earth with the Church in heaven in the one great communion of saints. Though separated from the living, the dead are still at one with the community of believers on earth and benefit from their prayers and intercession. At the rite of final commendation and farewell, the community acknowledges the reality of separation and commends the deceased to God. In this way it recognizes the spiritual bond that still exists between the living and the dead and proclaims its belief that all the faithful will be raised up and reunited in the new heavens and a new earth, where death will be no more.

7. The celebration of the Christian funeral brings hope and consolation to the living. While proclaiming the Gospel of Jesus Christ and witnessing to Christian hope in the resurrection, the funeral rites also recall to all who take part in them God's mercy and judgment and meet the human need to turn always to God in times of crisis.

MINISTRY AND PARTICIPATION

8. "If one member suffers in the body of Christ which is the Church, all the members suffer with that member" (1

Corinthians 12:26). For this reason, those who are baptized into Christ and nourished at the same table of the Lord are responsible for one another. When Christians are sick, their brothers and sisters share a ministry of mutual charity and "do all that they can to help the sick return to health, by showing love for the sick, and by celebrating the sacraments with them."[3] So too when a member of Christ's Body dies, the faithful are called to a ministry of consolation to those who have suffered the loss of one whom they love. Christian consolation is rooted in that hope that comes from faith in the saving death and resurrection of the Lord Jesus Christ. Christian hope faces the reality of death and the anguish of grief but trusts confidently that the power of sin and death has been vanquished by the risen Lord. The Church calls each member of Christ's Body—priest, deacon, layperson—to participate in the ministry of consolation: to care for the dying, to pray for the dead, to comfort those who mourn.

COMMUNITY

9. The responsibility for the ministry of consolation rests with the believing community, which heeds the words and example of the Lord Jesus: "Blessed are they who mourn; they shall be consoled" (Matthew 5:3). Each Christian shares in this ministry according to the various gifts and offices in the Church. As part of the pastoral ministry, pastors, associate pastors and other ministers should instruct the parish community on the Christian meaning of death and on the purpose and significance of the Church's liturgical rites for the dead. Information on how the parish community assists families in preparing for funerals should also be provided.

By giving instruction, pastors and associate pastors should lead the community to a deeper appreciation of its role in the ministry of consolation and to a fuller understanding of the significance of the death of a fellow Christian. Often the community must respond to the anguish voiced by Martha, the sister of Lazarus: "Lord, if you had been here, my brother would never have died" (John 11:21) and must console those who mourn, as Jesus himself consoled Martha: "Your brother will rise again. . . . I am the resurrection and

---

[3]See Roman Ritual, *Pastoral Care of the Sick: Rites of Anointing and Viaticum,* General Introduction, no. 33.

the life: those who believe in me, though they should die, will come to life; and those who are alive and believe in me will never die" (John 11:25–26). The faith of the Christian community in the resurrection of the dead brings support and strength to those who suffer the loss of those whom they love.

10. Members of the community should console the mourners with words of faith and support and with acts of kindness, for example, assisting them with some of the routine tasks of daily living. Such assistance may allow members of the family to devote time to planning the funeral rites with the priest and other ministers and may also give the family time for prayer and mutual comfort.

11. The community's principal involvement in the ministry of consolation is expressed in its active participation in the celebration of the funeral rites, particularly the vigil for the deceased, the funeral liturgy, and the rite of committal. For this reason these rites should be scheduled at times that permit as many of the community as possible to be present. The assembly's participation can be assisted by the preparation of booklets that contain an outline of the rite, the texts and songs belonging to the people, and directions for posture, gesture, and movement.

12. At the vigil for the deceased or on another occasion before the eucharistic celebration, the presiding minister should invite all to be present at the funeral liturgy and to take an active part in it. The minister may also describe the funeral liturgy and explain why the community gathers to hear the word of God proclaimed and to celebrate the eucharist when one of the faithful dies.

Pastors, associate pastors and other ministers should also be mindful of those persons who are not members of the Catholic Church, or Catholics who are not involved in the life of the Church.

13. As a minister of reconcilation, the priest should be especially sensitive to the possible needs for reconciliation felt by the family and others. Funerals can begin the process of reconciling differences and supporting those ties that can help the bereaved adjust to the loss brought about by death. With attentiveness to each situation, the priest can

help to begin the process of reconciliation when needed. In some cases this process may find expression in the celebration of the sacrament of penance, either before the funeral liturgy or at a later time.

LITURGICAL MINISTERS
Presiding Minister
14. Priests, as teachers of faith and ministers of comfort, preside at the funeral rites, especially the Mass; the celebration of the funeral liturgy is especially entrusted to pastors and associate pastors. When no priest is available, deacons, as ministers of the word, of the altar, and of charity, preside at funeral rites. When no priest or deacon is available for the vigil and related rites or the rite of commital, a layperson presides.

Other Liturgical Ministers
15. In the celebration of the funeral rites laymen and laywomen may serve as readers, musicians, ushers, pallbearers, and, according to existing norms, as special ministers of the eucharist. Pastors and other priests should instill in these ministers an appreciation of how much the reverent exercise of their ministries contributes to the celebration of the funeral rites. Family members should be encouraged to take an active part in these ministries, but they should not be asked to assume any role that their grief or sense of loss may make too burdensome.

MINISTRY FOR THE MOURNERS AND THE DECEASED

FAMILY AND FRIENDS
16. In planning and carrying out the funeral rites the pastor and all other ministers should keep in mind the life of the deceased and the circumstances of death. They should also take into consideration the spiritual and psychological needs of the family and friends of the deceased to express grief and their sense of loss, to accept the reality of death, and to comfort one another.

17. Whenever possible, ministers should involve the family in planning the funeral rites: in the choice of texts and rites

provided in the ritual, in the selection of music for the rites, and in the designation of liturgical ministers.

Planning of the funeral rites may take place during the visit of the pastor or other minister at some appropriate time after the death and before the vigil service. Ministers should explain to the family the meaning and significance of each of the funeral rites, especially the vigil, the funeral liturgy, and the rite of committal.

If pastoral and personal considerations allow, the period before death may be an appropriate time to plan the funeral rites with the family and even with the family member who is dying. Although planning the funeral before death should be approached with sensitivity and care, it can have the effect of helping the one who is dying and the family face the reality of death with Christian hope. It can also relieve the family of numerous details after the death and may allow them to benefit more fully from the celebration of the funeral rites.

DECEASED

18. Through the celebration of the funeral rites, the Church manifests its care for the dead, both baptized members and catechumens. In keeping with the provisions of *Codex Iuris Canonici*, can. 1183, the Church's funeral rites may be celebrated for a child who died before baptism and whose parents intended to have the child baptized.

At the discretion of the local Ordinary, the Church's funeral rites may be celebrated for a baptized member of another Church or ecclesial community provided this would not be contrary to the wishes of the deceased person and provided the minister of the Church or ecclesial community in which the deceased person was a regular member or communicant is unavailable.

19. Since in baptism the body was marked with the seal of the Trinity and became the temple of the Holy Spirit, Christians respect and honor the bodies of the dead and the places where they rest. Any customs associated with the preparation of the body of the deceased should always be marked with dignity and reverence and never with the despair of those who have no hope. Preparation of the body should include prayer, especially at those intimate moments

reserved for family members. For the final disposition of the body, it is the ancient Christian custom to bury or entomb the bodies of the dead; cremation is permitted, unless it is evident that cremation was chosen for anti-Christian motives.

20. In countries or regions where an undertaker, and not the family or community, carries out the preparation and transfer of the body, the pastor and other ministers are to ensure that the undertakers appreciate the values and beliefs of the Christian community.

The family and friends of the deceased should not be excluded from taking part in the services sometimes provided by undertakers, for example, the preparation and laying out of the body.

LITURGICAL ELEMENTS

21. Since liturgical celebration involves the whole person, it requires attentiveness to all that affects the senses. The readings and prayers, psalms and songs should be proclaimed or sung with understanding, conviction, and reverence. Music for the assembly should be truly expressive of the texts and at the same time simple and easily sung. The ritual gestures, processions, and postures should express and foster an attitude of reverence and reflectiveness in those taking part in the funeral rites. The funeral rites should be celebrated in an atmosphere of simple beauty, in a setting that encourages participation. Liturgical signs and symbols affirming Christian belief and hope in the paschal mystery are abundant in the celebration of the funeral rites, but their undue multiplication or repetition should be avoided. Care must be taken that the choice and use of signs and symbols are in accord with the culture of the people.

THE WORD OF GOD
Readings

22. In every celebration for the dead, the Church attaches great importance to the reading of the word of God. The readings proclaim to the assembly the paschal mystery, teach remembrance of the dead, convey the hope of being gathered together again in God's kingdom, and encourage

the witness of Christian life. Above all, the readings tell of God's designs for a world in which suffering and death will relinquish their hold on all whom God has called his own. A careful selection and use of readings from Scripture for the funeral rites will provide the family and the community with an opportunity to hear God speak to them in their needs, sorrows, fears, and hopes.

23. In the celebration of the liturgy of the word at the funeral liturgy, the biblical readings may not be replaced by nonbiblical readings. But during prayer services with the family nonbiblical readings may be used in addition to readings from Scripture.

24. Liturgical tradition assigns the proclamation of the readings in the celebration of the liturgy of the word to readers and the deacon. The presiding minister proclaims the readings only when there are no assisting ministers present. Those designated to proclaim the word of God should prepare themselves to exercise this ministry.[4]

Psalmody

25. The psalms are rich in imagery, feeling, and symbolism. They powerfully express the suffering and pain, the hope and trust of people of every age and culture. Above all the psalms sing of faith in God, of revelation and redemption. They enable the assembly to pray in the words that Jesus himself used during his life on earth. Jesus, who knew anguish and the fear of death, "offered up prayer and entreaty, aloud and in silent tears, to the one who had the power to save him out of death. . . . Although he was Son, he learned to obey through suffering; but having been made perfect, he became for all who obey him the source of eternal salvation . . ." (Hebrews 5:7–9). In the psalms the members of the assembly pray in the voice of Christ, who intercedes on their behalf before the Father.[5] The Church, like Christ, turns again and again to the psalms as a genuine expression of grief and of praise and as a sure source of trust and hope in times of trial. Pastors and other ministers are, therefore, to make an earnest effort through an effective catechesis to lead their communities to a clearer and

---

[4]See Lectionary for Mass (2nd *editio typica*, 1981), General Introduction, nos. 49, 52, and 55.
[5]See General Instruction of the Liturgy of the Hours, no. 109.

deeper grasp of at least some of the psalms provided for
the funeral rites.

26. The psalms are designated for use in many places in
the funeral rites (for example, as responses to the readings,
for the processions, for use at the vigil for the deceased).
Since the psalms are songs, whenever possible, they should
be sung.

Homily

27. A brief homily based on the readings is always given
after the gospel reading at the funeral liturgy and may also
be given after the readings at the vigil service; but there is
never to be a eulogy. Attentive to the grief of those present, the homilist should dwell on God's compassionate love
and on the paschal mystery of the Lord, as proclaimed in
the Scripture readings. The homilist should also help the
members of the assembly to understand that the mystery of
God's love and the mystery of Jesus' victorious death and
resurrection were present in the life and death of the deceased and that these mysteries are active in their own lives
as well. Through the homily members of the family and
community should receive consolation and strength to face
the death of one of their members with a hope nourished
by the saving word of God. Laypersons who preside at the
funeral rites give an instruction on the readings.

PRAYERS AND INTERCESSIONS

28. In the presidential prayers of the funeral rites the presiding minister addresses God on behalf of the deceased
and the mourners in the name of the entire Church. From
the variety of prayers provided the minister in consultation
with the family should carefully select texts that truly cap-
ture the unspoken prayers and hopes of the assembly and
also respond to the needs of the mourners.

29. Having heard the word of God proclaimed and
preached, the assembly responds at the vigil and at the funeral liturgy with prayers of intercession for the deceased
and all the dead, for the family and all who mourn, and for
all in the assembly. The holy people of God, confident in
their belief in the communion of saints, exercise their royal

priesthood by joining together in this prayer for all those who have died.[6]

Several models of intercessions are provided within the rites for adaptation to the circumstances.

MUSIC

30. Music is integral to the funeral rites. It allows the community to express convictions and feelings that words alone may fail to convey. It has the power to console and uplift the mourners and to strengthen the unity of the assembly in faith and love. The texts of the songs chosen for a particular celebration should express the paschal mystery of the Lord's suffering, death, and triumph over death and should be related to the readings from Scripture.

31. Since music can evoke strong feelings, the music for the celebration of the funeral rites should be chosen with great care. The music at funerals should support, console, and uplift the participants and should help to create in them a spirit of hope in Christ's victory over death and the Christian's share in that victory.

32. Music should be provided for the vigil and funeral liturgy and, whenever possible, for the funeral processions and the rite of committal. The specific notes that precede each of these rites suggest places in the rites where music is appropriate. Many musical settings used by the parish community during the liturgical year may be suitable for use at funerals. Efforts should be made to develop and expand the parish's repertoire for use at funerals.

33. An organist or other instrumentalist, a cantor, and, whenever possible, even a choir should assist the assembly's full participation in singing the songs, responses, and acclamations of these rites.

SILENCE

34. Prayerful silence is an element important to the celebration of the funeral rites. Intervals of silence should be observed, for example, after each reading and during the final

[6]See *de Oratione communi seu fidelium* (2nd ed., Vatican Polyglot Press, 1966), chapter 1, no. 3, p. 7: tr., *Documents on the Liturgy* (The Liturgical Press, 1982), no. 1893.

commendation and farewell, to permit the assembly to reflect upon the word of God and the meaning of the celebration.

SYMBOLS

Easter Candle and Other Candles

35. The Easter candle reminds the faithful of Christ's undying presence among them, of his victory over sin and death, and of their share in that victory by virtue of their initiation. It recalls the Easter Vigil, the night when the Church awaits the Lord's resurrection and when new light for the living and the dead is kindled. During the funeral liturgy and also during the vigil service, when celebrated in the church, the Easter candle may be placed beforehand near the position the coffin will occupy at the conclusion of the procession.

According to local custom, other candles may also be placed near the coffin during the funeral liturgy as a sign of reverence and solemnity.

Holy Water

36. Blessed or holy water reminds the assembly of the saving waters of baptism. In the rite of reception of the body at the church, its use calls to mind the deceased's baptism and initiation into the community of faith. In the rite of final commendation the gesture of sprinkling may also signify farewell.

Incense

37. Incense is used during the funeral rites as a sign of honor to the body of the deceased, which through baptism became the temple of the Holy Spirit. Incense is also used as a sign of the community's prayers for the deceased rising to the throne of God and as a sign of farewell.

Other Symbols

38. If it is the custom in the local community, a pall may be placed over the coffin when it is received at the church. A reminder of the baptismal garment of the deceased, the pall is a sign of the Christian dignity of the person. The use of the pall also signifies that all are equal in the eyes of God (see James 2:1–9).

A Book of the Gospels or a Bible may be placed on the coffin as a sign that Christians live by the word of God and that fidelity to that word leads to eternal life.

A cross may be placed on the coffin as a reminder that the Christian is marked by the cross in baptism and through Jesus' suffering on the cross is brought to the victory of his resurrection.

Fresh flowers, used in moderation, can enhance the setting of the funeral rites.

Only Christian symbols may rest on or be placed near the coffin during the funeral liturgy. Any other symbols, for example, national flags, or flags or insignia of associations, have no place in the funeral liturgy (cf. 132).

Liturgical Color

39. The liturgical color chosen for funerals should express Christian hope but should not be offensive to human grief or sorrow. In the United States, white, violet, or black vestments may be worn at the funeral rites and at other offices and Masses for the dead.

RITUAL GESTURES AND MOVEMENT

40. The presiding minister or an assisting minister may quietly direct the assembly in the movements, gestures, and posture appropriate to the particular ritual moment or action.

41. Processions, especially when accompanied with music and singing, can strengthen the bond of communion in the assembly. For processions, ministers of music should give preference to settings of psalms and songs that are responsorial or litanic in style and that allow the people to respond to the verses with an invariable refrain. During the various processions, it is preferable that the pallbearers carry the coffin as a sign of reverence and respect for the deceased.

42. Processions continue to have special significance in funeral celebrations, as in Christian Rome where funeral rites consisted of three "stages" or "stations" joined by two processions. Christians accompanied the body on its last journey. From the home of the deceased the Christian community pro-

ceeded to the church singing psalms. When the service in the church concluded, the body was carried in solemn procession to the grave or tomb. During the final procession the congregation sang psalms praising the God of mercy and redemption and antiphons entrusting the deceased to the care of the angels and saints. The funeral liturgy mirrored the journey of human life, the Christian pilgrimage to the heavenly Jerusalem.

In many places and situations a solemn procession on foot to the church or to the place of committal may not be possible. Nevertheless at the conclusion of the funeral liturgy an antiphon or versicle and response may be sung as the body is taken to the entrance of the church. Psalms, hymns, or liturgical songs may also be sung when the participants gather at the place of committal.

SELECTION OF RITES FROM THE ORDER OF CHRISTIAN FUNERALS

43. The *Order of Christian Funerals* makes provision for the minister, in consultation with the family, to choose those rites and texts that are most suitable to the situation: those that most closely apply to the needs of the mourners, the circumstances of the death, and the customs of the local Christian community. The minister and family may be assisted in the choice of a rite or rites by the reflections preceding each rite or group of rites.

44. Part I, "Funeral Rites," of the *Order of Christian Funerals* provides those rites that may be used in the funerals of Christians and is divided into three groups of rites that correspond in general to the three principal ritual moments in Christian funerals: "Vigil and Related Rites and Prayers," "Funeral Liturgy," and "Rite of Committal."

45. The section entitled "Vigil and Related Rites and Prayers" includes rites that may be celebrated between the time of death and the funeral liturgy or, should there be no funeral liturgy, before the rite of committal. The vigil is the principal celebration of the Christian community during the time before the funeral liturgy. It may take the form of a liturgy of the word (see nos. 54–97) or of some part of the

office for the dead (see Part IV, nos. 348–395). Two vigil services are provided: "Vigil for the Deceased" and "Vigil for the Deceased with Reception at the Church." The second service is used when the vigil is celebrated in the church and the body is to be received at this time.

"Related Rites and Prayers" includes three brief rites that may be used on occasions of prayer with the family: "Prayers after Death," "Gathering in the Presence of the Body," and "Transfer of the Body to the Church or to the Place of Committal." These rites are examples or models of what can be done and should be adapted to the circumstances.

46. The section entitled "Funeral Liturgy" provides two forms of the funeral liturgy, the central celebration of the Christian community for the deceased: "Funeral Mass" and "Funeral Liturgy outside Mass." When one of its members dies, the Church especially encourages the celebration of the Mass. When Mass cannot be celebrated (see no. 178), the second form of the funeral liturgy may be used and a Mass for the deceased should be celebrated, if possible, at a later time.

47. The section entitled "Rite of Committal" includes two forms of the rite of committal, the concluding rite of the funeral: "Rite of Committal" and "Rite of Committal with Final Commendation." The first form is used when the final commendation is celebrated as part of the conclusion of the funeral liturgy. The second form is used when the final commendation does not take place during the funeral liturgy or when no funeral liturgy precedes the committal.

48. Part II, "Funeral Rites for Children," provides an adaptation of the principal rites in Part I: "Vigil for a Deceased Child," "Funeral Liturgy," and "Rite of Committal." These rites may be used in the funerals of infants and young children, including those of early school age. The rites in Part II include texts for use in the case of a baptized child and in the case of a child who died before baptism.

In some instances, for example, the death of an infant, the vigil and funeral liturgy may not be appropriate. Only the rite of committal and perhaps one of the forms of prayer with the family as provided in "Related Rites and Prayers" may be desirable. Part II does not contain "Related Rites and Prayers," but the rites from Part I may be adapted.

49. Part III, "Texts from Sacred Scripture," includes the Scripture readings and psalms for the celebration of the funeral rites. Part IV, "Office for the Dead," includes "Morning Prayer," "Evening Prayer," and "Additional Hymns." Part V, "Additional Texts," contains "Prayers and Texts in Particular Circumstances," and "Holy Communion outside Mass." The texts that appear in the various rites in Parts I, II, and IV may be replaced by corresponding readings and psalms given in Part III and by corresponding prayers and texts given in Part V.

PART I

FUNERAL RITES
God is not the God of the dead but of the living; for in him all are alive.

50. Part I of the *Order of Christian Funerals* is divided into three groups of rites that correspond in general to the three principal ritual moments in the funerals of Christians: "Vigil and Related Rites and Prayers," "Funeral Liturgy," and "Rite of Committal." The minister, in consultation with those concerned, chooses from within these three groups of rites those that best correspond to the particular needs and customs of the mourners. This choice may be assisted by the reflections given in the General Introduction and in the introduction to each rite or group of rites.

VIGIL AND RELATED RITES AND PRAYERS
Do not let your hearts be troubled; trust in God still.

51. The rites provided here may be celebrated between the time of death and the funeral liturgy or, should there be no funeral liturgy, before the rite of committal. Two forms of the vigil are presented here: "Vigil for the Deceased," and "Vigil for the Deceased with Reception at the Church," for convenient use in accord with the circumstances.

"Related Rites and Prayers" includes three brief rites that may be used on occasions of prayer with the family: "Prayers after Death," "Gathering in the Presence of the Body," and "Transfer of the Body to the Church or to the Place of Committal." These rites are examples or models of what can be done and should be adapted to the circumstances.

52. The time immediately following death is often one of bewilderment and may involve shock or heartrending grief for the family and close friends. The ministry of the Church at this time is one of gently accompanying the mourners in their initial adjustment to the fact of death and to the sorrow this entails. Through a careful use of the rites contained in this section, the minister helps the mourners to express their sorrow and to find strength and consolation through faith in Christ and his resurrection to eternal life. The members of the Christian community offer support to the mourners, especially by praying that the one they have lost may have eternal life.

53. Ministers should be aware that the experience of death can bring about in the mourners possible needs for reconciliation. With attentiveness to each situation, the minister can help to begin the process of reconciliation. In some cases this process may find expression in the celebration of the sacrament of penance, either before the funeral liturgy or at a later time.

1.   VIGIL FOR THE DECEASED

Happy now are the dead who die in the Lord; they shall find rest from their labors.

54. The vigil for the deceased is the principal rite celebrated by the Christian community in the time following death and before the funeral liturgy, or if there is no funeral liturgy, before the rite of committal. It may take the form either of a liturgy of the word (nos. 69–81, 82–97) or of some part of the office for the dead (see Part IV, nos. 348–395). Two vigil services are provided: "Vigil for the Deceased" and "Vigil for the Deceased with Reception at the Church." The second service is used when the vigil is celebrated in the church and begins with the reception of the body.

55. The vigil may be celebrated in the home of the deceased, in the funeral home, parlor or chapel of rest, or in some other suitable place. It may also be celebrated in the church, but at a time well before the funeral liturgy, so that the funeral liturgy will not be lengthy and the liturgy of the word repetitious. Adaptations of the vigil will often be suggested by the place in which the celebration occurs. A celebration in the home of the deceased, for example, may be simplified and shortened.

If the reception of the body at church is celebrated apart from the vigil or the funeral liturgy, the "Vigil for the Deceased with Reception at the Church" may be used and simplified.

56. At the vigil the Christian community keeps watch with the family in prayer to the God of mercy and finds strength in Christ's presence. It is the first occasion among the funeral rites for the solemn reading of the word of God. In this time of loss the family and community turn to God's word as the source of faith and hope, as light and life in the face of darkness and death. Consoled by the redeeming word of God and by the abiding presence of Christ and his Spirit, the assembly at the vigil calls upon the Father of mercy to receive the deceased into the kingdom of light and peace.

STRUCTURE

57. The vigil in the form of the liturgy of the word consists of the introductory rites, the liturgy of the word, the prayer of intercession, and a concluding rite.

INTRODUCTORY RITES

58. The introductory rites gather the faithful together to form a community and to prepare all to listen to God's word. The introductory rites of the vigil for the deceased include the greeting, an opening song, an invitation to prayer, a pause for silent prayer, and an opening prayer.

In the vigil for the deceased with reception at the church, the rite of reception forms the introductory rites (nos. 82–86). In this case the family and others who have accompanied the body are greeted at the entrance of the church. The body is then sprinkled with holy water and, if it is the custom, the pall is placed on the coffin by family members, friends, or the minister. The entrance procession follows, during which a hymn or psalm is sung. At the conclusion of the procession a symbol of the Christian life may be placed on the coffin. Then the invitation to prayer, a pause for silent prayer, and an opening prayer conclude the introductory rites.

The opening song or entrance song should be a profound expression of belief in eternal life and the resurrection of the dead, as well as a prayer of intercession for the dead.

LITURGY OF THE WORD

59. The proclamation of the word of God is the high point and central focus of the vigil. The liturgy of the word usually includes a first reading, responsorial psalm, gospel reading, and homily. A reader proclaims the first reading. The responsorial psalm should be sung, whenever possible. If an assisting deacon is present, he proclaims the gospel reading. Otherwise, the presiding minister proclaims the gospel reading.

60. The purpose of the readings at the vigil is to proclaim the paschal mystery, teach remembrance of the dead, convey the hope of being gathered together in God's kingdom, and encourage the witness of Christian life. Above all, the readings tell of God's designs for a world in which suffering and death will relinquish their hold on all whom God has called his own. The responsorial psalm enables the community to respond in faith to the reading and to express its grief and its praise of God. In the selection of readings the needs of the mourners and the circumstances of the death should be kept in mind.

61. A homily based on the readings is given at the vigil to help those present find strength and hope in God's saving word.

PRAYER OF INTERCESSION

62. In the prayer of intercession the community calls upon God to comfort the mourners and to show mercy to the deceased. The prayer of intercession takes the form of a litany, the Lord's Prayer, and a concluding prayer.

After this prayer and before the blessing or at some other suitable time during the vigil, a member of the family or a friend of the deceased may speak in remembrance of the deceased.

CONCLUDING RITE

63. The vigil concludes with a blessing, which may be followed by a liturgical song or a few minutes of silent prayer or both.

MINISTRY AND PARTICIPATION

64. Members of the local parish community should be encouraged to participate in the vigil as a sign of concern and support for the mourners. In many circumstances the vigil will be the first opportunity for friends, neighbors, and members of the local parish community to show their concern for the family of the deceased by gathering for prayer. The vigil may also serve as an opportunity for participation in the funeral by those who, because of work or other reasons, cannot be present for the funeral liturgy or the rite of committal.

65. The full participation by all present is to be encouraged. This is best achieved through careful planning of the celebration. Whenever possible, the family of the deceased should take part in the selection of texts and music and in the designation of liturgical ministers.

66. Besides the presiding minister, other available ministers (a reader, a cantor, an acolyte) should exercise their ministries. Family members may assume some of these liturgical roles, unless their grief prevents them from doing so.

The presiding minister and assisting ministers should vest for the vigil according to local custom. If the vigil is celebrated in the church, a priest or deacon who presides wears an alb or surplice with stole.

67. As needs require, and especially if the funeral liturgy or rite of committal is not to take place for a few days, the vigil may be celebrated more than once and should be adapted to each occasion.

68. Music is integral to any vigil, especially the vigil for the deceased. In the difficult circumstances following death, well-chosen music can touch the mourners and others present at levels of human need that words alone often fail to reach. Such music can enliven the faith of the community gathered to support the family and to affirm hope in the resurrection.

Whenever possible, an instrumentalist and a cantor or leader of song should assist the assembly's full participation in the singing.

In the choice of music for the vigil, preference should be given to the singing of the opening song and the responsorial psalm. The litany, the Lord's Prayer, and a closing song may also be sung.

VIGIL FOR THE DECEASED

INTRODUCTORY RITES

GREETING

69. Using one of the following greetings, or in similar words, the minister greets those present.

A

May the God of hope give you the fullness of peace, and may the Lord of life be always with you.
℟. And also with you.

B

The grace and peace of God our Father and the Lord Jesus Christ be with you.
℟. And also with you.

C

The grace and peace of God our Father, who raised Jesus from the dead, be always with you.
℟. And also with you.

D

May the Father of mercies, the God of all consolation, be with you.
℟. And also with you.

OPENING SONG

70. The celebration continues with a song.

INVITATION TO PRAYER

71. In the following or similar words, the minister invites those present to pray.

My brothers and sisters, we believe that all the ties of friendship and affection which knit us as one throughout our lives do not unravel with death.

Confident that God always remembers the good we have done and forgives our sins, let us pray, asking God to gather N. to himself:

Pause for silent prayer.

OPENING PRAYER

72. The minister says one of the following prayers or one of those provided in nos. 398–399.

A

Lord our God,
the death of our brother/sister N.
recalls our human condition
and the brevity of our lives on earth.
But for those who believe in your love
death is not the end,
nor does it destroy the bonds
that you forge in our lives.
We share the faith of your Son's disciples
and the hope of the children of God.
Bring the light of Christ's resurrection
to this time of testing and pain
as we pray for N. and for those who love him/her,
through Christ our Lord.
℟. Amen.

B

O God,
glory of believers and life of the just,
by the death and resurrection of your Son, we are
  redeemed:
have mercy on your servant N.,
and make him/her worthy to share the joys of
  paradise,
for he/she believed in the resurrection of the dead.
We ask this through Christ our Lord.
℟. Amen.

171

LITURGY OF THE WORD

73. The celebration continues with the liturgy of the word. Other readings, psalms, and gospel readings are given in Part III, nos. 343–346.

FIRST READING

74. A reader proclaims the first reading.

2 Corinthians 5:1, 6–10
We have an everlasting home in heaven

RESPONSORIAL PSALM

75. Psalm 27 is sung or said or another psalm or song. ¹¹⁰

R̸. **The Lord is my light and my salvation.**

Or:

R̸. **I believe that I shall see the good things of the Lord in the land of the living.**

GOSPEL

76. The gospel reading is then proclaimed.

Luke 12:35–40
Be prepared. ¹³⁴

HOMILY

77. A brief homily on the readings is then given.

PRAYER OF INTERCESSION

LITANY

78. The minister leads those present in the following litany.

Let us turn to Christ Jesus with confidence and faith in the power of his cross and resurrection:

Assisting minister:
Risen Lord, pattern of our life for ever:
Lord have mercy.
R̸. **Lord, have mercy.**

Assisting minister:
Promise and image of what we shall be:
Lord have mercy.
R̸. **Lord, have mercy.**

Assisting minister:
Son of God who came to destroy sin and death:
Lord, have mercy.
R̸. **Lord, have mercy.**

Assisting minister:
Word of God who delivered us from the fear of death:
Lord, have mercy.
℟. **Lord, have mercy.**

Assisting minister:
Crucified Lord, forsaken in death, raised in glory:
Lord, have mercy.
℟. **Lord, have mercy.**

Assisting minister:
Lord Jesus, gentle Shepherd who brings rest to our souls, give peace to N. for ever:
Lord, have mercy.
℟. **Lord, have mercy.**

Assisting minister:
Lord Jesus, you bless those who mourn and are in pain. Bless N.'s family and friends who gather around him/her today:
Lord, have mercy.
℟. **Lord, have mercy.**

THE LORD'S PRAYER

79. Using one of the following invitations, or in similar words, the minister invites those present to pray the Lord's Prayer.

A
Friends [Brothers and sisters], our true home is heaven. Therefore let us pray to our heavenly Father as Jesus taught us:

B
With God there is mercy and fullness of redemption; let us pray as Jesus taught us:

C
Let us pray for the coming of the kingdom as Jesus taught us:

All:
Our Father . . .

CONCLUDING PRAYER

80. The minister says one of the following prayers or one of those provided in nos. 398–399.

A

Lord Jesus, our Redeemer,
you willingly gave yourself up to death,
so that all might be saved and pass from death to
life.
We humbly ask you to comfort your servants in their
grief
and to receive N. into the arms of your mercy.
You alone are the Holy One,
you are mercy itself;
by dying you unlocked the gates of life for those
who believe in you.
Forgive N. his/her sins,
and grant him/her a place of happiness, light, and
peace
in the kingdom of your glory for ever and ever.
R̶. Amen.

169

B

Lord God,
you are attentive to the voice of our pleading.
Let us find in your Son
comfort in our sadness,
certainty in our doubt,
and courage to live through this hour.
Make our faith strong
through Christ our Lord.
R̶. Amen.

A member or a friend of the family may speak in remembrance of the deceased.

CONCLUDING RITE

BLESSING

81. The minister says:

Blessed are those who have died in the Lord;
let them rest from their labors for their good deeds
   go with them.

A gesture, for example, signing the forehead of the deceased with the sign of the cross, may accompany the following words.

Eternal rest grant unto him/her, O Lord.
℞. And let perpetual light shine upon him/her.

May he/she rest in peace.
℞. Amen.

May his/her soul and the souls of all the faithful departed, through the mercy of God, rest in peace.
℞. Amen.

A   A minister who is a priest or deacon says:
May the peace of God,
which is beyond all understanding,
keep your hearts and minds
in the knowledge and love of God
and of his Son, our Lord Jesus Christ.
℞. Amen.

May almighty God bless you,
the Father, and the Son, ✠ and the Holy Spirit.
℞. Amen.

B   A lay minister invokes God's blessing and signs himself or herself with the sign of the cross, saying:
May the love of God and the peace of the Lord Jesus
   Christ
bless and console us
and gently wipe every tear from our eyes:
in the name of the Father,
and of the Son, and of the Holy Spirit.
℞. Amen.

The vigil may conclude with a song or a few moments of silent prayer or both.

VIGIL FOR THE DECEASED WITH RECEPTION AT THE CHURCH

INTRODUCTORY RITES

GREETING

82. The minister, with assisting ministers, goes to the door of the church. See no. 69.

SPRINKLING WITH HOLY WATER

83. The minister then sprinkles the coffin with holy water, saying:

**In the waters of baptism
N. died with Christ and rose with him to new life.
May he/she now share with him eternal glory.**

PLACING OF THE PALL

84. If it is the custom in the local community, the pall is then placed on the coffin by family members, friends, or the minister.

ENTRANCE PROCESSION

85. The Easter candle may be placed beforehand near the position the coffin will occupy at the conclusion of the procession. The minister and assisting ministers precede the coffin and the mourners into the church. During the procession a psalm, song, or responsory is sung (see no. 403).

PLACING OF CHRISTIAN SYMBOLS

86. A symbol of the Christian life, such as a Book of the Gospels, a Bible, or a cross, may be carried in procession, then placed on the coffin, either in silence or as a text from no. 400 is said.

INVITATION TO PRAYER

87. In the following or similar words, the minister invites those present to pray.

My brothers and sisters, we believe that all the ties
of friendship and affection which knit us as one
throughout our lives do not unravel with death.

Confident that God always remembers the good we
have done and forgives our sins, let us pray, asking
God to gather N. to himself:

Pause for silent prayer.

OPENING PRAYER

88. The minister says one of the following prayers or one
of those provided in nos. 398–399.

A
Lord, in our grief we turn to you.   33
Are you not the God of love
who open your ears to all?

Listen to our prayers for your servant N.,
whom you have called out of this world:
lead him/her to your kingdom of light and peace
and count him/her among the saints in glory.

We ask this through Christ our Lord.
R̷. Amen

B
Lord Jesus, our Redeemer,   169
you willingly gave yourself up to death,
so that all might be saved and pass from death to
 life.
We humbly ask you to comfort your servants in their
 grief
and to receive N. into the arms of your mercy.
You alone are the Holy One,
you are mercy itself;
by dying you unlocked the gates of life for those
 who believe in you.
Forgive N. his/her sins,
and grant him/her a place of happiness, light, and
 peace

in the kingdom of your glory for ever and ever.
℟. **Amen.**

LITURGY OF THE WORD

89. The celebration continues with the liturgy of the word. Other readings, psalms, and gospel readings are given in Part III, nos. 343–346.

FIRST READING

90. A reader proclaims the first reading.

1 John 3:1-2   103
We shall see God as he really is.

RESPONSORIAL PSALM

91. Psalm 103 is sung or said or another psalm or song.
Psalm 103
℟. **The Lord is kind and merciful.**   113

   Or:
℟. **The salvation of the just comes from the Lord.**

GOSPEL

92. The gospel reading is then proclaimed.

John 14:1-6   143
There are many rooms in my Father's house.

HOMILY

93. A brief homily on the readings is then given.

PRAYER OF INTERCESSION

LITANY

94. The minister leads those present in the following litany. See no. 78.

THE LORD'S PRAYER

95. Using one of the following invitations, or in similar words, the minister invites those present to pray the Lord's Prayer. See no. 79.

CONCLUDING PRAYER

96. The minister says one of the following prayers or one of those provided in nos. 398–399.

A

Lord God, in whom all find refuge,
we appeal to your boundless mercy:
grant to the soul of your servant N.
a kindly welcome,
cleansing of sin,
release from the chains of death,
and entry into everlasting life.

175

We ask this through Christ our Lord.
R͞. Amen.

B   See no. 80B.

A member or a friend of the family may speak in remembrance of the deceased.

CONCLUDING RITE

BLESSING

97. See no. 81.

The vigil may conclude with a song or a few moments of silent prayer or both.

2. RELATED RITES AND PRAYERS

If we have died with Christ, we believe we shall also live with him.

98. The section entitled "Related Rites and Prayers" contains three brief rites, "Prayers after Death," "Gathering in the Presence of the Body," and "Transfer of the Body to the Church or to the Place of Committal." These rites are presented to help the minister and others pray with the family and close friends in the period soon after death. "Prayers after Death" may be used when the minister first meets with the family, "Gathering in the Presence of the Body," when the family first gathers together around the body of the deceased, and "Transfer of the Body to the Church or to the Place of Committal," when the family and friends prepare to accompany the body of the deceased in the procession to the church or to the place of committal.

99. These rites are signs of the concern of the Christian community for the family and close friends of the deceased. The compassionate presence of the minister and others and the familiar elements of these simple rites can have the effect of reassuring the mourners and of providing a consoling and hopeful situation in which to pray and to express their grief.

100. The circumstances for the celebration of these rites may vary from place to place and from culture to culture. The rites as given are only models, for adaptation by the minister according to the circumstances.

PRAYERS AFTER DEATH
Blessed are the sorrowing; they shall be consoled.

101. This rite provides a model of prayer that may be used when the minister first meets with the family following death. The rite follows a common pattern of reading, response, prayer, and blessing and may be adapted according to the circumstances.

102. The presence of the minister and the calming effect of familiar prayers can comfort the mourners as they begin to face their loss. When the minister is present with the family

at the time death occurs, this rite can be used as a quiet and prayerful response to the death. In other circumstances, for example, in the case of sudden or unexpected death, this form of prayer can be the principal part of the first pastoral visit of the minister.

103. The initial pastoral visit can be important as the first tangible expression of the community's support for the mourners. A minister unfamiliar with the family or the deceased person can learn a great deal on this occasion about the needs of the family and about the life of the deceased. The minister may also be able to form some preliminary judgments to help the family in planning the funeral rites. If circumstances allow, some first steps in the planning may take place at this time.

PRAYERS AFTER DEATH

INVITATION TO PRAYER

104. Using one of the following greetings, or in similar words, the minister greets those present.

A
In this moment of sorrow
the Lord is in our midst
and consoles us with his word:
Blessed are the sorrowful; they shall be comforted.

B
Praised be God, the Father of our Lord Jesus Christ,
the Father of mercies,
and the God of all consolation!
He comforts us in all our afflictions
and thus enables us to comfort those who grieve
with the same consolation
we have received from him.

The minister then invites those present to pray in silence.

READING

105. The minister or one of those present proclaims the reading. A reading from Part III, nos. 343–346, or one of the following may be used.

A **Matthew 18:19–20**
B **John 11:21–24**
C **Luke 20:35–38**

THE LORD'S PRAYER

106. Using one of the following invitations, or in similar words, the minister invites those present to pray the Lord's Prayer.

A
With God there is mercy and fullness of redemption; let us pray as Jesus taught us:

B
Let us pray for the coming of the kingdom as Jesus taught us:

All:
Our Father . . .

CONCLUDING PRAYERS

107. A prayer for the deceased person is then said. This prayer may be followed by a prayer for the mourners.

For the deceased person: The minister says the following prayer or one of those provided in no. 398.

Holy Lord, almighty and eternal God,
hear our prayers for your servant N.,
whom you have summoned out of this world.
Forgive his/her sins and failings
and grant him/her a place of refreshment, light, and
**   peace.**
Let him/her pass unharmed through the gates of
**   death**
to dwell with the blessed in light,
as you promised to Abraham and his children for
**   ever.**
Accept N. into your safekeeping
and on the great day of judgment
raise him/her up with all the saints
to inherit your eternal kingdom.

167

We ask this through Christ our Lord.
℟. Amen.

For the mourners: The minister may then say the following prayer or one of those provided in no. 399.

Father of mercies and God of all consolation,
you pursue us with untiring love
and dispel the shadow of death
with the bright dawn of life.

[Comfort your family in their loss and sorrow.
Be our refuge and our strength, O Lord,
and lift us from the depths of grief
into the peace and light of your presence.]

Your Son, our Lord Jesus Christ,
by dying has destroyed our death,
and by rising, restored our life.
Enable us therefore to press on toward him,
so that, after our earthly course is run,
he may reunite us with those we love,
when every tear will be wiped away.

We ask this through Christ our Lord.
℟. Amen.

BLESSING
108. See no. 81.

GATHERING IN THE PRESENCE OF THE BODY

If we have died with Christ, we believe we shall also live with him.

109. This rite provides a model of prayer that may be used when the family first gathers in the presence of the body, when the body is to be prepared for burial, or after it has been prepared. The family members, in assembling in the presence of the body, confront in the most immediate way the fact of their loss and the mystery of death. Because cultural attitudes and practices on such occasions may vary, the minister should adapt the rite.

110. Through the presence of the minister and others and through the celebration of this brief rite, the community seeks to be with the mourners in their need and to provide an atmosphere of sensitive concern and confident faith. In prayer and gesture those present show reverence for the body of the deceased as a temple of the life-giving Spirit and ask, in that same Spirit, for the eternal life promised to the faithful.

111. The minister should try to be as attentive as possible to the particular needs of the mourners. The minister begins the rite at an opportune moment and, as much as possible, in an atmosphere of calm and recollection. The pause for silent prayer after the Scripture verse can be especially helpful in this regard.

SIGN OF THE CROSS

112. The minister and those present sign themselves with the sign of the cross as the minister says:

In the name of the Father, and of the Son, and of the Holy Spirit.
R̸. Amen.

SCRIPTURE VERSE

113. One of the following or another brief Scripture verse is read.

A   Matthew 11:28–30
B   John 14:1–3

Pause for silent prayer.

SPRINKLING WITH HOLY WATER

114. Using one of the following formularies, the minister may sprinkle the body with holy water.

A
The Lord is our shepherd
and leads us to streams of living water.

B
Let this water call to mind our baptism into Christ,
who by his death and resurrection has redeemed us.

C
The Lord God lives in his holy temple yet abides in
**   our midst.**
Since in baptism N. became God's temple
and the Spirit of God lived in him/her,
with reverence we bless his/her mortal body.

PSALM

115. One of the following psalms is sung or said or another psalm provided in Part III, nos. 343–344.

A   Psalm 130
℟. **I hope in the Lord, I trust in his word.**

B   Psalm 115 and 116
℟. **I will walk in the presence of the Lord, in the**
**   land of the living.**

THE LORD'S PRAYER

116. See no. 106

CONCLUDING PRAYER

117. The minister says one of the following prayers or one of those provided in nos. 398–399.

A
God of faithfulness,
in your wisdom you have called your servant N. out
**   of this world;**
release him/her from the bonds of sin,
and welcome him/her into your presence,

30

so that he/she may enjoy eternal light and peace
and be raised up in glory with all your saints.

We ask this through Christ our Lord.
℟. Amen.

B
Into your hands, O Lord,   168
we humbly entrust our brother/sister N.
In this life you embraced him/her with your tender
    love;
deliver him/her now from every evil
and bid him/her enter eternal rest.

The old order has passed away:
welcome him/her then into paradise,
where there will be no sorrow, no weeping nor pain,
but the fullness of peace and joy
with your Son and the Holy Spirit
for ever and ever.
℟. Amen.

BLESSING

118. The minister says:

Blessed are those who have died in the Lord;
let them rest from their labors for their good deeds
    go with them.

A gesture, for example, signing the forehead of the deceased with the sign of the cross, may accompany the following words.

Eternal rest grant unto him/her, O Lord.
℟. And let perpetual light shine upon him/her.

May he/she rest in peace.
℟. Amen.

May his/her soul and the souls of all the faithful
    departed,
through the mercy of God, rest in peace.
℟. Amen.

A A minister who is a priest or a deacon says:
May the peace of God,
which is beyond all understanding,
keep your hearts and minds
in the knowledge and love of God
and of his Son, our Lord Jesus Christ.
R̸. Amen.

May almighty God bless you,
the Father, and the Son, ✠ and the Holy Spirit.
R̸. Amen.

B A lay minister invokes God's blessing and signs himself or herself with the sign of the cross, saying:
May the love of God and the peace of the Lord Jesus
   Christ
bless and console us
and gently wipe every tear from our eyes:
in the name of the Father,
and of the Son, and of the Holy Spirit.
R̸. Amen.

TRANSFER OF THE BODY TO THE CHURCH OR TO THE PLACE OF COMMITTAL

Your life is hidden now with Christ in God.

119. This rite may be used for prayer with the family and close friends as they prepare to accompany the body of the deceased in the procession to the church or to the place of committal. It is a model, for adaptation by the minister according to the circumstances.

120. The procession to the church is a rite of initial separation of the mourners from the deceased; the procession to the place of committal is the journey to the place of final separation of the mourners from the deceased. Because the transfer of the body may be an occasion of great emotion for the mourners, the minister and other members of the community should make every effort to be present to support them. Reverent celebration of the rite can help reassure the mourners and create an atmosphere of calm preparation before the procession.

INVITATION

121. In the following or similar words, the minister addresses those present.

Dear friends in Christ, in the name of Jesus and of his Church, we gather to pray for N., that God may bring him/her to everlasting peace and rest.

We share the pain of loss, but the promise of eternal life gives us hope. Let us comfort one another with these words:

SCRIPTURE VERSE

122. One of the following or another brief Scripture verse is read.

A   Colossians 3:3–4
B   Romans 6:8–9

LITANY

123. The minister leads those present in the following litany.

Dear friends, our Lord comes to raise the dead and comforts us with the solace of his love. Let us praise the Lord Jesus Christ.

Assisting minister:
Word of God, Creator of the earth to which N. now returns: in baptism you called him/her to eternal life to praise your Father for ever:
Lord, have mercy.
R⁄. Lord, have mercy.

Assisting minister:
Son of God, you raise up the just and clothe them with the glory of your kingdom:
Lord, have mercy.
R⁄. Lord, have mercy.

Assisting minister:
Crucified Lord, you protect the soul of N. by the power of your cross, and on the day of your coming you will show mercy to all the faithful departed:
Lord, have mercy.
R⁄. Lord, have mercy.

Assisting minister:
Judge of the living and the dead, at your voice the tombs will open and all the just who sleep in your peace will rise and sing the glory of God:
Lord, have mercy.
R⁄. Lord, have mercy.

Assisting minister:
All praise to you, Jesus our Savior, death is in your hands and all the living depend on you alone:
Lord, have mercy.
R⁄. Lord, have mercy.

THE LORD'S PRAYER

124. In the following or similar words, the minister invites those present to pray the Lord's Prayer.

With faith and hope we pray to the Father in the words Jesus taught his disciples:

All:

Our Father . . .

CONCLUDING PRAYER

125. The minister says one of the following prayers or one of those provided in nos. 398–399.

A

Lord,

N. is gone now from this earthly dwelling

and has left behind those who mourn his/her absence.

Grant that as we grieve for our brother/sister

we may hold his/her memory dear,

and live in hope of the eternal kingdom

where you will bring us together again.

We ask this through Christ our Lord.

R̶. Amen.

B

Lord, in our grief we turn to you.   33

Are you not the God of love

who open your ears to all?

Listen to our prayers for your servant N.,

whom you have called out of this world:

lead him/her to your kingdom of light and peace

and count him/her among the saints in glory.

We ask this through Christ our Lord.

R̶. Amen.

C

God of all consolation,   176

open our hearts to your word,

so that, listening to it, we may comfort one another,

finding light in time of darkness

and faith in time of doubt.

We ask this through Christ our Lord.

R̶. Amen.

The minister invites those present to pray in silence while all is made ready for the procession.

INVITATION TO THE PROCESSION

126. In the following or similar words, the minister invites those present to join in the procession.

**The Lord guards our coming in and our going out.
May God be with us today
as we make this last journey with our brother/sister.**

PROCESSION TO THE CHURCH OR TO THE PLACE OF COMMITTAL

127. During the procession, psalms and other suitable songs may be sung. If this is not possible, a psalm is sung or recited either before or after the procession. The following psalm and others provided in Part III, no. 347 may be used.

Psalm 122
R̸. I rejoiced when I heard them say: let us go to the house of the Lord.

Or:
R̸. Let us go rejoicing to the house of the Lord.

If the reception of the body at the church is celebrated apart from the vigil or the funeral liturgy, the "Vigil for the Deceased with Reception at the Church" (nos. 82–97) may be used and simplified.

FUNERAL LITURGY
All will be brought to life in Christ.

128. The funeral liturgy is the central liturgical celebration of the Christian community for the deceased. Two forms of the funeral liturgy are presented here: "Funeral Mass" and "Funeral Liturgy outside Mass."

When one of its members dies, the Church encourages the celebration of the Mass. But when Mass cannot be celebrated (see no. 178), the second form of the funeral liturgy is used. When the funeral liturgy is celebrated outside Mass before the committal, a Mass for the deceased should be scheduled, if possible, for the family and friends at a convenient time after the funeral.

129. At the funeral liturgy the community gathers with the family and friends of the deceased to give praise and thanks to God for Christ's victory over sin and death, to commend the deceased to God's tender mercy and compassion, and to seek strength in the proclamation of the paschal mystery. Through the Holy Spirit the community is joined together in faith as one Body in Christ to reaffirm in sign and symbol, word and gesture that each believer through baptism shares in Christ's death and resurrection and can look to the day when all the elect will be raised up and united in the kingdom of light and peace.

STRUCTURE AND CONTENT OF THE FUNERAL LITURGY

130. The funeral Mass includes the reception of the body, if this has not already occurred, the celebration of the liturgy of the word, the liturgy of the eucharist, and the final commendation and farewell. The funeral liturgy outside Mass includes all these elements except the liturgy of the eucharist. Both the funeral Mass and the funeral liturgy outside Mass may be followed by the procession to the place of committal.

RECEPTION AT THE CHURCH

131. Since the church is the place where the community of faith assembles for worship, the rite of reception of the body at the church has great significance. The church is the

place where the Christian life is begotten in baptism, nourished in the eucharist, and where the community gathers to commend one of its deceased members to the Father. The church is at once a symbol of the community and of the heavenly liturgy that the celebration of the liturgy anticipates. In the act of receiving the body, the members of the community acknowledge the deceased as one of their own, as one who was welcomed in baptism and who held a place in the assembly. Through the use of various baptismal symbols the community shows the reverence due to the body, the temple of the Spirit, and in this way prepares for the funeral liturgy in which it asks for a share in the heavenly banquet promised to the deceased and to all who have been washed in the waters of rebirth and marked with the sign of faith.

132. Any national flags or the flags or insignia of associations to which the deceased belonged are to be removed from the coffin at the entrance of the church. They may be replaced after the coffin has been taken from the church.

133. The rite of reception takes place at the beginning of the funeral liturgy, usually at the entrance of the church. It begins with a greeting of the family and others who have accompanied the coffin to the door of the church. The minister sprinkles the coffin with holy water in remembrance of the deceased person's initiation and first acceptance into the community of faith. If it is the custom in the local community, a funeral pall, a reminder of the garment given at baptism, and therefore signifying life in Christ, may then be placed on the coffin by family members, friends, or the minister. The entrance procession follows. The minister precedes the coffin and the mourners into the church. If the Easter candle is used on this occasion, it may be placed beforehand near the position the coffin will occupy at the conclusion of the procession.

134. If in this rite a symbol of the Christian life is to be placed on the coffin, it is carried in the procession and is placed on the coffin by a family member, friend, or the minister at the conclusion of the procession.

135. To draw the community together in prayer at the beginning of the funeral liturgy, the procession should be ac-

companied, whenever possible, by the singing of the entrance song. This song ought to be a profound expression of belief in eternal life and the resurrection of the dead as well as a prayer of intercession for the deceased (see, for example, no. 403).

136. If the rite of reception has already taken place, the funeral Mass begins in the usual way and the funeral liturgy outside Mass begins with the entrance song, followed by the greeting and an invitation to prayer.

LITURGY OF THE WORD

137. The reading of the word of God is an essential element of the celebration of the funeral liturgy. The readings proclaim the paschal mystery, teach remembrance of the dead, convey the hope of being gathered together again in God's kingdom, and encourage the witness of Christian life. Above all, the readings tell of God's design for a world in which suffering and death will relinquish their hold on all whom God has called his own.

138. Depending on pastoral circumstances, there may be either one or two readings before the gospel reading. When there is a first and second reading before the gospel reading, it is preferable to have a different reader for each.

139. The responsorial psalm enables the community to respond in faith to the first reading. Through the psalms the community expresses its grief and praise, and acknowledges its Creator and Redeemer as the sure source of trust and hope in times of trial. Since the responsorial psalm is a song, whenever possible, it should be sung. Psalms may be sung responsorially, with the response sung by the assembly and all the verses by the cantor or choir, or directly, with no response and all the verses sung by all or by the cantor or choir. When not sung, the responsorial psalm after the reading should be recited in a manner conducive to meditation on the word of God.[1]

140. In the *alleluia*, or the gospel acclamation, the community welcomes the Lord who is about to speak to it. If the *alleluia* is not sung, it is omitted. The cantor or choir sings

[1]See Lectionary for Mass, (2nd *editio typica*, 1981), General Introduction, no. 22.

the *alleluia* or Lenten acclamation first and the people repeat it. The verse is then sung by the cantor or choir and the *alleluia* or Lenten acclamation is then sung once more by all.

141. A brief homily based on the readings should always be given at the funeral liturgy, but never any kind of eulogy. The homilist should dwell on God's compassionate love and on the paschal mystery of the Lord as proclaimed in the Scripture readings. Through the homily, the community should receive the consolation and strength to face the death of one of its members with a hope that has been nourished by the proclamation of the saving word of God.

142. In the intercessions the community responds to the proclamation of the word of God by prayer for the deceased and all the dead, for the bereaved and all who mourn, and for all in the assembly. The intercessions provided may be used or adapted to the circumstances, or new intercessions may be composed.

LITURGY OF THE EUCHARIST

143. At the funeral Mass, the community, having been spiritually renewed at the table of God's word, turns for spiritual nourishment to the table of the eucharist. The community with the priest offers to the Father the sacrifice of the New Covenant and shares in the one bread and the one cup. In partaking of the body of Christ, all are given a foretaste of eternal life in Christ and are united with Christ, with each other, and with all the faithful, living and dead: "Because there is one bread, we who are many are one body, for we all partake of the one bread" (1 Corinthians 10:17).

144. The liturgy of the eucharist takes place in the usual manner at the funeral Mass. Members of the family or friends of the deceased should bring the gifts to the altar. Instrumental music or a song (for example, Psalm 18:1–6, Psalm 63, Psalm 66:13–20, or Psalm 138) may accompany the procession with the gifts. Before the priest washes his hands, he may incense the gifts and the altar. Afterward the deacon or other minister may incense the priest and the congregation.

Eucharistic Prayer II and Eucharistic Prayer III are especially appropriate for use at the funeral Mass, because they provide special texts of intercession for the dead. Since music gives greater solemnity to a ritual action, the singing of the people's parts of the eucharistic prayer should be encouraged, that is, the responses of the preface dialogue, the Sanctus, the memorial acclamation, and the Great Amen.

To reinforce and to express more fully the unity of the congregation during the communion rite, the people may sing the Lord's Prayer, the doxology, the Lamb of God, and a song for the communion procession (for example, Psalm 23, Psalm 27, Psalm 34, Psalm 63, or Psalm 121).

FINAL COMMENDATION AND FAREWELL

145. At the conclusion of the funeral liturgy, the rite of final commendation and farewell is celebrated, unless it is to be celebrated later at the place of committal.

146. The final commendation is a final farewell by the members of the community, an act of respect for one of their members, whom they entrust to the tender and merciful embrace of God. This act of last farewell also acknowledges the reality of separation and affirms that the community and the deceased, baptized into the one Body, share the same destiny, resurrection on the last day. On that day the one Shepherd will call each by name and gather the faithful together in the new and eternal Jerusalem.

147. The rite begins with the minister's opening words and a few moments of silent prayer. The opening words serve as a brief explanation of the rite and as an invitation to pray in silence for the deceased. The pause for silence allows the bereaved and all present to relate their own feelings of loss and grief to the mystery of Christian hope in God's abundant mercy and his promise of eternal life.

Where this is customary, the body may then be sprinkled with holy water and incensed, or this may be done during or after the song of farewell. The sprinkling is a reminder that through baptism the person was marked for eternal life and the incensation signifies respect for the body as the temple of the Holy Spirit.

The song of farewell, which should affirm hope and trust in the paschal mystery, is the climax of the rite of final commendation. It should be sung to a melody simple enough for all to sing. It may take the form of a responsory or even a hymn. When singing is not possible, invocations may be recited by the assembly.

A prayer of commendation concludes the rite. In this prayer the community calls upon God's mercy, commends the deceased into God's hands, and affirms its belief that those who have died in Christ will share in Christ's victory over death.

PROCESSION TO THE PLACE OF COMMITTAL

148. At the conclusion of the funeral liturgy, the procession is formed and the body is accompanied to the place of committal. This final procession of the funeral rite mirrors the journey of human life as a pilgrimage to God's kingdom of peace and light, the new and eternal Jerusalem.

149. Especially when accompanied with music and singing, the procession can help to reinforce the bond of communion between the participants. Whenever possible, psalms or songs may accompany the entire procession from the church to the place of committal. In situations where a solemn procession on foot from the church to the place of committal is not possible, an antiphon or song may be sung as the body is being taken to the entrance of the church. Psalms, hymns, or liturgical songs may also be sung by the participants as they gather at the place of committal.

MINISTRY AND PARTICIPATION

150. Because the funeral liturgy is the central celebration for the deceased, it should be scheduled for a time that permits as many of the Christian community as possible to be present. The full and active participation of the assembly affirms the value of praying for the dead, gives strength and support to the bereaved, and is a sure sign of faith and hope in the paschal mystery. Every effort, therefore, should be made by the various liturgical ministers to encourage the active participation of the family and of the entire assembly.

151. The priest is the ordinary presiding minister of the funeral liturgy. Except for Mass, a deacon may conduct the funeral liturgy. If pastoral need requires, the conference of

bishops, with the permission of the Apostolic See, may decide that laypersons also preside at the funeral liturgy outside Mass.

152. Whenever possible, ministers should involve the family in the planning of the funeral liturgy: in the choice of readings, prayers, and music for the liturgy and in the designation of ushers, pallbearers, readers, acolytes, special ministers of the eucharist, when needed, and musicians. The family should also be given the opportunity to designate persons who will place the pall or other Christian symbols on the coffin during the rite of reception of the body at the church and who will bring the gifts to the altar at Mass.

153. An organist or other instrumentalist, a cantor, and, whenever possible, a choir should be present to assist the congregation in singing the songs, responses, and acclamations of the funeral liturgy.

3. FUNERAL MASS

Until the Lord comes, you are proclaiming his death.

154. When one of its members dies, the Church encourages the celebration of the Mass. In the proclamation of the Scriptures, the saving word of God through the power of the Spirit becomes living and active in the minds and hearts of the community. Having been strengthened at the table of God's word, the community calls to mind God's saving deeds and offers the Father in the Spirit the eucharistic sacrifice of Christ's Passover from death to life, a living sacrifice of praise and thanksgiving, of reconciliation and atonement. Communion nourishes the community and expresses its unity. In communion, the participants have a foretaste of the heavenly banquet that awaits them and are reminded of Christ's own words: "Whoever eats my flesh and drinks my blood shall live for ever" (John 6:55). Confident in Jesus' presence among them in the living word, the living sacrifice, the living meal, those present in union with the whole Church offer prayers and petitions for the deceased, whom they entrust to God's merciful love.

155. The funeral Mass is ordinarily celebrated in the parish church.

156. The Mass texts are those of the Roman Missal and the Lectionary for Mass, "Masses for the Dead." The intercessions should be adapted to the circumstances. Models are given in place and in Part V, no. 401.

157. In the choice of music for the funeral Mass, preference should be given to the singing of the acclamations, the responsorial psalm, the entrance and communion songs, and especially the song of farewell at the final commendation.

158. If the rite of reception of the body takes place at the beginning of the funeral Mass, the introductory rites are those given here and the usual introductory rites for Mass, including the penitential rite, are omitted. If the rite of reception of the body has already taken place, the Mass begins in the usual way.

INTRODUCTORY RITES

GREETING

159. The priest, with assisting ministers, goes to the door of the church and using one of the following greetings, or in similar words, greets those present.

A

The grace of our Lord Jesus Christ and the love of God and the fellowship of the Holy Spirit be with you all.
℟. **And also with you.**

B See no. 69 B
C See no 69 C
D See no. 69 D.

SPRINKLING WITH HOLY WATER

160. The priest then sprinkles the coffin with holy water, saying the words noted in no. 83.

PLACING OF THE PALL

161. If it is the custom in the local community, the pall is then placed on the coffin by family members, friends, or the priest.

ENTRANCE PROCESSION

162. The Easter candle may be placed beforehand near the position the coffin will occupy at the conclusion of the procession. The priest and assisting ministers precede the coffin and the mourners into the church. During the procession a psalm, song, or responsory is sung (see no. 403).

PLACING OF CHRISTIAN SYMBOLS

163. See no 86.

On reaching the altar, the priest, with the assisting ministers, makes the customary reverence, kisses the altar, and (if incense is used) incenses it. Then he goes to the chair.

OPENING PRAYER

164. When all have reached their places, the priest invites the assembly to pray.

Let us pray.

After a brief period of silent prayer, the priest sings or says one of the following prayers or one of those provided in no. 398.

A   Outside the Easter season   170

Almighty God and Father,
it is our certain faith
that your Son, who died on the cross, was raised
   from the dead,
the firstfruits of all who have fallen asleep.
Grant that through this mystery
your servant N., who has gone to his/her rest in
   Christ,
may share in the joy of his resurrection.

We ask this through our Lord Jesus Christ, your Son,
who lives and reigns with you and the Holy Spirit,
one God, for ever and ever.
℟. Amen.

B   Outside the Easter season

O God,
to whom mercy and forgiveness belong,
hear our prayers on behalf of your servant N.,
whom you have called out of this world;
and because he/she put his/her hope and trust in you,
command that he/she be carried safely home to
   heaven
and come to enjoy your eternal reward.

We ask this through our Lord Jesus Christ, your Son,
who lives and reigns with you and the Holy Spirit,
one God, for ever and ever.
℟. Amen.

C   Outside the Easter season

O God,
in whom sinners find mercy and the saints find joy,
we pray to you for our brother/sister N.,
whose body we honor with Christian burial,
that he/she may be delivered from the bonds of
   death.
Admit him/her to the joyful company of your saints

and raise him/her on the last day
to rejoice in your presence for ever.

We ask this through our Lord Jesus Christ, your Son,
who lives and reigns with you and the Holy Spirit,
one God, for ever and ever.
R̸. Amen.

D During the Easter Season 173
God of loving kindness,
listen favorably to our prayers:
strengthen our belief that your Son has risen from
the dead
and our hope that your servant N. will also rise
again.

We ask this through our Lord Jesus Christ, your Son,
who lives and reigns with you and the Holy Spirit,
one God, for ever and ever.
R̸. Amen.

LITURGY OF THE WORD

READINGS

165. After the introductory rites, the liturgy of the word is celebrated. Depending upon pastoral circumstances, either one or two readings may be read before the gospel reading.

HOMILY

166. A brief homily is given after the gospel reading.

GENERAL INTERCESSIONS

167. One of the following intercessions or those given in no. 401 may be used or adapted to the circumstances, or new intercessions may be composed.

A The priest begins:
Brothers and sisters, Jesus Christ is risen from the
dead and sits at the right hand of the Father, where
he intercedes for his Church. Confident that God
hears the voices of those who trust in the Lord Jesus,
we join our prayers to his:

Assisting minister:

**In baptism N. received the light of Christ. Scatter the darkness now and lead him/her over the waters of death.
Lord, in your mercy:
R/. Hear our prayer.**

Assisting minister:

**Our brother/sister N. was nourished at the table of the Savior. Welcome him/her into the halls of the heavenly banquet.
Lord, in your mercy:
R/. Hear our prayer.**

Assisting minister:

[For a religious: **Our brother/sister N. spent his/her life following Jesus, poor, chaste, and obedient. Count him/her among all holy men and women who sing in your courts.
Lord, in your mercy:
R/. Hear our prayer.]**

Assisting minister:

[For a bishop or priest: **Our brother N. shared in the priesthood of Jesus Christ, leading God's people in prayer and worship.
Bring him into your presence where he will take his place in the heavenly liturgy.
Lord, in your mercy:
R/. Hear our prayer.]**

Assisting minister:

[For a deacon: **Our brother N. served God's people as a deacon of the Church. Prepare a place for him in the kingdom whose coming he proclaimed.
Lord, in your mercy:
R/. Hear our prayer.]**

Assisting minister:

**Many friends and members of our families have gone before us and await the kingdom. Grant them an everlasting home with your Son.
Lord, in your mercy:
R/. Hear our prayer.**

Assisting minister:

Many people die by violence, war, and famine each day. Show your mercy to those who suffer so unjustly these sins against your love, and gather them to the eternal kingdom of peace.
Lord, in your mercy:
℟. Hear our prayer.

Assisting minister:

Those who trusted in the Lord now sleep in the Lord. Give refreshment, rest, and peace to all whose faith is known to you alone.
Lord, in your mercy:
℟. Hear our prayer.

Assisting minister:

[For the mourners: The family and friends of N. seek comfort and consolation. Heal their pain and dispel the darkness and doubt that come from grief.
Lord, in your mercy:
℟. Hear our prayer.]

Assisting minister:

We are assembled here in faith and confidence to pray for our brother/sister N. Strengthen our hope so that we may live in the expectation of your Son's coming.
Lord, in your mercy:
℟. Hear our prayer.

The priest then concludes:

Lord God,
giver of peace and healer of souls,
hear the prayers of the Redeemer, Jesus Christ,
and the voices of your people,
whose lives were purchased by the blood of the
    Lamb.
Forgive the sins of all who sleep in Christ
and grant them a place in the kingdom.

We ask this through Christ our Lord.
℟. Amen.

B The priest begins:
God, the almighty Father, raised Christ his Son from the dead; with confidence we ask him to save all his people, living and dead:

Assisting minister:
**For N. who in baptism was given the pledge of eternal life, that he/she may now be admitted to the company of the saints.
We pray to the Lord
℟. Lord, hear our prayer.**

Assisting minister:
**For our brother/sister who ate the body of Christ, the bread of life, that he/she may be raised up on the last day.
We pray to the Lord
℟. Lord, hear our prayer.**

Assisting minister:
[For a deacon: **For our brother N., who proclaimed the Good News of Jesus Christ and served the needs of the poor, that he may be welcomed into the sanctuary of heaven.
We pray to the Lord:
℟. Lord, hear our prayer.**]

Assisting minister:
[For a bishop or priest: **For our brother N., who served the Church as a priest, that he may be given a place in the liturgy of heaven.
We pray to the Lord
℟. Lord, hear our prayer.**]

Assisting minister:
**For our deceased relatives and friends and for all who have helped us, that they may have the reward of their goodness.
We pray to the Lord:
℟. Lord hear our prayer.**

Assisting minister:
For those who have fallen asleep in the hope of rising again, that they may see God face to face.

We pray to the Lord:
℟. Lord hear our prayer.

Assisting minister:
[For the mourners: **For the family and friends of our brother/sister N., that they may be consoled in their grief by the Lord, who wept at the death of his friend Lazarus.**
We pray to the Lord:
℟. Lord hear our prayer.]

Assisting minister:
For all of us assembled here to worship in faith, that we may be gathered together again in God's kingdom.
We pray to the Lord:
℟. Lord hear our prayer.

The priest then concludes:
God, our shelter and our strength,
you listen in love to the cry of your people:
hear the prayers we offer for our departed brothers
  and sisters.
Cleanse them of their sins
and grant them the fullness of redemption.
We ask this through Christ our Lord.
℟. Amen.

LITURGY OF THE EUCHARIST

168. The liturgy of the eucharist is celebrated in the usual manner.

169. If the final commendation is to be celebrated at the place of committal, the procession to the place of committal (no. 176) begins following the prayer after communion.

FINAL COMMENDATION

170. Following the prayer after communion, the priest goes to a place near the coffin. The assisting ministers carry the censer and holy water, if these are to be used.

A member or a friend of the family may speak in remembrance of the deceased before the final commendation begins.

INVITATION TO PRAYER

171. Using one of the following invitations, or one of those provided in no. 402, or in similar words, the priest faces the people and begins the final commendation.

A

Before we go our separate ways, let us take leave of our brother/sister. May our farewell express our affection for him/her; may it ease our sadness and strengthen our hope. One day we shall joyfully greet him/her again when the love of Christ, which conquers all things, destroys even death itself.   185

B

Trusting in God, we have prayed together for N. and now we come to the last farewell. There is sadness in parting, but we take comfort in the hope that one day we shall see N. again and enjoy his/her friendship. Although this congregation will disperse in sorrow, the mercy of God will gather us together again in the joy of his kingdom. Therefore let us console one another in the faith of Jesus Christ.   186

SILENCE

172. All pray in silence.

SIGNS OF FAREWELL

173. The coffin may now be sprinkled with holy water and incensed, or this may take place during or after the song of farewell. If the body was sprinkled with holy water during the rite of reception at the beginning of Mass, the sprinkling is ordinarily omitted in the rite of final commendation.

SONG OF FAREWELL

174. The song of farewell is then sung. The following or other responsories chosen from no. 403 may be used or some other song may be sung.

Saints of God, come to his/her aid!   47

Hasten to meet him/her, angels of the Lord! 66
R̷. Receive his/her soul and present him/her to God
  the Most High.

May Christ, who called you, take you to himself;
may angels lead you to the bosom of Abraham. R̷.

Eternal rest grant unto him/her, O Lord,
and let perpetual light shine upon him/her.R̷.

PRAYER OF COMMENDATION

175. The priest then says one of the following prayers.

A

Into your hands, Father of mercies, 48
we commend our brother/sister N.
in the sure and certain hope
that, together with all who have died in Christ,
he/she will rise with him on the last day.

[We give you thanks for the blessings
which you bestowed upon N. in this life:
they are signs to us of your goodness
and of our fellowship with the saints in Christ.]

Merciful Lord,
turn toward us and listen to our prayers:
open the gates of paradise to your servant
and help us who remain
to comfort one another with assurances of faith,
until we all meet in Christ
and are with you and with our brother/sister for ever.

We ask this through Christ our Lord.
R̷. Amen.

B

To you, O Lord, we commend the soul of N. your
  servant; 192
in the sight of this world he/she is now dead;
in your sight may he/she live for ever.
Forgive whatever sins he/she committed through human weakness
and in your goodness grant him/her everlasting
  peace.

We ask this through Christ our Lord.
℟. Amen.

PROCESSION TO THE PLACE OF COMMITTAL

176. The deacon or, in the absence of a deacon, the priest says:

In peace let us take our brother/sister to his/her place
of rest.

If a symbol of the Christian life has been placed on the coffin, it should be removed at this time.

The procession then begins: the priest and assisting ministers precede the coffin; the family and mourners follow.

One or more of the following texts or other suitable songs may be sung during the procession to the entrance of the church. The singing may continue during the journey to the place of committal.

A   The following antiphon may be sung with verses from Psalm 25, no. 347, 2 or separately.
May the angels lead you into paradise;   50
may the martyrs come to welcome you
and take you to the holy city,
the new and eternal Jerusalem.

B   The following antiphon may be sung with verses from Psalm 116, no. 347, 7, or separately.
May choirs of angels welcome you   50
and lead you to the bosom of Abraham;
and where Lazarus is poor no longer
may you find eternal rest.

C
Whoever believes in me,
even though that person die, shall live.   166
℟. I am the resurrection and the life.
Whoever lives and believes in me shall never die. ℟.

D   The following psalms may also be used.

Psalm 118, no. 347, 8; Psalm 42, no. 347, 3; Psalm 93, no. 347, 5; Psalm 25, no. 347, 2; Psalm 119, no. 347, 9.

4. FUNERAL LITURGY OUTSIDE MASS

I am the resurrection and the life; whoever believes in me shall never die.

177. In the funeral liturgy outside Mass the community gathers to hear the message of Easter hope proclaimed in the liturgy of the word and to commend the deceased to God.

178. This rite may be used for various reasons:

   1. when the funeral Mass is not permitted, namely, on solemnities of obligation, on Holy Thursday and the Easter Triduum, and on the Sundays of Advent, Lent, and the Easter Season;[1]
   2. when in some places or circumstances it is not possible to celebrate the funeral Mass before the committal, for example, if a priest is not available;
   3. when for pastoral reasons the parish priest (pastor) and the family judge that the funeral liturgy outside Mass is a more suitable form of celebration.

179. The funeral liturgy outside Mass is ordinarily celebrated in the parish church, but may also be celebrated in the home of the deceased, a funeral home, parlor, chapel of rest, or cemetery chapel.

180. The readings are those of the Lectionary for Mass, "Masses for the Dead." The intercessions should be adapted to the circumstances. Models are given in place and in Part V, no. 401. The celebration may also include holy communion.

181. In the choice of music for the funeral liturgy, preference should be given to the singing of the entrance song, the responsorial psalm, the gospel acclamation, and especially the song of farewell at the final commendation.

182. The minister who is a priest or deacon wears an alb with stole (a cope may be used, if desired); a layperson who presides wears the liturgical vestments approved for the region.

[1]See General Instruction of the Roman Missal, no 336.

183. If the rite of reception of the body takes place at the beginning of the funeral liturgy, the introductory rites are those given here. If the rite of reception of the body has already taken place, the liturgy begins with an entrance song and the greeting (no. 184), followed by the invitation to prayer (no. 189).

INTRODUCTORY RITES

GREETING

184. The presiding minister, with assisting ministers, goes to the door of the church and using one of the following greetings, or in similar words, greets those present.

A
The grace of our Lord Jesus Christ and the love of God and the fellowship of the Holy Spirit be with you all.
℟. **And also with you.**
B   See no. 69 B.
C   See no. 69 C.
D   See no. 69 D.

SPRINKLING WITH HOLY WATER

185. The presiding minister then sprinkles the coffin with holy water, saying the words noted in no. 83.

PLACING OF THE PALL

186. If it is the custom in the local community, the pall is then placed on the coffin by family members, friends, or the minister.

ENTRANCE PROCESSION

187. The Easter candle may be placed beforehand near the position the coffin will occupy at the conclusion of the procession. The presiding minister and assisting ministers precede the coffin and the mourners into the church. During the procession a psalm, song, or responsory is sung (see no. 403).

PLACING OF CHRISTIAN SYMBOLS

188. See no. 86.

On reaching the altar, the presiding minister, with the assisting ministers, makes the customary reverence and goes to the chair.

INVITATION TO PRAYER

189. When all have reached their places, the presiding minister, using the following or similar words, invites the assembly to pray.

My brothers and sisters,
we have come together to renew our trust in Christ
who, by dying on the cross, has freed us from eternal
death
and, by rising, has opened for us the gates of
heaven.

Let us pray for our brother/sister,
that he/she may share in Christ's victory,
and let us pray for ourselves,
that the Lord may grant us
the gift of his loving consolation.

OPENING PRAYER

190. After a brief period of silent prayer, the presiding minister sings or says one of the following prayers or one of those provided in no. 398.

A   Outside the Easter season   170
Almighty God and Father,
it is our certain faith
that your Son, who died on the cross, was raised
from the dead,
the firstfruits of all who have fallen asleep.
Grant that through this mystery
your servant N., who has gone to his/her rest in
Christ,
may share in the joy of his resurrection.

We ask this through our Lord Jesus Christ, your Son,
who lives and reigns with you and the Holy Spirit,
one God, for ever and ever.
R̸. Amen.

B Outside the Easter season

**O God,
to whom mercy and forgiveness belong,
hear our prayers on behalf of your servant N.,
whom you have called out of this world;
and because he/she put his/her hope and trust in you,
command that he/she be carried safely home to
heaven
and come to enjoy your eternal reward.**

**We ask this through our Lord Jesus Christ, your Son,
who lives and reigns with you and the Holy Spirit,
one God, for ever and ever.
R̷. Amen.**

C Outside the Easter season

**O God,
in whom sinners find mercy and the saints find joy,
we pray to you for our brother/sister N.,
whose body we honor with Christian burial,
that he/she may be delivered from the bonds of
death.
Admit him/her to the joyful company of your saints
and raise him/her on the last day
to rejoice in your presence for ever.**

**We ask this through our Lord Jesus Christ, your Son,
who lives and reigns with you and the Holy Spirit,
one God, for ever and ever.
R̷. Amen.**

D During the Easter season   173

**God of loving kindness,
listen favorably to our prayers:
strengthen our belief that your Son has risen from
the dead
and our hope that your servant N. will also rise
again.**

**We ask this through our Lord Jesus Christ, your Son,
who lives and reigns with you and the Holy Spirit,
one God, for ever and ever.
R̷. Amen.**

LITURGY OF THE WORD

READINGS

191. After the introductory rites, the liturgy of the word is celebrated. Depending upon pastoral circumstances, either one or two readings may be read before the gospel reading.

HOMILY

192. A brief homily should be given after the gospel reading.

GENERAL INTERCESSIONS

193. One of the following intercessions or those given in no. 401 may be used or adapted to the circumstances, or new intercessions may be composed.

A The presiding minister proceeds as noted in no. 167B.
B See no. 167 A.

THE LORD'S PRAYER

194. Using one of the following invitations, or in similar words, the minister invites those present to pray the Lord's Prayer.

A
Now let us pray as Christ the Lord has taught us:

B
With longing for the coming of God's kingdom, let us offer our prayer to the Father:

All say:
Our Father . . .

195. The celebration may include holy communion (Part V, nos. 409–410).

196. If the final commendation is to be celebrated at the place of committal, the procession to the place of committal (no. 203) begins following the Lord's Prayer or the prayer after communion.

FINAL COMMENDATION

197. Following the Lord's Prayer (or the prayer after communion), the presiding minister goes to a place near the coffin. The assisting ministers carry the censer and holy water, if these are to be used.

A member or a friend of the family may speak in remembrance of the deceased before the final commendation begins.

INVITATION TO PRAYER

198. Using one of the following invitations, or one of those provided in no. 402, or in similar words, the presiding minister faces the people and begins the final commendation.

A   See no. 171 A.
B   See no. 171 B.

SILENCE

199. All pray in silence.

SIGNS OF FAREWELL

200. The coffin may now be sprinkled with holy water and incensed, or this may take place during or after the song of farewell. If the body was sprinkled with holy water during the rite of reception at the beginning of the funeral liturgy, the sprinkling is ordinarily omitted in the rite of final commendation.

SONG OF FAREWELL

201. See no. 174.

PRAYER OF COMMENDATION

202. The presiding minister then says one of the following prayers.

A   See no. 175 A.
B   See no. 175 B.

PROCESSION TO THE PLACE OF COMMITTAL

203. An assisting minister, or in the absence of an assisting minister, the presiding minister says:

In peace let us take our brother/sister to his/her place of rest.

If a symbol of the Christian life has been placed on the coffin, it should be removed at this time.

The procession then begins: the presiding minister and assisting ministers precede the coffin; the family and mourners follow.

One or more of the following texts or other suitable songs may be sung during the procession to the entrance of the church. The singing may continue during the journey to the place of committal. See no. 176 A—D.

RITE OF COMMITTAL

Joseph took Jesus down from the cross, wrapped him in a shroud, and laid him in a tomb.

204. The rite of committal, the conclusion of the funeral rites, is the final act of the community of faith in caring for the body of its deceased member. It may be celebrated at the grave, tomb, or crematorium and may be used for burial at sea. Whenever possible, the rite of committal is to be celebrated at the site of committal, that is, beside the open grave or place of interment, rather than at a cemetery chapel.

205. Two forms of the rite of committal are provided here: "Rite of Committal" and "Rite of Committal with Final Commendation." The first form is used when the final commendation is celebrated as part of the conclusion of the funeral liturgy. The second form is used when the final commendation does not take place during the funeral liturgy or when no funeral liturgy precedes the committal rite.

206. In committing the body to its resting place, the community expresses the hope that, with all those who have gone before marked with the sign of faith, the deceased awaits the glory of the resurrection. The rite of committal is an expression of the communion that exists between the Church on earth and the Church in heaven: the deceased passes with the farewell prayers of the community of believers into the welcoming company of those who need faith no longer but see God face to face.

STRUCTURE AND CONTENT OF THE RITE OF COMMITTAL

207. Both forms of the committal rite begin with an invitation, Scripture verse, and a prayer over the place of committal. The several alternatives for the prayer over the place of committal take into account whether the grave, tomb, or resting place has already been blessed and situations in which the final disposition of the body will actually take place at a later time (for example, when the body is to be cremated or will remain in a cemetery chapel until burial at a later time).

208. The rite of committal continues with the words of committal, the intercessions, and the Lord's Prayer.

The rite of committal with final commendation continues with an invitation to prayer, a pause for silent prayer, the sprinkling and incensing of the body, where this is customary, the song of farewell, and the prayer of commendation (see nos. 227–231).

209. The act of committal takes place after the words of committal (in the rite of committal with final commendation, after the prayer of commendation) or at the conclusion of the rite. The act of committal expresses the full significance of this rite. Through this act the community of faith proclaims that the grave or place of interment, once a sign of futility and despair, has been transformed by means of Christ's own death and resurrection into a sign of hope and promise.

210. Both forms of the rite conclude with a prayer over the people, which includes the verse *Eternal rest,* and a blessing. Depending on local custom, a song may then be sung and a gesture of final leave-taking may be made, for example, placing flowers or soil on the coffin.

ADAPTATION

211. If there is pastoral need for a longer committal rite than those provided here, for example, when the funeral liturgy has been celebrated on a previous day or in a different community, the minister may use the appropriate form of the committal rite and adapt it, for example, by adding a greeting, song, one or more readings, a psalm, and a brief homily. When there has been no funeral liturgy prior to the committal rite, the "Rite of Committal with Final Commendation" may be used and similarly adapted.

212. The rite of committal may be celebrated in circumstances in which the final disposition of the body will not take place for some time, for example, when winter delays burial or when ashes are to be interred at some time after cremation. The rite of committal may then be repeated on the later occasion when the actual burial or interment takes

place. On the second occasion the rite may include a longer Scripture reading as well as a homily.

In the case of a body donated to science, the rite of committal may be celebrated whenever interment takes place.

MINISTRY AND PARTICIPATION

213. The community continues to show its concern for the mourners by participating in the rite of committal. The rite marks the separation in this life of the mourners from the deceased, and through it the community assists them as they complete their care for the deceased and lay the body to rest. The act of committal is a stark and powerful expression of this separation. When carried out in the midst of the community of faith, the committal can help the mourners to face the end of one relationship with the deceased and to begin a new one based on prayerful remembrance, gratitude, and the hope of resurrection and reunion.

By their presence and prayer members of the community signify their intention to continue to support the mourners in the time following the funeral.

214. The singing of well-chosen music at the rite of committal can help the mourners as they face the reality of the separation. At the rite of committal with final commendation, whenever possible, the song of farewell should be sung. In either form of the committal rite, a hymn or liturgical song that affirms hope in God's mercy and in the resurrection of the dead is desirable at the conclusion of the rite.

215. In the absence of a parish minister, a friend or member of the family should lead those present in the rite of committal.

The minister should vest according to local custom.

5. RITE OF COMMITTAL

INVITATION

216. When the funeral procession arrives at the place of committal, the minister says the following or a similar invitation.

Our brother/sister N. has gone to his/her rest in the peace of Christ. May the Lord now welcome him/her to the table of God's children in heaven. With faith and hope in eternal life, let us assist him/her with our prayers.

Let us pray to the Lord also for ourselves. May we who mourn be reunited one day with our brother/ sister; together may we meet Christ Jesus when he who is our life appears in glory.

SCRIPTURE VERSE

217. One of the following verses or another brief Scripture verse is read. The minister first says:

We read in sacred Scripture:

A	**Matthew 25:34**	119
B	**John 6:39**	121
C	**Philippians 3:20**	124
D	**Revelation 1:5–6**	126

PRAYER OVER THE PLACE OF COMMITTAL

218. The minister says one of the following prayers or one of those provided in no. 405.

A If the place of committal is to be blessed:
Lord Jesus Christ,   53
by your own three days in the tomb,
you hallowed the graves of all who believe in you
and so made the grave a sign of hope
that promises resurrection
even as it claims our mortal bodies.

Grant that our brother/sister may sleep here in peace until you awaken him/her to glory, for you are the resurrection and the life.

Then he/she will see you face to face
and in your light will see light
and know the splendor of God,
for you live and reign for ever and ever.
℟. Amen.

B If the place of committal has already been blessed:
All praise to you, Lord of all creation.
Praise to you, holy and living God.
We praise and bless you for your mercy,
we praise and bless you for your kindness.
Blessed is the Lord, our God.
℟. Blessed is the Lord, our God.

You sanctify the homes of the living
and make holy the places of the dead.
You alone open the gates of righteousness
and lead us to the dwellings of the saints.
Blessed is the Lord, our God.
℟. Blessed is the Lord, our God.

We praise you, our refuge and strength.
We bless you, our God and Redeemer.
Your praise is always in our hearts and on our lips.
We remember the mighty deeds of the covenant.
Blessed is the Lord, our God.
℟. Blessed is the Lord, our God.

Almighty and ever-living God,
remember the mercy with which you graced your servant N. in life.
Receive him/her, we pray, into the mansions of the
saints.
As we make ready our brother's/sister's resting place,
look also with favor on those who mourn
and comfort them in their loss.

Grant this through Christ our Lord.
℟. Amen.

C When the final disposition of the body is to take place
at a later time:

Almighty and ever-living God,
in you we place our trust and hope,
in you the dead whose bodies were temples of the
    Spirit find everlasting peace.

As we take leave of our brother/sister,
give our hearts peace in the firm hope
that one day N. will live
in the mansion you have prepared for him/her in
    heaven.

We ask this through Christ our Lord.
℟. Amen.

COMMITTAL

219. The minister then says the words of committal. One
of the following formularies or one provided in no. 406 may
be used.

A
Because God has chosen to call our brother/sister N.   55
    from this life to himself,
we commit his/her body to the earth [or the deep *or*
    the elements *or* its resting place],
for we are dust and unto dust we shall return.

But the Lord Jesus Christ will change our mortal
    bodies to be like his in glory,
for he is risen, the firstborn from the dead.

So let us commend our brother/sister to the Lord,
that the Lord may embrace him/her in peace
and raise up his/her body on the last day.

B
In sure and certain hope of the resurrection to eternal
    life through our Lord Jesus Christ,
we commend to Almighty God our brother/sister N.,
and we commit his/her body to the ground
    [or the deep *or* the elements *or* its resting place]:
earth to earth, ashes to ashes, dust to dust.

The Lord bless him/her and keep him/her,
the Lord make his face to shine upon him/her
and be gracious to him/her,
the Lord lift up his countenance upon him/her
and give him/her peace.

The committal takes place at this time or at the conclusion
of the rite.

INTERCESSIONS

220. One of the following intercessions or that given in
no. 407 may be used or adapted to the circumstances, or
new intercessions may be composed.

A   The minister begins:
For our brother/sister, N., let us pray to our Lord Jesus   56
Christ, who said, "I am the resurrection and the life.   75
Whoever believes in me shall live even in death and
whoever lives and believes in me shall never die."

Assisting minister:
Lord, you consoled Martha and Mary in their dis-
tress; draw near to us who mourn for N., and dry the
tears of those who weep.
We pray to the Lord:
R̸. Lord, have mercy.

Assisting minister:
You wept at the grave of Lazarus, your friend; com-
fort us in our sorrow.
We pray to the Lord:
R̸. Lord, have mercy.

Assisting minister:
You raised the dead to life; give to our brother/sister
eternal life.
We pray to the Lord:
R̸. Lord, have mercy.

Assisting minister:
You promised paradise to the repentant thief; bring
N. to the joys of heaven.
We pray to the Lord:
R̸. Lord, have mercy.

Assisting minister:
**Our brother/sister was washed in baptism and
anointed with the Holy Spirit; give him/her fellow-
ship with all your saints.
We pray to the Lord:**
R̄. Lord, have mercy.

Assisting minister:
**He/she was nourished with your body and blood;
grant him/her a place at the table in your heavenly
kingdom.
We pray to the Lord:**
R̄. Lord, have mercy.

Assisting minister:
**Comfort us in our sorrow at the death of N.; let our
faith be our consolation, and eternal life our hope.
We pray to the Lord:**
R̄. Lord, have mercy.

B The minister begins:
**Dear friends, in reverence let us pray to God, the
source of all mercies.**

202

Assisting minister:
**Gracious Lord, forgive the sins of those who have
died in Christ.
Lord, in your mercy:**
R̄. Hear our prayer.

Assisting minister:
**Remember all the good they have done.
Lord, in your mercy:**
R̄. Hear our prayer.

Assisting minister:
**Welcome them into eternal life.
Lord, in your mercy:**
R̄. Hear our prayer.

Assisting minister:
**Let us pray for those who mourn.
Comfort them in their grief.**

Lord, in your mercy:
R̸. Hear our prayer.

Assisting minister:
Lighten their sense of loss with your presence.
Lord, in your mercy:
R̸. Hear our prayer.

Assisting minister
Increase their faith and strengthen their hope.
Lord, in your mercy:
R̸. Hear our prayer.

Assisting minister:
Let us pray also for ourselves on our pilgrimage
through life.
Keep us faithful in your service.
Lord, in your mercy:
R̸. Hear our prayer.

Assisting minister:
Kindle in our hearts a longing for heaven.
Lord, in your mercy:
R̸. Hear our prayer.

THE LORD'S PRAYER

221. In the following or similar words, the minister invites those present to pray the Lord's Prayer.

With longing for the coming of God's kingdom, let
us pray:

All say:
Our Father . . .

CONCLUDING PRAYER

222. The minister says one of the following prayers or one of those provided in no. 408.

A
God of holiness and power,   56
accept our prayers on behalf of your servant N.;
do not count his/her deeds against him/her,
for in his/her heart he/she desired to do your will.

As his/her faith united him/her to your people on
   earth,
so may your mercy join him/her to the angels in
   heaven.

We ask this through Christ our Lord.
℟. Amen.

B
Almighty God,   199
through the death of your Son on the cross
you destroyed our death;
through his rest in the tomb
you hallowed the graves of all who believe in you;
and through his rising again
you restored us to eternal life.

God of the living and the dead,
accept our prayers
for those who have died in Christ
and are buried with him in the hope of rising again.
Since they were true to your name on earth,
let them praise you for ever in the joy of heaven.

We ask this through Christ our Lord.
℟. Amen.

PRAYER OVER THE PEOPLE

223. The assisting minister says:
Bow your heads and pray for God's blessing.

All pray silently. The minister, with hands outstretched,
prays over the people:

Merciful Lord,
you know the anguish of the sorrowful,
you are attentive to the prayers of the humble.
Hear your people
who cry out to you in their need,
and strengthen their hope in your lasting goodness.

We ask this through Christ our Lord.
℟. Amen.

The minister then says the following:
Eternal rest grant unto him/her, O Lord.
℟. **And let perpetual light shine upon him/her.**

May he/she rest in peace.
℟. **Amen.**

May his/her soul and the souls of all the faithful departed, through the mercy of God, rest in peace.
℟. **Amen.**

A A minister who is a priest or deacon says:
May the peace of God,
which is beyond all understanding,
keep your hearts and minds
in the knowledge and love of God
and of his Son, our Lord Jesus Christ.
℟. **Amen.**

May almighty God bless you,
the Father, and the Son, ✠ **and the Holy Spirit.**
℟. **Amen.**

B A lay minister invokes God's blessing and signs himself or herself with the sign of the cross, saying:
May the love of God and the peace of the Lord Jesus
**   Christ**
bless and console us
and gently wipe every tear from our eyes:
in the name of the Father,
and of the Son, and of the Holy Spirit.
℟. **Amen.**

The minister then concludes:
Go in the peace of Christ.
℟. **Thanks be to God.**

A song may conclude the rite. Where it is the custom, some sign or gesture of leave-taking may be made.

6. RITE OF COMMITTAL WITH FINAL COMMENDATION

INVITATION

224. When the funeral procession arrives at the place of committal, the minister says one of the following or a similar invitation.

A
We gather here to commend our brother/sister N. to God our Father and to commit his/her body to the earth/elements. In the spirit of faith in the resurrection of Jesus Christ from the dead, let us [raise our voices in song and] offer our prayers for N.

B
As we gather to commend our brother/sister N. to God our Father and to commit his/her body to the earth/elements, let us express in [song and] prayer our common faith in the resurrection. As Jesus Christ was raised from the dead, we too are called to follow him through death to the glory where God will be all in all.

SCRIPTURE VERSE
225. See no. 217.

PRAYER OVER THE PLACE OF COMMITTAL
226. The minister says one of the following prayers or one of those provided in no. 405. See no. 218

INVITATION TO PRAYER
227. Using one of the invitations provided in no. 171, or no. 402, or in similar words, the minister faces the people and begins the final commendation.

SILENCE
228. All pray in silence.

SIGNS OF FAREWELL
229. See no. 173.

SONG OF FAREWELL
230. See no. 174.

PRAYER OF COMMENDATION
231. The minister then says one of the following prayers. See no. 175.

COMMITTAL
232. The act of committal takes place at this time or at the conclusion of the rite.

PRAYER OVER THE PEOPLE
233. See no. 223.

A song may conclude the rite. Where it is the custom, some sign or gesture of leave-taking may be made.

PART II

FUNERAL RITES FOR CHILDREN

Let the little children come to me; it is to such as these that the kingdom of God belongs.

234. Part II of the *Order of Christian Funerals* provides rites that are used in the funerals of infants and young children, including those of early school age. It includes "Vigil for a Deceased Child," "Funeral Liturgy," and "Rite of Committal."

Part II does not contain "Related Rites and Prayers," nos. 98–127, which are brief rites for prayer with the family and friends before the funeral liturgy. The rites as they are presented in Part I are models and should be adapted by the minister to the circumstances of the funeral for a child.

235. The minister, in consultation with those concerned, chooses those rites that best correspond to the particular needs and customs of the mourners. In some instances, for example, the death of an infant, only the rite of committal and perhaps one of the forms of prayer with the family may be desirable.

236. In the celebration of the funeral of a child the Church offers worship to God, the author of life, commends the child to God's love, and prays for the consolation of the family and close friends.

237. Funeral rites may be celebrated for children whose parents intended them to be baptized but who died before baptism.[1] In these celebrations the Christian community entrusts the child to God's all-embracing love and finds strength in this love and in Jesus' affirmation that the kingdom of God belongs to little children (see Matthew 19:14).

---

[1] In the general catechesis of the faithful, pastors and other ministers should explain that the celebration of the funeral rites for children who die before baptism is not intended to weaken the Church's teaching on the necessity of baptism.

238. In its pastoral ministry to the bereaved the Christian community is challenged in a particular way by the death of an infant or child. The bewilderment and pain that death causes can be overwhelming in this situation, especially for the parents and the brothers and sisters of the deceased child. The community seeks to offer support and consolation to the family during and after the time of the funeral rites.

239. Through prayer and words of comfort the minister and others can help the mourners to understand that their child has gone before them into the kingdom of the Lord and that one day they will all be reunited there in joy. The participation of the community in the funeral rites is a sign of the compassionate presence of Christ, who embraced little children, wept at the death of a friend, and endured the pain and separation of death in order to render it powerless over those he loves. Christ still sorrows with those who sorrow and longs with them for the fulfillment of the Father's plan in a new creation where tears and death will have no place.

240. The minister should invite members of the community to use their individual gifts in this ministry of consolation. Those who have lost children of their own may be able in a special way to help the family as they struggle to accept the death of the child.

241. Those involved in planning the funeral rites for a deceased child should take into account the age of the child, the circumstances of death, the grief of the family, and the needs and customs of those taking part in the rites. In choosing the texts and elements of celebration, the minister should bear in mind whether the child was baptized or died before baptism.

242. Special consideration should be given to any sisters, brothers, friends, or classmates of the deceased child who may be present at the funeral rites. Children will be better able to take part in the celebration if the various elements are planned and selected with them in mind: texts, readings, music, gesture, processions, silence. The minister may wish to offer brief remarks for the children's benefit at suitable points during the celebration.

If children will be present at the funeral rites, those with requisite ability should be asked to exercise some of the liturgical roles. During the funeral Mass, for example, children
may serve as readers, acolytes, or musicians, or assist in
the reading of the general intercessions and in the procession with the gifts. Depending upon the age and number of
children taking part, adaptations recommended in the *Directory for Masses with Children* may be appropriate.

7.   VIGIL FOR A DECEASED CHILD

It is good to wait in silence for the Lord.

243. The vigil for the deceased is the principal celebration of the Christian community during the time before the funeral liturgy or, if there is no funeral liturgy, before the rite of committal. The vigil may take the form of a liturgy of the word, as described in Part I, nos. 57–68, or of some part of the office for the dead (see Part IV, nos. 348–372, 384, 385, 395).

244. The vigil may be celebrated at a convenient time in the home of the deceased child, in the funeral home, parlor or chapel of rest, or in some other suitable place. The vigil may also be celebrated in the church, but at a time well before the funeral liturgy, so that the funeral liturgy will not be lengthy and the liturgy of the word repetitious. When the body is brought to the church for the celebration of the vigil, the vigil begins with the rite of reception (see no. 58). Otherwise the vigil begins with a greeting, followed by an opening song, an invitation to prayer, and an opening prayer.

245. After the opening prayer, the vigil continues with the liturgy of the word, which usually includes a first reading, responsorial psalm, gospel reading, and homily. If there is to be only one reading, however, it should be the gospel reading. The prayer of intercession, which includes a litany, the Lord's Prayer, and a concluding prayer, then follows. Alternative concluding prayers are provided for use in the case of a baptized child or of a child who died before baptism. The vigil concludes with a blessing, which may be followed by a song or a few moments of silent prayer or both.

246. The minister should adapt the vigil to the circumstances. If, for example, a large number of children are present or if the vigil is held in the home of the deceased child, elements of the rite may be simplified or shortened and other elements or symbols that have special meaning for those taking part may be incorporated into the celebration. If custom and circumstances suggest, a member or a friend of the family may speak in remembrance of the deceased child.

247. The vigil celebrated at the church may begin with the rite of reception (nos. 248–252) which then serves as the introductory rite. Otherwise the vigil may begin with an opening song followed by a greeting (no. 248) and the invitation to prayer (no. 253).

INTRODUCTORY RITES

GREETING

248. The minister, with assisting ministers, goes to the door of the church and using one of the following greetings, or in similar words, greets those present.

A
May Christ Jesus, who welcomed children and laid his hands in blessing upon them, comfort you with his peace and be always with you.
R̸. And also with you.

B See no. 69 A.
C See no. 69 B.
D See no. 69 C.

SPRINKLING WITH HOLY WATER OR BRIEF ADDRESS

249. If the child was baptized, the minister sprinkles the coffin with holy water (option A). If the child died before baptism, the sprinkling with holy water is omitted and a brief address is given (option B).

A *Sprinkling with Holy Water*—If the child was baptized, the minister then sprinkles the coffin with holy water, saying:
In the waters of baptism
N. died with Christ and rose with him to new life.
May he/she now share with him eternal glory.

B *Brief Address*—If the child died before baptism, the minister may then address the mourners in the following or similar words.
My brothers and sisters, the Lord is a faithful God who created us all after his own image. All things are of his making, all creation awaits the day of salva-

tion. We now entrust the soul of N. to the abundant mercy of God, that our beloved child may find a home in his kingdom.

PLACING OF THE PALL

250. If it is the custom in the local community and the child was baptized, the pall is then placed on the coffin by family members, friends, or the minister.

ENTRANCE PROCESSION

251. The Easter candle may be placed beforehand near the position the coffin will occupy at the conclusion of the procession. The minister and assisting ministers precede the coffin and the mourners into the church. During the procession a psalm, song, or responsory is sung (see no. 403).

PLACING OF CHRISTIAN SYMBOLS

252. A symbol of the Christian life, such as a cross, may be carried in procession, then placed on the coffin, either in silence or as a text from no. 400 is said.

INVITATION TO PRAYER

253. In the following or similar words, the minister invites those present to pray.

Let us pray for this child and entrust him/her to the care of our loving God.

Pause for silent prayer.

OPENING PRAYER

254. The minister says one of the following prayers or one of those provided in nos. 398–399.

A A baptized child
To you, O Lord, 224
we humbly entrust this child,
so precious in your sight.
Take him/her into your arms
and welcome him/her into paradise,
where there will be no sorrow, no weeping nor pain,
but the fullness of peace and joy
with your Son and the Holy Spirit

for ever and ever.
℟. Amen.

B   A baptized child
Lord, in our grief we call upon your mercy: 223
open your ears to our prayers,
and one day unite us again with N.,
who, we firmly trust,
already enjoys eternal life in your kingdom.

We ask this through Christ our Lord.
℟. **Amen.**

C   A child who died before baptism
God of all consolation,   236
searcher of mind and heart,
the faith of these parents [N. and N.] is known to
   you.

Comfort them with the knowledge
that the child for whom they grieve
is entrusted now to your loving care.

We ask this through Christ our Lord.
℟. **Amen.**

LITURGY OF THE WORD

255. The celebration continues with the liturgy of the word. Other readings, psalms, and gospel readings are given in Part III, nos. 343 and 344.

FIRST READING

256. A reader proclaims the first reading.

1 John 3:1–2   103
We shall see God as he really is.

RESPONSORIAL PSALM

257. The following psalm is sung or said or another psalm or song.

℟. **The Lord is my shepherd; there is nothing I shall want.**

Psalm 23

GOSPEL

258. The gospel reading is then proclaimed.

Mark 10:13–16
The kingdom of God belongs to little children.

HOMILY

259. A brief homily on the readings is then given.

PRAYER OF INTERCESSION

LITANY

260. The minister leads those present in the following litany.

The Lord Jesus is the lover of his people and our only sure hope. Let us ask him to deepen our faith and sustain us in this dark hour.

Assisting minister:
**You became a little child for our sake, sharing our human life.
To you we pray:**
℟. **Bless us and keep us, O Lord.**

Assisting minister:
**You grew in wisdom, age, and grace and learned obedience through suffering.
To you we pray:**
℟. **Bless us and keep us, O Lord.**

Assisting minister:
**You welcomed children, promising them your kingdom.
To you we pray:**
℟. **Bless us and keep us, O Lord.**

Assisting minister:

You comforted those who mourned the loss of children and friends.

To you we pray:

R̸. Bless us and keep us, O Lord.

Assisting minister:

You took upon yourself the suffering and death of us all.

To you we pray:

R̸. Bless us and keep us, O Lord.

Assisting minister:

You promised to raise up those who believe in you, just as you were raised up in glory by the Father.

To you we pray:

R̸. Bless us and keep us, O Lord.

THE LORD'S PRAYER

261. Using one of the following invitations, or in similar words, the minister invites those present to pray the Lord's Prayer.

A

Together let us pray for strength, for acceptance, and for the coming of the kingdom in the words our Savior taught us:

B

In love, God calls us his children, for that indeed is what we are. We ask for the strength we need by praying in the words Jesus gave us:

All say:

Our Father . . .

CONCLUDING PRAYER

262. The minister says one of the following prayers or one of those provided in nos. 398–399.

A A baptized child

Lord of all gentleness,
surround us with your care

225

and comfort us in our sorrow,
for we grieve at the loss of this [little] child.

As you washed N. in the waters of baptism
and have welcomed him/her into heaven,
so call us one day
to be united with him/her
and share for ever the joy of your kingdom.

We ask this through Christ our Lord.
Ry. Amen.

B   A child who died before baptism
Lord Jesus,
whose Mother stood grieving at the foot of the cross,
look kindly on these parents
who have suffered the loss of their child [N.].
Listen to the prayers of Mary on their behalf,
that their faith may be strong like hers
and find its promised reward,
for you live for ever and ever.
Ry. Amen.

CONCLUDING RITE

BLESSING

263. The minister says:

Jesus said: "Let the children come to me. Do not
keep them from me. The kingdom of God belongs to
such as these."

A gesture, for example, signing the forehead of the deceased child with the sign of the cross, may accompany the
following words.

Eternal rest grant unto him/her, O Lord.
Ry. And let perpetual light shine upon him/her.

May he/she rest in peace.
Ry. Amen.

May his/her soul and the souls of all the faithful departed, through the mercy of God, rest in peace.

R̶. **Amen.**

A   See no. 81 A.
B   See no. 81 B.

The vigil may conclude with a song or a few moments of silent prayer or both.

FUNERAL LITURGY
The Lord will wipe away the tears from every cheek.

264. The funeral liturgy, as described in nos. 128–153, is the central liturgical celebration of the Christian community for the deceased. Two forms of the funeral liturgy are provided: "Funeral Mass" and "Funeral Liturgy outside Mass." If the second form is used, Mass may be celebrated at a later date.

265. The funeral Mass includes the reception of the body, if this has not already occurred, the celebration of the liturgy of the word, the liturgy of the eucharist, and the final commendation and farewell. The funeral liturgy outside Mass includes all these elements except the liturgy of the eucharist. Both the funeral Mass and the funeral liturgy outside Mass may be followed by the procession to the place of committal.

266. The rite of reception of the body begins with a greeting of the family and others who have accompanied the body to the door of the church. The minister may give brief explanations of the symbols in this rite for the benefit of any children who may be present for the celebration. In the case of a baptized child, the minister sprinkles the coffin in remembrance of the deceased child's acceptance into the community of faith. If it is the custom in the local community, a funeral pall, a reminder of the garment given at baptism and therefore signifying life in Christ, may then be placed on the coffin by family members, friends, or the minister. In the case of a child who died before baptism, the minister addresses the community with a few words. The entrance procession follows. The minister precedes the coffin and the mourners into the church, as all sing an entrance song. If the Easter candle is used on this occasion, it may be placed beforehand near the position the coffin will occupy at the conclusion of the procession.

If in this rite a symbol of the Christian life is to be placed on the coffin, it is carried in the procession and is placed on the coffin by a family member, friend, or the minister at the conclusion of the procession.

267. The rite of final commendation and farewell is celebrated at the conclusion of the funeral liturgy unless it is

deferred for celebration at the place of committal. The rite begins with the invitation to prayer, followed by a pause for silent prayer. In the case of a baptized child, the body may then be sprinkled with holy water and incensed. Or this may be done during or after the song of farewell. The song of farewell is then sung and the rite concludes with the prayer of commendation.

FUNERAL MASS

268. The funeral Mass is ordinarily celebrated in the parish church, but, at the discretion of the local Ordinary, it may be celebrated in the home of the deceased child or some other place.

269. The Mass texts are those of the Roman Missal and the Lectionary for Mass, "Masses for the Dead." The intercessions should be adapted to the circumstances; models are given in place and in Part V, no. 401.

270. In the choice of music for the funeral Mass, preference should be given to the singing of the acclamations, the responsorial psalm, the entrance and communion songs, and especially the song of farewell at the final commendation.

FUNERAL LITURGY OUTSIDE MASS

271. The funeral liturgy outside Mass may be celebrated for various reasons:

1. when the funeral Mass is not permitted, namely, on solemnities of obligation, on Holy Thursday and the Easter Triduum, and on the Sundays of Advent, Lent, and the Easter season;[1]
2. when in some places or circumstances it is not possible to celebrate the funeral Mass before the committal, for example, if a priest is not available;
3. when for pastoral reasons the pastor and the family decide that the funeral liturgy outside Mass is a more suitable form of celebration for the deceased child.

272. The funeral liturgy outside Mass is ordinarily celebrated in the parish church, but may also be celebrated in the home of the deceased, a funeral home, parlor, chapel of rest, or cemetery chapel.

[1]See General Instruction of the Roman Missal, no. 336.

273. The readings are those of the Lectionary for Mass, "Masses for the Dead." The intercessions should be adapted to the circumstances; models are given in place and in Part V, no. 401. The celebration may include holy communion.

274. In the choice of music for the funeral liturgy, preference should be given to the singing of the entrance song, the responsorial psalm, the gospel acclamation, and especially the song of farewell at the final commendation.

275. The minister who is a priest or deacon wears an alb or surplice with stole (a cope may be used, if desired); a layperson who presides wears the liturgical vestments approved for the region.

8. FUNERAL MASS

276. If the rite of reception of the body takes place at the beginning of the funeral Mass, the introductory rites are those given here and the usual introductory rites for Mass, including the penitential rite, are omitted. If the rite of reception of the body has already taken place, the Mass begins in the usual way.

INTRODUCTORY RITES

GREETING

277. The priest, with assisting ministers, goes to the door of the church and using one of the following greetings, or similar words, greets those present.

A
The grace of our Lord Jesus Christ and the love of God and the fellowship of the Holy Spirit be with you all.
℟. And also with you.

B   See no. 69 B.
C   See no. 69 C.
D   See no. 69 D.

SPRINKLING WITH HOLY WATER OR BRIEF ADDRESS

278. If the child was baptized, the priest sprinkles the coffin with holy water (option A). If the child died before baptism, the sprinkling with holy water is omitted and a brief address is given (option B).

A   *Sprinkling with Holy Water*—If the child was baptized, the priest then sprinkles the coffin with holy water, saying:
In the waters of baptism
N. died with Christ and rose with him to new life.
May he/she now share with him eternal glory.

B   *Brief Address*—If the child died before baptism, the priest may then address the mourners in the following or similar words.
My brothers and sisters, the Lord is a faithful God
who created us all after his own image. All things are
of his making, all creation awaits the day of salva-

tion. **We now entrust the soul of N. to the abundant mercy of God, that our beloved child may find a home in his kingdom.**

PLACING OF THE PALL
279. See no. 250.

ENTRANCE PROCESSION
280. The Easter candle may be placed beforehand near the position the coffin will occupy at the conclusion of the procession. The priest and assisting ministers precede the coffin and the mourners into the church. During the procession a psalm, song, or responsory is sung (see no. 403).

PLACING OF CHRISTIAN SYMBOLS
281. See no. 252.

On reaching the altar, the priest, with the assisting ministers, makes the customary reverence, kisses the altar, and (if incense is used) incenses it. Then he goes to the chair.

OPENING PRAYER
282. When all have reached their places, the priest invites the assembly to pray.

Let us pray.

After a brief period of silent prayer, the priest sings or says one of the following prayers or one of those provided in nos. 398–399.

A A baptized child
Merciful Lord,
whose wisdom is beyond human understanding,
you adopted N. as your own in baptism
and have taken him/her to yourself
even as he/she stood on the threshold of life.
Listen to our prayers and extend to us your grace,
that one day we may share eternal life with N.,
for we firmly believe that he/she now rests with you.

We ask this through our Lord Jesus Christ, your Son,
who lives and reigns with you and the Holy Spirit,
one God, for ever and ever.
R̸. Amen.

B A baptized child

Lord God,
from whom human sadness is never hidden,
you know the burden of grief
that we feel at the loss of this child.

As we mourn his/her passing from this life,
comfort us with the knowledge
that N. lives now in your loving embrace.

We make our prayer through our Lord Jesus Christ,
your Son,
who lives and reigns with you and the Holy Spirit,
one God, for ever and ever.
R̸. Amen.

C A child who died before baptism   235

O Lord, whose ways are beyond understanding,
listen to the prayers of your faithful people:
that those weighed down by grief at the loss of this
[little] child
may find reassurance in your infinite goodness.

We ask this through our Lord Jesus Christ, your Son,
who lives and reigns with you and the Holy Spirit,
one God, for ever and ever.
R̸. Amen.

D A child who died before baptism   236

God of all consolation,
searcher of mind and heart,
the faith of these parents [N. and N.] is known to
you.

Comfort them with the knowledge
that the child for whom they grieve
is entrusted now to your loving care.

We ask this through our Lord Jesus Christ, your Son,
who lives and reigns with you and the Holy Spirit,
one God, for ever and ever.
R̸. Amen.

LITURGY OF THE WORD

READINGS

283. After the introductory rites, the liturgy of the word is celebrated. Depending upon pastoral circumstances, either one or two readings may be read before the gospel reading.

HOMILY

284. A brief homily is given after the gospel reading.

GENERAL INTERCESSIONS

285. The following intercessions or those given in no. 401 may be used or adapted to the circumstances, or new intercessions may be composed.

The priest begins:

Let us pray for N., his/her family and friends, and for all God's people.

Assisting minister:

For N., child of God [and heir to the kingdom], that he/she be held securely in God's loving embrace now and for all eternity.
We pray to the Lord.
℟. Lord, hear our prayer.

Assisting minister:

For N.'s family, especially his/her mother and father [his/her brother(s) and sister(s)], that they feel the healing power of Christ in the midst of their pain and grief.
We pray to the Lord.
℟. Lord, hear our prayer.

Assisting minister:

For N.'s friends, those who played with him/her and those who cared for him/her, that they be consoled in their loss and strengthened in their love for one another.
We pray to the Lord.
℟. Lord, hear our prayer.

Assisting minister:

For all parents who grieve over the death of their chil-

dren, that they be comforted in the knowledge that
their children dwell with God.
We pray to the Lord.
℟. **Lord, hear our prayer.**

Assisting minister:
**For children who have died of hunger and disease,
that these little ones be seated close to the Lord at his
heavenly table.
We pray to the Lord.**
℟. **Lord, hear our prayer.**

Assisting minister:
**For the whole Church, that we prepare worthily for
the hour of our death, when God will call us by
name to pass from this world to the next.
We pray to the Lord.**
℟. **Lord, hear our prayer.**

The priest then concludes:
**Lord God,
you entrusted N. to our care
and now you embrace him/her in your love.**

**Take N. into your keeping
together with all children who have died.**

**Comfort us, your sorrowing servants,
who seek to do your will
and to know your saving peace.**

We ask this through Christ our Lord.
℟. **Amen.**

LITURGY OF THE EUCHARIST

286. The liturgy of the eucharist is celebrated in the usual
manner.

287. If the final commendation is to be celebrated at the
place of committal, the procession to the place of committal
(no. 294) begins following the prayer after communion.

FINAL COMMENDATION

288. Following the prayer after communion, the priest goes to a place near the coffin. The assisting ministers carry the censer and holy water, if these are to be used.

A member or a friend of the family may speak in remembrance of the deceased child before the final commendation begins.

INVITATION TO PRAYER

289. Using one of the following invitations, or one of those provided in no. 402, or in similar words, the priest faces the people and begins the final commendation.

A   A baptized child

God in his wisdom knows the span of our days; he has chosen to call to himself this child, whom he adopted as his own in baptism. The body we must now bury will one day rise again to a new and radiant life that will never end. 227

Our firm belief is that N., because he/she was baptized, has already entered this new life; our firm hope is that we shall do the same. Let us ask God to comfort his/her family and friends and to increase our desire for the joys of heaven.

B   A baptized child

With faith in Jesus Christ, we must reverently bury the body of N. 228

Let us pray with confidence to God, in whose sight all creation lives, that he will raise up in holiness and power the mortal body of this [little] child, for God has chosen to number his/her soul among the blessed.

C   A child who died before baptism

Let us commend this child to the Lord's merciful keeping; and let us pray with all our hearts for N. and N. Even as they grieve at the loss of their [little] child, they entrust him/her to the loving embrace of God. 237

SILENCE

290. All pray in silence.

SIGNS OF FAREWELL

291. The coffin of a baptized child may now be sprinkled with holy water and incensed, or this may take place during or after the song of farewell. If the body was sprinkled with holy water during the rite of reception at the beginning of Mass, the sprinkling is ordinarily omitted in the rite of final commendation.

SONG OF FAREWELL

292. The song of farewell is then sung. The following or other responsories chosen from no. 403 may be used or some other song may be sung.

A

I know that my Redeemer lives:
on the last day I shall rise again.
℟. And in my flesh I shall see God.

189

Or:
℟. On the last day I shall rise again.

I shall see him myself, face to face;
and my own eyes shall behold my savior. ℟.

Within my heart this hope I cherish:
that in my flesh I shall see God. ℟.

B

Saints of God, come to his/her aid!
Hasten to meet him/her, angels of the Lord!
℟. Receive his/her soul and present him/her to God
the Most High.

47

May Christ, who called you, take you to himself;
may angels lead you to the bosom of Abraham. ℟.

Eternal rest grant unto him/her, O Lord,
and let perpetual light shine upon him/her. ℟.

PRAYER OF COMMENDATION

293. The priest then says one of the following prayers or one of those provided in no. 404.

A   A baptized child

You are the author and sustainer of our lives, O God.
You are our final home.
We commend to you N., our child.

In baptism he/she began his/her journey toward you.
Take him/her now to yourself
and give him/her the life
promised to those born again of water and the Spirit.

Turn also to us who have suffered this loss.
Strengthen the bonds of this family and our
    community.
Confirm us in faith, in hope, and in love,
so that we may bear your peace to one another
and one day stand together with all the saints
who praise you for your saving help.

We ask this in the name of your Son,
whom you raised from among the dead,
Jesus Christ, our Lord.
℟. Amen.

B   A child who died before baptism

You are the author and sustainer of our lives, O God,
you are our final home.
We commend to you N., our child.

Trusting in your mercy
and in your all-embracing love,
we pray that you give him/her happiness for ever.

Turn also to us who have suffered this loss.
Strengthen the bonds of this family and our
    community.
Confirm us in faith, in hope, and in love,
    so that we may bear your peace to one another
and one day stand together with all the saints
who praise you for your saving help.

We ask this in the name of your Son,
Jesus Christ, our Lord.
℟. Amen.

PROCESSION TO THE PLACE OF COMMITTAL

294. The deacon or, in the absence of a deacon, the priest says:

In peace let us take N. to his/her place of rest.

If a symbol of the Christian life has been placed on the coffin, it should be removed at this time.

The procession then begins: the priest and assisting ministers precede the coffin; the family and mourners follow.

One or more of the following texts or other suitable songs may be sung during the procession to the entrance of the church. The singing may continue during the journey to the place of committal.

A   See no. 176 A.
B   See no. 176 B.
C   See no. 176 C.
D   See no. 176 D.

9. FUNERAL LITURGY OUTSIDE MASS

295. If the rite of reception of the body takes place at the beginning of the funeral liturgy, the introductory rites are those given here. If the rite of reception of the body has already taken place, the liturgy begins with an entrance song and the greeting (no. 277), followed by the invitation to prayer (no. 301).

INTRODUCTORY RITES

GREETING
296. See no. 277.

SPRINKLING WITH HOLY WATER OR BRIEF ADDRESS
297. If the child was baptized, the presiding minister sprinkles the coffin with holy water (option A). If the child died before baptism, the sprinkling with holy water is omitted and a brief address is given (option B).

A *Sprinkling with Holy Water*—If the child was baptized, the presiding minister then sprinkles the coffin with holy water, saying:
In the waters of baptism
N. died with Christ and rose with him to new life.
May he/she now share with him eternal glory.

B *Brief Address*—If the child died before baptism, the presiding minister may then address the mourners in the following or similar words.
My brothers and sisters, the Lord is a faithful God who created us all after his own image. All things are of his making, all creation awaits the day of salvation. We now entrust the soul of N. to the abundant mercy of God, that our beloved child may find a home in his kingdom.

PLACING OF THE PALL
298. If it is the custom of the local community and the child was baptized, the pall is then placed on the coffin by family members, friends, or the minister.

ENTRANCE PROCESSION

299. The Easter candle may be placed beforehand near the position the coffin will occupy at the conclusion of the procession. The presiding minister and assisting ministers precede the coffin and the mourners into the church. During the procession a psalm, song, or responsory is sung (see no. 403).

PLACING OF CHRISTIAN SYMBOLS

300. See no. 252.

On reaching the altar, the presiding minister, with the assisting ministers, makes the customary reverence and goes to the chair.

INVITATION TO PRAYER

301. When all have reached their places, the presiding minister, using the following or similar words, invites the assembly to pray.

My brothers and sisters,
we have come together to renew our trust in Christ
who, by dying on the cross, has freed us from eternal
   death
and, by rising, has opened for us the gates of
   heaven.
Let us pray that the Lord may grant us
the gift of his loving consolation.

OPENING PRAYER

302. After a brief period of silent prayer, the presiding minister sings or says one of the following prayers or one of those provided in nos. 398–399.

A   A baptized child. See no. 282 A.

B   A baptized child. See no. 282 B.

C   A child who died before baptism. See no. 282 C.   235

D   A child who died before baptism. See no. 282 D.   236

LITURGY OF THE WORD

READINGS

303. After the introductory rites, the liturgy of the word is celebrated. Depending upon pastoral circumstances, either one or two readings may be read before the gospel reading.

HOMILY

304. A brief homily is given after the gospel reading.

GENERAL INTERCESSIONS

305. The following intercessions or those given in no. 401 may be used or adapted to the circumstances, or new intercessions may be composed.

The presiding minister begins:
The Lord Jesus is the lover of his people and our only sure hope.
Let us ask him to deepen our faith and sustain us in this dark hour.

Assisting minister:
You became a little child for our sake, sharing our human life.
To you we pray:
℟. Bless us and keep us, O Lord.

Assisting minister:
You grew in wisdom, age and grace, and learned obedience through suffering.
To you we pray.
℟. Bless us and keep us, O Lord.

Assisting minister:
You welcomed children, promising them your kingdom.
To you we pray:
℟. Bless us and keep us, O Lord.

Assisting minister:
You comforted those who mourned the loss of children and friends.
To you we pray:
℟. Bless us and keep us, O Lord.

Assisting minister:

You took upon yourself the suffering and death of us all.
To you we pray:
R̸. Bless us and keep us, O Lord.

Assisting minister:

You promised to raise up those who believe in you,
just as you were raised up in glory by the Father.
To you we pray:
R̸. Bless us and keep us, O Lord.

The presiding minister then concludes:

Lord God,
you entrusted N. to our care
and now you embrace him/her in your love.

Take N. into your keeping
together with all children who have died.

Comfort us, your sorrowing servants,
who seek to do your will
and to know your saving peace.

We ask this through Christ our Lord.
R̸. Amen.

THE LORD'S PRAYER

306. Using one of the following invitations, or in similar words, the minister invites those present to pray the Lord's Prayer.

A
Now let us pray as Christ the Lord has taught us:

B
With longing for the coming of God's kingdom, let us offer our prayer to the Father:

All say:
Our Father . . .

307. The celebration may include holy communion (Part V, nos. 409–410).

308. If the final commendation is to be celebrated at the place of committal, the procession to the place of committal (no. 315) begins following the Lord's Prayer or the prayer after communion.

FINAL COMMENDATION

309. Following the Lord's Prayer (or the prayer after communion) the presiding minister goes to a place near the coffin. The assisting ministers carry the censer and holy water, if these are to be used.

A member or a friend of the family may speak in remembrance of the deceased child before the final commendation begins.

INVITATION TO PRAYER
310. See no. 289.

SILENCE
311. All pray in silence.

SIGNS OF FAREWELL
312. The coffin of a baptized child may now be sprinkled with holy water and incensed, or this may take place during or after the song of farewell. If the body was sprinkled with holy water during the rite of reception at the beginning of the funeral liturgy, the sprinkling is ordinarily omitted at the rite of final commendation.

SONG OF FAREWELL
313. See no. 292.

PRAYER OF COMMENDATION
314. The presiding minister then says one of the following prayers or one of those provided in no. 404.

A   A baptized child. See no. 293 A.
B   A child who died before baptism. See no. 293 B.

PROCESSION TO THE PLACE OF COMMITTAL

315. An assisting minister, or in the absence of an assisting minister, the presiding minister says:

In peace let us take N. to his/her place of rest.

If a symbol of the Christian life has been placed on the coffin, it should be removed at this time.

The procession then begins: the presiding minister and assisting ministers precede the coffin; the family and mourners follow.

One or more of the following texts or other suitable songs may be sung during the procession to the entrance of the church. The singing may continue during the journey to the place of committal.

A   See no. 176 A.
B   See no. 176 B.
C   See no. 176 C.
D   See no. 176 D.

RITE OF COMMITTAL

The Lord is my shepherd; fresh and green are the pastures where he gives me repose.

316. The rite of committal, the conclusion of the funeral rites (see nos. 204–215), is celebrated at the grave, tomb, or crematorium and may be used for burial at sea.

Three forms of the rite of committal are provided for the funeral of a child: "Rite of Committal," "Rite of Committal with Final Commendation," and "Rite of Final Commendation for an Infant."

317. The rite of committal is used when the final commendation and farewell is celebrated within the funeral liturgy. The rite of committal with final commendation is used when the final commendation is not celebrated within the funeral liturgy.

When the funeral liturgy is celebrated on a day prior to the committal or in a different community, the minister may wish to adapt the rite of committal, for example, by adding a song, a greeting, one or more readings, a psalm, and a brief homily. When no funeral liturgy precedes the rite of committal, the rite of committal with final commendation is used and should be similarly adapted.

318. The "Rite of Final Commendation for an Infant" may be used in the case of a stillborn or a newborn infant who dies shortly after birth. This short rite of prayer with the parents is celebrated to give them comfort and to commend and entrust the infant to God. This rite is a model and the minister should adapt it to the circumstances. It may be used in the hospital or place of birth or at the time of the committal of the body.

10. RITE OF COMMITTAL

INVITATION

319. When the funeral procession arrives at the place of committal, the ministers says the following or a similar invitation.

The life which this child N. received from his/her parents is not destroyed by death. God has taken him/her into eternal life.

As we commit his/her body to the earth/elements, let us comfort each other in our sorrow with the assurance of our faith, that one day we will be reunited with N.

SCRIPTURE VERSE

320. See no. 217.   121

PRAYER OVER THE PLACE OF COMMITTAL

321. The minister says one of the following prayers or one of those provided in no. 405.

A   If the place of committal is to be blessed: 230
O God,
by whose mercy the faithful departed find rest,
bless this grave,
and send your holy angel to watch over it.

As we bury here the body of N.,
welcome him/her into your presence,
that he/she may rejoice in you with your saints for
    ever.

We ask this through Christ our Lord.
℟. Amen.

B   If the place of committal has already been blessed:
All praise to you, Lord of all creation.
Praise to you, holy and living God.
We praise and bless you for your mercy,
we praise and bless you for your kindness.
Blessed is the Lord, our God.
℟. Blessed is the Lord, our God.

You sanctify the homes of the living
and make holy the places of the dead.
You alone open the gates of righteousness
and lead us to the dwellings of the saints.
Blessed is the Lord, our God.
℟. Blessed is the Lord, our God.

We praise you, our refuge and strength.
We bless you, our God and Redeemer.
Your praise is always in our hearts and on our lips.
We remember the mighty deeds of the covenant.
Blessed is the Lord, our God.
℟. Blessed is the Lord, our God.

Almighty and ever-living God,
remember the love with which you graced your child
    N. in life.
Receive him/her, we pray, into the mansions of the
    saints.
As we make ready this resting place,
look also with favor on those who mourn
and comfort them in their loss.

Grant this through Christ our Lord.
℟. Amen.

C   When the final disposition of the body is to take place
at a later time:
Almighty and ever-living God,
in you we place our trust and hope,
in you the dead, whose bodies were temples of the
    Spirit, find everlasting peace.

As we take leave of N.
give our hearts peace in the firm hope
that one day he/she will live
in the mansion you have prepared for him/her in
    heaven.

We ask this through Christ our Lord.
℟. Amen.

COMMITTAL

322. The minister then says the words of committal. One of the following formularies or one provided in no. 406 may be used.

A   A baptized child
Into your hands, O merciful Savior, we commend N.
Acknowledge, we humbly beseech you,
a sheep of your own fold, a lamb of your own flock.
Receive him/her into the arms of your mercy,
into the blessed rest of everlasting peace,
and into the glorious company of the saints in light.

B   A child who died before baptism
Lord God,
ever caring and gentle,
we commit to your love this little one [N.],
who brought joy to our lives for so short a time.
Enfold him/her in eternal life.

We pray for his/her parents
who are saddened by the loss of their child [baby/
**   infant].**
Give them courage
and help them in their pain and grief.
May they all meet one day
in the joy and peace of your kingdom.

We ask this through Christ our Lord.
℟. Amen.

The committal takes place at this time or at the conclusion of the rite.

INTERCESSIONS

323. The following intercessions or those given in no. 407 may be used or adapted to the circumstances, or new intercessions may be composed.

The minister begins:
Dear friends, let us turn to the Lord, the God of hope and consolation, who calls us to everlasting glory in Christ Jesus.

Assisting minister:
**For N., that he/she may now enjoy the place prepared
for him/her in your great love.
We pray to the Lord.
℟. Lord, hear our prayer.**

Assisting minister:
**For N.'s father and mother [brother(s) and sister(s)],
that they may know our love and support in their grief.
We pray to the Lord.
℟. Lord, hear our prayer.**

Assisting minister:
**For his/her friends [and teachers], that they may love
one another as you have loved us.
We pray to the Lord.
℟. Lord, hear our prayer.**

Assisting minister:
**For this community, that we may bear one another's
burdens.
We pray to the Lord.
℟. Lord, hear our prayer.**

Assisting minister:
**For all those who mourn their children, that they
may be comforted.
We pray to the Lord.
℟. Lord, hear our prayer.**

Assisting minister:
**For all who are in need, that the fearful may find
peace, the weary rest, and the oppressed freedom.
We pray to the Lord.
℟. Lord, hear our prayer.**

THE LORD'S PRAYER

324. Using the following or similar words, the minister invites those present to pray the Lord's Prayer.

**As sons and daughters of a loving God, we pray in
the confident words of his Son:**

All say:
Our Father . . .

CONCLUDING PRAYER

325. The minister says one of the following prayers or one
of those provided in no. 408.

A   A baptized child
Tender Shepherd of the flock,
N. has entered your kingdom
and now lies cradled in your love.
Soothe the hearts of his/her parents,
bring peace to their lives.
Enlighten their faith
and give hope to their hearts.

Loving God,
grant mercy to your entire family in this time of
**   suffering.**
Comfort us in the knowledge that this child [N.]
lives with you and your Son Jesus Christ
and the Holy Spirit,
for ever and ever.
R̸. Amen.

B   A baptized child   196
Listen, O God, to the prayers of your Church
on behalf of the faithful departed,
and grant to your child, N.,
whose funeral we have celebrated today,
the inheritance promised to all your saints.

We ask this through Christ our Lord.
R̸. Amen.

C   A child who died before baptism
God of mercy,
in the mystery of your wisdom
you have drawn this child [N.] to yourself.
In the midst of our pain and sorrow,
we acknowledge you as Lord of the living and the
**   dead**
and we search for our peace in your will.
In these final moments we stand together in prayer,
believing in your compassion and generous love.

**Deliver this child [N.] out of death
and grant him/her a place in your kingdom of peace.**

**We ask this through Christ our Lord.
R̸. Amen.**

PRAYER OVER THE PEOPLE
326. See no. 223.

A song may conclude the rite. Where it is the custom, some sign or gesture of leave-taking may be made.

11. RITE OF COMMITTAL WITH FINAL COMMENDATION

INVITATION

327. When the funeral procession arrives at the place of committal, the minister says the following or a similar invitation.

The life which this child N. received from his/her parents is not destroyed by death. God has taken him/her into eternal life.

As we commend N. to God and commit his/her body to the earth/elements, let us express in [song and] prayer our common faith in the resurrection. As Jesus Christ was raised from the dead, we too are called to follow him through death to the glory where God will be all in all.

SCRIPTURE VERSE

328. See no. 217.

PRAYER OVER THE PLACE OF COMMITTAL

329. The minister says one of the following prayers or one of those provided in no. 405.

A If the place of committal is to be blessed: 230
O God,
by whose mercy the faithful departed find rest,
bless this grave,
and send your holy angel to watch over it.

As we bury here the body of N.,
welcome him/her into your presence,
that he/she may rejoice in you with your saints for
     ever.

We ask this through Christ our Lord.
℟. Amen.

B If the place of committal has already been blessed:
All praise to you, Lord of all creation.
Praise to you, holy and living God.

We praise and bless you for your mercy,
we praise and bless you for your kindness.
Blessed is the Lord, our God.
℟. Blessed is the Lord, our God.

You sanctify the homes of the living
and make holy the places of the dead.
You alone open the gates of righteousness
and lead us to the dwellings of the saints.
Blessed is the Lord, our God.
℟. Blessed is the Lord, our God.

We praise you, our refuge and strength.
We bless you, our God and Redeemer.
Your praise is always in our hearts and on our lips.
We remember the mighty deeds of the covenant.
Blessed is the Lord, our God.
℟. Blessed is the Lord, our God.

Almighty and ever-living God,
remember the love with which you graced your child
   N. in life.
Receive him/her, we pray, into the mansions of the
   saints.
As we make ready this resting place,
look also with favor on those who mourn
and comfort them in their loss.

Grant this through Christ our Lord.
℟. Amen.

C   When the final disposition of the body is to take place
at a later time:
Almighty and ever-living God,
in you we place our trust and hope,
in you the dead, whose bodies were temples of the
   Spirit, find everlasting peace.

As we take leave of N.
give our hearts peace in the firm hope
that one day he/she will live
in the mansion you have prepared for him/her in
   heaven.

We ask this through Christ our Lord.
R̂. Amen.

INVITATION TO PRAYER

330. Using one of the following invitations or one of those provided in no. 402, or in similar words, the minister faces the people and begins the final commendation. See no. 289.

SILENCE

331. All pray in silence.

SIGNS OF FAREWELL

332. See no. 291

SONG OF FAREWELL

333. See no. 292

PRAYER OF COMMENDATION

334. The minister then says one of the following prayers or one of those provided in no. 404.

A   A baptized child. See no. 293 A.
B   A child who died before baptism. See no. 293 B.

COMMITTAL

335 The act of committal takes place at this time or at the conclusion of the rite.

PRAYER OVER THE PEOPLE

336. The assisting minister says:

Bow your heads and pray for God's blessing.

All pray silently. The minister, with hands extended, prays over the people:
Most merciful God,
whose wisdom is beyond our understanding,
surround the family of N. with your love,
that they may not be overwhelmed by their loss,
but have confidence in your goodness,
and strength to meet the days to come.

We ask this through Christ our Lord.
R̂. Amen.

The minister then says the following:
Eternal rest grant unto him/her, O Lord.
R̟. And let perpetual light shine upon him/her.

May he/she rest in peace.
R̟. Amen.

May his/her soul and the souls of all the faithful departed, through the mercy of God, rest in peace.
R̟. Amen.

See no. 223 A and B

The minister then concludes:
Go in the peace of Christ.
R̟. Thanks be to God.

A song may conclude the rite. Where it is the custom, some sign or gesture of leave-taking may be made.

12. RITE OF FINAL COMMENDATION FOR AN INFANT

BRIEF ADDRESS

337. In the following or similar words, the minister addresses those who have assembled.

Dear friends, in the face of death all human wisdom fails.

Yet the Lord teaches us, by the three days he spent in the tomb, that death has no hold over us. Christ has conquered death; his dying and rising have redeemed us. Even in our sorrow for the loss of this little child, we believe that, one short sleep past, he/she will wake eternally.

SCRIPTURE VERSE

338. The minister then introduces the Scripture verse.

The Lord speaks to us now of our hope for this child in these words of consolation.

A member of the family or one of those present reads one of the following verses.

A   Romans 5:5
B   1 John 3:2

BLESSING OF THE BODY

339. Using the following words, the minister blesses the body of the deceased child.

Trusting in Jesus, the loving Savior
who gathered children into his arms
and who blessed the little ones,
we now commend this infant [N.] to that same embrace of love,
in the hope that he/she will rejoice
and be happy in the presence of Christ.

Then all join the minister, saying:
May the angels and saints lead him/her
to the place of light and peace

where one day
we will be brought together again.

The minister continues:
Lord Jesus,
lovingly receive this little child;
bless him/her
and take him/her to your Father.
We ask this in hope,
and we pray:

Lord, have mercy.
℟. Lord, have mercy.

Christ, have mercy.
℟. Christ, have mercy.

Lord, have mercy.
℟. Lord, have mercy.

THE LORD'S PRAYER

340. Using the following or similar words, the minister invites those present to pray the Lord's Prayer.

When Jesus gathered his disciples around him, he taught them to pray:

All say:
Our Father . . .

PRAYER OF COMMENDATION

341. The minister then says the following prayer, or see no. 325 A.

Tender Shepherd of the flock,
N. now lies cradled in your love.
Soothe the hearts of his/her parents,
bring peace to their lives.
Enlighten their faith
and give hope to their hearts.

Father,
grant mercy to your entire family in this time of
   suffering.

Comfort us with the hope that this child [N.]
lives with you and your Son Jesus Christ,
and the Holy Spirit,
for ever and ever.
R̸. Amen.

BLESSING

342. Using one of the following blessings, the minister
blesses those present.

A   A minister who is a priest or deacon says:
May the God of all consolation
bring you comfort and peace,
in the name of the Father,   ✛   and of the Son,
and of the Holy Spirit.
R̸. Amen.

B   A lay minister invokes God's blessing and signs himself or herself with the sign of the cross, saying:
May the God of all consolation
bring us comfort and peace,
in the name of the Father, and of the Son,
and of the Holy Spirit.
R̸. Amen.

PART III

TEXTS OF SACRED SCRIPTURE

We shall not live on bread alone, but on every word that comes from God.

343. Part III, "Texts of Sacred Scripture," contains the Scriptural readings and psalms for the celebration of the funeral. It is divided into four sections: "Funerals for Adults" (no. 344.13), "Funerals for Baptized Children" (no. 346.14), "Funerals for Children Who Died before Baptism" (no. 346.15), "Antiphons and Psalms" (no. 347).

344. As a general rule, all corresponding texts from sacred Scripture in the funeral rites are interchangeable. In consultation with the family and close friends, the minister chooses the texts that most closely reflect the particular circumstances and the needs of the mourners.

13. FUNERALS FOR ADULTS

OLD TESTAMENT READINGS

1. Job 19:1, 23–27   83
I know that my Redeemer lives.

2. Wisdom 3:1–9 (longer) or 3:1–6, 9 (shorter)   84
He accepted them as a holocaust.

3. Wisdom 4:7–15   85
A blameless life is a ripe old age.

4. Isaiah 25:6a, 7–9   86
The Lord God will destroy death for ever.

5. Lamentations 3:17–26   87
It is good to wait in silence for the Lord God to save.

6. Daniel 12:1–3   88
Of those who lie sleeping in the dust of the earth many will awake.

7. 2 Maccabees 12:43–45   89
It is good and holy to think of the dead rising again.

NEW TESTAMENT READINGS

345. During the Easter season, reading 1, 17, 18, or 19 is used as the first reading instead of a reading from the Old Testament.

1. Acts of the Apostles 10:34–43 (longer) or 10:34–36, 42–43 (shorter)
God has appointed Jesus to judge everyone, alive and dead.

2. Romans 5:5–11   91
Having been justified by his blood, we will be saved from God's anger through him.

3. Romans 5:17–21   92
Where sin increased, there grace abounded all the more.

4. Romans 6:3–9 (longer) or 6:3–4, 8–9 (shorter)   93
Let us walk in newness of life.

5. **Romans 8:14–23**
We groan while we wait for the redemption of our bodies. ₉₄

6. **Romans 8:31b–35, 37–39** ₉₅
Who can ever come between us and the love of Christ?

7. **Romans 14:7–9, 10b–12** ₉₆
Whether alive or dead, we belong to the Lord.

8. **1 Corinthians 15:20–23, 24b–28** (longer) **or 15:20–
23** (shorter) ₉₇
All people will be brought to life in Christ.

9. **1 Corinthians 15:51–57** ₉₈
Death is swallowed up in victory.

10. **2 Corinthians 4:14—5:1**
What is seen is transitory; what is unseen is eternal.

11. **2 Corinthians 5:1, 6–10** ₉₉
We have an everlasting home in heaven.

12. **Philippians 3:20–21** ₁₀₀
Jesus will transfigure these wretched bodies of ours to be
like his glorious body.

13. **1 Thessalonians 4:13–18.** ₁₀₁
We shall stay with the Lord for ever.

14. **2 Timothy 2:8–13** ₁₀₂
If we have died with him, we shall live with him.

15. **1 John 3:1–2** ₁₀₃
We shall see God as he really is.

16. **1 John 3:14–16** ₁₀₄
We have passed from death to life, because we love our
brothers and sisters.

17. **Revelation 14:13** ₁₀₅
Happy are those who die in the Lord.

18. **Revelation 20:11–21:1** ₁₀₆
The dead have been judged according to their works.

19. **Revelation 21:1–5a, 6b–7**   107
There will be no more death.

RESPONSORIAL PSALMS

1. Psalm 23   108
℟. **The Lord is my shepherd; there is nothing I shall want.**

Or:
℟. **Though I walk in the valley of darkness, I fear no evil, for you are with me.**

2. Psalm 25   109
℟. **To you, O Lord, I lift my soul.**

Or:
℟. **No one who waits for you, O Lord, will ever be put to shame.**

3. Psalm 27   110
℟. **The Lord is my light and my salvation.**

Or:
℟. **I believe that I shall see the good things of the Lord in the land of the living.**

4. Psalm 42 and 43   111
℟. **My soul is thirsting for the living God: when shall I see him face to face?**

5. Psalm 63   112
℟. **My soul is thirsting for you, O Lord my God.**

6. Psalm 103   113
℟. **The Lord is kind and merciful.**

Or:
℟. **The salvation of the just comes from the Lord.**

7. Psalm 116   114
℟. **I will walk in the presence of the Lord in the land of the living.**

Or:
℟. **Alleluia.**

8. Psalm 122   115

℞. **I rejoiced when I heard them say: let us go to the
house of the Lord.**

Or:

℞. **Let us go rejoicing to the house of the Lord.**

9. Psalm 130   116

℞. **Out of the depths, I cry to you, Lord.**

Or:

℞. **I hope in the Lord, I trust in his word.**

10. Psalm 143   117

℞. **O Lord, hear my prayer.**

ALLELUIA VERSES AND VERSES BEFORE THE
GOSPEL

1. Matthew 11:25   118

**Blessed are you, Father, Lord of heaven and earth;
you have revealed to little ones the mysteries of the
kingdom.**

2. Matthew 25:34   119

**Come, you whom my Father has blessed, says the
Lord;
inherit the kingdom prepared for you since the foundation of the world.**

3. John 3:16   120

**God loved the world so much, he gave us his only
Son,
that all who believe in him might have eternal life.**

4. John 6:39   121

**This is the will of my Father, says the Lord,
that I should lose nothing of all that he has given to
me,
and that I should raise it up on the last day.**

5. John 6:40   122

This is the will of my Father, says the Lord,

**that all who believe in the Son will have eternal life
and I will raise them to life again on the last day.**

6. John 6:51a

**I am the living bread from heaven, says the Lord;
whoever eats this bread will live for ever.**

7. John 11:25–26   123

**I am the resurrection and the life, says the Lord;
whoever believes in me will not die for ever.**

8. See Philippians 3:20   124

**Our true home is in heaven,
and Jesus Christ, whose return we long for,
will come from heaven to save us.**

9. 2 Timothy 2:11b–12a   125

**If we die with Christ, we shall live with him,
and if we are faithful to the end, we shall reign with
    him.**

10. Revelation 1:5a, 6b   126

**Jesus Christ is the firstborn from the dead;
glory and kingship be his for ever and ever. Amen.**

11. Revelation 14:13   127

**Blessed are those who have died in the Lord;
let them rest from their labors for their good deeds
    go with them.**

GOSPEL READINGS

1. **Matthew 5:1–12a**   128

Rejoice and be glad, for your reward will be great in
heaven.

2. **Matthew 11:25–30**   129

Come to me . . . and I will give you rest.

3. **Matthew 25:1–13**   130

Look, the bridegroom comes. Go out to meet him.

4. **Matthew 25:31–46**   131
Come, you whom my Father has blessed.

5.   **Mark 15:33–39; 16:1–6** (longer) or **15:33–39**
(shorter)   132
Jesus gave a loud cry and breathed his last.

6. **Luke 7:11–17**   133
Young man, I say to you, arise.

7. **Luke 12:35–40**   134
Be prepared.

8. **Luke 23:33, 39–43**   135
Today you will be with me in paradise.

9. **Luke 23:44–46, 50, 52–53; 24:1–6**a (longer) **or**
23:44–46, 50, 52–53 (shorter)   136
Father, I put my life in your hands.

10. **Luke 24:13–35** (longer) **or 24:13–16, 28–35**
(shorter)   137
Was it not necessary that the Christ should suffer and so
enter into his glory?

11. **John 5:24–29**
Whoever hears my word and believes, has passed from
death to life.

12. **John 6:37–40**   138
All who believe in the Son will have eternal life and I will
raise them to life again on the last day.

13. **John 6:51–58**   139
All who eat this bread will live for ever; and I will raise
them up on the last day.

14. **John 11:17–27** (longer) **or John 11:21–27** (shorter)   140
I am the resurrection and the life.

15. **John 11:32–45**   141
Lazarus, come out.

16. **John 12:23–28** (longer) **or John 12:23–26** (shorter)   142
If a grain of wheat falls on the ground and dies, it yields a
rich harvest.

17. **John 14:1–6**   143
There are many rooms in my Father's house.

18. **John 17:24–26**   144
Father, I want those you have given me to be with me
where I am.

19. **John 19:17–18, 25–30**
Jesus bowed his head and gave up his spirit.

14.   FUNERALS FOR BAPTIZED CHILDREN

OLD TESTAMENT READINGS

1. **Isaiah 25:6a, 7–9**   203
The Lord God will destroy death for ever.

2. **Lamentations 3:22–26**   204
It is good to wait in silence for the Lord God to save.

NEW TESTAMENT READINGS

346. During the Easter season reading 6 or 7 is used as the
first reading instead of a reading from the Old Testament.

1. **Romans 6:3–4, 8–9**   205
We believe that we shall return to life with Christ.

2. **Romans 14:7–9**   206
Whether alive or dead, we belong to the Lord.

3. **1 Corinthians 15:20–23**   207
All people will be brought to life in Christ.

4. **Ephesians 1:3–5**   208
The Father chose us in Christ, before the creation of the
world, to be holy.

5. **1 Thessalonians 4:13–14, 18**   209
We shall stay with the Lord for ever.

6. **Revelation 7:9–10, 15–17**   210
God will wipe away all tears from their eyes.

7. **Revelation 21:1a, 3–5a**   211
There will be no more death.

RESPONSORIAL PSALMS

1. Psalm 23   212
℟. **The Lord is my shepherd; there is nothing I shall
want.**

2. Psalm 25   213
℟. **To you, O Lord, I lift my soul.**

3. Psalm 42

℟. **My soul is thirsting for the living God: when shall I see him face to face?**

214

4. Psalm 148

℟. **Let all praise the name of the Lord.**

215

Or:

℟. **Alleluia.**

ALLELUIA VERSES AND VERSES BEFORE THE GOSPEL

1. See Matthew 11:25

Blessed are you, Father, Lord of heaven and earth; you have revealed to little ones the mysteries of the kingdom.

216

2. John 6:39

This is the will of my Father, says the Lord, that I should lose nothing of all that he has given to me, and that I should raise it up on the last day.

217

3. 2 Corinthians 1:3b–4a

Blessed be the Father of mercies and the God of all comfort, who consoles us in all our afflictions.

218

GOSPEL READINGS

1. **Matthew 11:25–30**
You have hidden these things from the learned and the clever and revealed them to children.

219

2. **Mark 10:13–16**
The kingdom of heaven belongs to little children.

3. **John 6:37–40** (longer) **or John 6:37–39** (shorter)
This is the will of my Father, that I should lose nothing of all that he has given to me.

220

4. **John 6:51–58**
All who eat this bread will live for ever, and I will raise them up on the last day.

221

5. **John 11:32–38, 40**
If you believe, you will see the glory of God.

6. **John 19:25–30**
This is your mother.

15. FUNERALS FOR CHILDREN WHO DIED BEFORE BAPTISM

OLD TESTAMENT READINGS

1. **Isaiah 25:6a, 7–8b**   231
The Lord God will destroy death for ever.

2. **Lamentations 3:22–26**   232
It is good to wait in silence for the Lord God to save.

RESPONSORIAL PSALM

Psalm 25   233
℟. **To you, O Lord, I lift my soul.**

Or:
℟. **No one who waits for you, O Lord, will ever be put to shame.**

ALLELUIA VERSES AND VERSES BEFORE THE GOSPEL

1. 2 Corinthians 1:3b–4a
Blessed be the Father of mercies and the God of all comfort,
who consoles us in all our afflictions.

2. Revelation 1:5a, 6b
Jesus Christ is the firstborn from the dead;
glory and kingship be his for ever and ever. Amen.

GOSPEL READINGS

1. **Matthew 11:25–30**
You have hidden these things from the learned and the clever and have revealed them to children.

2. **Mark 15:33–46**   234
Jesus gave a loud cry and breathed his last.

3. **John 19:25–30**
This is your mother.

16. ANTIPHONS AND PSALMS

347. The following psalms with their antiphons may be
chosen for use in various places within the rites.

1. Psalm 23
Ant.: **Remember me in your kingdom, Lord.**   146

2. Psalm 25
Ant.: **Look on my grief and my sorrow: forgive all**   147
my sins.
   Or:
Ant.: **May the angels lead you into paradise; may
the martyrs come to welcome you and take you to the
holy city, the new and eternal Jerusalem.**

3. Psalm 42
Ant.: **I will go to the dwelling of God, to the won-**   147
derful house of my Savior.

4. Psalm 51
Ant.: **Eternal rest, O Lord, and your perpetual light.**   148
   Or:
Ant.: **Caught up with Christ, rejoice with the saints**   149
in glory.
   Or:
Ant.: **The bones that were broken shall leap for joy.**   150

5. Psalm 93
Ant.: **From clay you shaped me; with flesh you
clothed me; Redeemer, raise me on the last day.**   151

6. Psalm 114 and 115:1–12
Ant.: **May Christ welcome you into paradise.**   152
   Or:
Ant.: **Alleluia.**

7. Psalm 116
Ant.: **May choirs of angels welcome you and lead**   153
**you to the bosom of Abraham. May you find eternal
rest where Lazarus is poor no longer.**

Or:

Ant.: **I heard a voice from heaven: Blessed are those**   154
who die in the Lord.

Or:

Ant.: **Alleluia.**

8. Psalm 118

Ant.: **Open for me the holy gates; I will enter and**   155
praise the Lord.

Or:

Ant. **This is the gate of the Lord: here the just shall enter.**   156

9. Antiphon 1 may serve as the common antiphon for
Psalm 119 or an antiphon proper to each part of Psalm 119
may be used.

Psalm 119:1–8

Ant. 1: **They are happy who live by the law of God.**

Psalm 119:9–16

Ant. 2: **May you be for ever blessed, O Lord; teach**
me your holy ways.

Psalm 119:17–24

Ant. 3: **Open my eyes, O Lord, that I may see the**
wonders of your law.

Psalm 119:25–32

Ant. 4: **Lightly I run in the way you have shown, for**
you have opened my heart to receive your law.

Psalm 119: 33–40

Ant. 5: **Lead me, Lord, in the path of your commands.**

Psalm 119:41–48

Ant. 6: **Blessed are those who hear the word of God**
and cherish it in their hearts.

Psalm 119:49–56

Ant. 7: **In the land of exile I have kept your commands.**

Psalm 119:57–64

Ant. 8: **I have pondered my ways and turned back to**
your teaching.

Psalm 119:65–72

Ant. 9: **More precious than silver or gold is the law**
you teach us, O Lord.

Psalm 119:73–80
Ant. 10:   **Let your loyal love console me, as you promised your servant.**

Psalm 119:81–88
Ant. 11:   **Heaven and earth will pass away, but my words will not pass away.**

Psalm 119:89–96
Ant. 12:   **I have sought to do your will, O Lord; for this you give me life.**

Psalm 119:97–104
Ant. 13:   **Law finds its fulfillment in love.**
   Or:
Ant.:   **How sweet your promise, richer than honey from the comb.**

Psalm 119:105–112
Ant. 14:   **Whoever follows me will not walk in the dark, but will have the light of life.**

Psalm 119:113–120
Ant. 15:   **Receive me, Lord, as you promised, that I may live.**

Psalm 119:121–128
Ant. 16:   **Give your servant a loving welcome, O Lord.**

Psalm 119:129–136
Ant. 17:   **Guide my steps according to your promise, O Lord.**

Psalm 119:137–144
Ant. 18:   **Do the things you have learned, and you will be blessed.**

Psalm 119:145–152
Ant. 19:   **I cry for your help, O Lord; your word is my hope.**

Psalm 119:153–160
Ant. 20:   **If you love me, keep my commandments, says the Lord.**

Psalm 119:161–168
Ant. 21: **Great is the peace of those who keep your love, O Lord.**

Psalm 119:169–176
Ant. 22: **I have chosen to do your will; may your hand be always there to give me strength.**

10. Psalm 121
Ant.: **My help is from the Lord who made heaven and earth.**   158

11. Psalm 122
Ant.: **Let us go to the house of the Lord.**   159
Or:
Ant.: **I rejoiced when I heard them say: Let us go to the house of the Lord.**

12. Psalm 123.
Ant.: **Our eyes are fixed on the Lord, pleading for his mercy.**   160
Or:
Ant.: **To you, O Lord, I lift up my eyes.**

13. Psalm 126
Ant.: **Those who sow in tears shall sing for joy when they reap.**   161

14. Psalm 130
Ant.: **I cry to you, O Lord.**   162
Or:
Ant.: **My soul has hoped in the Lord.**   163

15. Psalm 132
Ant.: **Let your holy people rejoice, O Lord, as they enter your dwelling place.**   164

16. Psalm 134
Ant.: **Bless the Lord, all you servants of the Lord.**   165
Or:
Ant.: **In the stillness of the night, bless the Lord.**

PART IV

OFFICE FOR THE DEAD
With the Lord there is mercy and fullness of redemption.

348. The vigil for the deceased may be celebrated in the form of some part of the office for the dead. To encourage this form of the vigil, the chief hours, "Morning Prayer" and "Evening Prayer," are provided here. When the funeral liturgy is celebrated the evening before the committal, it may be appropriate to celebrate morning prayer before the procession to the place of committal.

349. In the celebration of the office for the dead members of the Christian community gather to offer praise and thanks to God especially for the gifts of redemption and resurrection, to intercede for the dead, and to find strength in Christ's victory over death. When the community celebrates the hours, Christ the Mediator and High Priest is truly present through his Spirit in the gathered assembly, in the proclamation of God's word, and in the prayer and song of the Church.[1] The community's celebration of the hours acknowledges that spiritual bond that links the Church on earth with the Church in heaven, for it is in union with the whole Church that this prayer is offered on behalf of the deceased.

350. At morning prayer the Christian community recalls "the resurrection of the Lord Jesus, the true light enlightening all people (see John 1:9) and 'the sun of justice' (Malachi 4:2) 'rising from on high' (Luke 1:78)."[2] The celebration of morning prayer from the office for the dead relates the death of the Christian to Christ's victory over death and affirms the hope that those who have received the light of Christ at baptism will share in that victory.

351. At evening prayer the Christian community gathers to give thanks for the gifts it has received, to recall the sacrifice of Jesus Christ and the saving works of redemption, and to call upon Christ, the evening star and unconquer-

---

[1] See General Instruction of the Liturgy of the Hours, no. 13.
[2] See General Instruction of the Liturgy of the Hours, no. 38.

able light.[3] Through evening prayer from the office for the dead the community gives thanks to God for the gift of life received by the deceased and praises the Father for the redemption brought about by the sacrifice of his Son, who is the joy-giving light and the true source of hope.

STRUCTURE AND CONTENT OF MORNING PRAYER AND EVENING PRAYER

352. Morning prayer and evening prayer from the office for the dead include the introduction (or the reception of the body), hymn, psalmody, reading, response to the word of God, gospel canticle, intercessions, concluding prayer, and dismissal.

INTRODUCTORY VERSE OR RECEPTION OF THE BODY

353. Morning prayer and evening prayer begin with the introductory verse, *God, come to my assistance,* except when the invitatory replaces it, or when the rite of reception of the body is celebrated, since this replaces both the introductory verse and the hymn.

HYMN

354. To set the tone for the hour, a hymn is sung.

PSALMODY

355. In praying the psalms of the office for the dead, the assembly offers God praise and intercedes for the deceased person and the mourners in the words of prayer that Jesus himself used during his life on earth. Through the psalms the assembly prays in the voice of Christ, who intercedes on its behalf before the Father. In the psalms of petition and lament it expresses its sorrow and its firm hope in the redemption won by Christ. In the psalms of praise the assembly has a foretaste of the destiny of its deceased member and its own destiny, participation in the liturgy of heaven, where every tear will be wiped away and the Lord's victory over death will be complete.

356. Since the psalms are songs, whenever possible, they should be sung. The manner of singing them may be:

[3] See General Instruction of the Liturgy of the Hours, no. 39.

    1. antiphonal, that is, two groups alternate singing the stanzas; the last stanza, the doxology, is sung by both groups;

    2. responsorial, that is, the antiphon is sung by all before and after each stanza and the stanzas are sung by a cantor;

    3. direct, that is, the stanzas are sung without interruption by all, by a choir, or by a cantor.

The rubrics for each psalm in morning prayer and evening prayer indicate a way for singing it; other ways may be used.

357. The psalmody of morning prayer from the office for the dead consists of Psalm 51, a psalm of lament and petition, Psalm 146 or Psalm 150, a psalm of praise, and an Old Testament canticle from Isaiah.

358. The psalmody of evening prayer consists of Psalm 121 and Psalm 130, two psalms of lament and petition, and a New Testament canticle from the letter of Paul to the Philippians.

359. For pastoral reasons, psalms other than those given in the office for the dead may be chosen, provided they are appropriate for the time of day and suitable for use in the office for the dead (see, for example, antiphons and psalms in Part III, no. 347).[4]

READING

360. The reading of the word of God in the office for the dead proclaims the paschal mystery and conveys the hope of being gathered together again in God's kingdom. The short reading in place in the hour or a longer Scripture reading from Part III, following no. 344, may be used.[5] For pastoral reasons and if circumstances allow, a nonbiblical reading may be included at morning or evening prayer in addition to the reading from Scripture, as is the practice in the office of readings.

RESPONSE TO THE WORD OF GOD

361. A period of silence may follow the reading, then a brief homily based on the reading. After the homily the

---

[4] See General Instruction of the Liturgy of the Hours, no. 252.
[5] See General Instruction of the Liturgy of the Hours, no. 46.

short responsory or another responsorial song (see, for example, no. 403) may be sung or recited.

GOSPEL CANTICLE

362. After the response to the word of God, the Canticle of Zechariah is sung at morning prayer and the Canticle of Mary at evening prayer as an expression of praise and thanksgiving for redemption.[6]

363. During the singing of the gospel canticle, the altar, then the presiding minister and the congregation may be incensed.

INTERCESSIONS

364. In the intercessions of the office for the dead, the assembly prays that the deceased and all who die marked with the sign of faith may rise again together in glory with Christ. The intercessions provided in the hour may be used or adapted to the circumstances, or new intercessions may be composed.

The presiding minister introduces the intercessions. An assisting minister sings or says the intentions. In keeping with the form of the intentions in the liturgy of the hours, the assembly responds with either the second part of the intention or the response. After a brief introduction by the presiding minister the assembly sings or says the Lord's Prayer.

CONCLUDING PRAYER AND DISMISSAL

365. The concluding prayer, proclaimed by the presiding minister, completes the hour.

366. After the concluding prayer and before the dismissal a member of the family or a friend of the deceased may be invited to speak in remembrance of the deceased.

367. When the funeral liturgy is celebrated the evening before the committal, it may be appropriate to celebrate morning prayer before the procession to the place of committal. In such an instance the dismissal is omitted and the rite continues with the procession to the place of committal.

[6] See General Instruction of the Liturgy of the Hours, no. 50.

MINISTRY AND PARTICIPATION

368. The celebration of the office for the dead requires careful preparation, especially in the case of communities that may not be familiar with the liturgy of the hours. Pastors and other ministers should provide catechesis on the place and significance of the liturgy of the hours in the life of the Church and the purpose of the celebration of the office for the dead. They should also encourage members of the parish community to participate in the celebration as an effective means of prayer for the deceased, as a sign of their concern and support for the family and close friends, and as a sign of faith and hope in the paschal mystery. This catechesis will help to ensure the full and active participation of the assembly in the celebration of the office for the dead.

369. The office for the dead may be celebrated in the funeral home, parlor, chapel of rest, or in the church. In special circumstances, when the office is combined with the funeral liturgy, care should be taken that the celebration not be too lengthy.[7]

370. The place in which the celebration occurs will often suggest adaptations. A celebration in the home of the deceased, for example, may be simplified or shortened.

371. A priest or deacon should normally preside whenever the office for the dead is celebrated with a congregation; other ministers (a reader, a cantor, an acolyte) should exercise their proper ministries. In the absence of a priest or deacon, a layperson presides.

Whenever possible, ministers should involve the family of the deceased in the planning of the hour and in the designation of ministers.

The minister vests according to local custom. If morning prayer or evening prayer is celebrated in the church, a priest or a deacon who presides wears an alb or surplice with stole (a cope may also be worn).

372. The sung celebration of the liturgy of the hours "is more in keeping with the nature of this prayer, and a mark

[7] See General Instruction of the Liturgy of the Hours, nos. 93–97.

of both higher solemnity and closer union of hearts in offering praise to God."[8] Whenever possible, therefore, singing at morning or evening prayer should be encouraged.

In the choice of music preference should be given to the singing of the hymn, the psalmody, and the gospel canticle. The introductory verse, the responsory, the intercessions, the Lord's Prayer, and the dismissal may also be sung.

An organist or other instrumentalist and a cantor should assist the assembly in singing the hymn, psalms, and responses. The parish community should also prepare booklets or participation aids that contain an outline of the hour, the texts and music belonging to the people, and directions for posture, gesture, and movement.*

373 – 383. The texts are found in the Liturgy of the Hours, Office of the Dead.

After the dismissal of the office the procession to the place of committal may follow.

PROCESSION TO THE PLACE OF COMMITTAL

384. The deacon, or in the absence of a deacon, the minister says:

In peace let us take our brother/sister to his/her place of rest.

If a symbol of the Christian life has been placed on the coffin, it should be removed at this time.

The procession then begins: the minister and assisting ministers precede the coffin; the family and mourners follow.

One or more of the following texts or other suitable songs may be sung during the procession to the entrance of the church. The singing may continue during the journey to the place of committal.

A The following antiphon may be sung with verses from Psalm 25, or separately.

---

[8] Congregation of Rites, Introduction *Musicam Sacram*, 5 March 1967, no. 37: AAS 59 (1967), 310; DOL 508, no. 4158.
*The texts are found in the Liturgy of the Hours, Office of the Dead.

May the angels lead you into paradise;
may the martyrs come to welcome you
and take you to the holy city,
the new and eternal Jerusalem.

B   The following antiphon may be sung with verses from Psalm 116, or separately.

May choirs of angels welcome you
and lead you to the bosom of Abraham;
and where Lazarus is poor no longer
may you find eternal rest.

C
Whoever believes in me, even though that person
    die, shall live.
℟. I am the resurrection and the life.
Whoever lives and believes in me shall never die. ℟.

D   The following psalms may also be used.

Psalm 118, Psalm 42, Psalm 93, Psalm 25, and Psalm 119.

18. EVENING PRAYER

385. When the celebration begins with the rite of reception of the body at the church (nos. 82–86) the introductory verse (no. 386) and the hymn (no. 387) are omitted and the celebration continues with the psalmody (no. 388).*

389–395. The texts are found in the Liturgy of the Hours Office of the Dead.

*The texts are found in the Liturgy of the Hours, Office of the Dead.

PART V

ADDITIONAL TEXTS
The one who raised Christ Jesus from the dead will give your mortal bodies life through his Spirit living in you

20. PRAYERS AND TEXTS IN PARTICULAR CIRCUMSTANCES

397. The following prayers for the dead and prayers for the mourners are for use in the various rites of Parts I, II, and IV.

The prayers are grouped as follows:

Prayers for the Dead (No. 398)

Prayers for the Mourners (No. 399)

PRAYERS FOR THE DEAD

398. The following prayers for the dead may be used in the various rites of Parts I and II and in Part IV. The prayers should be chosen taking the character of the text into account as well as the place in the rite where it will occur. All of the prayers in this section end with the shorter conclusion. When a prayer is used as the opening prayer at the funeral liturgy, the longer conclusion is used.

1. General

God of faithfulness, 30
in your wisdom you have called your servant N. out
  of this world;
release him/her from the bonds of sin,
and welcome him/her into your presence,
so that he/she may enjoy eternal light and peace
and be raised up in glory with all your saints.

We ask this through Christ our Lord.
R̸. Amen.

2. General

Lord, in our grief we turn to you. 33
Are you not the God of love
who opens your ears to all?

Listen to our prayers for your servant N.,
whom you have called out of this world:
lead him/her to your kingdom of light and peace
and count him/her among the saints in glory.

We ask this through Christ our Lord.
R̸. Amen.

3. General

Holy Lord, almighty and eternal God,   167
hear our prayers for your servant N.,
whom you have summoned out of this world.
Forgive his/her sins and failings
and grant him/her a place of refreshment, light, and
   peace.

Let him/her pass unharmed through the gates of
   death
to dwell with the blessed in light,
as you promised to Abraham and his children for
   ever.
Accept N. into your safekeeping
and on the great day of judgment
raise him/her up with all the saints
to inherit your eternal kingdom.

We ask this through Christ our Lord.
R̸. Amen.

4. General

Into your hands, O Lord,   168
we humbly entrust our brother/sister N.
In this life you embraced him/her with your tender
   love;
deliver him/her now from every evil
and bid him/her enter eternal rest.

The old order has passed away:
welcome him/her then into paradise,
where there will be no sorrow, no weeping nor pain,
but the fullness of peace and joy
with your Son and the Holy Spirit
for ever and ever.
R̸. Amen.

5. General, see no. 164A.

6. General

O God,   171
glory of believers and life of the just,
by the death and resurrection of your Son, we are
   redeemed:

have mercy on your servant N.,
and make him/her worthy to share the joys of
    paradise,
for he/she believed in the resurrection of the dead.

We ask this through Christ our Lord.
R̸. Amen.

7. General
Almighty God and Father, 172
by the mystery of the cross, you have made us
    strong;
by the sacrament of the resurrection
you have sealed us as your own.
Look kindly upon your servant N.,
now freed from the bonds of mortality,
and count him/her among your saints in heaven.

We ask this through Christ our Lord.
R̸. Amen.

8. General, see no. 164 D.

9. General
To you, O God, the dead do not die, 174
and in death our life is changed, not ended.
Hear our prayers
and command the soul of your servant N.
to dwell with Abraham, your friend,
and be raised at last on the great day of judgment.
In your mercy cleanse him/her of any sin
which he/she may have committed through human
    frailty.

We ask this through Christ our Lord.
R̸. Amen.

10. General
Lord God, in whom all find refuge, 175
we appeal to your boundless mercy:
grant to the soul of your servant N.
a kindly welcome,
cleansing of sin,

release from the chains of death,
and entry into everlasting life.

We ask this through Christ our Lord.
℞. **Amen.**

11. General
God of all consolation,
open our hearts to your word,
so that, listening to it, we may comfort one another,
finding light in time of darkness
and faith in time of doubt.

We ask this through Christ our Lord.
℞. **Amen.**

12. General. See no. 164 B.

13. General. See no. 164 C.

14. A pope
O God,
from whom the just receive an unfailing reward,
grant that your servant N., our Pope,
whom you made vicar of Peter and shepherd of your
**   Church,**
may rejoice for ever in the vision of your glory,
for he was a faithful steward here on earth
of the mysteries of your forgiveness and grace.

We ask this through Christ our Lord.
℞. **Amen.**

15. A diocesan bishop
Almighty and merciful God,
eternal Shepherd of your people,
listen to our prayers
and grant that your servant, N., our bishop,
to whom you entrusted the care of this Church,
may enter the joy of his eternal Master,
there to receive the rich reward of his labors.

We ask this through Christ our Lord.
℞. **Amen.**

16. Another bishop
**O God,
from the ranks of your priests
you chose your servant N.
to fulfill the office of bishop.
Grant that he may share
in the eternal fellowship of those priests
who, faithful to the teachings of the apostles,
dwell in your heavenly kingdom.**

**We ask this through Christ our Lord.
R̷. Amen.**

17. A priest
**God of mercy and love,
grant to N., your servant and priest,
a glorious place at your heavenly table,
for you made him here on earth
a faithful minister of your word and sacrament.**

**We ask this through Christ our Lord.
R̷. Amen.**

18. A priest
**O God,
listen favorably to our prayers
offered on behalf of your servant and priest.
and grant that N.,
who committed himself zealously to the service of
    your name,
may rejoice for ever in the company of your saints.**

**We ask this through Christ our Lord.
R̷. Amen.**

19. A priest
**Lord God,
you chose our brother N. to serve your people as a
    priest
and to share the joys and burdens of their lives.**

**Look with mercy on him
and give him the reward of his labors,**

the fullness of life promised to those who preach
  your holy Gospel.

We ask this through Christ our Lord.
℟. Amen.

20. A deacon
God of mercy,
as once you chose seven men of honest repute
to serve your Church,
so also you chose N. as your servant and deacon.
Grant that he may rejoice in your eternal fellowship
with all the heralds of your Gospel,
for he was untiring in his ministry here on earth.

We ask this through Christ our Lord.
℟. Amen.

21. A deacon
Lord God,
you sent your Son into the world
to preach the Good News of salvation
and to pour out his Spirit of grace upon your Church.

Look with kindness on your servant N.
As a deacon in the Church
he was strengthened by the gift of the Spirit
to preach the Good News,
to minister in your assembly,
and to do the works of charity.

Give him the reward promised
to those who show their love of you
by service to their neighbor.

We ask this through Christ our Lord.
℟. Amen.

22. A religious
All-powerful God,
we pray for our brother/sister N.,
who responded to the call of Christ
and pursued wholeheartedly the ways of perfect love.
Grant that he/she may rejoice
on that day when your glory will be revealed

and in company with all his/her brothers and sisters
share for ever the happiness of your kingdom.

We ask this through Christ our Lord.
℟. Amen.

23. A religious
God of blessings,
source of all holiness,
the voice of your Spirit has drawn countless men and
    women
to follow Jesus Christ
and to bind themselves to you
with ready will and loving heart.

Look with mercy on N.
who sought to fulfill his/her vows to you,
and grant him/her the reward promised to all good
    and faithful servants.
May he/she rejoice in the company of the saints
and with them praise you for ever.

We ask this through Christ our Lord.
℟. Amen.

24. One who worked in the service of the Gospel
Faithful God,   178
we humbly ask your mercy for your servant N.,
who worked so generously to spread the Good News:
grant him/her the reward of his/her labors
and bring him/her safely to your promised land.

We ask this through Christ our Lord.
℟. Amen.

25. A baptized child. See no. 254 B.

26. A baptized child. See no. 254 A.

27. A young person
Lord,   177
your wisdom governs the length of our days.
We mourn the loss of N.,
whose life has passed so quickly,

and we entrust him/her to your mercy.
Welcome him/her into your heavenly home
and grant him/her the happiness of everlasting
   youth.

We ask this through Christ our Lord.
℟. Amen.

28. A young person
Lord God,
source and destiny of our lives,
in your loving providence
you gave us N.
to grow in wisdom, age, and grace.
Now you have called him/her to yourself.

As we grieve the loss of one so young
We seek to understand your purpose.

Draw him/her to yourself
and give him/her full stature in Christ.
May he/she stand with all the angels and saints
who know your love and praise your saving will.

We ask this through Christ our Lord.
℟. Amen.

29. Parents
Lord God, who commanded us to honor father and
   mother,
look kindly upon your servants N. and N.,
have mercy upon them
and let us see them again in eternal light.

We ask this through Christ our Lord.
℟. Amen.

30. A parent
God of our ancestors in faith,
by the covenant made on Mount Sinai
you taught your people to strengthen the bonds of
   family
through faith, honor, and love.
Look kindly upon N.,

181

a father/mother who sought to bind his/her children
to you.
Bring him/her one day to our heavenly home
where the saints dwell in blessedness and peace.

We ask this through Christ our Lord.
R̸. Amen.

31. A married couple

Lord God, whose covenant is everlasting,   182
have mercy upon the sins of your servants N. and N.;
as their love for each other united them on earth,
so let your love join them together in heaven.

We ask this through Christ our Lord.
R̸. Amen.

32. A married couple

Eternal Father,
in the beginning you established the love of man and
woman
as a sign of creation.
Your own Son loves the Church as a spouse.
Grant mercy and peace to N. and N. who,
by their love for each other,
were signs of the creative love
which binds the Church to Christ.

We ask this in the name of Jesus the Lord.
R̸. Amen.

33. A married couple

Lord God,
giver of all that is true and lovely and gracious,
you created in marriage a sign of your covenant.
Look with mercy upon N. and N.
You blessed them in their companionship,
and in their joys and sorrows you bound them
together.
Lead them into eternal peace,
and bring them to the table
where the saints feast together in your heavenly
home.

We ask this through Christ our Lord.
℟. Amen.

34. A wife
Eternal God,
you made the union of man and woman
as a sign of the bond between Christ and the Church.

Grant mercy and peace to N.,
who was united in love with her husband.
May the care and devotion of her life on earth
find a lasting reward in heaven.
Look kindly on her husband and family [children]
as now they turn to your compassion and love.
Strengthen their faith and lighten their loss.

We ask this through Christ our Lord.
℟. Amen.

35. A husband
Eternal God,
you made the union of man and woman
as a sign of the bond between Christ and the Church.

Grant mercy and peace to N.,
who was united in love with his wife.
May the care and devotion of his life on earth
find a lasting reward in heaven.
Look kindly on his wife and family [children]
as now they turn to your compassion and love.
Strengthen their faith and lighten their loss.

We ask this through Christ our Lord.
℟. Amen.

36. A deceased non-Christian married to a Catholic
Almighty and faithful Creator,
all things are of your making,
all people are shaped in your image.
We now entrust the soul of N. to your goodness.
In your infinite wisdom and power,
work in him/her your merciful purpose,
known to you alone from the beginning of time.
Console the hearts of those who love him/her

in the hope that all who trust in you
will find peace and rest in your kingdom.

We ask this in the name of Jesus the Lord.
R̸. Amen.

37. An elderly person
God of endless ages,
from one generation to the next
you have been our refuge and strength.
Before the mountains were born
or the earth came to be,
you are God.
Have mercy now on your servant N.
whose long life was spent in your service.
Give him/her a place in your kingdom,
where hope is firm for all who love
and rest is sure for all who serve.

We ask this through Christ our Lord.
R̸. Amen.

38. An elderly person
God of mercy,
look kindly on your servant N.
who has set down the burden of his/her years.
As he/she served you faithfully throughout his/her
  life,
may you give him/her the fullness of your peace and
  joy.
We give thanks for the long life of N.,
now caught up in your eternal love.
We make our prayer in the name of Jesus who is our
  risen Lord
now and for ever.
R̸. Amen.

39. One who died after a long illness
God of deliverance,
you called our brother/sister N.
to serve you in weakness and pain,
and gave him/her the grace of sharing the cross of
  your Son.

179

Reward his/her patience and forbearance,
and grant him/her the fullness of Christ's victory.

We ask this through Christ our Lord.
R⁄. Amen.

40. One who died after a long illness
Most faithful God,
lively is the courage of those who hope in you.
Your servant N. suffered greatly
but placed his/her trust in your mercy.
Confident that the petition of those who mourn
pierces the clouds and finds an answer,
we beg you, give rest to N.
Do not remember his/her sins
but look upon his/her sufferings
and grant him/her refreshment, light, and peace.

We ask this through Christ our Lord.
R⁄. Amen.

41. One who died after a long illness
O God,
You are water for our thirst,
and manna in our desert.
We praise you for the life of N.
and bless your mercy
that has brought his/her suffering to an end.
Now we beg that same endless mercy
to raise him/her to new life.
Nourished by the food and drink of heaven,
may he/she rest for ever,
in the joy of Christ our Lord.
R⁄. Amen.

42. One who died suddenly
Lord,   180
as we mourn the sudden death of our brother/sister,
show us the immense power of your goodness
and strengthen our belief
that N. has entered into your presence.

We ask this through Christ our Lord.
R⁄. Amen.

43. One who died accidentally or violently
Lord our God,
you are always faithful and quick to show mercy.
Our brother/sister N.
was suddenly [and violently] taken from us.
Come swiftly to his/her aid,
have mercy on him/her,
and comfort his/her family and friends
by the power and protection of the cross.

We ask this through Christ our Lord.
℟. Amen.

44. One who died by suicide
God, lover of souls,
you hold dear what you have made
and spare all things, for they are yours.
Look gently on your servant N.,
and by the blood of the cross
forgive his/her sins and failings.

Remember the faith of those who mourn
and satisfy their longing for that day
when all will be made new again
in Christ, our risen Lord,
who lives and reigns with you for ever and ever.
℟. Amen.

45. One who died by suicide
Almighty God and Father of all,
you strengthen us by the mystery of the cross
and with the sacrament of your Son's resurrection.
Have mercy on our brother/sister N.
Forgive all his/her sins and grant him/her peace.
May we who mourn this sudden death be comforted
   and consoled by your power and protection.

We ask this through Christ our Lord.
℟. Amen.

46. Several persons
O Lord,
you gave new life to N. and N.
in the waters of baptism;

show mercy to them now,
and bring them to the happiness of life in your
   kingdom.

We ask this through Christ our Lord.
R̰. Amen.

47. Several persons
All-powerful God,
whose mercy is never withheld
from those who call upon you in hope,
look kindly on your servants N. and N.,
who departed this life confessing your name,
and number them among your saints for evermore.

We ask this through Christ our Lord.
R̰. Amen.

PRAYERS FOR THE MOURNERS
399. The following prayers for the mourners may be used
in the various rites of Parts I and II. The prayers should be
chosen taking the character of the text into account as well
as the place in the rite where it will occur.

1. General
Father of mercies and God of all consolation,   34
you pursue us with untiring love
and dispel the shadow of death
with the bright dawn of life.

[Comfort your family in their loss and sorrow.
Be our refuge and our strength, O Lord,
and lift us from the depths of grief
into the peace and light of your presence.]

Your Son, our Lord Jesus Christ,
by dying has destroyed our death,
and by rising, restored our life.
Enable us therefore to press on toward him,
so that, after our earthly course is run,
he may reunite us with those we love,
when every tear will be wiped away.

We ask this through Christ our Lord.
R̰. Amen.

2. General

Lord Jesus, our Redeemer,   169
you willingly gave yourself up to death,
so that all might be saved and pass from death to
**   life.**
We humbly ask you to comfort your servants in their
**   grief**
and to receive N. into the arms of your mercy.
You alone are the Holy One,
you are mercy itself;
by dying you unlocked the gates of life for those
**   who believe in you.**
Forgive N. his/her sins,
and grant him/her a place of happiness, light, and
**   peace**
in the kingdom of your glory for ever and ever.
℟. Amen.

3. General

God, all-compassionate,   202
ruler of the living and the dead,
you know beforehand
those whose faithful lives reveal them as your own.
We pray for those who belong to this present world
and for those who have passed to the world to come:
grant them pardon for all their sins.
We ask you graciously to hear our prayer
through the intercession of all the saints
and for your mercy's sake.

For you are God, for ever and ever.
℟. Amen.

4. General

Lord our God,
the death of our brother/sister N.
recalls our human condition
and the brevity of our lives on earth.
But for those who believe in your love
death is not the end,
nor does it destroy the bonds
that you forge in our lives.

We share the faith of your Son's disciples
and the hope of the children of God.
Bring the light of Christ's resurrection
to this time of testing and pain
as we pray for N. and for those who love him/her,
through Christ our Lord.
℟. Amen.

5. General
Lord God,
you are attentive to the voice of our pleading.
Let us find in your Son
comfort in our sadness,
certainty in our doubt,
and courage to live through this hour.
Make our faith strong
through Christ our Lord.
℟. Amen.

6. General
Lord,
N. is gone now from this earthly dwelling,
and has left behind those who mourn his/her
     absence.
Grant that as we grieve for our brother/sister
we may hold his/her memory dear
and live in hope of the eternal kingdom
where you will bring us together again.

We ask this through Christ our Lord.
℟. Amen.

7. General
Most merciful God,
whose wisdom is beyond our understanding,
surround the family of N. with your love,
that they may not be overwhelmed by their loss,
but have confidence in your goodness,
and strength to meet the days to come.

We ask this through Christ our Lord.
℟. Amen.

8. A baptized child. See no. 262 A.

9. A baptized child
Eternal Father,   226
through the intercession of Mary,
who bore your Son and stood by the cross as he died,
grant to these parents in their grief
the assistance of her presence,
the comfort of her faith,
and the reward of her prayers.

We ask this through Christ our Lord.
R̸. Amen.

10. A baptized child
Lord God,
source and destiny of our lives,
in your loving providence
you gave us N.
to grow in wisdom, age, and grace.
Now you have called him/her to yourself.

We grieve over the loss of one so young
and struggle to understand your purpose.

Draw him/her to yourself
and give him/her full stature in Christ.
May he/she stand with all the angels and saints,
who know your love and praise your saving will.

We ask this through Jesus Christ, our Lord.
R̸. Amen.

11. A baptized child. See no. 282 A

12. A baptized child. See no. 282 B

13. A child who died before baptism. See no. 282 C

14. A child who died before baptism. See no. 282 D

15. A stillborn child
Lord God,
ever caring and gentle,

we commit to your love this little one,
quickened to life for so short a time.
Enfold him/her in eternal life.

We pray for his/her parents
who are saddened by the loss of their child.
Give them courage
and help them in their pain and grief.
May they all meet one day
in the joy and peace of your kingdom.

We ask this through Christ our Lord.
R̸/. Amen.

PLACING OF CHRISTIAN SYMBOLS

400. The following texts may be used during the "Reception at the Church" when placing Christian symbols on the coffin. Numbers 1 and 2 are for deceased persons who were baptized; number 3 is for a child who died before baptism.

1.   *Book of the Gospels or Bible*—While the Book of the Gospels or Bible is placed on the coffin, the minister says in these or similar words:

In life N. cherished the Gospel of Christ.
May Christ now greet him/her with these words of
**   eternal life:**
Come, blessed of my Father!

2.   *Cross*—While a cross is placed on the coffin, the minister says in these or similar words:

In baptism N. received the sign of the cross.
May he/she now share
in Christ's victory over sin and death.

3.   *Cross*—During the presentation of a cross in the case of a child who died before baptism, the minister says in these or similar words:

The cross we have brought here today was carried by
**   the Lord Jesus in the hour of his suffering.**
We place it now on [near] this coffin as a sign of our
**   hope for N.**

As the cross is placed on (or near) the coffin, the minister says:

Lord Jesus Christ,
you loved us unto death.
Let this cross be a sign of your love for N.
and for the people you have gathered here today.

GENERAL INTERCESSIONS AND LITANIES

401. The following intercessions and litanies may be used during a liturgy of the word or at Mass and should be adapted according to the circumstances.

1. See no. 167 B.   200

2.
                                                                                           201

My dear friends, let us join with one another in pray-
ing to God, not only for our departed brother/sister,
but also for the Church, for peace in the world, and
for ourselves.

That the bishops and priests of the Church, and all
    who preach the Gospel,
may be given the strength to express in action the
    word they proclaim.
We pray to the Lord:
℟. Lord, hear our prayer.

That those in public office may promote justice and
    peace.
We pray to the Lord:
℟. Lord, hear our prayer.

That those who bear the cross of pain
in mind or body may never feel forsaken by God.
We pray to the Lord:
℟. Lord, hear our prayer.

That God may deliver the soul of his servant N. from
punishment and from the powers of darkness.
We pray to the Lord:
℟. Lord, hear our prayer.

That God in his mercy may blot out all his/her offenses.
We pray to the Lord:
℟. Lord hear our prayer.

That God may establish him/her in light and peace.
We pray to the Lord:
℟. Lord, hear our prayer.

That God may call him/her to happiness in the company of all the saints. We pray to the Lord:
℟. Lord, hear our prayer.

That God may welcome into his glory those of our family and friends who have departed this life.
We pray to the Lord:
℟. Lord, hear our prayer.

That God may give a place in the kingdom of heaven to all the faithful departed.
We pray to the Lord:
℟. Lord, hear our prayer.

O God,
Creator and Redeemer of all the faithful,
grant to the souls of your departed servants
release from all their sins.
Hear our prayers for those we love
and give them the pardon they have always desired.

We ask this through Christ our Lord.
℟. Amen.

3. See no. 167A.

4.
Let us turn to Christ Jesus with confidence and faith in the power of his cross and resurrection:

Risen Lord, pattern of our life for ever:
Lord, have mercy.
℟. Lord, have mercy.

Promise and image of what we shall be:
Lord, have mercy.
℟. Lord, have mercy.

Son of God who came to destroy sin and death:
Lord, have mercy.
℞. Lord, have mercy.

Word of God who delivered us from the fear of
  death:
Lord, have mercy.
℞. Lord, have mercy.

Crucified Lord, forsaken in death, raised in glory:
Lord, have mercy.
℞. Lord, have mercy.

Lord Jesus, gentle Shepherd who brings rest to our
souls, give peace to N. for ever:
Lord, have mercy.
℞. Lord, have mercy.

Lord Jesus, you bless those who mourn and are in
pain. Bless N.'s family and friends who gather
around him/her today:
Lord, have mercy.
℞. Lord, have mercy.

5. A baptized child

Jesus is the Son of God and the pattern for our own creation. His promise is that one day we shall truly be like
him. With our hope founded on that promise, we pray:

That God will receive our praise and thanksgiving
for the life of N.:
Let us pray to the Lord.
℞. Lord, have mercy.

That God will bring to completion N.'s baptism into
Christ:
Let us pray to the Lord.
℞. Lord, have mercy.

That God will lead N. from death to life:
Let us pray to the Lord.
℞. Lord, have mercy.

That all of us, N.'s family and friends, may be comforted in our grief:

Let us pray to the Lord.
℟. Lord, have mercy.

That God will grant release to those who suffer:
Let us pray to the Lord.
℟. Lord, have mercy.

That God will grant peace to all who have died in
the faith of Christ:
Let us pray to the Lord.
℟. Lord, have mercy.

That one day we may all share in the banquet of the
Lord, praising God for victory over death:
Let us pray to the Lord.
℟. Lord, have mercy.

6. A baptized child
The Lord Jesus is the lover of his people and our
    only sure hope.
Let us ask him to deepen our faith and sustain us in
this dark hour.

You became a little child for our sake, sharing our
human life.
To you we pray:
℟. Bless us and keep us, O Lord.

You grew in wisdom, age, and grace, and learned
obedience through suffering.
To you we pray:
℟. Bless us and keep us, O Lord.

You welcomed children, promising them your
kingdom.
To you we pray:
℟. Bless us and keep us, O Lord.

You comforted those who mourned the loss of chil-
dren and friends.
To you we pray:
℟. Bless us and keep us, O Lord.

You took upon yourself the suffering and death of us
all.

To you we pray:
℟. Bless us and keep us, O Lord.

You promised to raise up those who believe in you
just as you were raised up in glory by the Father.
To you we pray:
℟. Bless us and keep us, O Lord.

Lord God,
you entrusted N. to our care
and now you embrace him/her in your love.

Take N. into your keeping
together with all children who have died.

Comfort us, your sorrowing servants,
who seek to do your will
and to know your saving peace.

We ask this through Christ our Lord.
℟. Amen.

7. A deceased child. See no. 285.

FINAL COMMENDATION AND FAREWELL

INVITATION TO PRAYER

402. The following are alternatives to the invitation to prayer.

1.

With faith in Jesus Christ, we must reverently bury   46
the body of our brother/sister.   65

Let us pray with confidence to God, in whose sight all creation lives, that he will raise up in holiness and power the mortal body of our brother/sister and command his/her soul to be numbered among the blessed.

May God grant him/her a merciful judgment, deliverance from death, and pardon of sin. May Christ the Good Shepherd carry him/her home to be at peace with the Father. May he/she rejoice for ever in the presence of the eternal King and in the company of all the saints.

2.

Our brother/sister N. has fallen asleep in Christ. Con-   183
fident in our hope of eternal life, let us commend him/her to the loving mercy of our Father and let our prayers go with him/her. He/she was adopted as God's son/daughter in baptism and was nourished at the table of the Lord; may he/she now inherit the promise of eternal life and take his/her place at the table of God's children in heaven.

Let us pray also on our own behalf, that we who now mourn and are saddened may one day go forth with our brother/sister to meet the Lord of Life when he appears in glory.

3.

Because God has chosen to call our brother/sister N.   184
from this life to himself,

we commit his/her body to the earth,
for we are dust and unto dust we shall return.

But the Lord Jesus Christ will change our mortal bodies to be like his in glory,
for he is risen, the firstborn from the dead.

So let us commend our brother/sister to the Lord,
that the Lord may embrace him/her in peace
and raise up his/her body on the last day.

4.

Before we go our separate ways, let us take leave of
our brother/sister. May our farewell express our affection for him/her; may it ease our sadness and
strengthen our hope. One day we shall joyfully greet
him/her again when the love of Christ, which conquers all things, destroys even death itself.

185

5.

Trusting in God, we have prayed together for N. and
now we come to the last farewell. There is sadness in
parting, but we take comfort in the hope that one day
we shall see N. again and enjoy his/her friendship.
Although this congregation will disperse in sorrow,
the mercy of God will gather us together again in the
joy of his kingdom. Therefore let us console one another in the faith of Jesus Christ.

186

SONG OF FAREWELL

403. The following may be used as alternatives for the
song of farewell. These responsories may also be used during the entrance procession in the celebration of the funeral
liturgy.

1. See no. 292 B.

2.

Lord our God, receive your servant, for whom you
shed your blood.
Ry. Remember, Lord, that we are dust: like grass,
like a flower of the field.

187

Merciful Lord, I tremble before you,
ashamed of the things I have done. ℟.

3.

You knew me, Lord, before I was born.   188
You shaped me into your image and likeness.
℟. I breathe forth my spirit to you, my Creator.

Merciful Lord, I tremble before you:
I am ashamed of the things I have done;
do not condemn me when you come in judgment. ℟.

4. See no. 292 A.

5.

I know that my Redeemer lives,   189
And on that final day of days,
His voice shall bid me rise again:
Unending joy, unceasing praise!

This hope I cherish in my heart:
To stand on earth, my flesh restored,
And, not a stranger but a friend,
Behold my Savior and my Lord.

6.
Lazarus you raised, O Lord, from the decay of the   190
    tomb.
℟. Grant your servant rest, a haven of pardon and
    peace.

Eternal rest, O Lord,
and your perpetual light. ℟.

7.
You shattered the gates of bronze   191
and preached to the spirits in prison.
℟. Deliver me, Lord, from the streets of darkness.

A light and a revelation
to those confined in darkness. ℟.

"Redeemer, you have come,"
they cried, the prisoners of silence. ℟.

Eternal rest, O Lord,
and your perpetual light. ℟.

PRAYER OF COMMENDATION

404. The following prayers may be used as alternative
forms of the prayer of commendation.

1. A baptized person

Into your hands, Father of mercies,
we commend our brother/sister N.
in the sure and certain hope
that, together with all who have died in Christ,
he/she will rise with him on the last day.

[We give you thanks for the blessings
which you bestowed upon N. in this life:
they are signs to us of your goodness
and of our fellowship with the saints in Christ.]

Merciful Lord,
turn toward us and listen to our prayers:
open the gates of paradise to your servant
and help us who remain
to comfort one another with assurances of faith,
until we all meet in Christ
and are with you and with our brother/sister for ever.

We ask this through Christ our Lord.
℟. **Amen.**

2. A baptized child

Lord Jesus,
like a shepherd who gathers the lambs
to protect them from all harm,
you led N. to the waters of baptism
and shielded him/her in innocence.

Now carry this little one
on the path to your kingdom of light
where he/she will find happiness
and every tear will be wiped away.

To you be glory, now and for ever.
℟. **Amen.**

3. A baptized child

Into your gentle keeping, O Lord,
we commend this child, [N.].
Though our hearts are troubled,
we hope in your loving kindness.

By the sign of the cross
he/she was claimed for Christ,
and in the waters of baptism
he/she died with Christ to live in him for ever.

May the angels, our guardians,
lead N. now to paradise
where your saints will welcome him/her
and every tear will be wiped away.
There we shall join in songs of praise for ever.

We ask this through Christ our Lord.
℟. Amen.

RITE OF COMMITTAL

PRAYER OVER THE PLACE OF COMMITTAL

405. One of the following may be used to bless the tomb or grave.

1. See no. 218 A.

2.

O God,

by whose mercy the faithful departed find rest,
bless this grave,
and send your holy angel to watch over it.

As we bury here the body of our brother/sister,
deliver his/her soul from every bond of sin,
that he/she may rejoice in you with your saints for
    ever.

We ask this through Christ our Lord.
R̷. Amen.

193

3.

Almighty God,

you created the earth and shaped the vault of heaven;
you fixed the stars in their places.
When we were caught in the snares of death
you set us free through baptism;
in obedience to your will
our Lord Jesus Christ
broke the fetters of hell and rose to life,
bringing deliverance and resurrection
to those who are his by faith.
In your mercy look upon this grave,
so that your servant may sleep here in peace;
and on the day of judgment raise him/her up
to dwell with your saints in paradise.

We ask this through Christ our Lord.
R̷. Amen.

194

4.

God of endless ages, 195
through disobedience to your law
we fell from grace
and death entered the world;
but through the obedience and resurrection of your
    Son
you revealed to us a new life.
You granted Abraham, our father in faith,
a burial place in the promised land;
you prompted Joseph of Arimathea
to offer his own tomb for the burial of the Lord.
In a spirit of repentance
we earnestly ask you
to look upon this grave and bless it,
so that, while we commit to the earth the body of
    your servant N.
his/her soul may be taken into paradise.

We ask this through Christ our Lord.
R̸. Amen.

COMMITTAL
406. The following are alternative forms of the committal.

1. General. See no. 219 A.

2. General. See no. 219 B.

3. For ashes

My friends,
as we prepare to bury [entomb]
    the ashes of our brother/sister,
we recall that our bodies bear the imprint of the first
    creation when they were fashioned from dust;
but in faith we remember, too, that by the new
    creation we also bear the image of Jesus who was
    raised to glory.

In confident hope that one day God will raise us and
    transform our mortal bodies, let us pray.

Pause for silent prayer.

Faithful God,
Lord of all creation,
you desire that nothing redeemed by your Son
will ever be lost,
and that the just will be raised up on the last day.

Comfort us today with the word of your promise
as we return the ashes of our brother/sister to the
earth.

Grant N. a place of rest and peace
where the world of dust and ashes has no dominion.
Confirm us in our hope that he/she will be created
anew
on the day when you will raise him/her up in glory
to live with you and all the saints
for ever and ever.
℟. Amen.

4. For burial at sea

Lord God,
by the power of your Word
you stilled the chaos of the primeval seas,
you made the raging waters of the Flood subside,
and calmed the storm on the sea of Galilee.
As we commit the body of our brother/sister N. to
the deep,
grant him/her peace and tranquility
until that day when he/she and all who believe in
you
will be raised to the glory of new life
promised in the waters of baptism.

We ask this through Christ our Lord.
℟. Amen.

INTERCESSIONS

407. The following may be used as an alternative form of
the intercessions.

1. See no. 220 A.

2.
Dear friends, our Lord comes to raise the dead and comforts us with the solace of his love. Let us praise the Lord Jesus Christ.

Word of God, Creator of the earth to which N. now returns: in baptism you called him/her to eternal life to praise your Father for ever:
Lord, have mercy.
R̶̸. Lord, have mercy.

Son of God, you raise up the just and clothe them with the glory of your kingdom:
Lord, have mercy.
R̶̸. Lord, have mercy.

Crucified Lord, you protect the soul of N. by the power of your cross, and on the day of your coming you will show mercy to all the faithful departed:
Lord, have mercy.
R̶̸. Lord, have mercy.

Judge of the living and the dead, at your voice the tombs will open and all the just who sleep in your peace will rise and sing the glory of God:
Lord, have mercy.
R̶̸. Lord, have mercy.

All praise to you, Jesus our Savior, death is in your hands and all the living depend on you alone:
Lord, have mercy.
R̶̸. Lord, have mercy.

CONCLUDING PRAYER
408. One of the following may be used as an alternative to the concluding prayer.

1.
Listen, O God, to the prayers of your Church
on behalf of the faithful departed,
and grant to your servant N.,

whose funeral we have celebrated today,
the inheritance promised to all your saints.

We ask this through Christ our Lord.
℞. Amen.

2.

Loving God, from whom all life proceeds   197
and by whose hand the dead are raised again,
though we are sinners, you wish always to hear us.
Accept the prayers we offer in sadness for your servant N.:
deliver his/her soul from death,
number him/her among your saints
and clothe him/her with the robe of salvation
to enjoy for ever the delights of your kingdom.

We ask this through Christ our Lord.
℞. Amen.

3.

Lord God,   198
whose days are without end
and whose mercies beyond counting,
keep us mindful
that life is short and the hour of death unknown.
Let your Spirit guide our days on earth
in the ways of holiness and justice,
that we may serve you
in union with the whole Church,
sure in faith, strong in hope, perfected in love.
And when our earthly journey is ended,
lead us rejoicing into your kingdom,
where you live for ever and ever.
℞. Amen.

21. HOLY COMMUNION OUTSIDE MASS

INVITATION TO COMMUNION

409. If there is to be communion, the minister shows the eucharistic bread to those present, saying:

This is the Lamb of God
who takes away the sins of the world.
Happy are those who are called to his supper.

All then respond:

Lord, I am not worthy to receive you,
but only say the word and I shall be healed.

Those present then receive communion in the usual way.

PRAYER AFTER COMMUNION

410. When all have received communion, the minister then says one of the following prayers after communion:

Let us pray.

All pray in silence for a brief period.

A   Outside the Easter season
Lord God,
your Son Jesus Christ gave us
the sacrament of his body and blood
to guide us on our pilgrim way to your kingdom.
May our brother/sister N., who shared in the
**   eucharist,**
come to the banquet of life Christ has prepared for
**   us.**

We ask this through Christ our Lord.
R̸. Amen.

B   Outside the Easter season
Father, all-powerful God,
we pray for our brother/sister N.
whom you have called from this world.
May this eucharist cleanse him/her,
forgive his/her sins,
and raise him/her up to eternal joy in your presence.

We ask this through Christ our Lord.
℟. Amen.

C   During the Easter season
Lord God,
may the death and resurrection of Christ
which we celebrate in this eucharist
bring our brother/sister N. the peace of your eternal
    home.

We ask this in the name of Jesus the Lord.
℟. Amen.

D   A baptized child
Lord,
hear the prayers of those who share in the body and
    blood of your Son.
Comfort those who mourn for this child
and sustain them with the hope of eternal life.

We ask this through Christ our Lord.
℟. Amen.

E   A baptized child
Lord,
you feed us with the gift of your eucharist.
May we rejoice with this child
at the feast of eternal life in your kingdom.

We ask this through Christ our Lord.
℟. Amen.

F   A child who died before baptism
Lord,
hear the prayers of those who share in the body and
    blood of your Son.
By these sacred mysteries
you have filled them with hope of eternal life.
May they be comforted in the sorrows of this present
    life.

We ask this in the name of Jesus the Lord.
℟. Amen.

APPENDIX

"ORDO EXSEQUIARUM," 1969

INTRODUCTION*

1. At the funerals of its children the Church confidently celebrates Christ's paschal mystery. Its intention is that those who by baptism were made one body with the dead and risen Christ may with him pass from death to life. In soul they are to be cleansed and taken up into heaven with the saints and elect; in body they await the blessed hope of Christ's coming and the resurrection of the dead.

The Church, therefore, offers the eucharistic sacrifice of Christ's Passover for the dead and pours forth prayers and petitions for them. Because of the communion of all Christ's members with each other, all of this brings spiritual aid to the dead and the consolation of hope to the living.

2. As they celebrate the funerals of their brothers and sisters, Christians should be intent on affirming their hope for eternal life. They should not, however, give the impression of either disregard or contempt for the attitudes or practices of their own time and place. In such matters as family traditions, local customs, burial societies, Christians should willingly acknowledge whatever they perceive to be good and try to transform whatever seems alien to the Gospel. Then the funeral ceremonies for Christians will both manifest paschal faith and be true examples of the spirit of the Gospel.

3. Although any form of empty display must be excluded, it is right to show respect for the bodies of the faithful departed, which in life were the temple of the Holy Spirit. This is why it is worthwhile that there be an expression of faith in eternal life and the offering of prayers for the deceased, at least at the more significant times between death and burial.

Depending on local custom, such special moments include the vigil at the home of the deceased, the laying out of the

*As emended by the Congregation for the Sacraments and Divine Worship, 12 September 1983.

body, and the carrying of the body to the place of burial. They should be marked by the gathering of family and friends and, if possible, of the whole community to receive in the liturgy of the word the consolation of hope, to offer together the eucharistic sacrifice, and to pay last respects to the deceased by a final farewell.

4. To take into account in some degree conditions in all parts of the world, the present rite of funerals is arranged on the basis of three models:

1. The first envisions three stations, namely, at the home of the deceased, at the church, and at the cemetery.

2. The second covers only two stations, at the church and at the cemetery.

3. The third involves only one station, which is at the home of the deceased.

5. The first model for a funeral is practically the same as the former rite in the Roman Ritual. It includes as a rule, at least in country places, three stations, namely, at the home of the deceased, at the church, and at the cemetery, with two processions in between. Especially in large cities, however, processions are seldom held or are inconvenient for various reasons. As for the stations at home and at the cemetery, priests sometimes are unable to lead them because of a shortage of clergy or the distance of the cemetery from the church. In view of these considerations, the faithful must be urged to recite the usual psalms and prayers themselves when there is no deacon or priest present. If that is impossible, the home and cemetery stations are to be omitted.

6. In this first model the station at the church consists as a rule in the celebration of the funeral Mass; this is forbidden only during the Easter triduum, on solemnities, and on the Sundays of Advent, Lent, and the Easter season. Pastoral reasons may on occasion require that a funeral be celebrated in the church without a Mass (which in all cases must, if possible, be celebrated on another day within a reasonable time); in that case a liturgy of the word is prescribed absolutely. Therefore, the station at the church always includes a liturgy of the word, with or without a Mass, and the rite hitherto called "absolution" of the dead and henceforth to be called "the final commendation and farewell."

7. The second funeral plan consists of only two stations, namely, at the cemetery, that is, at the cemetery chapel, and at the grave. This plan does not envision a eucharistic celebration, but one is to take place, without the body present, before the actual funeral or after the funeral.

8. A funeral rite, following the third model, to be celebrated in the deceased's home may perhaps in some places be regarded as pointless. Yet in certain parts of the world it seems needed. In view of the many diversities, the model purposefully does not go into details. At the same time it seemed advisable at least to set out guidelines so that this plan might share certain elements with the other two, for example, the liturgy of the word and the rite of final commendation or farewell. The detailed directives will be left to the conferences of bishops to settle.

9. In the future preparation of particular rituals conformed to the Roman Ritual, it will be up to the conference of bishops either to keep the three models or to change their arrangement or to omit one or other of them. For it is quite possible that in any particular country one model, for example, the first with its three stations, is the only one in use and as such the one to be kept. Elsewhere all three may be needed. The conference of bishops will make the arrangements appropriate to what particular needs require.

10. After the funeral Mass the rite of final commendation and farewell is celebrated.

The meaning of the rite does not signify a kind of purification of the deceased; that is what the eucharistic sacrifice accomplishes. Rather it stands as a farewell by which the Christian community together pays respect to one of its members before the body is removed or buried. Death, of course, always has involved an element of separation, but Christians as Christ's members are one in him and not even death can part them from each other.[1]

The priest's opening words are to introduce and explain this rite, a few moments of silence are to follow, then the sprinkling with holy water and the incensation, then a song of farewell. Not only is it useful for all to sing this song, composed of a pertinent text set to a suitable melody, but

[1] See Simeon of Thessalonica, *De ordine sepulturae*: PG 155, 685 B.

all should have the sense of its being the high point of the entire rite.

Also to be seen as signs of farewell are the sprinkling with holy water, a reminder that through baptism the person was marked for eternal life, and the incensation, signifying respect for the body as the temple of the Holy Spirit.

The rite of final commendation and farewell may only be held during an actual funeral service, that is, when the body is present.

11. In any celebration for the deceased, whether a funeral or not, the rite attaches great importance to the readings from the word of God. These proclaim the paschal mystery, they convey the hope of being gathered together again in God's kingdom, they teach remembrance of the dead, and throughout they encourage the witness of a Christian life.

12. In its good offices on behalf of the dead, the Church turns again and again especially to the prayer of the psalms as an expression of grief and a sure source of trust. Pastors are, therefore, to make an earnest effort through an effective catechesis to lead their communities to a clearer and deeper grasp of at least some of the psalms provided for the funeral liturgy. With regard to other chants that the rite frequently assigns on pastoral grounds, they are also to seek to instill a "warm and living love of Scripture"[2] and a sense of its meaning in the liturgy.

13. In its prayers the Christian community confesses its faith and makes compassionate intercession for deceased adults that they may reach their final happiness with God. The community's belief is that deceased children whom through baptism God has adopted as his own have already attained that blessedness. But the community pours forth its prayers on behalf of their parents, as well as for all the loved ones of the dead, so that in their grief they will experience the comfort of faith.

14. The practice of reciting the office of the dead on the occasion of funerals or at other times is based in some places on particular law, on an endowment for this purpose, or on

[2]Vatican Council II, Constitution on the Liturgy *Sacrosanctum Concilium*, art. 24.

custom. The practice may be continued, provided the office is celebrated becomingly and devoutly. But in view of the circumstances of contemporary life and for pastoral considerations, a Bible vigil or celebration of God's word may be substituted.

14bis. Funeral rites are to be celebrated for catechumens. In keeping with the provisions of CIC, can. 1183, celebration of funeral rites may also be granted to:

1. children whose baptism was intended by their parents but who died before being baptized;

2. baptized members of another Church or non-Catholic Ecclesial Community at the discretion of the local Ordinary, but not if it is known that they did not wish this nor if a minister of their own is available.

15. Funeral rites are to be granted to those who have chosen cremation, unless there is evidence that their choice was dictated by anti-Christian motives.

The funeral is to be celebrated according to the model in use in the region. It should be carried out in a way, however, that clearly expresses the Church's preference for the custom of burying the dead, after the example of Christ's own will to be buried, and that forestalls any danger of scandalizing or shocking the faithful.

The rites usually held in the cemetery chapel or at the grave may in this case take place within the confines of the crematorium and, for want of any other suitable place, even in the crematorium room. Every precaution is to be taken against the danger of scandal or religious indifferentism.

OFFICES AND MINISTRIES TOWARD THE DEAD

16. In the celebration of a funeral all the members of the people of God must remember that to each one a role and an office is entrusted: to relatives and friends, funeral directors, the Christian community as such, finally the priest, who as the teacher of faith and the minister of comfort presides at the liturgical rites and celebrates the eucharist.

17. All should also be mindful, and priests especially, that as they commend the deceased to God at a funeral, they have a responsibility as well to raise the hopes of those present and to build up their faith in the paschal mystery and the resurrection of the dead. They should do so in such a way, however, that as bearers of the tenderness of the Church and the comfort of faith, they console those who believe without offending those who grieve.

18. In preparing and planning a funeral, priests are to keep in mind with delicate sensitivity not only the identity of the deceased and the circumstances of the death, but also the grief of the bereaved and their needs for a Christian life. Priests are to be particularly mindful of those who attend the liturgical celebration or hear the Gospel because of the funeral, but are either non-Catholics or Catholics who never or seldom take part in the eucharist or have apparently lost the faith. Priests are, after all, the servants of Christ's Gospel on behalf of all.

19. Except for the Mass, a deacon may conduct all the funeral rites. As pastoral needs require, the conference of bishops, with the Apostolic See's permission, may even depute a layperson for this.

When there is no priest or deacon, it is recommended that in funerals according to the first model laypersons carry out the stations at the home and cemetery; the same applies generally to all vigils for the dead.

20. Apart from the marks of distinction arising from a person's liturgical function or holy orders and those honors due to civil authorities according to liturgical law,[3] no special honors are to be paid in the celebration of a funeral to any private persons or classes of persons.

ADAPTATIONS BELONGING TO THE CONFERENCES OF BISHOPS

21. In virtue of the Constitution on the Liturgy (art. 63 b), the conferences of bishops have the right to prepare a section in particular rituals corresponding to the present section of the Roman Ritual and adapted to the needs of the different parts of the world. This section is for use in the regions concerned, once the *acta* of the conferences have been reviewed by the Apostolic See.

[3]See Vatican Council II, Constitution on the Liturgy *Sacrosanctum Concilium*, art. 32.

In making such adaptations it shall be up to the conferences of bishops:

1. to decide on the adaptations, within the limits laid down in the present section of the Roman Ritual;

2. to weigh carefully and prudently which elements from the traditions and culture of individual peoples may be appropriately admitted and accordingly to propose to the Apostolic See further adaptations considered to be useful or necessary that will be introduced into the liturgy with its consent;

3. to retain elements of particular rituals that may now exist, provided they are compatible with the Constitution on the Liturgy and contemporary needs, or to adapt such elements;

4. to prepare translations of the texts that are truly suited to the genius of the different languages and cultures and, whenever appropriate, to add suitable melodies for singing;

5. to adapt and enlarge this Introduction in the Roman Ritual in such a way that the ministers will fully grasp and carry out the meaning of the rites;

6. in editions of the liturgical books to be prepared under the direction of the conferences of bishops, to arrange the material in a format deemed to be best suited to pastoral practice; this is to be done in such a way, however, that none of the contents of this *editio typica* are omitted.

When added rubrics or texts are judged useful, these are to be set off by some typographical symbol or mark from the rubrics and texts of the Roman Ritual.

22. In drawing up particular rituals for funerals, it shall be up to the conferences of bishops:

1. to give the rite an arrangement patterned on one or more of the models, in the way indicated in no. 9;

2. to replace the formularies given in the basic rite with others taken from those in Chapter VI, should this seem advantageous;

3. to add different formularies of the same type whenever the Roman Ritual provides optional formularies (following the rule given in no. 21, 6);

4. to decide whether laypersons should be deputed to celebrate funerals (see no. 19);

5. to decree, whenever pastoral considerations dictate,

omission of the sprinkling with holy water and the incensation or to substitute another rite for them;

6. to decree for funerals the liturgical color that fits in with the culture of peoples, that is not offensive to human grief, and that is an expression of Christian hope in the light of the paschal mystery.

FUNCTION OF THE PRIEST IN PREPARING AND PLANNING THE CELEBRATION

23. The priest is to make willing use of the options allowed in the rite, taking into consideration the many different situations and the wishes of the family and the community.

24. The rite provided for each model is drawn up in such a way that it can be carried out with simplicity; nevertheless the rite supplies a wide selection of texts to fit various contingencies. Thus, for example:

1. As a general rule all texts are interchangeable, in order to achieve, with the help of the community or the family, a closer reflection of the actual circumstances of each celebration.

2. Some elements are not assigned as obligatory, but are left as optional additions, as, for example, the prayer for the mourners at the home of the deceased.

3. In keeping with liturgical tradition, a wide freedom of choice is given regarding the texts provided for processions.

4. When a psalm listed or suggested for a liturgical reason may present a pastoral problem, another psalm may be substituted. Even within the psalms a verse or verses that seem to be unsuitable from a pastoral standpoint may be omitted.

5. The texts of prayers are always written in the singular, that is, for one deceased male. Accordingly, in any particular case the text is to be modified as to gender and number.

6. In prayers the lines within parentheses may be omitted.

25. Like the entire ministry of the priest to the dead, celebration of the funeral liturgy with meaning and dignity presupposes a view of the priestly office in its inner relationship with the Christian mystery.

Among the priest's responsibilities are:

1. to be at the side of the sick and dying, as is indicated in the proper section of the Roman Ritual;

2. to impart catechesis on the meaning of Christian death;

3. to comfort the family of the deceased, to sustain them amid the anguish of their grief, to be as kind and helpful as possible, and, through the use of the resources provided and allowed in the ritual, to prepare with them a funeral celebration that has meaning for them;

4. finally, to fit the liturgy for the dead into the total setting of the liturgical life of the parish and his own pastoral ministry.

BIBLICAL INDEX FOR THE ORDER OF CHRISTIAN FUNERALS